PERFECT?

NATURE

UTOPIA

AND THE

GARDEN

black dog publishing
london uk

CONTENTS

Dedicated to all lovers of nature.

ACKNOWLEDGMENTS

This project originated at a meeting of the Society for Utopian Studies at Wrightsville Beach, North Carolina. Our audience's enthusiasm, and our own appreciation for each other's conference papers, led us to conceive a collection of essays focused at the intersection of three resonant topics: Nature, Utopia, and the Garden.

The heart of the project is our own love for plants and for nature. We cultivate two very different domestic gardens. Annette's is a garden in the woods. Her contemporary home is sheltered by great swaths of oakleaf hydrangea and azalea, as well as by the native woodland plants of Pennsylvania. Naomi's is a town garden in Maine, an old clapboard house with informal flower beds, a dilettantish vegetable garden, a weedy lawn, and an undisciplined collection of shrubs defined by the 'survival of the fittest'.

In a project of this scale, a debt of gratitude is owed to a great many people. We wish to thank: Donald Dunham, who was asked for his advice regarding every aspect of this project; Nathan Stormer, for his steady encouragement and wonderful cooking; Ann Ardis for her unflagging support; Peter Buchanan, Fernando Caruncho, Nicholas Horsfall, Patrick Hunt, Tom Moylan, and Lyman Tower Sargent, mentors and friends; and, importantly, all those who so generously contributed essays and donated images.

This book would not have been possible without funding from the University of Delaware's Interdisciplinary Humanities Research Center and Department of Foreign Languages and Literatures in the College of Arts and Sciences; the University of Maine's College of Liberal Arts and Sciences under the leadership of Dean Jeff Hecker, and Regular Faculty Research Funds; and Robert H. Richards, III.

For practical advice and/or assistance we are indebted to Michael Alpert and Stella Santerre of the University of Maine as well as Nadine Bangerter, Jane Wessell, Bonnie Robb, and Almondo Ciaffi of the University of Delaware.

At Black Dog Publishing, we thank Adriana Caneva for realizing the potential of this project, and Rachel Pfleger for her phenomenal book design.

Last but not least, we are grateful to Maia, Kura, McLovin, and Bueller—the animal companions with whom we share our lives—and to all the growing things.

There was a poor fisherman of Wuling who lived in a time of violence and corruption. One day he was out in his boat, rowing upstream to look for a place where the fish would bite, and keeping his eyes on the water. Then a luscious fragrance filled the air. Looking up, he realized that he was entering an immense grove of blossoming peach trees, covering both banks for as far as he could see. Intrigued, he rowed up the stream to its source, a crystalline spring bubbling up from a mossy basin and carpeted all around with peach blossom petals. Behind it was an opening in the mountain. Leaving his boat, he squeezed through the narrow crevasse and was amazed to see before him a vast, peaceful valley with elegant houses and well-tended fields, orchards, and ponds. The cheerful villagers greeted him kindly and fed him well. Long ago, their ancestors had taken refuge in this place from the war and chaos of their time. Still following the old ways, the villagers didn't even know how much time had passed, and they sighed to hear that the world outside had not improved. The fisherman decided that he would be a happy man if he could live in this place, but first he wanted to retrieve his possessions. Promising the villagers that he wouldn't reveal the existence of their utopia, he left the valley, leaving markers along the way to help him find the place again. But as soon as he had returned to civilization, he went directly to the prefect to tell what he had seen. Accompanied by soldiers and curiosity-seekers, he tried in vain to find his way back to this bucolic paradise. The way was lost, and never found again.

NATURE, UTOPIA, AND THE GARDEN

6 /ANNETTE GIESECKE
/NAOMI JACOBS

Figure 1/ *Peach Blossom Spring*, detail. Qiu Ying, Chinese, c. 1494–1552.
A garden place where people live in harmony with nature. Photograph © 2012, the Museum of Fine Arts, Boston.

In this beloved tale of the "Peach Blossom Spring", the Chinese fable first written down by Tao Yuanming in 421 CE, we encounter a familiar vision of utopia as a perfect place, set apart from the complexities and difficulties of modern life. Significantly, it is also a garden place, where human beings live in harmony with nature. They work the land, but the labor is not burdensome, and their care is abundantly rewarded with good food, physical comforts, and beautiful surroundings [Figure 1].[1] The way to the secret entrance is marked by blossoming fruit trees—plants that are not only useful, but pleasing to the eye, nose, and taste buds. In China, the peach is known as the "Fairy Fruit"; its tree is associated with long life and protection from evil. One magical peach tree of Chinese legend blooms only once every 3,000 years and brings immortality to those who taste its fruit, recalling the Tree of Life in the book of Genesis. Like Eden, the paradise of the Peach Blossom Spring is forfeited if one does not treasure it; the fisherman breaks his promise and breaks the faith because he is too attached to the things of his world and cannot be satisfied with what this paradise offers. His punishment is to live out his life as an exile, knowing that somewhere in the mountains, the gardens of a lost utopia continue to bloom.

THE GARDEN

The links between gardening and utopian dreaming are ancient and deep. In Judeo-Christian mythology, and also in the beliefs of Islam, the Garden of Eden was the site where the first man and woman lived in harmony with nature and with God—a place and condition lost, and therefore replete with nostalgic yearning. Justifiably so, for in the words of the Syrian monk John the Damascene (c. 676–749 CE) this garden, planted by the hands of God,

> is temperate and the air that surrounds it is the rarest and purest: evergreen plants are its pride,

Figure 2/ Eden transformed into a *hortus conclusus* (enclosed garden) symbolic of the Virgin Mary's fecund chastity.
Das kleine Paradiesgärtlein (*The Little Garden of Paradise*). Master of the Upper Rhine, c. 1410.
Photograph, The Art Archive at Art Resource, NY.

> sweet fragrances abound, it is flooded with light, and in sensuous freshness and beauty it transcends imagination... a suitable home for him who was created in God's image.[2]

So great has been this yearning for the original paradise that, since antiquity, Eden has repeatedly been identified with the heavenly paradise of the hereafter.[3] This evocative place of creation was seen as the ideal place of redemption, though only in the teachings of the Qur'an has the heavenly paradise, *djanna*, unambiguously remained a garden.[4] It is a place abounding in shade-giving and fruit-bearing trees, green pastures dotted with cool pavilions, and fountains of gushing water.

Far from a unique concept, the idealized, Biblical sacred garden has parallels and connections with the sacred gardens of a range of ancient Near Eastern civilizations, among them those recounted in the Sumerian myths of the god Enki and of the hero Gilgamesh as well as the mountaintop garden of the mythical Persian king Jima.[5] Indeed, the roots of Eden likely extend to tales such as these from the kingdoms of the western Orient in the third and second millennia BCE. Once formed, the idea of Eden would fuse readily and seamlessly with Greco-Roman beliefs in a lost Golden Age—a belief also very probably stemming from Near Eastern sources—when a generous nature provided for human needs. And it would fuse as well with Classical visions of the Elysian Fields and the Isles of the Blessed, landscapes blessed by the gods. Both were originally earthly paradises, relocated in the netherworld only in the passage of time.[6] These remote places, enjoying as they did Golden Age conditions, could be reached only by a select, pious or heroic few and that, for the most part, only after death. In the fifth century BCE, the Greek lyric poet Pindar extolled the Blessed Isles for their profusion of golden flowers and sea breezes. The Roman poet Horace (65–8 BCE) fleshed out this description, focusing on the Islands' abundance and preternatural fertility:

> ... every year the land, unploughed, yields corn, and ever blooms the vine unpruned, and buds the shoot of the never-failing olive; the dark fig graces its native tree; honey flows from hollow oak; from the lofty hill, with plashing foot, lightly leaps the fountain.[7]

Similarly, the Elysian Fields, as described in Virgil's *Aeneid* (c. 30–19 BCE), are beatific "lands of gladness, glades of gentleness" graced by "dazzling light" and fragrant, shady groves of laurel as well as by "soft riverbanks and meadows where fresh streams flow".[8]

It has been observed that "paradise in its Judeo-Christian form has to be accepted as the deepest archaeological layer of the Western utopia".[9] Thus vestiges of Eden and of the ancient myths closely related to it may be sought in every Western utopian endeavor. It has also been observed that every garden may be viewed as a reflection of Eden [Figure 2]. A garden is always a utopian construct, for its creation is predicated on hope—hope that what one has planted will grow, that one's plantings will provide nourishment for the body and for the soul. But what precisely is a garden, and what is meant by the term "utopia"? Both concepts are instinctively comprehensible and readily used in conversation and print, but are not often actually defined.

Though humans are necessarily part of nature, the relation of humanity to nature has never been a simple one. The Roman statesman Cicero (106–43 BCE) called the garden a "second nature" (*altera natura*), and so indeed it is.[10] For the garden is a human creation driven by the desire to find an ideal place in nature—a second, kinder nature as opposed to a nature that can be unpredictable and harsh. Whether it takes the form of a field of wheat, a Zen exercise, or a collection of exotic plants, the garden is what the ancient Greeks termed a *temenos*, an off-cut from the larger natural environment. The very word "paradise" derives from an ancient Persian word for a walled enclosure; it came to take on a more specific reference to an enclosed natural area, whether orchard, ornamental garden, or wild animal park.[11] All such enclosures were designed to bring nature under human control and to fence out those natural elements that might endanger people as well as the plants and animals upon which their sustenance depended. It is instructive in this context to reflect that Eden had not only mythological but also physical models or parallels, in walled gardens such as those created in the sixth century BCE by Persian king Cyrus the Great at Pasargadae in Iran. Cyrus' lush, amply watered gardens would have been an improbable oasis of intoxicating fragrance, bright blooms, abounding orchard produce, and refreshing shade in a vast, inhospitable desert. As such they embodied the ruler's godlike status, his defiance of the elements and the change of seasons, as well as his consequent ability to feed his people. Cyrus was not the first Near Eastern monarch to use the garden as a symbol of his divine fecundity; among his predecessors were Assurbanipal II (883–859 BCE), who founded the Neo-Assyrian Empire; Assyrian king Sargon II (722–705 BCE) together with his successor Sennacherib (704–681 BCE); and King Nebuchadnezzar II (604–562 BCE) of Babylon, famous for his elusive hanging gardens.[12]

By contrast, an overriding fear of wild nature, discouraging love even of its gentler counterpart, is perhaps the reason why gardens have no place in the ideal society represented by Greek philosopher Plato (c. 429–347 BCE) in his *Republic*, a work often cited as the *de facto* origin of the utopian tradition in literature. The characteristic form of social organization in Plato's Classical Greece was the city-state or *polis*, comprising a town and the surrounding countryside that sustained it. Realizing an ideal mapped out by Homer in the eighth century BCE at the dawning of 'urbanism' in Greece, the *polis* contained few gardens within its walls.[13] Gardens in Classical Athens, for instance, were located almost exclusively in the urban periphery and were entirely utilitarian; outside the fortified urban center lay market gardens in which fruit, vegetables, herbs, and flowers were grown. Temples contained plantings that were pleasing to the gods and served to secure their continued favor. Trees were planted in *gymnasia* not for aesthetic purposes but in order to provide shade for those at exercise and rest. There were no pleasure gardens. Greeks of the Classical period, particularly the Athenians, celebrated humanity and its triumphs over both nature and the barbarian, which were believed—not coincidentally—to be closely aligned.

THE GARDEN AND UTOPIA

A garden, then, is the result of humanity's attempt to carve out an ideal place in nature, thereby fashioning a 'perfect' Earth. But what of utopia? In common parlance, utopia is regarded as an unrealizable dream of a perfect place—such as the idyllic village of the Peach Blossom Spring. Utopian thinkers have been considered wild-eyed dreamers at best, and dangerous megalomaniacs at worst. Utopian communities have been seen as laughable, utopian hopes as futile. This collection is grounded in an understanding of utopia *as process* that is set expressly against this dismissal of utopianism as foolish or deluded.

In the discipline of utopian studies, the utopian impulse is seen as an essential element of the human drive toward a better life. The concept of utopia and the practice of utopian projection have had a remarkably lively history in Western culture since Thomas More coined the term in his 1516 *Utopia.*[14] This founding text, a description of a society supposedly existing in the New World, was not intended to be taken as a blueprint. The very word "utopia" is a neologism evoking both *eu-topia* (Greek for "good place") and *ou-topia* (Greek for "no place"). More further signaled that his work was a thought experiment, a *jeu d'esprit*, by such sly hints as naming its river *Anydrus* (waterless) and its ruler *Anander* (without people). And no one could regard as a serious proposal the utopians' practice of making chamberpots and prisoners' chains out of gold. Over the subsequent centuries, thousands of writers and thinkers have proffered their own visions of an ideal society, solemn or satirical, and some have even attempted to bring them into being. In addition to literary utopias, a great many political philosophies, social movements, intentional communities, and cultural phenomena can be understood as fuelled by utopian longings.

A number of flexible and capacious taxonomies have been proposed for understanding utopia as more than a literary form. The field of utopian studies' premier bibliographer, Lyman Tower Sargent, has defined utopianism as "social dreaming", an activity manifesting "three faces": literary utopias, political programs, and intentional communities.[15] Political theorist Ruth Levitas argues that utopia must be variously understood as a literary form, a specific kind of content, and a specific cognitive function, all of which arise from and express "desire for a better way of life".[16] Perhaps the most influential theorist of utopianism in postmodern culture, Fredric Jameson, addresses the ways in which utopian works bring us face to face with our inability to break free of our assumptions and fully imagine the transformed reality for which we long.[17]

Central to these new understandings is the link between *ou-topia* and *eu-topia*. To envision the "no place", whether eutopian or dystopian, is a way to move toward the "good place", or at least, a better place. One need not accept a eutopian vision in all its details in order to be so moved; rather, one must simply remain open to what that vision tells us about the insufficiencies of 'our place': the way things are, which we need not take as inevitable. Similarly, one need not believe that the horrors depicted in a futuristic dystopia will come to pass in order to be moved to take action against the tendencies that such a work illuminates in the present day. For East German philosopher Ernst Bloch (1885–1977) this "Principle of Hope" could be traced in phenomena as varied as fashion, film, music, and religion.[18] He argued that unconscious longing for the "not yet" (*noch-nicht-beworden*) motivates every emancipatory social change, and visions of better ways of life always arise from a critique of the "something missing" in the present.[19] Crisis, not contentment, breeds utopias. It follows that eutopia and dystopia are versions of the same mental operation. The eutopian dream of a better world can be assessed and appreciated only against the backdrop of the less-perfect world we inhabit. The nightmare of dystopia implies a possible better world that has been lost and might be found again, if the darker tendencies of the present can be defeated. In both forms, the desire for a better world is the driving force.

Whether its expression takes a literary, concrete, or purely speculative form, utopia is the expression of a social ideal, and it is inextricably entwined with the garden. In the Western world, the formal 'invention' of utopia by Thomas More went hand in hand with a waning belief in the enduring physical existence of Eden, an earthly, God-given paradise that could be recovered by humankind.[20] Utopia is a form of paradise created not by a god or gods but by 'man'. From More's *Utopia* onward, most utopian fictions, proposals, and experiments have recognized the importance of the cultivation of plants for human happiness as well as human survival [Figure 3]. More himself was an enthusiastic gardener, and his utopian traveler Raphael Hythloday tells his tale while sitting on a grassy bank in an Antwerp garden. The householders in Utopia all love to garden, not only because of the pleasure they find in the activity itself but also because of their desire to outdo their neighbors. We are told that "he who founded the town seems to have taken care of nothing more than of their gardens", such that "every house has both a door to the street, and a back door to the garden". Raphael notes that the utopians "cultivate their gardens with great care, so that they have vines, fruits, herbs, and flowers in them; and all is so well ordered, and so finely kept, that I never saw gardens anywhere that were both so fruitful and so beautiful as theirs... there is indeed nothing belonging to the whole town that is both more useful and more pleasant".[21] More's models for these gardens were both sacred and secular: the enclosed monastery gardens of his time and the river gardens of London, including his own.[22] Similarly, in Francis Bacon's *The New Atlantis*, 1626, the narrator notes the "large and various orchards and gardens" cultivated by the scientists of Bensalem, who devote their efforts to improving existing varieties of useful plants.[23]

When Scottish industrialist Robert Owen (1771–1858) created his model village at New Lanark, he encouraged self-sufficiency through domestic gardens and allotments. Magnificent gardens on a larger scale were an important feature of Harmony, the utopian system envisioned by French Socialist Charles Fourier (1772–1837). The imagined day of his typical working-class Harmonian Lucas was to include a 5 AM pre-breakfast session with a group of gardeners, and a 9:30 AM session with the "vegetable growers' group, under a tent". The wealthy Mondor would have a morning session with a group of horticulturalists and afternoon sessions with the "greenhouse group" and the "group of exotic plant growers".[24] Whatever one's class level, Fourier stipulated that "workshops, field, and gardens

12 VTOPIAE INSVLAE TABVLA.

Figure 3/ Map of the Island of Utopia. Frontispiece to *Utopia*, Sir Thomas More. Woodcut by Ambrosius Holbein, 1518. Image, Private Collection/ The Bridgeman Art Library.

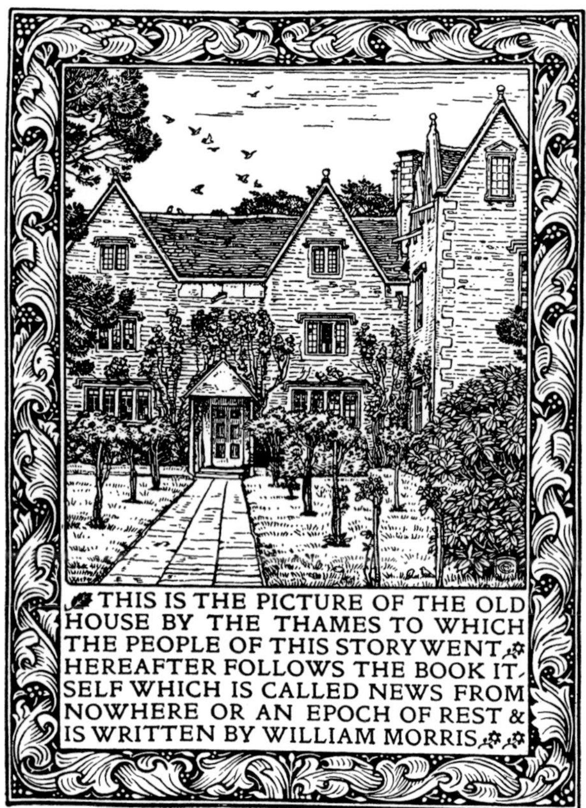

Figure 4/ Gardens of the east front of Kelmscott Manor, home of William Morris. Frontispiece to *News from Nowhere*, William Morris. Woodcut by W. H. Hooper, 1892, after a design by C. M. Gere. Photograph, Private Collection/ The Bridgeman Art Library.

must offer the worker the enticements of elegance and cleanliness".[25] For Fourier, time spent tending to plants was an essential element in a happy life and a prime example of "attractive labor" designed to combine social and sensual pleasures with productive activity.

By the late nineteenth century, the garden appears as a central metaphor for the ideal society envisioned in William Morris' *News from Nowhere*, 1890. Gardens are mentioned 56 times, and gardening is named among the pleasant kinds of work that keep people from becoming too bookish. The houses are all surrounded by flowers as well as vegetables, herbs, and fruit trees [Figure 4]. Morris' narrator mentions cabbage, strawberries, apricots, plums, pears, and lavender, as well as many gardens "stuffed" with flowers. Even the mills have gardens that are "marvels of loveliness". Indeed, in Morris' ideal future, the fields themselves were "everywhere treated as a garden made for the pleasure as well as the livelihood of all", and all England has become "a garden, where nothing is wasted and nothing is spoilt".[26]

Morris' book had been written in reaction to Edward Bellamy's *Looking Backward*, 1888, whose vision was largely an urban and industrialized one. Yet even Bellamy had hoped for a world in which "the earth would bloom like one garden".[27] Bellamy's book strongly influenced British visionary Ebenezer Howard, who put forward his ideas for a utopian community combining the best of city and country in *To-Morrow: A Peaceful Path to Real Reform*, 1898, later reprinted as *Garden Cities of Tomorrow*, 1902.[28] Howard's ideas would provide the guiding principles for urban and suburban housing developments in the English-speaking world throughout the twentieth century, and continue to find expression in town planning schemes today. Meanwhile, as Howard and his followers sought to unify the garden and the city, others had abandoned urban settings to re-create an Eden in the countryside. The Cambridge-educated Socialist Edward Carpenter (1844–1929) made a life for himself as a market gardener in Derbyshire; his home became a pilgrimage site for intellectuals including novelist D. H. Lawrence and 'sexologist' Havelock Ellis. The impulse to 'return to the soil' was expressed on a more modest scale in the allotment gardens to be found outside many European cities in this period.

In their darkened mirrors, the dystopian novels of the twentieth century also reflect the importance of gardens to the good life, for the absence of gardens, or indeed of any vegetation, is a prominent feature of works such as Evgeny Zamyatin's *We*, 1921, and George Orwell's *Nineteen Eighty-Four*, 1948.[29] The nightmare city of *We* is made of glass; Orwell's is made of steel and concrete. But for the rebellious citizens of both cities, a beautiful and fertile natural world—the wilderness outside the Green Wall in the former, and the more domesticated "Golden Country" in the latter—provides glimpses of an ideal life in contrast to the oppression of the dystopian society.

The utopian energies of the 1960s in the United States fueled a revived Back to the Land movement for which home vegetable gardening was an essential element of rural self-sufficiency. Many of these hippie homesteaders were inspired by elders such as Helen and Scott Nearing, whose books advocating the "simple life" dated back to the 1950s.[30] This was the time of the 'flower children', who found in the beauty of nature an inspiration to peace and harmony and sang about getting "back to the garden". Such views and practices inform the utopian fictions of the period. The villages of Marge Piercy's *Woman on the Edge of Time*, 1976, are rich with bloom and mostly "own-fed"—self-sustaining in food production. Their collaboration with nature extends to the breeding of spiders that spin and mend garden fences.[31] In Ernest Callenbach's *Ecotopia*, 1975, there are roof gardens in the large cities, children work gardens to produce food for their school meals, and home gardens are placed next to bathrooms so that grey water can be used for irrigation.[32] Utopian citizens in fiction of this period tend to be expert composters, avid botanists, and eloquent opponents of waste. They protect nature for its spiritual and aesthetic qualities as well as for its essential role in supporting human life.

The ethos expressed in these works of fiction was hardly confined to the United States. The Findhorn spiritual community in Scotland, founded in 1962, became famous for the enormous vegetables it succeeded in growing on formerly barren ground. Today, the 450 residents of the contemporary eco-village at Findhorn are said to have the lowest ecological footprint in the industrialized world.[33] A 25-acre organic farming enterprise provides the majority of the residents' fresh vegetables and also feeds over a hundred families in the area.[34]

In today's popular discourse, the representation of gardening as a utopian activity has taken on a new insistence as domestic gardening is linked to larger issues of ecology. The Slow Food and Locavore movements indicate a lively desire to engage with the production of plants, whether as home gardener or as farmer's market customer, along with a conviction that the world would be a better place if it included more or different kinds of gardens. Influential chefs like Alice Waters as well as authors such as Michael Pollan, Barbara Kingsolver, and Eric Schlosser have written eloquently of the damage that the industrial production of food inflicts upon the environment and on our bodies.[35] The Obama White House has its organic garden, and Peter Lamborn Wilson (aka Hakim Bey of the *Temporary Autonomous Zone*) has advocated "avant gardening" as an act of resistance that is simultaneously a work of art, a positive praxis conjuring up an autonomous zone outside the mediations and commodification of capitalism.[36] Tim Hodgkinson, author of *How to Be Idle*, has written that "digging is anarchy in action" and has called upon revolutionaries to "put down their weapons and take up their spades".[37] A "Guerrilla Gardening" website offers the slogan, "Fight the Filth with Forks and Flowers."[38] And Douglas Tallamy exhorts suburban gardeners to favor native plants in order to better support the web of life.[39]

A good deal of sociological evidence does confirm that gardening can serve utopian ends. Garden projects at prisons, schools, nursing homes, and hospitals have all been shown to have a beneficial effect on participants. The establishment of community vegetable gardens on abandoned city lots and at housing projects has led to decreased crime, drug use, vandalism, and littering, created friendlier relations between neighbors, and even increased self-esteem among the urban poor. Studies in the UK have shown community gardens to "promote social inclusion, and give rise to health benefits".[40] A Denver study found that community gardens foster "high levels of collective efficacy", which "at the neighborhood level are associated with decreased risky sexual behaviors, asthma prevalence, obesity, and premature mortality, as well as improved self-appraisal of health".[41]

With health benefits, social benefits, psychological benefits, physical benefits, economic benefits and the ecological benefits that come with reducing our reliance on industrial agriculture, it might seem there can be no dark side to the enterprise of gardening, and it is tempting to think of the garden as a space of innocence and simplicity. It can be precisely that. But, as has been shown above, like all works of human artfulness, gardens are complicated places. They can be used to express the power of a monarch or a regime, to impress one's neighbors, or to glorify the human control of nature. They can be toxic places as well as sacred spaces, regions of conflict as well as realms of harmony. The gardener's very love for the plant world's amazing diversity can lead to unwelcome side effects, as when the nursery industry introduces to home gardens a beautiful plant that promptly invades the woodlands nearby. Some gardens, whether in art or reality, catalyze our anxieties about the power of nature and the unruliness of our own natural impulses. Some gardens are enclosed by walls topped with broken glass, intended to keep out the hungry and the angry.

THE GARDEN, UTOPIA, AND NATURE

As the number of people living on our garden planet approaches seven billion—perhaps to reach nine billion by the middle of the century—the possibility of sustaining a harmonious life in nature seems ever more remote. Cities spread across the landscape like a cancer, claiming forests and meadows, draining water tables, destroying wildlife habitat, and generating new miles of asphalt and power lines. Activities necessary to human nourishment, shelter, and movement foul the water and air. Industrial agriculture damages the web of insect and bird life, as well as the microorganisms that inhabit healthy soils. As the climate warms, some fertile areas are expected to become too dry to support plant life—or human life. Many fear the Earth will become little more than a gigantic garbage dump, covered with mountains of discarded consumer goods, plastic bags, rusting vehicles, and old computers, unless humanity profoundly changes inured forms, patterns, and modes of habitation.

These concerns are far from new. Over the millennia there have been repeated passionate calls for the absolute necessity of reducing humanity's footprint on the planet: if we aspire to garden and recklessly reap a harvest from the entire Earth, no uncompromised nature will remain. One such call issued some two thousand years ago from

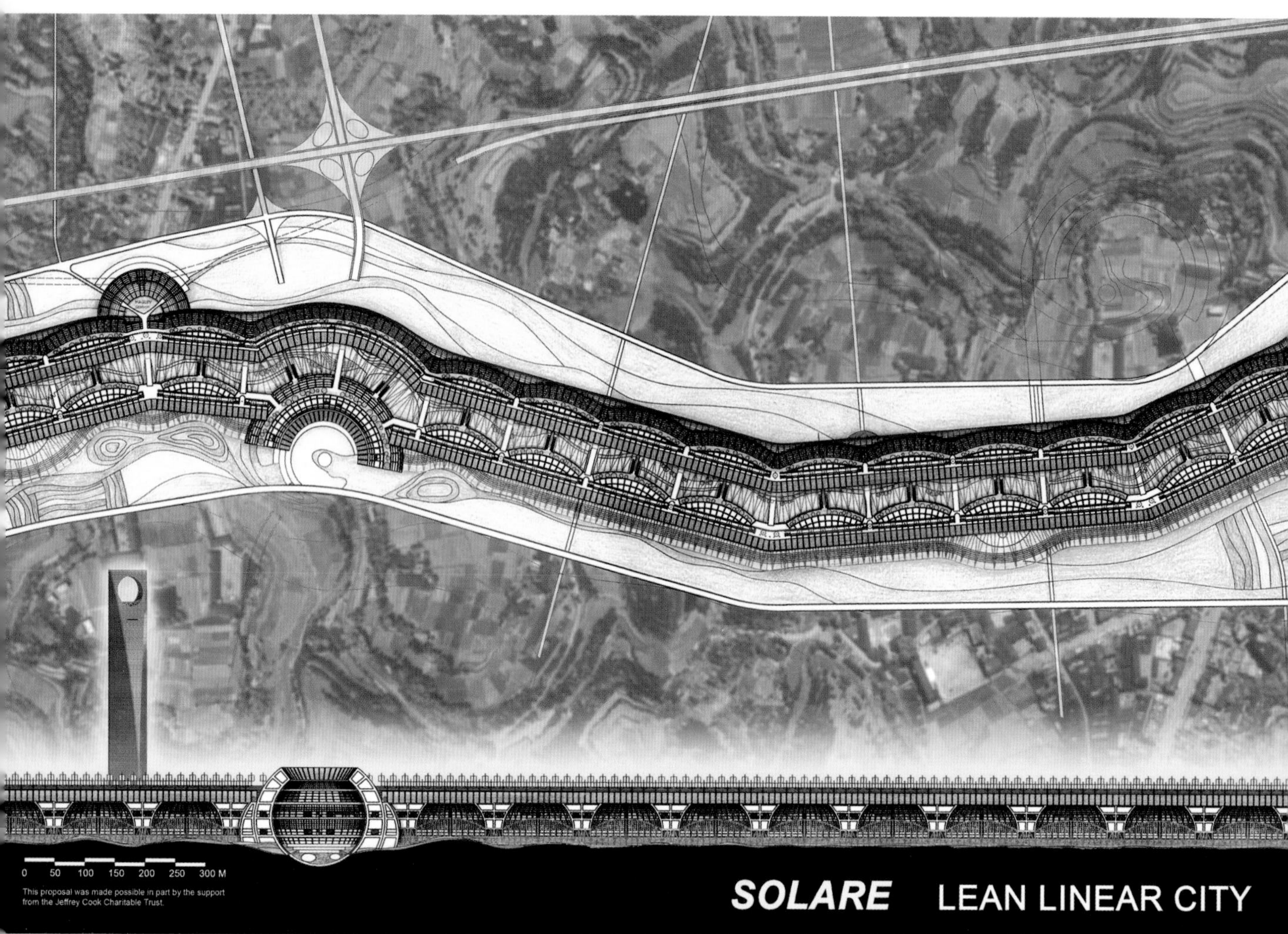

the Roman poet and ardent utopian Lucretius (c. 99–55 BCE). A follower of the philosopher Epicurus and of the school he called "The Garden", Lucretius stated that the Earth is in decline, a process hastened by humanity's relentless use and abuse of nature's resources. While the Earth's depletion and ultimate passing cannot be reversed, the process can be slowed if we embrace the fact of the essential, atomic unity of all life on the planet. Harmony with the very nature that people had come to consider 'other' and remote from the human endeavor, Lucretius wrote, is the key to a good life and happiness.[42]

Today, architect and utopian theorist Paolo Soleri delivers a similar message, arguing that it is not merely reform—of urban and suburban patterns in particular—but thoroughgoing reformulation that is required. A lifelong proponent of sustainable urban efforts that reduce impact on the natural environment while promoting improved quality of life, Soleri has proposed "Solare: the Lean Linear City". Consisting of two urban ribbons on either side of a continuous urban park, the linear city would concentrate residential commercial, industrial, institutional, cultural, recreational, and health maintenance spaces, leaving the surrounding environment intact [Figures 5, 6].[43] Notably, the garden is key in Soleri's utopian scheme, as it was in Lucretius'.

For many of us, the creation of a garden is a small candle lit in the darkness of impending ecological collapse. But how can the humble garden possibly make a difference in the face of such apocalyptic scenarios, the results of misguided gardening efforts on a global scale? With every passing day, this question becomes more timely and the anticipation of a response more pressing. Since the garden and gardening practices define humanity's relation to the natural environment, it is of utmost importance to retrace and re-examine the garden's symbolism, history, and life-sustaining potency. The contributors to this volume do so

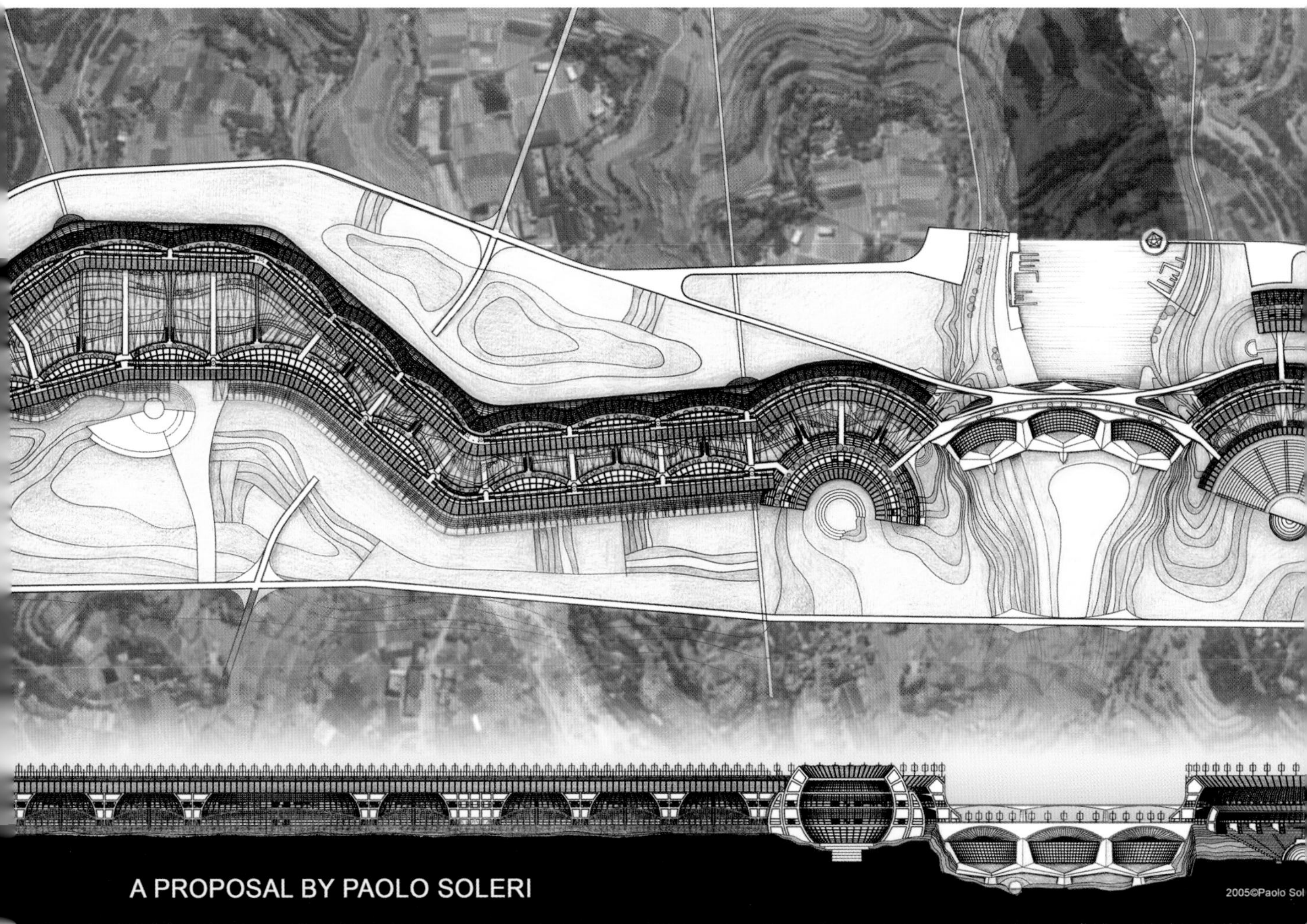

Figure 5/ SOLARE: the Lean Linear City, Paolo Soleri, 2005. At the base of the city on the southerly side are greenhouse aprons, and orchard aprons are on the northerly side. Image courtesy of the Cosanti Foundation.

by exploring both sides of the utopian dynamic—utopian desires and dystopian fears, utopian hope and dystopian despair—in relation to the garden. They consider the garden as an escape from harsh reality, a site for the practice of virtues, an emblem of the ideal human relationship to nature, and an intimate setting that helps us to find hope even in the 'garbage dump' of the present. But they also recognize that the garden can express fear of nature or a desire to control its unruly powers. They demonstrate that the garden is a reflection at once of our unavoidable separation from wild nature and of the gardener's intimate relation of care with the natural world.

Necessarily possessing many points of contact, the essays in this collection are grouped in accordance with their particular emphases: the garden's spiritual dimension, touching on questions of the sacred, of healing, and of creative agency; the garden as subject of human creativity that explores its representational limits; the garden as a critical natural space of peace and beauty that enfolds the home; the social and political forces at work in the creation of gardens as repositories of hope; the essential economic value of gardens to a humanity that survives by virtue of the exploitation of nature; and the garden as a place to learn how to live with the nature that sustains us. The gardens featured here range from the domestic gardens of ancient Rome to zoological and botanic gardens of the present day, from Versailles to the English Picturesque, from Hieronymus Bosch's Eden to a small Connecticut organic farm, and from a war-scarred Bohemia to pharaonic Egypt. Each represents the innate human drive to perfect the Earth, and each in its own way signals how delicate is this venture. In the words of Jean-

Figure 6/ The Lean Linear City in summer, a garden space flanked by two urban ribbons. 3D rendering by Young Soo Kim. Image courtesy of the Cosanti Foundation.

Jacques Rousseau, we are undone if we "forget that the fruits of the Earth belong to us all, and the Earth itself to nobody".[44] A perfect Earth necessarily comprises humanity, nature, and the garden in unison.

Notes

1. Figure 1 is further identified by the following: "Peach blossom spring" [*Taohua yuan*], poem by Tao Qian (365–427). Chinese, Ming dynasty, 1368–1644. Ink and color on paper. Overall: 33 x 762 cm (13 x 300 in.) Image: 33 x 472 cm (13 x 185 13/16 in.). Museum of Fine Arts, Boston. Keith McLeod Fund, 56.494. For the Cyril Birch translation of the original text, go to http://afe.easia.columbia.edu/ps/china/taoqian_peachblossom.pdf, and to learn more about the Peach Blossom Spring legend in relation to Chinese utopian traditions, see Sing-chen Lydia Chiang, "Visions of Happiness: Daoist Utopias and Grotto Paradises in Early and Medieval Chinese Tales", *Utopian Studies* vol. 20, no. 1, 2009, pp. 97–120.
2. As quoted in Markus Bockmuehl, "Locating Paradise", *Paradise in Antiquity: Jewish and Christian Views,* Markus Bockmuehl and Guy G. Stroumsa eds., Cambridge: Cambridge University Press, 2010, p. 200.
3. The bibliography on this point is vast. See, for instance Asma Afsaruddin, "Garden", *Encyclopaedia of the Qur'an,* Vol. II, Jane Dammen McAulife ed., Leiden, Boston, and Köln: Brill, 2002, pp. 282–287; Bochmuehl, "Locating Paradise", pp, 195 and 209; Chaim Cohen, "Eden, Garden of", *The Oxford Dictionary of the Jewish Religion,* R. J. Werblowsky and Geoffrey Wigodu eds., Oxford: Oxford University Press, 1997, p. 214; The Rev. John McClintock, D. D. and James Strong, S. T. D. eds., "Paradise", *Encyclopaedia of Biblical, Theological, and Ecclesiastical Literature,* Vol. VII, New York: Arno Press, pp. 652–660; Robert W. Rogers, "Eden", *The New Schaff-Herzog Encyclopedia of Religious Knowledge,* Vol. IV, Samuel Macauley Jackson, D. D., L. L. D. ed., New York and London: Funk and Wagnalls Co., 1909, pp. 74–75; and Alessandro Scafi, "Epilogue: A Heaven on Earth" in Bochmuehl and Stroumsa eds., *Paradise in Antiquity,* pp. 212 and 219.
4. See, for example, Leah Kinberg, "Paradise" in Dammen McAulife ed., *Encyclopaedia of the Qur'an,* Vol. IV, 2004, pp. 12–19; and L. Gardet, "*Djanna*", *The Encyclopaedia of Islam,* Vol. II, B. Lewis, C. Pellat, and J. Schacht eds., Leiden and London: Brill, 1965, pp. 447–452.
5. See Jean Delumeau, *The History of Paradise: The Garden of Eden in Myth and Tradition,* Matthew O'Connell trans., New York: Continuum, 1995, pp. 5–15; Elizabeth B. Moynihan, *Paradise as a Garden in Persia and Mughal India,* New York: George Braziller, 1979, pp. 2–12; and Alessandro Scafi, *Mapping Paradise: A History of Heaven on Earth,* Chicago: The University of Chicago Press, 2006, p. 12.
6. For the Blessed Isles, Elysium, and the Golden Age, see note 5, particularly Delumeau, *The History of Paradise,* p. 8 for reference to Pindar's second Olympian ode, which is referenced here. See also James S. Romm, *The Edges of the Earth in Ancient Thought: Geography, Exploration, and Fiction,* Princeton: Princeton University Press, 1992; and Lindsay C. Watson, *A Commentary on Horace's Epodes,* Oxford: Oxford University Press, 2003, p. 483.
7. Quoted from the sixteenth epode in C. B. Bennett trans., *Horace: The Odes and Epodes,* Cambridge, MA: Harvard University Press, 1934, p. 405.
8. Quotations stem from the sixth book of the *Aeneid,* lines 846–850, Allen Mandelbaum trans., *The Aeneid of Virgil,* New York: Bantam, 1961, p. 151.
9. Manuel, Frank E. and Fritzie P. Manuel, *Utopian Thought in the Western World,* Cambridge, MA: Belknap Press of Harvard University Press, 1979, p. 33.
10. See John Dixon Hunt, *Greater Perfections: The Practice of Garden Theory,* Philadelphia: The University of Pennsylvania Press, 2000, pp. 32–75. The phrase "*altera natura*" is used by Cicero in the second book of his *De Natura Deorum* (*On the Nature of the Gods*), section 152.
11. Bremmer, Jan, "Paradise from Persia, via Greece, into the *Septuagint*", *Paradise Interpreted: Representations of Biblical Paradise in Judaism and Christianity,* G. P. Luttikhuizen ed., Leiden: Brill, 1999, pp. 1–20.
12. See Patrick Hunt, "Persian Paradise Gardens: Eden and Beyond as

Chahar Bagh", www.electrummagazine.com/2011/07/paradise-gardens-of-persia-eden-and-beyond-as-chahar-bagh/; Joachim Schaper, "The Messiah in the Garden: John 19.38–41, (Royal) Gardens, and Messianic Concepts" in Bochmuehl and Stroumsa eds., *Paradise in Antiquity*, pp. 17–27; and David Stronach, "The Garden as a Political Statement: Some Case Studies from the Near East in the First Millennium B.C.", *Bulletin of the Asia Institute*, New Series Vol. 4, 1990, pp. 171–180.
13. Giesecke, Annette L., *The Epic City: Urbanism, Utopia, and the Garden in Ancient Greece and Rome*, Cambridge, MA: Harvard University Press, 2007, pp. xi–78.
14. More, Sir Thomas, *Utopia*, 1516. Electronic Text Center, University of Virginia Library. http://etext.lib.virginia.edu/toc/modeng/public/MorUtop.html.
15. Sargent, Lyman Tower, "The Three Faces of Utopianism Revisited", *Utopian Studies*, vol. 5, no. 1, 1994, pp. 1–37.
16. Levitas, Ruth, *The Concept of Utopia*, Syracuse, New York: Syracuse University Press, 1990.
17. Jameson, Fredric, "Of Islands and Trenches: Neutralization and the Production of Utopian Discourse", *Diacritics*, vol. 7, no. ii, 1977, pp. 2–21. For more on Jameson and utopia, see the special issue of *Utopian Studies*, vol. 9, no. 2, 1998.
18. Bloch, Ernst, *The Principle of Hope*, Neville Plaice, Stephen Plaice and Paul Knight trans., Boston: MIT Press, 1995. See also Douglas Kellner's helpful overview and assessment of Bloch at http://pages.gseis.ucla.edu/faculty/kellner/Illumina%20Folder/kell1.htm.
19. Bloch, Ernst and Theodor Adorno, "Something's Missing: A Discussion between Ernst Bloch and Theodor W. Adorno on the Contradictions of Utopian Longing", *The Utopian Function of Art and Literature: Selected Essays*, Jack Zipes and Frank Mecklenburg trans., MIT Press, 1989, pp. 1–17.
20. Delumeau, *History of Paradise*, p. 120; and Manuel and Manuel, *Utopian Thought*, p. 112.
21. More, *Utopia*, Book II, Chapter 2. n.p.
22. Christianson, C. Paul, *The Riverside Gardens of Thomas More's London*, New Haven: Yale University Press, 2005.
23. Bacon, Francis, *The New Atlantis*, Project Gutenberg, http://www.gutenberg.org/ebooks/2434, n.p.
24. Fourier, Charles, in Jonathan Beecher, *Charles Fourier: The Visionary and His World*, Berkeley: University of California Press, 1990, pp. 281–282.
25. Fourier, in Beecher, *Charles Fourier*, p. 277.
26. Morris, William, *News from Nowhere, in News from Nowhere and Other Writings*, edited and with an introduction by Clive Wilmer, London: Penguin, 1993, p. 211, p. 105.
27. Bellamy, Edward, *Looking Backward, 2000–1887*, pp. 216–217.
28. Howard, Ebenezer, *Garden Cities of To-Morrow*, London: Swan Sonnenschein, 1902.
29. Zamyatin, Evgeny, *We*, Gregory Zilboorg trans., New York: E. P. Dutton, 1924; George Orwell, *Nineteen Eighty-Four*, London: Secker and Warburg, 1949.
30. Nearing, Scott and Helen Nearing, *Living the Good Life: How to Live Sanely and Simply in a Troubled World*, New York: Schocken Books, 1970.
31. Piercy, Marge, *Woman on the Edge of Time*, New York: Alfred A. Knopf, 1976, p. 62.
32. Callenbach, Ernst, *Ecotopia: the Notebooks and Reports of William Weston*, New York: Bantam, 1977.
33. Tinsley, S. and H. George, *Ecological Footprint of the Findhorn Foundation and Community*, Moray: Sustainable Development Research Centre, UHI Millennium Institute, 2006.
34. http://www.ecovillagefindhorn.com/.
35. Pollan, Michael, *The Omnivore's Dilemma: A Natural History of Four Meals*, New York, Penguin, 2006; Barbara Kingsolver, *Animal, Vegetable, Miracle: A Year of Food Life*, New York, HarperCollins, 2007; Eric Schlosser, *Fast Food Nation*, New York: Houghton Mifflin, 2001.
36. Wilson, Peter Lamborn, "Avant Gardening", *Avant Gardening: Ecological Struggle in the City & the World*, Peter Lamborn Wilson and Bill Weinberg eds., Brooklyn: Autonomedia, 1999, pp. 7–34.
37. Hodgkinson, Tim, "Digging for Anarchy", *Vista: the culture and politics of gardens*, Noël Kingsbury and Tim Richardson eds., London: Frances Lincoln Limited, 2005, pp. 66–73.
38. http://www.guerrillagardening.org/
39. Tallamy, Douglas W., *Bringing Nature Home: How Native Plants Sustain Wildlife in Our Gardens*, Portland, Oregon: Timber Press, 2007.
40. Teig, Ellen et al., "Collective efficacy in Denver, Colorado: Strengthening neighborhoods and health through community gardens", *Health and Place*, vol. 15, 2009, p. 1120.
41. Teig et al., "Collective efficacy", p. 1115.
42. Lucretius, *De Rerum Natura*, W. H. D. Rouse trans., Cambridge, MA: Harvard University Press, 1982. For Lucretius and the Roman 'green movement', see Giesecke, *The Epic City*, pp. 79–159.
43. For a formal presentation of Solare, see http://www.youtube.com/watch?v=xX_GD7omON4 and also http://www.arcosanti.org/project/background/soleri/commissions.html.
44. Rousseau, Jean-Jacques, *The Social Contract and Discourses*, G. D. H. Cole trans., New York: Dutton, 1950, p. 235.

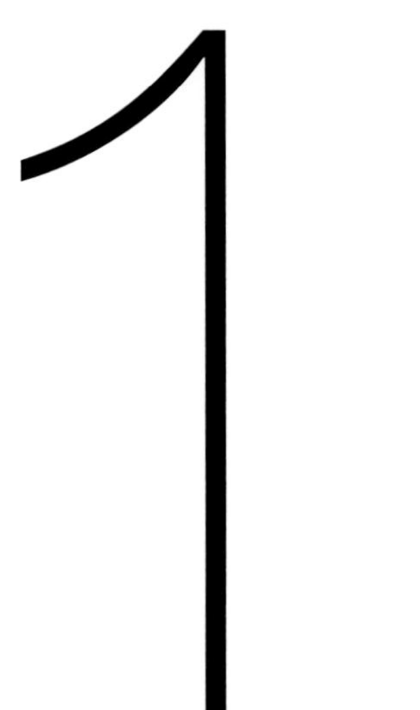

BEING IN NATURE

GARDENS AND THE WAY OF THINGS

/DAVID E. COOPER

The idea that the garden might be a site or an inspiration for an ideal human life is perhaps almost as old as garden making itself. Certainly it is one that has endured, in various forms, through the history of gardening. The perception, for example, of the garden as depicting a place—a 'Paradise' or a 'Pure Land'—where life is perfected recurs throughout this history, in Buddhist and Islamic writings especially, but in secular ones too. In *The Decameron*, Boccaccio describes a group of young revellers in a garden who agree that "if a Paradise might be created upon earth, they could not conceive any form, other than that of this garden, which it might have" [Figure 1].[1]

GARDENS, VIRTUES, AND TRUTH

One recurrent and influential thought has been that of the garden as a place especially suited to both inviting and cultivating the exercise of the virtues. Epicurus' garden was designed to encourage diligence and effort, but also enjoyment of the austere, simple, and fret-free life valued by the philosopher. Pliny's ambition in creating his two gardens was to "cultivate myself" and to lead "a good life and a genuine one".[2] The purpose of the landscaped scenic sites (*bajing*) in Song dynasty China was as much a moral as an aesthetic one—or, better, these purposes were not regarded as separate. As a Song official in Huzhou put it, enjoyment of a pavilion, its surroundings, and a nearby lake will "moralise people" more effectively than "preaching to them".[3]

This kind of thought, stretching back to ancient times, has on the surface at least continued to flourish in the modern period. General LaFayette's garden near Paris, like Thomas Jefferson's in Virginia, was intended to evoke and instill the republican virtues of liberty and self-reliance for which both men had fought. In England, a few years later, the garden writing couple, John and Jane Loudon, were exhorting members of the newly emerging middle class to create small, urban gardens in which the 'Victorian values' of industry, self-discipline, and devotion to home and family could be nurtured. And in our contemporary context, enthusiasm for community gardens, city farms, allotments, and organic gardening is inspired as much by ethical concerns as by ones for economy and the quality of food. According to contemporary rhetoric, gardens which are motivated by these concerns represent moral resistance to the darker aspects of modernity—the atrophy of communities, the hegemony of technology, the degradation of natural environments.

It is not clear, however, how closely these modern conceptions of the idea of gardens as theaters of virtue correspond to more ancient ones. What looks to be missing from the later versions is a connection that was central to ancient discourses of virtue. This is the connection between virtue and wisdom, between the good and the true. For the authors of these discourses, the genuinely virtuous person must be 'in the truth', just as one who genuinely understands the way of things is necessarily a virtuous person. For Socrates, famously, a failure to act well is always a failure of understanding. For Aristotle also—though he rejected the Socratic equation—"full" virtue, as distinct from a natural inclination to behaving virtuously, belongs only to a person possessed of "understanding and practical wisdom".[4] This intimate connection between virtue and wisdom is made, too, by the ancient thinkers of India and China. According to the Buddha, for example, people have not properly internalized doctrines like that of 'not-self' and the ubiquity of 'suffering' (*dukkha*) unless they renounce the vices. "What, bikkhus, is full understanding? The extinction of greed, aversion and delusion."[5] Further east, the *Daodejing* spoke of a "profound virtue" (*xuande*) which, in contrast with simply acting well, presupposes "deep and far-reaching" understanding, and, because of this, leads to "compliance" with the *dao*, the Way.[6]

This unity of the good and the true has an important implication for utopian conceptions of the garden as a site for the exercise and cultivation of the virtues. The implication is that the garden must also be a site of truth. Unless, in some manner, it exemplifies or evokes the truth of things, the garden cannot be an appropriate arena for the exercise of virtue. Unless, one might say, the gardener is "in the truth"—or, as Daoists would say, "on the Way"—he or she cannot be the exemplar of the good life as imagined in utopian discourses. This is an implication which ancient thinkers who concerned themselves with the garden surely recognized. As one commentator explains, the garden of Epicurus—in order for it to invite moral "self-cultivation"—was designed by the philosopher to be "a form of education in the ways of nature" which communicated, for example, the "greater harmonies" of the cosmos and the soul's "essential connection to matter".[7]

Figure 1/ *The Decameron*. Tales in the garden, a paradise on Earth. John William Waterhouse, 1916.

The example of the Epicurean garden is apposite, since it illustrates the kind—or scale—of truth which gardens must express or evoke if they are to serve as sites for living well, for lives in which virtue and wisdom are jointly cultivated. Clearly, there are many ways in which a garden, or part of one, could be described as truthful. Maybe it accurately depicts a famous mountain, or perhaps it faithfully registers the emotions of the person who made it. But it is difficult to see how truthfulness of these sorts, or on this scale, could have a general connection with the good life. The truth which the garden needs to possess must, so to speak, be a 'big' one—indicative, say, of cosmic "harmonies" or spirit's "connection to matter" in the manner, it was suggested, of Epicurus' garden. In the following section, we encounter other candidates which, over the centuries, have been proposed as the large truths that the garden is suited to communicate. This will not only render more concrete the idea of the relevant kind of truth, but prepare for my own proposal concerning a significant way in which, as I see it, the garden may be 'in the truth'.

GARDENS AS 'DISCLOSIVE': SOME HISTORY

The main emphasis of this essay is not historical, but my own account of gardens as communicating the way of things does not spring from nowhere, and it will be helpful briefly to consider earlier accounts on which it may then draw. For these are accounts in which the garden is an important means for "disclosing" the world, for rescuing its "visibility".[8]

Early conceptions of the garden as disclosing truth are found in the related East Asian traditions of Daoism and Ch'an or Zen Buddhism. Indeed, these are related not least through a shared perception of the garden as an epitome of the true relationship between human beings and their world. It is not surprising, perhaps, that in China, Buddhist and Daoist priests often cooperated in landscaping the areas around their temples. In both traditions, the garden is a place for teaching and exercising the virtues. The gentle, freely flowing contours of Chinese 'literati' gardens, it is sometimes said, reflected and inspired the central Daoist virtue of *wu wei*, literally "not acting", but better understood as unforced, flexible and spontaneous behavior. And while it may be exaggerated to hold that, for Zen Buddhists, looking after it was "the very point of having a garden in the first place", the gardener's daily exercise of care and humility was a significant dimension of Buddhist spiritual life.[9]

In both traditions, crucially, the garden and gardening are held to be expressive of the truth of things. The idea of Chinese and Japanese gardens as microcosms of the world is familiar; but often, too much attention is directed to the emblematic role of these gardens, the manner in which particular stones and other ingredients represented certain objects or places—isles of the gods, famous mountains, or whatever. More interesting was the way in which the gardens were regarded as "a miniaturization of the natural structure of the world" as a whole, or—as by the seventeenth century author of the famous *Yuan Ye* (*The Craft of Gardens*) —as distilling the essence of things or indeed "the very universe" [Figure 2].[10]

But if Daoist and Zen gardens epitomized "the natural structure of the world"—by, for example, rendering salient the ephemeral character of everything—they were also intended to point to the mysterious, indeed ineffable, source or ground of nature as a whole. The Daoist garden, Maggie Keswick argued, endeavors in its quiet way to make "the inexpressible experience of the *dao* possible".[11] For an earlier author, the sixteenth century gardener and monk, Soami, the Zen garden in its simplicity serves to "portray... the mystery of nature", especially the 'emptiness' that is held to be a precondition for the emergence of things.[12]

Figure 2/ The Gardens of Activity, Harmony, and Peace. Distilling the very universe. The Royal Botanic Gardens, Kew, UK. Photograph by Annette Giesecke.

In both these Asian spiritual traditions, moreover, gardens and gardening encapsulate the true relationship between people and the natural world. There is much talk, in the secondary literature, of the 'unity' and 'inseparability' of human beings and nature emphasized by Daoists and Buddhists alike. It is rarely made clear, however, what such talk amounts to. Still, it is certainly true that, in the primary texts, the authors insist on an intimacy and reciprocity between the human and natural spheres. This is enough, perhaps, to justify references by commentators to gardening, in these Asian traditions, as exemplifying "a dialectic of cooperation between humans and the natural world" or an "unbroken whole" of "nature and spirit".[13]

In short, the reflective Daoist or Zen Buddhist gardener is not only exercising the virtues associated with a spiritual dispensation but does so, in significant part, through recognition of large truths intimated by the work in which he is engaged. These are truths about the very nature of nature, the source or well-spring of the natural world, and the dialectical relationship between nature and people.

This perception of the garden and the gardener has not been confined to Asia. For all the obvious differences of religious sensibility and metaphysical doctrine, a comparable perception prevailed in parts of Europe during the Renaissance period. As in China and Japan, Renaissance gardens—those created by or for the Medicis, for example—were theaters for the exercise of virtue, of the dignity, decorum, and humane civility belonging to the humanist ideal of *virtù*. Again, however, this was not virtue of a kind that could be attained independently of knowledge—of the world, its source, and the place of humans within it—which the garden could itself help to teach and advance.

The Italian Renaissance garden, as Eugenio Battisti points out, was among much else a "measured and well-ordered model of the universe", displaying in a salient way the symmetries and forms which, according to thinkers like Marsilio Ficino, constituted the structure of reality.[14] But in doing this, the garden was at the same time reminding those who experienced it of the source, the creator, of the natural world: God. For Alberti, the garden maker, like the architect, attempts in his works to realize *concinnitas*, a 'congruity' or harmony. This congruity, though it is "the principal law of nature", has its "true seat... in the mind and in reason"—in, that is, the

Figure 3/ Piccolomini Palace Garden. Contrasting artifact and wild nature. Bernardo Rosselino, 1459. Pienza, Italy. Photograph courtesy of Stephen Bartlett, Kennesaw State University.

logos or divine mind, which is responsible for all that is; gardens, like buildings, owe their "dignity and value" to this capacity to communicate the divine.[15]

Just as there is *concinnitas* among the components of a beautiful work and among the constituents of nature, so there is between human beings, the world they inhabit, and God. These days one often reads that Renaissance and Early Modern philosophers were guilty of dualistic doctrines that set human beings apart from the rest of reality. But while these philosophers, Descartes included, may indeed have thought that people are very different beings from anything else in creation, they were typically anxious to demonstrate that human beings and the natural world were, through God's arrangements, fitted to one another in a maximally harmonious way. Thus, while it was the intention of gardens like those of the Piccolomini Palace to contrast an artifact with the wild terrain beyond, it was also their purpose to convey the overall congruity of human existence with the wider universe and, thereby, to "place Man at harmony with his [and the universe's] Maker" [Figure 3].[16]

The reflective Renaissance garden maker, then, is a person of virtue, possessed of a decorum and dignity that owes, in a significant way, to an appreciation of the garden and the work done in it as congruous with the harmonious order of the world and thereby with the divine *logos* that gives structure to nature and the human mind alike.

A few centuries later, during the great period of eighteenth century English gardening, no one vision of the garden's role was dominant. Respective champions of an older formalist style, of 'improvement' in the manner of 'Capability' Brown, and of Picturesque design proclaimed very different views of this role. These proclamations frequently reflected competing moral perceptions. William Gilpin, for example, explicitly contrasted the values expressed by the Picturesque garden with that of utility, while Vicesimus Knox argued, in an Epicurean spirit, that gardens could encourage an "amiable disposition" which is as integral to ethical life as a "severe" sense of duty.[17]

An ethical discourse of the garden was a component in larger disputes over the garden as a mirror of nature and of the relationship of human beings to nature. There is a tendency today to regard the champions of formalism and of 'improvement' as guilty of hubristic dominion of the natural world for the pleasure and convenience of human beings. This is not, however, the way that matters were viewed by these champions, many of whom followed William Chambers in drawing a distinction between "vulgar" and "true" nature.[18] The gardener's intrusions into nature were necessary, as Horace Walpole put it, to "restore" to nature her "honours"—to reveal the true or essential aspects of nature that are typically opaque to human perception.[19] As the American garden writer, A. J. Downing, noted a few decades later, competing tendencies in English gardening registered conflicting visions of nature's "subtle essence". Where some identified an underlying symmetry and proportion in nature which it was the gardener's job to render salient, others experienced a wilder "energy" and "power" that it should be his ambition to capture. These competing perceptions of nature's essence encouraged, Downing continues, contrasting accounts of humanity's fundamental relationship to the natural world. On some accounts, human beings belong in and to the ordered, harmonious whole, which, in the eyes of many Enlightenment thinkers, nature as the product of a divine designer must be. On other accounts, they are engaged in a struggle between "spirit and matter", a battle to harness the "rough" energy revealed to the "Picturesque" gaze.[20]

Contemporary garden writers, by and large, tend not to dwell, like Downing, on the capacity of gardens to express or encapsulate large truths about the world and humanity, but there are still garden makers for whom this capacity remains a central focus. A well-known example is Charles Jencks's *Garden of Cosmic Speculation* in southwest Scotland, which is intended to communicate, among much else, the fractal geometrical forms of nature, the genetic structures of life, and even—through the device of a cascade—the story of evolution.[21] The "spiritual and cognitive experience" afforded by the garden is also the primary concern of the Spanish gardener, Fernando Caruncho.

Figure 4/ Mas de les Voltes.
A place to encounter space and invoke it through the garden.
Fernando Caruncho, Wheat and cypresses parterre, Catalonia, Spain.
Photograph courtesy of Fernando Caruncho.

Primarily by means of its geometry and grid forms—like those apparent in a wheat and cypress parterre he designed —a person is "enabled... to encounter space and to invoke it through the garden" [Figure 4]. More importantly, perhaps, the garden—as an extension of philosophy—is a location for studying and disclosing "the mythical-spiritual relation of man and the universe", for "reveal[ing] the analogies between man and the universe" and retrieving an innocent intimacy with nature that most people have lost.[22] Caruncho's remarks give modern voice to older ambitions to render the truth of the world, and of ourselves, through making and working in gardens

These ambitions have taken diverse forms, as this brief survey has shown. Different traditions have employed different conceptions of the truths that the garden is apt for conveying—contrasting views, for example, of the relationship between human beings and the world they occupy. Different proposals, too, have been made concerning the means by which gardens might convey truth—whether by symbolic representation, by intimating the source of things, by embodying the fundamental relationship between mind and nature, or in some other way.

Despite these differences, there are common themes among the approaches considered. To begin with, they share the thought that, among human creations, the garden is *especially* suited for communicating important truths about the world—particularly apt, say, to convey the ephemerality of things or the immense power of natural processes. There has been agreement, too, that the garden's special role has to do with gardening's obvious and immediate involvement with the natural world—with the elements, with plants, with creatures. Even in traditions where mind and nature are regarded as radically distinct, or where human beings are portrayed as engaged in a struggle with nature, it is recognized that there are essential connections between the human and the natural that gardens can disclose. There has been agreement, finally, that experience of gardens—especially, perhaps, the gardener's own experience—may be transformative, inducing a fresh understanding of people and nature, and thereby a new perspective on the good life. Caruncho speaks for many when he remarks that, appropriately experienced, gardens and gardening have a "power of transformation" which is able to shape reinterpretations of life [Figure 5].[23]

GARDENS AND MEANINGS

To claim that the garden may communicate large truths is to attribute great significance or meaning to the garden. Before I elaborate an account of what this meaning might be, I need to respond to voices that are skeptical about talk of the meaning of gardens. If it is justified, this skepticism not only threatens the idea of gardens as being 'in the truth', but of gardens as making an important contribution to the good life. For it is reasonable to hold that it is only in creations and practices which men and women find meaningful that such a contribution is made.

The story is told of an eminent British gardener who, visiting the *Garden of Cosmic Speculation*, remarked that he did not care about "the meaning of gardens" provided

Figure 5/ L'Amastuola. Horticulture with a power of transformation and able to shape reinterpretations of life. Fernando Caruncho, Vineyard project, Puglia, Italy. Photograph courtesy of Fernando Caruncho.

they looked nice. On this negative, anti-intellectual, and even philistine attitude towards gardens, we need not dwell, but more serious challenges to garden meaning may be found, in, for example, an erudite essay by the classicist, G. R. F. Ferrari, uncompromisingly titled "The Meaninglessness of Gardens". "When considered as works of art", Ferrari contends, "gardens have no meaning. They communicate nothing... they operate at the degree zero of meaning. And this is part of their charm."[24] Ferrari does not deny that parts of a garden may be intended to mean or symbolize something—a plant which is a traditional emblem of love, say, or a grotto representing the underworld. Nor does he deny that a whole tracts of a garden, as at Stourhead, may be "co-opted in order to produce something other than a work of garden art: a narrative".[25] But none of this gainsays the claim that, as an art work, the garden as a whole means nothing.

In order to avoid contentious issues about the status of gardens as art works, it is advisable, perhaps, to recast Ferrari's point as follows: to focus on what is meant by parts of gardens, or on the narratives which gardens may be co-opted to tell, is to fail to appreciate gardens for what they are, essentially 'a society of plants'—and to treat them, instead, as open-air museums or sculpture parks. So expressed, Ferrari's contention is one with which I sympathize. I have already remarked on the excessive emphasis, as I see it, on the references—to islands, mountains, or whatever—of rocks in Zen gardens. Where I demur

Figure 6/ Donnell Garden. Bodying forth the essential components of Modernism. Thomas Church, Sonoma, California. Photograph courtesy of Peter Frankel.

from Ferrari is in allowing a richer understanding of the notion of meaning than he does. As his examples indicate, Ferrari equates garden meaning with depiction, representation, and allusion—with, one might say, the referential functions of garden components. For him, it is because the garden as such—the garden as an artwork, he would say—has no such intended function that it is without a meaning.

However, the term "meaning" is a generous one: there are many different modes of meaning, many different ways in which something can be said to mean or communicate. A garden may not depict or represent some place or object, but it may express the feeling or mood of its maker. Or, it may be symptomatic of political or other currents of its time. Or, it may be significant for someone in virtue of the personal associations it evokes. And so on. These and many other modes of meaning may be exhibited by a garden.[26] Indeed, most of the claims considered above about the truths communicated by gardens, were not claims that the garden depicts or serves as an emblem of a truth. It is not, for instance, through picture-like representation or narrative device that, for Zen Buddhists, the garden is apt for evoking the impermanence of things.

Even if one were more enthusiastic over the emblematic, depictive, or narrative ambitions of gardens than Ferrari or myself, it cannot be meaning in these modes which the garden, to be 'in the truth', must have. And the same can be said about other modes of meaning just identified—meaning as emotional expression, for example. This is because what gardens depict, narrate, or express varies from garden to garden. As one admirer of the garden's representational role in Renaissance and eighteenth century tradition stresses, "fundamental to this perception of the garden was the belief that local circumstances would dictate the extent and modes of representation".[27] The garden's significance as communicating a fundamental truth of things, however, is something that the garden as such possesses. It does not vary according to the particular symbolic aims of gardeners and the traditions in which they work. Such, at any rate, is the claim I want to make good in this essay.

Someone will reasonably ask, at this point, what mode of meaning it could be that the garden as such possesses. How could a meaning be shared by *all* gardens? Well, this second question betrays a misunderstanding, which I need to correct. When I refer to the garden, I do not refer to all gardens, to gardens in general. I refer, rather, to 'exemplary' gardens—those that are good, paradigmatic instances of their kind and not, say, ones that have gone to seed, been buried beneath rubbish, or are made entirely of concrete. (To take an analogy, when I speak of the piano as a versatile instrument, or as one worth learning to play, I am not talking about all pianos—broken down ones and honky-tonks included—but only those which typify their kind.)

The answer to the question concerning the mode of meaning which the garden as such—exemplary gardens, in other words—can have is quick: exemplification. The idea, less quickly, is as follows. Something may signify or stand for something through being an especially salient instance of it—through, one might say, exemplifying or epitomizing it. Thus one might speak of a building like the Bauhaus as 'standing for' Modernist architecture: for it is not only a Modernist building, but one which, as it were, bodies forth the essential components of Modernism. Gardens, too, may signify through exemplifying. Like the Bauhaus, the Californian gardens of Thomas Church epitomize Modernist design, for they wear on their sleeve the functionality broadcast in Church's slogan "Gardens are for people" [Figure 6].

The question remains, however, what the exemplary garden as such might exemplify and thereby signify. How does one get from an account of what a garden designed by Thomas Church—or Humphrey Repton or Ji Cheng—exemplifies to a characterization of what *the* garden exemplifies? Rather than debate this question abstractly, it is better to let an answer emerge from the characterization for which I shall now argue.

CREATIVITY AND THE EXPERIENCE OF NATURE

In this section, I try to identify a fundamental aspect of reality which the garden and engagement with gardens exemplify or epitomize and, in virtue of so doing, may be described as being 'in the truth', as 'in the way of things'. Precedents for my proposal are found in claims—some of which we heard earlier—to the effect that gardens convey something about the relationship between humanity and the natural world. This is especially the case with claims that the garden 'mediates' between, 'reconciles', or demonstrates a 'unity' of human beings and nature. Claims like these are, however, only promissory notes: they call out for elucidation. What follows may be thought of as an attempt at elucidation.

The relationship between people and the natural world I want to expose is intimated by remarks of the Daoist thinker, Zhuangzi, around 300 BCE. In Chapter Six of the book attributed to him, Zhuangzi considers the questions of "what is done by the Heavenly" and what "is done by the Human". Here "Heaven" may be translated as "nature", and the philosopher's answer is that, in the final analysis, it is impossible to separate out the contributions of nature and man. "How could I know whether what I call the Heavenly is not really the Human?" The sage comes to see that, in the explanation of things, "neither the Heavenly nor the Human wins out over the other". In Chapter Two, the reason for this has been anticipated. Without the world, it is explained, "there would be no me... but without me there would be nothing selected out from it all [the world]".[28] Zhuangzi's point, I shall take it, is that it is impossible, even in principle, to determine what in our experience owes to human activity and what to our encounter with nature. And this is because, while there would be no experience, no 'me', without the natural world; nor could nature be encountered except through human practice, for without this, nothing in nature would be 'selected', nothing would stand out and figure for us. Human practice and nature as it is encountered are, therefore, deeply co-dependent: neither can be without the other, and it makes no sense to isolate their respective contributions to experience.

It is this thesis, I suggest, which is the real import of claims about the 'unity' of human beings and nature. I shall elaborate and defend it later, but I first want to indicate its bearing on the significance of the garden. Much ink has been spilled over the question of whether the garden is 'art' or 'nature', the favorite answer being that it is a combination or mixture of the two. But talk of combination and mixture—or of art 'added' to nature—is liable to mask the essential intimacy of the human and the natural that occurs in the garden. So salient is this occurrence that the garden exemplifies the deep co-dependence of human creativity and nature indicated above. As such, it epitomizes a large truth about the relationship of people to their world.

There is no need to labor the obvious, that gardening physically impacts nature just as natural processes physically affect the garden. Whether the flowers grow well depends partly on the efforts of the gardener, just as the outcome of such endeavors depends on the weather, soil composition, and other natural phenomena. No garden is able to flourish without cooperation between human skill and nature. But the mutual dependence between endeavor and nature is not confined to these physical exchanges. Of greater interest are what might be termed phenomenological exchanges—ways in which perceptions of nature influence the gardener's art and, conversely, ways in which this art shapes experience of nature.

Consider, for example, the use of stones in a gardening tradition like that found in the surrounds of Zen temples. As a Japanese gardening manual famously put it, the placing of a stone should heed "the request of the stone" [Figure 7].[29] How and where the stone is placed will be a response to a way of experiencing natural objects and places—beaches on which stones are found, mountains from which they have tumbled. Conversely, the placing of the stone affects further experience of the natural environment—by, for example, rendering salient a distant, previously inconspicuous hill whose contours resembles the stone's.

Or consider the relationships between a gardener's creations and an experience of wildness in nature. As with the Piccolomini Palace mentioned earlier, it may be the intention of the designer to emphasize a terrain's wildness by forcing the viewer to see it from within a formal, unmistakeably artifactual garden. Conversely, a characteristically modern perception of birds and other creatures as endangered wildlife, rather than as pests, may encourage the gardener to place bird-baths or bee-friendly bushes around the lawn.

One could keep piling up examples of, say, statuary which alters a perception of the orientation of trees and plants, or of the 'borrowed' scenery beyond the garden wall which gives to the garden within a mood or texture which it would not otherwise have had. But the point made is that, in the garden, co-dependence between human creativity and encountering or receiving nature is perspicuous, salient. The garden, more perhaps than any other art, displays the creative receptivity which humane practices presuppose. It is no accident, surely, that—whether in ancient China, Medieval Japan, or modern France—painters have taken inspiration from their work in the garden. Cézanne, who liked portraying his own gardener, Vallier, was speaking of gardening as much as of painting when he referred to creative work as "the union of the world [nature] and the individual".[30]

It is worth adding that co-dependence does not operate only at the individual level, between a particular garden and its creator's experience of the natural world. Whole styles or movements in garden-making may discernibly owe to, and in turn reinforce and educate ways of encountering nature. Indeed, we have already encountered examples of this, in the Picturesque movement, for instance. Innovations in garden making—and in landscape painting—helped to inspire a perception of craggy mountains, not as deviations from the essentially regular geometrical structure of nature, but as expressions of an unbounded natural energy.

Figure 7/ Japanese Garden. Heeding the request of the stone. Cornwall, UK. Photograph by David E. Cooper.

Figure 8/ Temple of Poseidon. Enabling earth to emerge. Sounion, Greece. Photograph by Annette Giesecke.

This, it was held by advocates of the Picturesque, is an energy to which creative artists, including gardeners, should be receptive and which they should seek to register in their works.

Granted that it is important to recognize the garden as a site of co-dependence, some readers might worry that it is nevertheless hyperbolic to speak of the garden as therefore communicating 'the way of things' and being 'in the truth'. In response, I want to emphasize just how fundamental is the co-dependence of which I have been speaking. Put dramatically, without it there could be neither ourselves nor a natural world for us to encounter. To accept this, one needs to appreciate that co-dependence between human practice and experience of nature goes, so to speak, all the way down and all the way back.

It helps foster this appreciation to think about cultural practices and experiences of nature remote from our own—ones that we do not take for granted and therefore fail to attend to. Consider, for instance, the sixteenth century Japanese tea ceremony and the building and garden in which it took place. To attain proper understanding of the ceremony and of the design of the building and garden requires exploration of a whole culture and a whole way of experiencing the natural world. It requires, more exactly, reflection on practices that presuppose ways of receiving the natural world—ways which in turn are shaped by these and related practices. A heightened sense of the ephemeral character of natural phenomena is, in the ceremony and its setting, intimately tied to a style of practice, to the cultivation of a stillness that makes possible attention to the evanescent and fugitive.

When I speak of co-dependence going all the way down, I mean that there is no level at which experience of nature is raw, uninformed by human practice, and no level at which practice is uninformed by ways of experiencing nature. Oscar Wilde exaggerates, of course, in calling nature "our creation". But in his insistence—against those who postulated "an innocent eye" for detecting nature in the raw,—that "how we see it, depends on the Arts that have influenced us", he is right.[31] There is, as William James put it, no way of "weeding out" the "human contribution" to the perception of the natural world, for this perception presupposes a process of selection grounded in our purposes and practices.[32]

When I speak of co-dependence going all the way back, I mean that there never was a time when creative engagement with the world was not already informed by ways of experiencing nature, nor a time when these were not already responsive to that engagement. Practice and experience of nature are 'always already' interfused. Again, it helps to think of a culture remote from our own, as Martin Heidegger does in a celebrated passage on an ancient Greek temple. The temple—or, more generally, Greek art—gave to natural things, such as eagles, rocks, and trees their "look": in effect, it enabled "earth" to "emerge" for the Greeks as it did [Figure 8]. But, at the same time, the look of natural things and the way in which Earth was experienced helped to forge the Greek people's "outlook on themselves"—an outlook which imbued their politics, their literature, and their cultural practices, including the building of temples.[33] Heidegger's point is that, at no stage, did culture precede experience of nature or *vice-versa*, so there is no way, even in principle, of isolating them from one another. In his later writings, Heidegger applies this point to modern technology and a complicit way of "revealing" nature. Technological innovation, and the arts and crafts associated with it, served to shape a perception of nature as "equipment" to be employed for industrial and agricultural purposes. This mode of revealing nature, in turn, encourages or dictates further innovations and technically creative interventions into forests, oceans, and other natural environments.[34] Here, as in ancient Greece and indeed everywhere, human endeavor and human reception of the natural world are always already together in mutual dependence.

It is not hyperbolic to describe this co-dependence as a fundamental aspect of existence. Indeed, "fundamental" is the apt term, for co-dependence is the ground on which human practice and people's experience of nature stand—the condition for the very possibility, therefore, of human life as we know it. It is not hyperbolic to describe a human activity as 'in the truth', as showing 'the way of things', if it exemplifies or epitomizes this fundamental aspect, this relationship between the human and the natural. And it is this, I have argued, which is achieved when we make and work in gardens. The point is not that the garden is unique in manifesting co-dependence. On the contrary, since co-dependence goes all the way down and back, then *every* human practice presupposes it. What is special about the garden is not that it is an example of co-dependence (for so is every human product), but that it exemplifies it, in the sense explained earlier. The garden, appropriately contemplated or engaged with, renders co-dependence salient, bodies it forth, shows it up.

But can this explain the garden's place in utopian thought, in incorporating and conveying visions of the good life? The question is a request, in effect, for connecting my claims on behalf of the garden's significance with the topic of the virtues that have figured in garden discourses. This connection is made in the next and final section of the essay.

CO-DEPENDENCE AND THE VIRTUOUS GARDENER

In making the connection between co-dependence and virtue, I am also trying to answer another question that some readers will be asking. Even ones sympathetic to the idea of the garden as a site and epitome of co-dependence will wonder if this does much to explain why so many people over the millennia have invested such significance in the garden. Isn't the thesis of co-dependence too 'abstract', too 'philosophical', to account for why more than a few people have discerned in the garden a place of truth and goodness?

The question perhaps underestimates the number of people who explicitly assent to *something like* the idea of co-dependence. My proposal was intended to lend greater precision and substance to what, after all, is a long-standing and popular rhetoric of gardens as reconciling, even uniting, culture and nature, human beings and the natural world. Some idea of unity, we noted, has imbued all the traditions of gardening sketched earlier in this essay. But let's grant that, if the idea of co-dependence explains recognition of the garden as a site of virtue and truth, this is not generally because the idea is explicitly articulated and endorsed. Appreciation of co-dependence, typically, is something more implicit. But implicit in what? My answer is that it is implicit in virtuous garden practice—in gardening which exhibits virtues whose status *as* virtues presupposes a sense of the garden as exemplifying co-dependence. And this answer, in effect, helps one to gain a view of the connection between the garden as a site of truth and the garden as an integral part of the good life. It is because the garden, as an epitome of co-dependence, is 'in the truth' that certain garden practices can be virtuous, and hence constituents in a good life.

All sorts of alleged virtues have been attributed to gardening, including some rather Promethean and 'macho' ones. (The ex-army Scottish creator of the Villa Taranto, near Lake Maggiore, clearly regarded the site he had purchased as terrain for the exercise of such military virtues as bold attack [on trees] and technological initiative.) However, in several great traditions of gardening—and in much garden writing of the last hundred years—the pre-eminent virtues associated with gardening have been of a gentler kind: they include care and compassion, humility and gratitude, hope and respect.[35]

It is possible, no doubt, for someone to exercise such virtues, in the context of the garden, in an unreflective way, without recognition even of their being virtues. The reflective gardener, conversely, will have a sense of the care or gratitude that he or she exercises as appropriate attitudes, ones called for by the very practice of gardening—as virtues of gardening, in effect. It is difficult, in my judgement, to explain or understand this sense without appealing to an implicit appreciation of the co-dependent relationship between human craft and nature.

Consider, first, care and compassion. Caring for plants and other ingredients in a garden is, of course, a precondition of having a flourishing garden at all. But if care is to be a virtue, and not simply a requirement of horticultural prudence, it involves an awareness of responsibility for beings whose good depends on one's

Figure 9/ Contemporary Topiary. Care and compassion, or violation of a plant's integrity? Shanghai Century Park. Photograph courtesy of Wendy Kershaw.

actions. This dependence is not only of a simple physical kind, but phenomenological too. To flourish, a flower must not only be watered and kept free from weeds: it must also be placed appropriately, so that, for example, it is properly visible to be enjoyed, and allowed to show itself for what it is, not overwhelmed by neighboring flowers whose vivid reds 'kill' its quieter color. Compassion, as a virtue, is not simply a feeling aroused by the fate of living things: it is a disposition to step in—to help, to cure—when a living being is seen to be suffering. So compassion, too, requires recognition of a practical dependence upon human activity of natural beings in the garden. These beings need not be sentient. There is nothing absurd in the Buddhist idea that living beings, even when they do not feel, may 'suffer': for they have a good—a way they should be if they are to flourish as things of their kind—which can be threatened. When they are perceived to be thus threatened, compassion is an appropriate, not a merely sentimental or anthropomorphic response. (Ferrari's metaphor, alluded to earlier, of the garden as a society of plants, of living beings, deserves attention in this connection.)

If care and compassion presuppose recognition of a dependence of natural life on human practice, then humility and gratitude rest on appreciation of the gardener's dependence on the natural world [Figure 9]. According to Alexander Pope, it is a gardener fallen victim to the hubristic pride that "misguide[s] the mind" who fails to acknowledge the "grace beyond the reach of art" that enables him to succeed in his efforts.[36] It is easy to fall victim to this, since it is easy to forget just how much the grace of nature contributes to the success of even the simplest act of gardening—to forget, say, the cooperation of the weather, the quality of soil in which the seeds were planted, the help of the worms and other subterranean creatures necessary for the plants to grow, and so on. Nor, once again, is this dependence solely a physical one. For the planting to achieve its desired effect on the viewer, a glimpse of distant scenery, appropriate atmospheric conditions, and the chirping of birds or insects may all be necessary. Traditional Japanese craftsmen did not put their name to the things they made, thereby acknowledging the degree of "Other Power" on which the quality of what they made relied.[37] Humility calls for a similar acknowledgment on the part of the gardener.

Humility, combined with appreciation of the worth of what the gardener may achieve in cooperation with natural processes, yields the Epicurean virtue of gratitude. A life goes well, Epicurus judged, only when it is free both of resentment at past misfortunes and of an exclusive (and stressful) focus on future goals. The gratitude of the wise and happy person is an acknowledgment that, calmly observed, the life which is given to one is typically something to celebrate.[38] In the language of those Japanese craftsmen, the "Other Power" on which the fortune of the garden depends calls for gratitude on the part of the person who is able to enjoy the garden, free from anger at last winter's storm and from anxiety about the size of next summer's marrows.

A further virtue does refer to the future: hope. As a virtue, hope is not the making of cheerful predictions, but a quiet (and qualified) confidence that skilled, reflective, and virtuous human practice will yield good results. Without hope—without faith in their efficacy—it is hard to see why any other virtues should be cultivated or exercised. The gardener who plants and tends in hope is, in fact, acknowledging co-dependence in both its aspects. There must, on the one hand, be appreciation that this work is effective, that natural processes in the garden will respond to it, that flowers will prosper, and vegetables grow fat. But hope involves appreciation, too, that despite the fragile prospects of success, nature will generally favor the gardener's undertakings when these are sensible and benign. The gardener's dependence on nature is like that of someone on a stern, but finally fair and benevolent guardian.

The virtue, finally, of respect for nature also contains an acknowledgment of co-dependence in both its dimensions. Or better, perhaps, respect is not a single virtue, but two distinguishable ones. There is respect, first, in the sense of acknowledgment of something's independence, power, and integrity. In respecting nature's processes in this sense, the gardener is once again acknowledging and admiring what, it is conceded, exceeds human control and purpose. Perhaps one should say what *ought* to exceed human control: for respect for integrity may demand that one refrains from imposing certain purposes on living beings. The objection to some topiary, for instance, is that the form imposed on a shrub—that of a phallus, say, or of Mickey Mouse—violates the integrity of the plant. But respect is shown, too, when the needs of someone or something are acknowledged, alongside an obligation to intervene when these needs are not being met. The gardener's respect for wildlife would be respect only in name, unless exhibited in the form of a readiness to protect creatures when their lives are threatened by freezing weather, drought or whatever. This readiness registers recognition of the dependence of natural beings on the gardener's practice.

One could go on identifying further virtues of gardening that owe their status as virtues to their consonance with a co-dependent relationship between human practice and nature. But the ones I have identified are sufficient, I hope, to secure this conclusion. The exercise of the gardener's virtues is at once a vehicle for and especially suited to appreciation of this relationship between practice and nature. Precisely because the gardener's practices of care, humility, hope, and the rest are, when undertaken in appreciation of that relationship, genuinely virtuous ones, they belong in the economy of a good life. Because of this, in turn, they reasonably figure in utopian discourses of the garden.

Doubtless there will remain people for whom, as for Dr. Johnson, gardening is only an "innocent amusement", even when it is conducted with care, humility, respect, and the like. But this would be to ignore the reflective gardener's sense that, when gardening is so conducted, it is replete with significance as an epitome of the way of things. To be engaged in something that one knows to be possessed of meaning, even if one struggles to articulate that meaning, is to be engaged in more than an amusement.

Notes

1. Quoted in Tom Turner, *Garden History: Philosophy and Design 2000 BC–2000 AD*, London: Spon, 2005, p. 138.
2. Pliny, *The Letters of the Younger Pliny*, Betty Radice ed., London: Penguin, 1963, pp. 43, 112.
3. Quoted in Kairan Li, *Landscape improvement and Scenic Sites in Pre-modern China: a critical review*, Ph.D. Thesis, Sheffield University, 2009, p. 152.
4. Aristotle, *Nicomachean Ethics*, Terence Irwin trans., Indianapolis: Hacket, 1999, p. 1144b.
5. See David E. Cooper and Simon James, *Buddhism, Virtue and Environment*, Aldershot: Ashgate, 2005, pp. 79–80.
6. Keping, Wang, *The Classic of the Dao: A New Investigation*, 2004, p. 250.
7. Harrison, Robert Pogue, *Gardens: An Essay on the Human Condition*, Chicago: University of Chicago Press, 2008, pp. 73–74.
8. Harrison, *Gardens*, p. 124.
9. Keane, Marc, *Japanese Landscape Design*, Boston: Tuttle, 1996, p. 128.
10. The concept of "miniaturization" is discussed in Jeffrey Meyer,

"Salvation in the garden: Daoism and ecology", *Daoism and Ecology*, N. J. Girardot, James Miller, and Xiaogan Liu eds., Boston: Harvard University Press, 2001, p. 224. For the *Yuan Ye*, see Ji Cheng, *The Craft of Gardens*, Alison Hardie trans., New Haven: Yale University Press, 1988, p. 121; and for the "distillation of the universe", Thomas Hoover, *Zen Culture*, New York: Random House, 1977, Kindle loc. 2176.
11. Keswick, Maggie, *The Chinese Garden: History, Art and Architecture*, London: Academy, 1978, p. 82.
12. Quoted in Zdenek Hrdlička, *The Art of Japanese Gardening*, London: Hamlyn, 1989, p. 11.
13. Meyer, "Salvation in the garden", p. 223; Herrigel, Gustie, *Zen and the Art of Flower Arrangement*, R. F. C. Hull trans., London: Souvenir, 1999, p. 88.
14. Quoted in William Howard Adams, *Nature Perfected: Gardens through History*, New York: Abbeville Press, 1991, p. 92.
15. Alberti, Leon, *The Ten Books of Architecture*, Giacomo Leoni trans., New York: Dover, 1986, p. 195.
16. Strong, Roy, "Renaissance Gardens", *The Oxford Companion to the Garden*, Patrick Taylor ed., Oxford: Oxford University Press, 2006, p. 403.
17. Mabey, Richard, *Beechcombings: The Narratives of Trees*, London: Vintage, 2008, p. 134; Knox quoted in John Dixon Hunt and Peter Willis, *The Genius of the Place: The English Landscape Garden 1620–1820*, Cambridge, MA: MIT Press, 1988, pp. 330–331.
18. Quoted in Hunt and Willis, *The Genius of the Place*, p. 322.
19. Quoted in Hunt and Willis, *The Genius of the Place*, p. 316.
20. Downing, Andrew, *Landscape Gardening and Rural Architecture*, New York: Dover, 1991, pp. 57, 61. See also Mabey, *Beechcombings*, pp. 133–145.
21. Jencks, Charles, *The Garden of Cosmic Speculation*, London: Frances Lincoln, 2003.
22. Caruncho, Fernando, "The Spirit of the Geometrician", *Vista: The Culture and Politics of Gardens*, Noël Kingsbury and Tim Richardson eds., London: Frances Lincoln, 2005, pp. 111–116.
23. Caruncho, "The Spirit of the Geometrician", p. 114.
24. Ferrari, G. R. F., "The Meaninglessness of Gardens", *The Journal of Aesthetics and Art Criticism*, vol. 68, no. 1, Winter 2010, p. 37.
25. Ferrari, "The Meaninglessness of Gardens", pp. 38–39.
26. See David E. Cooper, *A Philosophy of Gardens*, Oxford: Clarendon Press, 2006, pp. 108–128; and Mara Miller, *The Garden as an Art*, Albany: State University of New York Press, 1993.
27. Hunt, John Dixon, "Gardens: Historical Overview", *Encyclopedia of Aesthetics*, Michael Kelly ed., New York: Oxford University Press, 1998, p. 273.
28. Zhuangzi, *Zhuangzi: The Essential Writings*, Brook Ziporyn trans., Indianapolis: Hackett, 2009, pp. 10, 41–42.
29. See Jiro Takei and Marc Keane, *Sakuteiki: Visions of the Japanese Garden*, Boston: Tuttle, 2001, p. 4.
30. Kendall, Richard, *Cézanne by Himself: drawings, paintings, writings*, Edison, NJ: Chartwell Books, 1994, p. 289; "Creative receptivity" is Gabriel Marcel's phrase.
31. Wilde, Oscar, "The Decay of Lying", *Complete Works of Oscar Wilde*, London: Collins, 1968, p. 986.
32. James, William, "Pragmatism and Humanism", *The Writings of William James*, John McDermott ed., Chicago: University of Chicago Press, 1977, p. 45.
33. Heidegger, Martin, *Poetry, Language, Thought*, Albert Hofstadter trans., New York: Harper and Row, 1971, pp. 41ff.
34. See the essays in Martin Heidegger, *The Question Concerning Technology and Other Essays*, William Lovitt trans., New York: Harper and Row, 1977.
35. See Isis Brook, "The Virtues of Gardening", *Gardening Philosophy for Everyone: Cultivating Wisdom*, Dan O'Brien ed., Chichester: Wiley-Blackwell, 2010; and Cooper, *A Philosophy of Gardens*, Chapter 5.
36. Pope, Alexander, *Essay on Man and Other Poems*, New York: Dover, 1994, pp. 8f.
37. See Muneyoshi Yanagi, *The Unknown Craftsman: a Japanese Insight into Beauty*, Bernard Leach trans., Tokyo: Kodansha, 1989.
38. See Harrison, *Gardens*, pp. 78f. and Annette L. Giesecke, *The Epic City: Urbanism, Utopia, and the Garden in Ancient Greece and Rome*, Cambridge MA: Harvard University Press, 2nd ed. 2010, pp. 81f. and Chapter 3.

ON SACRED GROUND: THE SOMMERBERGER GARDEN

/UWE CLAUS
/ANNETTE GIESECKE, TRANS.

When you walk into the forest, don't forget to knock.
/ Bengt af Klintberg

The path up and the path down are one and the same.
/ Heraclitus

Beside my Zen practice I plant rare trees and set particularly expressive rocks; so it is that I achieve the impression of a landscape.
/ Kogaku Soko[1]

Above the German Baroque city Amorbach im Odenwald, along the Sommerberg's southwestern slope, lie the ancient agrarian plots Im Heiligen (On Sacred Ground) and Im Obern Mäurich. Upon arrival of the new millennium, it was here that, just above a popular hiking path that ascends to the Medieval Gotthardsruine (a Gothic column basilica), a strolling garden was created on a sloping, rectangular plot of forest approximately a hectare in size.[2]

Towards the end of the twentieth century, art collector Michael Berger invited me to visit this forest plot above Amorbach, which he had acquired some 40 years earlier as a young man.[3] As he explained to me, this landscape conjured happy memories of his childhood, a time in which he spent long days of boisterous play with his friends. As the decades passed, the property was left undisturbed, enshrouded by lush vegetation. A myriad of fallen trees, entwined with climbing hop, blackberry, rose, honeysuckle, and ivy, had been transformed into a nearly impenetrable thicket—a closed, truly magical wilderness concealing at its core the buried traces of agriculture.

Fruit trees, some gnarled and others shattered by the weight of years, as well as the remnants of ancient terraces braced by sandstone walls and linked by steps—relics of human cultivation—serve as reminders of times in which vineyards, orchards, and vegetable gardens were laboriously tended here. Indeed, vineyards, stocked with Riesling and a bit of Elbling, were cultivated here for hundreds of years until the middle of the nineteenth century when they were abandoned upon the catastrophic infestation of grape phylloxera.[4]

Michael Berger explained to me that he wished to make something of this wilderness again and asked if I could imagine ways of doing this. Finding the atmosphere of this impassible terrain moving—"trees and undergrowth grow in profusion around the ruins"—and finding the prospect of immersing myself more deeply in such an enchanted, mystical place thoroughly compelling, I accepted [Figure 1].[5]

In terms of my self-conceptualization as an artist, exposure to those unique gardens that for hundreds of years served as material expressions of Far Eastern aesthetics had proven formative.[6] And for me they have remained a source of endless wonder. Since the 1980s, the experience of their enchanting atmosphere has prompted me to pursue the relationship of powers residing in rocks, crags, and plants through my art. It was Buddhist and Daoist monks, as well as learned aristocratic creators of gardens in China, Korea, and Japan, who subtly employed the existing landscape and its various aspects as the basis for their memorable creations. Both the philosophical underpinnings of these gardens, themselves expressions of a poetic world view, and the historical background of the Sommerberg, together with its physical condition, would serve as inspiration for my treatment of this wooded mountain slope.

SITE CONDITION

An initial inventory of the site's trees revealed an unusually broad range of species. Nearly 30 different native and exotic trees were found within the boundaries of this, in part, steep wooded site. Oak (*Quercus robur*) and hornbeam (*Carpinus betulus*) formed groves of varied density alongside the lofty forest at its eastern boundary. One of these oaks is the largest and surely the oldest tree on the property. Beneath its mighty, low-growing limbs runs the path up to the garden's entrance.

The groves themselves are interspersed with ancient fruit trees that Johann Philip Bronner mentioned in his critical discussion of Amorbach's viticulture. In the course of a visit to the Sommerberg region in 1839, the Grand Ducal privy counselor from Baden, himself a vineyard owner and chemist, remarked upon "whole stands of fruit trees that interrupt the planted grapevines' usual uniformity and lend the whole a pleasing aspect". Here he found "walls... so filled with grapes, peaches, figs, and pome fruit that they appear veritably overcrowded".[7]

Figure 1/ Entrance to the Sommer Berger Garden.
A part of the UNESCO Geo-Naturepark, Bergstrasse-Odenwald, Germany. Photograph courtesy of Matthias Hubert.

Of the trees he mentioned, one may still find: apple (*Malus spec.*), cherry (*Cerasus spec.*), plum (*Prunus spec.*), sloe (*Prunus spinosa*), quince (*Cydonia oblonga*), and hazelnut (*Corylus avellana*). One may also find solitary exemplars of linden (*Tilia cordata*), ash (*Fraxinus excelsior*), sycamore (*Acer pseudo-platanus*), and Norway maple (*Acer platanoides*) as well as, on higher ground, several birch (*Betula pendula*) and pine (*Pinus sylvestris*). The varieties of chestnut (*Castanea sativa*) and walnut (*Juglans regia*) appearing in this area have established themselves with seedlings in the underbrush.

By contrast, the western and uppermost areas of the property are dominated by a stand of black locust (*Robinia pseudoacacia*), a species imported from North America since the seventeenth century. In their sparse understory grow hawthorn (*Crataegus spec.*), elder (*Sambucus nigra*), American snowberry (*Symphoricarpos rivularis*), ivy (*Hedera helix*), and wild common hop (*Humulus lupulus*). Black locust and snowberry were presumably first introduced to the region in 1806/1807, likely in connection with the Amorbach castle's Lake Garden, which was redesigned by Friedrich Ludwig von Sckell (1750–1823), the most important proponent of the English and Anglo-Chinese styles of landscape design in southern Germany at the time. Sckell was deeply influenced by British landscape architects Capability Brown (1716–1783) and William Chambers (1723–1796). Looking down from the Sommer Berger Garden to the valley's floor, one can sometimes descry the sun's reflection in the tree-ringed waters of the lake garden on clear winter and spring afternoons.

Walls, stairways, and drainage channels constructed in the olden days of red sandstone—and so too a small grotto dating from the vineyard's time—have survived as remains in the Baroque city's periphery. Johann Phillip Bronner's description of the condition of the structures on the Sommerberg's slopes in 1839 reads as follows:

> One could almost believe that a certain indifference to this form of cultivation had already taken root at some stage in the past, since most of the vineyards have irregular divisions and boundaries dating to

> earlier times. The furrows—the boundaries, that is—that are in part points of entry and in part water conduits are also usually crooked and zigzagging, which is why the field lots and terraces that every vineyard has in abundance, are carefully marked with boundary stones. Every terrace has its own stairway consisting of rocks protruding from the side of the wall.[8]

By the year 2000, entire sections of this sandstone construction had been completely buried under the red, sandy soil or had crumbled utterly; only parts were still in good repair. It appeared logical to incorporate, secure, and, where necessary, restore these testimonies of prior cultivation in the new garden's design.

Figure 2/ View of Amorbach from the Beuchner Mountain. Attributed to Ludwig Müller, c. 1881, artist and mayor of Amorbach 1862–1881. Archiv Bernhard Springer, Amorbach. Courtesy of Bernhard Springer.

DESIGN METHODOLOGY

It appeared more appropriate to employ an intuitive, experiential methodology inspired by Japanese garden designers than to base the new garden's conception on a grand master plan. Thus one would make one's way slowly through the landscape, considering detail after unfolding detail and carefully weighing progressively emerging possibilities. As landscape architect Marc Peter Keane had realized, "if one were to divide off a portion of forest and tend it for several years, or even decades, by raking and weeding, it would ultimately manifest all the aesthetic characteristics of the Japanese garden".[9] His words contained a spiritual design approach that could be productively applied at the Sommerberg.

I decided to devote myself to the Sommerberg's sacred ground for a period of several years, spending a few weeks in spring and fall there accompanied by a trusted assistant, and in the course of this free, unrestrained working process, design results would emerge. Only a design template consisting of nine equal squares, itself modeled on the Lo Shu diagram that the Chinese had applied to the layout of architecture and gardens for thousands of years, was employed at the commencement of the design process:[10]

4	9	2
3	5	7
8	1	6

This diagram (referred to henceforth as LS) made it possible to map the distribution of various species of trees. Having studied the site carefully, we were able to conclude that hornbeam dominates two of the nine squares (LS 2 and 7), oak dominate three (LS 8, 1, and 6), and black locust dominate four (LS 4, 9, 3, and 5). The black locusts' excess determined the removal of all specimens in the central square 5, where their seeds and root suckers had spread some 20 years earlier. The slopes of square 5 were then cleared and transformed into a terraced meadow traversed by footpaths. The meadow, its southwesterly terracing reminiscent of the ancient vineyard, became a central, focal clearing for the entire property. From the grotto located at the clearing's uppermost edge a wide view emerged once more: over the tops of the old oaks at the garden's base, over Amorbach into the Mud-Bach Valley and onto the wooded ridges of Wolkmann Mountain as well as of the Beuchner and Preunschener Mountains to the southwest [Figure 2]. The meadow's strategic creation therefore enabled the inclusion of valley and distant summits as elements in the upper garden's composition once more. Such 'borrowed' landscapes are expressions of the integrating principle known in Japanese garden design as *shakkei* and in Chinese, *chie ching*, which may be defined as "borrowed scenery" or "landscape captured alive".[11]

GARDEN ELEMENTS

Garden elements will be described in the order in which a garden visitor would ideally encounter them, namely in an experiential succession. Naturally, this ideal itinerary constitutes just one of many possible ways to experience and enjoy this garden; repeated visits would surely lead to the discovery of favorite side paths and resting places as well as of entirely new ways up and down. The various components of this garden bear the mark of literary and art historical allusions that served as inspirations for its conception. These allusions may serve as experiential stimuli, to be contemplated individually or as landmarks in a spiritual journey, itinerant dreams, set against the garden's scenic backdrop. Should this remote garden serve the visitor as a place to read undisturbed or as a locus for poetic rendezvous, either would be most welcomingly enhanced.

A loosely constructed wooden fence on the garden's lower terraces (LS 6, 1, 8) accompanies the path along the mountain's uphill slope. Catching sight of this simple, minimal enclosure may awaken a desire—certainly more strongly in some ascending hikers than in others—to discover for themselves what secrets may lie hidden at the grove's very heart. "Following the line of a fence, he arrived at an entrance gate."[12] So reads the Ming Dynasty erotic story, "Tale of a Spring Dream", which, through its elegant diction, relates the chance discovery of a mythical garden realm. Here the poet's sensual experience as he wanders through the wooded surroundings of his hometown ultimately manifests itself as a supernatural encounter with two enchanting fairies who dwell in a plum and an apple tree.

Above all, it is this enclosure, consisting of wooden fences and gates of stone, that defines this place 'on sacred ground' as a garden. The fence itself was constructed employing hemp cord and wooden posts derived from the black locust that had been removed to create the central clearing. In style, the garden's simple fence is reminiscent of a Japanese 'four-eyed' bamboo lattice fence, *Yotsume-gaki*.[13] Having reached the old, mighty oak at the path's edge, the visitor, walking beneath it, arrives at two simple gates, one of them stone and the other wooden (LS 8). The latter suggests the *torii* erected at Japanese Shinto shrines to demarcate the sacred space's boundary. Beyond this gate, a winding path running parallel to the slope leads to the lowest of the garden's terrace plateaus. Here spring yields expansive drifts of yellow daffodils blooming where trees grow less densely. The second gate, that of stone, opens onto a stairway leading up to the garden's higher elevations (LS 8, 3, 4).

As religious historian Mircea Eliade observed, entrance into any sacred precinct constitutes an initiation, as a result of which it is not possible for everyone to reemerge unchanged:

> The enclosure, wall, or circle of stones surrounding a sacred place—these are among the most ancient of known forms of man-made sanctuary.... The enclosure does not only imply and indeed signify the continued presence of a kratophany or hierophany within its bounds; it also serves the purpose of preserving profane man from danger to which he would expose himself by entering it without due care. The sacred is always dangerous to anyone who comes into contact with it unprepared, without having gone through the gestures of approach that every religious act demands.[14]

Turning to the narrow stone entrance gate leading upwards, the visitor descries an epigram carved into the lintel: "WHEN YOU WALK INTO THE FOREST, DON'T FORGET TO KNOCK. BENGT AF KLINTBERG".[15] The Swedish anthropologist and poet's lovely directive calls upon all who enter to heed and respect the forest and its inhabitants. Having crossed the threshold, the ascending visitor encounters the Sommer Berger Garden's elevated terraces. Here a network of paths some 700 meters in length winds its way up the slope through the groves and clearing, but all levels may also be accessed via the stone stairway that serves as a link to a walking path higher up in the woods and that marks the garden's upper boundary.

The narrow stairway, lying largely in ruins, was overgrown and only partially preserved intact. Steps still remaining *in situ* were set anew, and missing sections were reconstructed with steps and short runs of paving to create a long, rugged stair of archaic character over 80 meters in length. The stair's base is marked by a newly planted gingko tree (*Gingko biloba*), an important inclusion in Chinese and Japanese temple gardens. This unique tree has the potential of reaching a very old age in this location. Some of the original sections of stair are steep, so steep that one should avail oneself of them only for ascent. It is a veritable stairway to heaven, and every step taken becomes a metaphor of incarnations one has previously lived. "The ritual climbing up to heaven is a *durohana*, a 'difficult climb'", as Eliade describes it.[16] The ascent is necessarily a steep path, full of dangers, for it is a rite of passage from profane to sacred, from the ephemeral and illusionistic to the real and everlasting, from death to life, from man to god; "Every ascent is a breakthrough, as far as different levels of existence are concerned, a passing to what is beyond, an escape from profane space and human status." Thus a mortal "can enter the heavens which are impregnated with holiness, and become like gods. Their contact with the starry heavens makes them divine".

Heraclitus had once postulated that "the path up and the path down are one and the same". Yet the physically demanding ascent appears a very different experience from the descent. Every step of this stairway differs in size and shape from that which precedes it, and the ascent demands the visitor's fullest attention. The heart beats faster, inducing a keener mental acuity. With every deepening breath, the visitor's surroundings assume a greater clarity. Time's passage slows, veritably decelerating the visitor's pace. Halfway up, the visitor encounters a bench of stone set amongst the airy growths of black locust (LS 3). Even early in the year, this bench is warmed by the sun's vernal rays, sources of an absorbed energy that exclaims: "WARM UP AND GIVE A KISS! U WE." For "energy stems from two poles, male and female".[17] Without a burning heart, no ascent to heaven is possible. Appropriately, box, originating from the Mediterranean, runs along the stairway to heaven. The box's hard, horn-like, densely-growing wood has, since time immemorial, been the source of Cupid's arrows—or so the story goes. So potent are Cupid's arrows that none whom they strike, whether god or goddess, nymph or human, can withstand the flames he ignites.

Small paths running parallel to the slope cross back and forth over the ascending heaven's stairway: again, "ascents, the climbing of mountains or stairs, ... always signify a transcending of the human and a penetration into higher cosmic levels" [Figure 3].[18] On high, greater celandine (*Chelidonium majus*), grape hyacinth (*Muscaria latifolium*), and wood hyacinth (*Hyacinthoides hispanica*) appear. Yellow fawn lilies (*Erythronium californicum 'Pagoda'*) peek timidly from under fallen trees, thickly covered with ivy. One path branches off, soon disappearing into the impassable wilderness. "Sweet it is in hallowed wilderness to wander... taking respite in solitude", wrote Friedrich Hoelderlin (1770–1843), yearning to become one with Nature.[19]

Progressing to still greater elevations, the visitor, now nearly at the stairway's end, reaches a small earthen terrace ringed and shaded by hawthorn. Here evergreen Chinese clematis (*Clematis armandii*) entwines thorny shrubbery. Its white blossoms, opening in the early spring or late winter—so too the flower umbels appearing later in May—lend their thorny hosts a distinctive odor. According to old European traditions, particularly the Celtic, passed down to the present day, hawthorn marks fairies' dwelling places. It is an inviting place, sheltered by protective powers: a shady spot perfect to linger in, to enjoy an alfresco meal on a hot summer afternoon, to enjoy an undisturbed read, to play a game of chess, or to play an instrument. There are just enough small fragments of red sandstone with which to perform the finale of Nam June Paik's *Symphony Nr. 5*: "behold how a tiny pebble grows to a rocky mountain! Play on...".[20]

Everywhere red rock: from slabs of red stone to the red sand of the footpaths, up and down the mountain. Other sorts of rock appear, but only sporadically, having been transported here. Everywhere allusions to T. S. Eliot's "shadow of red rock", or, even more pronounced, to Buddhist poet and saint Milarepa's classic "The Tale of Red Rock Jewel Valley" from his *Hundred Thousand Songs*. Sculptor Constantin Brancusi felt the influence of this Tibetan Repa-Yogi. Here in this garden Tibetan Kagypa nuns were heard singing sacred mantras that resounded through the garden and also garden masters, at the break of day, ringing their bells and chanting Tibetan rituals amidst the cool stones.

Should one wish to leave this place, a variety of paths present themselves. One may proceed up the last steep section of stair, up to the wooden gate that marks the garden's boundary and thence, beyond the garden's realm, out into the mountain's forest. Or, one may follow a narrow path that leads to the eastern part of the garden and to its lower areas. Thrice daily, with the exception of Sundays, a ship's horn may be heard on the mountain: at seven in the morning, at noon, and at two in the afternoon. It is a hissing steam whistle whose penetrating echo resounds from the surrounding mountains. Indeed, looking down the steep slope from this terrace, the visitor may—"Ship Ahoy !"—catch a glimpse of an ocean liner between the black locust reaching towards the light. It appears to float through the forest. Who may be traveling upon it? What enigmatic odyssey unfolds so boldly upon the forest's billowing trees? "Who must be operating this dreaming vessel so softly parting harbor waters off its steel-shin bow with snout pointed to the Four Winds of the World you see nothing, no one, not a soul?"[21]

One should draw nearer to it and go back down the last bit of stair to the terrace lying below (LS 9). Viewed from a closer vantage point, against the backdrop of the factory on the valley floor and its chimneys, one sees white steam rising, like puffs of smoke rising from three ship's smokestacks painted black, red, and white. The breeze seems to carry the sounds of a cruise band just audible against the gentle rustling of leaves: jazz rhythms... "Blue Bird"... wafting from inside the ship. This ocean liner is the work of Anna Tretter, an artist who resides at the foot of the Sommerberg and who, from an early stage, was involved in the shaping of the garden. Hers are two site-specific sculptural installations and also a video piece entitled *Sunday Morning* that, through dual cameras suspended at waist level, presents the garden's winding paths as viewed through an animal's lateral eyes.

To the east of the ocean liner the visitor, still following the path, comes upon a campsite at which tea was brewed daily over a fire during the garden's creation. From the first, a functional fire pit was conceived of as the social nucleus of this forest garden. Joseph Beuys had characterized his famous installation *The Hearth* as a locus of 'permanent conference'.[22] The hearth's role as an image-generating, living medium for creative transformations and metamorphoses in the sense of Goethe and Ovid cannot be overstated—to say nothing of the blessings of hospitality that may be enjoyed at a hearth's side. Beuys' aforementioned work is, for me, also indelibly suggestive of a garden sculptor's praxis: in his essay on the

Figure 3/ Ascending and Forking Paths. The Sommer Berger Garden. Photograph courtesy of Matthias Hubert.

philosophy of gardens, "The Art of Setting Stones", Mark Peter Keane describes a morning ritual in a Kyoto garden at the beginning of the third millennium, and what he describes is fundamentally the same as what took place when the Sommer Berger Garden was created. "At the end of the path, amid piles of tools, three gardeners huddle over an old iron can.... Gardeners have their rituals, like breaks for tea at ten and three, and on chill mornings a fire always precedes the beginning of work."[23] Here, at this small campsite, grows *Helleborus niger*, blooming white in winter: perhaps Homer's 'Moly', the flower Odysseus employed to cast a spell upon the enchantress Circe.

Two paths cross in the grove of hornbeam east of the campsite, and here another stone bench awaits the visitor. From here, gazing between the slender trunks of hornbeam, aspen, birch, and also holly (*Ilex aquifolium*) that were planted as markers adjacent to boundary stones, one overlooks a shaded portion of inner forest dappled but sparsely with flecks of sunlight and leading ultimately to the high forest of old oak and red beech.[24] Inscribed on the bench are words uttered by the garden's patron, words left for future visitors to discover....

From their point of crossing, one of the paths follows the slope to the region above the central clearing. At the path's head, a throne-like grouping of stone, set 'spontaneously' between hornbeam trunks by one of the gardeners while constructing the path, nestles against the slope. The visitor acquainted with garden history may recall the austere throne built for John Ruskin in his famed forest garden Brantwood in England's Cumbrian lake district.[25] Ruskin—author, artist, critic, philosopher, social reformer, and ecological visionary—believed that happiness and good fortune stem from the size not of one's property but of one's heart.

A few steps further on, the visitor emerges from the forest's twilight into the light at the edge of the woods. Beneath the gently bowing, twisting trunk of an ancient hornbeam, lies a platform of stone covering a grotto beneath. Here too is a bench of stone that offers the visitor a vista out into the distance: over the forest's glade and beyond Amorbach to wooded peaks to the southwest. In letters of blue, this bench also bears an inscribed directive, "FLY", an allusion to Yoko Ono's *Fly Piece*.[26]

This place is an ideal one at which to observe the swift, dizzying flight of bats seeking insects hovering above the wooded glade as dusk falls. In the Far East, the bat became a symbol of an enterprising spirit's good fortune. Guillaume Apollinaire's proverbial utterance is apt:

> "Come to the edge", he said.
> They said, "We are afraid."
> "Come to the edge", he said.
> They came.
> He pushed them... and they flew.

But who were those that flew beyond the edge? Here once again, Eliade may serve as a guide:

> Exponents of *yoga* and Indian alchemists fly in the air, and cover vast distances in a few moments. To be able to fly, to have wings, becomes a symbolic formula for transcending human status; the ability to rise into the air indicates access to the ultimate realities... Yogis, ascetics, magicians, "fly" by their own efforts.... It is their ascent that sets them apart from the mass of ordinary uninitiated souls: they can enter the heavens which are impregnated with holiness, and become like gods. Their contact with the starry spaces makes them divine.[27]

Should one not depart from this place by taking flight, one may descend a narrow stone stair running through fragrant sage (*Salvia spec.*), lavender (*Lavandula spec.*), and thyme (*Thymus spec.*). This stair leads to the entrance of the red sandstone grotto that is the topographical center of this garden 'on sacred ground'. A blue muscat grapevine (*Vitis vinifera*) growing at the base of a black elderberry serves to mark this spot. The face-edge of the massive sandstone plate that covers the plain, unadorned grotto bears an inscribed epigram. Here, at the wishes of the garden's patron, appear words once directed by the Greek god Apollo to the Spartan statesman Chilon, one of the Seven Sages. These very words would become the cornerstone of Socratic philosophizing and were inscribed at the entrance of Apollo's temple at Delphi: "GNOTHI SAUTON" (Know Thyself).[28]

The grotto, lined with slabs of stone, provides just enough space for one or two people to recline therein. It is a sanctuary within the mountain, a space or 'vessel' for meditation. In reference to the Delphic utterance, the Roman statesman Cicero wrote in his *Tusculan Disputations*: "When, therefore, he says 'Know thyself', he says this, 'Know the nature of your soul'; for the body is a kind of vessel, or receptacle of the soul."[29] It is said that the inner sanctum of Apollo's temple—the place that housed Apollo's priestess the Pythia who, enraptured by the god's aura, made pronouncements to the god's petitioners in riddling meters—contained a grove of sacred laurel (*Laurus nobilis*).[30] Chewing laurel leaves, permitted to no other on this sacred ground, enhanced the priestess's mantic power.[31] As the laurel could not survive the Odenwald's harsh winter unprotected, there are trees in the proximity of the grotto that produce an equivalent atmosphere. Its foliage and stature quite similar to the laurel, evergreen cherry laurel (*Prunus laurocerasus*) grows at the wood's edge to the east. Above the grotto, meanwhile, grows a chaste tree (*Vitex agnus castus*), a rarity in Central Europe, and also a bitter orange (*Poncirus trifoliata*). As the laurel is sacred to Apollo, so the chaste tree is sacred to the god's sister Artemis. Ranging mountain forests to hunt with her nymphs, she, a virgin goddess, is mistress and protectress of the creatures of the wild. Still today, aromatic chaste trees surround the ruins of the goddess's massive temple at Ephesus, one of the ancient world's Seven Wonders, and the goddess' chaste priestesses strewed their beds with the chaste tree's leaves. In China, an aromatic charcoal that burns very hot, and longer than that derived from other wood, was produced from the chaste tree's roots.[32] Our restoration of the grotto yielded pieces of anthracite coal as well as horseshoe nails from the upper soil layer, which indicates that the grotto had once been used as a smithy.

All this, together with the newly created fire pit, bears reference to Joseph Beuys' installation and artistic 'action' bearing as its title the name of the shrub, *Vitex Agnus Castus*. Beuys' performative action, which drew on alchemy and shamanistic practices, took place in the summer of 1972 at the opening of his show *Arena. Dove sarei arrivato se fossi stato intelligente!* in Naples. Beuys' performance consisted of lying on the ground for hours in front of two stacks of beeswax blocks in a trancelike state but wracked by convulsive twitches. Short pieces of copper and iron protruded from these blocks just above ground level. Rubbing the metals continuously, Beuys derived an electric charge, their polarized Mars-Venus energy. Pinned to his hat was a branch of chaste tree together with a cobalt blue ribbon bearing the botanic name of this sacred plant written in sulfur paste. Beuys later said of his human battery: "Energy emanates from the two poles, male and female. My action drew them together. I mean a different concept of chastity produced by this reaction and the conflict of elements."[33]

What is it that links this particular plant next to the "Fly" bench above the grotto with the work of Joseph Beuys? Art historian Armin Zweite wrote: "As repulsive and enigmatic as the 'action' might be, it was, in fact, nothing other than a compelling metaphor for a means of dealing with Nature that does not strive for subjugation and exploitation but rather embraces *Temperantia* and *Castitas*."[34] True as this may be, is there not something quite apart from a demonstration of virtues, namely an ascent to heaven? A 'still' from this filmed performance presents an 'ascending Beuys'. Similarly, in his artistic 'multiple' *Levitazione in Italia*, the artist vanishes through the picture's upper edge: merely his legs, elevated above the ground and easily identifiable as the artist's through his typical combination of boots and blue jeans, next to which dangled a cobalt ribbon with the words "Agnus Castus".[35]

In the Middle Ages the chaste tree, whose seeds were called "monk's pepper", became a *Parzival* symbol for Christian monks. And looking to the southwest from the place by the grotto where the chaste tree stands, one can just make out the Preunschner Mountain as a *point de vue* beyond the Mud Valley. Upon foothills of this mountain lies Wildenburg Castle, a ruin of the Staufer era (1138–1254) and the location where, it is said, Wolfram von Eshenback wrote parts of his romance *Parzival*, the courtly tale of a quest for the Holy Grail that people in the Middle Ages, finding therein reflections of themselves, used to 'find' or determine their place in the world.

Somewhat above the Sommerberg's grotto grows an evergreen, trifoliate bitter orange. Native to the eastern part of Eurasia, Korea, and northern China, this shrub emits the scent of citrus when its snow-white blossoms appear in April and May. Its green fruit, changing from yellow to orange, is also aromatic and, though unpalatable raw, is treasured in China as medicine and spice. Armed as it is with long green thorns, this shrub may well mature here to a tree. "How often am I laced in drops of dew fallen from the leaves, as I/ enjoying the moonlit night—sit upon a bench/ beneath the trees." So read the last lines of a poet by Tang lyricist Du Fu (712–770), in which he describes the delicious atmosphere beneath a grove of orange trees.[36]

To either side of the grotto is an old, dry-laid stone wall, and where necessary, it was reconstructed in the course of this garden's re-creation (LS 5). Mediterranean plants and herbs have been planted on the wall's top, and beneath it unfolds the meadow-covered clearing of the terraced slope. Running parallel to the slope, 'dead hedges' line the wall. Comprised of brittle twigs, cleared blackberry vine, and branches from the thinning of the forest as well as of cuttings from the mowed meadows and foliage from swept paths and terraces, these hedges have become an integral part of the garden's life-cycle. Growing annually with an accumulation of biomass and, in turn, shrinking as this mass compresses, these 'dead' materials are, with the occasional addition of lime, transformed into aromatic, vital humus. Heat sculptures *par excellence* are what the hedges actually are. I had received instruction in this method of composting from farmer and philosopher Masanobu Fukuoka in 1985 while working with him on his mandarin and orange orchards in Ohira on the island of Shikoku where, over decades he had developed his '*Mahajana*-cultivation' and 'do-nothing' natural farming methods. Another point of reference here: some 20 years earlier, in 1961, Joseph Beuys had created an 'earthwork', a five-cornered compost heap, in the forest without any participants or spectators. Having interviewed Beuys, art historian Dieter Koepplin reported as follows:

> Beuys had gathered and assembled the branches of various trees and bushes to create a 'hearth' of approximately two meters in diameter—a hearth without flames, a potential hearth, a heat-sculpture. Every incineration, whether resulting from decay or open, consuming fire, has a transformational effect both in a physical and the

> metaphysical sense. So, for instance, Rudolf Steiner characterized the development of human spiritual life as something progressing from a flame that, as it were, consumes the body.[37]

Concentrated in the embankments is the garden's biological reservoir. They are covered by a web of hop, false buckwheat (*Polygonum dumetorum*), and spreading honeysuckle, all growing wild on this slope. A myriad of birds, small animals, amphibians, and insects find refuge and sustenance here. Even phosphorescing microorganisms and luminescent fungi may be observed here glowing at night.

Five trees were planted at the edge of the clearing (LS 5) marking the corners of a pentagon. These are young exemplars of a species of conifer that has been planted in German parks, and to a lesser degree in the woods, since the middle of the nineteenth century. This species of tree had already been planted on this mountainside, namely in the garden of the Prinzenpalais (princely palace) to the west beneath the Gotthard Ruin. The tree is the Californian giant sequoia (*Sequoiadendron giganteum*). The five sequoia planted in the Sommer Berger Garden will, one day, tower over their neighboring oak and black locust, thereby making the garden easily recognizable from the valley below. Thus in the space of half a century, these trees and the quintessence of their majestic bearing will have significantly impacted the character of the garden. These massive and long-lived trees once also grew in Central Europe in the Cretaceous Period. In their current home, California's Sierra Nevada Mountains, they grow in isolated groves. Since the nineteenth century only the few specimens that had been placed under protection as natural monuments have survived humanity's relentless, consumer-driven pursuit in the Western world.

The dynamic shape of the pentagonal planting is befitting the garden's function as a point of contact between Heaven and Earth. It is a locus where the transition between separate realms becomes possible and palpable. Here cosmic divinity is poetically inscribed 'on sacred ground'. As the pentagon's trees grow, so too does the garden's role of intermediary between extremes. As those five majestic trees, their trunks enveloped in soft, red-brown bark, rise from the mountain's red-brown sandstone, the bedrock is transformed, pressed beyond its mineral limits, to ensure that, as they drink in the rays of the sun, these wondrous specimens achieve due prominence.

Inscribed within a pentagram star, the pentagon is, on a philosophical or spiritual level, associated with the emancipation of the 'Ego', for it is a symbol of movement and the negation of dualistic principles. For this reason it served as a signifier of Christ on the Gnostic Rose Cross. This five-fold planting of sequoia was of particular significance to the garden's patron Elk Michael Berger; an admirer and collector of the work of Joseph Beuys, he was aware that the artist had done an entire series of drawings in which one or more moose appear beneath the massive form of a sequoia.[38]

Leaving the grotto and proceeding eastward towards the edge of the woods, the garden visitor comes upon a second installation by Anna Tretter via a diagonally descending path. Here the artist has secured two flat mirrors, both at the same height, to the slender trunks of two oaks. This is an ingenious device whereby, (from an elevated vantage point), to view oneself in attempted flight. The topos of flight, familiar to the garden visitor from the "FLY" inscription encountered earlier, is taken up again, now to be experienced more deeply—physically.

In the words of Joseph Beuys, "movement results from a provocation, from an empowerment, from an initiation of the purpose of the movement. One arouses the principle of motion itself."[39] First one steps onto the "H" inscribed on a slab of stone on the path beneath the mirrors. Then, leaning forward towards the valley floor and moving one's arms up and down rhythmically, like a bird's wings, one can see oneself 'suspended', like Icarus in flight, as one looks up into the smaller mirror. Such a tragic figure, Icarus. His father, Daedalus, had, by making wings of wax and feathers, been the first to enable human flight. Skilled craftsman though he was, Daedalus was unable to prevent the death of his only son who, reveling in his new-found powers, flew too close to the sun. But it is not the tale of Icarus to which the mirror installation alludes; rather, it references the fifteenth proposition of Heron of Alexandria. This Greek mathematician, physicist, and engineer, whose work is dated variously to the first century CE and the second century BCE, authored volumes on mechanics, pneumatics, and measurements, as well as on automated devices for the theater. The theoretical underpinnings of his *Mechanica* are based, in part, on the work of the Greek mathematician Archimedes, in particular upon his theory for calculating the area of a triangle. Regarding his construction employing plane mirrors that showed people 'flying', Heron wrote:

> Let there be an equilateral triangle '*abg*' that is divided at the base '*bg*' into two equal parts by a '*t*'. Let a plane mirror '*zh*' be attached to '*ag*' and another such '*ed*' to '*ab*'. Let a subject, who is standing on '*t*', look towards one of the mirrors. Let the mirror at which he gazes remain motionless, but let the other that is behind him be raised or lowered until its reflection reaches the subject's heels (*k*). The subject then will believe that he is flying.[40]

In her installation, Anna Tretter left the movement of the mirror to the natural movement of the trees.

In the late Middle Ages and in the Renaissance, Heron's prescription for flying found repeated application.

Thus Vitellius, writing in about the year 1270, wrote: "It is possible to construct a mirror in which one may see oneself flying from a grouping of plane mirrors."[41] Physician, astrologer, and alchemist Aprippa von Nettersheim (1486–1535), a distinctly Faustian character, thought he saw demons in such flying bodies. Italian philosopher, physician, and mathematician Geronimo Cordano (1501–1576) for his part, described Heron's method point for point in 1550 and compared the resultant effects with the flight of birds.

A little below the mirror installation another stone bench has been set between the hornbeams' slender trunks. This bench also bears an inscription in blue capitals, "DIE PFLANZEN SIND EIN ORGAN DES MENSCHEN. JOSEPH BEUYS" (plants are a human organ); Beuys had remarked that "the forest is a part of the human body; trees are an extended human organ".[42] This particular spot in the forest induces the visitor to come to this very realization and to experience it meditatively. Again in the words of Beuys:

> We must gain the ability to perceive that Nature—physical Nature in the form of plants, trees, and the planet itself—is in actuality an external organ without which human existence is not possible. Just as a person cannot live without a heart, liver, kidney, brain, and lung, so the heart, liver, kidney, brain, and lung are not capable of sustaining life without the oxygen that trees produce. And when a species of animal becomes extinct, a significant spiritual and astral spark is extinguished in humankind.[43]

From the aforementioned bench, the visitor glimpses a grouping of stones on somewhat lower ground. The constellation of stones set between the trunks of young hornbeam is yet another garden element that harbors associations with flight. These stones suggest a crane flying from the east. In the Far East the crane was viewed as a mount appropriate for the Immortals and accordingly became an allegory for long life. In Japan such a grouping of stones is called a *tsurushima*, a "crane's island", and in the garden, it is a direct reference to ancient Chinese myth of the island of the Immortals. Yet this island lies in the sea no more than the ocean liner in the upper portion of the garden actually crosses the ocean. Rather, this lapidary island provides the vehicle for an aesthetically-driven, spiritual flight whereby to attain the paradisiacal realms of the Immortals. And these may lie closer than one imagines.

A bit lower down the slope is a small, nearly square area beneath the canopy of oak and hornbeam (LS 7). This site, formerly overgrown by hazel thickets, is framed by old retaining walls. The ground here had been crudely paved with broken rock and must once have served as a covered shelter for pack animals. At any rate, as this pad was exposed, a donkey's shoe came to light in addition to the ceramic sherds that were also found

Figure 4/ Inscribed Stone Table. The Sommer Berger Garden. Photograph courtesy of Matthias Hubert.

elsewhere in the garden. "This common or garden is now in stiller realithy the/ starey sphere of an oleotorium for broken pottery and ancient/ vegetables."[44]

We edged this pad with large sandstone pavers, setts, and provided it with a floor of beaten earth. Here a low table of black granite was set, an allusion to those plain stone tables that stood in philosophers' gardens in ancient China to serve as centerpieces for gatherings or as a locus of quiet, contemplative withdrawal [Figure 4]. On these tables, the denizens of such gardens had written poems, unrolled scrolls, or displayed rare artifacts for contemplation, and arranged cups of wine, flowers, and meals for themselves and their guests.[45] The table in the Sommer Berger Garden bears an inscription of eight Chinese characters in silver:

止 動 無 動

動 止 無 止

This inscription is the fifty-second epigram from the *Hsin-Hsin-Ming , Credence Inscribed*, a condensed presentation of the Mahayana of Seng T'san, the third patriarch of Zen Buddhism in China.

From this tree-shaded spot, the epigram and the poetic wisdom it offers span a vast geographical and temporal divide. In their laconic brevity, its few, secretive symbols contain a worldview comprising the perception of the continuous flux between the poles of activity and rest residing in the natural world that surrounds us and in the nature of our intellect. The cyclical play of light beneath the trees' canopy—the light, in turn, of sun and moon—is reflected in the table's black, polished stone as well as in its silver lettering. Here too may be felt the unhindered presence of wind and clouds, or of light rain and snow. Palpable here are the cyclical rhythms of creation and preservation as well as of destruction and quiescence. It is a metaphor of the spirit's continuum.

A four-language limited edition of Seng Ts'an's *Hsin-Hsin-Ming* appeared in 1980 in Brussels.[46] The publication resulted from the cooperation of four artist-poets who succeeded in connecting the threads of a philosophical text composed some 1,500 years earlier with the essence of the twentieth century Fluxus art movement, of which they themselves were a part. Those 37 epigrams are each composed of two sets of four symbols, and they were translated from Chinese into English by George Brecht. The English version was then translated into French by Robert Filliou and into German by Albrecht Fabri. Japanese Fluxus artist Takako Saito wrote the calligraphy in the Chinese *K'iai-schu* script.

George Brecht's English translation, entitled *Credence Inscribed*, was later published with a commentary by Dick Higgins, founder of the avant-garde Something Else Press and an early member of the Fluxus movement.[47] Producing a commentary of this kind was itself in the Buddhist tradition. Higgins' commentary was then later itself released in 1991 by Generator Press in Ohio under the title *the autobiography of the moon—a commentary on the hsin-hsin-ming by dick higgins*. The following are translations of the fifty-second epigram, together with Higgins' commentary thereon:

Brecht	Arresting movement: no moving Moving rest: no rest
Filliou	Inactive activité: non-activité Active inactivité: non-inactivité
Fabri	Aus Bewegung, die man anhält, wird Nicht-Bewegung; Aus Nicht-Bewegung, die man in Bewegung setzt, Bewegung.
Higgins	to follow: the inner way pursued. to earn: the giving and gaining and flowing.

Next to the trunk of an oak, somewhat lower than the stone table, a dark, hexagonal stone stele protrudes from the forest floor [Figure 5]. The stele is basalt of volcanic origin and stems from the Westerwald. Standing here by an oak alongside a path above Amorbach, is this stele a *pierre d'amour* (love stone)? The combination of rock and tree present the garden visitor with a cultic binome. In Eliade's view, such a combination is a microcosm of those places where the deepest roots of religious sensibility reside, ranging from the Aegean beyond India and Indonesia to China and Australia.[48] For example, in the Mohenjo-daro culture of the third century BCE Indus Valley, sacred space consisted of a wall around a tree; such places could be found throughout India at the time that the Buddha delivered his sermons. Over time, the microcosmic landscape became reduced to a tree and an altar, and the stone pillar. Old Indian Pali inscriptions often mention the stone or the altar next to a holy tree, together forming the basis of traditional cults of the fertility goddess Yaksha. The Buddhist *caitya* 'sacred place' was sometimes just a tree without an altar and sometimes a primitive structure erected in a tree's vicinity. In the Greek world too sacred trees are found beside a rock from Minoan times to the twilight of Hellenism. A stone may represent reality *par excellence*: indestructibility and endurance. With its capacity for periodic regeneration, the tree, for its part, evinced its sacred power in the realm of the living.

Like a veritable leitmotif, this cultic binome pervades a work of literary Modernism that appeared in 1939, "Lo behold! La arboro, lo petrusu. The augustan peacebetothem oaks, the monolith rising stark from moonlit pinebarren."[49] For Joseph Beuys, who loved and was deeply inspired by *Finnegan's Wake*, these lines proved prophetic. The artist revived and monumentalized the ancient link between tree and stone in his art 'action' *7000 Eichen* (*7000 Oaks*); and at the same time, this ancient conceit assumed new relevance in an age of ecological disaster. This socio-ecological 'action',

Figure 5/ Basalt Stele. The Sommer Berger Garden. Photograph courtesy of Michael Förtsch.

Figure 6/ *Elegant Gathering in the Western Garden.* Copy c. 1600 of Qui Ying, Chinese c. 1482–1559. Ink and color on silk. Indianapolis Museum of Art, Gift of Mrs. John H. Roberts, Jr. Image courtesy of the Indianapolis Museum of Art.

which was publicly presented in 1982 at Documenta 7 in the city of Kassel, comprised the planting within the city of 7,000 trees, each with a basalt stele beside it, and it has henceforth both won worldwide recognition and has been variously expanded or continued.[50] The sacred nature of this garden 'on sacred ground' emanates from the microcosmic pairing of oak and stele that is simultaneously an ideal link to and physical realization of Beuys' intention: expressed in the motto "*Difessa Della Natura*" Beuys planned to undertake a wide-ranging network of projects "in the defense of Nature". It is to this philosophy that the creators of the Sommer Berger Garden are dedicated. Indeed, some 20 years earlier, the garden's founder dedicated himself to Beuys' cause through donations towards the artistic installation of trees and basalt markers in Kassel.[51]

In the lower part of the garden reside further 'heat sculptures' constructed from heaped-up brush. They are hiding places for the frogs that are denizens of this garden. As Japanese poet Kobayashi Issa recounted in his frog tales, frog geniuses were the teachers of Daoist geniuses whom they instructed in the art of flying. One of his Haiku verses would appropriately have been written here 'on sacred ground':

> Serenely
> Gazing up at the mountain
> A frog.[52]

An old rose climbs up an even older apple tree, and beneath it one last stone bench awaits the visitor. If descending, the bench's inscription is legible from the apple tree:

> THE MOON IS THE OLDEST TV
> NAM JUNE PAIK[53]

Chinese scroll paintings provide illustrations and descriptions of garden gatherings that have become famous. Composers, poets, painters, Daoist and Buddhist monks, as well as other important persons invited one another to such gatherings. Notable gatherings of this sort included the "gathering at the orchid pavilion" of 35 CE, the "poetic gathering in the west garden" of 1080, and the "elegant gathering in the apricot garden" that took place in April 1437 when Yang Rong, a high-ranking scholar-official serving the emperor of China, invited eight important officials and dignitaries to his famous garden to view paintings and calligraphy, compose poetry, and play chess [Figure 6]. A number of the scroll paintings depicting such musical/philosophical gatherings in gardens bore inscriptions recording both poetry that had been produced and the distinguished guests present. Evidently, it was believed that the presence of such persons enhanced a garden's inspirational aura. Visiting artists and intellectuals have had a similar effect on the Sommer Berger Garden.

Figure 7/ Elk Michael Berger, Anna Tretter, and U We Claus, left to right. 5 October, 2003, in the Sommer Berger Garden. Photograph courtesy of Matthias Hubert.

At length, leaving the garden for the valley below, the visitor steps over the threshold of a stone gate inscribed with a 'word event' by George Brecht: "EXIT!" [Figure 7].[54]

Listing of plants in the garden

WOODY PLANTS/ ***Acer campestre***, Hedge Maple, original stock as well as later plantings. Native to Europe, Near East, and Africa. ***Acer platanoides***, Norway Maple, original stock. Native to Europe and West Asia/ ***Acer pseudoplatanus***, Sycamore Maple, original stock. Native to Europe/ ***Betula pendula***, Silver Birch, original stock (four specimens remaining). Native to Europe, Siberia, and West Asia. ***Buxus sempervirens***, European Boxwood, planted (ten specimens). Native from Northern Spain to the Caucasus/ ***Campsis radicans***, Trumpet vine, one specimen planted in 2010/ ***Carpinus betulus***, European Hornbeam, original stock. Native to Europe and West Asia/ ***Castanea sativa***, Sweet or Spanish Chestnut, original stock as seedlings. Native to Southern Europe, West Asia, and North Africa/ ***Cerasus vulgaris***, Cherry tree, old stock (two specimens remaining). Native from the Northern Balkan to Northern Indian/ ***Clematis armandii***, Evergreen Clematis, one specimen planted. Native to China/ ***Corylus avellana***, Common Hazel (Hazelnut), original stock. Native to Central Europe/ ***Crataegus laevigata***, Smooth or Midland Hawthorn, original stock. Native to Europe/ ***Crataegus monogyna***, One Seed or Common Hawthorn, original stock. Native from Europe to Siberia, and North Africa/ ***Cydonia oblonga***, Common Quince, old stock (a bushy specimen). Native to the South Caucasus, Persia, and Turkestan/ ***Euonymus europaea***, European Spindle Tree, original stock. Native from Europe to the Caucasus and Western Siberia/ ***Euonymus fortunei***, Winter Creeper, one specimen planted 2010. Native from Pakistan to China, Korea, Japan, and Indonesia/ ***Fagus sylvatica***, European Beech, original as seedlings self-propagated from old stock. Native to Europe/ ***Fraxinus excelsior***, European Ash, original stock. Native to Europe, the Caucasus, and West Asia/ ***Gingko biloba***, Gingko Biloba, planted (one specimen). Native to Zhejiang and Guizhou Provinces of China; planted in Europe since 1727/ ***Hedera helix***, English Ivy, original stock. Native from Europe to the Caucasus/ ***Ilex aquifolium***, English Holly, planted (about 10 specimens). Native to Europe, North Africa, the Caucasus, North Persia, and Central China/ ***Ilex aquifolium 'JC van Tol'***, English Holly, planted (one specimen), Garden variety/ ***Jasminum nudiflorum***, Winter Jasmine, planted (one specimen). Native to North China; introduced in Europe in 1844 through Robert Fortune/ ***Juglans regia***, English or Persian Walnut, original stock as seedlings. Native to Southeast Europe and Southwest and Central Asia/ ***Juglans nigra***, Black Walnut, seedlings. Native to North America/ ***Lavandula angustifolia***, English Lavender, planted. Native to the Mediterranean region/ ***Lonicera caprifolium***, Italian Honeysuckle, original stock as well as later plantings. Native from Europe to Crimea, and the Caucasus/ ***Lonicera periclymenum***, Woodbine Honeysuckle, planted (three specimens). Native to Central and Western Europe/ ***Mahonia aquifolium***, Mahonia or Oregon Grape, old stock (one specimen). Native to Pacific North America; planted in Europe since 1823/ ***Malus domestica***, Apple Tree, self-propagated from old stock (still about five specimens). Garden varieties/ ***Parthenocissus quinquefolia***, Virginia Creeper, planted (one specimen). Native to Atlantic North America; grown in Europe since 1629/ ***Pinus sylvestris***, Scotch Pine, native (three specimens). Native from Europe to Central Asia/ ***Poncirus trifoliata***, Hardy or Trifoliate Orange, planted (one specimen). Native to North China and Korea; grown in Europe since 1850/ ***Popolus tremula***, European Aspen, native. Native to Europe, North Africa, West Asia, the Caucasus, Siberia, China, and Japan/ ***Prunus laurocerasus***, Cherry Laurel, planted in two varieties. Native to Southeast Europe and West Asia; grown in Central Europe since the sixteenth Century/ ***Prunus spinosa***, Blackthorn, native. Native to Europe, West Asia, and North Africa/ ***Prunus domestica***, Plum Tree, a grove self-propagated from old stock. Native from

Central Asia to Syria, and the Caucasus/ ***Quercus robur***, English Oak, original stock. Native to Europe, West Asia, and the Caucasus/ ***Ribes uva-crispa***, European Gooseberry, original stock. Native from Europe to the Caucasus, Manchuria, and Morocco/ ***Robinia pseudoacacia***, Black Locust, original stock. Native to Atlantic North America and Mexico; grown in Europe since 1601/ ***Rosa spec.***, Rose, original stock, one old specimen and seedlings/ ***Rubus fruticosus***, Shrubby Blackberry, native. Native to Europe/ ***Salvia nemorosa x pratensis***, Woodland Sage, planted. The garden variety is a cross of Forest- and Meadow Clary/ ***Salvia officinalis***, Sage, planted, died out winter 2009/2010. Native to the Mediterranean Region and North Africa/ ***Sambucus nigra***, Black Elderberry, original stock. Native to Europe/ ***Sequoiadendron giganteum***, Giant Sequoia, planted (five specimens). Native to California; grown in Europe since 1853/ ***Symphoricarpos rivularis***, Snowberry, original stock. Native to Pacific North America; grown in Europe since 1817/ ***Syringa vulgaris***, French Lilac, original stock. Native to Southeast Europe/ ***Taxus baccata***, English Yew, planted. Native from Europe to the Caucasus and North Africa/ ***Thymus vulgaris***, Thyme, planted. Native to the Mediterranean Region/ ***Tila cordata***, Littleleaf Linden, original stock (one specimen, one more planted). Native from Europe to Western Siberia/ ***Ulmus minor***, Field Elm, original stock as seedlings. Native to Europe, West Asia, and North Africa/ ***Vinca minor***, Common Periwinkle, planted, present elsewhere in the region. Native to Europe and West Asia/ ***Vitex agnus castus***, Lilac Chaste-tree, one specimen. Native from the Mediterranean region to Central Asia/ ***Vitis vinifera 'Muscat Bleu'***, Muscat Grape, one specimen planted. Cultivar from Switzerland/ ***Wisteria sinensis 'Alba'***, Chinese Wisteria, planted. Native to China; garden variety grown in Europe since 1816.

HERBACEOUS AND CLIMBING PLANTS AND SHRUBS/ ***Agrostemma githago***, Common Corncockle, sown 2010/ ***Alcea rosea***, Hollyhock/ ***Alliaria petiolata***, Garlic Mustard, original stock. Native to Europe and West Asia/ ***Allium spec.***, Garlic, original stock/ ***Allium cepa***, Onion, planted. Garden variety/ ***Amaranthus paniculata***, Purple Amaranth/ ***Antennaria dioica***, Mountain Everlasting or Pussytoes/ ***Anthemis tinctoria 'E. C. Buxton'***, Chamomile/ ***Anthericum liliago***, St. Bernard's Lily/ ***Antirrhinum majus***, Snapdragon/ ***Aquilegia vulgaris***, Columbine/ ***Bergenia purpurascens***, Elephant's Ears/ ***Bryonia dioica***, White Bryony, original stock/ ***Calamintha sylvatica***, Woodland Calamint/ ***Calendula officinalis***, Marigold/ ***Campanula carpatica***, Carpathian or Tussock Bellflower/ ***Campanula glomerata***, Clustered Bellflower/ ***Chelidonium majus***, Greater Celandine, original stock. Native to Europe and West Asia/ ***Convallaria majalis***, Lily of the Valley, planted/ ***Corydalis solida***, Fumewort, planted. Native to Northern Europe and Asia/ ***Crocus vernus***, Common Crocus, planted. Native to Eastern Europe/ ***Delphinium consolida***, Larkspur/ ***Dianthus gratianopolitanus***, Cheddar Pink/ ***Digitalis purpurea***, Foxglove/ ***Dracocephalum moldavica***, Dragonhead/ ***Echium vulgare***, Viper's Bugloss/ ***Eranthis hyemalis***, Winter Aconite, planted. Native from Southern France to Bulgaria/ ***Erythronium 'Pagoda'***, Fawn Lily, Trout Lily, Dog's-tooth Violet, planted. Garden variety/ ***Fragaria vesca***, Woodland Strawberry, native. Native to Europe/ ***Fritillaria persica***, Persian Fritillary/ ***Galanthus nivalis***, Common Snowdrop, planted. Native from the Pyrenees to Ukraine/ ***Gentiana tibetica***, Tibetan Gentian/ ***Geranium robertianum***, Robert Geranium, original stock. Native to Europe, Northwest Africa, Western Asia, the Himalayas, and Southwest China/ ***Helleborus niger***, Christmas Rose, planted. Native to Germany, Austria, Switzerland, Italy, and Slovenia/ ***Hieracium aurantiacum***, Orange Hawkweed/ ***Hieracium pilosella***, Mouse-ear Hawkweed/ ***Humulus lupulus***, Common Hop, original stock. Native to Europe, Western Asia, and North America/ ***Hyoscyamus niger***, Black Henbane/ ***Juncus***, Rush/ ***Leucojum aestivum***, Summer Snowflake, planted. Native from Europe to the Caucasus, Western Asia, and Northern Persia/ ***Lychnis flos-cuculi***, Ragged Robin or Cuckoo Flower/ ***Lychnis flos-jovis***, Flower of Jove/ ***Majorana horteensis***, Marjoram/ ***Malva sylvatica atropurpurea***, Mallow/ ***Meconopsis cambricum***, Welch Poppy/ ***Muscaria latifolium***, Grape Hyacinth, planted. Native to Southwest Asia/ ***Narcissus pseudonarcissus***, Daffodil, planted. Native to Europe/ ***Narcissus pseudonarcissus 'Carlton'***, Daffodil, planted. Garden variety/ ***Narcissus cyclamineus***, Cyclamen-flowered Daffodil, planted. Native to Northwest Spain and Northwest Portugal/ ***Origanum vulgare***, Common Oregano/ ***Papaver rhoeas***, Shirley Poppy, Corn Poppy, Flanders Poppy or Field Poppy/ ***Polygonum dumetorum***, Climbing False Buckwheat, original stock. Native to Europe and Asia/ ***Primula elatior***, Primrose, original stock/ ***Ranunculus ficaria***, Fig Buttercup, original stock. Native to Europe, Northwest Africa, and Southwest Asia/ ***Rhinanthus alectorolophus***, European Yellow Rattle/ ***Rhinanthus minor***, Yellow Rattle/ ***Saxifraga Arendsii-Hybr. 'Harter Zwerg'***, Mossy Saxifrage or Rock Foil, planted. Garden variety/ ***Saxifraga granulate***, Meadow Saxifrage/ ***Scandix pecten-veneris***, Venus's Comb/ ***Scilla nutans***, Bluebell, planted. Native to Western Europe/ ***Scilla siberica***, Siberian Squill or Spring Beauty, planted. Native from Ukraine to Azerbaijan and North Persia/ ***Scutellaria galericulata***, Marsh Skullcap/ ***Sedum pachyclados***, White Diamond/ ***Sedum sexangulare***, Tasteless Stonecrop, planted. Native to Europe/ ***Sedum spurium***, John Creech/ ***Sedum telephium***, Autumn Joy/ ***Sempervivum***, Houseleeks or Liveforever, planted. Native to Europe/ ***Silene alba***, White Campion/ ***Solanum nigrum***, Wonderberry or Sunberry/ ***Symphytum officinale***, Comfrey/ ***Urtica dioica***, Stinging Nettle, native/ ***Verbena officinalis***, Common Verbena/ ***Viola canina***, Dog-violet or Heath, native. Native to Europe and Western Asia/ ***Viola tricolor***, Johnny Jump-Up. As well as many other, not more precisely defined, types of ferns, grasses, mosses, and fungi.

Notes

* The translator wishes to thank U We Claus, Hans-Joerg Busch, and Herwarth Giesecke for their invaluable comments on and corrections of the translation from the original German.

1. The first quote is the seventh of the "Seven Forest Events" in Bengt af Klintberg, *The Cursive Scandinavian Slave*, New York: Something Else Press, 1967 (also in *The Fluxus Performance Workbook*, Ken Friedman, Owen Smith, and Lauren Sawchyn eds., Trondheim, Norway: Guttorm Nord, 1990, p. 28). For Heraclitus in the original Greek, see fragment B60 in Hermann Diels ed., *Die Fragmente der Vorsokratiker*, Berlin: Weidmann, 1906–1910. The words of Kogaku

Soko are recorded in Hans Günther Wachtmann and Ingrid von Kruse, *Daisen-in: Ein Zen-Tempel des 16. Jahrhunderts in Kyoto* (bilingual German and English), Munich: Hirmer Verlag, 2000, p. 48.

2. This is a path that Theobald 'Teddy' Wiesengrund Adorno (1903–1969) enjoyed, saying of Amorbach and its surroundings that they reflect "the eternal, holy paradise that no one ever possessed but everyone hoped to enter one day".

3. Michael Elk Berger is an entrepreneur, collector, and humorist who grew up in Amorbach.

4. This is on the authority of Johann Philip Bronner, *Der Weinbau des Main- und Taubergrundes under Würzburger Gegend* (1839) as cited in Guntram Kunz, "Weinbau in Amorbach", *Amorbach 750 Jahre Stadt 1253–2003*, pp. 255ff.

5. The citation is taken from the work of lyricist and composer Dschjang Kue (c. 1155–1235), specifically the poem "The city Yangdschou after the departure of the Jurchen" collected in Ernst Schwarz ed., *Chrysanthemen im Spiegel: Klassische chinesische Dichtung*, Berlin: Rütten and Leoning, 1988.

6. Among the Japanese shrines and temple gardens that I visited in 1985, and that proved to be particularly influential, are the Shinto shrines of Ise in Mie, the temple grounds of Tôdai-ji in Nara, the imperial parks and country residence Katsura of Prince Toshihito, Emperor Gomizuoö's Shugaku-in villa in Kyoto, Yoshimasa Ashikaga's Ginkaku-ji (Temple of the Silver Pavilion), Yoshimitsu Ashikaga's Kinkaku-ji (Temple of the Golden Pavilion), the Daitoku-ji Temple and Kogaku Soko's Daisen-in, Soami's Ryôan-ji temple garden, and the Kiyomizu Temple, all in Kyoto, together with the Sanzen-in Temple on the Takano River in Ohara.

7. The source of the quotations is Bronner, *Der Weinbau*, pp. 255ff.

8. Here too, the source of these words is Bronner, *Der Weinbau*, pp. 255ff.

9. See Mark Peter Keane's "Gärten", *Zen: Interieurs & Gärten*, David Scott ed., Munich: Heyne Verlag, 1999, pp. 86–123. The quote itself is from page 122.

10. According to Karl Henning, *Japanische Gartenkunst*, Cologne: DuMont, 1980, pp. 121ff., this cosmogram is said to date back to the time of the emperor Yü, who was the founder of the Hsia-dynasty and reigned 2205–2197 BCE. The Lo River, which flows along the city of Lo-yang, is reputed to have washed this numbers game ashore.

11. This principle is described in detail in Teiji Itoh, *Space and Illusion in the Japanese Garden*, Ralph Friedrich and Masajiro Shimamura trans., New York: Weatherhill, 1973.

12. Of unknown authorship, "The Tale of the Spring Dream" may be found in Martin Gimm trans., *Das schöne Mädchen Yingying: Erotische Novellen aus China*, Zürich: Manesse Verlag, 2001, pp. 94–128. The material quoted here appears on page 98.

13. See Osamu Suzuki and Isao Yoshikawa, *The Bamboo Fences of Japan*, Tokyo: Books Nippon, 1989, pp. 52ff.

14. See Mircea Eliade, *Patterns in Comparative Religion*, Rosemary Sheed trans., Lincoln, NE and London: University of Nebraska Press, 1996, p. 381. For the quoted text, see section 141, "The 'Construction' of the Sacred Space", pp. 370–371.

15. The seventh of the "Seven Forest Events" in Klintberg, *The Cursive Scandinavian Slave*.

16. For the quotes in this line and the following, see Eliade, *Patterns*, pages 104, 101, and 108 respectively. For Eliade's discussion on ascent generally, see sections 31–34 in "The Sky and Sky Gods", pages 38-123. The video entitled "THE WAY UP IS THE WAY DOWN" was produced by U We Claus in 2007 for the Venice Biennale. It can be viewed at http://www.youtube.com/watch?v=73gQVRUjgT4.

17. The words are those of Joseph Beuys as recorded in his conversation with Caroline Tisdall in her work *Joseph Beuys*, London and New York: Thames and Hudson, 1979, p. 225.

18. See Eliade, *Patterns*, p. 108.

19. The Hölderlin quotation is derived from Horst Dieter Rau, *Heilige Wildniss: Naturaesthetik von Hölderlin bis Beuys*, Munich: W. Fink Verlag, 1998, pp. 100, 101, and 252.

20. Decker, Edith ed., *Nam June Paik: Niederschriften eines Kulturnomaden Aphorismen Briefe Texte*, Cologne: Du Mont, 1992, p. 44.

21. These words are those of Jack Kerouac in "Slobs of the Kitchen Sea" from the collection *Lonesome Traveller*, London: Andre Deutsch Ltd., 1962, p. 84. At the time of its creation, the creator of this garden was heavily influenced by the work of Jack Kerouac, Allen Ginsberg, and Gary Snyder.

22. For more information on *The Hearth*, see Dieter Koepplin ed., *Joseph Beuys in Basel, Bd. 1, Feuerstätte: "THE HEARTH (Feuerstätte) 1968–1974" und "Feuerstätte II 1978–1979 von Joseph Beuys*, Munich: Schirmer/Mosel, 2003.

23. Keane, Marc Peter, *The Art of Setting Stones and Other Writings from the Japanese Garden*, Berkeley: Stone Bridge Press, 2002, p. 122.

24. In the spring of 2001, the Sommer Berger Garden was freshly surveyed, and missing property markers were replaced.

25. For a good photograph of Ruskin's throne, see Tim Richardson ed., *The Garden Book*, London and New York: Phaidon Press, 2000, p. 392.

26. For Yoko Ono's *Fly Piece* of 1963, see Ken Friedman ed., *The Fluxus Performance Workbook* (*El Djarida*, special edition), Trondheim, Norway: Editions Conz, 1990, p. 43.

27. See Eliade, *Patterns*, p. 108.

28. Referenced here as well are Joseph Beuys' meditations on the 'being' or existence of humankind in pantheistic thought. See Beuys' conversation with Elisabeth Pfister of 10 November 1984 which is reproduced in Gunda Hinrichs, *Der Heilige Wald von Bomarzo*, Berlin: Mann, 1996, p. 32.

29. Cicero *Disp. Tusc.* 1, 52. *"Nosce te," dicit, hoc dicit: "nosce animum tuum". Nam corpus quidem quasi vas est aut aliquod animi receptaculum....*

30. A bronze by Joseph Beuys entitled *Pythia Sybilla* (1954–1959) is today part of the Block Beuys in the Hessisches Landesmuseum, Darmstadt (room 3). See Tisdall, *Beuys*, pp. 56 ff.

31. As observed by Marianne Beuchert in *Symbolik der Pflanzen*, Frankfurt am Main and Leipzig: Insel Verlag, 1995, pp. 193 ff.

32. See the Chinese folktale "Die Ginkofee" collected in Walter Müller and Ernst Pöppel eds., *Ginko: Der Baum des Lebens*, Frankfurt am Main and Leipzig: Insel Verlag, 2003, p. 11.

33. See note 17.

34. Zweite, Armin, "Prozesse entlassen Strukturen, die keine Systeme sind. Anmerkungen zu einigen raumbezogenen Arbeiten von Joseph Beuys", *Joseph Beuys Skulpturen und Objekte*, Heiner Bastian ed., Berlin: G. Hatje Verlag, 1988, p. 76. See also: Uwe Schneede, *Joseph Beuys: Die Aktionen*, Ostfildern-Ruit: G. Hatje Verlag, 1994; Tisdall, *Beuys*, p. 225;

Lynne Cooke and Karen Kelly eds., *Joseph Beuys Arena—wo wäre ich hingekommen, wenn ich intelligent gewesen wäre!*, Stuttgart and New York: Dia Center for the Arts, 1994. Refer also to the following of Beuys' works classed as 'Multiples': *Vitex Agnus Castus* 1973 (an exemplar of which resides in the collections of Ute and Michael Berger, Wiesbaden and U We Claus, St. Tönis-Vorst), *APOLLO mit Beuys* 1977, *Denkend Sehend (APOLLO)* 1977, and *Levitazione in Italia* 1978, all of which are depicted in J. Schellmann ed., *Joseph Beuys: Die Multiples*, Munich: Edition Schellmann and Schirmer/Mosel Verlag, 1992, nrs. 73, 212, 213, and 237. The 'action' *VITEX AGNUS CASTUS* itself took place on the evening of June 15, 1972 in the Modern Art Agency of Lucio Amelio in Naples on the occasion of the opening of the exhibition *Arena. Dove sarei arrivato so fossi stato intelligente.* A film by Nino Longobardi and nine further works by Beuys were created with respect to this plant.
35. See note 34.
36. Cited after Ruth Schneebeli-Graf ed., *Blütenland China: Botanische Berichte und Bilder*, Basel, Boston and Berlin: Birkhaüser, 1995.
37. For the citation, see Koepplin, *Feuerstätte*, p. 40. Woods that Beuys employed in this work include hawthorn, hornbeam, and mountain ash. A drawing ———? (*Feuerstelle*) of 1961 provided the plan for this 'action' and is today part of the Secret Block for a Secret Person in Ireland, Collection Erich Marx, Nationalgalerie, Berlin.
38. See Dieter Koepplin ed., "Hirschdenmäler im Werk von Joseph Beuys", *Joseph Beuys Symposium Kranenburg 1995*, Basel: Wiese Verlag, 1996, pp. 44 and 48 (notes 4 and 51).
39. Beuys' words as cited in Friedhelm Menneke, *Joseph Beuys MANRESA. eine Aktion as geistliche Übung zu Ignatius von Loyola*, Frankfurt am Main and Leipzig:1992, p. 65.
40. *Propositio XV* as cited in Jurgis Baltrusaitis, *Der Spiegel: Entdeckungen, Täuschungen, Phantasien*, 2nd German ed., Gabriele Ricke and Ronald Vouillé trans., Giessen: Anabas Verlag, p. 251
41. See Baltrusaitis, *Der Spiegel*, p. 252 for the quote and pp. 247–271 for the following remarks and citations regarding artificial or 'created' specters.
42. As remarked by the artist in his conversation with Elisabeth Pfister, recorded in Hinrichs, *Der Heilige Wald*, p. 89. Beuys had presented these very ideas to a public in Tokyo after the concert entitled Coyote III, which he performed in conjunction with his friend Nam June Paik. See Eva, Wenzel, and Jessyka Beuys with Eugen Blume, *Konzert Joseph Beuys COYOTE III Nam June Paik Piano Duet 2. Juni 1984 Sôgetsu Hall, Tokyo* 1815–1915, Medien Archiv JOSEPH BEUYS I, Nationalgalerie Berlin, 1996, p. 36. (Nr. 1 of the publications of the Medien-Archiv). See further Beuys' similar remarks in Joseh Beuys, Jannis Knounellis, Anselm Kiefer, and Enzo Cucchi, *Ein Gespräch*, Jacqueline Burkhardt ed., Zurich and Ostfildern, Hatje Cantz Verlag, 1986, p. 102.
43. See Albert Lutz and Alexandra von Przychowski, *Wege ins Paradies: oder die Liebe zum Stein in China. Felsen und Steine in der chinesischen Malerei*, Zurich: Museum Rietberg, 1998.
44. Joyce, James, *Finnegans Wake*, London: Faber and Faber, 1939, 503.
45. At the Sommer Berger Garden's opening, 15 white chrysanthemums in a painted, blue Chinese vase stood upon the table.
46. Sengcan, George Brecht, Albrecht Fabri, Robert Filliou, Takako Saito, *Seng Ts'an Hsin Hsin Ming*, Brussels and Hamburg: Editions Lebeer Hossmann, 1980.
47. A largely unknown but very lovely installation by Dick Higgins is part of the collection of Eva-Maria Berger in the Mutter Museum in Amorbach.
48. For Eliade's discussion of the consecration of space and the construction of sacred space, see Eliade, *Patterns*, pp. 369–374.
49. Joyce, *Finnegans Wake*, p. 53.
50. See U We Claus, *Der Baum, der Stein*, Förderverein "Museum Schloss Meuland e.V.", Bedburg-Hau, in collaboration with the Stiftung Schloss Meuland—Sammlung van der Grinten—Joseph Beuys Archiv Des Landes Nordrhein Westfalen, 1998. Oaks and basalt stelai were installed for the Free International University Italia in Venice in 2007 and 2008 in Bolognano by the FIU Amsterdam. In York, England, U We Claus and the FIU Amsterdam placed an oak with stele in 2010 (see http: //www.crunchtime2010.org/pages/catalogue.html).
51. With reference to this, see U We Claus, "PERMANENTE KOOPERATION—vom gemeinsamen erarbeiten des Weltbestandes bei Joseph Beuys", *Joseph Beuys ÜBERSINNLICHES GELÄCHTER aus der Sammlung Ute & Michael Berger im Fluxeum Wiesbanden*, Wiesbaden-Erbenheim: Harlekin Art, 1998, pp. 10–18.
52. Issa, Kobayashi, *Mein Frühling*, G.S. Dombrady trans., Manesse Bibliothek der Weltliterature Bd. 24059, Wiesbaden: Manesse Verlag, 1983, pp. 45ff.
53. The work *The Moon is the Oldest TV*, created from 12 black and white television sets, is depicted in Nam June and Charlotte Moorman, *Nam June Paik*, New York: Whitney Museum of Art, 1982. Nam June Paik (1932–2006) was a Korean-born American composer and Fluxus artist as well as video pioneer.
54. See *The Fluxus Performance Workbook*, p. 13.

Figure 1/ The Planet Earth.
Image of Earth floating in space as photographed by the Apollo 17 crew as they traveled toward the moon. Photograph © NASA.

PARADISE LOST?

/LYNDA H. SCHNEEKLOTH

"Imagine we live in a garden." Those of us who live in Western culture can imagine this. In fact, imagining living in the Garden is at the root of much of our cultural production and practices. Now... "Imagine we live on a planet."[1] This imagination is very new in human thought, a perspective tied to the rise of modernity and science, and made visible to all in the Apollo image of the small blue planet floating in the blackness of space [Figure 1].

Both the Garden and the Planet are "place types" rooted in the discourse of typology and naming.[2] A place type has three aspects: a material aspect manifest as a physical presence in the world; a conceptual dimension that describes, analyzes, and sets criteria for inclusion and exclusion as a kind of thing; and an imaginal aspect, most often embedded in stories, that ties that kind of place into the world of beliefs, desires, hope, and visions of utopia and dystopia. A pragmatic culture like ours focuses on the material and conceptual aspects of place, and often denies the imaginal power of places to structure attitudes and practices in the world. That, of course, does not mean the imaginal does not exist, but on the contrary, points to its underlying power.

The Garden as an imaginal type is the vision of paradise, the place of desire in Western culture. The Creation story told in the first chapters of Genesis places humans at the center of Creation in the Garden of Eden. Enter the Planet, the globe, the imagination of the whole Earth. This new imaginal place, the Planet, has turned our vision inside out. Instead of being the center of the universe, we now know we inhabit a very small planet on the edge of our solar system in a vast universe. We are both more unique and more inconsequential.

These two place types frame the modern project as manifest in Western beliefs and attitudes about *homo sapiens*. The Garden and the Planet, however, have different origins and times: the one is an ancient story rooted in the Judeo-Christian-Islamic cosmology, and the other is newborn, having emerged conceptually and empirically through the practice of science in the last few hundred years. In spite of their uneasy relationship, both imaginations play a significant role in our activities and perceptions as a culture and as a species.

Because an imaginal type is best understood in the form of stories, the first section of this essay, "The Stories", offers readings of three texts that explore the use of the imaginal Garden and Planet. The first story is the Biblical account of the creation of the Earth and the Garden of Eden. The second story is Margaret Atwood's *The Year of the Flood*, 2009, the second novel in her MaddAdam trilogy. The third is the emerging story of climate change on the planet Earth based in science and ecology. My concluding section, "Suicide or Adoration", explores consequences of the imaginal Garden and Planet, and proposes that the place type, 'Planet', a singular entity in a heliocentric world, has the capacity to transform and enlarge our cultural concept of Garden. To understand the power and potential of these imaginal places is urgent in the face of the current and future impact of global climate destabilization. If we take on this project, we might create a new imagination of human life in the Garden, Planet Earth.

THE STORIES

THE GARDEN, OH THE GARDEN

This word, this place type, is thick with meaning. The garden brings to mind the healing place, the source of food and sustenance, and the space of beauty. For cultures grounded in the Judaic-Christian-Islamic tradition, the garden has been here since the dawn of the world [Figure 2].[3]

There are two accounts of Creation in the book of Genesis, but it is the more ancient story of the Garden of Eden that has framed the cosmology of Western culture. In Genesis 2 and 3, God created the Earth, the land and water, and all the plants. In that garden,

> He put the man whom he had formed. And out of the ground made the Lord God to grow every tree that is pleasant to the sight, and good for food;

the Tree of Life also in the midst of the garden and the Tree of Knowledge of Good and Evil.[4]

God put Adam "into the Garden of Eden to dress it and keep it" and according to the text, the man was alone in a verdant world of plants.[5] The Lord God, seeing that the man was lonely, made all the animals—those of the land, the water and the air—and brought them before Adam, who named them all. But the Lord God saw that this was not enough, and so he made Eve as Adam's helpmate.

Adam and Eve were provided all they needed, including the invitation to eat from the abundance of the garden. There was only one rule: "But of the Tree of Knowledge of Good and Evil thou shalt not eat for in that day that thou eatest thereof thou shalt surely die."[6] The wily snake hissed into Eve's ear and told her that if she ate of the fruit of the Tree of Knowledge, she would not die, but would be like the gods, knowing good and evil. She convinced Adam it was a good thing to do—and so they ate of the fruit of the Tree of Knowledge, knowingly disobeying their creator, but not willing, or perhaps not able, to understand the consequences of this action.

As Jack Miles reminds us in *God: A Biography*, the snake was right. Immediately, they were like the gods with an awareness of good and evil. They knew they were naked, they experienced separateness, and they were ashamed.

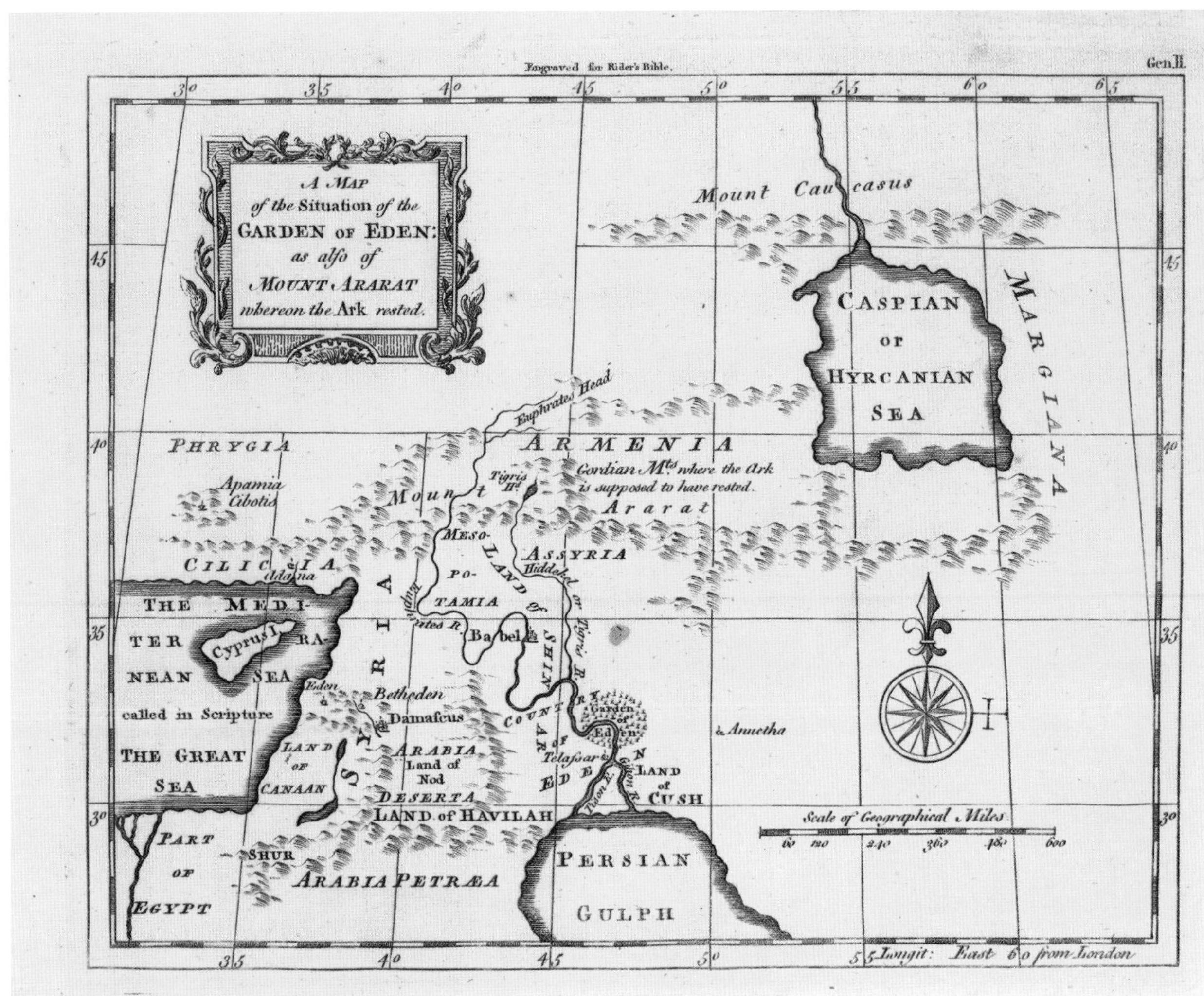

Figure 2/ The Garden: archetypal place of desire.

A Map of the Situation of the Garden of Eden: as also of Mount Ararat whereon the Ark Rested. Map with the "Persian Gulph" at the base, the "Caspian or Hyrcanian Sea" in upper right and the "Gordian Mts. where the Ark is supposed to have rested. / Ararat" in the center. Illustration to *The Christian's Family Bible* (1763–1767), print made by Charles Grignion. Image © The Trustees of the British Museum.

They tried, unsuccessfully, to hide. God's response was swift. Fearing that Adam and Eve would also seek the Tree of Life in the garden and achieve immortality, "the Lord God sent [Adam] forth from the Garden of Eden, to till the ground from whence he was taken".[7] From this time forward, the humans would experience scarcity, would have to work for their sustenance, and would experience pain. They were tempted, they disobeyed, and they were cast out of Eden.

According to the Biblical texts, this was not the only time that God punished the humans he had created. His second act against men and women is told in the story of Noah and the Flood, which is said to have occurred not many generations after Adam and Eve's expulsion.[8] God saw the continued disobedience and evil of the people. This time He decided to expel people not only from the precious Garden, but from the Earth itself. Yet God did find one righteous man and agreed to save Noah and his family and two of each of the animals of the world. Noah and his sons, in spite of ridicule, built an ark on dry land to God's specifications. They gathered the creatures of the world together and marched them onto the boat that survived 40 days and nights of rain. According to the story, the world was drowned.

After the Flood, God begins all over again with his creation and his human creatures. He promises that He will never again destroy the whole Earth because of man. "And I will remember my covenant, which is between me and you and every living creature of all flesh; and the waters shall no more become a flood to destroy all flesh."[9] Because the flood destroyed all life on Earth except for those on the ark, this event could be considered the second Creation, the remaking of the world after the great extinction.

Like all origin stories, these narratives explain why we are on the Earth and how the world came to be. These stories tell us many things at the very foundation of our culture, beginning with the premise that the Earth is the result of a great making, and humans are unique and special. We also learn that as humans, we are powerful and we are disgraced; we have free will and there are consequences; we are curious and we refuse to accept constraints.

The lesson that the Western world seems to remember best is that we, the Adams and the Eves who were once a part of everything, are now separate. For an act of disobedience, for the desire to know and be like the gods, we were thrown out of utopia, our given home in the Garden of Eden. And we long to return. This often unspoken desire has framed our culture, whether we locate the Garden in heaven, in the founding of the 'New World' and nations such as the United States, in the protection of wilderness in our parks, or in the suburban yards that have carpeted the United States.

The Garden, verdant and bounteous, is at the center of this origin story. As imagined in Western culture, it is beautiful, green, nourishing, and fertile; the Garden is generous and provides. The place type embodies a refuge and refers to an enclosed space, an inside. Everything outside is the shadow, the not-garden, wild, untended, and suitable for use. This dialectic of inside and outside has made and unmade the world with increasing intensity since the dawn of modernity with its science, technological tools, and seemingly unlimited energy. The sacred Garden, enclosed and set aside, renders everything else profane and therefore subject to different rules and practices. The consequences of the imaginal garden and the assignment of everywhere else as non-garden, have generated a world that retains only a few precious protected places set in the midst of ruin.

Scholars such as Karen Armstrong and William Schniedewind report that these Judeo-Christian-Islamic origin stories about the Garden of Eden and The Flood were written by various authors between 8000 and 6000 BCE.[10] One has to wonder what experiences and deep fears would cause the small population of people in the Middle East to recount their origin as a 'fall', as an expulsion from paradise. What could they have done that made it appear impossible to go back to the place of their origin? We can never know for certain, but two significant transformations during those millennia might have reset a vision of the place of humans on the Earth: agriculture and individuation.

Evolutionary biologists and theorists have suggested that the stories found in Genesis recount the long transition from a hunting/gathering culture to a life of agriculture after the last global ice age and mark the beginning of the Holocene epoch.[11] The idea of the garden as a place denied to us emerged as a cultural response to the cultivation of land as a way of life. In Genesis, God tells humans:

> Cursed is the ground for thy sake; in sorrow shalt thou eat of it all the days of thy life; Thorns also and thistles shall it bring forth to thee; and thou shalt eat the herb of the field; In the sweat of thy face shalt thou eat bread, till thou return until the ground; for out of it wast thou taken; for dust thou art, and unto dust shalt thou return.[12]

During the millions of years we as a species inhabited the Earth before agriculture and cities, tribes of humans moved across territories as foragers, plucking and digging the fruits of the Earth, trapping and hunting to sustain small decentralized populations. If current research on existing forager cultures reflects the life of our early ancestors, they led a culturally rich existence that was filled with social and community life, while working only about 20 hours a week to provide food and shelter for themselves. Imaginally, it might be said that early humans lived in the Garden of Eden, where the Earth itself provided everything they needed. Even today, the few remaining hunter/gatherer societies live within the constraints of their gardens and therefore, have not been thrown out, at least, not until modern humans arrive. Chellis Glendinning provides a timeline:

> A mere 300 generations ago, or 0.03 percent of our time on earth, humans in the Western world began the process of controlling the natural world through agriculture and animal domestication. Just five or six generations have passed since the industrial societies emerged out of this domestication process.[13]

We have been taught that the transition from a hunting/gathering life into city life and agricultural settlements is the tale of *progress* that created civilization. But what if this transition, slow and generational as it must have been, was rather a deep humiliation for humans? Urban and settled life brought not only the toil of agriculture and an increase of physical labor, but also food insecurity, hierarchal society, and loss of community life. And so began the search for a return to paradise to reclaim the lost garden.

Some scholars have argued that during this same period of transition from foraging to agriculture, the human psyche was evolving because of the radically different social relationships that resulted from settled life in villages and cities.[14] Lacking the rootedness of inviolate kinship systems that characterize forager cultures, agrarian societies saw the "perception of the self as an individual" become more distinct. This transition from community-focused culture to individual-focused culture has reached its zenith in modernity. One consequence has been an unrelenting experience of "separateness". Such self-reflexive knowledge comes with an acute awareness of limits, of loneliness, and of death; this knowledge may be too much to bear:[15]

> It is indeed the illusion of bodily separation that is the genuine sorrow, that accounts for our loneliness, that isolates us and leads us to exploit and violate one another, the world we live in, and ultimately ourselves.... The sorrowful illusion of separateness is expressed in Judeo-Christian thinking as estrangement from God; it is what the fruit of the tree of knowledge–consciousness–condemns us to.[16]

We cannot know why these particular origin stories were constructed over eons by different authors in the early civilizations of the Fertile Crescent, but we do know some of the consequences. The shift from gathering from the Earth and adoring the Earth, to setting ourselves apart and extracting from the Earth, set the stage for modern industrial culture and the world we find ourselves in today. We have used the given world to meet our needs, as all creatures do. However, we alone of all creatures are using the planet to such an extent that we are destroying the fabric of the Earth on which our very lives depend. And we do know that the extreme individuation of modern life, made possible through the power of humans over the natural world, has not made us happy, has not healed the perceived rift, and has not given us any cosmology as fulfilling as the vision of the garden.

THE GARDENERS OF ATWOOD'S FUTURE

The story of the Garden of Eden is thought to describe the world during the radical transformation from a life in a garden, in which humans gathered bounty from the Earth, to life in a world of agriculture, in which they worked the land. Margaret Atwood's novel, *The Year of the Flood*, takes place in a near future Toronto that offers insights into the radical transformation from modernity to an undetermined and conflicted future.

The collapse of the structure of everyday life is the background for Atwood's dystopia. The violent and dysfunctional urban neighborhoods she describes are imaginal place types more reminiscent of hell than garden. Everyone is controlled by the CorpSeCorps, a powerful private security force that has totally replaced any semblance of public security or governance. The privileged few are protected in gated compounds, while 'outside', on the streets of the "pleebmobs", it is dangerous and often deadly.

But within the degenerated neighborhood of Sinkhole, a utopian enclave is maintained by a community calling itself the Gardeners, who have created an 'inside', a series of protected spaces in abandoned buildings scattered through the neighborhood [Figure 3]. They tend what gardens they can through their own efforts at growing

Figure 3/ Making Gardens.

The Massachusetts Avenue Project (MAP) works with urban youth in a distressed community in Buffalo, NY. Young people grow, harvest, and sell the food, and in addition, have begun a small business making products from their gardens to sell in local supermarkets. Photographs by Erin Sharkley, used by permission of MAP.

Figure 4/ Garbage to Gardens, Guatemala City, Guatemala.
The largest garbage dump in Central America was transformed into three gardens by the Safe Passage, an NGO, and community members with the assistance of a design/build studio under the supervision of Daniel Winterbottom, Associate Professor, University of Washington, Department of Landscape Architecture. The landfill (left). The Garden of Hope (right). Photographs by Daniel Winterbottom, 2006.

food on vacant lots, on roofs, and in the basements of abandoned buildings. They make use of every available resource secured from the streets while living with as little as possible [Figure 4].

The Gardeners practice sustainable forms of agriculture in make-shift and unpretentious gardens carved out of the decaying city. Their vision of life is based on the ecological and evolutionary knowledge of the planet Earth. And yet the cosmology that guides their faith and grounds their spatial and cultural practices maintains deep connections with the Biblical account of the Judaic-Christian-Islamic tradition. Indeed, their elders are all named 'Adam' or 'Eve', differentiated only by numbers to indicate their primacy in the group.

Adam One, the leader, gives insight into this vision that blends the ancient Biblical stories with the newer story of science:

> Our Fall from the original Garden was a Fall from the innocent acting-out of such patterns and impulses to a conscious and shamed awareness of them; and from thence comes our sadness, our anxiety, our doubt, our rage against God.... Why do we think that everything on Earth belongs to us, while in reality, we belong to Everything?[17]

His words echo both the ancient Garden of Eden and the discipline and practice of ecology. For the Gardeners, knowledge is critical to their practices, but equally important is the adoration of the very presence and function of the Earth.

The Year of the Flood is narrated in flashback by two survivors, Toby and Ren, after a mysterious "Waterless Flood" has swept over the planet. Toby has sequestered herself in a spa where she had been working. Ren had been isolated in a highclass brothel, "Scales and Tails". Both had earlier lived with the Gardeners. When they find each other toward the end of the novel, Toby and Ren leave their places of refuge/captivity; only then do they, and we, discover the fate of the other Gardeners.

Toby had been rescued from an extremely abusive situation by Adam One and the children of the Gardeners. Her description of the Gardeners' primary home, Edencliff, and her emotions upon joining them reflect an image of the Garden of Eden and suggest a sense of coming home:

> She gazed around it in wonder: it was so beautiful, with plants and flowers of many kinds she'd never seen before. There were vivid butterflies; from nearby came the vibration of bees. Each petal and leaf was fully alive, shining with awareness of her. Even the air of the Garden was different. She found herself crying with relief and gratitude. It was as if a large, benevolent hand had reached down and picked her up, and was holding her safe.[18]

Atwood teaches us about the faith of the Gardeners through a whimsical set of rhymes, hymns, saints and their festivals, and sermons by Adam One. Their origin story borrows heavily from Genesis as recorded in "The God's Gardeners Oral Hymnbook":

> THE GARDEN
> Who is it tends the Garden,
> The Garden oh so green?
>
> T'was once the finest Garden
> That ever has been seen.
>
> And in it God's dear Creatures
> Did swim and fly and play:

But then came greedy Spoilers,
And killed them all away.

And all the Trees that flourished
And gave us wholesome fruit,

By waves of sand are buried,
Both leaf and branch and root.

And all the shining Water
Is turned to slime and mire,

And all the feathered Birds so bright
Have ceased their joyful choir.

Oh Garden, oh my Garden,
I'll mourn forevermore

Until the Gardeners arise,
And you to Life restore.

Interesting: no snake, no Tree of Knowledge, no expulsion. This account of Creation does not tell us we were thrown out of the garden. Rather, it is the "Spoilers" who have destroyed the "The Garden oh so Green". The Gardeners of Sinkhole daily witness the destruction of the Earth and its community; they are reminded every day of the total disregard for life and the intentional killing of the planet, of humans, and of the nearly extinct animals for food and fun. They have every reason to believe that God will visit his vengeance upon the human species, for it is humans who have broken the covenant of the last flood:

> We have taken the World given to us and carelessly destroyed its fabric and its Creatures. Other religions have taught that this World is to be rolled up like a scroll and burnt to nothingness, and that a new Heaven and a New Earth will then appear. But why would God give us another Earth when we have mistreated this one so badly? No, my Friends. It is not this Earth that is to be demolished: it is the Human Species. Perhaps God will create another, more compassionate race to take our place. For the Waterless Flood has swept over us... it is a plague—a plague that infects no Species but our own and that will leave all other Creatures untouched.[19]

The Gardeners know that the next great extinction is under way. In anticipation of the Waterless Flood, they are building an Ark to save themselves and other creatures. They see themselves as "the plural Noah: we too have been called, we too forewarned".[20] Like the Noah of Genesis, they endure ridicule and are, in truth, protected by it. As Adam tells Toby: "They [the larger culture] view us as twisted fanatics who combine food extremism with bad fashion sense and a puritanical attitude toward shopping. But we own nothing they want, so we don't qualify as terrorists."[21]

Atwood creates a rich sense of the daily life and practices that tie the community together. They eat no flesh, refrain from killing any creature, and rely totally on plants and occasional insects for their sustenance; their lives are filled with labor in the production of food, including mushrooms and vegetables. The arduous labor required for agricultural production is lightened and sustained through rituals, festivals, and saint days. For example, on St. Farley of the Wolves day, the young people move out into the "plebe" streets to collect anything thrown out and bring their findings back to make soap or vinegar or to reuse for whatever purpose. They collect and find uses for what others conceived to be waste. One of their principles is that "Nothing should be carelessly thrown away, not even wine from sinful places. There is no such thing as garbage, trash, or dirt, only matter that hadn't been put to a proper use."[22] Part of what they produce is saved for the caches or "Ararats", to be stored for use after the Flood when they, like Noah, will start again to care for the garden Earth, to preserve, protect, and rebuild it.

The Gardeners' adoration of plants through the book is detailed and delightful. On St. Euell of Wild Foods week, the entire community moves out into the surrounding area, especially Heritage Park (an actual park in present-day Toronto), to gather fungi and plants, singing, "Oh sing we now the Holy Weeds / That flourish in the ditch, / For they are for the meek in needs, / They are not for the rich." Every life form is celebrated, from the giant whales to the "tiny perfect Moles / That garden underground / The Ant, the Worm, the nematode / Wherever they are found."[23]

One of the most important teachings of the Gardeners regards the intimacy of life and death. Ren, in her isolation, recalls their endless talk about death: "The Gardeners were strict about not killing Life, but on the other hand they said Death was a natural process, which is sort of a contradiction, now that I think about it. They had the idea that turning into compost would be just fine. Not everyone might think that having your body become part of a vulture was a terrific future to look forward to, but the Gardener did."[24] After Eve Six dies, she is 'composted' in Heritage Park so that she may now nourish the ground.

The community is governed by a small group of the elders, whose deliberations are communal, extensive, and secret. This group resembles a cult in its 'end of the world is coming' attitude, but their belief is grounded in the experiences of the individuals who truly knew what was occurring in the larger world. Many of the members had participated in the corporate compound culture as scientists, doctors, and even secret police. When they discovered that the goal of their corporate research was the development of

a final plague that would wipe out the human species, they disappeared into the Gardeners. Others like them who were less fortunate met with mysterious accidents.

Even intentional communities like the Gardeners have disagreements and conflict between members and resentment by the young people toward the adults. But the Gardeners' most fundamental tension is between Adam One and another member, Zeb. The faction led by Adam One believe that their purpose is to prepare for the Flood and second great extinction. They decry the violence of the world, and believe their work is to "bear witness" to the dissolution of the fabric of the Earth rather than take action. They ask, "What is it about our own Species that leaves us so vulnerable to the impulse to violence? Why are we so addicted to the shedding of blood?" But they "take comfort in the thought that this history will soon be swept away by the Waterless Flood.... For all works of Man will be as words written in water." Others, under the leadership of Zeb, believe that decisive action must be taken: "Peace goes only so far.... There's at least a hundred new extinct species since this time last month. They got fucking eaten! We can't just sit here and watch the lights blink out."[25] Zeb encourages others to join him in 'bio-resistance' and counter-terrorism designed to impede and frustrate the work of the corporations. He refuses to simply witness the coming Flood that would destroy the world.

In spite of the differences in strategy, all of the Gardeners believe in, and plan for, the end. All expect some event that will wipe humans off the face of the Earth. When it arrives, they recognize that:

> This was the Waterless Flood.... It had all the signs: it travelled through the air as if on wings, it burned through cities like fire, spreading germ-ridden mobs, terror, and butchery. The lights were going out everywhere, the news was sporadic: systems were failing as their keepers died. It looked like total breakdown.[26]

When the novel begins, Toby and Ren, not even knowing of the other's existence, are apparently the only two humans alive. In their terrifying isolation, these women are consoled, in part, by the simple rhymes, songs, festivals, and lessons they had each learned in the utopian community, devices that remind them of their place in the world. The slogan, "It is better to hope than to mope" rings in Ren's head.[27] The sustained, ritualized celebration of life reminds them that even now, after the Waterless Flood, they are Gardeners, and that thought leaves a small hope that other Adams and Eves are alive, just as Noah and his family survived the first Flood.

In the midst of a dysfunctional and violent world, the Gardeners created their own paradise—not a perfect space, but a material and imaginal garden. They borrowed from the stories we already know, the Garden, the Flood, science and ecology, and wove them into a worldview that was seductive and oppositional, grounding these systems of thoughts as practices embedded in daily life. The Gardeners' rhymes and songs, festival and lessons affirmed their place in the world and their responsibilities to the Earth and life itself.

Atwood's dystopian future recasts the story of the Genesis that has framed Western culture's belief and practices. Only this time, humanity faces not an imaginal expulsion from the Garden, but something more like the Flood, the total annihilation of the species. The degenerate human society, driven by consumption, violence, and exploitation, is swept away in the Waterless Flood, leaving readers to ponder whether or not the Earth would be better off without the cruel, self-exiled humans.

MEANWHILE, BACK ON PLANET EARTH

According to the narrative of modernity, humans have finally achieved power over nature and can provide a rich and pleasurable life—a life in the garden, for many in Western industrialized nations. However, this modern life, which began around the sixteenth century, has had unintended consequences for all of Earth's creatures that we are only now beginning to understand. One of these consequences, the very recent story of climate change framed by the discourse of science, has permeated the globe in this age of international communications.

Hence, the poignancy of Atwood's fiction is not only in its story of loss, but in its plausibility, as the fast approaching dystopia is made manifest in the actual

transformation of this planet. Bill McKibben, one of the great storytellers of the current cultural crisis, tells us that global climate destabilization is closer to Atwood's narrative than we would like to hear. He and most scientists have confirmed that this massive change is not something that will happen in the future, but it is happening right now. Modern life has brought an end to the Holocene epoch and the garden-like world that engendered ten thousand years of human culture. This change has been so swift and so profound that McKibben suggests we rename our planet and call it "Eaarth". As is spoken in the Bhagavad Gita, and quoted by J. Robert Oppenheimer at the first nuclear explosion, "We have become as gods, destroyers of the world" [Figure 5].[28]

According to McKibben, "Eaarth represents the deepest of human failures."[29] Humans have pushed and exploited the natural world, destroying life support systems that sustain us and other creatures—the air, the land, the water, and living things. We have been running Genesis backwards, in essence, 'uncreating' the given world.

Figure 5/ On the 'Outside': the Legacy of Toxic Waste. The Buffalo River was used as a repository of waste by the industry that grew along its banks during the nineteenth and early twentieth centuries. The river was invisible and 'outside' the legitimate city. In 1985 the International Joint Commission declared it an Area of Concern, one of the 42 toxic hot spots on the Great Lakes. The legacy is 600,000 cubic yards of contaminated sediment and debris that must be removed for the Buffalo River to reclaim its life as a living body of water. Photograph by Jill Jedlicka, used by permission of the Buffalo Niagara Riverkeeper.

The tipping point was the last energy shift into hydrocarbon, a form of energy that provides enormous and invisible power.[30] The life we have formed around fossil fuels is unprecedented and unsustainable. Consider that "[O]ne barrel of oil yields as much energy as 25,000 hours of human manual labor—more than a decade of human labor per barrel. The average American uses 25 barrels each year, which is like finding 300 years of free labor annually" for each person.[31] Imagine for a moment what that means. Each year every American uses the equivalent of 300 years of free human labor; we are living as if each of us had an endless stream of slaves at our call. No wonder it is so hard to conceive of living differently.

During the Holocene geological epoch, which began about 12,000 years ago, the Earth's temperature has averaged between 58 and 60 degrees Fahrenheit, giving us stable seas and ice sheets, favorable conditions for farming, and the climate control of many diseases.[32] Only in the last 200 years have we brought up ancient plants and animals from the depths of the Earth—literally fossil fuels—burned them and dispersed them into the atmosphere. This practice, especially since the 1950s, has brought us to a new reality—a more capricious, violent, and unstable planet. Nature is pushing back. Here are some of the consequences as told by McKibben and others:

- Because of the Earth's warming, more water in the atmosphere is increasing rainfall and extreme weather events.
- Rivers, the source of fresh water for most of the Earth, are drying up.
- Droughts are increasing and are predicted to expand across southwest United States, Northern China, Brazil, and Argentina.
- Ice is disappearing quickly, already 40 percent less than when Apollo flew in 1968. The disappearance of land-based glaciers means the elimination of drinking water for millions.
- One degree Celsius is enough to cause 6 percent increase in lightning, resulting in mega-fires.
- The ocean is becoming more acid, killing coral; higher temperatures reduce the absorption of the sea and plants.
- Modern industrialized agricultural systems are failing, while at the same time contributing as much as 40 percent to warming.
- "One-fifth of Earth's plant life is under threat of extinction", and this era may well be the end of the Age of Large Mammals.[33]
- "History shows that whenever humans have faced a choice between starving or raiding, they raid."[34] We are already seeing an increase in the number of environmental refugees and fights over water and land, threatening peace and security worldwide.
- Worldwide wealth is used for the military; 48 percent of the world's total military spending is in the Pentagon.[35]
- If everyone in the world lived as citizens of the USA, we would need the resources of five planet Earths.

Figure 6/ Water Bodies, 2009.
A dance in celebration of our relationship to water was choreographed by Gerald Trentham and performed by Amy Taravella on the shores of Lake Erie. It was commissioned by the Canadian Consulate of Buffalo in celebration of the one hundredth Anniversary of the Boundary Waters Treaty that created a joint US/Canadian Commission responsible for the Great Lakes. Photograph by Lynda Schneekloth.

These facts, no longer predictions, are impossible to truly hear. We have been unable to bring these conditions together into a story that makes sense to our perceptions and experience. Regardless of our beliefs, the challenges ahead are vast, and so much greater than anyone has led us to believe. The science of climate change is unassailable.[36] At some deep level, people know in their hearts. You hear it in the anger expressed about everything and in the violence toward one another. Anger can be righteous and appropriate. But often, psychologists say, anger is an emotional reaction to fear or to grief. The world as we know it is dying, much of the life on Earth is dying. How can we not be afraid? How can we not grieve?

The landscapes we have inhabited for thousands of years are changing; even the places we have known in our own lifetimes are changing. Glenn Albrecht describes what is happening to Australians who experienced a severe drought followed by unprecedented flooding; they seem to be 'homesick', although they are still at home. Albrecht suggests it is a type of nostalgia—a new kind of sadness, "solastalgia"—defined as "[a] form of homesickness one gets when one is still at 'home'". The drought deepened, the floods ravaged the Earth, and the land and weather changed. "Familiar plants don't grow any more. Gardens won't take. Birds are gone."[37] People experience serious and lasting depression at the loss of their home as the world around them is dying.

The solastalgia of Albrecht's Australians is similar to that of Atwood's Gardeners, who daily mourn the loss of the Earth's species. The changing earth, this new planet *Eaarth*, brings not only physical, political and economic changes, but personal, deeply emotional responses that we have not even begun to consider. Toby's account of her earlier life resembles all too closely our world today:

> I knew there were things wrong in the world... but the wrong things were wrong somewhere else.... [Later] the wrongness had moved closer. She remembers the oppressive sensation, like waiting all the time for a heavy stone footfall, then the knock at the door. Everybody knew. Nobody admitted to knowing. If other people began to discuss it, you tuned them out, because what they were saying was both so obvious and so unthinkable. *We're using up the Earth. It's almost gone.* You can't live with such fears and keep on whistling.[38]

Like the people in *The Year of the Flood*, it is almost impossible for us to imagine that we are using up the Planet Earth. This story cannot be true; surely there is always some place outside the garden for us to use. The knowledge and imagination of the Planet is so new that we have not had time, culturally, to absorb the vast cosmological insight that everything is inside. We continue to function under our origin story of the Garden of Eden, in which precious inside places are surrounded by the profane 'everywhere else' that is open to human exploitation rather than protection. We are the people of ancient beliefs playing with powers we cannot comprehend or responsibly employ. We are, in a sense, reenacting the willful act of Adam and Eve in the Garden of Eden.

How does an individual, a community, a world, respond to the changes we are seeing on the planet we inhabit? Through the new practices of biological and ecological sciences that have grown since modernity, we are confronted with a new imagination of the Earth and the evolution of life on this planet. Indeed, we see that there can be no Garden, biologically speaking, because the inside cannot be separated from the outside. Everything is connected to everything else. The origin stories of the Garden, the Fall and the Flood cannot help us know what to do [Figure 6].

SUICIDE OR ADORATION

According to Teilhard de Chardin, "The day is not far when humanity will realize that biologically it is faced with a choice between suicide and adoration."[39] To one from a future generation looking back at our time, the verdict would be clear—we have chosen suicide. The current world trajectory is the continuation of an addiction to fossil fuels, if by addiction one means continuing some behavior in spite of knowing that "it is destructive to self, family, work or social relationships".[40] We seem unable to stop our suicidal and 'eco-cidal' behavior. All of our energy, wealth, technology, and might is being using to puncture and slice open the Earth to extract the last drop of oil, lump of coal, or ounce of natural gas. Strong nations go to war against people across the globe to secure their access to this powerful drug; environmental destruction is occurring at an unimaginable scale; and the increase of carbon and methane in the atmosphere continues to drive up the Earth's temperatures at a rate inconceivable only ten years ago. In spite of this destructive path, the extraction of fossil fuels continues as corporations proceed to hydro-frack for natural gas in formerly preserved forests and farmland, drill wells deep in the ocean, and extract oil from the tar sands at great financial and environmental costs. For what purpose is not asked. This is our reality—but it was not inevitable.

> We will stand before whoever is able and willing to judge, or perhaps the silence of extinction, as a generation that willfully and unnecessarily imposed egregious wrongs on all future generations, depriving them of liberty, property, and life.[41]

There is a great divide between the culture of modernity that fragments the world into Garden and not-Garden and the perspective embodied in a holistic ecological imagination.[42] David Orr suggests that there is also a cultural divide in how we imagine the future. If we believe we all share one place both now and in the future, then we are compelled to "lay the foundation for a durable and just global civilization, to secure the gift of life and pass it on undiminished to unnumbered generations. No previous generation could have said that, and none ever had greater work to do."[43] If, however, we believe that the spaces of the protected Garden permit the exploitation of the rest of the Earth, and if, like the people of Atwood's novel, we do not assume a responsibility to future generations, we will continue to add to the legacy of ecological and financial debt and deficits.

This is not just a failure of individuals; it is a failure of the collective. We have failed to establish institutions to protect posterity, failed to orient ourselves to the generations to come who will bear the consequences of our actions and inactions, and failed to understand the inadequacy of our vision of the Garden. Unlike many native cultures—such as the Haudenosaunee (Iroquois), whose cosmology is based on a vision of responsibility for seven generations —we do not recognize the rights of future human generations on this planet. Only a few nations, Ecuador among them, even acknowledge the rights of nature in their constitutions.[44]

In Atwood's trilogy, there do exist people other than the Gardeners who share a desire to stop the lunacy of human's destruction. But their way is a perversion of modernity's faith in human ingenuity and creativity and in the tools of science and technology. The scientist Crake of the novel *Oryx and Crake* believes he could improve on God's design and describes his work as focused on the "biggest problem of all, which was human beings—their cruelty and suffering, their wars and poverty, their fear of death. What would you pay for the design of a perfect human being?"[45] Under his direction, the corporate project, "Paradice", is successful in eliminating the old model, God's creation, in the Waterless Flood.

Crake and his team also successfully create an 'improved human model' to replace the original flawed one. This new human is peaceful, docile, and cooperative: "[T]hey don't need clothes, they eat leaves, they purr like cats."[46] This genetically engineered species is the human solution to the flawed 'image of God'. Crake, like modern culture itself, has taken on the role of the gods, ignoring the fabric of life with which humans evolved. Yes, this is speculative fiction, but it also reflects the world of biotechnology conducted within our contemporary corporate compounds.

Teilhard de Chardin offered us an alternative: adoration. This is a sense of awe in the face of the miracle that is the Earth. The Gardeners in *The Year of the Flood*,

though preparing for the end, live in a state of wonder and celebration. And even in the face of despair after the Flood, when Ren believes she may be the last person alive on the Earth, she finds strength in such celebration, telling herself, "Ren, your life is a precious gift, and where there's a gift there is a Giver, and when you've been given a gift, you should always say thank you."[47]

Adoration as expressed in Atwood's book has two foundations: a knowledge-based understanding of the Earth's ecology, and a cosmology based in gratitude and celebration of something beyond any understanding—a profoundly incomprehensible divine creation. The Earth is a garden and the garden is a gift. We are a part of the garden; our being is interwoven into the presence of the whole Earth. This oneness, however, does not mean we are unaware of our separateness and aloneness, including the recognition of the presence of death not just as an idea, but as personal extinction. Adam One incorporates both science and wonder in his final words in the book:

> All Souls [Festival] is not restricted to Human Souls: among us, it encompasses the Souls of all the living Creatures that have passed through Life, and have undergone the Great Transformation, and have entered that state sometimes called Death, but more rightly known as Renewed Life. For in this our World, and in the eye of God, *not a single atom that has ever existed is truly lost*."[48] [italics added]

Humans, like all living beings, are a part of the Great Transformation and the conservation of energy and matter. There is no life without death, and what brief immortality exists belongs to the species, not to the individual. But unlike the Gardeners, modern culture has yet to integrate what we know and what we allow ourselves to know about life and death. In truth, we have yet to believe in the fiber of our beings, or maybe have only forgotten, that we are totally dependent on the generosity of the Earth and the biodiversity of the planet for our very lives. As Douglas Tallamy cautions,

> Humans cannot live as the only species on this planet because it is other species that create the ecosystem services essential to our survival. Every time we force a species to extinction we promote our own demise. Biodiversity is not optional.[49]

"Ecosystem services" is the phrase used in the discipline of ecology to describe those things we are given simply by being a part of the Earth community: air, water filtration in the Earth, bacteria that break down waste, and so on [Figure 7]. The Gardeners of Atwood's novel would completely understand this concept and encourage us to cease the war we are waging on the home and food supply of the plants and animals that feed us.

At one level, the basis of life is very simple. As Evan Eisenberg puts it, "What all hunters, all farmers, all plants and animals do is hunt the sun and eat it. The trick is to find the most efficient path between the sun and the mouth."[50] Humans, like almost all other creatures on this Earth, are dependent on plants, the kingdom of beings that has evolved to turn sunlight into nutrients for all the rest of us. Plants have done this for eons and certainly much longer than the brief time *homo sapiens* have been on this planet. Even though we interact with plants every day as we breath their oxygen, benefit from their use of our CO_2, eat them, admire them, excrete them, plant them, tend them, and cut them down, we have failed to understand plants and their role in the garden that is the planet. The result is that the green mantle of the Earth, on which all life depends, is endangered.

Millions of years of patient evolution created our planet Earth. We are only beginning to understand the impact of human actions on these generative and interdependent systems, and have only begun to act on that knowledge. The stories recounted tell us that, unlike the Gardeners who lived with an ecological imagination, we do not recognize the interdependency of all beings. Rather, the people of modern culture, like Adam and Eve, like the people of Noah's day, refuse to be bound by any constraint, whether the laws of ecology or the proposition that we have a responsibility to posterity.

Yet, we still long to live in the Garden. We tell ourselves that we have been making replicas of the Garden by developing parks and preserves, but we do not acknowledge that these are isolated islands of limited biodiversity. In the name of making 'gardens' we invented the suburbs, a landscape that has destroyed the ecological fabric of this country with endless lawns, the monoculture non-productive green carpet, populated with plants treated as isolated beings.[51] Plants cannot function as individual species any more than humans can. Each plant belongs to an entire community that includes photosynthesizing materials, insects, worms, bacteria, minerals, waters, other plants, birds, and so on. In our quest to make gardens, we have used biotechnology to improve on the created world, discovering, again, that our actions have created more problems than we have solved. And mostly, in our attention to the Garden, we have used up the outside, the not-garden.

The imaginal Garden has maintained its power over centuries; it is still a vision of paradise, the precious place, the source of nourishment, and the enclosed space. But the vision of the Garden cannot hold in the face of *Eaarth*. The Garden now resides uneasily within an imagination of another place, the Planet, the image of the small blue globe floating in space: one place, one ecology, one home.

Figure 7/ Cheonggye River Restoration in Seoul, Korea.

This river, once channeled, piped, and covered with a highway, was daylighted and now is a part of the stormwater management system in the city of over ten million people. This ecological imagination provides not only environmental services, but a green respite in the gray city. Photograph by Lynda Schneekloth.

Given the power of the imaginal Garden, we cannot and should not abandon or reject it as place of desire. Rather, we must find a way to reframe it through the new place type of the Planet. *Eaarth* is the same Garden—almost—that was given to us at the dawn of the world. And even though we have behaved as if we were thrown out and denied, the Garden has never disappeared and we have never been denied. We have just been blinded to its gifts. Now that the blessings we have taken for granted for millions of years are really endangered, as paradise is about to be lost, will we be able to see that we have truly been living in the Garden? As one of Atwood's characters asks, "Why are we designed to see the world as supremely beautiful just as we're about to be snuffed?"[52]

It is possible to rethink the origin story, not of the Garden itself, but our imagination of it. As recently as 50 years ago we didn't understand the implications of our collective path of progress and resource consumption. Because we didn't understand or imagine that there is only one place, one Garden Planet, we failed to see that the activities of modern life were destructive beyond our imagination. But today we do know. We of this generation are faced with a choice that our forebears did not have to face: suicide or adoration. Toby begins for us when she prays:

> Dear Adams, dear Eves, dear Fellow Mammals and Fellow Creatures, all those now in Spirit—keep us in your view and lend us your strength, because we are surely going to need it.[53]

Notes

1. McKibben, Bill, *Eaarth: Making a Life on a Tough New Planet*, New York: Times Books, Henry Holt and Company, 2010, p. 1.
2. Schneekloth, Lynda H. and Karen A. Franck, *Ordering Spaces: Types in Architecture and Design*, New York: Van Nostrand Reinhold, 1994.
3. I am using the familiar Creation story of Genesis without critique as a generative narrative and will not attempt to resolve difference and contradictions of the two Creation stories told in Genesis 1, 2, and 3 or the inconsistencies in the story of the Flood in Genesis 6–9. The five books of Moses are sacred texts for Judaism, Christianity, and Islam and serve as foundational stories for these religious traditions. Four different authors or traditions have been identified in the first five books of the religious text. The Garden of Eden version told in Genesis 2 and 3 was written by a tradition known as "J" (who called God "Yahweh") around the eighth century BCE. The six-day account from Genesis 1 and 2 is purported to have been written almost two thousand years later by the "P" (Priestly) tradition probably in the sixth century BCE. See Karen Armstrong, *A History of God*, New York: Balletin Books, 1993; Jack Miles, *God: A Biography*, NY: Vintage Books, 1995; and William M. Schneidewind, *How the Bible Became a Book*, London: Cambridge University Press, 2004.
4. Genesis 2: 8–9.
5. Genesis 2: 15.
6. Genesis 2: 17.
7. Genesis 3: 23–24.
8. Genesis 6–9.
9. Genesis 9: 15.
10. See Armstrong, *A History of God* and Schneidewind, *How the Bible Became a Book*.
11. See David Christian, *This Fleeting World: A Short History of Humanity*, Great Barrington, MA: Berkshire Publishing Group, 2008; Evan Eisenberg, *The Ecology of Eden*, New York: Vintage Books, 1998; Robert Pogue Harrison, *Forests: The Shadow of Civilization*, Chicago: University of Chicago Press, 1992; and Paul Shepard, *Coming Home to the Pleistocene*, Washington, D.C.: Island Press, 1998.
12. Genesis 3: 17–19.
13. Glendinning, Chellis, "Technology, Trauma and the Wild", *Ecopsychology: Restoring the Earth, Healing the Mind*, Theodore Rosak, Mary E. Gomes, and Allen D. Kanner eds., San Francisco: Sierra Club Books, 1995, p. 52.
14. Julian Jaynes, author of *The Origin of Consciousness in the Breakdown of the Bicameral Mind*, NY: Houghton Mifflin, 1976, argues that reflexive consciousness only appeared in humans around 1200 BCE—coincidental with the end of the last Ice Age and the emergence of agriculture. There have been many critiques of his work (see for example, Andrea Cavanna, Michael Trimble, Federico Cinti, and Francesco Monaco, "Bicameral Mind 30 Years on: A Critical Reappraisal of Julian Haynes' Hypothesis", *Functional Neurology*, vol. 22, no. 1, 2007, pp. 11–15) but it has remained as a point of departure for research in many fields. Even without a physiological shift in the human brain as proposed by Jaynes, significant transformation of human psychological and cultural consciousness would grow out of the radical transformation of spatial practices to accommodate agriculture and the settled life. More recently, Yi Fu Tuan, *Segmented Worlds and Self: A Study of Group Life and Individual Consciousness*, Minneapolis: University of Minnesota Press, 1982, has argued that it is modernity that has fixated on the individual at the expense of community life. This transformation, occurring over the last 500 years, is obviously not a biological shift but a cultural one, and has led to the hyper-individuation that characterizes modern Western industrialized nations.
15. Harrison, *Forests*, p. 249.
16. Barrows, Anita, "The Ecopsychology of Child Development", *Ecopsychology: Restoring the Earth, Healing the Mind*, Theodore Rosak, Mary E. Gomes, and Allen D. Kanner eds., San Francisco: Sierra Club Books, 1995, p. 109.
17. Atwood, Margaret, *The Year of the Flood*, New York: Anchor Books, 2009, pp. 52–53.
18. Atwood, *The Year of the Flood*, p. 43.
19. Atwood, *The Year of the Flood*, p. 424.
20. Atwood, *The Year of the Flood*, p. 91.
21. Atwood, *The Year of the Flood*, p. 48.
22. Atwood, *The Year of the Flood*, p. 69.
23. Atwood, *The Year of the Flood*, pp. 127 and 162.
24. Atwood, *The Year of the Flood*, p. 59.
25. Atwood, *The Year of the Flood*, pp. 312 and 252.
26. Atwood, *The Year of the Flood*, p. 20.

27. Atwood, *The Year of the Flood*, p. 89.
28. McKibben, Bill, *Eaarth: Making a Life on a Tough New Planet*, New York: Times Books, 2010, p. 106.
29. McKibben, *Eaarth*, p. 212.
30. For example, each gallon of gas we put into our cars represents a hundred tons of ancient plants, according to McKibben, *Eaarth*, p. 28.
31. McKibben, *Eaarth*, p. 27.
32. McKibben, *Eaarth*, p. 1.
33. Report on a study by Kew Royal Botanical Gardens, National History Museum and IUCN: http://www.rawstory.com/rs/2010/09/281.
34. McKibben, *Eaarth*, p. 85.
35. McKibben, *Eaarth*, pp. 144–145.
35. See James Howard Kunstler, *The Long Emergency: Surviving the Converging Catastrophes of the Twenty-First Century*, New York: Atlantic Monthly Press, 2005.
37. Thompson, Clive, "Global Mourning: How the next victim of climate change will be our minds", *WIRED*, January 2008.
38. Atwood, *The Year of the Flood*, p. 239.
39. Teilhard de Chardin, Pierre, *The Divine Milieu*, New York: Harper and Row Publishers, 1957: pp. 40–41.
40. Metzner, Ralph, "The Psychopathology of Human-Nature Relationship", *Ecopsychology: Restoring the Earth, Healing the Mind*, Theodore Rosak, Mary E. Gomes, and Allen D. Kanner eds., San Francisco: Sierra Club Books, 1995, p. 60.
41. Orr, David W., *Down to the Wire: Confronting Climate Collapse*, London: Oxford University Press, 2009, p. 73.
42. Peter Bishop, *The Greening of Psychology*, Dallas: Spring Publications, 1990, p. 3, writing from the standpoint of archetypal psychology, speaks of an ecological imagination. "The idea of *ecology*—no matter how sophisticated, how pertinent and 'right' it seems for these desperate times—is an imaginal fiction. Nevertheless, the creation of such a fiction, such an important symbol, is a major psychological event. Through this symbol, concern for images of the *Other* is becoming more important than concern for images of *Self*."
43. Orr, *Down to the Wire*, p. 151.
44. See http://climateandcapitalism.com/?p=479
45. Atwood, *The Year of the Flood*, p. 305.
46. Atwood, *The Year of the Flood*, p. 396.
47. Atwood, *The Year of the Flood*, p. 227.
48. Atwood, *The Year of the Flood*, p. 423.
49. Tallamy, Douglas W. and K. J. Shropshire, "Ranking Lepidopteran use of native versus introduced plants", *Conservation Biology*, vol. 23, 2009.
50. Eisenberg, Evan, *The Ecology of Eden*, New York: Vintage Books, 1999, p. 3.
51. The United States has turned millions of acres of diverse croplands into mono-cultures, factories of plants and animals in the twentieth century. These practices are suicidal, but not irreparable. Douglas W. Tallamy, *Bringing Nature Home: How You Can Sustain Wildlife with Native Plants*, Portland, OR: Timber Press, 2007, argues that planting native plants in our gardens across this country and the world would do more to protect our food supply that will be endangered by global warming than all technological innovations and gene splicing together.
52. Atwood, *The Year of the Flood*, p. 415.
53. Atwood, *The Year of the Flood*, p. 431.

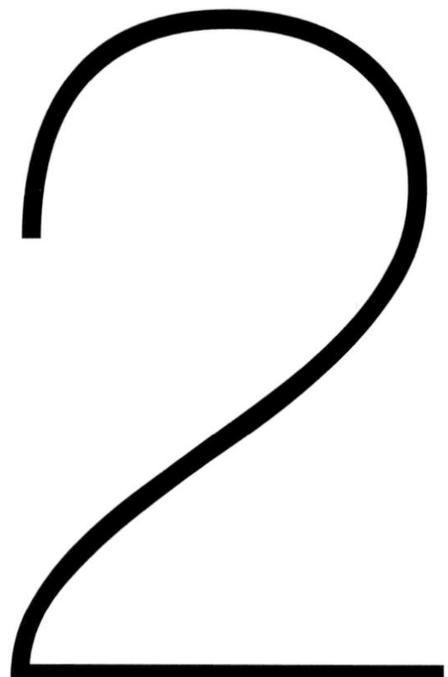

INSCRIBING THE GARDEN

THE GARDEN OF EARTHLY DELIGHTS

/PATRICK HEALY

Eden, cast as Earth's first garden—its splendors eternally longed for after humanity's sinful Fall—is emblematic of the complex nature of utopias and utopian yearning. While utopian visions strive to express an ideal, these same visions, necessarily fallible because they are human constructs, contain the seeds of their own destruction.[1] Perhaps the most vivid attempt to express the complexity both of Eden itself and its relation to postlapsarian existence in this world and in the hereafter is *The Garden of Earthly Delights*, the creation of Dutch painter Hieronymus Bosch. Displayed in the Museo Nacional del Prado, Madrid, *The Garden of Earthly Delights*, c. 1500–1505, is the most complex and mesmeric of Bosch's known works. It is also the most enigmatic, its dream-like representation of carnal delights amidst the bounty of nature and the garden having elicited innumerable interpretations.[2]

The Garden of Earthly Delights is generally recognized as one of Bosch's late works and its migration to the Prado reasonably well known.[3] For the contemporary viewer, it is the work's situation in a major museum collection that opens up the first of the interpretative challenges: how much does our consumption of the work in the pedagogic context of the museum hinder our ability to understand it? In the current self-advertising of the Prado—doubtless a reflex of the increased use of culture by cities in competition for economic resources and as means of branding or defining urban image—the triptych is given 'star' status and is used to attract more visitors to an already over-crowded museum. Then, beyond its physical presence in a gallery, the painting is also available to be viewed on the museum's website with a closeness never available when standing physically before it. This perspective inscribes both visual confusion and incalculable distance; the process of pixilation involves the kind of constructive logic of the jig-saw puzzle, and at the same time distorts the whole/part relationship of the work, rendering multi-layered aspectual seeing impossible.[4]

It is not easy to deconstruct one's own viewing and at the same time offer an account of the different interpretative responses to Bosch's work that have accumulated since the early sixteenth century. Indeed, in the recent past, the reception of art has undergone particularly marked changes due, in turn, to significant changes in the practice and theory of art. The problem of viewing itself has a commitment to critique and reason that is characteristically modern. Regardless of how we ultimately come to terms with the effect of an artwork's current setting on our seeing of it, and regardless of how we can recover from our own contexts of visual consumption and aesthetic concerns, the challenge of art-historical method remains: how should one talk about the role of imagination in responding to art-works, and how give an account of the respective roles of imagination, thinking, and technique, which involves questions of composition, line, color, and so forth? At this point, the fundamental questions of "what is an art-work" and "what is history" still remain in abeyance. In this essay I will rely on iconographical and other resources in order to illuminate the meaning of Bosch's work, but with the caveat that sometimes remote sources are more significant for understanding than those more immediately contemporary to the work. The current of influences does not emerge in a linear way. Style history can be more of a hindrance than help in appreciating the particular achievement of an artist and, further, often reduces a singular work to the status of mere *epiphenomenon* (secondary phenomenon).

THE WILY FOX

We are always viewing a work of art from 'somewhere'; it is a convenient fiction that viewing can be from 'nowhere'. Art historical accounts often suppress the construction of viewing. This suppression has vitiated the power of image and often neutralized the impact of works into a mere pendant to technical development, or the simple congealing of social and other processes (economic, technological) as a kind of ensemble and assemblage of other phenomena.[5] The question of an image's fatal destiny—its ownership and circumstances of its preservation, for example—remains key to how we respond to works of art. Indeed, that destiny is key to our ability to engage a work of art directly, not in a passive, however refined form of consuming, but in a literal immersion in the creative process, a creative co-creation that we struggle to achieve by way of understanding and reason, ultimately guided by imagination. And then there is the the enigmatic fact that, in the passage of time, a work can continue to shape social agency, and continue to communicate under different ideological circumstances. In the end, our problem of access to works of the past remains keyed to the account we give of the imagination. It is in reading Pico della Mirandola's *De Imaginatione*—almost contemporary with Bosch's work—and Gilles Deleuze's account of the imagination that we can gain a better insight into the dangers of seeing and the power of image, which nevertheless remains inaccessible and lives in depths of affectivity we never fully grasp.[6]

When we look at *The Garden of Earthly Delights* in the Prado we accept that it is set against a wall, and that its two wings are visible, without the painting on the obverse being viewable directly. The format of the triptych may or may not have theological significance, as a reference to the dogma of the triune nature of God, or to the structure of the cross on which Jesus was nailed. Yet when looking at other instances of the triptych format, say for example in the work of the painter Francis Bacon, such thoughts are unlikely to occupy the viewer's mind. We do not think of Bosch's work as portable, as an altar piece, nor indeed as having the structure of a slim box: the wings can be folded in, and the lid—showing the painting of the world and its creator, accompanied by a banderole text—could be opened and closed, and literally spread out on different supports. We also readily accept that the text hanging by the Bosch triptych, describing artist and work, is part of the viewing experience. Indeed, in the case of some viewers, this text completely determines what is seen.

Here the phenomenon of historical production is placed before us in the interplay of visitor and host institution. In his *Museum Memories*, Didier Maleuvre has detailed the means by which the public museum gathers history and summons it as image in the modern period. The fundamental form of museum typology was established from 1793–1852: the Louvre opened its doors in 1793, the Prado in 1820, the National Gallery in London in 1824, the Altes Museum, Berlin, in 1830, and the British Museum in 1852.[7] The work of Bosch illustrates very well a primary phenomenon of museum culture, namely that it has become immobile. The essential task of the museum is to translate a primary phenomenon of art into the secondary language of cultural and finally commercial consumption. The immobility also points to a transcendental history of invariability, where in the accretion of cultural *spolia* (spoils)—of which the Louvre was an egregious example, with works taken from private ownership and displayed as property of the nation—the museum also settles accounts with the historical. Culture sides with the freezing of the past, and cultural authenticity is invented as nostalgia. Art is also affected. It is referenced as an 'aesthetic' object, and is to be understood through an objectifying mode of seeing. A further consequence of the displaying and storage of the newly valorized object is the abstraction of the work from immediacy. The museum provides minimal context, and thereby constructs the work as an image that belongs to the aesthetic dimension of 'beautiful illusion'. This effectively glosses over the ambiguity and instability of the subject/object relation and indeed, what Nicolas Bourriaud recently has pointed to as the precariousness of the world.[8]

The museum works as a capturing prism which secures the abstract universal claim of disinterestedness for the realm of aesthetic detachment. The fashioning of a stable image also de-realizes the ability to see a work of art, and instead the work becomes merely a means of 'seeing by'. The work now serves a secondary function in terms of the wider purpose of the museum itself. This is a curious form of annihilation, whereby the role of memory and the object is inverted. Thus by being taken out of historical process and being submitted instead to the discourse practice of stylistics, or organization according to epoch, periodization, and influences, the event of the past is not in need of an actual community of memory. A form of scopic substitution allows every fragment the role of the historical, and thus the historical is also doomed to the positivist delusion of endless significance. It is of some relevance that both Kant's third Critique, *The Critique of Judgment*, and Hegel's *Lectures on Aesthetics* were formulated and published in the very decades that museum culture and the reformulation of the concepts of *Bildung* (culture) were taking place in Germany, as a kind of conciliatory gesture to the emerging middle classes and a means of protecting Prussian political interests. A particular version of the Greek past was co-opted in this project. Art and the State came into a fatal collusion, guided by the newly emerging historicism and the growth of art history as a university discipline.

The museum, then, is a constructed place of memory where the market and scholarship are joined to eliminate any of memory's milieu. Here the past is presented as a frozen theater of object-defining practices, in which the final substitution is the valorizing of the inorganic in place of or over the human. The retrieval and exhibition of the historical object is marked, as Walter Benjamin shows, by its inapproachability. As it happens, this loss of aura is fully captured in the pixilation of an image when it is viewed 'virtually', because the physical denigration of the material and real object has been transformed into the epiphenomenal, and instead of communion, there is the unique manifestation of distance. Works of art become historical documents, their appearance an historical phenomenon, or simply a ruin.[9]

In the museum context, art is removed from the domain of forces of action and reaction, of bodies and encounters, of slippage and excess, disaster and blessing in which the historical is eventuated, and is reduced to being a bearer of representation. This process intensifies the elimination of the human subject by its reduction to thinghood, as *res cogitans* (thinking object). It also concentrates the parameters of visibility to an increasing scopic abstraction and need for disenchantment and exclusion, in which the thing's 'gathering' is simply the act of projective and sustained meaning within disciplinary boundaries. The subject must participate in its own neutralization. In the pseudo-religious atmosphere of the museum the subject stays silent, does not touch, and is compliant. The lesson of self-abnegation is as perfectly structured here as in the most remote penitential texts aimed at human perfection, a phenomenon which Nietzsche identifies as the secret of Christian slave-morality in his virulent and stunning polemical accounts in *Beyond Good and Evil* and *The Genealogy of Morals*.[10]

Among the bibelots, trinkets, ornaments, and gimcracks of the imagined *Wunderkammer* (cabinet of curiosities)—which is the new constellation of the past, the product of cultural plundering (Elgin Marbles), stylistic farrago, and simple pastiche (neo-Gothic architecture)—there is only historical regression. The image of the past is a clutter and consortium, where the broad metaphysical character of the epoch (the advent of nihilism) is diverted by the human subject: like a wily fox, thinking to play dead, even though it will end up as a fur around the neck of time, or, as a fearful host seeking to divert the 'uncanny guest at the door', by pretending not to be at home—both failing to realize that they are faced with the inevitable.[11]

DIVINE SPHERE

Let us begin by thinking of the outer panels of Bosch's triptych and the literal function of the wings as the opening flaps to a box [Figure 1]. The image of the Creator outside of his Creation and the text of Psalm 33 then figure as initial keys to understanding the work, and guide one in the beginning of an interpretation. The calligraphic flourish of the text—which might lend support to the view that Bosch had worked in a scriptorium in Utrecht—reminds one that the Gothic is still present in the letter shapes, whether the text is in Latin or the vernacular. The figure on the upper left corner is that of God the Father, who literally is diminutive, and lying outside of the created world, which is shown as spherical and crystalline. This is the case, at least, if we take the figure with its papal tiara and book lying open on his lap in conjunction with the quotation from Psalm 33, which says the Creator ordered the world to be made.

The *ipse dixit* or "he said" is also the securing of Creation through the *fiat* of the word. The same insistence is found in Genesis: "and God said: 'Let there be light'". "Saying" is then followed by "seeing": "and God saw it was good". The psalmist asks the righteous to sing to the Lord, to praise the Lord with music, to "sing to Him a new song". They are so enjoined because they thereby align themselves with the Creation, that is, with the word of God, which made the heavens: "and by the breath of his mouth were made the starry host". The act of creation is physical and issues in a bodily form. The problem outside of a providential history is that the singular body remains irascible and defiant to any generalization.

The reflection on Creation in the psalm invites fear on the part of the people before the power of the word that 'forms': "for He spoke and it came to be, He commanded, and it stood firm". That fear is further intensified with the description of the firmness of the plan of God, and the all-seeing nature, the celestial panopticon of the Lord, who "looks down and sees all mankind, who forms the heart of all". But the eyes of the Lord are especially on those who fear him, or on those who hope that in his unfailing love he will deliver them from death. The psalmist is among those who put their hope in the Lord. Fear of death and hope of deliverance become the mainstay of the righteous towards God. It is, as we will see, the key to what has been prepared for those that love Him. This *dabar Yahweh* (Word of God) is as much deed as semantic item; it is the saying of "let it be". God offers freedom within being, and allows being to occur as event.

The account of Creation in Genesis repeats this fundamentally active view of the word, in which the word is emergent and fully temporalized, securing a *novum* (new thing) that will later be seen as providential. The argument that the Creation is from 'nothing' is an extra-Biblical interpretation. The verb "*bara*" in the Hebrew is exclusive to divine making. The Latin meaning of "*creatio*", from which "to create" and "creation" derives, has the meaning of "growth" and is related in a direct way to the idea of emergence and event (from "*cresco*"). This word would have translated the Greek "*physis*" better than the use of "*natura*", which is of specific Ciceronian input to the philosophical vocabulary of the West. An analogous sense was developed by Julius Scaliger, in his *Poetices* published in Lyon in 1561, where the poet is said to make things like a second God ("*sed velut alter Deus condere*"). Clearly it is a key component in the first registering of an historical account of art by Vasari.[12] In the Credo of mass in the West, the first item was the belief that God was the maker of Heaven and Earth, although no special fast day was set aside for this auspicious act: "*Credo in unum Deum Patrem omnipotentem, factorem coeli et terrae, visibilium omnium et invisibilium*" (I believe in one God, the omnipotent Father, creator of the sky and the earth, of all things visible and invisible). Further, it is held that the Incarnation is also a product of making, "*homo factus est*" (and the word was made flesh).[13]

In Bosch's painting, that which is created, the world, is a transparent sphere. This crystalline sphere shows us a pre-human world. It is the pre-lapsarian place of mineral and possible vegetable extrusions. The whole is suspended and seems as weightless as a dream. It is a remarkable feature of Bosch's development that the crystallization and mineralizing of his vision goes in tandem with complexity of human and bodily concentration, and, one could even say, density in other parts of the painting. Significantly, this panel is painted in green-gray *grisaille*, the neutral tones suggesting that the Earth is not inhabited, although it has its shape. One strand of theological thinking of some interest here is that of Alain of Lille (c. 1128–1202), who, making use of the emanationist, ultimately neo-Platonic view of Creation

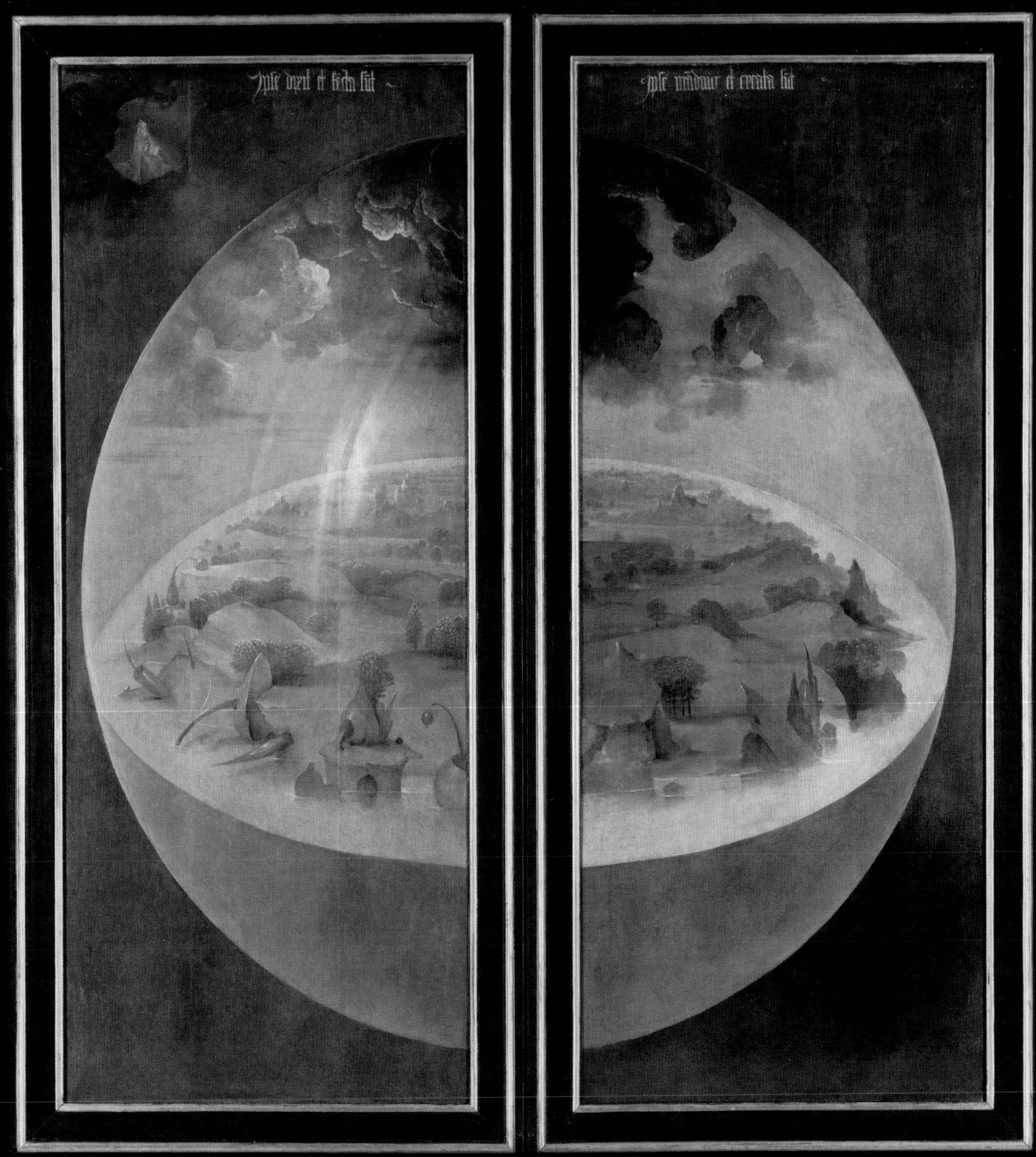

Figure 1/ The Creation. *The Garden of Earthly Delights*, obverse, the tryptich with wings closed. Hieronymus Bosch, Flemish, 1500–1505. Oil on wood, 220 x 194.5 cm. Museo Nacional del Prado, Madrid. Photograph courtesy of the Museo del Prado.

1500–1505. Oil on wood, 220 x 389 cm. Museo Nacional del Prado, Madrid. Photograph courtesy of the Museo del Prado.

Figure 2/ Paradise, the Garden of Earthly Delights, and Hell. *The Garden of Earthly Delights*. Hieronymus Bosch, Flemish,

as expressed by Augustine (354–430) in the *Confessions* and more precisely in the *City of God*, Bk. 9, 17, made the claim that God was a sphere, but that unlike the mathematical construction, the divine sphere was created not with a dimensionless point at the center, but rather with a center everywhere and its circumference nowhere.

The act of creation is also a moment of divine effulgence, abundance, and illumination. However, the further from the source the emanation, the further from God in the outpouring and streaming of his divine life. Thus that which is created, the 'creature', is an apex and profoundly abject.[14] Created things were therefore the most distant from the divine, and yet participated in and were indeed images of the divine. This problem of creatureliness, and the image of the divine, was one of the most vexing for all theologians and philosophers. To take one significant source from the Christian tradition, and one of its most polemically powerful: Clement of Alexandria's (c. 150–215) arguments against the Greeks and their tradition of imaging the gods are unrelenting in the service of the claim that human facture of images is "demonic" and that true *gnosis* is from the word and the recognition of Christ as the divine *Logos* (word).[15] The conquering of demons required the abjuration of matter. This the Greeks could not do, and Clement delights in the use of sophisticated syntax and language to remind them of this—they with the mincing affectation of their speech and lack of sober-mindedness, in close affinity with madness. Clement delivers a constant mocking reproach to the Greeks' worship of statues and images. Irrational minds were set on idols. They, the image makers, were in bitter bondage to tyrannizing demons. It was childish willfulness that gave the mystic rites and their symbols their force: the dice, the ball, the apples, the spinning top, the looking glass and tufts of wool—all giving evidence that the goddess Aphrodite was really just a lover of *virilia* (the male member) and a projection of unbridled lust. For Clement, the pitch of licentiousness and wantonness was evident in the vile practice of the debauching of boys; his contempt echoes the strictures of Philo of Alexandria (c. 20 BCE–40 CE) against the defilement of same-sex *eros*. Superstition became the fountain of insensate wickedness. Beauty defiled by vice was loathsome, and the institution of same-sex *eros* offered only insult to youth in its bloom, exhibiting the tyranny of man over beauty. Such lust was not easily restrained as it was destitute of fear.

Clement insists that unlike the "pagans", Christians have no image that was in fact only dead matter shaped by the craftsman's hand; rather they had an image perceived by the mind alone. The forms of images are stamped with the characteristic nature of demons. And while art is powerful in its capacity to delude, it is not so powerful as to deceive reason or those who are agreeable to reason. Those who bear within themselves the living and moving image of human nature, the likeness of God, cannot be deceived by the turning of Heaven into a stage where what is divine has become a spectacle or drama, and what is sacred has been acted in comedies under the masks of demons. The image of God was ultimately his incarnate word, the Son of Man, and this divine word was the archetypal light of light. The image of this word is the mind of man, assimilated to the divine word in the affections of the soul and therefore rational, whereas effigies sculpted in material things are but perishable impress of humanity, manifestly devoid of truth. Ultimately, for Clement, a life occupied with so much 'matter' is no different than one given over to insanity.

While such a tirade pointed to a rejection of the man-made image, the problem of the image itself, the image of a Trinitarian God in human form, remained. It is in the ninth book of the *De Trinitate* that Augustine pursues the question of the image of the Trinity in man most fully. As Manuel Brito Martins has demonstrated, Augustine is engaged in a hermeneutic circle by showing that the triadic structure of the human points to the nature of the blessed Trinity.[16] Within human knowing Augustine describes two triadic structures. The first, namely that of perception, or "perception of", has the following three-fold structure: firstly, that which we see (*primo ipsa res quam videmus*); second, that perception which does not exist other than by the object which is sensed by the senses (*visio quae non erat priusquam rem illam obiectam sensui sentiremus*), and thirdly there is an *intentio animi* (intellectual intention) which maintains the senses in the direction of the object perceived—this is the notion of "intentionality". This first triad has the function of uniting (*coniungit*), or better to say, gathering into unity the visible thing, the singular body as viewed by the senses. The resulting vision therefore belongs to the activity of the spirit. This is an activity and force of uniting (*vis copulandi*) the actual form of the object and its image as produced by the senses.

The second triad, which is referred to as "interior", is also made up of three elements: memory, internal vision or "image", and will (*voluntas*). This second triad unites in its activities what is then united in thinking. In the internal working there is a different temporality than in the external perception, and this allows one to speak of a *memoria retiens*, which is a memory of the image as past. In the modern period, Husserl and Bergson, as well as Wittgenstein, developed different readings from what Augustine presents. In a wider context it may well be that a less complex reading was also active and influential.

What emerges from the account of Augustine is that the image is produced in two ways: as an external synthetic unity—such as Kant will later suggest—and as the product of image in the temporality of memory, which also includes the present. The upshot is that there can be a distinction between *phantasmata* (appearances or visions) and the rational created image. This latter consideration, that the rational mind was most likely the mirror of the divine, ran into considerable difficulties in counting man as a being in the image of God. The image of the mirror, or better to say the metaphor of the mirror, pointed to both the virtual and therefore merely possible, and to the need for polishing and so difference and ambivalence, and finally to the impossibility of showing itself.[17]

THE PROBLEM OF PARADISE

Opening the panel, one is faced with a triptych that we read from left to right [Figure 2]. When closed, it should be noted that the two wings read as Paradise and Hell are folded over the central panel, that of the Garden of Earthly Delights itself. It is a well-established procedure that the panels are read from left to right, which follows the direction of reading practice in the West. However, unlike with text, there is no need to read from top to bottom, and as with the nature of the mental image—for example thinking of how we would look at a building seen by the mind's eye—no precise direction is necessary. We have before us an ambient field of vision in which we select significant features in light of how we actually interpret the scene before us.

The scene on the left is taken as depicting the creation of Adam and Eve in the Garden of Eden, referred to as Paradise. This is the first garden of two with which the work is concerned. That the two gardens are visually interconnected can be seen from the run-on or cross-over of the horizon from the left to the central panel. This creates a split vision, and forces the reading towards the center. The visualization of Paradise is, of the three panels, the simplest. It is the least crowded with figures, and the one which is most fully and evenly illuminated. The organization of the visual field is also different in composition from the other two panels, where the intensity and accumulation of details press against the viewer, creating a literal de-routing of the senses. The hallucinative interval activated by visual swarming requires that one looks in sections against the thick grain of the various scenes and figures and objects. This is especially true of the composition of the right panel.

The issue of the Son as image of the Father is immediately apparent in the Edenic scene, and the various problems of imaging can concretely be seen in action. The animals shown point to the complex sources in visual culture available for reference. Eden is the primal Garden, and it is also the place of divine making of human bodies. In Bosch's work the imaging of God the Father has also undergone a subtle transformation: the depiction being proleptic for an incarnational theology. The Son has taken on flesh, and the contiguity of Adam to God, whose garment touches the foot of the created creature, contrasts with the pointing, but not touching, of the creation of Adam in Michelangelo's Sistine Chapel [Figure 3].

Figure 3/ Eden, divine making of human bodies.
The Garden of Earthly Delights, detail. Hieronymus Bosch, Flemish, 1500–1505. Museo Nacional del Prado, Madrid. Photograph courtesy of the Museo del Prado.

As for imagining Paradise and landscapes, this is every bit as difficult as imagining monsters, since none of these exist except as imaginative constructs. Bosch's gardens set in train the whole pictorializing tradition of landscape from this time onward in European art, establishing as well the possibility of viewing from an idealized point of view. That there is a conflation of various forms of imagining in showing the paradisiacal is a moot point. For a thinker such as Origen (185–259) the problem of locating Paradise points to the imagining of sacred geography. The specific tradition of geographical speculation was highly theoretical, and accordingly, no clear image of Paradise exists. Early Christian speculation moved towards confirming it was a real place on Earth. The position of Paradise on the left panel of Bosch's work—therefore given our reading of up as north, and south as down, left as east and right as west—confirms that the Christian location of Paradise was in the East. The recent work of Gordon Lindsay Campbell suggests that in the writings of Clement of Alexandria and Origen there is an association of ancient philosophical sacred lands and utopias with the Christian Paradise. In the *De Principis* Origen insists that the situation of Paradise had to be corporeal, and thus he speculates that it is on Earth. Paradise was to be sought in the East, but also near the open gate of Heaven.[18]

In a developed sense, Campbell's argument points out that the theoretical positing of such a place would eventually lead to its creation. The fabrication of Paradise was a complex result of different kinds of physical imagining, so that the space/time of Paradise is imagined like the ancient view of blessed islands and various Classical tropes, or *topoi*, literal place-holders for a syncretic and abstract notion. The author who captures this best is Lactantius (c. 240–320). Campbell suggests that in the poem attributed to him, *On the Phoenix*, the account is effectively a cut-and-paste job from many sources. These sources allow one to grasp many significant moves in imagined geographies and a profound shift in the relation between Garden and Utopia that occurs and is shown in Bosch. In this poem there are clearly versions of the Golden Age from Homer and Ovid; Paradise is a blend of the Elysian Fields, the Isles of the Blessed, the Golden Age, and Mount Olympus, but now situated in the East. In Lactantius, the addition of the image of a fountain to Paradise complements the remote setting:

> there is a wood planted with trees blooming with the beauty of perpetual foliage, and bitter grief is absent; there is neither tempest nor torrent, and the frost does not cover the Earth with frozen dew. But a fountain is in the middle, called by the name of life, transparent, gentle, rich with sweet waters gushing once a month and irrigating the whole grove with its stream.[19]

Here one can hear direct echoes of Homer's description of Mount Olympus in *Odyssey* 6.42–46:

> ... Olympus, where the abode of the gods stands firm and unmoving / forever, they say, and is not shaken with winds nor spattered / with rains, nor does snow pile ever there, but the shining bright air / stretches cloudless away, and the white light glances upon it.[20]

A major source for Paradise in Bosch may very well be the *Navigatio Sancti Brendani*, which is replete with details that depart from the more Classically toned account of Lactantius. This is confirmed by the elements of the animal and mineral life included by Bosch. In Saint Brendan's voyage to the the earthly Paradise, both the ethnographic imaginings with their roots in the work of Herodotus (c. 484–425 BCE) and the Biblical account in Genesis, deeply influenced by Berossus (fourth century BCE), underlie the figuring of the Other and the exotic in terms of distantiality, or far-awayness. The sailing across Ocean, and thus in a westerly direction, brings Brendan to an island shrouded in darkness. Yet upon the travelers' approach, the clouds part, and the paradisiacal island reveals itself as a kind of fabulous jewel box. Not unlike the town halls of many Gothic cities, the island is surrounded by a high wall which, reaching to the sky, contained materials unknown to the travelers:

> [with] a whiteness brighter than the snow, [the structure] gave witness to the fact that it had been created by God, that Architect who made all things from nothing. It was free of all sculptures, but shone on all sides with precious stones. Chrysolites set in lumps of gold threw off great radiance. With topaz and chrysoprase, jacinth and chalcedony, with berylls and other precious stones the wall shone equally on all sides, as if the stones had been set with great art and industry.[21]

Figure 4/ Fountain of Life.
The Garden of Earthly Delights, Paradise, detail. Hieronymus Bosch, Flemish, 1500–1505. Museo Nacional del Prado, Madrid.
Photograph courtesy of the Museo del Prado.

The island's physical setting is directly related to Genesis 2:10–14, where we read that a river flowed out of Eden and then divided into four: "A river went out of Eden to water the garden; and from there it was parted, and became four heads. The name of the first is Pishon; it is the one which flows around the whole land of Havi-lah, where there is gold; and the gold of that land is good; bedellium and onyx stone are there."

In some sense the attempt to locate Paradise geographically confirmed the shift which the Victorine had inaugurated against the Augustinian heritage, namely a shift to concentration on the material world of manifestation, and the making precise of the geographical locus. Thus in his *Excerptiones priores*, Hugo of Saint Victor (c. 1096–1141) makes clear:

> Asia has many provinces and regions whose names and locations I shall set forth briefly, beginning with Paradise. Paradise is a place in the East, planted with every kind of timber and fruit trees. It contains the Tree of Life. No cold is there nor excessive heat, but a constantly mild climate. It contains a fountain which runs off in four rivers. It is called Paradise in Greek, Eden in Hebrew, both of which words in our language mean a Garden of Delight.[22]

The sourcing of minerals had been one of the chief agents for trade and exploration from a Europe that was not rich in such resources. This point was especially apt for painters, who relied on precious stones and pigments from distant lands.[23] In any event, these various imaginings of Paradise clearly converge on the problem of imagining both the utopian and the dystopian spaces, Paradise and Hell, which in the case of Bosch's painting function as mirror images on the wings, leaving only the earthly Garden of Delights as an actual place.

Figure 5/ Music in Hell.
The Garden of Earthly Delights, Hell, detail. Hieronymus Bosch, Flemish, 1500–1505. Museo Nacional del Prado, Madrid.
Photograph courtesy of the Museo del Prado.

ANIMAL OTHERNESS AND HELL INCARNATE

In *The Garden of Earthly Delights*, the luminous landscape and the triune group of God the Creator and Adam and Eve are punctuated by fabulous beasts. The bestiary of Bosch will expand and contract in the course of the work, at the same time as the human body with its instability and *punctum* (point) of weakness, which—via curiosity—allowed sin to enter the world, is shown in light and relative perfection. In a pure moment of desire, the longing look of Adam towards Eve points to the significance of generation in maintaining the divine economy, the covenantal plan for Abraham and his seed. Then, at the other extreme, bodies have become monstrous, chimeras that are bludgeoned in fire and darkness, human and bestial in a constellation of infernal and loathsome corruption and denigration.

The only true otherness for the human is the animal, and, at the same time, the only unmediated knowledge is that of carnal consumption. The Creation and the view of Paradise are already haunted by such premonitions, in two directions. First, the cat with the mouse in the lower register points to a *topos* of theological bestiary in which the cat is taken as a diabolical animal ferrying souls to Satan, and, further, the strange figure of the animal points to a kind of exotic hybridity, which suggests the remote and strange, namely the East or India.[24]

The second prefiguring that takes place is the indication of the Godhead as the incarnate, human/divine Christ, which is in turn related to the theme of the fountain of life signified by the structure of the middle ground [Figure 4]. The shapes of structures in this painting, both in Paradise and in the central panel, indicate something constantly liminal, as it is difficult to interpret these structures as being either mineral or vegetable. This ambivalence is also seen in the spherical world on the painting's obverse. The loss of significance of direction within such a sphere can only lead to suggestions of an atmosphere and a torsion of forces that just barely hold together, such that the sphere's dissolution appears imminent. Indeed it can be noted that the discord that is hinted at in Paradise points to one of the most significant readings of the nature of Hell on the opposite panel, and of the relation of music to human desire. The mystery of the musical instruments in Hell becomes a key to a deeper if more abstract consideration; after all, the introduction of the pentatonic scale was referred to as the *modus lascivius* (lustful meter) [Figure 5]. The musical theory of modes and harmonies had been deployed by exegetes to create a harmony even from discordant elements, which was said to advance the soul's aspiration to the divine order of things. Doubtless the impact of Plato's *Timaeus* lies behind much of this theorizing, where the micro-/macrocosmic balance is a Pythagorean musical metaphor and analogy.[25]

Remarkably, the harmonious nature of the Paradise scene is maintained despite the presence of discordant elements. This is not just a compositional requirement but points directly to the significance of exegetical practice as a means of holding highly discordant, even antithetical beliefs together in unity. In Hell the temporalizing of punishment as eternal indicates that the eternal recurrence of pain is its most perspicuous feature. An expansion of the principle of the body as an open system of circulation, the "constant return of the same" is the principle of punishment that dominates the infernal region. The deeper context of this is surely the awful ambivalence towards the body, which on the one hand is the mystery of the incarnation, in which the word is made flesh, while on the other, the human is asked to be divine. To understand some of the wider affective context in which images such as Bosch created are to be followed, it is necessary to take seriously the fear of Hell, death, and the Last Judgment, which has ancient roots but was promoted by the 'advance' of the notion of Purgatory. As Jacques Le Goff's research on Purgatory shows—and as will become clear in deciphering some of the panel to the right—there was an elision that was underway between the conceptions of Purgatory as a place and as a condition. In Purgatory the punishing of sinners was expiated by the intercession of the living, granting to the Church a power and intercession over a domain that, quite remarkably, remained contiguous to Hell.

One of the direct effects of this development was a renewed emphasis on dying and on the eternal pain of the souls consigned to Hell. Various buffer zones had been created (Limbo, Purgatory), which in no way diminished either the exaltation of the blessed in Heaven, or the excruciating and coruscating suffering of the damned. Indeed, renewed focus on these extremes resulted in direct physicalization of the divine and a renewed consideration of the nature of the 'human limit'.[26] This process can be traced in the direction of devotional piety in this period in The Netherlands, where popular devotion increasingly venerated the sheer corporality of the human/divine person of Christ, with a concomitant literal aggression towards the frailty of the human body itself.[27] Two sources worth considering would be the intense veneration of the Sacred Heart among the Beguines, and the increased somatizing of the notion of folly, which is a theme of Bosch's work in the *Ship of Fools* and has its literary analogue in the poetry of Sebastian Brant.[28]

The early Christian practice of bringing dead bodies into the city had an enormous impact on the creation of the notion of sacred space.[29] Clearly, the more fragile the sense of the continuity of the body—and the more, in turn, flesh is seen as vulnerable to innumerable attacks from nature and especially from the almost innumerable demonic realm—the less any sense of continuity of identity can be posited. Within the theological matrix, the salvific claim that, after the resurrection, bodies could be changed and glorified had to be set against the actual mortal nature of the human and the innate inclination to sinfulness. For Christ in his incarnation had taken on bodily human form, and was like to the human in all things but sin.

If bodies are produced by discourse, they have the obtuse and unremitting habit of also impacting on social agency and cannot simply be viewed as just artifacts, or indeed as the specular theater of display. The social matrix and the theological discussions are highly volatile.[30] What is clear in Bosch is that the whole gamut of physicality, ranging from the human to the bestial to the divine, is visible and interchanging through the work. With something of the clutter of a Hindu temple, Bosch's work is replete with the kind of polycorporeal intertwining that can be seen in some of the earliest Germanic art and within early Medieval manuscript production, the most intricate example of which is surely the *Book of Kells*.

BODY COMPLEX

The awareness of the body as the place-holder of change and corruption, as something volatile and mortal, comes directly from Aristotle's study *On Generation and Corruption*, which had been commented on by Thomas Aquinas (1225–1274). Such reflections underscored the awareness of the body's fatality—as did the riveting awareness of decay and change transferred from mediating the wounds of the crucified—which is a much more emphatic aspect of Western spirituality, and specifically Northern European, than of the spirituality of the East. For example, Byzantine art, not unlike Ancient Greek tragedy, eschews the sensationalist showing of extreme forms of mutilation or physical deformity.[31]

Precariousness and marginality, volatility and metamorphosis convey the fear and trembling of these late-Medieval persons, riven with the fear of death, judgement, and eternal damnation.[32] That something so *nuisible* or noxious as a body could merit this punishment, led to the sense that soul and matter were inextricably bound to each other. Further, one literally didn't know the day or the hour of one's death, and the mutability of things and bodies makes the body increasingly something so Other that it needs constant monitoring. Finally, the body as Other is perceived as the locus of an interplay of forces, among them growth and corruption, a notion that also impacted all manner of discourse.

One of the remarkable features of this complex around the body was the insistence on penitential practice as a means of perfecting the individual soul. Sinning was a form of deicide, and consequently, mortification of the flesh was harnessed as penitence under scriptural commands. Penitence consisted of renunciation and was based on the calling of the Apostles in Luke Chapter 5, in which the Apostles were commanded to renounce all and follow Jesus. Self-abnegation is also a necessary part of the strategy of mortification: "*Si quis vult post me venire, abneget semetipsum, et tollat crucem suam quotidie et sequatur me*" (Luke 9:23–24, if someone wishes to follow me, let him deny himself and let him raise his cross daily and follow me).[33]

For the Dutch writer Thomas à Kempis in the *De Imitatione Christi* (*On the Imitation of Christ*, c. 1418–1427), this text from Luke is of crucial importance, as nothing is more of an obstacle to the perfection of the soul than self-love. The texts from Paul in Colossians 111:5 and Romans 8:13 enjoin one directly to "*mortificare ergo membra vostra*" (therefore mortify your limbs). This injunction is intensified by Paul as a requirement for Christians to literally crucify themselves: "*Qui sunt Christi carnem suam crucifixerunt... cum vitiis et concupiscentia*" (Galatians 5:24, Those who are followers of Christ have crucified their flesh with its vices and desires). The consequences to the 'self' of such a death are indicated in Colossians 3:3 and predicated a release to a new life. Spiritual death was also death to the 'old man', a sloughing off of old ways and a renewal, for which see Colossians 3:9, "*exspoliantes vos veterem hominem*" (putting aside your old self). The Christian is an athlete of the chastizing of the body.

The ultimate goal of this practice of abnegation is 'submission' to the will of God. This submission is also a central notion of Islam, the word "*islam*" itself meaning "submission". As in all monotheistic religions, the question of chastity was uppermost. Where in polytheism, abandoned multiplicity was thinkable, for Christians the scriptural basis in the New Testament was unequivocal. The text of Matthew 5:28 indicates that a look was equivalent to the deed; a man who lusts after a woman in looking has already committed adultery: "*Ego autem dico vobis: quia omnis, qui videret mulierem ad concupiscendum eam, iam moechatus est eam in corde suo*" (However I say [this] to you, since everyone who looks at a woman in desire has already committed adultery in his heart).

The work of Heaven and of Hell were both pitted in combat within the human body. Aquinas had argued that the demons could not act directly on the higher faculties, intelligence and will: "*Deus solus animae illabitur*" (only God can enter the soul).[34] However, demons could work on the body, on imagination and memory, and thus indirectly on the will after all.[35] But not all attacks were demonic; the concupiscence of the flesh also did its work on de-railing the soul. The struggle is continual. The principal enemies of Christian perfection are the world and the demon. À Kempis gives the long reprise of the Christian life from its incorporation through baptism in Jesus as, "*at tota vita Christi crux fuit et martyrium*" (but the whole life of Christ, and of the martyrs, was the cross).[36] According to this view, life is the long martyrdom. One must not only abnegate the self, but also carry the cross of Christ. Zeal to share in the suffering of the crucified was also a co-opting of others' sins to save the fallen. Thus mortification was the best means to preserve oneself from sin, and to deliver the soul from the easy temptations of vice. Sensuality and *amour-propre* (self-love) were the twin obstacles to perfecting the life.[37]

What allows one to speak of the sublime in Bosch—and of the entire work as being a general metamorphosis of the body in an open system of connection—is precisely the contrast between the beauty of the paradisical landscape, and the horror, darkness, and inexpressible, ultimately non-representable quality of Hell. Hell becomes 'oneself' in the intricate imaginings that are prompted for the mind and also in the play of location and dislocation—and where, as in the central panel, human bodies lurk in bestiality from which they are also cut off, literally overwhelming the very nature to which they are most connected. For Nature too is reconfigured in its presentation as secondary to the theological drama of souls. Meaning and affectivity are concurrent: sign and object do not belong simply to a decipherable code. This mobilization is even consequent in Bosch's non-concealing of brushwork, the way in which, with a limited tonal range, he communicates such intense visual values, thereby addressing the viewer in a form of communication so direct and powerful that it does not not require learned interpretation. Rather, the whole network of fear and the *sensorium* (sensory faculties) of the body are given a hallucinative possibility in which feeling and meaning, especially toward a virtual future state, takes on an intense certainty precisely because it does not need any interpretative strategy. What is shown is always more than what could be said. It is the irreducible element of Bosch's work that sets the truth of belief and religious fervor into forms.[38]

Le Goff has shown how relevant this 'actualization' of one's future is for considering both the development of the notion of Purgatory, which he sees as emerging in the late twelfth century, and the localization and expansion of the importance of the afterlife, which could now benefit from the actual intervention of the Church and the living. The effect of the attempt to localize Purgatory—traceable from the Irish tradition, which still continues on St. Patrick's Purgatory pilgrim site in County Donegal—gave way to a shift in the understanding of death and repentance as well as to a politicizing of the realm of the 'other-world'. Irish missionaries had also introduced to continental Christianity a renewed concern with penitential and eschatological themes. Although the Church has never named anyone as being in Hell, the function of Hell was in fact to mobilize fear. The function of rigorous ascetic practices was a kind of auto-terrorism, devised to maintain the restraint of one's *phantasia* (imaginings) and to promote constant vigilance and self-policing as a result of the imagining of horror. Papal control of Purgatory was the source of the doctrine of indulgences, which assures remission before God of post-mortem punishment through the prior forgiveness of one's sins, and which involved colonizing of the other-world and claiming power over the dead. Purgatory moved in the direction of infernalization because—as Le Goff insists—the Church relied on the preaching of fear to "allow its inquisitors to wield instruments of torture in this world as well as the next".[39] The veneration of the *arma Christi* (weapons of Christ) became the template for a sadic theology of punishment and retribution, which resulted in a reign of calculation and instrumental reason to confine and delimit. Fear always depends on possibility, on that which is about to take place.

Again hybridity and liminality, by their very ambiguity, would inevitably lead to strict imaginings of invisible realms, which served to enhance the hatred of the world, the despising of the senses, and the suspicion of human desire. Aquinas had made it clear that in life there was penance, but after death there could only be punishment. Thus physical death became more important than life, and Le Goff agrees with medievalist and historian Philippe Ariès in seeing the extension of the liminal relation between Purgatory and Hell as the increased dramatization of the moment of death.[40]

SATAN'S PIT AND THE CAULDRON OF DREAD

Turning to one literary source that had direct influence on Bosch's imagining may help one to understand the expressive power of his pictorial invention. A contemporary illuminated manuscript from the last decades of the fifteenth century, commissioned by Margaret of York and illustrated by Simon Marmion, confirms both the currency of one of the most popular texts of Medieval infernal literature and its circulation in the Burgundian court. Dated to around 1474, the manuscript now in the Getty Collection and happily available to viewing and reading online—even in its finest miniatures—points to the vast difference in the achievement of Bosch when dealing with essentially the same subject, Paradise and Hell. The text, known as the *Visio Tnugdali* (in English as *Tundale's Vision*), is said to have been composed for its dedicatee Giselda, the abbess of the Benedictine convent of St. Paul in Regensburg, after 1149, and its narration is set in Cork, Ireland, around 1148. The *Visio Tnugdali* belongs to what has been called the *immram* genre in old Irish literature, a genre dealing with otherworldly voyage, the ultimate mixture of sailors' yarns and supernatural speculation.[41] The vision is itself indebted to the *Navigatio Sancti Brendani*, and constitutes one of the most developed visions of the place of punishment in the afterworld before Dante's *Inferno*.

The knight Tundale, who collapses and almost dies, is taken by a guardian angel initially to a gloomy valley where the burning souls of murderers reside [Figure 6], and to a mountain that stinks of tar and sulphur, where snow and fire are alternating forms of torture for those captive there. In the course of his voyage, the knight encounters fiends with gaping mouths like packs of wolves, with black dirty bodies and eyes sparking with fire, leering tongues and claws of sharpened metal—fiends who upon seeing Tundale want to sing a song of death, because he is envisioned as one of their own. The *visio* emphasizes the acoustic din and foul odor of the infernal place, as Tundale is led from yet another gloomy valley to another mountain. Along the way he comes upon a bridge that is almost impossible to cross—one in fact of several—except by a priest who had lived a blameless life and carried holy water and a palm frond. The specific forms of torture Tundale encounters are geared to particular kinds of sin, venial and mortal, and the bridge is a case in point: it is the punishment for the proud and boastful.

Later Tundale comes upon the figure of the enormous boar, its mouth so large that it could accommodate 9,000 armed, mounted men entering simultaneously in a single

Figure 6/ The Torment of Murderers.
Manuscript illumination of *The Visions of Tundale*, detail. Attributed to Simon Marmion, c. 1475. Tempera colors, gold leaf, gold paint, and ink on parchment; leaf 36.3 x 26.2 cm. The J. Paul Getty Museum, Los Angeles, Ms. 30, fol. 13v. Photograph courtesy of the J. Paul Getty Museum.

Figure 7/ The Beast Acheron. Manuscript illumination of *The Visions of Tundale*, detail. Attributed to Simon Marmion, c. 1475. Tempera colors, gold leaf, gold paint, and ink on parchment; leaf 36.3 x 26.2 cm. The J. Paul Getty Museum, Los Angeles, Ms. 30, fol. 17. Photograph courtesy of the J. Paul Getty Museum.

row [Figure 7]. Two giants, figures recongnizable from Irish legend, stand between the creature's teeth holding its awful jaws agape. Demons are shepherding souls towards this gaping pit of torment; this is the punishment for the covetous. Tundale is forced to enter the boar's mouth, where his bones are gnawed and his vital organs are pulled out by dragons. Here venomous snakes consume his body, and he is burned by fire and then frozen by ice; the stink of sulphur mixes with the fetid smell of self-laceration. Suddenly, however, he is released and finds the angel beside him. They leave his place of torment, but there is still more to come. For next Tundale and the angel come upon a lake spanned by a booby-trapped bridge set with spikes that penetrate the soles of the feet of those who try to cross. Monsters await in the water below. There is a man making the crossing with a sack of corn slung over his back, his punishment for theft from the church. Tundale too is consigned by the angel to cross the bridge—and this leading a nervous cow. The precariousness of the situation, as well as the protagonist's anxiety, makes for one of the finest narrative moments, when the two men meet in the middle with blood from their feet dripping into the lake below, and there is a pitiful stand-off of the two parties.

The angel intervenes, as throughout, and suddenly Tundale is returned to dry land, his swollen feet healed, and he is taken to a large building as high as a mountain. This detail is directly reminiscent of the *Navigatio* of Saint Brendan. However, Tundale's reprieve does not yield to a vision of Paradise, but rather to a demented charnel house. The building is built like a large oven, with an aperture at the front with shooting flames licking outwards constantly; it contains butchers wielding disproportionately large saws and forks and instruments of carnage for cleaving of flesh. The significant detail is that when the butchering is done, the afflicted and decimated are restored, and the procedure starts all over again. Within the fire of this building there is also a terrifying dog, and Tundale, in a moment that anticipates Dante most directly, recognizes persons he has known among the clergy who are being fed on by parasites and vermin, their genitalia devoured and torn apart.

Figure 8/ The Forge of Vulcan. Manuscript illumination of *The Visions of Tundale*, detail. Attributed to Simon Marmion, c. 1475. Tempera colors, gold leaf, gold paint, and ink on parchment; leaf 36.3 x 26.2 cm. The J. Paul Getty Museum, Los Angeles, Ms. 30, fol. 27. Photograph courtesy of the J. Paul Getty Museum.

The most vivid depiction of the whole *visio* is the 'imagining' of the hideous creature encountered in the Cauldron of Dread. The narrative is now difficult to follow, having increased in difficulty as it progresses due to the need to sustain the journey motif, and to add new details, each surpassing in its horror that which has been previously described. Pain is intensified by the addition of detail. In the cauldron resides a hideous creature with black wings and claws and with a long, slender neck, upon which rested a massive head with huge, red eyes and a mouth that blazes with fire. The creature sits in the middle of a frozen lake consuming bodies that are then expelled in its excrement, where they are left until they have recovered and become whole again. At this stage the narrative moves away from the graphic description to suggest the real truth of the punishment: that it is eternal, without end. The gnawing of the flesh, the internal evisceration by snakes and rats, the flaying of the skin, the screams of terror, will abate only when the figures are exuded from the monster, but these torments will recur eternally. This torment is especially directed towards monks and clerics who have strayed from their vows and the rule of obedience.

It is from this section and the next of the vision that Bosch has most clearly learned, and if he cannot suggest smell, he is in a position to indicate the deafening noise and screaming by the brilliant device of the musical instruments. The cacophony of the place of death to which Tundale is now transported is emphasized by the fact that souls are being beaten on anvils, and the master blacksmith is Vulcan [Figure 8].[42] This horror behind him, Tundale is assailed by fiends with long, black teeth and tusks, and with eyes burning like lamps. They have bodies of dragons and tails of scorpions; each claw is hooked like a ship's anchor and is as tempered as damascened steel. Possessed of large black wings, they could fly anywhere. Even in the excoriating moment facing these malign and ferocious demons, Tundale is assured by the angel that soon "he will explode into the light", but not before encountering a vision which is also one of the most inventive in this work. For the last vision is that of Satan on the floor of the pit of Hell, held in immobility of suffering, a pain from which he never escapes, for Satan "is the heart of suffering", the angel exclaims [Figure 9]. Now the narrative shifts from its almost unbearable descriptions and Tundale is taken to where different forms of blessed life are shown.

In the early part of the vision, the way in which the calculus of pain and punishment is given in Purgatory/Hell indicates that these places have literally morphed into each other. The difficulty of distinguishing belongs to the chaos and confusion. Again, this is precisely what occurs in the Hell of Bosch. As with the imagining of blessed islands, gardens of Paradise, or the utopian, a form of active hybridization has taken place. This hybridization, constituting a shift in the visualization of Hell, occurs hand in hand with the hybridization of Paradise, its utopian counterpart, both visions now being projections of the future versus retrojections to the past.[43]

THE GARDEN OF EARTHLY DELIGHTS

The whole of Bosch's work turns on the dramatic confrontation of the projected future pains of Hell with the ambivalent relation between two gardens, the Garden of Eden and the Garden of Delights. For apart from the density of figures, the differences between the gardens are relatively subtle. In both resides the strange ambivalence of a world shown as androgynous and even sexless. There is a careful, almost complete absence of the *membrum virile*, and the inner suggestion of androgyny points to a deeper alchemical reading such as attempted by Lynda Harris.[44] In both there is no old age, nor are there any children. In the Garden of Earthly Delights, its colors somewhat brighter and high-keyed, the roseate pink of Eden and its luminous blues are markedly retained. In both, blanched flesh tones are set against bright vegetation—though the Garden of Delights adds the contrast of pale flesh with dark in the juxtaposition of 'Ethiopians', possibly symbols of demonic lust. The background line of hills, which are delicately blurred with slight *sfumato* effects, link the horizon line of the left with the central panel, and also suggest something dreamlike and evanescent.

Inevitably the carrousel of riders around a pool of women attracts attention in the middle ground of the central panel. The play of the crystalline and the spherical in the

Figure 9/ The Gates of Hell and Lucifer. Manuscript illumination of *The Visions of Tundale*, detail. Attributed to Simon Marmion, c. 1475. Tempera colors, gold leaf, gold paint, and ink on parchment; leaf 36.3 x 26.2 cm. The J. Paul Getty Museum, Los Angeles, Ms. 30, fol. 30v. Photograph courtesy of the J. Paul Getty Museum.

Figure 10/ Fleshy pleasures: fish, fruit, and fowl.
The Garden of Earthly Delights, Garden of Earthly Delights, detail.
Hieronymus Bosch, Flemish, 1500–1505. Museo Nacional del Prado, Madrid. Photograph courtesy of the Museo del Prado.

almost frolicking pavilions, which become piscean, isolates and protects the atmosphere of mussel shell and fish. The piscean presence surely belongs pre-eminently to the *symbolorum salacitatis* (symbols of lust). The apparent innocence, which has led to the panel being seen as a kind of gamboling exordium to the innocent joys of hedonism, is, as with Paradise, stalked by the animal. But in the Garden of Delights in particular the avian and piscean realms overload the suggestion of the body's ripeness, projected by the inclusion of fruit [Figure 10]. This, together with the presence of vermin and even the diabolical owl, lends the scene a hortatory and didactic end, where what is figured is Lust.

There is no gainsaying that the teeming profusion of concupiscence is on show in the Garden of Earthly Delights: the figures in the mussel shell, the man in the water and what must be called "*les fleurs du mal*", the showing of a young man penetrating the rectum of a companion with flowers. Walter Gibson has also suggested that in the strawberries themselves, there may be an allusion to the very insubstantiality of fleshly pleasures.[45] The strong imputation of the accumulation of fish, fruits, birds, multiple vernacular symbols of the phallic and sexual, including even the rinds and shells in which lovers or pairs are enclosed, is that love is also a part of the agony of body, its strife and conflict, and it is also worthless in light of lovers who, instead of availing of penance, must inevitably prepare for punishment. The figures in the shell from which a blue thistle-like flower emerges are literally being consumed by the emptiness of the fruit, and behind them a group of faces look up in what seems like painful rather than ecstatic expression.

The double inner circle of the central part of women bathing and the cavalcade of circus-like figures all add to the profusion of Bosch's satire on courtly love, and the insidious way in which physical metamorphosis, especially seen in the hybridization of the animals on which the riders are cavorting, points directly to the ferocity of the underlying ambivalence. Bosch has heaped symbol upon symbol, and used the strange and the exotic as a form of moral warning; the placing of the 'Ethiopians' at the lower 'entry' to the scene and again the co-mingling of the white and black bodies in the pool of the center perhaps communicate a further play on the theme of erotic dissolution, outdoors and lesbian, a lewd exhibitionism providing entertainment for the damned who ride around in circles, inevitably. The circling animals, especially the swine and goats, are of course associated with fecundity and animal lustfulness. The men and women are segregated. It is altogether likely that the reference here has been inspired by Augustine's descriptions of the obscene customs of the ancient Romans in *The City of God*. Here the struggle of the overpowering creatures of nature and the human bodies inevitably brings to mind the death which awaits and the punishment that is due. The world of excess and the miring in matter of flesh and bone, the mixture of fruit and fish in this moralizing allegory is just the antechamber to Hell; the deep consequences of the expulsion from Paradise are the chaotic, ultimately meaningless diversions of pleasures of the body. Pleasure without limit, as in Plato's *Philebus*, is chaos and thus the equivalent to utter meaninglessness. The material singularity of the body in its excess leads to nihilism and destruction. Without limit there can be no virtue.

Between these visions and the work of, for example, Theresa of Avila and Catherine of Genoa, one must grant to Bosch the most visually complete showing of Hell in the entire Western tradition. Followers such as Breughel remain in his shadow. His figuring alone of the infernal and diabolical, his linking it to the didactic satire on the pleasures of the flesh, the shift in focus from a nostalgia for a 'past-time Paradise', and the grotesque and monstrous viewing of Satan remain consequent until Goethe turns the Devil into an urbane gentleman with sophisticated manners and a heart of cold deception, a disguise which tricks out the last deception: namely to convince the world that the Devil does not exist, a fact strangely less lightly borne than the proclaimed death of God for the post-human subject.

In the work of Bosch, the power of the imagination had gone beyond any bounds to control, and risked the dangers of which Mirandola was fearful: distortion of the truth and corruption of the soul. For the painting suggested that the Garden of Eden, Earth's primordial, most perfect state and the constant focus of nostalgic utopian yearnings, contained dystopian elements that precluded any hope for a return to Paradise. The artist, like the theologians, was caught in the dilemma of a medium that transcended its message. The Reform's anti-iconicism eviscerated the world of inherited images, and the Jesuits' control of image in the Counter-reformation, though motivated by a different psychology, ultimately produced the same result. Both sought to control the power of the image and thus attempted to harness the free play of imagination into the realm of propaganda.

Notes

1. For a good overview of utopias and utopianism, see Ronald Schaer, Gregory Claeys, and Lyman Tower Sargent eds., *Utopia: The Search for the Ideal Society in the Western World*, New York and Oxford: Oxford University Press, 2000, particularly Lyman Tower Sargent "Utopian Traditions: Themes and Variations", pp. 8–17 and Ronald Schaer, "Utopia: Space, Time, History", pp. 3–7.

2. Among the vast range of publications, the following are of direct interest, remaining provocative and controversial: L. S. Dixon, *Alchemical Imagery in Bosch's Garden of Earthly Delight*, Anne Arbor, Michigan: UMI Research Press, 1981; William Fraenger, *The Millenium of Hieronymous Bosch: Outlines of a New Interpretation*, London: Faber, 1952; Walter Gibson, *Hieronymus Bosch*, London: Thames and Hudson, 1973; and Lynda Harris, *The Secret Heresy of Hieronymus Bosch*, Edinburgh: Floris Books, 1995. For the earliest descriptions of the painting see the article of E. H. Gombrich, "The Earliest Description of Bosch's Garden of Delights", *Journal of the Warburg and Courtauld Institutes*, vol. 30, 1967, pp. 403–406. For the most detailed attempt to interpret individual elements in the works of Bosch, see Dirk Bax, *Hieronymus Bosch: His Picture-Writing Dechiphered*, Rotterdam: A. A. Balkema, 1979. The work of Ludwig von Baldas, *Hieronymous Bosch*, Vienna: A. Schroll, 1943, p. 230, gives earlier literature in one page of bibliography, much of which is still relevant. The article by P. Gerlach, reviewing the sources for the biography of Bosch, in *Gazette des Beaux-Arts*, LXXI, 1968, pp. 109–116, is still valuable.

3. Walter Gibson has provided the main dates for the rapid diffusion of Bosch's work. *The Garden of Earthy Delights* had been owned by Hendrick III of Nassau, and came into the possession of one of his descendants, William the Silent, when during the occupation of the Netherlands by the Spanish it was confiscated by the Duke of Alva, eventually coming into the hands of Phillip II. By 1542, tapestry copies of *The Garden of Earthly Delights* are listed in an inventory of the furnishing of Francis I of France. For these, see Otto Kurz, "Four Tapestries after Hieronymus Bosch", *Journal of the Warburg and Courtauld Institutes*, vol. 30, 1967, pp. 150–163.

4. A further question that might be borne in mind: in what way does the current debate on image help or hinder access to this work? Or in Wittgenstein's significant distinction, what are the consequences for viewers and their relation to the art-work in terms of the difference between perception, and "perception as"? Do we need a genealogy not only of how we come to see the work in its current physical emplacement, but also of the contexts of seeing in which we view it as an "art-work"? Should we consider it in terms of visual rather than textual culture, moving out of what the recently deceased Leo Steinberg once called the "textism" bias of art-historical research? On perception, see Chantal Bax, *Subjectivity after Wittgenstein: the Post-Cartesian Subject and the Death of Man*, London: Continuum, 2011, especially section 3.7: "Wittgenstein on Aspect Perception", pp. 63–67. Textism is also central to the Boschian panel, as the only other appearance of 'text', apart from the scriptural quotation, is the letter "M" on a knife in Hell. There may be a real sense in which the visual alone comes to communicate what the word cannot tell. For a contemporary play on water and letters, see Dutch writer and visual artist Hilarius Hofstede, *De Markies van Water*, available online: http://www.demarkiesvanwater.org.

5. In anthropological studies, especially in the work of Gell, the relational positioning of works and their impact on social actions, what has been called a social-relational agency, suggests that only those works which have complex intentionalities are "art-works" as opposed to artifacts. An excellent discussion can be found in Dusan Boric's "Body Metamorphosis and Animality: Volatile Bodies and Boulder Artworks from Lepenski Vir", *Cambridge Archaeological Journal*, vol. 15, no.1, 2005, pp. 35–69. See also Alfred Gell, *Art and Agency: An Anthropological Theory*, Oxford: Clarendon Press, 1998, and the writings of Tim Ingold, especially *The Perception of the Environment*, London: Routledge, 2000.

6. The *De Imaginatione* of Pico della Mirandola was published in Venice for the first time in 1501. An English translation was published by Harry Caplan, Cornell Studies in English, no. XVI, 1930, and the text he established was used in the Eckhard Kessler German edition of 1984, Fink Verlag, Munich, and also forms the basis of a recent edition in French. For Deleuze on the imagination, see Gilles Deleuze, "The Idea of Genesis in Kant's Esthetics", *Desert Islands and Other Texts*, David Lapoujade ed., Michael Taormina trans., New York: Semiotext(e) Foreign Agents Series, 2002, pp. 56–71. For Carl Einstein, and the relation with surrealism, Bataille and a gnostic interpretation of materiality, see Conor Joyce, *Carl Einstein in Documents*, Philadelphia: Xlibris, 2003.

7. Maleuvre, Didier, *Museum Memories: History, Technology, Art*, Stanford, CA: Stanford University Press, 1999.

8. The current debate between Nicolas Bourriaud and Jacques Rancière can be followed in Bourriaud, *The Radicant*, James Gussen and Lili Porten trans., New York: Lukas and Sternberg, 2009. Bourriaud stresses the fictionality of the domains of engagement, art/politics, their 'as-if' structure, and also the precariousness of the world which art continues to affirm.

9. Maleuvre, *Museum Memories*.

10. See the work of Nandita Biswas Mellamphy, *The Three Stigmata of Friedrich Nietzsche: Political Physiology in the Age of Nihilism*, London: Palgrave, 2011. The genealogical project was developed as a

challenge to the pursuit of 'origin'. It is the body which is the primal scene of the inscribed events traced by language, and in perpetual disintegration. (Foucault in his reading of Nietzsche). The task of philosophy is to read the body as the primary scene of conflict and emergence, of the repeated play of domination that makes up history. The body is an "emergence", not an ontological state. The body is a prosthesis, with no essence, and "its essence was first fabricated from alien forms". See p.43 for discussion.

11. For Benjamin, see Alex Coles ed., *The Optic of Walter Benjamin*, London: Black Dog Publishing, 1999, specifically his essay "The Ruin and the House of Porosity", pp. 140–168.

12. I have followed the translation in *The Holy Bible*, New International Version, Grand Rapids, Michigan: Zondervan, 1973. The discussion on creation can be followed with further amplification in Sven Rune Havsteen, Nils Holger Petersen, Heinrich Schwab, and Eyolf Østrem eds., *Creations: Medieval Rituals, The Arts, and the Concept of Creation*, Turnhout, Belgium: Brepols, 2007. The article "*Deus Artifex and Homo Creator*: Art between the Human and the Divine", by Eyolf Østrem, pp.15–48, is replete with references.

13. I have followed the text as given in M. O'Callaghan and Felice Zualdi, *The Sacred Ceremonies of Low Mass according to the Roman Rite*, Dublin: Browne and Nolan, 1899, pp. 64–66.

14. The theme of abjection has been of enormous contemporary interest, especially in French psychoanalytic writing, as well as in the recent novels of Michel Houellebecq and Christine Angot, and in the cinema of Bertrand Bonello, Jean-Luc Godard, and Marco Ferreri, for which see Keith Reader, *The Abject Object: Avatars of the Phallus in Contemporary French Theory, Literature and Film*, Amsterdam: Rodopi, 2006.

15. For this admittedly trunctated and skimming summary, I have drawn on the texts of Clement in the *Stromata*, available online at: www.newadvent.org/fathers/0210.htm.

16. These arguments can be followed in greater detail in the important work of Manuel Brito Martins: *L'herméneutique originaire d'Augustin en relation avec une ré-appropriation Heideggerienne*, Porto: Fundaçao Eng. António de Almeida, 1998. In light of Augustine's ontotheology, the idea of human *mutatio* was repugnant to reason.

17. A significant addendum to this argument can be found in Jeffrey F. Hamburger and Anne-Marie Bouche eds., *The Mind's Eye: Art and Theological Argument in the Middle Ages*, New Jersey: Princeton University Press, 2006, and especially the article by Brigitte Miriam Bedos-Rezak, "Replica, Images of Identity and the Identity of Image in Prescholastic France", pp. 46–65.

18. The argument in this work and its sources are invaluable for the discussion being followed here: Gordon Lindsay Campbell, *Strange Creatures: Anthropology in Antiquity*, London: Duckworth, 2006.

19. As cited in George Boas, *Primitivism and Related Ideas in the Middle Ages*, Baltimore and London: Johns Hopkins University Press, 1948, pp. 157–158. On Lactantius, see also Jackson Bryce, "*De Ave Phoinice* and the Religious Policy of Constantine the Great", *Studia Patristica*, Elizabeth A. Livingstone ed., Oxford: Oxford University Press, 1987, pp. 73–79, as well as Bryce's online bibliography at http: www.carleton.edu/curricular/CLAS/lactantius/biblio.htm.

20. This is Richmond Lattimore's translation from *The Odyssey of Homer*, New York: HarperCollins, 1965, p. 103.

21. As quoted in Boas, *Primitivism*, p. 159.

22. The *Navigatio* was enormously influential on the development of Dutch literature. The quotation from the *Excerptiones priores* can be found in Jacques Paul Migne, *Patrologia Latina*, vol. 177, Paris: Garnier, p. 209, which can be accessed online at http://pld.chadwyck.co.uk/; see Campbell, *Strange Creatures*, for details, chapter 7, and p. 173. *The Seafaring Saint*, published by Strijbosch in 2000, contains relevant analysis and comparanda of the Brendan Voyage, and in popular culture Severin has attempted a reconstruction of the voyage and fueled the legend of the 'Irish' discovery of America.

23. For a discussion of pigments and trade contacts see Christopher Michael Woolgar, *The Senses in Late Medieval England*, New Haven: Yale University Press, 2006. The chapter on "Vision", pp. 147–190, is of particular interest.

24. For a review of the material from Pliny on India, *Natural History*, 7.21–23, and the island of Panachia in Euhemerus, see Campbell, *Strange Creatures*, pp.112–136. For the sources of bestiaries and images possibly available to Bosch, see the informative L. A. J. R. Houwen ed., *Animals and the Symbolic in Medieval Art and Literature*, Groningen: Egbert Forsten, 1997, particularly the article by Lesley Kordecki, "Losing the Monster and Recovering the Non-Human in Fable(d) Subjectivity", pp. 29–35. On page 30 a list is provided of Biblical citations referring to monsters, dragons, basilisks, lamis, onocentaurs, griffins, pilosusses, etc., as well as a list of authors in which monsters figure most prominently, e.g. Ratramnus of Corbie, Marco Polo, Odoric of Pordenone, John Mandeville, the references to Pliny and the Physiologus, along with works of Thomas de Cantimpré, Pseudo-Hugh of St. Victor, Vincent of Beauvais. Not included is Cyriac of Ancona, the reception of whose work needs to be considered in relation to the period in which Bosch is working, c. 1450–1516.

25. For this, see especially Anna C. Esmeijer, *Divina Quaternitas: a Preliminary Study in the Method and Application of Visual Exegesis*, Amsterdam: Van Gorcum, 1978, pp. 117–128. For Plato-reception in this period, see James Hankins, *Plato in the Italian Renaissance*, Leiden: Brill, 1991. Ernest G. McClain, *The Pythagorean Plato: Prelude to the Song Itself*, York Beach, Maine: Nicolas-Hays Inc., 1984, has much detail on the musical trigonometry of Plato, and the impact of the *Timaeus* on musical theory.

26. Le Goff, Jacques, *La naissance du purgatoire*, Paris: Gallimard, 1981. I have drawn for convenience on Arthur Goldhammer's English translation, *The Birth of Purgatory*, London: Scolar Press, 1984.

27. For further details see the invaluable article of Caroline Walker Bynum, "The Female Body and Religious Practice in the Later Middle Ages", *Fragments for a History of the Human Body*, New York: Zone, 1989, pp. 161–219. Many of these religious groups, including the confraternity to which Bosch belonged, were between the lay and clerical states, and thus a kind of affiliation in liminality to both. They increasingly emphasized the nature of personal penance and private devotion, and the main handbook of their ascetic orientation was the *Imitatio Christi* of Thomas à Kempis.

28. The study of this material has been intensified because of Foucault's *Birth of the Clinic*, and the fascinating work of Henri

Hubert Beek, *Waanzin in de Middeleeuwen*, Haarlem: De Toorts, 1969.
29. The phenomenon of bringing the dead into the city in late antiquity has been studied by Beatrice Caseau in her article "Sacred Landscapes", *Interpreting Late Antiquity: Essays on the Post-classical World*, G. W. Bowersock, Peter Brown, and Oleg Grabar eds., Cambridge, MA: Belknap Press, 2001, pp. 21–60. One could also consult Dawn Marie Hayes, *Body and Sacred Place in Medieval Europe*, 1100–1389, London: Routledge, 2003.
30. For a study of Heidegger on early Christianity, see Martins, *L'herméneutique originaire d'Augustin*, which is still the most detailed study to date. The fear and trembling and individual existential awareness emphasized by Heidegger have a kind of compulsive physicalism for the early Christians.
31. For Aristotle's *On Generation and Corruption*, see Frans de Haas and Jaap Mansfeld eds., *Oxford Symposium Aristotelicum 1, Aristotle's On Generation and Corruption*, 15th Symposium 1999, Oxford: Oxford University Press, 2004.
32. For material on the Last Judgment, see Kees Veelenturf, *Dia Brátha: Eschatological Theophanies and Irish High Crosses*, Amsterdam: Stichting Amsterdamse Historische Reeks, 1997, pp. 69–95. On page 96 he lists the significant Biblical passages.
33. All New Testament quotations are from Erwin Nestle and Kurt Aland eds., *Novum Testamentum*, 22nd edition, Stuttgart: Deutsche Bibelgesellschaft, 1964.
34. Durbin, Paul T., ed., *St. Thomas Aquinas Summa Theologiae, Volume 12: Human Intelligence*, Cambridge: Cambridge University Press, 2006 p. 142. (STh 1a.89.2).
35. A point made by Aquinas in the *Summa Theologiae*, 1a. III.3: "*voluntas semper remanet libera ad consentiendum vel resistendum passioni*" (the will always remains free with regard to consenting to or resisting passion), and adding that God did not allow us to be tempted beyond our available force of resistance. See M. J. Charlesworth ed., *St. Thomas Aquinas Summa Theologiae, Volume 15: The World Order*, Cambridge: Cambridge University Press, 2006, p. 24.
36. Thomas à Kempis, *De Imitatione Christi Libri Quatuor*, Parma: Ex Imperiali Typographia, 1807, p. 185.
37. I have for the most part followed Adolphe Tanquerey's *Précis de Théologie Ascétique et Mystique*, Paris: Desclée and CIE, 1923.
38. For a study of the allegorical, especially see Richard Goulet and Gilbert Dahan eds., *On the Allegory of Poets and of Philosophers*, Paris: Vrin, 2005.
39. Quoted from Le Goff, *The Birth of Purgatory*, p. 259.
40. See Le Goff, *The Birth of Purgatory*, pp. 217, 259.
41. For this and much else on Hell, see the work of Eileen Gardiner, whose edition of the *Visio Tnugdali* remains the best available: Gardiner, Eileen, *The "Vision of Tundale": a Critical Edition of the Middle English Text*, Ann Arbor, Michigan: University Microfilms, 1980. Gardiner further maintains the site "Hell online", and this also provides invaluable bibliographies and summaries of recent work: http://www.hell-on-line.org/index.html. Paraphrases here are derived from Gardiner's text. See also Thomas Kren and Roger S. Wiek, *The Visions of Tondal from the Library of Margaret of York*, Malibu CA: The Getty Museum, 1990 for background information and beautifully illustrated text excerpts.
42. This of course points directly to the influence of Plutarch (*Moralia*) on this tale, and some of the salient details of the fiends here are directly taken over for Bosch's grimoire of forms and depiction of the demonic realm.
43. This hybridizing shift is seen also in the near contemporary of Bosch, Erasmus.
44. See Gibson, *Hieronymus Bosch*, p. 81.
45. See Harris, *The Secret Heresy*, passim.

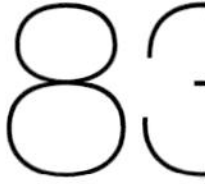

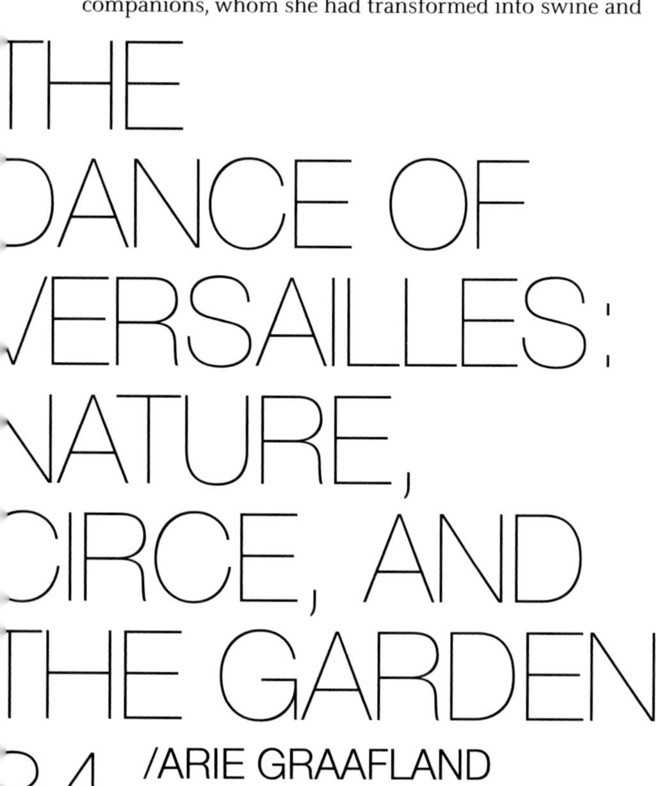

THE DANCE OF VERSAILLES: NATURE, CIRCE, AND THE GARDEN

34 /ARIE GRAAFLAND

Versailles is a park, but it is equally a book. *It is the bible through whose pages the god-king, resorting to every possible mode of narrative (allegories, digressions, secrets, surprises...) and flinging into the grand mix every sort of personage, whether divine, human or animal, tells who he is and fathers his own being.*
/ Érik Orsenna[1] [Figure 1]

Circé est le naturel de l'homme. *(Circe is the Nature of man.)*
/ Balthazar de Beaujoyeulx[2]

As Homer tells the tale, Odysseus, cleverest and most resilient of heroes, endures ten years of fighting at Troy and a further ten years of wandering to make his way home to his wife and kingdom on the island of Ithaka. Among the perils he faces in the course of his protracted travels is the island-dwelling goddess Circe, daughter of the sun god Helios. Versed in the dark arts, this seductive enchantress-goddess lures the unsuspecting Greeks with a false semblance of feminine submissiveness and domesticity, for they find the goddess at work at the loom, the very picture of an ideal Greek wife. Yet, strangely and ominously, Circe is surrounded by wild animals: wolves and lions fawn about her like domesticated dogs. This Nature goddess, Mistress of Animals and the Wild, poses the greatest threat to Odysseus and patriarchal Greece.[3] So great is the threat she poses, that Odysseus must draw his sword to overpower her. Only then can he force her to restore to human form those of his companions, whom she had transformed into swine and

held captive in her palace. Homer's Circe epitomizes that which patriarchal Greece, and every patriarchal society thereafter, feared most: the oneness of the irrational, chaotic 'Feminine' with Nature, bearing with it control over life and death.

ISLANDS, WATER, AND THE GARDEN

Islands play an important role in the ancient myths of Asia and Europe. The island as the *terra firma* rising up out of the infinite seas is a model of the creation of the world and is the place of everything that must become new. It was not only new life that was presented in this way; death as birth, as the transition to a different existence, was also connected to the island. Advancing Christianity replaced these images on the grounds that they reflected a naive and yearning hedonism. Accordingly, dream islands became models of positive and negative perfection, guiding models for the Christian life.

The island as the place of renewal and longing was first given a geographic depiction in the fifteenth century in Italy and in the sixteenth century in Northern Europe. The opening up of new continents as well as new sea roads, which revealed new experiences, made this geographic view possible, and the drive to spatial expansion and experience

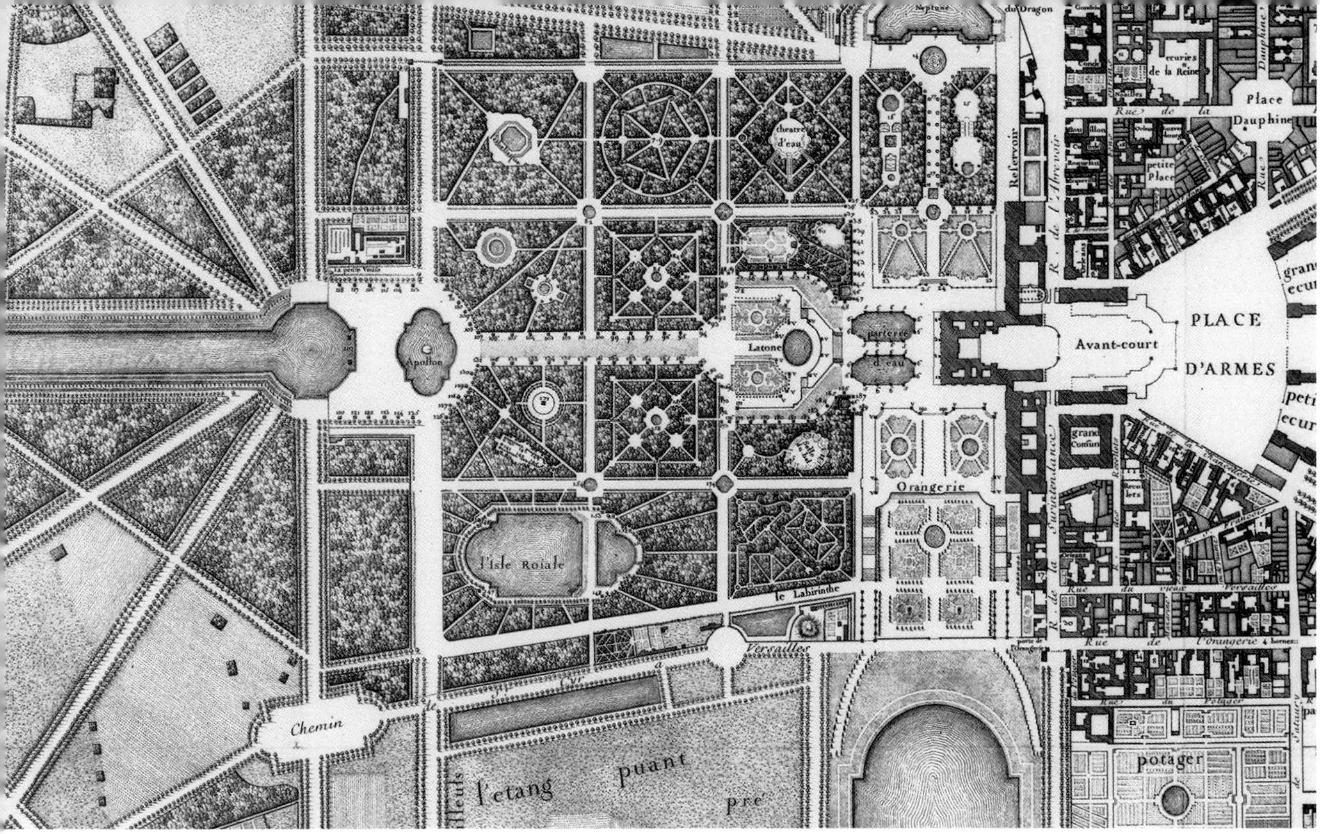

Figure 1/ *Plan de Versailles*, 1746. Jean Delagrive.

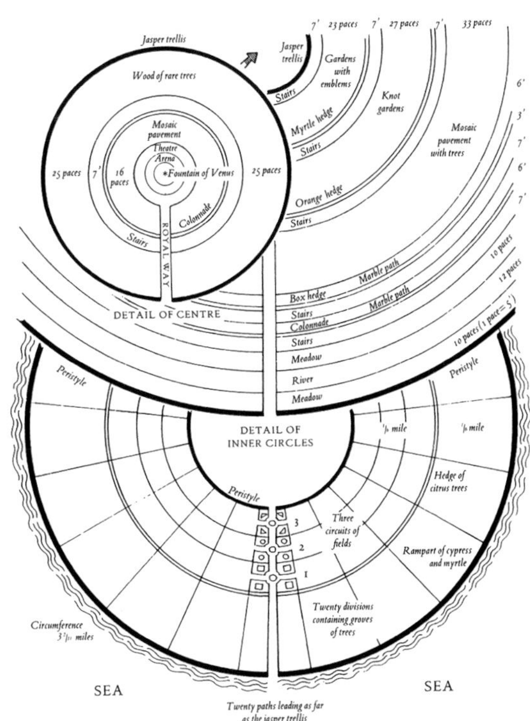

Figure 2/ Island of Cytherean Venus.
Based on Francesco Colonna's *Hypnerotomachia Poliphili.*

determined the images. For example, in Francesco Colonna's *Hypnerotomachia Poliphili* (*Strife of Love in a Dream*), the Isola di Citera (Island of Cytherean Venus) stands for the place where everything forms a strict geometric whole [Figure 2].[4] The circular island with 20 radial streets, intersected by concentric roads, probably has its origin in Plato's description of Atlantis. The hero Poliphilo describes it as an earthly paradise where man and beast live in perfect harmony:

> It was so benign and pleasing to the senses, so delectable and beautiful with unusual ornamental trees, that the eye had never seen anything so excellent and voluptuous.... This heavenly and delicious place, all planted and decorated, combined a vegetable garden, a herbarium, a fertile orchard, a convenient plantation, a pleasant arboretum and a delightful shrubbery.... The trees were sweet of scent, plentiful of fruit, and broad of branch. It was a garden yielding incomparable pleasure, extremely fertile, decked with flowers, free from obstacles and traps, and ornamented with playing fountains and cool rivulets.[5]

Indeed, here water and its various erotically charged delights abound:

On the rivers are boats and skiffs rowed by many maidens with lovely hair interwoven with various scented flowers, wearing flimsy crêpe tunics or shifts of saffron yellow slashed or eyeleted with gold, trimmed and belted over their nymph-like nakedness with lascivious ornaments, and voluptuously offering their rose-tinted flesh to the unimpeded gaze.[6]

In the center of the island is a round amphitheater at the heart of which stands an ornate fountain house, its seven columns carved of precious stones and its cupola of crystal. When Poliphilo and his love Polia finally arrive at the fountain, itself a wonder to behold, they must, as a symbolic gesture, rend a velvet curtain that hangs between the columns, thereby revealing the divine figure of Venus:

> The divine Venus stood naked in the middle of the transparent and limpid waters of the basin, which reached up to her ample and divine waist, reflecting the Cytherean body without making it seem larger, smaller, doubled or refracted; it was visible simple and whole, as perfect as it was in itself. And all around, up to the first step, there was a foam that gave the scent of musk. The divine body appeared luminous and transparent, displaying its majesty and venerable aspect with exceptional clarity and blazing like a precious and coruscating carbuncle in the rays of the sun; for it was made from a miraculous compound which humans have never conceived of, much less seen.[7]

Not only this image, but the entire book is characterized by nostalgia for the past, both the Classical and Christian. The lovers' quest amidst architectural fantasies and gardens was very appealing, probably because in many respects it resembled its predecessor, *Le Roman de la Rose* (*Story of the Rose*), written by Guillaume de Lorris in 1235, a Medieval meditation on love in which battle is joined between sensual desire and Christian asceticism.[8] In Colonna's epic, which John Summerson called "the romantic, haunted, introverted side of the Renaissance", the pagan gods of the ancient world remain alive in the cultural setting and ritual of the late Middle Ages.[9] Classical fantasies of architecture become the setting for Christian ritual in Colonna's garden. The Medieval 'Fountain of Salvation' becomes the backdrop of a garden love scene, and the *nympheum* (grotto) of antiquity becomes a Platonic baptistery, according to W. H. Adams.[10]

In the second half of the sixteenth century, with the help of large fountains and cascades, Italian garden architecture was in a position to give expression to a more active spatial thinking and, in this way, introduce the island motif into garden art. The Medieval source of life—*fons salutis* (fount of salvation)—changed in meaning, and now stood for the forces and joys of the rural life in nature. Arabic and Persian influences were probably the cause of this shift. Water, and particularly the specific treatment of water in fountains and cascades, now acquired a special significance. Thus, in a number of cases, water features deliberately deviated from the dominant symmetry of numbers, size, and arrangement characterizing the geometric plan of Italian Renaissance villas. The pond and park at Villa Lante near Viterbo are an expression of this.

The Villa Lante, 1568, was laid out by the Bishop of Viterbo, Cardinal Gambara, about 50 kilometers to the north of Rome, on a spur of a range of hills running on a north–south axis [Figure 3]. The town of Bagnaia occupied the strategic northern point of the range. The villa's main element, the axis of symmetry, followed the natural direction of the chain of hills from north to south. The axis began high on the slope where a spring rises from a grotto deep in the *bosco* (woods). C. M. Steenbergen shows that the falling water was increasingly subject to architectural treatment as it descended until it ultimately came to rest in the large reflecting pond on the lower terrace.[11] The villa's garden expands from the grotto above to the terrace below. The location of the buildings follows this line; the house itself is split into two casinos positioned symmetrically with regard to the axis. According to John Shepherd and Geoffrey Jellicoe the position of the two casinos indicates a power that far surpasses the life of the mortals who eat,

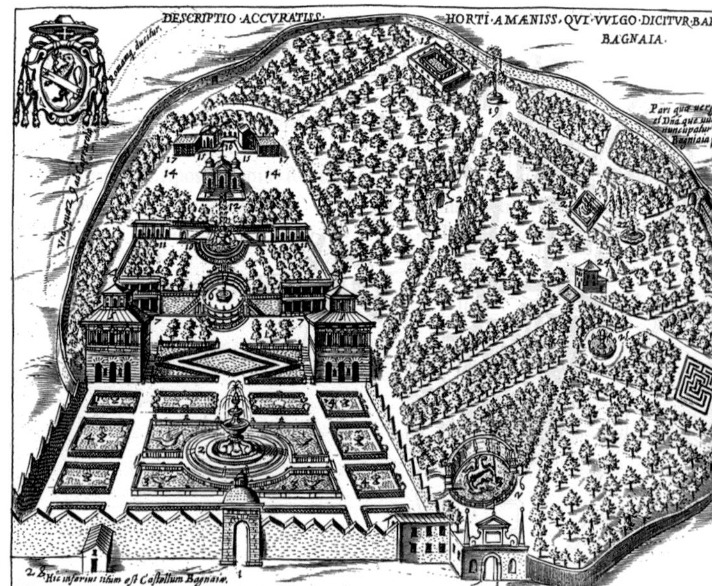

Figure 3/ Plan of the Villa Lante, detail, 1596. Tarquinio Ligustri.

sleep, grow up and die here. The casinos bow down before Giovanni da Bologna's fountains, symbol of an ideal order.[12] The cascade which links grotto and pond is the most deviant element. The water apparently does not allow itself to be confined by geometry, a theme I will develop later on. The source of the water, the grotto, also has a divergent meaning:

> In the Renaissance the grottoes almost became deceptions, the human work being hidden; the material is natural, stalagmites and stalactites that are gathered and carried from distant sites. We are told directly by Alberti that the most complete mimesis was the principal goal, but it should not be assumed that this was for reasons of modesty, because, as in theatrical performances the most faithful imitation corresponds to the highest ability and the result is not banality but surprise. It is not by chance that this legerdemain coincides with the early concept of the first illustrated scientific encyclopedia. A new ingredient, geology, accompanies botany and a new emotion, wonder, is combined with pleasure.[13]

The significance of these diverse, irregular, 'naturalistic' elements such as *boschetto* (grove) and *nymphaeum* (grotto) is often overlooked. The Villa Lante itself is often described in terms of the formal terraced gardens in front of and behind the two casinos, while the informal park to the side is ignored.[14] However, Elizabeth MacDougall, who points to the Villa Lante as a model, shows that the gardens dating from after 1520 are dynamic:

> The early Renaissance garden was primarily static and could be viewed in its entirety from a fixed point of view. To borrow from literary terminology, it had a unity of space and time. The gardens after the 1520s consisted of a series of successive spaces, isolated from each other physically and visually. They could only be experienced through movement, and the relationship between spectator and garden became active rather than passive. The arrangement of terraces at Castello, the planting and the position of the connections between the terraces called for movement from one space to another and from one level to another, as did the succession of courtyards at the Villa Giulia.[15]

Yet 'wild nature' only came to be properly developed in French landscape art; in France, the Italian influences fell on fertile ground. Not without reason Gerold Weber says that in the tradition of the French grotto art, these deviations from the rationalist pattern only have a place as an 'image' in a much greater whole.[16]

FRANCE

In a way, every castle surrounded by water forms its own island. With the passage of time, the water, together with the castle itself, lost its effectiveness as fortification and since 1350 had acquired an aesthetic effect. One of the so-called Valois Tapestries, which celebrate the sixteenth century royal court of France, exemplifies such an aestheticization of danger. Here a forested island appears in the middle of an elongated basin of water, and on the basin's short side a Renaissance castle is set against the backdrop of a fantastic mountain landscape. The whole is complemented by ships in an ancient style. Closely packed together on the shore, spectators follow the dramatic sea battle that ended in the conquest of the island. But, judging from a preliminary sketch for this tapestry by Antoine Caron, this is no battle scene at all but rather a festive game set at the carp pond of Fontainebleau.[17]

Ultimately, in seventeenth century France the Palais d'Apolidon (Palace of Apolidon) would become the usual formula to denote a residence as picturesque or enchanting. This enchanted, miraculous castle is described in the immensely popular chivalric romance *Amadis de Gaule*, which had been translated from the original Spanish into French, Italian, German, Dutch, and Hebrew by the end of the sixteenth century. Built on the Isle Ferme (Steadfast Island) by the Byzantine emperor's heir Apolidon in memory of the bliss he had enjoyed with his beloved, the castle was distinguished by the precious materials—gemstones, gold, bronze, alabaster, coral, and cypress included—of which it was built, as well as by a series of magical defenses:

> All the portals of this palace were of damascene alabaster, with mouldings, tympana, and pediments in amber stone and red agate, all sculpted in the classical manner.... And Apolidon had the mouldings of these portals made expressly from magnetic stone and the doors of steel so that when they were opened they would close again on their own by virtue of this stone.[18]

In Renaissance gardens, the continuing geometrification of the overall plan, which increasingly came to dominate all the parts, could do little with the dream island. With growing frequency this artificially laid-out Île Enchantée (Enchanted Isle) was displaced to the side areas of the park, where intimacy provided by such islands could still be done justice. The Île d'Amour (Isle of Love), built by Le Nôtre in 1643 with a pavilion in the park of Dampierre, is one example. Others include the Île de Bois Vert (Isle of the Green Wood) and Île d'Amour in the canals of Chantilly.

The island motif is also familiar in European literature. In particular, new moral and social orders were

Figure 4/ *Salle du Conseil,* Versailles. c. 1688. Étienne Allegrain.

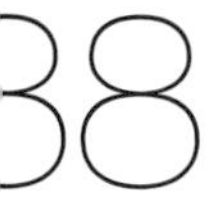

represented on distant islands. A primary example is Thomas More's *De optimo rei publicae statu, deque nova insula Utopia*, 1516, more commonly known as *Utopia*, in which the state is founded on natural law. So too Campanella's *Civitas Solis* (*City of the Sun*) features the island of Taprobane where the strict harmonic construction of the state is reflected in the form of a terraced, circular city crowned by a cylindrical temple and surrounded by concentric walls. The themes of erotic love and death also came to be connected to the island motif. The sixteenth century explorer, cosmographer, and cleric André Thevet was the first to give the island an erotic dimension by having a pair of lovers stranded there.[19] In the seventeenth century, the secretary of la Grande Mademoiselle, Jean Regnauld de Segrais, dedicated his Arcadian *Relation de l'Île imaginaire* (*Tale of the Imaginary Isle*) to his mistress. Meanwhile, we find the theme of death on the deserted island of Philippe Habert's "*Temple de la Mort*" ("Temple of Death").

Figures 5, 6, 7/ *Île Royale* (top), *Vue du Théâtre d'Eau* (middle), *Plan du Bassin d'Apollon* (bottom), Versailles. Jacques Rigaud, 1681–1754.

While the island revealed the image of the ideal city in Italy, France was the only country in Europe that kept this ideal of beauty alive until the seventeenth century. This idea of the island was realized in the garden, specifically in the Île Enchantée. Gardens, fountains, and ponds are related; the island motif and hydraulic installations for fountains and cascades are linked. The motif of the artificial island occurs in three different forms, as the naturalistic but inaccessible wooded island in Versailles (Le Marais), as the stylized Salle du Conseil (Council Chamber) where the geometry is universally preponderant [Figure 4], and as an island surrounded by a moat, as in Liancourt. Until the nineteenth century, actual isolation by water in a pond was called an Île Royale [Figure 5], Île d'Amour, or Île de Mars (Royal Isle, Isle of Love, or Isle of Mars). Hamilton Hazlehurst sees a *bosquet* (open-air room cut out of the woodland) like Le Marais as an intimate spot in the middle of the formal layout of the gardens. The bosquets—Le Marais was also called "Bosquet du Buffet"—were literally 'hewed out' of the trees. André Félibien called it "*un salon de verdure*" (a chamber of greenery), in his *Description sommaire*, 1674, the "summary description" serving as official guide to Versailles. The Marais is the first bosquet, probably invented by Louis XIV's mistress, Madame de Montespan.[20] Here too the island motif is linked to the water, with the Théâtre d'Eau (Theater of Water) emerging at the Marais; here water is the chief protagonist [Figure 6]. The Théâtre d'Eau would be replaced by the Bains d'Apollon (Baths of Apollo) in 1704 [Figures 6, 7].[21]

BALLETS

The island motif is scenery demanding a performance. This it finds in ballet. Jean Rousset provides a chart of *Ballets magiciens et métamorphoses* (ballets of magic and transformation) that were performed between 1581 and 1664 in Italy, France, The Netherlands, and England. Of the 27 ballets, there are 12 in which the scene includes an island or grotto. Four names are central in these ballets: Circe, Calypso, Alcina, and Armida, all of whom were represented as "capricious fabricators of an unstable creation that they change at whim".[22] Of these ballets, the Circe ballet is the most common. Indeed, the Circe motif was central to the 1581 *Balet Comique*, performed at the Louvre before Henri III, which is considered by many as the beginning of ballet history. But before analyzing this originary work in detail, we will turn to a series of

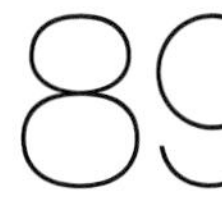

royal festivities at Versailles between 1664–1674, all of which enact the triumph of 'masculine' reason over the 'irrational' powers of nature represented by the Circe figures, and all of which served not so much to reflect as intensify and stabilize royal power.

Louis XIV himself was an excellent dancer, just like his predecessors Henri III, Henri IV, and Louis XIII. He first danced in 1651, at the age of 13, in the *Balet de Cassandre.*[23] Between 1661 (the year he began keeping a diary) and 1670, the King danced in 12 ballets, assuming approximately 29 roles. The court ballets were immensely popular and often took months to prepare. As the first performance approached, rehearsals were held three times a day, bringing Louis to a state of exhaustion. Dancing means attaining a high degree of perfection, expressing a state of harmony with one's body. Further, dancing with virtuosity is a duty for a king. "One cannot allow oneself to be the laughing stock of the court when one is king."[24] Unquestionably, the dance is a key to a better understanding of the sixteenth and seventeenth centuries in France. The ballet has particularly close ties with the gardens of Versailles which, as Philippe Beaussant remarks, "was born for music".[25] Indeed, the palace's gardens proved ideal for the ballets in which Louis was sometimes a principal performer [Figure 8]. That he excelled as a dancer can only have enhanced the magic of the ballet, with a backdrop of lawns, statues, pools, and fountains for the dancers' stately minuets. More significantly, we may see in these performances a social metaphor of control and balance.[26] Via their physical engagement with the dance itself, participants would

Figure 8/ *Vue perspective du château et des jardins de Versailles*, 1668. Pierre Patel.

Figure 9/ Louis XIV as the Sun God Apollo.
Joseph Werner, 1642–1708.

receive an impression of the harmony of Louis' ideal universe, of the subjection of all, dancers and spectators alike, to Apollo, god of culture, harmony, light, and life—and so to the Sun King himself [Figure 9]. But there was more involved than a social metaphor.

LES PLAISIRS DE L'ÎLE ENCHANTÉE

The first great festivities took place at Versailles during the spring of 1664, from 7 to 13 May. These were entitled *Les Plaisirs de l'Île Enchantée* (*The Pleasures of the Enchanted Isle*). *The Enchanted Isle* was officially held for the pleasure of Louis' mother Anne of Austria, who had been married to Louis XIII and whose Spanish niece, Infanta Marie-Thérèse, was Louis' wife and Queen. Unofficially, however, this first festival was mounted in honor of the King's love for Louise de la Vallière. Louis had married Marie-Thérèse d'Autriche on June 1660, but his mistress, La Vallière, was already on the scene in July of 1661. Louise was madly in love with the King, feelings that were in fact mutual. On 20 January 1662 Louis would write in his diary: "L. is more and more dear to me; she is young, pure, sincere, and lacking all ambition" (L. is La Vallière).[27] For the time being, the King but newly wed, their meetings had to be in secret, and there were no trysts during the day. These took place in the evening, when the King took his wife's carriage and met La Vallière's carriage in the dark. Nor did it stop there: he borrowed a room in the castle from his *premier gentilhome* (first gentleman), Comte de Saint-Aignan. On 15 July 1661 the King wrote in his diary: "At Fontainebleau there are too many people, and there is not an appropriate venue. I required a secret apartment, and thank God, Saint-Aignan gave me his room for an hour or two."[28] The outcome is well-known, for this relationship brought forth four children, two of whom survived. The *Île enchantée* is thus specifically linked to La Vallière. She was part of that '*jeunesse dorée*' (golden youth) involved in moonlight promenades, concerts, balls, and love that surrounded the King and his court.

For the first *fêtes* of Versailles, held between 1664 and 1668 in the open air, the gardens, verdure, and fountains provided the decor. Slowly but surely this setting seems to have ceded in the years that followed to marble and bronze. In characterizing the *fêtes*, Beaussant stresses their similarity to the *carrousel*, a procession, or rather cavalcade, on horseback in which the nobility could show off their power and wealth. Like the *carrousel*, the festival of the *Île enchantée* lasted several days. The two most famous *carrousels* from the seventeenth century were that of 1662 (which lasted three days) and that of 1612 (two days). The main difference is that the *fête* of the *Île enchantée* was no longer enacted in the public sphere. The *carrousel* of 1612 had been held at what is now called Place des Vosges, and that of 1662 between the Louvre and the Tuileries, now Place du Carrousel. The *Île enchantée* of 1664, meanwhile, took place in a private setting.

The *Île enchantée* was a thematic festival, a significant collaboration between playwright Molière, composer Jean-Baptiste Lully, and Carlo Vigarani, who served as set designer. The festival, whose climax occurred on the third day, would last a full seven days and, as Louis recorded in his secret diary, was attended by 600 persons: "I came to Versailles with my Court, and for this celebration of the Pleasures of the Enchanted Isle, there will be some six hundred persons that require feeding, but mercifully, not lodging".[29] It must be remembered that Versailles was not, at that time, a grand edifice but rather a relatively modest château that hosted the festival's cavalcades, declamations, pageants, tiltings, ballets, music composed and arranged by Lully, plays by Molière, fireworks, and banquets. The plays performed by Molière and his company were *La Princesse d'Élide*, *Les Fâcheux*, *Le Mariage Forcé*, and a version of *Tartuffe*, but the over-arching theme of the festival was the magic of the sorceress Alcina, who used her witchcraft to hold brave warriors captive in her castle.

The King played a leading role in the festivities, of course. On the day of the opening he rode into the gardens of Versailles on his horse preceded by the sound of trumpets. He looked like an armed Greek fighter "wearing a richly

Figure 10/ *Les Plaisirs de l'Île Enchantée*, Second Day: the 'ephemeral' theater installed in the gardens of Versailles for the production of *La Princesse d'Élide*, 1664. Israël Silvestre.

Figure 11/ *Les Plaisirs de l'Île Enchantée*, Third Day: theater constructed in the middle of the Rond d'Eau basin for the production of *Alcina*, 1664. Israël Silvestre. Photograph © The Trustees of the British Museum.

embroidered breastplate of gold lamé and a helmet decorated with feathers the color of fire".[30] In the case of the Alcina ballet, which took place on the festival's third day, the court was actively involved in the performance. The King himself represented Rugiero, who was brought to the island to save his friend Astolf, and in doing so, his own virtue. The royal household took the other heroic roles and appeared in 'Greek' costumes. On Friday, 9 May, the King wrote in his diary:

> This was the day of Alcina, sister of the fairy Morgana, and here Molière wanted to flatter his king:
> Let us say that at the pinnacle of absolute power
> Without pomp and without pride, his grandeur manifested itself...
> Let us praise his grand works, let us praise the just laws
> Of this son known as the greatest of kings.
> In the evening, marvelous fireworks completed the festivities.[31]

Israël Silvestre's engravings of *Les Plaisirs de l'Île Enchantée* vividly demonstrate the extent to which the avenues of the park were relied on to achieve theatrical perspective in the staging of the festivities. Theater art and garden art were inextricably related.[32] Certainly the gardens were indispensable for the staging of *La Princesse d'Élide*; they were the most important décor [Figure 10]. Indeed, Silvestre depicted King and court sitting with their backs to the castle and facing a temporary, tapestry-flanked stage that had been erected at a point where avenues in the garden crossed. Another of Silvestre's engravings portrays the Alcina spectacle, which took place in the middle of the great quatrefoil basin, the Rond d'Eau (Circle of Water), that would later become the Apollo Basin. In this instance once again the entire garden became part of the theatrical experience. The large rectangular pond with rounded corners contained an artificial island that was positioned off-center [Figure 11]. On the island stood the Castle of Alcina. The building consisted of a middle section with open vestibule, and on both sides large, semi-circular arches created the wings that framed a trapezoidal terrace where the ballet took place. The portrayal was not realistic, but was intended to stimulate the imagination. The elaborately decorated screens placed to the sides of the water feature were intended to accentuate, if not accelerate, the perspective in the direction of Alcina's palace. This is an oft-applied theatrical technique, with the screens achieving an effect of depth. As was shown in the engraving, key scenes are often enacted not in the immediate foreground, but more to the rear in the stage scene.[33] On one side of the perspective screens were the violinists, and on the other side the trumpeters and kettledrummers. In the water were three sea monsters; the first carried Alcina (played by Mlle du Parc) and the other two Célie and Dircé, two nymphs from her retinue (played by Mlle de Brie and Mlle Molière).

As mentioned earlier, the theme of the Alcina spectacle was largely commensurate with that of the Circe ballet: a magical seductress whose charms must be resisted and her powers overcome by the heroic male. Further, as in the case of the Circe ballet, the Alcina spectacle demanded

Figure 12/ *Les Plaisirs de l'Île Enchantée*, Third Day: explosion of the palace of Alcina, 1664. Israël Silvestre. Photograph © The Trustees of the British Museum.

an enchanted palace on a rocky isle, creatures to defend the island, and the fiery destruction of the sorceress' palace marking the dissipation of her powers [Figure 12]. In other words, the performances would have had strong parallels both in theme and setting. In terms of thematic significance specifically, the seventeenth century image of Arcadian life as expressed in the *Île Enchantée* allowed the sensory itself to become an island. A place of bliss, this '*lieu enchanté et de plaisir*' (place of enchantment and delight), became a place of repentance, practice, and control, a true '*école de vertu*' (school of virtue). Just how deeply run these thematic parallels to the Circe ballet is a subject to which I will return shortly.

LES DIVERTISSEMENTS DE VERSAILLES

Immediately after the festivities of *The Enchanted Isle* the King left with his retinue, as he did not yet live at Versailles. Shortly afterwards in 1668 came the second great festival. Then, in 1674, the garden's ponds and bosquets were ready for the most spectacular festivities ever held in Versailles, *Les Divertissements de Versailles donnés par le Roi à toute sa cour* (*The Entertainments of Versailles Given by the King to His Entire Court*). This festival far surpassed the previous two. The festive entourage was devised by painter Charles Le Brun and Vigarani. The old castle at Versailles had been rebuilt as Château-Neuf (New Castle) by architect Louis Le Vau and now consisted of two wings and a central block with a terrace on the garden side and, on the other side, the Cour de Marbre (Court of Marble). The palace's great wings had not yet been built—in fact had not even been designed. To the far left, seen from the garden, the Thétis Cave was still present. In 1670 the Apollo basin had been excavated and the monumental group put in place.

This festival of 1674 was in truth not a singular event but a number of celebrations in succession.[34] Beaussant typifies it as an optical illusion, a false perspective. Like the festival of 1664, it encompassed six days, spread over two months, from 4 July to 31 August. On that 4th of July, Le Vau's rebuilding work was accomplished and the Grand Canal complete. The festival took place at different locations: on 4 July the opera *Alceste* was staged at the Cour de Marbre. On 19 July it was the bosquets, the Marais, the Théâtre d'Eau, and the Thétis Cave that served as settings for the ballet-pastorale *Fêtes de l'amour et de Bacchus* (the pastoral ballet *Festivals of Love and of Bacchus*). The performance was followed by a supper at the Cour de Marbre. On 18 August, *Iphigénie* was performed in the Orangerie. For the last evening, 31 August, a sumptuous spectacle was planned in which the King, his park, his newly trenched canal, and his '*machiniste*', Carlo Vigarani, played the principal roles. At one hour past midnight, the entire court stepped into gondolas and ornately decorated boats. The park, lit with torches, resounded with music through the greenery. Gondolas, boats, statues... everything was magically lit on this most extraordinary night. André Félibien's account of this occasion is breathtaking in itself. In the still of the night His Majesty's boat sailed up the canal with violin music wafting after him from the gardens. An impressive silence prevailed that night; the women softly stroked the hair of their children who had, out of sheer fatigue, fallen asleep in their laps. Only the torches on the banks illuminated the water, with the statues showing in the faint torchlight. "*Les effets de croyance*", "the effects of belief", is what Louis Marin calls this: "the effects of belief provoked in the imagination of those who, on that night of 31 August to 1 September 1674, saw the King of France on the Grand Canal, in the park of his Palace of Versailles".[35] At the end of the spatial sequence, and built especially for this occasion, there was a picturesque castle very like that described in Colonna's *Hypnerotomachia Poliphili*. In the eyes of Félibien it was, "*un palais de cristal bâti dans l'eau*" (a palace of crystal built on the water), a prototype of the '*lieu enchanté*' (enchanted place). Once again an enchanted palace, just one of many links with Circe.

The gardens of Versailles, so intimately linked with music and performance, are a pure reflection of the Sun King and the ideals of his regime. The festivals staged at Versailles provide important clues, but an even clearer picture of these ideals emerges when the gardens are viewed through the lens of the first Circe ballet, the so-called *Balet Comique* of 1581. When applied as a provisional frame to the geometries of Louis' gardens, the themes and structures of the early ballet reveal much about the utopian desires of this period, which, in turn, inform us more deeply about the purpose of both gardens and ballets.

NIGHT AGAIN, OCTOBER 15, 1581; THE CIRCE BALLET

The *Balet Comique* of 1581, as earlier stated, is often seen as the beginning of known ballet history. The large-scale study *L'Art du ballet de cour en France, 1581–1643* (*The Art of the Court's Ballet in France*), by Margaret M. McGowan begins with it, and the noted scholar of social philosophy and aesthetics Rudolf zur Lippe also treats this ballet extensively.[36] While choreographic details of the dancing were not recorded, and the costumes of those who actually danced were not illustrated in the ballet's manuscript, the ballet's choreographer is known to be Balthazar de Beaujoyeulx (his Italian name was Baldassarino da Belgiojoso). The ballet's central theme was the subjugation of the sensual enchantress Circe to the principles of the new absolutist state power in France. In a letter accompanying his manuscript, Beaujoyeulx refers to the religious disputes then occurring in France and offers his ballet as a remedy.[37] The ballet clearly symbolizes the subjection of those who resist the modern centralist state power. At the same time, the King Henri III is depicted as liberator and conqueror. The sovereign is the representative of history; he holds the course of history in his hand like a scepter.[38] The countless comparisons of the prince with the sun in the literature of the epoch were intended to stress the exclusiveness of this ultimate authority.

Essentially a new art form, the ballet of sixteenth century France brought together poetry, music, and dance in the mythological form usual at that time. The notion of '*comique*' in the *Balet Comique* refers to the 'structural' combination of these. But in political terms, this art form reflected the deepening and broadening of the state power of the French king, Henri III. Jean Rousset describes this age (from 1580 to 1670) as being in flux, changeable and unstable. His book, bearing the subtitle *Circé et le paon* (Circe and the peacock) presents *le paon*, which symbolizes metamorphosis, as well as ostentation or display as the defining characteristics of the Baroque.[39] "The religious man of the Baroque era clings so tightly to the world because of the feeling that he is being drawn along with it to a cataract", writes Walter Benjamin.[40] The French *Balet Comique* was thus intended not only to amuse the King; Circe was 'desire' (*le désir en général*), a mixture of divinity and sensuality (*mestié de la divinité et du sensible*). The ballet depicts not the banishing of desire, but the unraveling and transforming of its productive energy. In this the ballet embodies what Michel Foucault describes as a hallmark of disciplinary power: the principal function being not to remove or eliminate an opposing power, but to train it. Circe is, as such, deployed to enlarge the King's power.

The immediate reason for the staging of the 1581 Circe Ballet was the marriage of Anne d'Arques, the King's favorite minion, to his sister-in-law Margaret de Lorraine Vaudemont of the house of Lorraine, the sister of Queen Louise. Anne d'Arques, who was born in the Ardèche in 1560, grew up in Avignon and later attended the College de Navarre in Paris. Since 1577 he had been the King's inseparable companion. In August 1581 he was given the title Anne, Duc de Joyeuse. As the King's protégé he was the right person to marry the queen's sister. The marriage was an appropriate way of lending new impetus to the power and certainly also the popularity of the French king among the nobility. The festivities lasted about two weeks. Thursday 14 September was kept free for the official marriage ceremony; on Sunday there was a competition of tilting at the ring (*course de bague*). On Tuesday there was a great banquet under the guidance of the Duc de Mercoeur. On Thursday this was repeated, and on Saturday there were various dances in the Great Court of the Louvre. The next day there was a festive procession, and the same evening a masquerade with musicians dressed as fauns and men and women disguised as exotic trees. The following day, in the evening and into the night, the *Balet Comique de la Royne* (The Queen's Royal Ballet), as the ballet's full title reads, was performed at the Louvre. The following Tuesday there came a series of banquets, the first in the house of the Cardinal de Bourbon, another held by the Duc de Guise, and finally one at the queen mother's home. A total of 17 banquets were given, all with music, fireworks, and the ever-popular water spectacles.

Rousset sketches the significance of water and the Tritons in the royal festivities. In one of the wedding events, prepared by the Cardinal de Bourbon, a great ferry in the form of a war chariot drifted down the Seine with the King, Queen, princes and princesses, and, naturally, the newly-wed pair aboard. Tritons, Sirens, dolphins, and sea monsters played an important role on the various other vessels. In this pageant on the Seine, the water itself became the theater. Royal entries of this kind, blending pageantry and propaganda, were regularly occurring events in those days, both in France and England.[41] Considerable sums of money, raised by the townships, were invested in them, and such investments carried with them the welcome bonus of civic rights and privileges granted.

Henri II and his wife Catherine de Medici, for example, had availed themselves of a pageant of entry in Rouen in 1550. The entry into Rouen was unquestionably one of the most impressive that ever took place. Gladiators in action, a parade of elephants, nymphs and muses, and an imitation sea battle between France and Portugal were among its attractions. Michael Wintroub emphasizes another interesting aspect of this pageant, namely the transition between the Old World and the New, symbolized by a Brazilian village that was erected in a small provincial town nearby. A Rouen merchant imported 50 'savages' into France for the occasion. The rest were disguised Norman sailors who were evidently indistinguishable from 'real savages'. A group of Tobajara assembled round their leader, after which they attacked another group, the Tupinambás, and a vicious struggle ensued. The Tupinambá Indians retaliated ferociously and burned down the entire Tobajara settlement. The Tupinambás were associated with the French, the Tobajaras with the Portuguese.

The royal entry is seen by Wintroub as "an allegorical voyage capable of establishing a reconciliation between two opposed conceptions of the nobility in the sixteenth century—the one, feudal, of the nobility of the sword, and the other of the new urban nobility, the nobility of the robe".[42] The nobility of the robe owed their titles to political or financial services to the crown, and not, like the nobility of the sword, to military power and more important, bloodlines. It seems that Henri's entry was accompanied by a cultural offensive, for it is Orpheus who opens up the town for Henri II. On leaving behind the 'Brazilian village' and preparing to enter Rouen, the King first had to cross the old bridge over the Seine. In the rock, apparently blocking his way, we see the cave of Orpheus, the son of the god Apollo (Oiagros is usually named as the father) and Calliope, the goddess of epic poetry. Orpheus is able not only to tame wild beasts with his harp, but also to transform the 'savage' into a cultivated person.

The engraving of Henri's entry shows us the sea battle and the allegorical ships on the Seine. Once again, water plays a key role. And just as in the *Hypnerotomachia Poliphili*, there is an earthly paradise, such as will recur in the later Circe ballet. In the final pageant Henri II discovers a magnificent garden full of rare trees, plants, and fruits. In the center of this earthly paradise is Henri's father, François I, flanked by a representation of the *Bonne Mémoire*, the benevolent memory. In his hands he holds the symbol of his patronage of knowledge, a book written in Latin, Hebrew, and Greek. Exotic gardens, water, and fountains are the ingredients that appear regularly. According to Wintroub, the entire course of the entry can be understood as a cultural transition from a condition of savagery to the earthly paradise of the exotic garden. He does, however, warn against reading the logic of the event as a simple linear schema from barbarism to civilization. The reverse is also possible, with the savages representing a critique of the new *noblesse de robe* (nobility of the robe).

A similar water motif occurs in the festivals of Fontainebleau in 1564 when Sirens sailed around in the canal and Neptune's chariot was drawn by sea horses.[43] Why use water as a stage? Rousset is clear about it: water is the element of mobility, instability, and metamorphosis par excellence. The theme of water bears the same connotations as the theme of 'woman', as we will see.[44] Let us return, then, to our ballet scenes and Henri III's role in them.

Beaujoyeaulx's Circe ballet was performed in a rectangular room in the Louvre, the Grande Salle de Bourbon, on the night of 15 October 1581.[45] Here everything had its symbolic place. The short sides of the salon had a special significance: King Henri III sat in the center of one, and on the other a sort of stage had been constructed. Some spectators sat on the long sides and others behind the King. Under the galleries, approximately in the middle and within the King's line of sight, a Hain de Pan (Grove of Pan) had been constructed, and opposite it a place for musicians and singers, camouflaged by clouds. Although there was no water present, and it is not mentioned in the manuscript, the symbolism is clear; the entire central space was meant to suggest a stretch of water. Circe's castle is on an island, as are Pan's woods and grotto. In the course of the ballet this would become clear as sea horses pulled the carriages and the naiad nymphs sported fish tails. The entire space was, in fact, a vast illusory sea. That it was also possible to walk and dance on it presented no real disruption of the island theme for the spectators. The whole was lit so cleverly using oil lamps, torches, and fires that it manifested a likeness to a summer's day. A hundred torches illuminated the castle of Circe alone, and, as Beaujoyeulx remarks, the innumerable series of torches in the hall produced "*le plus beau et serein jour de l'année*" (the most beautiful and serene day of the year).[46]

The staging made evident two poles—two antagonistic directions are to be seen in the proceedings. The whole must be seen from this perspective and assessed in terms of the spectators and their positions. In fact, the whole stage was erected from the point of view of the monarch.[47] Seated on his throne, he was "probably the only spectator/player who could view the designs correctly", as McGowan notes.[48] Upon entering the hall, each carriage made its way along its periphery through the crowd of spectators, coming to a halt before the King. Each actor made a point of acknowledging the King directly with his praises, his complaints, his songs, and so on. The spectator felt him or herself to be behind the King and identified, or conflated, the monarch with the scenes enacted before him. The spectators were selected by the guards at the entrances; only people of '*marque et cogneuses*' (of distinction and note) were let through, so that this crowd itself became a conspicuous object. Beside the King sat the Queen Mother, Catherine de Medici, who with her special influence over the King confirmed a charged relationship with him. On the little stage opposite the King, the entire wealth of sensory perception was present. This is a typical

Renaissance motif, a true '*cabinet de curiosités*' (cabinet of curiosities) in which all the treasures of this world were displayed to the King. The King's gaze was an act of appropriation, a prerogative here meant primarily for him. The garden in front of the imitation castle united everything: rare plants (with medicinal effects), fruit, flowers, strawberries, melons, lemon trees, everything that nature has to offer, including sparkling jewels and exotic animals. Here dwells the goddess Circe—"who changes [men's] bodies into monstrous form"; her name is Nature.[49] As daughter of the sun god Helios and of Perseis, goddess of the sea, she represents the mingling of the elements of fire and water, through which all things are formed. She is both *causa formalis* (the formal cause) and *causa materialis* (material cause).

> Circe—signifying mixture—
> Is daughter of the Sun
> Which is warmth,
> And daughter of the sea, which is moisture:
> Because all things are created of warmth and moisture,
>
> Thus Circe is the mixture of the elements,
> Achieved only through the movement of the Sun,
> Who is father & form,
> And Perseis being mother and matter.[50]

The performance served two ends: to discipline those groups who attempted to resist the modern, centralist power, and to portray the King as liberator and conqueror. Circe represents human nature, inclined to everything evil. Ulysses, known to the Greeks as Odysseus, is her heroic foe and stands for that part of humanity which implies reason. To break the power of Circe a whole collection of counter-forces is required: "To combat the power of Circe, one needed not only the virtues and the eloquence of Mercury but also the intellect of Minerva and the power of Jupiter and the King."[51]

Music announced the beginning of the ballet and linked the dance to the poetry according to the principles of the Académie de Poésie et de Musique founded by Jean-Antoine de Baïf at the King's instigation in 1570. Ulysses, the narrator, played by the queen's servant Le Sieur de la Roche, rushes on from behind the castle. He is looking in different directions, to see whether Circe has followed him. In his hand is a handkerchief embroidered with gold—*un mouchoir ouvré d'or*—to wipe his face. He proceeds to the King. Out of breath, he stands before the King who is sitting in the center of the hall. He describes how Circe changed him and his companions into wild animals, but ultimately returned him to his original form.

> And I saw my limbs changed into the body of a Lion,
> And I was captive in a garden amid her flock:
> But by some circumstance the witch was appeased,
> And I found myself returned to my original state.[52]

Ulysses throws himself at the feet of the King and begs him for help. This chamberlain of the queen mother acts as a knight who has fled from the garden of Circe. The meaning is clear: Henri III is the central actor, the only human figure who can take the place of Ulysses. Only the sovereign is immune to the magic power of Circe. For Circe is the chaotic natural state of the world, back into which man threatens to subside if he heeds his own nature. Poliphilo repeatedly sighs in the *Hypnerotomachia Poliphili*:

> Why ever did desire and lust cohabit there with wisdom, power and will? By Jupiter, it was so pleasurable to my amorous eyes that I desired nothing else than to be able to gaze perpetually at these splendid nymphs—so beautiful, so shapely and so delightful with their lively glances, decked out so sumptuously and lasciviously, with their snow-white garments radiantly shining. With such enticement, a man could give himself up willingly to cruel death.

The captured animals/men are "prisoners of the palace of Circe who demonstrate the wretched servitude of those led by the brutal desire of sensual delight".[53] When Ulysses has told his story, Circe appears for the first time, looking for her subject who, indeed, has fled. She is furious and resolves to act much more cruelly and uncompromisingly in the future. After her appearance she withdraws into her castle.

The power of the King is represented by sea gods and monsters. In a dialogue with the musicians, Sirens sing of his power. During their procession they pass the naiads, played by the queen, bride, and ladies-in-waiting. Together with eight Tritons they form the train of the sea deities Glaucus and Thetys. Glaucus complains of being under the spell of Circe and asks in duet with his wife for help. Thetys is powerless because she has transferred her powers to the earthly goddess, the French queen Louise.

Then an ornate fountain—a most elaborate prop—is brought in, drawn by sea horses, and on it are seated 12 naiads, all members of the royal household and court. The whole scene is a model of a garden, symbol of the flowering kingdom of the Great King. The monarch's wife, Louise, does not sit next to him, but is one of the leading actresses. In the dance that now follows, the 12 naiads dance 12 different geometric schemes. At the end everyone takes the same position again as in the beginning, two triangles with the queen at their apex, pointing at the King.

> In the first entering passage there were six abreast,
> Forming a line across the room,

And three in front, in a very large triangle:
With the queen at their head,
And likewise there were three in back.[54]

The naiads stand for the powers that are represented by the garden and the spring. Their social function underlines that they are on the King's side.

In France lives only one King,
Henry, great King of the French,
In subjects, in justice, and in laws
Leaves nothing to the other Gods.[55]

It is significant that the French duchesses and the Queen herself perform a dance for the King as white-clad naiads. This is the overt staging of the subjugation of female productive power as the court sees it, not as previously thought:

> The new construction of the bourgeois absolutist state concentrates on the principle of a new formation of the sexuality of the 'lofty woman', which will stand as model for all the others. The flow of the streams is imprisoned in a fountain which for the benefit of pleasure in the garden of the man spouts de-sensualized 'white' water, good for the irrigation of the new organizing state.[56]

Nature is there to be exploited, what is implied by sensual pleasure is combated, and at the same time the sensual woman is controlled. Seldom is the consolidation of power in the patriarchy represented in as tangible a way as here.

Circe waits until the naiads have abandoned their geometric formations, in order, together with the musicians, to become frozen in unmoving figures. Now Mercury, Jupiter's messenger, makes his appearance, bringing the antidote, the mixture of herbs or 'moly', which Ulysses needs as a defense against the magical powers. Mercury himself announces in his opening song which historical forces he personifies:

I have taught people to obey the law,
The sciences, the arts and also the cities belong to me,
And with the treasures I bestow the art of speaking:
In order to heal the disarmed spirit of reason which,
Abandoned by virtue, has been seduced by pleasures,
I bring 'moly', that excellent root.[57]

Mercury's remedy awakes the naiads once more to well-organized movement. The geometric ballet and music revive. But Mercury is nevertheless no match for the magic powers of Circe, and she brings everything to a standstill again:

I am the only cause for all this change
Proceeding step by step, from moment to moment:
My father, restless he tosses and he turns,
Announcing the end of a season and the birth of a new century,
The sun alone can change the ages
Thus through destiny all things shall be linked.[58]

In a long song she paints the natural state of affairs that prevailed in paradise. Her second appearance ends in a victory over Mercury, whom she takes by the hand and brings into her garden. Her animals come and take him into their midst. These animals are the men whom Circe has transformed.

I will detain this frivolous Mercury,
Who, presumptuous of skills and courage
Intends to liberate these nymphs
Expecting to have power against my golden rod,
And to disrupt my plans with a root
that served Ulysses once as remedy
Against my poisons.[59]

The fear of man in the face of sensual woman is also symbolized here. The woman as *instrumentum diaboli* (instrument of the devil) can also be the woman as *courtisane*, as *femme fatale*. Only now is it really clear how great her power is. Until now the greatest part of her world was hidden by a curtain, but at the moment it falls, the beauty of her garden is revealed. Eight satyrs then enter, led by the Sieur de Saint Laurent. He expresses an emotion which is general in the hall when he sings the praises of Jupiter and the French King, both famous for their power and virtue. While the satyrs move through the hall, they pass the woods of Pan, which are also inhabited by four dryads. Pan's help must be enlisted to defeat Circe. He is very suitable for this because he too is able to change everything. The alliance into which he enters with Minerva joins his microcosm to Minerva's macrocosm, one of the important themes of Neoplatonic thought from that period.[60] While the forest god promises to come and help, the four Virtues enter the scene. The god Pan, whose nature is the opposite of Circe's, and the four (royal) virtues of *Prudence*, *Tempérance modérée*, *Fortitude*, and *Justice* reinforce the battle forces against Circe.

Gods of whom we are daughters,
Oh Gods, protectors of mankind,
From the skies with us descend;
And for the benefit of France
Powerful Gods do follow closely these Virtues,
Who are your kin,[61]

With every entry a greeting is given to the King. Finally, Minerva, played by Mlle de Chaumont, enters in a war chariot. Her words to the King and to Pan, and her appeal to Jupiter the god of thunder, occupy much space. As McGowan remarks,

> Hope and fear lie at the heart of human weakness, and such fallible states can be counteracted not by the mere eloquence of Mercury, but by reason itself. The glorious deeds of the king have freed France from most trials, and Minerva proposes to liberate the country from its last source of strife—Circe.[62]

When the chariot has come to rest before the King, Minerva stands up and tells him why she is a key figure in the struggle against Circe. She is not born of woman, not from a body, but came forth from the head of Jupiter. In this manner she symbolizes the theoretical intelligence of man. History, reason, and the principle of achievement flow together into one. She turns to the King to say she has come to help defeat Circe.

> I received very rare gifts from his hands,
> Reason, which rules the mild and human spirit,
> He gave me the reins of the vistas of thought,
> With which I can control human understanding.[63]

When Jupiter enters, a new music sounds, which contains more voices and instruments than before. In his address to Pallas (Minerva), Jupiter refers to Henri III as his son:

> Dear Pallas, daughter, look at me;
> Remain here, as you are sister of this King,
> This King, my son the pride of French authority:
> May the gaze of Medusa transform
> His enemies and order his people
> Under his righteous law, humble and obedient.[64]

With this mention of the *moderator mundi* (king of the heavens), the ballet's reference to politics is made concrete. In the sovereignty of Jupiter, that of the crown is doubled, not reflected. Divine gifts are bestowed on the King; his person represents a universal order.[65]

The campaign against Circe begins. An imposing machinery is set in motion. The marvels of technology serve the royal ballet and, also mythologically, the royal state. Circe's castle is stormed. Circe's army of transformed men throw themselves furiously at the attackers. She herself calmly waits. In fact she fears only one opponent, the King of France.

> I shall resist you. Even if destiny
> Has drained my golden rod of power
> do not believe this in your favor, Jupiter.
> If anyone must soon triumph over me
> It will be the King of France.
> And, like myself, you must surrender to him
> The skies that you possess.[66]

Jupiter throws his lightning. Minerva reaches the vestibule of the castle. Then, Jupiter offers to extend mercy to Circe. She refuses, and her fortress is destroyed. Fire breaks out. Circe is taken prisoner and dragged through the hall in triumph to be handed over by Pallas as a gift, ultimately, for the King. The battle against chaos is almost over. Minerva and Mercury throw themselves at the King's feet, and Circe is defeated. *Le Roi* (the King) and *la Géometrie* (geometry) are identical. At the end of each scene, the naiads, with Queen Louise in their midst, turn their gaze on the King. They dance geometric figures, such as squares, circles, and triangles: Archimedes could not have defined the proportions better. The Queen then hands the King a gold medallion bearing the image of a dolphin, Dauphin, an heir to the French Crown. All other women follow her example with other images. Finally, the performance goes into the 'Grand ballet', "a geometrical one, whose figures formed and un-formed themselves, symbolizing the eternity of matter and the soul, the transmutation of the elements".[67] The court danced in the entire space, including the stage. The ballet lasted from ten in the evening to half past three in the morning: by the end, "the power game... has been resolved predictably in favor of the monarch."[68]

GEOMETRIES AND MEANING

Giving a geometric character to the body, as Beaujoyeulx intended with his ballet, also characterizes the models of planned absolutist cities. Hence the geometric town planning

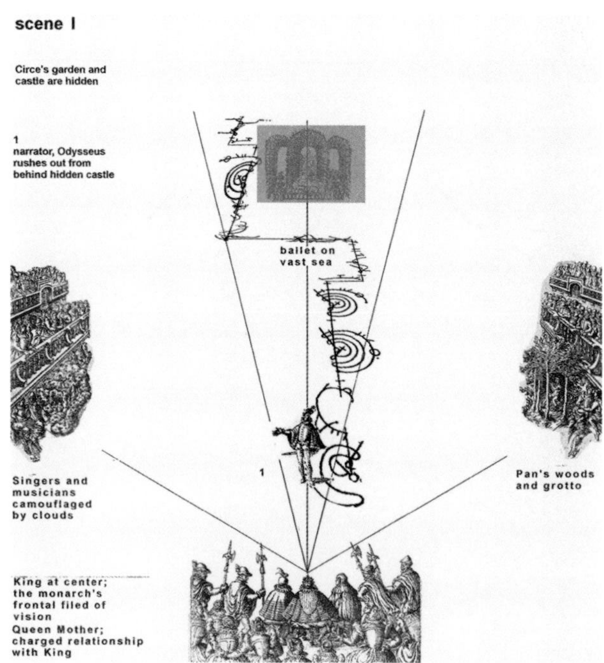

of the France of Louis XIV. The *'rond point'* (round point, 'circular area whence paths or avenues radiate') structure was used for the first time for a city plan in Versailles and possibly taken later to Italy by Bernini when he returned from France.

Space, as in the seventeenth century theater, is completely dominated and understood from a static standpoint at which all perceptions melt into a single perfect illusion. This is the position found in front of the mirrors in the Grand Salon at Versailles. From that place the King could not only look through infinite space but also keep it under control. The entire construction is that of a telescope trained on the landscape, bringing infinite space within reach of the eye. Joseph Rykwert mentions that the notion of the garden as a framed picture is implicit here, being reflected in that vast mirror wall, the greatest expanse of mirror in the world at the time and a triumph of French technology.[69]

As revealed in the Circe ballet, the hidden meaning of Versailles, its pageants, and its gardens can only be discovered from the standpoint of the monarch: "This gaze is a pure gaze, doubtless attentive, but lacking affect; unemotional, theoretical, ultimately empty, with no expression other than the spectacle that it creates."[70] For whatever holds true for Vaux, holds equally true for Versailles; "the politics of the eye was now established, and its setting was Versailles".[71] There the illusion of perfect order reveals itself. In its turn, this confirms the monarch in his position as the mediator of God's plan, by definition 'ideal', in human society.

THE CIRCE BALLET IN SEVEN DRAWINGS; THE WAY TO PRESENT THE GARDENS OF VERSAILLES *LE BALET COMIQUE; MANIÈRE DE MONTRER LES JARDINS DE VERSAILLES*

The Way to Present the Gardens of Versailles exists in six versions, all written by Louis XIV between 1689 and 1705 to explain the beauty of his gardens and fountains, which as we know now, were only supposed to function when the King and his guests were passing by. *The Way to Present* was written as a kind of treatise to be referenced when the King was absent from court and unable to show guests around. These seven drawings, however, offer a different perspective on the presentation of the gardens by overlaying the gardens of Versailles with the geometries of the Circe ballet.[72] The layout of Versailles is now provided with an interpretative structure by way of Beaujoyeulx's *Balet Comique.*

scene II

1
King is represented by sea gods and monsters

2
Sirens sing of King's power

3
8 tritons appear

4
All form the train of Thetis and Glaucus

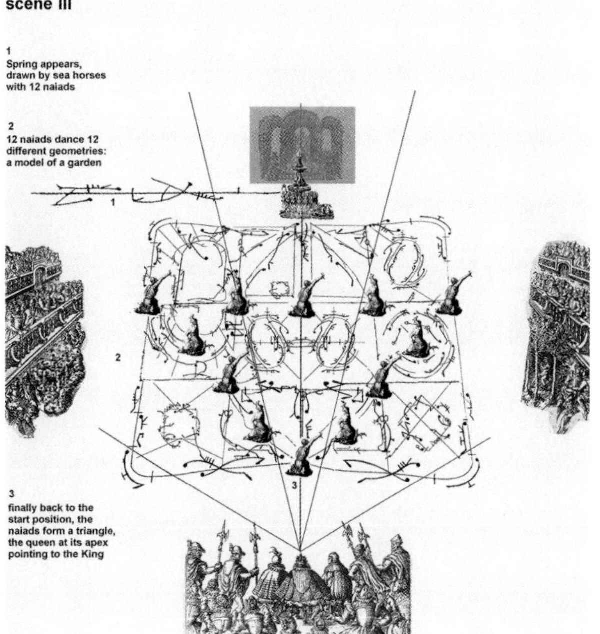

While Beaujoyeulx's manuscript gives us little in the way of real information on the dance and the setting, what we do know has been used in this reconstruction. The dance steps, the different scenes (which are difficult enough to distinguish as it is), the exact actions—these are the ingredients of an enterprise as uncertain as it is intriguing. This certainly holds true for the system of notation used for the dance. It remains a formidable task to this day to determine precisely how the different steps and figures are to be executed. This problem is little different, essentially, from that of an architectural notation, even though the latter is static and the former dynamic. Dance notations are much like tracks made in newly fallen snow; they exist only momentarily in their brief life, and the attendant movement of the body is even more difficult to capture in a static image. In spite of these challenges, the essay closes with seven drawings that give a picture of how we ourselves can regard the bosquets of Versailles, though unquestionably in a perspective other than that of the King. Even so, it would come as no surprise were he to be enthusiastic about these imagined dance-filled gardens of his beloved Versailles.

Notes

1. Orsenna, Érik, *André Le Nôtre: Gardener to the Sun King*, Moishe Black trans., New York: George Braziller, 2001, p. 55.
2. de Beaujoyeulx, Balthazar, *Le Balet Comique*, 1581, Margaret M. McGowan intro. and ed., Binghamton, New York: State University of New York, Binghamton, 1982, p. 74.
3. See Annette L. Giesecke, *The Epic City: Urbanism, Utopia, and the Garden,* Cambridge, MA.: Harvard University Press, 2007, pp. 21–24.
4. Colonna, Francesco, *Hypnerotomachia Poliphili: The Strife of Love in a Dream,* Joscelyn Godwin trans., London: Thames and Hudson, 1999. The work was originally published in Venice in 1499. In 1546 the *Hypnerotomachia* was translated into French by Jean Martin, as *Discours sur le Songe de Poliphile.*
5. Colonna, *Hypnerotomachia Poliphili*, p. 292.
6. Colonna, *Hypnerotomachia Poliphili*, p. 313.
7. Colonna, *Hypnerotomachia Poliphili*, p. 362.
8. Blunt, Anthony, "The *Hypnerotomachia Poliphili* in 17th century France", *Journal of the Warburg and Courtauld Institute*, vol. 1, no. 2, 1937, pp. 117–137.
9. Summerson, John, "Antitheses of the Quattrocento", *Heavenly Mansions and Other Essays on Architecture,* Kent Bloomer ed., New York: W. W. Norton, p. 46.
10. Adams, William Howard, *The French Garden, 1500–1800*, New York: Braziller, 1979, p. 15.
11. Steenbergen, Clemens Maria, *De stap over de horizon: Een ontleding van het formele ontwerp in de landschapsarchitectuur,* Dissertation, Delft: Technical University, Delft, 1990, p. 80.
12. Shepherd, John Chiene, and Geoffrey Jellicoe, *Italian Gardens of the Renaissance*, London: Alec Tiranti, 1966, p. 73.
13. Battisti, Eugenio, "Natura Artificiosa to Natura Artificialis", *The Italian Garden*, David R. Coffin ed., Washington D.C.: Dumbarton Oaks, 1972, p. 31.
14. MacDougall, Elizabeth, "*Ars hortulorum*: sixteenth century garden iconography and literary theory in Italy", *The Italian Garden*, David R. Coffin ed., Washington D.C.: Dumbarton Oaks, 1972, p. 43.
15. MacDougall, "*Ars hortulorum*", p. 46.
16. Weber, Gerold, *Brunnen und Wasserkunste in Frankreich im Zeitalter von Louis XIV*, Worms, Germany: Werner'sche Verlagsgesellschaft, 1985, p. 123.

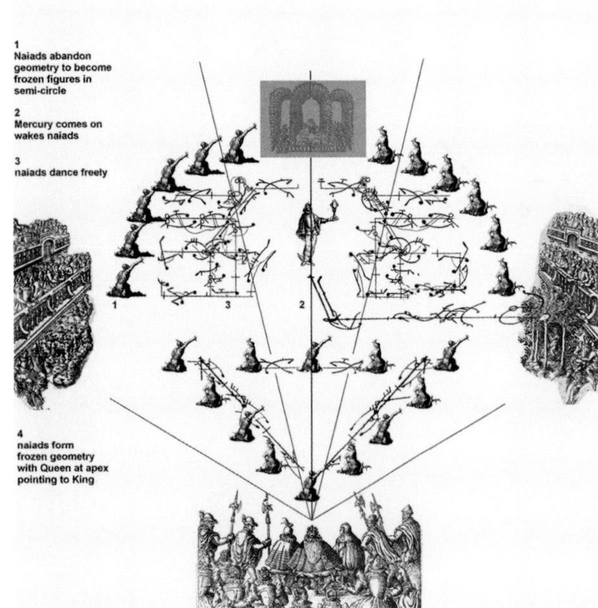

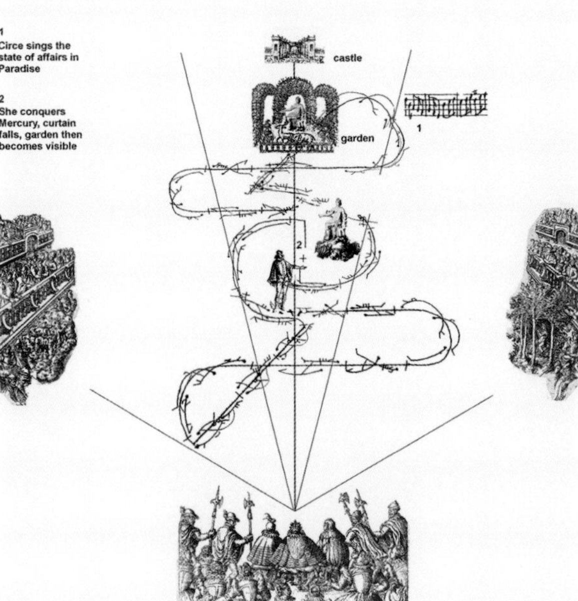

17. Junecke, Hans, *Montmorency: Der Landsitz Charles le Brun's*, Berlin: B. Hessling, 1960, pp. 73–110. See also Frances A. Yates, *The Valois Tapestries*, London: Warburg Institute, 1959.
18. These details are recounted in André Chastel, *The Palace of Apolidon*, Oxford: Clarendon Press, 1986, p. 12, as well as in David Thomson, *Renaissance Architecture: Critics, Patrons, Luxury*, Manchester: Manchester University Press, 1993, p. 85.
19. The island in question is the so-called Isle of Demons near Labrador. This is where Sieur de Roberval, who had been commissioned by Francis I to found the first colony in New France, marooned his niece Marguerite as punishment for a shipboard affair. Her lover jumped overboard to be with her but did not live long enough to witness the birth of his child.
20. Hazlehurst, F. Hamilton, *Gardens of Illusion*, Nashville, Tennessee: Vanderbilt University Press, 1980, p. 90.
21. Garrigues, Dominique, *Jardins et Jardiniers de Versailles au Grand Siècle*, Seyssel, France: Champ Vallon, 2001, p. 170.
22. According to Jean Rousset, *La littérature de l'âge baroque en France: Circé et le paon*, Paris: J. Corti, 1963, p. 16, Circe, Calypso, Alcina, and Armida were represented as "*demiurges capricieuses d'une creation instable qu'ils transforment à leur guise*".
23. de Benserade, Isaac, *Mascarade en forme de balet, Dansé par le Roy au Palais Cardinal, le 26em Fevrier 1651*, Paris: Bibliothèque Nationale.
24. "*On ne se permet pas d'être la risée de la cour quand on est le roi.*" Beaussant, Philippe, *Le Roi-Soleil se lève aussi*, Paris: Gallimard, 2000, p. 155.
25. "*est né de la musique*". Beaussant, Philippe, and Patricia Bouchenot-Déchin, *Les Plaisirs de Versailles: Théâtre et musique*, Paris: Fayard, 1996, p. 24.
26. Treasure, Geoffrey, *Louis XIV*, New York: Longman, 2001, p. 185.
27. "*L. m'est de plus en plus chère; elle est jeune, pure, sincère, dépourvue de toute ambition.*" Bluche, Francois, *Le Journal secret de Louis XIV*, Monaco: Editions de Rocher, 1998, p. 26.
28. "*A Fontainebleau, il y a trop de monde et la place manque. J'eus besoin d'un appartement secret; Dieu merci, Saint-Aignan me prêta sa chambre pour une heure ou deux.*" Bluche, *Le Journal secret*, p. 22.
29. "*Je vins à Versailles avec la Cour; il y aura, pour cette fête des Plaisirs de l'île enchantée, quelque 600 personnes à nourrir (non à loger, Dieu merci).*" Bluche, *Le Journal secret*, p. 38.
30. "*cuirasse de lames d'argent richement brodée et casque orné de plumes couleur feu*". For the quote see Patricia Bouchenot-Déchin, *Henry Dupuis, Jardinier de Louis XIV: Les métiers de Versailles*, Paris: Perrin, 2001, p. 36.
31. *Ce fut le jour d'Alcine, soeur de la fée Morgane, et ici Molière voulut flatter son roi: / Disons qu'au plus haut point de l'absolu pouvoir / Sans faste et sans orgueil, sa grandeur s'est fait voir... / Vantons les longs travaux, vantons les justes lois / De ce fils reconnu pour le plus grand des rois. / Le soir, un merveilleux feu d'artifice acheva les divertissements.* Bluche, *Le Journal secret*, p. 39.
32. Adams, *The French Garden*, pp. 67–69.
33. Dietrich, Margret, "Der Mensch und der szenische Raum", *Maske und Kothurn: Vierteljahrsschrift für Theaterwissenschaft*, no. 3, 1965, pp. 193–196.
34. Beaussant and Bouchenot-Déchin, *Les Plaisirs de Versailles*, p. 51.
35. "*les effets de croyance provoqués dans l'imagination de ceux qui ont vu, en cette nuit du 31 août au 1 er septembre 1674, le roi de France sur le Grand Canal, dans son parc de son château de Versailles*". Marin, Louis, *Le Portrait du Roi: Le sens commun*, Paris: Les Editions de Minuit 1981, p. 250.
36. McGowan, Margaret M., *L'art du Ballet de Cour en France, 1581–1643*, Paris: Editions du Centre National de la Recherche Scientifique,

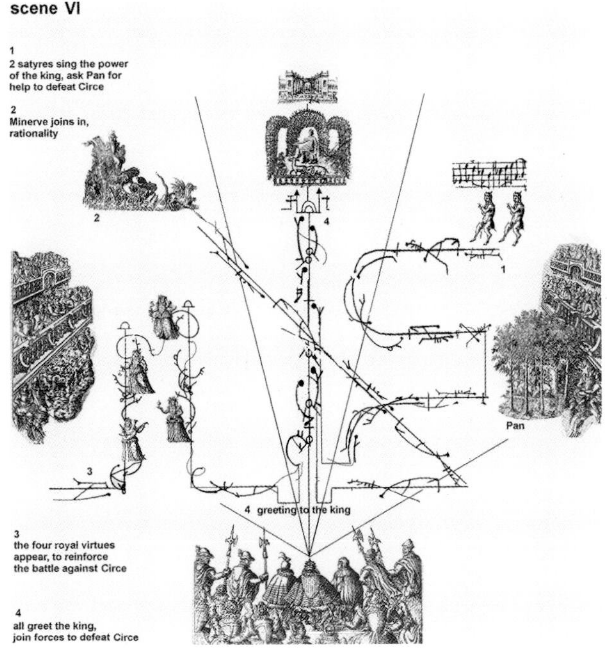

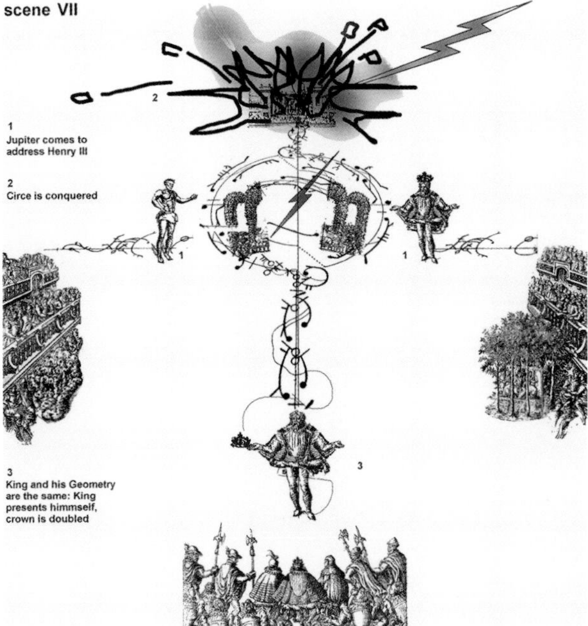

1978. McGowan gives a number of other sources, to be found in Mss. fr. 24352 to 24356, Ms. 15057. She also mentions a list prepared by Beauchamps: *Recherches sur les théâtres*, Paris 1735; Paul Lacroix, *Ballets et Mascarades*, Paris, 1868; Bibliothèque de Soleinne, Paris 1843; Bibliothèque de Pont de Vesle, Paris 1847; and M. de La Vallière, *Ballets, opéras et autres ouvrages lyriques*, Paris 1860. Her book *L'art du ballet de cour en France 1581–1643* gives in the appendix all the sources of the ballets in that period. See also Rudolf zur Lippe, *Naturbeherrschung am Menschen I und II: Geometrisierung des Menschen und Repräsentation des Privaten im französischen Absolutismus*, Frankfurt am Main: Suhrkamp, 1974.

37. Four years after the *Balet Comique* was written, a number of Catholic members of the aristocracy joined forces against the extravagances of Henri III. Their aim was to get the Duc de Guise on the French throne. After the murder of Henri III in 1588 a civil war broke out between the Catholic league under the leadership of the Duc de Mayenne and Henri de Navarre, the legitimate successor to the throne. The bloody religious and political battles lasted five years. Even after the succession of Henri IV, there was continued religious and political instability in France. This social political situation corresponds to the ballet. The scenes span the moral world of man. "In such a universe of mirrors and reflections any single element can be expanded to express the whole. Circe gives us a sense of a power able to disrupt an harmoniously organized world, a power whose magical effects are almost as great as the force of good originally responsible for the happy working of harmony. The disturbing power of magic and evil is not unique to the *Balet Comique*", writes McGowan in her "Introduction to de Beaujoyeulx", *Le Balet Comique*, p. 34. However, "the artistic ambitions behind the *Balet Comique* appear realized, though the political pretensions remain unfulfilled", she concludes, p. 42.

38. Benjamin, Walter, *The Origin of German Tragic Drama*, John Osborne trans., London: NLB, 1977, p. 65.

39. Rousset, Jean, "L'eau et les tritons dans les fêtes et ballets de cour", *Les Fêtes de la Renaissance: Études réunies et presentées par Jean Jacquot*, Paris: Editions du Centre National de la Recherche Scientifique, 1955, pp. 8, 181 and 182.

40. Benjamin, *The Origin of German Tragic Drama*, p. 66.

41. See for England, Clifford Geertz, *Local Knowledge*, New York: Basis Books, 1983, esp. chapter 6, "Centers, Kings, and Charisma: Reflections on the Symbolics of Power", pp. 121–129.

42. *"un voyage allégorique susceptible d'établir un rapprochement entre deux conceptions opposées de la noblesse au XVI e siècle—celle, féodale, de la noblesse d'epée et celle de la nouvelle noblesse urbaine de robe"*. Wintroub, Michael, "L'Ordre du Rituel et L'Ordre des Choses: l'entrée royale d'Henri II à Rouen", 1550, *Annales, Histoire, Sciences Sociales: La royauté française, Mises en scène du discours politique*, March–April 2001, p. 485. See also Lawrence Bryant, *The King and the City in the Parisian Royal Entry Ceremony: Politics, Ritual, and Art in the Renaissance*, Geneva: Librairie Droz, 1986, and Roy Strong, *Art and Power: Renaissance Festivals, 1450–1650*, Woodbridge, Suffolk: Boydell Press, 1984.

43. Rousset, "L'eau et les tritons", p. 236.

44. *"L'eau est par excellence l'élement de la mobilité, de l'instabilité, de la métamorphose."* Rousset, "L'eau et les tritons", p. 242.

45. Leclerc, Hélène, "Paper Seven: Circé ou Le Balet Comique de la Royne, 1581, Metáphysique du son et de la lumière", *Theatre Research, Recherches Théâtrales*, International Federation for Theatre Research, vol. III, no. II, 1961, pp. 101–120.

46. de Beaujoyeulx, *Le Balet Comique*, p. 7

47. Schöne, G., "Die Entwicklung der Perspektivbühne von Serlio bis Galli-Bibiena", *Theatergeschichtliche Forschungen* no. 43, Nendeln/Liechtenstein, 1977, p. 13.

48. The quote is from Margaret McGowan's "Introduction" (p. 30) to de Beaujoyeulx, *Le Balet Comique*.

49. *"qui changez de leurs corps en forme monstreuse."* de Beaujoyeulx, *Le Balet Comique*, p. 9. For the ballet's full manuscript, see also *Ballets et Mascarades de Cour, de Henri III à Louis XIV 1581–1652, recueillis et publiés, d'après les éditions originales*, I, Paul Lacroix ed., Geneva: J. Gay & fils, 1868–1870. Reprinted by Slatkine, Geneva 1968, pp. 1–87.

50. *Circé qui signifie mistion, est fille du Soleil, qui est la chaleur, & de la fille de la mer qui est l'humidité: pource que toutes choses sont creées de chaleur & d'humidité. Circé donc est la mistion des elemens, qui ne se peut faire que par le mouvement du Soleil qui est le pere & la forme, et Perseis la mere & la matiere.* From *"Allegorie de la Circé, que natalis comes a retire des commentaires des poetes Grecs"*, de Beaujoyeulx, *Le Balet Comique*, p. 74.

51. *"Pour combattre le pouvoir de Circe il fallait non seulement les Vertus, l'éloquence de Mercure, mais la raison de Minerve et la puissance de Jupiter et du roi"*. McGowan, *L'art du ballet de cour en France*, p. 47. See also Henry Prunières, *Ballet de Cour en France avant Lully et Benserade*, Paris 1914.

52. *Et en corps de Lyon mes membres transforma, / Et entre ses troupeaux dans un parc m'enferma: / Mais quelque occasion adoucit la sorciere / Qui m'a faict retourner en ma forme premiere.* de Beaujoyeulx, *Le Balet Comique*, p. 9.

53. *"prisonniers au palace de Circe (qui) montrent la servitude misérable de ceux menés du désir brutal de la volupté"*. Leclerc, "Paper Seven", p. 119.

54. *Au premier passage de l'entree estoyent six de front, toutes en un rang du travers de la salle, & trois devant en un triangle bien large: duquel la Royne marquoit la premiere pointe, & trois derriere de mesme.* de Beaujoyeulx, *Le Balet Comique*, p. 23.

55. *Un Roy seul en France habite, / Henry, grand Roy des François, / En peuple, en iustice, en loix / Rien aux autres Dieux ne quitte.* de Beaujoyeulx, *Le Balet Comique*, p. 14.

56. Theweleit, K., *Männerphantasien*, vol. I: *Frauen, Fluten, Körper, Geschichte*, Frankfurt am Main: Verlag Roter Stern, 1977, p. 401.

57. *J'ay aux hommes appris d'obeir à la loy, / Les sciences, les arts, les villes sont à moy, / Et avec les thresors ie donne l'eloquence: / Et pour guarir l'esprit de raison desarmé, / Que, laissé de vertu, les plaisirs ont charmé, / Je porte le Moly racine d'excellence.* de Beaujoyeulx, *Le Balet Comique*, p. 24.

58. *Seule cause ie suis de tout ce changement / Qui suit de rang en rang, de moment en moment: / Mon pere, sans repos qui se meut & se tourne, / La fin d'une saison d'un nouveau siècle bourne, / Le Soleil fait tout seul ces âges varier. / Ainsi veut le Destin toutes choses lier.* de Beaujoyeulx, *Le Balet Comique*, p. 26.

59. *Je vais emprisonner ce Mercure volage, / Qui vient, presomptueux, & d'art et de courage / Ces nymphes secourir, et se promet encor / D'avoir quelque pouvoir contre ma verge d'or, / Et rompre mes desseins avec une racine / Qui servit à Ulysse un iour de medecine / Encontre mes poisons...* de Beaujoyeulx, *Le Balet Comique*, p. 26.
60. Delmas, E., "Le Ballet Comique de la Reine, Structure et signification", *Revue d'Histoire du Théâtre* 2, 1970, p. 151. See also Indra Kagis McEwen, *Socrates' Ancestor: An Essay on Architectural Beginnings*, Cambridge, MA: MIT Press, 1993.
61. *Dieux, de qui les filles nous sommes, O dieux, les protecteurs des hommes, Du ciel avec nous descendez; Dieux puissans, suivez à la trace Les Vertus, qui sont vostre race, En la France que vous gardez.* de Beaujoyeulx, *Le Balet Comique*, lyric from the *Chant des quatre vertus*, p. 42.
62. McGowan, Margaret M., "Introduction" (p. 21) to de Beaujoyeulx, *Le Balet Comique.*
63. *De sort rares presens ie receuz de sa main, / La raison, qui regit l'esprit doux et humain, / Et des vistes pensers il me donna la bride, / Dont sur l'entendement des hommes ie preside.* de Beaujoyeulx, *Le Balet Comique*, p. 48.
64. *Chere Pallas, fille, regarde moy, / Demeure icy, tu es soeur de ce Roy, / Ce Roy mon fils, fleur du sceptre de France: / Fay des regards de Meduse changer / Ses ennemis, & son peuple ranger / Sous sa loy juste, humble d'obeissance.* de Beaujoyeulx, *Le Balet Comique*, p. 52.
65. According to Delmas, p. 153, the king appears as "*un personnage quasi-divin hors de l'humanité commune: aussi bien son éloge est-il chanté constamment par des divinités, et par les intermèdes qui sont étroitement associés au thème de l'âge d'or. Incarnation nationale de l'ordre universel comme ses prédécesseurs, c'est autour de lui que doit s'opérer la réconciliation générale à laquelle travaillait déjà l'Académie de Baïf.*" See also Frances A. Yates, "Charles-Quint et l'idée d'Empire", *Les fêtes de la Renaissance II*, Paris: Centre national de la recherche scientifique, 1960, pp. 92–97.
66. *Je vous resisteray; que si la destinee / A de ma verge d'or la force terminee, / Ce n'est en ta faveur, Jupiter, ne le croy: / Et si quelqu'un bientot doit triompher de moy, / C'est ce Roy des François & faut que tu luy cedes, / Ainsi que ie luy fais, le ciel que tu possedes.* de Beaujoyeulx, *Le Balet Comique*, pp. 54–55.
67. "*géometrique, dont les figures se formant et se défaisant, symbolisent l'éternité de la matière et de l'esprit, la transmutation des éléments*". Leclerc, "Paper Seven", p. 117.
68. McGowan, "Introduction" (p. 22) to de Beaujoyeulx, *Le Balet Comique.*
69. Rykwert, Joseph, *The First Moderns: The Architects of the Eighteenth Century*, Cambridge, MA: MIT Press, 1980, p. 54.
70. "*ce regard est un pur regard, attentif sans doute mais dépourvu de tout affect: regard apathique, regard théorique, en fin de compte vide, sans autre expression que le spectacle qu'il amène à apparaître.*" Marin, *Le Portrait du Roi*, p. 246.
71. Orsenna, *Le Nôtre*, p. 58.
72. Erwin Panofsky presented a more or less comparable method in his analysis of the Gothic. While I do not follow this approach, I have found Panofsky's book inspiring: Erwin Panofsky, *Gothic Architecture and Scholasticism. An inquiry into the analogy of the arts, philosophy, and religion in the Middle Ages*, New York: Meridian, 1951.

PLANTING MY CABBAGES

/STEVEN BROWN

When it comes to seeking perfection, Western culture is horticulturally obsessed, especially as it dreams of *the* Garden, capital G.[1] Our pastoral ideal goes something like this: once upon a time, our animal needs were met in abundance by the Earth, without struggle, without pain, without sorrow. Of course, in literature, to find utopia among the bud and bloom of one's garden is nothing unusual. The sixteenth century essayist, Michel de Montaigne, expressed this sentiment famously in his essay, "That to Philosophize Is to Learn to Die", when he said, "I want death to find me planting my cabbages", as if death were nothing more than a visitor to the agrarian paradise of Montaigne's own cultivation.[2] Montaigne's utopian impulse, however, differs slightly from the familiar Garden pastoral; for him, the Garden exists in the here-and-now, between the body's necessities and the buried seed—an intentional space near the dirt, captured by the eye, gripped by the hand. There's something almost child-like to this image of a man tending his cabbages in the face of death, something playfully detached from the commercial aura of those garden images we find on TV, in magazines, even on the walls of museums.

Montaigne's statement anticipates a shift in today's aesthetic approach to, and social criticism of, utopian representation. Part of this shift is grounded in a reaction against modern labor: the difficulty of finding work with meaning and, subsequently, work's lack of meaningful compensation. To make up for this loss, our gardens often provide a haven from the stress and unease of our daily professions. Growing a few cabbages in a furrow of my own might boost my sense of independence from an economy that does what it can to ensure long-term dependency on subpar wages, inflated health care costs, and nonrenewable energy.

More importantly, many people find something authentic in their relationships to their gardens. As a synonym for 'the good', authenticity suggests all sorts of upbeat virtues: validation, truth, wholeness, intimacy, and so on. But to the extent that our vision of the garden becomes more and more compositional or planned according to the forms of our ideals, we might pull from this poetry of authenticity certain images regarding our own place and purpose in life. I might feel, in other words, that this row of purple cabbages is where I belong, not because it feeds me or maintains my health, but because I imagine it as representing the source of my authentic experience in a world which capitalizes on inauthenticity. As a consequence, I may attribute to the garden a sense of perfection attainable by no other means than a pair of leather gloves, a trowel, and a tilled corner of the yard.

For this essay, I want to focus on the garden's visual image: how we read the garden through media like the photograph and how those readings often perpetuate a particular social consciousness ironically opposed to an authentic relationship to the garden. For the purpose of addressing utopianism and its ancient relationship to the garden, photography might seem an odd choice. It is, after all, a relatively young art form, having made its debut as a patented scientific and artistic tool in the hands of the French inventor, Louis-Jacques-Mandé Daguerre, less than 200 years ago. But it is, I think, precisely its youth that matters most. Unlike many other traditional arts (painting, sculpting, composing) in which the formal elements have been defined and refined over hundreds, if not thousands, of years, photography is free in its formal and technical naivety to idealize its surroundings with the reckless momentum of its youth. It has this characteristic of spontaneity and child-like indeterminacy in common with the image of the Garden. Does photography capture an instance of reality? Can it tell the truth? What if we tamper with the scene—paint it, retouch it, crop it, revise it by excising this or that object? Do we have an ethical responsibility to the camera? Does the camera have a responsibility to us? All of these questions and more persist as hot topics among critics of photography, and nothing, thankfully, seems to have been settled thus far.[3]

In photography, the utopian vision of the garden is often defined by what is absent from the image rather than what is present. And what is often most conspicuously absent from the garden photograph is not only the refuse gardens produce—the weeds, the excess rot, the dug-up stones—but precisely that which makes a garden a garden and not just a wilderness or field: us, people, human presence.

Whether it is a photo of the gardens at Versailles or a digital snapshot of one's own cabbages, nothing looks less threatening than a picture of a garden without people. Such erasures of human presence suggest a vacancy for the viewer's own ambitions, like an unbuilt parcel of land. But at a more subversive level, the image of the depopulated garden perpetuates the myth of our exile from a better world, rather than supporting our ambition for one. Laughably averse to its own ideal, it presents a record of our own extinction.

To be fair, what many of us value about photography is its capability to capture a moment and preserve it from time's ongoing amnesia. So whenever a garden, perfectly pruned and weeded, presents itself to the viewer photographically, we read in it our hopes for the future, as if it were a capsule sent back in time. But this capsule brings sad news: said future does not include us.

TRANSITORY GARDENS

Such a reading of the human absence from garden photographs may seem extravagant. For one thing, personal gardens outside the realm of folklore and fairytale bear very little, if any, quantifiable influence on historical social progress as such. Furthermore, the absence of people in any given image of a garden may reflect only an instance of inoccupancy, not a permanent vacancy. Every photograph evokes a connection to people, for the camera itself requires our influence in some capacity. But it is exactly that which we cannot imagine concerning our absence from this image that allows us to remain comfortably in the realm of ideology.

Using ideology in Marx's classic sense as a kind of 'opium of the masses', the social theorist Slavoj Žižek reads the rhetoric of ecology as the opium of the twenty-first century. In Astra Taylor's documentary, *Examined Life*, 2010, Žižek explains his position on ecology while walking and talking in the middle of a dumpsite. The setting of his interview is crucial to the argument he makes. For the believing eye's benefit, the scene is cinematically furnished with all the atrophied decor one would expect at a dumpsite. Horizons of rubbage, pits of tires, and scraping bulldozers assault our field of vision. Yet Žižek insists that such a place is exactly where we should find ourselves at home: visually, intellectually, even religiously. "What we expect from religion", Žižek tells us, "is a kind of unquestioned highest authority. It's God's work. So it is. You don't debate it."[4] Ecological ideology, he argues, dethrones that unquestionable authority and replaces it with Nature. "Don't mess with DNA, don't mess with Nature", ecology says, positing its own conservative "mistrust of change".

Part of Žižek's critique of ecological ideology stems from the way we think about waste, or better yet, the way we don't think about it. We know that the life nature provides is put at risk by our contributions to global warming and the like. Even so, Žižek says, we hide behind the psychological veil of disavowal, which is to say, "I know very well, but." We know very well that our industrial means of advancing civilization make the environment uninhabitable, but in our daily occupations and preoccupations, we don't believe that even something so devastating as an oil spill viewable from space (like the BP spill) can threaten civilization as we know it.[5]

Žižek's classic example is the magic toilet. Rationally, we know our feces go somewhere, that they collect and stagnate, but we normalize this everyday function and act as if flushing erases the waste we produce. In the immediate interplay between our minds and the world, we practice a holistic ecology, the logic of which says, *All is nature, all is connected.* As a result, we easily convince ourselves that our excrement, like an earthworm's expulsions, will take care of itself precisely because it is the byproduct of our own cyclical participation in nature. This totalizing view, according to Žižek, makes us unable to imagine catastrophes such as the one at Chernobyl, much as we cannot imagine our permanent exile from the Garden. Such events intrude upon our convictions regarding ecological unity; they disturb our vision of an impenetrable nature.

Rousing society from this ideological torpor is no easy task. Žižek's solution is to cut ourselves off from nature even more: "We need more alienation from our lifeworld. We need to be more artificial." If we see ourselves as a cyclical part of the garden, then we're like those romantic poets who attach themselves so emotionally to their subject matter (daffodils and roaming clouds) that they become blind to the sentimentality that kills their art. To be more artificial is to see both the daffodil and the trash heap in which it grows. Only from the terrible heights of the garbagetops do we find that our feces have not been 'flushed away', and have certainly not gone 'back to nature', wherever that may be. Only when faced with the immediate, material reminder of the dumpsite—the smell of fetid refrigerators and the noise of compactors—can we imagine a useful relationship to the Earth.

However, to live as complete aliens as Žižek advises would conflict with our attempts to create poetry in this world, and require us to adopt an aesthetic sensibility completely foreign to the Garden of our historical and ecological imagination. Again, it seems unimaginable that we could find beauty in that which we throw away, that which we clearly do not value, much less idealize. In his poem, "The Man on the Dump", Wallace Stevens raises a similar concern: even if the dumpsite reminds us of a truer, more immediate reality than the one we envision, how are we to survive without those great aesthetic tropes of the utopian spirit (hope, health, community)? "Is it peace, / Is it a philosopher's honeymoon, one finds / On the dump? Is it to sit among mattresses of the dead, / Bottles, pots, shoes and grass and murmur *aptest eve*?"[6]

Few would say that trash itself (the Styrofoam and baby diapers, the corroding landslide of batteries) is actually beautiful. However, we might find the conception and form of a particular work beautiful, as in photographer Edward Burtynsky's landscapes of tires [Figure 1]. Burtynsky's photograph creates formal tension between organization and chaos. Symmetrical piles of rubber emphasize a neatly cleared avenue of earth, a path through the waste, a visual escape from civilization's traffic and fast distractions toward quiet, open skies beyond. The black ash hue of the tires contrasts with the mineral dirt. The image shifts from dust to hints of green on the horizon. That ever so slight evocation of grass attracts the eye so intensely that the image urges us beyond the tires with tremendous

Figure 1/ *Oxford Tire Pile #8.*
Photograph © Edward Burtynsky, courtesy of Flowers, London & Nicholas Metivier, Toronto.

force—suggesting that all the industrial mobility in the world (embodied by the tires) cannot match the power of the persistent growth of a little spring sod. Burtynsky's dumpsite opens up like the Biblical parting of the Red Sea. This creates another level of formal tension, between the miraculous and the ordinary. But once again, it is the form rather than the trash itself that creates poetry in Burtynsky's tirescapes.

Just as Žižek's presence in the dumpsite helps us to visualize his ecological concern, the photograph-as-evidence can make concrete the ecological rhetoric of totality that Žižek says most of us cannot think beyond. Consider, for example, the classic gardens photographed by Eugène Atget. In Atget's Saint-Cloud series, a suggestion of utopian antiquity prevails, interrupted only here and there by hints of human agency: a bike leaning against a concrete vase (*Saint-Cloud, mars 1926, 9 h. matin*) or the conical topiaries of evergreens (*Saint-Cloud. 1921–22*).[7] Or consider the results of a simple internet search for garden images. When the occasional human cameo does appear, it is usually by way of synecdoche, as with Atget's bicycle. A sunhat shades a pair of pruning shears to let us know some man or woman attends the garden regularly, or an empty chair hints at a break between weedings. At times, to offer a sense of drama, a hand reaches into the frame to pluck a weed, à la Michelangelo's *Creation of Adam*. Such photographs need not depict any one person to account for the obvious human interventions they portray.

But the garden, as we know, requires more than weekend dilly-dally in the backyard. It is the product of utopian effort; it gives shape to those aspects of responsible ecology we borrow from various social ideals: law (order), education (life sciences, geography, history), economy (conservation, trade), and so forth. This is why historical gardens were once sites of academic study and spiritual pilgrimage.[8] The garden is the most basic of the images by which we establish a panorama of our own authenticity in the world. If we are not pictured, the hands and minds behind the social construct dissolve into the totality of ecology, no longer necessary or even relevant.

In his claim that the dumpsite is the garden for us, Žižek is only partly right—*partly* right because his argument depends upon the cyclical framework of ecology itself. After all, we can't neglect the fact that waste *is* the byproduct of an organic cycle, and humans *are* a part of that cycle. We are too dependent on the soil to ever become fully alien. Žižek participates, perhaps unwittingly, in an aesthetic push to reduce the dumpsite by way of critiquing the ideology that produces it. As Ernst Bloch, the renowned German thinker of art's relationship to utopia, once commented, "In every age two threads intertwine: first, 'the cultural heritage', that is, religion, art, and philosophy; and second, ideology."[9] So, too, culture and ideology are intertwined in Žižek's assertions.

Our cultural heritage contains the potential for dissent from ideology in the use value it ascribes to its arts, especially to images, which allow us to *see* the unfamiliar in the familiar. In the absence of aesthetic intervention, to alienate ourselves from the notion of totality just to see, objectively, where we stand would only increase that totality by driving it back further into the totalizing horizon. If we could de-ecologize ourselves, as Žižek advises, we'd be left paralyzed and static, like a statue without aesthetic purpose, a parody of human presence.

Margaret Morton and Diana Balmori's collaborative book, *Transitory Gardens, Uprooted Lives*, 1993, offers a visual criticism of the depopulated garden that anticipates Žižek's. For this book, Morton photographed the gardens of New York City's homeless. The streets, of course, are not what we typically associate with the garden image, for the very simple reason that the streets lack the verdure of that original depiction of *the* Garden. We like, after all, to keep our ideals pure. A transitory garden, however, may contain nothing organic whatsoever:

> Living plants are not the main feature of homeless gardens, primarily because of the scarcity of water and the difficulty in obtaining it; but also plant growth takes time, an element these planters, who may not stay on one lot long enough to see such growth, do not have. It is, in fact, surprising that under these extreme conditions any of the gardens have living plants at all.[10]

Figure 2/ *Guineo's Garden.*
Photograph courtesy of Margaret Morton.

Instead of plants, one might find stuffed animals and brick cairns. At the apex of Morton's photograph, *Guineo's Garden*, a plastic tree gives shade to the gardener's possessions. Its dominance in the frame represents a kind of power one might attribute to the fruit tree of the original Garden; but its artificial quality, its removal from the fertility it represents, suggests more emphatically our expulsion from paradise. The statue beneath it contributes to that sense of loss [Figure 2].

However, there is an important way in which Morton's transitory gardens defy the Garden exile. The typical image of the backyard flower bed implies a certain level of domestic security. After all, in the industrial world, money and leisure are the prerequisites for tilling up the lawn. Ironically, for many middle class people, the home and the garden sanctuaries that surround it exist independent of one another. For the suburbanite, the garden is merely an image of paradise seen through the frame of the window. By contrast, "[homeless] gardens are not a part of the historical tradition in which the vestiges of paradise are embedded"—nor are they part of the contemporary tradition of *self*-perpetuated exile, where a pane of glass keeps us safely distanced from the garden's reality.[11] The transient lives in the garden, not behind the glass. Morton's homeless do not simply come to visit or tend their gardens from afar; rather, they sustain themselves at the intersection of ecological ideology and ecological reality. Most walk back and forth to a fire hydrant for the water needed to sustain both themselves and their plants. The same is true for food and shelter. Materials used to roof a makeshift home may need daily reconstruction. Here there is no illusion of stability. Everything is transitory with an aim toward mediating the garden and its waste with a utopian aesthetic. But there's a catch: although everything is transitory in the homeless garden, the condition of homelessness is not. Like our images of Eden, these gardens evoke both domicile and exile.

Though Morton's photographs take us closer to an ecologically-oriented aesthetic where people matter, the realities of homelessness mean that Morton's subjects are pushed out of their gardens on a daily basis. Unlike Žižek's dumpsite, which is a form of self-exile, this is forced exile, transitory agency without the possibility of change, which is to say, without the possibility of changing the garden one tends into something sustainable.

The dumpsite is only useful as a viewing point if it becomes more than a site for minor social touch-ups; it must become a site for the manifestation of the impossible. Using the example of oil and the millions of years of biological deterioration required to make it, Žižek argues that the actual manifold catastrophes occurring in nature exceed the short temporal reach of our imaginations. But I think the opposite is true. Great catastrophe is the easiest evocation of the human mind. The image of the garden without people is haunted by the persistence of incalculable disaster. Anywhere rich, fertile, open land appears in photographs of the garden, the commercial surveyor licks his lips and posts his 'Coming Soon' signs. The garden then becomes the site of forced clearing and exclusion, like the transitory gardens in Morton's photographs.

Catastrophe is evoked by both the nostalgic utopianism of the depopulated garden and the productive utopianism of an image troubled by human presence and its consequences. But room remains between the two for an aesthetic mediation that we might call the seraphic mediation. The angel, after all, is a key image in the history of the Garden, gardens, dumpsites, and their human transients. We cannot speak of the garden without its fallen counterpart.

ECOLOGY OF ANGELS

"His eyes are staring, his mouth is open, his wings are spread": this is the visage of Paul Klee's famous watercolor, *Angelus Novus* [Figure 3], as described by Walter Benjamin in his short collection, "Theses on the Philosophy of History", 1940.[12] Shocked, indeed paralyzed by the storm of Western progress, the angel is driven backward, unable to turn away from the wasteland of a war-torn Europe. But Benjamin's reading emphasizes the angel's continued engagement with social catastrophe rather than a distanced engagement with the past alone. The angel represents the out-of-body experience of the body politic. We misunderstand the angel if we think of it as a living entity who gazes of its own volition. In fact, we may be mistaken if we believe the angel to be gazing at anything. Benjamin's description of fixed eyes, mouth ajar, and splayed wings resembles the description of a victim at a crime scene, already dead.

> This is how one pictures the angel of history. His face is turned toward the past. Where we perceive a chain of events, he sees one single catastrophe which keeps piling wreckage upon wreckage.... The angel would like to stay, awaken the dead, and make whole what has been smashed. But a storm is blowing from Paradise; it has got caught in his wings with such violence that the angel can no longer close them. This storm irresistibly propels him into the future to which his back is turned, while the pile of debris before him grows skyward. This storm is what we call progress.[13]

We know that Benjamin's aesthetic reading stems from his immediate social concerns. He looks at the damaged social body and finds in Klee's painting an image to reflect it. My approach reverses Benjamin's. I start from Klee's image and see the possibility of a new social body. This is not to negate the social implications of the image itself. Both approaches are grounded in the act of looking.

The first thing to point out here is that Benjamin stresses the difference between what the angel sees and what is possible for us to see. In Benjamin, *we* cannot rightly be understood as *we-the-individual-readers* who see themselves safely detached from catastrophe (via the suburban window) and in no particular need of rescue. This positioning, for Benjamin, would have been unthinkable. *We* is the assumed future inextricably linked to Benjamin's own theory of the historical body—that is, both his own endangered body and the equally endangered multitude represented by his body as a kind of *Everyman*, continuously in need of its guardian angel, its own history.

Paradoxically, "the angel would like to stay, awaken the dead, and make whole what has been smashed".[14] This need to "make whole" is only another death, another historicism where marginalized moments in history disappear into the linear historical narratives of the powerful. How then can the dead reform the dead? Or more to the point, how can the dead ever re-inhabit the garden? Benjamin claims, "We have been endowed with a weak Messianic power" to intervene in historical events: the ability to regenerate, revise, revive, resurrect ourselves out of our catastrophes—the catastrophes not only of progress but of progressive ideology taught by our institutions of power.[15] Saving ourselves from further wreckage requires a sacrifice on our part, as with certain messianic traditions where redemptive potential is unlocked through death.[16] The death of the angel, of historicism, of ideology, is necessary for our own self-resurrection.

In the essay, "A Native Hill", writer and social critic Wendell Berry critiques the linear model of history by contrasting the meandering paths of Native American communities with the linearity of our modern roadways. "A path is little more than a habit that comes with knowledge of a place", he says. "It is a sort of ritual of familiarity.... [The path] obeys the natural contours; such obstacles as it meets it goes around. A road, on the other hand,... embodies a resistance against the [land]. Its reason is not simply the necessity for movement, but haste."[17] By "haste", Berry

Figure 3/ Paul Klee, *Angelus Novus*, 1920.
Photograph © The Israel Museum, Jerusalem; photo by David Harris.

> In every era the attempt must be made anew to wrest tradition away from a conformism that is about to overpower it. The Messiah comes not only as the redeemer, he comes as the subduer of Antichrist. Only that historian will have the gift of fanning the spark of hope in the past who is firmly convinced that *even the dead* will not be safe from the enemy if he wins. And this enemy has not ceased to be victorious.[18]

means the progression from point A to point B in as little time and with as little friction as possible. This requires a straight line and the obliteration of all obstructions. If one moves forward without regard to one's surroundings, then one has no conception of the waste left behind, which is to say, no awareness of the past, and as a result, one cannot begin to correct past mistakes.

Benjamin's angel embodies Berry's cautionary criticism. Though its eyes "stare" as if aware of the waste, its perception of the waste as continuous history impedes its ability to act, as well as its ability to see into the material moment. For all practical purposes, the angel is dead. Yet it progresses linearly in the wake of its obliterations, like a dead leaf blown down the street.

Žižek's critique of ecology applies equally to the wasteland of modernity; for decades now, the reigning themes in art and literature have been disconnection, disorientation, and disaster, so much so that along with our angel of history, we have blown away any notion of human reconciliation with the garden. But there are always those after the hurricane who grab a rake and start again.

Benjamin's major critique of the ideology of linear progress to which we, under the auspices of global capitalism, are so accustomed is precisely the inability of its apologists to recognize themselves as dead and in need of resurrection —not into some extraterrestrial space, but into the very terrestrial waste that linear models of normativity have gifted to the future.

Our weak messianic power is, of course, the power needed to "wrest tradition away from a conformism that is about to overpower it"—that is, to wrest the material moments of reality from ideology. But even the dead, as Benjamin rightly adds, "will not be safe from the enemy" if the catastrophes win, if linear progress *stays its course* and continues to drive our history away without our own ability to intervene.

To the extent that they represent nonlinear alternatives to normative linear thinking, Benjamin's theses resonate with Berry's path/road critique. The claim that the path is healthier than the road might seem like a utopian fantasy of a time when social interactions were healthier than they are now. Not at all. History denies us the luxury of any such assertion. That both the internal (social productivity) and external (social byproduct: waste, etc.) operations of the garden are never linear, or never perpetually linear, is simply a fact neglected in the humanless garden.

THE IMAGE OF EXPECTATION

Robert and Shana ParkeHarrison's book of photographs, *The Architect's Brother*, 2000, is about catastrophe, fallen angels, and the reciprocities of the garden. In every picture, one man, referred to in most criticism of the book as the 'Everyman' (recalling Benjamin's own function in his theses) inhabits a place not unlike Žižek's poetry-deficient dumpsite and the transitory gardens of Morton's photographs, but with an important twist. What trees we see, what domestic comfort exists, what increment of civilization survives, all stem from this Everyman's aesthetic engagement with the ash and litter of a garden otherwise devoid of nature. Because these are photographs, we cannot know the cause of the losses they depict. But we see clearly in most images that smokestacks cough up smog, and it is as both survivors and forerunners of whatever catastrophe left the Everyman alone that these smokestacks read like the synecdoches of Atget's gardens. The resources used to counteract the smog in *The Architect's Brother* come from the detritus of a civilization undeniably human as well. Plastic bags, iron nails, light bulbs, and wires punctuate our line of sight through the Everyman's litter-equipped inventions.

Figure 4/ *The Clearing.*

Photograph courtesy of Robert and Shana ParkeHarrison.

Their work has three important characteristics in common with Benjamin's explication of the *Angelus Novus*. First: the "one single catastrophe which keeps piling wreckage upon wreckage" serves as a driving motif in their photography.[19] In most ParkeHarrison images, scattered ruin surrounds the Everyman. In *The Clearing* [Figure 4], for instance, garbage heaps and leans right out of the frame, as if to suggest that we see only one side of a larger pile, like a close-up of Burtynsky's tires taken from the clearing between the piles. Second, their photographs share a story in the middle of catastrophic progress, but also suggest a future inhabitation of that progress and therefore a sense of possibility. In this way, like Benjamin, they attribute a messianic power to our relationship to history. Finally, Benjamin and the ParkeHarrisons share a critique of linear progress as the accumulation of motion's aftermath: used time, used space, used resources, and used energy. In fact, the photograph *Visitation* [Figure 5] shows the severed wings of what might have been the very same angel of Benjamin's ninth thesis.

In *Landscape and Images*, 2005, John Stilgoe takes this critique of linear progress a step further. By distinguishing between what is meant by the German word for landscape, *Landschaft*, and what Americans mean by landscape, Stilgoe finds an image of the garden from which community, the Everyman, cannot be extracted. "[*L*]*andschaft* connote[s] the inhabitants of a place and their obligations to one another and to their land", a "spatial expression of identity, order, and value, a kind of collective self-portrait of small-group life".[20] Landscape, on the other hand, is where the Garden meets reality. Landscaping—using the image of perfection without people as a blueprint for real world design—is a staple of American values. By contrast, the depiction of *Landschaft* in the ParkeHarrisons' work promotes self-place reciprocity through a kind of diligent *onwardness* (as opposed to the *forwardness* of linear progress). It is an effort to reflect, in the everyday activity of communal husbandry, on those circulations both within our own bodies (as biological repetitions) and without (as seasonal cycles). Many of the ParkeHarrisons' photographs incorporate this circle/circulation model, as in *Turning to Spring* [Figure 6] where a Father Time figure keeps the garden's gears and cogs in repair. In other images, circulation takes on a hematological meaning, as in the bloodwork of reciprocity between person and place.

Figure 6/ *Turning to Spring.*
Photograph courtesy of Robert and Shana ParkeHarrison

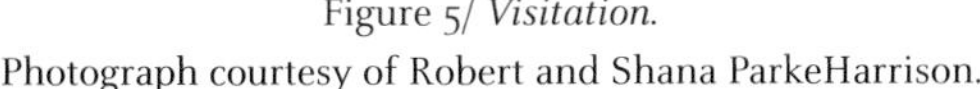

Figure 5/ *Visitation.*
Photograph courtesy of Robert and Shana ParkeHarrison.

Landscape indexes the tragedy of communal blood *loss*, especially in the face of global industrialization. Stilgoe pinpoints the problem: with the onslaught of road-networking, "[s]elf-sufficiency vanished.... Roads became ever more important to the places they linked, for along them flowed wealth and ideas greater than those of any one *Landschaft*"; consequently, "*Landschaft* surrendered its identity to the highway" and to the wasteland of linearity.[21]

In *Visitation*, we come to the place where the angel of history lies buried in the very same wasteland from which it was blown backward. Somewhere along the way, the disembodied experience of history re-embodied itself in the flesh and blood Everyman, standing with an air of devotion next to the wings. So what has happened? Exactly that which Benjamin knew could not be acknowledged by historicism: individual aesthetic intervention, or re-invention.

The photographic moment is something to which we can return again and again for perspective and for resistance against the linear passage of time. The ParkeHarrisons' representation of the angel embodies the idea of *return* in both craft and vision, while eschewing a purely nostalgic idea of a progression toward some sweet, green, and burdenless future.[22]

This messianic interaction between the Everyman and death has a much older visual antecedent than our literary Edens. We might think, for instance, of the Everyman painted on the caves at Lascaux, known better as The Shaft of the Dead Man [Figure 7], in which a human figure with the head of a bird lies next to a bison as if he has just been gored. Next to the birdman's body, we find a broken spear or totem topped with a bird as well. Again: an image of the Everyman's connection to history's seraphic failures. Lascaux counters the myth of the Golden Age with the image of tooth-and-claw catastrophes in the *original*, original Garden. That Garden was something to escape, which is why we found fire in it and dreamed of the wheel—which is why we painted on the walls against the ever-encroaching nothingness. Herein lies the significance of the communal nature of the Everyman as opposed to man or woman, singular. What it took to escape the Garden was communal effort, not competition; competition itself was the terror of the Garden.[23]

If death—be it death as biological terminus or death as any lived point of re-vision and resurrection—if death defines our meaningful encounters with who we really are, and if death (as *the* ultimate encounter with authenticity) alone defines our sense of purpose, then our standard for social progress remains fixed (like the angel's fixed gaze) in the inescapability, or historical continuity, of social conflict in the unholy Garden of Lascaux. What Benjamin tells us, and what the ParkeHarrisons show us, is that no amount of discourse, education, philosophy, or activism will save us from the effect of that social indoctrination which says we are born into a world dependent on violence. We must flee the Garden of historicism and move toward the garden where death is no longer the conclusion of progress—where, instead of us seeking death, death finds us, planting our cabbages.

The image of the depopulated garden asks this question: how do we *see* beyond lived experience as a series of catastrophes, necessary or otherwise? Žižek and others would say that such an understanding requires an aesthetic beyond our own limited critical powers and that we should embrace catastrophe as the reality of our artificial lives. The ParkeHarrisons' photographs show this view to be among our greatest delusions. Social conditioning cannot dictate the limits of vision. To say that it may be impossible to imagine a social system without some modicum of competition is, in some ways, to acknowledge the possibility of such a system. To photograph that impossibility, as the ParkeHarrisons do in *The Architect's Brother*, is to create the site of anomaly where such conduct thrives.

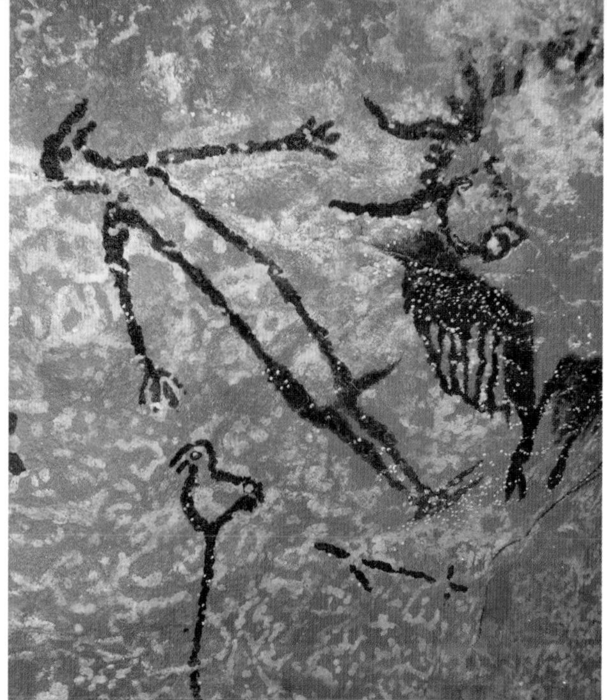

Figure 7/ The Shaft of the Dead Man.
Photograph © Christophe Brocas.

In this strange site, expectation makes us Argus-eyed, abolishing the blind spots that prevent us from seeing the communal Everyman at work in the garden. Both Bloch and Benjamin stress the importance of expectation to what we are capable of seeing. Bloch tells us, "truth is not the reflection of facts but of processes; it is ultimately the indication of the tendency or latency of that which has not yet become and needs its activator".[24] Where is the Everyman going in any of the ParkeHarrisons' images? Where is he walking, flying, floating? Bloch intuits that 'where?' is the wrong question, though it is the underlying question of the Western model of linear progress. To ask *where* is to look for the end and ignore the process. But only the process indicates what experiences the future will receive from us.

"This is the secret agreement between past generations and the present one", says Benjamin. "Our coming was *expected* on the earth" [emphasis added]—expected by those who employ their own messianic powers of aesthetic intervention, who carry with them the photographs of gardens with people in them.[25] The Everyman arrives at the site of anomaly as one who has journeyed toward death but without the expectation of death, only the expectation of ruin—the inevitable realization of the garden. Ruin in the garden is only the breaking down of form to be reused and recycled. This understanding brings us closer to the garden in which garden*ing* actually takes place—where Benjamin's messianic power is embodied in the act of seed-sowing and new growth.

The utopian element in *Visitation* is precisely its ecological situation. Past, present, and future merge into the form of a requiem on an ecological site of ruin. The Everyman (the resurrected body politic) offers flowers, renewal, ceremony: in short, creativity against vacuity, regeneration against the finality of death. And this, unlike the backward flight of the angel, can happen only on the ground.

THE NECESSARY FAILURE OF CABBAGES

The ParkeHarrisons' *Visitation* speaks to the necessity of a return to the garden of ruin where people matter, where death itself participates in ecological reciprocity with nature's manifold circulations. Here we revisit Montaigne's seminal statement: "I want death to find me planting my cabbages."

Let us imagine for a moment Montaigne's cabbages. No cabbage, to twist an old maxim, grows in a vacuum; therefore, our image needs place. It needs dirt, light, sky. It needs shape, not only its own but the measured borders, mounds, and rows which give it contour and emphasis. It needs the evidence of ecological manipulation—the kind of intentional sculpting found in any garden photograph. Indeed, the photograph itself is necessary, not only for its ability to rupture ideology, but because, as Montaigne tells us, death as an abstraction of the material Earth is not what we are looking for. Let abstraction find us! Montaigne concerns himself with snapshot and lens. "I want death to find *me*", which is to say, I want death to *picture* me as me: the blood and bone organism that is my thirsty, hungry, fallible, and finite body. And I want him to find me "planting my cabbages", absorbed in the sensual efforts of my body's intent. Without the intervention of *me*, we have only the catastrophe of abstraction.

If the gardener's localized interventions are erased from our images, the human role in the social garden becomes mysticized, ideologized, and in the truly social sense, globalized. Global capitalism idealizes the consumption, instead of the multiplication, of localized sites for productive communities and individuals everywhere. We think of it as a system detached from the guiding hand of any particular person, though the survival of capitalism depends on models of sustainability created by local hands.

Take the Green Movement, for instance, which has been an established political presence for the past three or four decades. Because capitalist enterprise depends on monitoring the trends of local consumption, corporate and government agencies are the first to appropriate and commodify alternatives to those trends when their trendiness is no longer profitable. And it is to the local community of dissent, the utopian or intentional community, that those powers must turn for fresh ideas.[26]

When Americans railed against hyper-inflated gas prices in 2008, we saw a 'Greenspeak' boom in the news, in the market, and in the political arena. The term "eco-friendly" tagged the product boxes of almost everything sellable, from the plastic handle of toothbrushes to the encasements of laptops. The branding of intentional living surfaced on the American billboard of consumer power like never before. The irony, however, is that many intentional communities have advocated careful ecology and self-sustainability for decades—for centuries in fact, if we think of groups like the Amish and Mennonites.[27] Recycling, alternative fuel and energy consumption, environmentally sound methods of production—these all have been standards of the cabbage culture whose historical footprint has coexisted with the dominant consumer culture since America's beginnings. When capitalism finally decides to appropriate the practices and values of the intentional community, it does so with its own values of sustainability in mind, the ethics of which revolve around a different kind of 'green'. By definition, capitalism cannot think outside its own safety deposit box.

In order to adapt to the needs of an ever-evolving public base, hegemonic powers need the intentional community. The local drives the global, and social power circulates in order to maintain the variations of interest within the much larger framework of something like a democracy. To preserve the overriding metaphor here, Death must copy Montaigne in order to perpetuate its own authority; it must return to the garden again and again to make its self-sustaining thefts.

The potential for revolution exists at any and every moment on the edges of linear progress where utopian experimentation survives, as at the edges of the garden, where mounds of expired vegetation and unused waste rot into next year's compost. These utopian moments at the edges, so rarely depicted in common images of the garden, are moments of compos[t]ing: a return, in the sense of both a turning under and a reversal, of the material social topsoil through localized, communal dissent, as well as of social composition: an aesthetic rewriting of the traditional power narrative through the arts, especially the image.[28]

In his essay, "Art, Fate, and the Disciplines", W. J. T. Mitchell speaks to the reversal that compos[t]ing aesthetics can employ:

> [T]he steady progress toward the empyrean of ideas is never that simple and is periodically interrupted by some form of dialectical reversal.... A consistent theme of modernist aesthetics is the notion, as

William Carlos Williams put it, that there are "no ideas but in things". And postmodern aesthetics has betrayed a stubborn refusal to give up on materiality, not in the name of modernist medium specificity, but in the formless scatter pieces, found objects, and detritus of 'trash art'.[29]

Mitchell's point is that art greatly influences dialectical progression. When the empyrean begins to move a little too far away, aesthetic representation regrounds itself in the dirt. The "trash art" to which Mitchell refers is not necessarily Žižek's dumpsite; it is, rather, the aesthetic site of compos[t]ing, where the *Angelus Novus* falls and is turned back under the earth for renewal by the Everyman in the ParkeHarrisons' photography. This is what Ruth Levitas has called "necessary failure" in her essay, "Looking for the Blue: The Necessity of Utopia".[30] The logic is as basic as compost itself: failure *necessarily* invites reconstructive dialogue, dialogue invites people, and people invite productive contributions to the social garden.

The ParkeHarrisons' photographs solicit no great lament. On the contrary, they are odes to reciprocity, re-imaging the human urge to productivity in opposition to Western history's failed doctrines of manifest destiny and industrial modes of rapid consumption. I read Benjamin's theses similarly as odes to reciprocity that incite us to moments of necessary failure, begging a return to the site of the angel's original departure—a return to the waste, but also a return to the waste's potential to become a productive garden. Here, the Everyman (Montaigne, *we*) mediates between the blue 'sight' and the green 'site'. In the garden, surrounded by catastrophe though it is, possibility survives the holocaust of impossibility and looks into itself for the future to see within itself new flight [Figure 8].

Notes

1. Throughout this essay, I differentiate between the real garden in the lowercase and the Garden of utopian myth in the uppercase.
2. de Montaigne, Michel, *The Complete Works*, Donald Murdoch Frame trans., New York: Knopf, 2003, p. 74.
3. For a particularly telling example of photography's naivety, one can refer to the SFMOMA conference entitled, "Is Photography Over?" (April 2010). Video of the event can be found here: http://www.sfmoma.org/pages/research_projects_photography_over.
4. Žižek quoted in Astra Taylor, *Examined Life*, New York: Zeitgeist Films, 2010.
5. For NASA images: http://www.nasa.gov/topics/earth/features/oilspill/index.html.
6. Stevens, Wallace, *The Collected Poems of Wallace Stevens*, New York: Knopf, 1989, lines 40–43.
7. See John Szarkowski's *Atget*, New York: MOMA, 2000.
8. See Robert Pogue Harrison's *Gardens: An Essay on the Human Condition*, Chicago: University of Chicago Press, 2008.
9. Bloch, Ernst, *The Utopian Function of Art and Literature: Selected Essays*, Jack Zipes and Frank Mecklenburg trans., Cambridge, MA: MIT Press, 1988, p. xii.
10. Balmori, Diana and Margaret Morton, *Transitory Gardens, Uprooted Lives*, New Haven: Yale University Press, 1993, p. 52.
11. Balmori and Morton, *Transitory Gardens*, p. 3.
12. Benjamin, Walter, "Theses on the Philosophy of History", *Illuminations*, Harry Zohn trans., Hannah Arendt ed., New York: Schocken Books, 2007, p. 257.
13. Benjamin, "Theses on the Philosophy of History", pp. 257–258.
14. Benjamin, "Theses on the Philosophy of History", p. 257.
15. Benjamin, "Theses on the Philosophy of History", p. 254.
16. For a salient example of Benjamin's theory in action, see Jennifer Roberts' *Mirror-Travels: Robert Smithson and History*, New Haven: Yale University Press, 2004.
17. Berry, Wendell, "A Native Hill", *Art of the Commonplace: The Agrarian Essays of Wendell Berry*, Norman Wirzba ed., Washington, D.C.: Counterpoint, 2002, p. 12.
18. Benjamin, "Theses on the Philosophy of History", p. 255.
19. Benjamin, "Theses on the Philosophy of History", p. 257.
20. Stilgoe, John R., *Landscape and Images*, Charlottesville: University of Virginia Press, 2005, pp. 30 and 35.
21. Stilgoe, *Landscape and Images*, p. 36.
22. See Lyle Rexer's *Photography's Antiquarian Avant-Garde: The New Wave in Old Processes*, New York: Abrams, 2002, in which he marks a contemporary trend in uses of old photographic methods.
23. See Martha C. Nussbaum's "Beyond the Social Contract: Capabilities and Global Justice", *Oxford Development Studies*, vol. 32, no. 1, March 2004, pp. 3–18.
24. Bloch, *The Utopian Function of Art and Literature*, p. xx.
25. Benjamin, "Theses on the Philosophy of History", p. 254.
26. For a parallel example, see Arjun Appadurai's introduction to *The Social Life of Things: Commodities in Cultural Perspective*, Cambridge: Cambridge UP, 1986, pp. 25–26, where he talks about "diversion" and "enclave" economies and the commodification of cultural exchange value.
27. See Ivonne Audirac's *Rural Sustainable Development in America*, New York: Wiley, 1997. See also Wendell Berry's *The Gift of Good Land: Further Essays Cultural and Agricultural*, Berkeley: Counterpoint, 2009. Berry has long advocated Amish agricultural methods in modern practices of sustainability.
28. In Paul S. Boyer's foreword to Donald Pitzer's *America's Communal Utopias*, Chapel Hill, University of North Carolina Press, 1997, Boyer emphasizes the historical view that nineteenth century utopianism had long-lasting effects on the future of American social reform. He quotes from Alice Felt Tyler's classic on antebellum utopias, *Freedom's Ferment: Phases of American Social History from the Colonial Period to the Outbreak of the Civil War*, Minneapolis: University of Minnesota Press, 1944: "while these communities failed, their ideals nevertheless entered 'the mainstream of American life... contributing their share to the democratic philosophy of the New World'" (Pitzer, pp. x–xi).
29. Mitchell, W. J. T., "Art, Fate, and the Disciplines: Some Indicators", *Critical Inquiry*, vol. 35, no. 4, 2009, p. 1025.
30. Levitas, Ruth. "Looking for the Blue: The Necessity of Utopia", *Journal of Political Ideologies*, vol. 12, no. 3, October 2007, p. 302.

Figure 8/ *Da Vinci's Wings.*
Photograph courtesy of Robert and Shana ParkeHarrison.

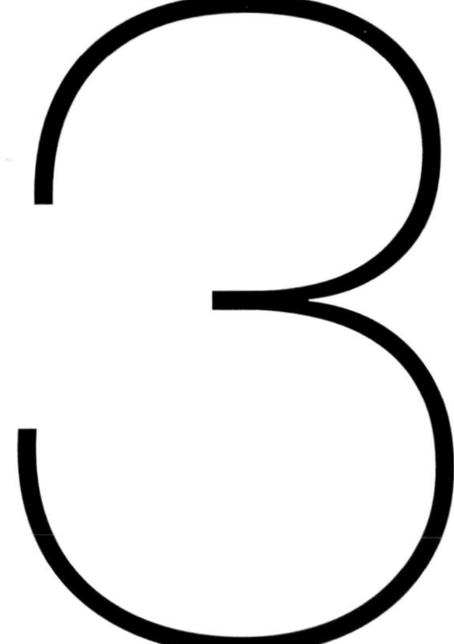

GREEN/ HOUSE

Figure 1/ Mount Vesuvius viewed from Pompeii's Forum. Photograph by Annette Giesecke, su concessione del Ministero per i Beni e le Attività Culturali—Soprintendenza Speciale per i Beni Archeologici di Napoli e Pompei.

OUTSIDE IN AND INSIDE OUT: PARADISE IN THE ANCIENT ROMAN HOUSE

/ANNETTE GIESECKE

It is 24 August, the very day on which Vesuvius buried Pompeii nearly 2,000 years ago. In spite of the sweltering heat intensified under a cloudless sky, the ancient city swarms with tourists; some wander alone, and others throng behind their intrepid leaders, hired guides identifiable by the brightly colored paddles that they hold aloft. Most will have commenced their experience by adhering closely to the itinerary recommended in the official archaeological guide: one is encouraged to enter the site via the Porta Marina, the city gate closest to the sea, progressing thence to the remains of the Temple of Venus, the Temple of Apollo, a capacious basilica, and the Forum, Pompeii's civic center. Walking to the north, with the verdant slopes of Vesuvius plainly in view [Figure 1], one comes to a bath complex, blocks of houses, an expansive extra-mural cemetery, and the Villa of the Mysteries, always a high point in any Pompeiian itinerary. Retracing one's steps and heading south, one winds one's way through seemingly endless blocks of housing to the theater district, and from there, one strolls—or rather jostles—eastward along the Via Dell'Abondanza, the main shopping avenue whose name, "Street of Abundance", promises a myriad of ancient marvels. Unless one is moving very quickly, by late afternoon this itinerary will lead one to Pompeii's amphitheater, gladiators' barracks, and exit, all of which lie at the city's eastern end. With the increasing onset of thirst and fatigue, it is easy to bypass the doorway to a most extraordinary house located just north of the gladiators' barracks: the so-called "Casa di D. Octavius Quartio" [Figure 2].[1]

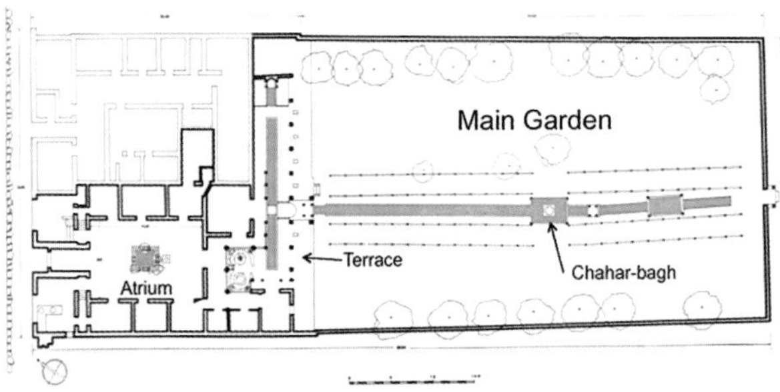

Figure 2/ Casa di D. Octavius Quartio, Pompeii. Plan of the house and gardens as remodeled after 62 CE. Plan and rendering by Annette Giesecke after an original drawing by Roberto Pane with students of the Facoltà di Architettura della R. Università di Napoli. From Amedo Maiuri and Roberto Pane, *I Monumenti Italiani Serie II Fasc. I: La Casa di Loreio Tiburtino e la Villa di Diomede in Pompei*, Roma: La Libreria dello Stato, 1947, Tav. I. Courtesy of L'Accademia Nazionale dei Lincei.

Figure 3/ Atrium garden of the Casa di D. Octavius Quartio, offering a glimpse of the truncated peristyle garden beyond. Photograph by Annette Giesecke, su concessione del Ministero per i Beni e le Attività Culturali—Soprintendenza Speciale per i Beni Archeologici di Napoli e Pompei.

The moment one steps over the threshold, heat, fatigue, and the din of voices from the road just outside are all forgotten, supplanted by an overwhelming sense of tranquility and an uncanny collapse of space and time as the house's succession of garden oases unfolds before one's eyes. Suddenly it is no stretch to imagine what it was like to enter and experience this house as a guest invited to dine on such a late-summer's eve. Here even the atrium, the house's formal entry, has been transformed into a garden: at its heart lies a catch basin for water, which is rimmed by a planter bursting with pink blossoms and equipped with a fountain [Figure 3]. At the atrium's far end, another garden beckons. As one draws near, this second garden, once populated by a group of Egyptian-themed statuettes, reveals itself to be a truncated peristyle garden, enclosed on three sides by a short colonnade [Figure 4].[2] Just beyond this, the visitor encounters a shaded terrace running the full length of the back of the house and overlooking park-like grounds that comprise roughly two thirds of the entire property. No ordinary terrace, it is fitted at its eastern end with an elaborate fountain flanked by masonry dining couches now lacking their comfortable, ornate cushions.

Figure 4/ Truncated peristyle garden and view of main garden beyond, Casa di D. Octavius Quartio. Reconstruction by Roberto Pane with students of the Facoltà di Architettura della R. Università di Napoli. From from Amedo Maiuri and Roberto Pane, *I Monumenti Italiani Serie II Fasc. I: La Casa di Loreio Tiburtino e la Villa di Diomede in Pompei*, Roma: La Libreria dello Stato, 1947, p. 5. Courtesy of L'Accademia Nazionale dei Lincei.

Cooled and soothed by the fountain's splashing waters, those reclining here to dine were surrounded by wall paintings drawn from the world of botanical myth [Figure 5]. On one side of the fountain sits Narcissus, so obsessed with his own reflection that he would waste away, transformed ultimately into the bloom that bears his name.[3] On the other side of the fountain appear Pyramus and Thisbe, two ill-starred young lovers from Babylon. As all contact between them had been forbidden by their parents, they agreed to meet clandestinely at nightfall. Thisbe arrived first but was frightened off by a lioness. The lioness, her jaws bloodied from a fresh kill, did not linger at this spot, staying just long enough to mouth the cloak that Thisbe had dropped in flight. But soon Pyramus arrived, and upon finding his beloved's bloodstained cloak, fell in grief upon his sword... just as Thisbe, in turn, would later do. In this cursed place stood a mulberry tree, its white fruit stained crimson by Pyramus' blood; and so it would remain, eternal testimony to a cruel fate.

Figure 5/ Botanical myths, frescoes from the terrace's alfresco dining area, Casa di D. Octavius Quartio. Narcissus (left). Pyramus and Thisbe (right). Photographs by Annette Giesecke, su concessione del Ministero per i Beni e le Attività Culturali—Soprintendenza Speciale per i Beni Archeologici di Napoli e Pompei.

At the opposite end of the terrace appears another myth that underscores the connectedness of humanity and nature. This is the tale of Diana and Actaeon, which is painted on the exterior walls of an entertainment room facing the dining couch.[4] While hunting in the forest with his dogs, Actaeon caught sight of Diana, goddess of the hunt, emerging naked from the bath. In punishment for his crime, Diana transformed Actaeon into a deer and sent a frenzy upon his dogs, who then mauled to death their master. The hunter, however unintended his infraction, thus became the hunted. Meanwhile, the walls running along the long northern side of the terrace bear other nature-related scenes now badly faded: Orpheus, who with his music charmed both animals and plants; the birth of Venus, her powers essential to the fertility of any garden; and a wild animal park, a *paradeisos*, such as those that belonged to the great kings of Persia.

This group of paintings, with their alluring blend of Greek and Near Eastern themes, is but one of the terrace garden's captivating decorative features. The terrace itself is shaded by a vine-clad pergola reminiscent of those in the sacred gardens depicted on the walls of Egyptian tombs.[5] Beneath this pergola once flowed a course of water, a miniature Nile, fed by the dining couch's fountain and lined by an array of statuettes no longer in situ: a lion and its prey, a greyhound attacking a hare, baby Hercules strangling the serpent sent to kill him, two busts of the god Dionysus, a satyr, a sphinx, and a reclining 'river god' usually identified as a personification of the Nile. Two of the Muses, patron goddesses of the arts, completed this sculptural tableau. The Muses did not, however, flank the terrace's watercourse but rather framed a small 'temple' deliberately built as a focal point for the house's grand interior dining room.

This temple, beyond which appears a lush landscape of trees, shrubs, and flowers, was enlivened by a semicircular fountain from which water, supplied by the terrace's watercourse, once cascaded down into a grotto. A sanctuary for the nymphs who populate wild places, the grotto, now largely bereft of its adornments, was itself a marvel. Its walls boasted paintings of a sacred landscape, of fish in a pool, and, once more, of Diana and Actaeon. Here too was the sculpted face of a river god, disgorging a stream of water onto steps upon which sat Cupid, a theater mask clenched in his chubby hands.

Perhaps most dramatic of all, a long, secondary water channel extends from the grotto nearly the entire length of this house's ample rear garden. Interrupting the linear flow of the channel's waters are three intriguing structures. The first is a rectangular pool, once filled with fish, at the center of which rises a stepped pyramidal fountain, like the pyramids of Egypt and the ziggurats of Mesopotamia, a divine mountain emerging from the Earth's primeval waters [Figure 6]. Enchantingly, the fountain's waters would have flowed in four cascading streams into the pool below, the whole a miniature *chahar-bagh*, the confluence of the four rivers of Creation. A feature of central importance to Islamic gardens, the *chahar-bagh* originated in ancient Persia, and, indeed, this house's water features resonate as much with Persian as with Egyptian influences.[6]

Figure 6/ Water features, rear garden, Casa di D. Octavius Quartio. Water channel, extending the length of the rear garden (left). Pyramidal fountain and fish pool (right). Photographs by Annette Giesecke, su concessione del Ministero per i Beni e le Attività Culturali—Soprinten denza Speciale per i Beni Archeologici di Napoli e Pompei.

The long channel's second structure is a baldachin bridge upon which a hermaphrodite once languorously reclined, and the third a plain rectangular pool, again likely having contained fish. This channel's various allurements, as well as the plethora of scents and sounds within this garden, could be enjoyed at close proximity by strolling around it along a lovely arbored path. One might also have lingered for a while, or for that matter hours, seated on benches or reclining under the vine-shaded dining couch that once stood near the pyramidal fountain.

The owner of this house must have been proud—justifiably so—of his horticultural achievement, for his gardens provided a veritable feast for all the senses. Not only this, but the dense assemblage of all its elements achieved a most astonishing synthesis of utopian attributes. His gardens blended the sacred and the profane. They provided a refuge, serving as a source of refreshment for body and soul. And though deeply rooted in the Romans' humble agricultural past, these gardens reached beyond Italian soil to the cultural splendors of Classical Greece as well as to the magnificent, lush gardens of Egyptian and Near Eastern kings that, growing as they did in desert soils, provided ample proof of their creators' divinity. Yet what, in the end, is most remarkable about this house's gardens is that while their particular combination of plantings, statuary, and paintings is unique, their multi-faceted paradisiacal resonances are, in fact, characteristic of Roman domestic gardens.

Figure 7/ View through the *fauces*, atrium, and *tablinum* to the garden beyond, Casa delle Nozze D'Argento (House of the Silver Wedding), Pompeii. Construction begun end of the second century BCE. Photograph by Annette Giesecke, su concessione del Ministero per i Beni e le Attività Culturali—Soprintendenza Speciale per i Beni Archeologici di Napoli e Pompei.

DOMUS: THE ROMAN HOUSE

Among the most famous and colorful personalities to have waxed lyrical about the Pompeiian house and garden was the architect Charles-Édouard Jeanneret, more commonly known as Le Corbusier. In his polemical architectural manifesto *Towards an Architecture*, Le Corbusier argues for a plan that "proceeds from within to without", as a house, in his words, is "comparable to a living being".[7] To illustrate his point, he describes a particular Roman dwelling in Pompeii whose thoughtful interior, enclosed by fortress-like exterior walls, effortlessly produces extraordinary effects of light, shade, and volume:

> Casa del Noce, at Pompeii. Again the little vestibule which frees your mind from the street. And then you are in the Atrium; four columns in the middle (four cylinders) shoot up towards the shade of the roof, giving a feeling of force and a witness of potent methods; but at the far end is the brilliance of the garden seen through the peristyle which spreads out this light with a large gesture, distributes it and accentuates it, stretching widely from left to right, making a great space. Between the two is the Tablinum, contracting this vision like the lens of a camera. On the right and on the left two patches of shade—little ones. Out of the clatter of the swarming street which is for every man and full of picturesque incident, you have entered the house of a *Roman*.[8]

Ironically, there is no Casa del Noce at Pompeii, and the house Le Corbusier describes in such detail is, instead, that known as the Casa delle Nozze d'Argento (House of the Silver Wedding) [Figure 7]. Yet the fact that the architect misremembered the house's name—or was misinformed about it—is, on a profound level, extremely telling, as the experience of entry is virtually the same in the case of every Pompeiian house.

We are fortunate to know quite a bit about Roman domestic architecture based on extensive finds at the ancient cities of Pompeii and Herculaneum, as well as other sites on the Bay of Naples, all fortuitously preserved by the eruption of Vesuvius in 79 CE. While there is a great deal

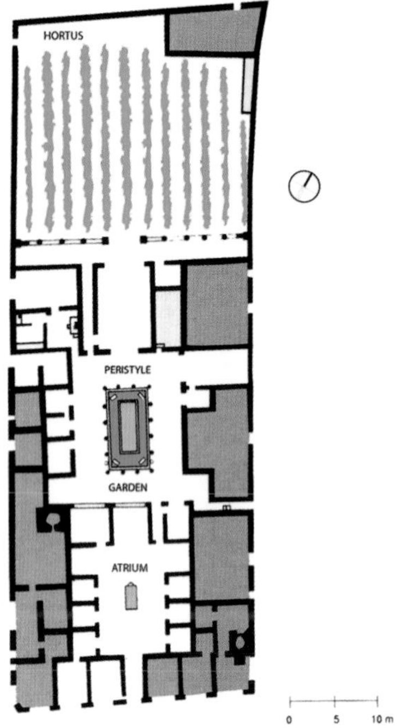

Figure 8/ Ground plan of the Casa di Pansa, Pompeii. Construction begun middle of the second century BCE. Rendering by Don Cowan after Wilhem Zahn, *Die schönsten Ornamente und merkwürdigsten Gemälde aus Pompeji*, vol. 2, Berlin: G. Reimer, 1842/1844, pl. 100.

of variation among individual ground plans, this variation occurs around a core of spaces that have a more or less formulaic arrangement [Figure 8]. Upon crossing the threshold of a Roman town house, one passes through a constricted entry passageway (the *fauces*, literally the 'jaws' of the house) into the atrium, a light-filled reception area, at the center of which lies an *impluvium*, a shallow rectangular pool for collecting rain water. The historic core of the Roman house, the atrium is surrounded by a variety of smaller chambers, some of them likely bedrooms. Beyond the atrium lies the *tablinum* (office) and beyond that, the peristyle garden, surrounded by a colonnade and a series of private rooms for dining, relaxing, and entertaining. The peristyle garden is frequently more or less on axis with the *fauces*, atrium, and *tablinum*, and it is for this reason that Le Corbusier remarks on the garden's visual prominence from the moment of entry. But not only that: the garden is actually visible, deliberately so, from every major room of the house [Figure 9]. Lushly planted with herbs, flowers, trees, and shrubs, both native and imported, gardens were adorned with fountains and eclectic collections of statuary: animals, gods, athletes, and philosophers primary among them.[9] As Le Corbusier notes, the atmosphere of these houses' interiors, pervaded by the sounds of chirping birds and splashing fountains, as well as by the colors and fragrance of plantings, would indeed have been quite a contrast to, and a welcome escape from, the noise and filth of city life just beyond its doors.

OUTSIDE INSIDE

The presence and visual prominence of the garden in the Roman town house has been amply remarked upon, but one should add that the house actually *became* a garden, its interior walls dissolved into the landscape by illusionistic painting.[10] In cases where a garden was particularly small, or the house's owner simply wanted to embellish the planted area, garden scenes of various kinds were painted on walls contiguous to it. For instance, the rear wall of the small garden in the Casa dei Ceii boasts illusionistically painted views into a wild animal park [Figure 10]. Here lions, boars, wolves, leopards, rams, and gazelles are visible beyond a painted garden in which flowering shrubs and fountains offer refuge to swallows, peacocks, and pigeons. Meanwhile, painted views into a statuary-filled garden of rose, oleander, and myrtle—and even vistas out to sea, where a just-born Venus floats beckoningly in a shell—appear beyond the plantings of the Casa della Venere in Conchiglia (House of Venus in the Shell) [Figure 11]. Still another kind of garden painting appears on the walls to the side and rear of the garden in the Casa della Fontana Piccola (House of the Small Fountain): here prospects into 'distant', hazy landscapes containing seaside and country villas alternate with views into a fenced, shrub and tree filled garden. However, landscape scenes such as these painted on walls adjacent to planted gardens represent far from the full extent of garden painting in a Roman house.

Figure 9/ Garden as focal point. Central peristyle garden, Casa degli Amorini Dorati (House of the Golden Cupids), the result of extensive remodeling c. the middle of the first century BCE, Pompeii. Photograph by Annette Giesecke, su concessione del Ministero per i Beni e le Attività Culturali—Soprintendenza Speciale per i Beni Archeologici di Napoli e Pompei.

Figure 10/ Wild animal park, a Roman *paradeisos*.
Garden fresco, detail, third quarter of the first century CE. Casa dei Ceii, Pompeii. Photograph by Annette Giesecke, su concessione del Ministero per i Beni e le Attività Culturali—Soprintendenza Speciale per i Beni Archeologici di Napoli e Pompei.

In fact, virtually any interior could be (illusionistically) deconstructed by the presence of painted gardens.

It was customary for Romans to decorate the walls of their built interiors less with hung works of art such as painted wooden panels—though we certainly hear of great 'master' paintings imported from Greece—than with frescoes, paint applied directly to the walls' plaster. Nineteenth century German archaeologist and art historian August Mau recognized a basic four-stage stylistic progression of Roman wall painting: an earliest style that he deemed the "First" followed by a Second, Third, and Fourth.[11] The earliest identifiable style in Roman wall painting, the so-called First or Masonry Style, is characterized by emulation in paint and modeled stucco of ashlar block masonry and other architectonic elements such as moldings and cornices. This style of painting, a form of literal illusion, served both to decorate and to solidify walls visually. Around 100 BCE, the First Style was replaced by the Second, also known as the "Architectural Style", which employed an arsenal of illusionistic devices pioneered by Greek painters in the fifth and fourth centuries BCE. It now became fashionable to 'pierce' walls to produce vistas into landscapes (temple precincts, colonnaded courts, and sacred grottoes among them) framed by a range of architectural forms.[12] The best preserved examples of paintings in the Second Style hail not from Pompeiian town houses but rather from larger country estates that inspired the décor of their more modest counterparts in Pompeii. In the Villa di Publius Fannius Synistor at Boscoreale, an astonishing sequence of paintings decorated the walls of one of its bedrooms, now fully re-created in New York's Metropolitan Museum. Here the viewer is confronted with vistas into a shrine

Figure 11/ Venus in the shell, a view out to sea.
Garden fresco, detail, after 62 CE. Casa della Venere in Conchiglia (House of Venus in the Shell), Pompeii. Photograph by Annette Giesecke, su concessione del Ministero per i Beni e le Attività Culturali—Soprintendenza Speciale per i Beni Archeologici di Napoli e Pompei.

Figure 12/ Shrine of Artemis, goddess of the wild, and circular temple. Second Style fresco, detail, c. 50–40 BCE. Bedroom, Villa di Publius Fannius Synistor, Boscoreale. The Metropolitan Museum of Art, New York, NY. Photograph © The Metropolitan Museum of Art/ Art Resource, NY.

dedicated to Artemis, the goddess of the wild [Figure 12]; into the sacred precinct surrounding a *tholos* (circular temple); and into a grotto embellished with a vine-draped pergola and stepped fountain. Another splendid example of the Architectural Style appears in a dining/reception room in the so-called "Villa di Poppea at Oplontis", modern Torre Annunziata [Figure 13]. This room is dominated by a fresco in which a grillwork gate, tantalizingly ajar, beckons the viewer into a garden enclosed by a two-tiered colonnade. This garden is presumably a sacred precinct, as the god Apollo's tripod, enveloped by vegetation, looms large just beyond the garden gate.

In the last decades before the Common Era, a change in taste supplanted bold illusionism with a more sedate form of decoration. The dramatic vistas and impressive architectural forms of the Second Style were now severely checked, resulting in the Third or Candelabra Style, in which fragile, delicate, candelabra-like pavilions framed central wall zones containing the equivalent of painted panels or canvases in a picture gallery. These central panels often offered prospects into the landscape and/or sacred gardens, but the prospects' diminished scale and their impressionistic quality affirmed a certain visual remoteness. Their relative remoteness was further enhanced by the fact that some of the landscapes portrayed served as backdrops for didactic mythological scenes; others provided the setting for dreamily nostalgic sacro-idyllic compositions featuring temples, statues of the gods, and also the shadowy figures of farmers,

Figure 13/ Garden sanctuary of Apollo. Second Style fresco, c. 50–40 BCE. Salon 5, Villa di Poppea at Oplontis, Torre Annunziata. Photograph by Annette Giesecke, su concessione del Ministero per i Beni e le Attività Culturali—Soprintendenza Speciale per i Beni Archeologici di Napoli e Pompei.

Figure 14/ Sacro-idyllic landscape. Third Style fresco, c. 10 BCE. Red room in the Villa di Agrippa Postumus at Boscotrecase. Museo Archeologico Nazionale, Naples. Photograph, The Bridgeman Art Library.

shepherds, goatherds, and other pious rustics [Figure 14]. The so-called "sacro-idyllic" was an iconography favored by Rome's first emperor Augustus, who ingeniously promoted his new regime as a return to the Old Republic and its reliance on a citizenry of pious farmers.[13]

Roughly in the middle of the Common Era's first century, prevalent forms of interior décor changed once again. Difficult to describe categorically because of the diverse forms that it took, the Fourth Style, also known as the "Flavian Baroque", was broadly eclectic. Architectural illusionism returned, often taking on the appearance of utterly fantastic stage facades [Figure 15], but it coexisted with more sedate monochromatic panels bearing delicate 'embroidered' borders. In surveying the evolution of Roman wall painting, it would appear, at first glance, that painted gardens and other landscape scenes progressively declined in prominence, but this is far from the truth.

THE GOD IN THE GARDEN

A survey of walls painted in the Second (Architectural), the Third (Candelabra), and the Fourth (Baroque) Styles reveals a noteworthy set of common features whose collective significance warrants investigation. First, it would not be wrong—and would very likely be more correct—to state that the Second Style and its garden vistas never actually faded into obsolescence. Rather, Second Style schemes, which had begun by offering glimpses of the sky and, over time, offered more expansive views into garden areas, continued to evolve. Ultimately, the walls on which illusionistic vistas were painted dissolved entirely into the garden-scapes. Putting it differently, the Second Style evolved in two directions, one naturalistic and the other architectural. Those naturalistic garden scenes that were painted on walls contiguous to planted gardens and enjoyed great popularity in the era of Third and Fourth Style painting surely exemplify bold illusionistic deconstruction of the walls on which they appear. Conventionally, garden-expanding paintings are assigned to their own genre, that of 'garden painting', as distinct from Second Style garden vistas in which architectural elements, rather than plants, are visually dominant.[14] However, such exemplars certainly had their origin in Second Style naturalism and garden scenography.

The earliest and most famous full-blown garden painting dates to the early 'reign' of Augustus, roughly 30–20 BCE, and is therefore viewed as contemporary with the Third (Candelabra) Style. This spectacular painting, now housed in the Museo Nazionale Romano, Palazzo Massimo, once decorated all four walls of a semi-subterranean dining room in a villa belonging to the emperor's wife, Livia [Figure 16].[15] Aptly described as paradisiacal, this painted

Figure 15/ Scenographic painting of the Fourth Style, third quarter of the first century CE. Central panel, Hercules on Mount Olympus at the completion of his twelve labors with Jupiter, Hera, and Athena. Sede degli Augustali, Shrine of the deified Augustus and headquarters of his cult, Herculaneum. Photograph by Annette Giesecke, su concessione del Ministero per i Beni e le Attività Culturali—Soprintendenza Speciale per i Beni Archeologici di Napoli e Pompei.

Figure 16/ Paradisiacal Garden.

Fresco from the Villa di Livia at Prima Porta, detail, c. 20 BCE. Museo Nazionale, Palazzo Massimo. Photograph by Annette Giesecke, su concessione del Ministero per I Beni e le Attività Culturali—Soprintendenza Speciale per i Beni Archeologici di Roma.

garden is filled with a preternatural abundance of plant life all tidily contained behind a low lattice fence: spruce, cypress, ilex, palm, pine, laurel, quince, box, arbutus, myrtle, oleander, viburnum, fern, ivy, quince, pomegranate, oak, acanthus, iris, chamomile, chrysanthemum, poppy, rose, violet, and daisy. The paradise effect is enhanced by the fact that many of these plants have associations with individual divinities; the laurel, palm, and acanthus, for example, were sacred to Apollo; the oak to Zeus, known to the Romans as Jupiter; and the rose and myrtle to Aphrodite, Roman Venus.[16] Further, this garden's plants bloom and/or produce fruit regardless of seasonality. Like other, later garden paintings, this one is populated by a wide variety of birds; pigeons, quails, blackbirds, jays, thrushes, magpies, orioles, buntings, and sparrows have all been counted in their number. Seldom remarked is the fact that a fringe of rock has been painted along the top of this paradise garden, giving the effect that the garden is viewed from a grotto.[17] As far as the painting's meaning is concerned, the paradisiacal associations of this garden were integral to the blatantly utopian propaganda of Augustus' regime. The first *de facto* emperor in a country intolerant of the monarchy, Augustus had to tread with care. Capitalizing on the fact that he had put an end to decades of civil war so intense and bloody that it threatened irreparably to rend the very fabric of Roman society, Augustus promoted himself as author of a new era of universal peace (*Pax Romana*). Under the auspices of her first citizen, as Augustus styled himself, Rome as well as her empire would now experience a Golden Age of harmony and plenty founded on piety and the agrarian values of old.[18]

While the various plants depicted in Livia's garden room had associations with specific deities and myths, there is one god in particular who was associated with all abundant plant life and the felicitous state that such afforded. That deity was Dionysus, called Bacchus by the Romans [Figure 17]. Regardless of the name by which one calls him, Dionysus, known primarily as the god of wine, immediately conjures images of drunken revelry; but his powers extended far beyond the oenetic. A god imported to Greece from the Near East (and later from Greece to Rome), Dionysus was in origin a god of liquid life, in particular of the life-sustaining fluids in plants (sap), hence his association with luxuriant plant growth.[19] Over time he became associated with other life-sustaining fluids as well, those derived both from plants and other sources in nature: wine, honey, milk, and blood. A desire to commune with the god by imbibing blood underlay the ritual of *sparagmos* (pulling apart) and *omophagia* (eating raw) of wild animals, as (in)famously documented in Euripides' classic Greek play

The Bacchae, which premiered in 405 BCE. This same play, our fullest source of information regarding the worship of Dionysus in ancient Greece, is also incidentally—but not coincidentally—key to the second century BCE description of an earthly Paradise in the third book of the *Oracula Sibyllina*, thought to be a product of Egyptian Judaism. In Euripides' text, the Earth streams with wine, milk, and honey where it is struck by the magical staffs of the god's devotees.[20] And the same triad of fluids reappears in the oracular paradise: "... then God will give great joy to men,/ for earth and trees and countless flocks of sheep/ will give to men the true fruit/ of wine, sweet honey and white milk/ and corn, which is best of all for mortals".[21]

Abundance in plant growth and life-sustaining fluids was not, however, the extent of Dionysus' gift to mortals. His worship offered a welcome release from the routine hardships and stresses of everyday life, and in his eyes, all were equal: young and old, male and female, slave and free, even animal and human. In certain respects, the god may be viewed as enabling the creation of a felicitous "alternative cohesive society", and it is little wonder, therefore, that Dionysus' worship spread like wildfire.[22] It is also fully appropriate that Dionysus and his usual entourage of satyrs (hybrid creatures part horse or goat and part man) and nymphs should have represented a substantial proportion of the statuary found in Roman domestic gardens. After all, these gardens were conceived as oases, offering respite and retreat from the hardships of daily life.

Figure 17/ The god of the garden, and his entourage: Dionysus, reclining in the lap of his wife Ariadne. Fresco from the Villa dei Misteri (Villa of the Mysteries), Pompeii, detail, c. 60–50 BCE. Photograph by Annette Giesecke, su concessione del Ministero per i Beni e le Attività Culturali—Soprintendenza Speciale per i Beni Archeologici di Napoli e Pompei.

While traditional forms of worshipping Dionysus lived on, particularly in remote rural areas in ancient Greece, a new, sanitized form more appropriate to cultured life in the city was introduced over time: performances in the theater. Athens was at the helm of these developments, and the theater, which fully engaged politics, became an important and popular utopian device. Through this institutionalized medium, playwrights could question social norms and international policy in an alternate, fictional world that, by virtue of its remove from reality, was relatively unthreatening.[23] Reflecting the popularity and influence of the theater in Classical antiquity, theater masks became favored iconographic elements, appearing on carved reliefs, in mosaics, and also on painted walls, all of which featured in the Roman house. Dionysus, the god who facilitated the blurring of distinctions between real and unreal, the god of the garden, accordingly appeared not only in planted areas but virtually everywhere in the Roman house.

Returning to Roman wall painting specifically, the presence of theater masks as a decorative feature is another one of the constants linking the Second, Third, and Fourth Styles. It has long been thought, and rightly so, that the architectural illusionism of the Second Style was inspired by scene painting for the Greek theater. Although there are no extant examples of scene painting from Greek theaters, literary sources record that Agatharchos of Samos, perhaps active in the middle of the fifth century BCE, was responsible for inventing rules for rendering spatial perspective in painting; Vitruvius in particular notes that perspectival renderings were first applied in the creation of stage sets for the theater in Athens.[24] In the absence of actual Greek scene painting, the Second Style paintings from the Boscoreale bedroom described above are generally cited as examples of sets for all types of Greek drama: tragedy (sanctuaries), comedy (cityscapes), and satyr play (views of the countryside).[25] The likelihood that the Boscoreale paintings were inspired by scenery for the stage is underscored by the presence of theatrical masks, which would otherwise be pictorially unmotivated.

Strictly speaking, the Third (Candelabra) and the Fourth (Baroque) Styles of wall painting were Roman creations with no Greek precedent, but one may surely see them as having evolved from theater-inspired Second Style painting. Architectural illusionism may have waned in the Third Style, but it reemerged, and forcefully so, in the Fourth. And again, theatrical inspiration for all three styles of wall painting would be suggested by the ubiquitous appearance of miniature theater masks among commonly applied decorative motifs. It is also the case that the abundant vegetal motifs found in exemplars of all three styles are conceptually linked to these masks: masks and vegetation both necessarily allude to the presence of Dionysus. Vitruvius provides a good sense of the application of such vegetal motifs in his complaints about the replacement of the Second Style's 'true' or believable architectural illusionism by the Third Style's nonsensical, pseudo-architectural monstrosities:

> But these, which were created in imitation of Reality, are now rejected due to our perversion of tastes and ways. For walls are painted with monstrosities rather than with truthful representations of definite things: thus in place of columns, fluted reeds appear as structural elements, and in place of pediments [there are] decorative attachments adorned with curled and twisting foliage, and also candelabra supporting shrines, atop their roofs clusters of thin stalks and volutes shooting up from their roots [and] in which, quite in defiance of logic, are nestled tiny figures, and frequently too, split tendrils harboring figures, some with human and others with animal heads.[26]

Roman wall paintings, then, may be viewed as backdrops or scenery for the drama of domestic life enabled by Dionysus, the fecund god of gardens, and played out under his watchful eye. Further, even walls not decorated with garden vistas *per se* were full of motifs drawn from the plant world. Thus the magic of Dionysus and the garden's delights pervaded the Roman house, lending the whole an Edenic quality.

SOCIO-POLITICAL UNDERPINNINGS

A comparison of the Classical Greek town house with its Roman counterpart readily reveals just how extraordinary was the transformation of the Roman house's interior into a virtual garden. Interior courtyards came to be characteristic of both Greek and Roman houses, yet these open spaces were radically different. In Greek towns, interior courtyards provided houses with light and air, but they were never, to our knowledge, planted. These were simply open-air rooms in which to work or play. The Greek town house functioned as a barrier against the penetration of the potentially threatening natural world, while the Roman house was built with an eye towards domesticating that world.[27]

It had not always been the case, however, that gardens formed the visual and ideological core of the Roman house, and it remains to consider the factors underlying this development. As exemplified by the Casa del Chirurgo (House of the Surgeon) in Pompeii, which likely dates to the second half of the third century BCE, early Italian town houses did certainly contain garden spaces; however, these gardens were relegated to the rear of the house and were what one would describe as kitchen gardens, *horti*, provisioning the household.[28] The kitchen gardens were important but clearly not fully integrated into the living experience. Two interrelated factors were pivotal in the change of the interior garden's emphasis from productive to primarily ornamental and from appendage to focal point. The first was the integration of the peristyle, an open court surrounded by a colonnade that had its origins in the public architecture of Greece, in the plan of the traditional Roman house from the late third century BCE. The second was the explosion, shortly thereafter, of the Roman villa phenomenon. Enriched by foreign conquests as well as by domestic opportunities for gain resulting from Rome's protracted civil wars—notably property made available by proscriptions and failed agricultural reforms—wealthy Romans acquired a taste for sprawling villas with lavish gardens, both ornamental and productive. These villas were outfitted with Greek masterpieces (originals and copies) of statuary, painting, and mosaic. Their grounds contained a wide range of architectural refinements, including Greek-style exercise grounds (*gymnasia*), bath complexes, covered walkways, aviaries, column-encircled halls, and chambers for storing fruit produced in the estates' orchards.[29] Water features such as fishponds and swimming pools, as well as towers and terraces for maximizing views, were also particularly popular. An exceptionally well-preserved example of such an estate is the aforementioned Villa di Poppea at Oplontis with its vast planted gardens, sculpture-lined swimming pool, and walls decorated with frescoes that suggested complete integration with nature in their depiction of gardens and landscape scenes of various kinds [Figure 18]. Such elite estates, initially built primarily on the Tyrrhenian coast as luxurious retreats from busy life in Roman politics, came to be constructed

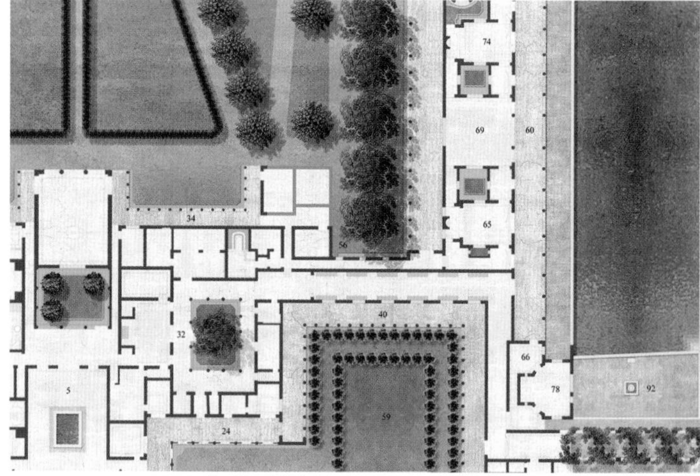

Figure 18/ The Villa di Poppea at Oplontis, Torre Annunziata, and its gardens. Plan of the excavated portion of the villa and its grounds, detail. Initial building phase c. 50 BCE, thereafter repeatedly remodeled. Plan courtesy of James Stanton-Abbott.

Figure 19/ Peristyle garden with a succession of ornamental fish ponds.
Praedia di Giulia Felice (Estate of Julia Felix), Pompeii, as expanded after the middle of the first century BCE. Photograph by Annette Giesecke, su concessione del Ministero per i Beni e le Attività Culturali—Soprintendenza Speciale per i Beni Archeologici di Napoli e Pompei.

not only in Rome's *sub-urbium*, the areas lying outside the city's wall, but also on coveted intramural parcels.[30] Not wanting to be left behind, householders in Pompeii apparently followed suit. And, to the extent that their personal resources allowed, they transformed their town houses into miniature villas containing statuary-filled ornamental gardens and walls painted to mimic views into their extensive imaginary grounds.[31] Two particularly lavish examples, both properly classifiable as urban villas, are the Casa di D. Octavius Quartio, with which this essay opened, and the Praedia di Giulia Felice (Estate of Julia Felix), which comprised living quarters, a bath complex, a peristyle garden, a swimming-pool garden, and an expansive 'park' [Figure 19].

The villa phenomenon was spurred on in the last decades of the Roman Republic by intensifying competition on the part of members of the Roman elite jockeying for social position and the political clout that social climbing inevitably carried.[32] One's villas—it was not uncommon to own more than one—and their accoutrements were an ideal way to impress others with one's power, wealth, and erudition, all clearly indicated by the quality and extent of one's art collection and range of ancillary structures. For example, in his letters the statesman Cicero (106–43 BCE), famous for his rise to prominence as a *Novus Homo* (a "New Man", his family new to the highest levels of political office), mentions the importance of building a sculpture collection appropriate for the 'replica' Academy on the grounds of one of his villas. The Academy referenced here is the gymnasium grounds and sanctuary housing Plato's famed school of philosophy just outside of Athens, a city frequented by Romans of means for instruction in philosophy.[33] Indeed, it was standard practice to include structures that mimicked or recalled a wide range of landmarks from around the increasingly Roman-controlled world, and this practice, in turn, suggested the villa owners' preeminent worldliness. Thus it was that the estates of the Roman elite came to contain such features as the river Nile,

Figure 20/ Royal garden complex, Pasargadae, Iran. Constructed for King Cyrus the Great of Persia, ruling 559–530 BCE. Aerial view, conjectural plantings of the *chahar-bagh*, fourfold garden looked onto from Palace P to the north (top). Axial view towards the exterior throne of Palace P (bottom left). Apple allée, east–west axis of the *chahar-bagh* (bottom right). Reconstruction concept and design by Annette Giesecke and Donald Dunham, rendering by Don Cowan after David Stronach's schematic reconstruction, by permission.

'Babylonian' hanging gardens, and Persian style hunting parks (*paradeisoi*), all in reduced scale.

It is telling that the direct models for these Roman estates were almost certainly the palaces of the Hellenistic monarchs and potentates who inherited administration of the massive empire forged by Alexander the Great. This empire, created between 336 and 323 BCE, stretched from the Ionian Sea to the Himalayas, uniting European Greece with the territories of the Persian Empire including Asia Minor, Syria, and Egypt. Entirely in line with the hybrid character of Alexander's new world, the design of the Hellenistic palaces and their grounds wedded Greek with local traditions.[34] Notably, Persian palaces and royal Egyptian temple/tombs contained a great many of the elements that would become fundamental to the design of Roman villa gardens: elaborate water features, planted interior courtyards, geometrically-arranged planting beds, and ornate garden pavilions among them. This should come as no surprise, as Near Eastern and Egyptian garden traditions were already thousands of years old at the time of Rome's birth in 753 BCE. Archaeological evidence for most of the parks and gardens that Assyrian, Babylonian, Persian, and Egyptian monarchs constructed has not survived the ravages of time. Nevertheless, enough material has been unearthed to reveal just how impressive and *affective* such gardens must have been. One such marvel of landscape design was the royal garden built by the Persian king Cyrus the Great (559–530 BCE) at Pasargadae in what is modern Iran [Figure 20]. This garden was a departure, very different from royal gardens in Assyria and Babylonia, for it was not an appendage to the structure of the palace. Instead, in the words of its excavator David Stronach, the garden was "an integral part of a comprehensive design in which, in a sense, the garden itself became the royal residence".[35] Of particular interest is Palace P, an open-sided structure with deep, pillared porches open to the palace grounds. In the palace's south-east colonnade was a throne oriented outwards and placed on axis with the garden just beyond—perhaps the earliest *chahar-bagh* or "four-part garden", defined by the confluence of Creation's four rivers. The layout of this inner garden, framed by Palace P and its two auxiliary pavilions, was determined by straight water channels of finely dressed limestone that served not only to articulate but also to irrigate and embellish the garden's plantings. Though extensive disturbance of the area has rendered recovery of organic matter and the accurate reconstruction of planting beds unlikely, literary sources as well as later Persian gardens would lead one to imagine a garden of plants such as cypress trees, apple trees, pomegranates, roses, jasmine, poppies, tulips, and native grasses in symmetrical, geometric arrangements.

Ancient Egypt, for its part, has yielded a wealth of tomb paintings depicting densely planted gardens teeming with wildlife.[36] A prominent water feature, often taking the form of a T-shaped pond, is ubiquitous in these gardens,

Figure 21/ Vine-covered arbor, painted interior of the Tomb of Sennefer, New Kingdom, Egyptian eighteenth Dynasty c. 1567–1320 BCE. Valley of the Nobles, Thebes, Egypt. Photograph, The Bridgeman Art Library.

and many contain arbors shaded by vines heavily laden with grapes. The Tomb of Sennefer, the interior of which was painted to resemble a tent inside a vine-covered arbor, provides a particularly evocative example of the garden delights awaiting the deceased in the life beyond [Figure 21]. This tomb also beautifully illustrates the extent to which the Egyptians sought to incorporate the natural world into their architectural environment, a tendency that persisted beyond the Pharaonic period into the Arab occupation. Individual parts of buildings regularly represented papyrus, water lilies, palm trees, flowers, and fruit. Thus walls of temple interiors were often decorated with carvings in relief of papyrus marshes, the plants symbolically emerging from the Earth to grow ever higher, rising towards the heavens in clumps to form the temples' columns. Planted areas in tomb and temple gardens were framed by painted or carved backdrops of vegetation that illusionistically dissolved walls and floors, providing bright blooms upon the fading of their living cousins. One such immortal garden, that within Tuthmosis III's Temple at Karnak, portrays a wide range of plants that the pharaoh brought back from his campaigns in Palestine and Syria and may be the first known botanic garden, a lasting memorial to its creator's might and to the extent of his good fortune.

In Persia and Egypt, rulers were considered living gods, and their gardens, improbably lush oases in a most inhospitable climate, were testimony not only to their creators' wonder-working divinity but also to their ability to nourish and sustain the lands beneath their sway.[37] It was imperative that these kings be more than merely good gardeners; they had to be, far and beyond, the best. Through botanic allusions to Egypt and the Near East, a lavish Roman villa could therefore suggest erudition, world dominion, and god-like status at once. All this was intensely troubling to that portion of the Roman psyche ingrained with belief in the innate virtues of the simple agricultural life lived by Rome's founder Romulus. Adding yet another layer of complexity to the ideology of the Roman villa, productive aspects were awarded particular value so that the owner could simultaneously preserve the images of gentleman farmer and of living god.[38]

EPICURUS' GARDEN

While opportunities for personal display in an atmosphere of intense competition for social standing are certainly key in the Roman villa's popularity among the elite—as well as in its ultimate imitation by householders of more modest means—there is another factor, already mentioned in passing, that is not sufficiently recognized. That factor is the opportunity for relaxation, contemplative or otherwise, which the Romans called "*otium*". In the Classical tradition, *otium* has a long association with gardens, and, most interestingly, it was the philosopher Epicurus (341–270 BCE) who, as the elder Pliny states in the first century CE, pioneered the notion of the garden as a locus of repose (*otium*) versus a utilitarian horticultural plot.[39] Epicurus' philosophy was understandably popular, for it was egalitarian and communal, offering solace and comfort in politically turbulent times. In fact, the high point of the philosopher's career coincided with the great, presumably unsettling changes that inevitably followed Alexander the Great's creation of a new 'world order' mingling peoples of so many different lands.[40] What Epicurus preached in the school he called "The Garden" was a utopian harmony with nature that was within everyone's reach and achievable by attaining a state of ataraxy, defined as lack of disturbance. Ataraxy, for its part, could be achieved by abstaining from that which complicates one's life and instead embracing simple pleasures such as friendship and the cool shade offered by a tree beside a babbling brook. Spending one's energies vying for political office and maximizing one's profits in business was to be avoided as much as possible, and withdrawal into the garden was greatly preferred. It is hardly surprising that Epicurus' disciples spread his philosophy to places far and wide, among them Roman Italy, where it gained particular momentum precisely in those turbulent times marked by the blossoming of the Roman villa phenomenon. On Italian soil, the Bay of Naples, a location favored for villas, became the epicenter of Epicureanism. The Roman elite who found Epicureanism attractive were not few in number, and, tailoring Epicurus' teachings to their own needs or circumstances, they could find the restorative communion with nature they desired in the gardens of their own estates.

While it would be unlikely that all or even most of Italy's population were Epicureans, the undeniable restorative quality of the garden experience, as well as its nostalgic associations with a lost Golden Age and/or simpler times when pre-urbanized humanity enjoyed a much greater proximity with nature, was surely central to the progressive 'greening' of Roman Italy and the longevity of the Roman garden movement.[41] In other words, quasi-Epicurean sentiments and the weight of Rome's agricultural past had much to do with both the creation of private and public garden spaces and with the transformation of the Roman house into a virtual garden. Just how prevalent gardens of all kinds were in the Roman world is indicated by Pompeii, in which roughly 17 percent of the excavated area, comparable to the space devoted to roads and public squares, was devoted to gardens. Gardens were not only everywhere in the typical Roman house, they were apparently everywhere in the city. In Pompeii, buildings of every size and type contained them, including shops, inns, theaters, temples, and apartments, which had planted window boxes and interior garden courtyards.[42]

PARADISE

The utopian aspects of the Roman house and its gardens are manifest. Gardens, under the auspices of a miracle-working Dionysus, were sources of pleasure, solace, and comfort, *and* they were widely accessible. They were also vehicles by which Romans might remember their ancestral traditions and rural origins. But how, precisely, were gardens 'paradise'? The answer to this is: "in every possible way".

The Romans borrowed the word "*paradeisos*" from the Greeks, but it does not have Hellenic origins. Instead, the word is derived from the Median *paridaeza* (a walled enclosure), which corresponded with Old Persian *paridaida* and Babylonian *pardesu*. Judging from extant Babylonian, Elamite, and Greek texts, the semantic range of this word was considerable, encompassing vineyards, orchards, nurseries, luxurious pleasure gardens, hunting parks, and storage spaces for produce. Even Plato's Academy was designated a *paradeisos*.[43] Overt suggestions of prosperity and pleasure associated with the royal parks (*paradeisoi*) of Persian kings would lead to the translation of Hebraic *Gan Eden* in Genesis (3:23) as *paradeisos tes tryphes* (paradise of pleasurable luxury) in Greek and to the conception of the Qur'an's paradise as gardens.[44] The Roman villa and house contained all of these paradises, whether physically realized or rendered in paint, and in all cases, the aim was pleasure, whether or not one defined it as the Epicureans did: absence of distress and pain.

Notes

The author owes a particular debt of gratitude to Patrick Hunt for supplying an invaluable bibliography on Persian gardens; to David Stronach for sharing his insights into the plan and constitution of Cyrus the Great's gardens at Pasargadae as well as for permitting the use of his plans of those gardens and their palaces as a basis for the reconstructions created for this essay; and to Stephen Forbes for verifying the plausibility of the garden's plantings as reconstructed here.

The ideas put forward in this essay are a development of arguments in Annette Giesecke, *The Epic City: Urbanism, Utopia, and the Garden in Ancient Greece and Rome*, Hellenic Studies 21, Cambridge, MA: Harvard University Press, 2007. Portions of this essay were presented at the International Association for the Study of Traditional Environments conference in Beirut, Lebanon, 2010, subsequently appearing in the IASTE *Traditional Dwellings and Settlements Working Papers Series*, vol. 230, *Environmental Utopias and the Green Ideal*, 2010, pp. 51–69 as conference proceedings.

1. The nomenclature of Pompeiian houses has become inconsistent over the years: some of the houses are known by several names, some are known by Italian names, and some are known by names that mix Latin and Italian, all subject to translation into a variety of different languages. In the interest of consistency, I refer to houses in Pompeii, Herculaneum, and other areas around the Bay of Naples using names assigned by the Soprintendenza Archeologica di Napoli e Pompei (http://www.pompeiisites.org/), which corresponds with usage in Fabrizio Pesandro and Maria Paola Guidobaldi, *Pompei, Oplontis, Ercolano, Stabiae*, Roma: Editori Laterza, 2006. Located in Pompeii's Regio II (*insula* or "block" ii, doorway 2), the Casa di D. Octavius Quartio, once known as the Casa di Loreio Tiburtino, is a favorite and has been much discussed in scholarly sources. Descriptions and analyses of the house include: John R. Clarke, *The Houses of Roman Italy, 100 B.C.–A.D. 250: Ritual, Space, and Decoration*, Berkeley: The University of California Press, 1991, pp. 23–25; Wilhelmina F. Jashemski, *The Gardens of Pompeii: Herculaneum, and the Villas Destroyed by Vesuvius*, New Rochelle, NY: Caratzas, 1979, pp. 44–47; Wilhelmina F. Jashemski, *The Gardens of Pompeii, Herculaneum, and the Villas Destroyed by Vesuvius*, Vol. II: Appendices, New Rochelle, NY: Caratzas, 1993, pp. 78–83; Amedo Maiuri and Roberto Pane, *La Casa di Loreio Tiburtino e La Villa di Diomede in Pompei*. I Monumenti Italiani Serie II, Fasc. I, Roma: La Libreria dello Stato, 1947, pp. 3–11 and tables I–VIII; Lauren Hackworth Petersen, *The Freedman in Roman Art and Art History*, New York: Cambridge University Press, 2006, pp. 129–136; Katharine T. von Stackelberg, *The Roman Garden: Space, Sense, and Society*, New York: Routledge, 2009, pp. 101–106, 111–125; and Paul Zanker, *Pompeii: Public and Private Life*, Deborah Schneider trans., Cambridge, MA: Harvard University Press, 1998, pp. 145–156.

2. Statuettes found in the truncated peristyle garden are representations of an ibis, a Pharaonic figure, and the Egyptian god Bes.

3. The myths of Narcissus and of Pyramus and Thisbe are preserved in Ovid's *Metamorphoses*. Narcissus features in Book III, lines 339–510. The tale of Pyramus and Thisbe is recounted in Book IV, lines 55–166. See Ovid, *Metamorphoses*, Rolphe Humphries trans., Bloomington: Indiana University Press, 1955, pp. 67–73 and 83–86.

4. Ovid also recounts the tale of Diana and Actaeon: Book III, lines 139–252 in Ovid, *Metamorphoses*, pp. 61–64.

5. Egyptian gardens are described in Alix Wilkinson, *The Garden in Ancient Egypt*, London: The Rubicon Press, 1998, and the vine is featured on pages 12, 24, and 109.

6. The history of Persian gardens, both their design and symbolism, is discussed and lushly illustrated in Penelope Hobhouse, *The Gardens of Persia*, London: Kales Press, 2004; and Medhi Khansari, M. Reza Moghtader, and Minouch Yavari, *The Persian Garden: Echoes of Paradise*, Washington, D.C.: Mage Publishers, 2004. Gardens, which are so integral to Persian architecture, are also featured in Arthur Pope, *Persian Architecture: The Triumph of Form and Color*, New York: George Braziller, 1965. The notion that the *chahar-bagh* (fourfold garden) can be traced to ancient Persia, specifically to the royal gardens of Cyrus the Great at Pasargadae, was put forward by the garden's excavator David Stronach in: "The Royal Garden at Pasargadae: Evolution and Legacy", *Archaeologia Iranica et Orientalis*, Leon de Meyer and Ernie Haerinck eds., Gent: Peeters Press, 1989, pp. 475–500; "The Garden as a Political Statement: Some Case Studies from the Near East in the First Millennium B.C.", *Bulletin of the Asia Institute*, vol. 4, 1990, pp. 171–180; and again in "The Building Program of Cyrus the Great at Pasargadae and the Date of the Fall of Sardis", *Ancient Greece and Ancient Iran: Cross-Cultural Encounters*, S. M. R. Darbandi and A. Zournatzi eds., Athens: National Hellenic Research Foundation, 2008, p. 165. Stronach's analysis is confirmed in Rémy Boucharlat, "Pasargadae", *Iran*, vol. 40, 2002, pp. 279–282.

7. Le Corbusier, *Towards a New Architecture* [sic], Frederick Etchtells trans., London: The Architectural Press, 1946, p. 166.

8. The description of the Casa del Noce stems from Le Corbusier, *Towards a New Architecture*, pp. 169–170.

9. The standard source on the appearance, plantings, and ornamentation of the Roman garden is Jashemski, *The Gardens of Pompeii*, vols. 1 & 2. The role of the garden and its integration into the architecture of the Roman house may be found in: Lise Bek, *Towards Paradise on Earth: Modern Space Conception in Architecture*, Odense, Denmark: Odense University Press, 1980; Jens-Arne Dickmann, "The Peristyle and the Transformation of Domestic Space in Hellenistic Pompeii", *Domestic Space in the Roman World: Pompeii and Beyond*, Ray Lawrence and Andrew Wallace-Hadrill eds., *Journal of Roman Archaeology*, Supplementary Series 22, Portsmouth, RI: JRA, 1997, pp. 121–136; H. Lauter-Bufe, "Zur architektonischen Gartengestaltung in Pompeji und Herculaneum", *Neue Forschungen in Pompeji und den anderen vom Vesuvausbruch 79 n. Chr. verschütteten Städten*, B. Andreae and H. Kyrieleis eds., Aurel Bongers Verlag, 1975, pp. 169–178; and von Stackelberg, *The Roman Garden*.

10. Approaching this idea are Ann Kuttner, "Looking Outside Inside: Ancient Roman Garden Rooms", *Studies in the History of Gardens and Designed Landscapes*, vol. 19, no. 1, pp. 7–35, whose argument is limited to Second Style painting and its garden "immersion rooms"; and Bettina Bergmann, "Staging the Supernatural: Interior Gardens of Pompeiian Houses", *Pompeii and the Roman Villa: Art and Culture around the Bay of Naples*, Carol Mattusch ed., Washington, D.C.: The National Gallery, 2008, pp. 53–69.

11. Though repeatedly challenged, Mau's basic schema has largely withstood the tests of time: see August Mau, *Geschichte der dekorativen*

Wandmalerei in Pompeji, Berlin: Reimer Verlag, 1882. A balanced summary of stylistic progression and genres in Roman wall painting is provided in Roger Ling, *Roman Painting*, Cambridge: Cambridge University Press, 1991. It should be added, however, that the stylistic and temporal boundaries between the Second, Third, and Fourth Styles are blurry and remain contested.

12. These celebrated Greeks had suggested volume by the use of highlights and shading, and they carried out experiments in linear perspective with increasing success. For these advances in Greek painting see Martin Robertson, *A Shorter History of Greek Art*, Cambridge: Cambridge University Press, 1981, pp. 60–79, 106–109, 147–156, 172–182, 204–208; and Mary Hamilton Swindler, *Ancient Painting*, New Haven: Yale University Press, 1929, pp. 195–416.

13. Important sources on the policies and iconography adopted by Augustus are: Karl Galinsky, *Augustan Culture*, Princeton: Princeton University Press, 1996; Andrew Wallace-Hadrill, *Augustan Rome*, London: Bristol Classical Press, 1993; and Paul Zanker, *The Power of Images in the Age of Augustus*, Alan Shapiro trans., Ann Arbor: The University of Michigan Press, 1990.

14. For garden paintings distinguished from landscapes and treated as a separate sub-genre of Roman painting, see Ling, *Roman Painting*, pp. 142–153.

15. The garden paintings of Livia's Prima Porta villa are extensively published in Mabel Gabriel, *Livia's Garden Room at Prima Porta*, New York: New York University Press, 1955; and Salvatore Settis, *La Villa di Livia: le pareti ingannevoli*, Milan: Electa, 2008.

16. For the divine associations of plants, see Hellmut Baumann, *The Greek Plant World in Myth, Art, and Literature*, William T. and Eldwyth R. Stearn trans., Portland, OR: Timber Press, 1993; Peter Bernhardt, *Gods and Goddesses in the Garden: Greco-Roman Mythology and the Scientific Names of Plants*, New Brunswick, NJ: Rutgers University Press, 2008; David Castriota, *The Ara Pacis Augustae and the Imagery of Abundance in Later Greek and Early Roman Imperial Art*, Princeton: Princeton University Press, 1995, pp. 87–123; as well as Dorothy Thompson and Ralph Griswold, *Garden Lore of Ancient Athens*, Princeton: American School of Classical Studies at Athens, 1982.

17. This point is made by Kuttner, "Looking Outside Inside", p. 27, who rightly sees this room as a development of Second Style landscapes, particularly those offering vistas into a grotto.

18. For further discussion of the paradisiacal and utopian associations of Augustan propaganda, see Giesecke, *The Epic City*, pp. 79–155.

19. Classic works on Dionysus and his powers are Walter Otto, *Dionysus: Myth and Cult*, Robert Palmer trans., Bloomington: Indiana University Press, 1965, as well as E. R. Dodds' introduction to his own edition of Euripides' *Bacchae*, 2nd edition, Oxford: Clarendon Press, 1960.

20. *Bacchae*, lines 142–143.

21. This quote from the *Oracula Sibyllina* III, lines 619–623, stems from Jan Bremmer, *The Rise and Fall of the Afterlife*, London: Routledge, 2002, p. 121, where this passage is linked with the *Bacchae*.

22. The notion of an alternative society stems from R. R. R. Smith, *Hellenistic Sculpture: a Handbook*, London: Thames and Hudson, 1991, p. 127, who also writes of the popularity of Dionysian statuary in the Roman villa garden, pp. 127–154. "Dionysian" refers to the god's entire entourage: satyrs, maenads, nymphs, fauns, and hermaphrodites.

23. The bibliography on the political nature of Greek tragedy is vast, but for a particularly good discussion, which also points to tragedy's essentially utopian character, see Paul Cartledge, "'Deep Plays': Theatre as Process in Greek Civic Life", *The Cambridge Companion to Greek Tragedy*, P. E. Easterling ed., Cambridge: Cambridge University Press, 1997, pp. 3–35.

24. In his writings on architecture, Vitruvius mentions Agatharchos and the latter's role in the development of scenic painting in *De Architectura* 7. praef. 11. For Vitruvius translated into English, see Vitruvius, *The Ten Books on Architecture*. M. H. Morgan trans., New York: Dover Publications, 1960, p. 198.

25. On the links of scenic painting with developments in Roman wall painting, see H. G. Beyen, "The Wall-decoration of the Cubiculum of the Villa of P. Fannius Synistor near Boscoreale in its Relation to Ancient Stage-painting", *Mnemosyne* 4th ser. 10, 1957, pp. 147–153; and Alan M. G. Little, *Roman Perspective Painting and the Ancient Stage*. Kennebunk, ME: Star Press, 1971.

26. This translation of Vitruvius, *De Architectura* 7.5.3, my own, deliberately sacrifices grammatical propriety in English in an effort to capture the full force of the original Latin as closely as possible. The translation is based on the standard Latin edition: Vitruvius, *Vitruvii De Architectura Libri Decem*, F. Krohn ed., Leipzig: Teubner Verlag, 1912.

27. A nicely illustrated book that allows ready comparison of Greek, Roman, and other house forms in antiquity is Erika Brödner, *Wohnen in der Antike*, Darmstadt: Wissenschaftliche Buchgesselschaft, 1989.

28. On the evolution of the Roman house, see, for instance: Alexander Gordon McKay, *Houses, Villas, and Palaces in the Roman World*, Ithaca: Cornell University Press, 1975, pp. 30–63; and Nicholas Purcell, "The Roman Garden as a Domestic Building", *Roman Domestic Buildings*, I. M. Barton ed., Exeter: University of Exeter Press, 1996, pp. 121–153. For recent archaeological data regarding the houses in Pompeii, see Pesandro and Guidobaldi, *Pompei, Oplontis, Ercolano, Stabiae*, pp. 166–167 for the Casa del Chirurgo in particular.

29. Ancient sources of primary importance for our understanding of the appearance of the Roman villa are the letters of Cicero and of Pliny the Younger as well as the writings of Varro on agriculture. It is Varro specifically who lists these particular villa outbuildings (*De Re Rustica* 2. Prologue 2), translated into English by William D. Hooper, *Cato and Varro: De Re Rustica*, Cambridge, MA: Harvard University Press, 1979, p. 307.

30. The classic description of the beginnings and spread of the Roman villa phenomenon is John H. D'Arms, *Romans on the Bay of Naples: A Social and Cultural Study of the Villas and Their Owners from 150 B.C. to A.D. 400*, Cambridge, MA: Harvard University Press, 1970.

31. This view was popularized by Zanker, *Pompeii*.

32. A lively description of the image-making potential of the Roman house may be found in T. P. Wiseman, "*Conspicui Postes Tectaque Digna Deo*: The Public Image of Aristocratic and Imperial Houses in the Late Republic and Early Empire", *L'Urbs: espace urbain et histoire (Ier siècle av. J.C.–IIIe siècle ap. J.C.)*. Actes du colloque international organisé par le Centre national de la recherche scientifique et L'École française de Rome, Rome, 8–12 mai 1985, Rome: L'École française de Rome, 1987, pp. 393–413.

33. The particular letter in which Cicero mentions wanting statuary

appropriate for his Academy is "Letter to Atticus, 5" in D. R. Shackleton Bailey, *Cicero's Letters to Atticus.* Vol. I (Books I–II), Cambridge: Cambridge University Press 1965, p. 115.
34. Among the best discussions of the Hellenistic palace and the derivation of its architectural forms (as well as a discussion of the Roman villa) is Inge Nielsen, *Hellenistic Palaces: Tradition and Renewal*, Aarhus: Aarhus University Press, 1999.
35. See David Stronach, *Pasargadae: A Report on the Excavations Conducted by the British School of Persian Studies from 1961 to 1963*, Oxford: Oxford University Press, 1978, on the various architectural influences upon, as well as the later influence *of*, the Palace of Cyrus the Great at Pasargadae. Speaking in particular to the palace and its garden as an important political vehicle, see also Stronach's "The Garden as a Political Statement" and "The Royal Garden at Pasargadae", the second of which is the source of the quote, p. 480.
36. On the Egyptian garden, see Wilkinson, *The Garden in Ancient Egypt.*
37. On the politics of planting in Egypt, see Wilkinson, *The Garden in Ancient Egypt*, especially pp. 3, 63; and in ancient Persia, see Pierre Briant, *From Cyrus to Alexander: A History of the Persian Empire*, Peter T. Daniels trans., Winona Lake, IN: Eisenbraun, 2002, pp. 234–235, 241, 329, 341, 526, 621, 713, 805, 873, 914, and 1014.
38. The complexity of ideological resonance in the Roman villa, particularly ostentatious display balancing rural virtue, is well-outlined in Nicholas Purcell "Dialectical Gardening", *Journal of Roman Archaeology* vol. 14, no. 2, 2001, pp. 546–556; Andrew Wallace-Hadrill, "Horti and Hellenization", *Horti Romani: Atti del Convegno Internazionale Roma, 4–6 maggio 1995*, Maddalena Cima and Eugenio La Rocca eds., Rome: L' Erma di Bretschneider, 1998, pp. 2–12; and Andrew Wallace-Hadrill, "The Villa as Cultural Symbol", *The Roman Villa: Villa Urbana*, Alfred Frazer ed., Philadelphia: University Museum, University of Pennsylvania, 1998, pp. 43–54.
39. As stated in Pliny the Elder's *Natural History* 19.50–51.
40. Howard Jones, *The Epicurean Tradition*, London: Routledge, 1989, provides a full discussion of Epicurus, his philosophy, and its influence.
41. Nostalgia, which is both backward and forward looking, as a dominant sensibility in Roman culture is treated more fully in Giesecke, *The Epic City*, pp. 126–155, the chapter entitled "Nostalgia and Virgil's Pastoral Dream".
42. These findings, including statistics, are Jashemski's, *The Gardens of Pompeii*, vol. I, pp. 1–24.
43. The derivation and semantic range of "*paradeisos*" is detailed in Bremmer, *The Rise and Fall of the Afterlife*, pp. 109–120 and also in the same author's previous work "Paradise from Persia, via Greece, into the *Septuagint*", *Paradise Interpreted: Representations of Biblical Paradise in Judaism and Christianity*, Gerald P. Luttikhuizen ed., Leiden: Brill, 1999, pp. 607–632.
44. As noted by Bremmer, *The Rise and Fall of the Afterlife*, p. 119.

Buildings replace the land. That is architecture's original sin.
/ Aaron Betsky[1]

What in heaven's name could she hope to accomplish with her frail arms? It was like trying to build a house in the sea by brushing the water aside.
/ Kobo Abé[2]

The opening frame of Hiroshi Teshigahara's 1964 cinematic adaptation of Kobo Abé's novel *Suna no Onna* (*The Woman in the Dunes*) reveals a close-up of a grain of sand; as the camera pans out, this minuscule particle of crushed rock melts into an abstract composition that appears to be sand raked in a wave pattern, reminiscent of a Japanese *karesansui* or dry landscape garden.[3] The grain's deceptive and foreboding purpose is slowly unearthed as the narrative unfolds. In Abé's existential and allegorical novel, sand is at once mysterious, merciless, and everywhere [Figure 1].

Figure 1/ *The Woman in the Dunes.*
Sand is at once mysterious, merciless, and everywhere.
Photograph by Donald Dunham.

The Woman in the Dunes centers around an amateur entomologist searching for insects among the sand dunes while on holiday near the seashore. Preoccupied with sand and insects, the man finds himself in a strange village where houses were built into large, deep depressions within the dunes. Having missed the last bus back to the railroad station, he is invited by the villagers to spend the night there. As darkness falls, the man is escorted to one of the sandpit houses, only accessible via a rope ladder that hangs down the sheer and unstable sand walls. At the bottom of the pit, its depth more than three times the height of the house, the man is met by a "smallish, nice sort of woman around 30".[4] While the man goes to sleep for the night, the woman shovels sand from around the small house into buckets that are hoisted up and out of the pit from above by village men. In the morning the man awakes to find the woman asleep, wearing only a coat of fine sand spread over her prostrate body. The rope ladder has vanished.

Unable to climb out of the sandpit without the aid of a ladder or rope, the man finds himself a captive; any attempt to scale the sand walls only results in an unclimbable avalanche of sand. Attempts to escape are in vain, and the man ultimately succumbs to the rigors of his new found destiny: shoveling sand alongside the woman into buckets that the villagers haul out of the sandtrap. The protagonist also realizes that without undertaking this constant nightly task, the house and the subterranean depression in which it sits will ultimately be completely immersed in sand. As the shifting winds continually blow sand into the hollow from the dunes above, the man slowly adjusts to his fate. He acknowledges that without this daily housekeeping ritual, nature will win out, and survival would be impossible. Yet in due course he discovers an additional facet of his predicament: there is another, more sinister purpose for his toil that is dictated not by an antagonistic 'nature' but by the human drive to exploit nature's bounty. Possessing a full understanding of nature's and society's demands—and bound by complex emotional ties—the man makes a surprising decision: when the rope ladder is inadvertently left down and he is given the chance to escape, he remains in the sand hole.

In Teshigahara's beautifully rendered and highly visual film, the man asks the woman, "Are you shoveling sand to live or living to shovel sand?"[5] This question, a conundrum for all those who contemplate it, is the basis for the following discussion, and as such, is the simple truth underlying humankind's relationship to the natural world, our world, the only world we can safely address. Abé's profoundly poetic construct, *The Woman in the Dunes*, also helps frame this discussion conceptually. Time, our ticking time bomb, is measured by the flow of sand intruding into the space that we have carved out of nature in order to live, and this relentless flow is also a metaphor for the simple hourglass. The seemingly dystopian task of clearing sand from around the hut in order to survive is partnered with the

ARCHITECTURE WITHOUT NATURE?

/DONALD DUNHAM

perceived belief of a better world beyond the sand dunes. This utopian vision—utopian at least from the point of view of a man captive within the sandpit—is shattered when the truth of his perceived Sisyphean circumstance is finally revealed: the village secretly sells the sand to construction companies to mix with cement to make concrete. The sand, which is saturated with salt, is sub-standard; this allows the villagers to sell the sand more cheaply. When the man questions the woman about the morality of this enterprise, explaining that buildings and dams will fail structurally through the use of tainted sand, the woman replies, "Why should we worry what happens to others?"[6]

In the face of this truth, could utopia and its adversarial complement, dystopia, actually reside elsewhere in this narrative? I suggest that the fluctuating space between the woman's hut and the ideologically corrupt dystopian village—along with the outside world—that so avidly exploits nature, is a mediated respite from competing visions. It is a utopian space commonly known as the garden.

THE SIMPLE LIFE?

The Utopians are very fond of their gardens.
/ Thomas More[7]

Once upon a time, life was simple, or was it? The answer to that question, of course, is impossible to know. From time immemorial the quest for survival has been fundamental to every life form, and, from a human perspective, survival often involves messy or complex endeavors. Humans have established an infinite number of metrics concerning what constitutes a good life, though a good life may or may not be a simple life. This disparity between good and simple shapes much of what humans do. The subject here, namely the relationship between architecture, nature, and the garden, is also messy and complex in its vastness. Constantly striving for constructs that contribute to a good if not better life, architecture is by its very nature utopian, but it is generally not what we might consider 'simple'. Hidden in the shadows of its making, architecture, for better or worse, leaves a nearly immeasurable debris field of discarded construction and manufacturing material, environmental damage, and unaccounted economic and human debt. But architecture, or at minimum, shelter, is fundamental to our being and our survival. The garden, it may be argued, like architecture, is also a utopian construct. From its most elaborate mythological incarnation, Eden, the garden has been perceived as nature perfected, a place where the glory and bounty of the Earth intersect, a place where all is provided. It goes without saying that Thomas More's Utopians would be and were "very fond of their gardens".[8] However, the garden, like architecture, is not a simple space, nor like architecture is it necessarily a 'good space'. But it is a necessary space.

Making is what humans do. We make offspring, shelter, food, excrement, clothing, weapons, war, money, art, energy, and misery; the list is of course endless. In fact our production far outpaces our needs: in highly-developed and developed countries most retail spaces overflow with items for sale while self-storage complexes continue to fill up with superfluous objects. Much of this production is designed to amuse or entertain, nothing else. This is not necessarily a bad thing; after all, the daily punishment of the 'real' often requires a lighter reality in the form of games, virtual realities, films, and music. Evidence of human tool-making stretches back at least 2.6 million years. And while much of this evidence points to the more pragmatic uses of tools, like hammering and cutting, it is also the case that some 40,000 years ago, musical instruments as well as two- and three-dimensional representations of the world were being made by humans. In any event, the evolution of making has certainly provided a multitude of successful and unsuccessful prototypes beyond the basic Paleolithic Oldowan toolkit, and while it may be argued by some that art and music making are endeavors unnecessary to human survival, anthropologists think otherwise.[9]

The purpose of making gardens, and garden history, are often misunderstood, misinterpreted, and inadequately documented. Architecture, on the other hand, has produced a far more extensive and 'transparent' historical record in literature and in physical remains. In the first century BCE, the Roman architect Vitruvius, exploring the substance and meaning of architecture in his book *De architectura*, wrote that buildings must exhibit the qualities of *firmitas, utilitas, venustas*—that is, architecture must exhibit strength, utility, and grace. Yet in his day, there was visible and tangible evidence that structures predating him possessed these qualities, and it still remains today.[10] By their very nature, gardens, as conventionally defined, quickly disappear, leaving little evidence of their existence if they are not maintained, while buildings, relying on durable exterior materials, enjoy greater longevity. It is true that garden remains can be forensically analyzed through radiocarbon dating, and that fossil remains provide some insight to their history, but the vast catalogue of gardens known to have existed throughout the ancient and modern eras has largely disappeared. The scant extant visual and literary evidence provides some useful clues but very little actual insight into what gardens may have afforded their users beyond utility, recreation, or the intellectual pursuit of beauty.

The earliest known literary description of a garden is found in the ancient Sumerian story *The Epic of Gilgamesh*. Three different versions were recorded on stone tablets over a period of 1,000 years, and all tell the stories of the well known deeds of the illustrious King of Uruk, Gilgamesh, c. 2700 BCE. Little doubt remains as to the existence of Gilgamesh, and the epic tale is ripe with adventure and unique encounters with the natural world as well as with god and human. Tablet IX finds Gilgamesh determined to discover the secret of eternal life, and after a dangerous journey complete with Scorpion-beings discouraging further adventure, Gilgamesh enters a garden. Of course this is no ordinary garden; here are trees that bear fruit in the form of precious stones and jewels. Interestingly, just as evidence of an untended garden's existence slips gracefully back into the earth, so too elemental nature has eroded the ancient tablets' legibility:

> [Before him there were] trees of precious stones,
> And he went straight to look at them.
> The tree bears carnelian as its fruit,
> Laden with clusters (of jewels), dazzling to behold,
> It bears lapis lazuli as foliage,
> Bearing fruit, a delight to look upon.

[25 lines are missing here, describing the garden in detail]

> ... cedar
> ... agate
> ... of the sea... lapis lazuli,
> Like thorns and briars... carnelian,
> ..., ... jasper
> Rubies, hematite, ...
> ...
> Like... emeralds (?)
> ... of the sea,
> ...
> Gilgamesh... on walking onward,
> Raised his eyes [and saw...].[11]

Pictorial representations also provide a small window into ancient horticultural gardens. For instance, a third century BCE relief in a tomb of Mereuka at Saqqara, Egypt, shows garden laborers irrigating subdivided planting beds. And physical remains of what appear to be similar planting beds dating from the second to third century BCE have been excavated at Mirgissa in present day Sudan. At what point the garden and house or settlement became more fully integrated, as opposed to the garden remaining well away from or auxiliary to domestic functions, is not known. However, archeological remains at Amarna, Egypt, suggest that horticultural gardens and orchards were contained within the city walls as early as the second century BCE. Meanwhile, excavations at Pasargadae, in present day Iran, have revealed a massive, walled palatial complex with gardens irrigated by a series of stone water channels that date to the sixth century BCE.[12] These ancient gardens demonstrate the human desire to live more closely to nature.

AN EMERALD PARADISE?

Beware of false prophets, which come to you in sheep's clothing, but inwardly they are ravening wolves.
/ Gospel of Matthew[13]

So what is a garden exactly? Is it an emerald paradise, or is it raked sand found in a Japanese *karesansui* garden? To some, of course, 'the garden' suggests gardening and whatever results from the manipulation of ground or space. The garden certainly involves planting, watering, nurturing, and cultivating, most often coupled with backbreaking work and disappointments. It can be a source of food as well as pleasure and contemplation. The garden can be a work of art. To others, the garden is a place to discover and unravel the history of a place and its people, providing an opportunity to analyze and to theorize; perhaps the results may tell us more about ourselves and what we do *outside* of the garden. I will admit here that I am not a gardener, but I have always admired this type of 'considered space' within the context of the built environment. I am an architect, and my relationship to the garden, gardeners, and landscape architects, has always been somewhat adversarial and murky at best. But I am married to a passionate gardener, who by making a garden has forced me to consider the garden in my work—not as a piece of design, but as a significant 'considered space'. I will also admit that not all gardens are things of beauty or pleasure to me. The generic front yard of mowed grass open to the street, overly manicured and uninspiring arrangements of specimen plantings, and difficult-to-maintain surfaces of groundcovers planted without attention to placemaking are gardens that do little to stir my interest or emotions. Aesthetically, a poorly executed planting might echo John Ruskin's words, "And the flower-garden is as ugly in effect as it is unnatural in feeling: it never will harmonize with anything, and if people will have it, should be kept out of sight till they get into it [*sic*]".[14] Other gardens, those that may have found their genesis on a landscape architect's drawing table or computer screen, are often overly pretentious in the precious and self-conscious way they are designed. That is not to say an abstract landwork cannot be both art and garden; a work that helps us connect with nature and alludes to several layers of discourse can be a rich experience. However, I prefer wild gardens, nature untamed encroaching on our patches of urbanity, the vagueness of reciprocity between the two in an uneasy balance, the threshold linking them constantly being negotiated, tended, and violated.

To begin to understand the garden conceptually, it is important to recognize which parameters *are crucial* to the garden. Without gardening, a garden cannot exist.

All gardeners, bent uncomfortably over their plants and their ground, will tell you this. Gardens only exist as a result of continuous human intervention, whether that intervention involves carving space out of a dark forest, or appropriating an empty space found between buildings in the city. This intervention quite likely has a very long history. When the first garden was made is open to conjecture, but the practice of enclosing exterior space goes back at least 10,000 years; the words "garden", "yard", "court", "park", and "paradise", all refer to enclosure etymologically.[15] Paradise more directly is derived from the ancient Persian *pairidaeza*, meaning "walled enclosure"; because of the magnificent qualities of such enclosures—often hunting parks and bountiful orchards—"paradise" became synonymous with the utopian qualities of any desirable place.

A garden also requires 'place'. By virtue of its sheer presence, a garden automatically activates a boundary condition. This boundary creates a specific site, or place. Martin Heidegger wrote, "A boundary is not that at which something stops but, as the Greeks recognized, the boundary is that, from which something begins its presencing [its 'being']".[16] Without 'place' the garden is not a willful construction. A deliberately planted tree in a clearing or space in the forest certainly reflects intentional action, but without continued acknowledgement of its existence, it becomes another tree in the forest, no longer able to claim right of place. It is at the complete mercy of nature untamed. Thus, the boundary condition must always be maintained or 'gardened' to establish 'place'. The precise nature of the boundary, whether established first or after the constructed intention, planted or otherwise, is immaterial. Often helter-skelter plantings or cultivation of nature determine the boundary condition after the fact. Remember, this is a space frequently in flux. 'Place' is also found in nature, as natural boundaries are formed by the line between sky and land or sea; between flat ground and hills or mountains; between ground and rivers or canyons; between woods and meadows, etc..

In their plans, landscape architects generally determine the boundary between nature and garden, and any other designed objects, such as buildings, pavilions, paths, or walls; architects usually envision the exterior face of their building as the boundary between it and nature. The purpose of the architectural boundary is two-fold: it clearly delineates the architect's responsibility, and through its making, is the edge of controlled or 'conditioned space' within.[17] Conditioned space is that part of a building that is designed to be thermally regulated for the comfort of occupants or for other reasons, although this control may be minimal. Needless to say, the materials used to make this external control barrier need to resist all forces of nature, and regular maintenance must be performed to insure the barrier's effectiveness. Beyond the architects'

Figure 2/

Beware of false prophets which come to you in sheep's clothing.
An untended garden quickly becomes nature's payback.
Photograph by Donald Dunham.

established line of intention is, to their minds, nature. Although architects generally consider site beyond the building 'envelope' or 'footprint', these gestures tend to be of less importance. Object-centric strategy is what architecture has always been about, and it persists today with very little opposition. For the architect, the garden is often less friend than foe, as an untended 'garden' quickly becomes nature [Figure 2]. While the architect designs with this likelihood in mind, structures can deteriorate rapidly due to an unruly garden's acting or encroaching on this boundary: "Beware of false prophets, which come to you in sheep's clothing, but inwardly they are ravening wolves."[18]

During a building's lifecycle, the natural weathering of its materials occurs. This sometimes graceful degradation of the architectural boundary is not always unwanted. It can be argued that this process is not only inevitable, but desirable. Mohsen Mostafavi and David Leatherbarrow caution us

> not to see finishing as the final moment of construction but to see the unending deterioration of a finish that results from weathering, the continuous metamorphosis of the building itself, as part of its beginning(s) and its ever-changing 'finish'.[19]

While corruption of the fragile dialogue between the building's exterior or 'skin' and nature is part of the natural lifecycle of materials (whether the material is used directly from the earth or after undergoing a manufacturing process), a tectonic demarcation line between the building's exterior and nature, however thin, must always remain under watch.

ARCHITECTURE *WITHOUT* NATURE?

Architecture is what nature is unable to do.
/ Louis I. Kahn[20]

Nature and the garden play a part, not only in contextualizing architecture, but also in organizing building functions, shaping building form, selecting materials, and ultimately, determining architecture's cultural and societal value. Architecture is inevitably an expression of its culture: building forms are a result of what is important, and not important to its makers. While this all may seem self-evident, it is nevertheless the case that in the design of buildings, nature is often substituted by its far tamer surrogate, the garden. This misstep has led to the demise of many structures, their ultimate state of neglect or unusable ruin from non-maintenance attributed to programmatic, political, or economic issues. The truth is that in such instances, the architecture has been considered without nature, not merely in the mechanical sense, but in the aesthetic.

The garden and its formal partners, nature and architecture, have had a long history. As the garden has become synonymous with nature, architecture has formed an uneasy but inseparable bond with the garden, which serves as the intermediary between nature and our built environment. Simply put, Laugier's 'primitive hut' mandated some type of clearing, pruning, and/or adjustment to nature, albeit minimal [Figure 3].[21] Another early example of this would be the ancient Greek *temenos*, which literally means "an off-cut". This refers to a marked-off exterior space, a cleared area of land within the woods, or a grove of trees defined by a parametrical clearing and dedicated to a god or holy purpose. The ancient temple building, a ring of columns surrounding an open space, may have been an imitation of this. As the clearing or 'garden paradise' gained traction, the utopian currency of this space increased. Architecture benefitted not only from the contextualizing aesthetic and new-found utopian qualities of the garden, but also from the pragmatic buffering it provided. Architecture has conveniently sought its place in the world *without* nature. Although structures are generally designed to withstand the forces of gravity, wind, and earthquake, and to resist the invasive nature of water, without periodic exterior maintenance, nature *will* intrude beyond the building's delineating boundary; as Betsky reminds us, "... nature always creeps in".[22] This 'formal' edge condition can be invisible, or disguised; this space, the negotiator between nature and human-made constructions, is at once considered

Figure 3/ The Primitive Hut.
The frontispiece of Marc-Antoine Laugier's *Essai sur l'Architecture*, 1755.

a mechanical and aesthetic barrier. The space may be vast or a mere incision, formal or informal, or in the most abstract sense, an idea of immeasurable dimension, or even a structural calculation. In all cases, it must be inspected and/or maintained.

What then *is* the space, if any, between human intentions and nature? The garden? And can architecture exist without this critical space and simultaneously not risk material degradation? The hard leaning and well-intentioned prophets of oneness with nature would have us believe we can go shoulder to shoulder with nature, the thin line between nature and ourselves barely discernible or even dissolved. Ian McHarg writes in *Design with Nature*, "It is indeed only the man who believes himself apart from nature who needs... a garden."[23] As a species, we are indeed part of the natural world; however, few, if given the choice, would prefer to bed down for the night *directly* with nature.

While it is true that many architects have struggled with the line between design and nature, others have seen the boundary as an advantage, making their work mimic nature and often fooling us into believing we are one big happy family. Although technology can and does allow for integrative bio-mimetic design, and certainly more sensible and sustainable architecture and urban strategies, ultimately a line between nature and our constructed interventions is present, even if invisible to the naked eye. From another perspective, architect Louis Kahn stated, "Architecture is what nature is unable to do."[24] That may be true, but as designers further appropriate nature, will nature further appropriate architecture? As William McDonough and Michael Braungart write in *Cradle-to-Cradle*:

> Nature doesn't have a design problem. People do.... Instead of using nature as a mere tool for human purposes, we can strive to become tools of nature who serve its agenda too.... What would it mean to become, once again, native to this place, the Earth —the home of all our relations?[25]

Discarded human artifacts do become armatures for natural constructions; purposefully sunken marine vessels form successful living artificial reefs. Apparently the fine line between nature and us may not be necessary from the point of view of nature, or is it? The Gaia Hypothesis perhaps correctly suggests that *all* of our planet's organic and inorganic systems are part of an integrated *cooperating* organization necessary to the maintenance of Earth. Hmmm....

WHAT THE HELL ARE WE TALKING ABOUT?

Architects could never explain space.
/ Rem Koolhaas[26]

Garden and landscape theorist and historian John Dixon Hunt provides an inclusive and thorough definition of what a garden is. His definition is so carefully constructed that it tends to read more like a contract written up by an attorney or solicitor, and is much too long to insert into the body of this text in its entirety:

> A garden will normally be out-of-doors, a relatively small space of ground (relative, usually, to accompanying buildings or topographical surroundings).... The specific area of the garden will be deliberately related through various means to the locality in which it is set: by the invocation of indigenous plant materials, by various modes of representation or other forms of reference (including association) to that larger territory.... Either it will have some precise boundary, or it will be set apart by the greater extent, scope, and variety of its design and internal organization; more usually, both will serve to designate its space and its actual or implied enclosure. A combination of inorganic and organic materials are strategically invoked for a variety of usually interrelated reasons—practical, social, spiritual, aesthetic—all of which will be explicit or implicit expressions or performances of their local culture. The garden will therefore take different forms and be subject to different uses....[27]

While there is no shortage of highly prescriptive texts on garden design and making from the Middle Ages onward, Hunt's specificity provides a broader, more inclusive explanation as to what a garden is.[28] By comparison, other definitions—the plant, soil, water, and sun variety—seem too limiting and ill-prepared to accept the challenges that landscape architects, architects, gardeners, and garden designers may propose and propagate. Simple or more classical definitions are also problematic here; they suggest that a garden is a self-contained space without the possibility of any outside interventions or hybridizing transformations:

> *Garden:* A plot of ground used principally for growing vegetables, fruits, or flowering and/or ornamental plants. / Cyril M. Harris, *Dictionary of Architecture and Construction*[29]

I would like to take Hunt's definition (which, by the way, I like very much) and add to it:

> *Garden:* [Hunt's definition]+ any declared space that is manipulated through human intention beyond that which is previously defined.

With that being said, I would like to explore the idea of architecture without nature (or, put differently, architecture and its unconditional dependence on the garden), by examining several examples of architecture, most of which will be well known, or perhaps recognizable, to the reader. This of course may take a leap of faith for those who may still believe the garden is for the most part, "A plot of ground used principally for growing vegetables, fruits, or flowering and/or ornamental plants." But the garden can be much more than that, just as architecture can be much more than an igloo or the Eiffel Tower. What is problematic here is that definitions of architecture are not quite as tidy as the aforementioned amended garden definition. But for the sake of this discussion I would like to put forward my own, which I am hoping will encompass the traditional boilerplate definition as well as the plethora of more contractual definitions, such as Hunt's garden definition.[30]

> *Architecture:* 1. The art and science of designing and building structures, communities, or open areas, in keeping with aesthetic and functional criteria. 2. Structures built in accordance with such principals./ Cyril M. Harris, *Dictionary of Architecture and Construction*[31]

My definition:

> *Architecture:* any declared space that is manipulated through human intention beyond that which is previously defined.

There is probably some truth to the observation by architect Rem Koolhaas that "architects could never explain space".[32] All of this 'spacetalk' is slippery stuff; ask ten architects, "What is 'space'?" The result would be ten never-ending works in progress; ask the same architects what constitutes a garden, and you might get a more concise reply, along the lines of "nature controlled"; however, they are just as likely to suggest that "nature is the garden", implying greater primeval authenticity (or beauty). This leaning toward eighteenth century philosopher Jean-Jacques Rousseau's ideas of the divine inherent in nature versus the more imitative control found in the gardens of the English Picturesque, makes it more difficult to clarify what a garden is in the context of the natural environment and architecture.[33] Landscape architects are not immune to the conflation of nature and garden either; during the mid-nineteenth century, Frederick Olmstead, pioneer of American landscape architecture, became the first overseer of Yosemite Valley in California and an advocate for a hands-off policy there. At the time, Yosemite "quickly gained the reputation of most beautiful natural landscape in America, the ideal garden of the New World", reinforcing the notion of nature as the garden.[34] However, according to Cyril Harris (and others), the garden, being part of the built environment, is clearly not 'natural':

> *Natural environment:* The aggregate of the natural external surroundings and conditions, in contrast to the built environment (i.e., those surroundings and conditions resulting from construction by human beings)./ Cyril M. Harris, *Dictionary of Architecture and Construction*[35]

It could be stated that anything not reliant on human intervention is part of nature; this classical assumption—'human' nature versus nature as the 'other'—suggests that human beings are apart from, rather than a part of, nature. Therefore, I will leave the definition of *nature* up to you.

VILLA VALS: THE GARDEN FENCE?

Good fences make good neighbors.
/ Robert Frost[36]

Vals, Switzerland, is a small alpine village in the southeast corner of the country, high in the Swiss Alps. This remote village lies virtually at road's end in the stunningly beautiful, fissured, and wild Valser Valley. With a population of just over 1,000, Vals is best known for its "*Valserwasser*" mineral water and thermal springs. The first spa hotel, Therme, opened in 1893; in 1996 a new thermal spa opened to replace the cramped and dilapidated bathing facilities of the 1960s era Therme hydro hotel. Pritzker Prize winning architect Peter Zumthor was commissioned to design a new separate spa building, resulting in a play of light, stone, mountain, and water. Built with horizontal Valser *gneiss* or quartzite, the dense stonework initiates a dialogue with the extreme geology and topography of the Valser Valley. Two years after the completion of the therme, the building was granted historic status, and Vals has since become a destination for architectural connoisseurs and those wishing to experience the therapeutic benefits of the thermal mineral springs and the drama of the narrow Valser Valley.

In the late 1990s, Dutch architect Bjarne Mastenbroek had visited Zumthor's therme and, overwhelmed by the landscape, was determined to build a holiday villa in Vals. Mastenbroek teamed with architect Christian Müller, and the two designed a house on a site adjacent to Zumthor's building. Unwilling to compete architecturally with either the powerful design of the therme, the vernacular timber and stone farmhouses found in Vals, or the 1960s architecture of the Hotel Therme, the pair submerged the villa into a steep hillside below the therme [Figure 4]. This effectively concealed the structure from the therme's view. Seen from below, however, the burrowed form is revealed as a hole in the face of the incline; this opening allows light and air into the villa. An elliptical patio set within the concavity of the quartzite stone front wall is the resultant focal point of the composition. Although this is not the first modern building excavated into the ground, here, by contrast, the cylindrical boring gives rise to a precise and minimalist expression that is seemingly void of any separation between object and nature. To further reinforce this geometric precision, entrance is via a tunnel accessed through an adjacent barn on the slope below the Villa.

In 1948, 60 years before Villa Vals took form, Frank Lloyd Wright's Herbert Jacobs House 2 was completed. In 1937, Jacobs and his family moved into the first Usonian house designed by Wright, the Herbert Jacobs House 1;

Figure 4/ Villa Vals.
Submerged. Photograph by Iwan Baan.

Jacobs had challenged Wright by asking the architect, "What this country needs is a decent five thousand-dollar house. Can you build it?"[37] Wright was able to deliver the completed house, including his fee, for $5,500. Subsequently, when the expanding city of Madison, Wisconsin began to encroach on the Jacobs' somewhat rural Usonian Shangri-La, Jacobs bought a 52 acre farm outside of Madison with the intention of having Wright design another house for his family. Wright had been toying for several years with what he would call "The Solar Hemicycle" house; with the Jacobs family anxious for a new design, Wright again tried out a prototype structure on his clients. The house, like Villa Vals, has a concave front wall facing south; the rear of the house is built into an earth-berm. Interestingly, like Vals, it too is accessed via a tunnel. Wright, who is well known for his designs that integrated architecture and nature, wanted the entry sequence to incorporate complete immersion into the earth while reinforcing ingress choreography through anticipation and surprise, prospect and refuge. This subterranean journey effectively takes the occupant from the more dominant natural environment into the realm of architectural spatial control, an experience shared by Villa Vals. Architects commonly use a physical threshold to disconnect the architectural experience from its contextual ground; for instance, Richard Meier's 1973 Douglas House, on Lake Michigan, USA, and Mario Botta's 1973 House at Riva San Vitale, Ticino, Switzerland, both employ entry footbridges spanning between elevated ground and the structure as disengagement devices.

Another burrowed house that bears resemblance to Vals is the 1996 House in Wales, UK [Figure 5]. Designed by the late Future Systems architects as a weekend retreat, the house sits partially buried within bermed ground high above the sublime expanse of St. Brides Bay, seemingly hermetically sealed off from the immediate environment. Two glazed walls akin to a 'glove box' allow access, air, daylight, and views. Here the berm is cleaved to allow entry into the structure, the drama of its context unfolding as one is drawn into the house; unlike at Vals, a physical threshold was seemingly unnecessary. However, if one looks closely at the highly controlled, flat turf roof covering, a faint line is visible at the perimeter of the berm's top edge. This line, a line of demarcation between nature and intent, is for all practical purposes, the garden's formal boundary. At Villa Vals, a similar line exists; however, where at Wales some ambiguity beyond the roof edge is present, blurring the transition between nature and garden, at Vals, no such ambiguity exists.

Figure 5/ House in Wales.
A garden exists between nature and intent.
Courtesy of Amanda Levete Architects.

Clearly the garden space at Villa Vals is the elliptical semi-walled exterior patio, a premeditated consequence of the coring exercise. As deliberate as a *karesansui* garden, this space not only frames views of the mountain backdrop in a most dramatic fashion, but also invites the occupants into the steeply inclined exterior space—on level ground. However, it is neither patio nor views that capture one's eye, but rather the edge of this alpine garden. At the upper conclusion of this continuous cylindrical coring, stretching around the perimeter rim from the highest point down to just below the ellipse's mid-point, is a fence [Figure 6]. This is no ordinary picket enclosure; the fence, a series of radiating steel tubes suggesting the axial coring angle, are connected by netting. Designed as a guardrail to protect against falls from above, the fence was also designed to help protect against avalanche. This crucial device, perhaps the most important part of the garden space, surgically separates nature from human intention.

Figure 6/ Villa Vals.
In the garden, good fences make good neighbors. Courtesy of SeARCH.

B018: INSCRIBING THE GARDEN?

A nation which lives a pastoral and innocent life never decorates the shepherd's staff or the plough-handle; but races who live by depredation and slaughter nearly always bestow exquisite ornaments on the quiver, the helmet, and the spear.
/ John Ruskin[38]

Seeing B018 by the light of day, it is hard for the uninitiated to imagine anything beyond what is visible: a derelict, forgotten space bordering a motorway in an industrial area of Beirut, Lebanon, known as the Quarantaine [Figure 7]. One does not expect to find mesmeric, powerful architecture, nor does one expect to find a garden. Yet lurking beneath the surface, with only its prehistoric, reptilian spine evident—much like a watchful and partially submerged crocodile—is a prince of darkness, music club B018.

The Quarantaine is located adjacent to Beirut's main port, and was once a quarantine area for arriving immigrants and ship crews. During the Lebanese Civil War, 1975–1990, the Quarantaine area was home to over 20,000 Palestinian, Kurdish, and South Lebanese refugees, and was largely destroyed during the Karantina Massacre by Lebanese Christian militias.[39] For more than 20 years the Quarantaine sector continued to remain isolated from the city until 1998 when underground club impresario Naji Gebran moved his clandestine night scene into a new 'building' designed by Lebanese architect Bernard Khoury. Gebran had begun his club in his apartment, code named B018, during some of the worst years of the Lebanese Civil War as a form of "musical therapy".[40] After the war ended, B018 moved into a warehouse before relocating to the Quarantaine. Khoury's design "refuses to participate to the naïve amnesia that governs the post-war reconstruction efforts"; the bunker-like structure and its exposed armor shielding recall the savage violence of war.[41] The below-grade interior space of the club is entered through 'airlocks' accessed via a slender stair from the radial parking area that circumscribes the buried

Figure 7/ B018.
Aerial view of the nightclub and garden.
Courtesy of Bernard Khoury/DW5.

structure. Within this subterranean space, coffinesque furniture serves as impromptu dance platforms; when the hinged top is opened, cushioned seating is revealed. Above the dancers, steel roof panels slide open to reveal the night sky and to help cool the interior space, while another steel panel, mirrored to the interior cavity below, hinges up to a 50 degree angle [Figure 8]. Headlights from encircling cars and from motorway traffic as well as lights from the city are reflected down into the club. Reciprocally, light from the club is projected on the mirrored panel, visible to the arriving club-goers and to those driving on the motorway. The mirrored surface is at once a screen, and a symbolic gesture akin to raising a flag as an act of defiance or an unwillingness to accept defeat; it not only reflects the reality of the city in real-time, but also reflects the memory of its history.

This is covert space-making to be sure; while exploiting the politics and history of its site, Bo18 is capable of remaining almost invisible, while at the same time being the dominant focal point within its own political boundary. The cavity and its protective *testudo*, or tortoise shell, is firmly pressed into the earth; at grade it is surrounded by a circular concrete disc ringed by an asphalt drive with parking spaces separated by small lights radiating in a concentric ring at the perimeter. At the site's boundary line is a small gap: here at the outer ring's edge, nature has attempted to intervene, to make its presence known. Plants struggle to form a defensive screen sandwiched between the motorway, the Quarantaine, and Bo18. Despite the perceived hostility to the 'natural environment', nature exists. So where is the garden here?

Landscape architects, architects, and garden designers have all pushed the boundaries of gardencraft. Inscribing gardens into the Earth's crust, whether through hardscaping or through more pliable and sometimes less durable materials, has often rendered spectacular place-making. These spaces, usually defined as "urban design" or "landscape architecture or design", are in fact garden spaces. For instance, while a sidewalk is a sidewalk, it can be, and usually is, a garden space. Examples of the sidewalk garden, or pedestrian thoroughfare garden, range from the dreary to the magnificent. Modernist landscape architect Roberto Burle Marx's design of the four kilometer long, highly abstract, wave-patterned Copacabana promenade garden, 1970, is an urban garden space of iconic proportions. The recent Seattle Olympic Sculpture Park is an art garden while at the same time solving pedestrian infrastructural needs in the city. As in these cases, at Bo18, the inscription of the project onto its site is clearly visible. Looking at satellite photographs of Beirut, it is quite easy to find Bo18 amidst several millennia of competing town planning strategies; the genesis of Khoury's plan suggests that it was born from determining place and then taking possession of it. This careful and yet potent placement

Figure 8/ Bo18.
Sutured into the city's memory by its garden.
Courtesy of Bernard Khoury/DW5.

of the project within Beirut, a city still haunted by the memory of a 15 year war and its aftermath, is etched into the city fabric, much like the infamous Green Line that once divided the city. Like Le Corbusier's plan for Chandigarh and Lucio Costa's plan for Brasília, which was "akin to a cosmic gesture for marking out a symbolic place on the vast virgin landscape of the Brazilian interior", Khoury has implanted a new history on ground where the future also remains uncertain.[42] These prototype utopias all negotiate their fragility between architecture and nature with garden spaces; at Brasília and Chandigarh the monumental horizontality of the garden landscape not only frames the buildings, but dominates them. At Bo18, it is the horizontal asphalt drive and radiating parking spaces between the concrete disc and perimeter gap that function effortlessly and magnificently as the garden.

It is impossible to enter the club without passage through this highly abstract garden space; it is an essential piece of the precise choreography that Khoury has designed. The garden is often part of a building's entry sequence, and many of Khoury's projects exploit the garden as an architectural element. Khoury's Centrale, 2001, in Beirut, is not only a restaurant, bar, and experience extraordinaire, but it is also a poetic study in historical shifts, decay, and like all of Khoury's work, a dynamic tectonic undertaking of the most fastidious and inventive kind. Entry to Centrale is off a small street from which the visitor passes first through a wall of trees before being confronted with the first of many architectonic surprises. Like Bo18, Centrale fails to succumb to amnesia, and it too is fully inscribed to place, sutured into the city's memory by its garden.[43]

FREY HOUSE: BLURRING THE LINE?

This dawning sense of the Within as reality when it is clearly seen as Nature will by way of glass, steel and concrete make the garden be the building as much as the building will be the garden: the sun and sky as treasured a feature of daily indoor life as the ground itself.
/ Frank Lloyd Wright[44]

In October 1928 at age 25, Swiss architect Albert Frey found work in the expanding atelier of Parisian architects Le Corbusier and Pierre Jeanneret. Frey had entered France on a student visa with the intention of working for Le Corbusier before ultimately travelling on to the United States; the USA was a country that Frey felt was at the forefront of progress and technology, issues important to young European architects at the time. However, Frey believed that Le Corbusier was more 'American' in his architecture than Frank Lloyd Wright, and for this reason the young architect wanted to work in his studio.[45] After Frey had shown Jeanneret his portfolio, Jeanneret told him, "We could use you", and within a short time, he was working on one of Le Corbusier's masterpieces, Villa Savoye.[46] Villa Savoye at Poissy, which lies in the western suburbs of Paris, was completed two years later in 1931. In essence the iconic structure acted as a laboratory for Le Corbusier's basic principles on architecture, the "Five Points". These five tenets of architectural aesthetics advocated the use of: 'pilotis' or column supports, roof gardens, an open plan, horizontal 'ribbon' windows, and a non-load-bearing facade. This manifesto codified a new style of architecture that has endured into the twenty-first century.

Villa Savoye is set well back from the roadway, initially hidden from view behind a dense cluster of trees. As the house comes into view, one cannot help but notice an elevated, horizontal white box floating above the long gravel drive. Upon closer inspection, this elevation reveals a vertical plane gently touching the ground, while on the three remaining elevations, slender pilotis reinforce the lightness of the structure. What the pilotis achieve is to effectively disengage the house from the ground, unlike Villa Vals or the Jacobs House 2, where the design intent was to fully immerse the building into the site, merging structure and earth. At Villa Savoye, the building becomes an object in a distinct and barren landscape, with nature-at-large well clear of the architect's intent [Figure 9]. Here a roof garden therapeutically brings nature-as-ornament directly into the house, much as ancient Roman villas, of which Le Corbusier was extraordinarily fond, incorporated gardens within their exterior walls. The ribbon windows and openings at Villa Savoye, which extend almost unbroken horizontally around the elevated box, provide uninterrupted framed views of nature and the distant horizon beyond; not unlike the house itself, nature—as if it were an object in a museum—is to be observed, considered, and experienced as an aesthetic exercise.

Figure 9/ Villa Savoye. Much like the house itself, as if it were an object in a museum, nature is to be observed, considered, and experienced—as an aesthetic exercise. Photograph: Scala/White Images/Art Resource, NY. © 2011 Artists Rights Society (ARS), New York/ ADAGP. Paris/FLC.

Frey would leave Le Corbusier and Jeanneret, and arrived in New York City in September of 1930. There he quickly found work in the office of A. Lawrence Kocher, with whom he designed and built the Aluminaire house, a low cost pre-fabricated demonstration house for the Allied Arts and Building Products annual exhibition in 1931. In 1932 the Aluminaire was selected to be included in the Museum of Modern Art's groundbreaking International Exhibition of Modern Architecture show; the house reflected the influence of Le Corbusier, especially that of Villa Savoye. Late in 1934, Frey left for Palm Springs, California, to oversee the construction of a modest garden office-apartment building that he had designed for Kocher's brother, a physician practicing in the small desert resort town about 100 miles east of Los Angeles. This humble, open-plan building integrated International Style architecture, small planted garden spaces, the desert sky, and the San Jacinto Mountains that project steeply above the desert floor. Frey returned to New York in 1938 only to depart a year later, again for Palm Springs, where he lived and worked until his death in 1998.

Frey, who kept up a correspondence with Le Corbusier, wrote to him in 1936: "The California desert continues to charm me.... It is a most interesting experience to live in a wild, savage, natural setting."[47] In 1940 Frey designed his first desert house, the Frey House I. This work would help establish a new desert Modernism, and was composed of an interplay of vertical and horizontal planes. Less Villa Savoye and more Barcelona Pavilion—the 1929 iconic Modernist work of German architect Ludwig Mies van der Rohe—the diminutive Frey House I blurred the line between interior and exterior spaces by extending interior walls out into the landscape, and by using glass as 'planes' of transparency. Frey would take this idea even further in the 1946 desert house for industrial

Figure 10/ Loewy House.
Nature creeping in. © J. Paul Getty Trust. Used with permission.
Julius Shulman Photography Archive, Research Library at the Getty Research Institute (2004.R.10).

designer Raymond Loewy; not only does the house move further out into the landscape, but the landscape actually moves into the house [Figure 10]. The house, built adjacent to a large desert boulder field, is at the same time part of the boulder colony; the massive rocks engage the pond-like swimming pool while a portion of the pool, along with another large boulder, 'enters' the house through a retractable wall of glass [Figure 11]. This garden, as it completes its metamorphic transformation from "a wild, savage, natural setting" to the carefully configured Modernist composition designed by Frey, more than blurs the line between nature and architecture. In a sense, the garden becomes a true surrogate for nature, although the threshold of responsibility is beautifully vague, dynamic, and serenely electrifying.

Frey is not the first Modern architect to attempt such overt co-mingling of nature, garden, and architecture; Frank Lloyd Wright's design for a weekend home for Edgar

Figure 11/ Loewy House.
Nature creeping in, all the way in. © J. Paul Getty Trust. Used with permission. Julius Shulman Photography Archive, Research Library at the Getty Research Institute (2004.R.10).

Figure 12/ Fallingwater.
Living alongside of nature. Photograph: Art Resource, NY. © 2011 Frank Lloyd Wright Foundation/Artists Rights Society (ARS), New York.

Figure 13/ Casa Malaparte.
Emerging from the rock to which it is married.
Photograph by Thomas Reichart.

Kaufmann, the 1936–1939 Fallingwater, is built steadfastly to its rock-strewn site while it hovers above a 30 foot waterfall. Wright made allowances in the structure to accommodate existing trees; at one time a large tree penetrated the terrace off of Kaufmann's bedroom. While Fallingwater fits hand-in-glove into the dramatic site, it is first and foremost a composition, seemingly unwilling to concede its dominance over place [Figure 12]. The line between nature and architecture is clearly defined and detailed. A less-known dwelling, Casa Malaparte on the island of Capri, is a more challenging and far more aggressive site-bound structure. As a composition of materiality and place, it is as organic as Michelangelo's *Atlas Slave*, yet far more composed. Unlike Villa Vals or even Future System's House in Wales, the line is not only vague and uncertain, but intentionally scrubbed clean. The authorship of the house has always been in doubt, but most agree the principal designer was client and original owner, Italian writer Curzio Malaparte. Construction of the house began in 1938 based on a plan by architect Adalberto Libera and was more or less completed in 1942; however, the design had deviated from Libera's original plans. Located on an isolated rock promontory on Capri's eastern edge, the house appears to "emerge from the rock to which it is married" [Figure 13].[48] Here, architecture confronts nature and at the same time accepts its conditions; when building so closely to nature, failure is always a risk. In 1940 Malaparte wrote from Capri:

> There was in Capri, in its wildest, most solitary and dramatic part, in that part completely oriented toward the south and east, where the human island becomes savage and nature expresses itself with incomparable and cruel strength, a promontory of extraordinary pure lines, lunging at the sea with its rocky spur.... For it is easy to let oneself be overcome by nature, to become its slave, to be crushed by those delicate and violent jaws, to be swallowed by nature like Jonah the whale. It became clear to me from the beginning that not only the outline of the house, its architecture, but also the building materials had to fit with that wild and delicate landscape. No bricks, no concrete, but stone, of the local kind, from which the cliff, the mountain is made.[49]

Without a doubt, the precipitous and spectacular coastline of Capri is subjected to the occasional wrath of nature; however, in the California desert, nature can and regularly does subject architecture to extremes in temperature, intense ultraviolet radiation exposure, and pitting from sand storms. It was in this desert environment that Viennese Modernist Richard Neutra, another transplanted European architect, found work. Neutra, like Frey, had made a pilgrimage to the United States, but unlike Frey, he was determined at least to meet, if not work for, Frank Lloyd Wright. In 1923, Neutra arrived in New York City, and just over a year later was working for Wright at Taliesin in Spring Green, Wisconsin. He would leave three months later. Neutra was consumed with nature

Figure 14/ Kaufmann Desert House.
A dynamic continuum. © J. Paul Getty Trust. Used with permission.
Julius Shulman Photography Archive, Research Library at the Getty Research Institute (2004.R.10).

and the place of human beings in the universe; in fact the very first word in chapter one of Neutra's 1954 *Survival Through Design* is "Nature".[50] For Neutra, nature was all-encompassing, a "dynamic continuum"; this meant that human beings lived as 'one with' nature, as opposed to Wright's notions of living closely 'alongside with' nature.[51] Neutra's work also manifested another crucial difference from Wright's; where Wright always considered the hearth to be the epicenter of the home, Neutra felt that the most important space in a house was the ambiguous threshold between inside and outside.[52] Evidence of this is seen in Neutra's own 1932 van der Leeuw (VDL) Research House in Los Angeles, California. Interior spaces stretch beyond opened folding glass and steel doors to reveal what appears to be interior/exterior space; the line of architectural control between inside and outside has vanished. Similarly, Neutra's 1937 Miller House in Palm Springs acknowledged the brutal sun and wind angles of the exposed desert site, while walls of transparent glazing suggested a seamless transition out to the landscape, though without the same determination as the VDL. However, it is in Neutra's design for Edgar Kaufmann's Palm Springs house that interior and exterior space, architecture, garden, and nature, merge at every opportunity [Figure 14]. Interestingly, Kaufmann had passed over Wright, apparently unimpressed with Taliesin West, and hired the former Wright disciple. The Kaufmann Desert House, 1946, sits atop the desert plane, in a sense extending the landscape through the house by exploiting the inherent horizontality of the site. Like Albert Frey's House I, the Kaufmann House borrows heavily from Mies van der Rohe's Barcelona Pavilion, the exchanging of spatial territories accomplished through planar extension and sliding glass walls. An open-air rooftop terrace, the 'gloriette' defined by another horizontal roof plane, is visually anchored to the masonry chimney mass; this terrace is enclosed on two sides by movable vertical louvers that deflect wind and the relentless invasion of sand. Nevertheless, while nature is front and center, a clear line defines what is what, and who is who: in places this line is etched into the site as carefully as a surgeon's first cut, in other places, as broadly and expansively as the generous site will allow. This line is defined by the track of the retractable glass walls, the plane of the closed aluminum louvers on the gloriette, and the tended lawn around the moonscape of intentionally placed desert boulders. This line is the garden. Without it, the carefully staged architectonics of the Kaufmann Desert House would soon succumb to the fate of Abé's literary house in the dunes.

Perhaps the most masterful blurring of nature and architecture occurs in Albert Frey's 1964 Frey House II, located on the steep lower slopes of San Jacinto Mountain overlooking the city of Palm Springs and the desert beyond. The focal point of the small glass and steel structure is not the commanding view of the city or the rugged mountainscape; it is a colossal boulder that appears to have tumbled down the mountain face and to have lodged itself between the underside of the roof and ground, penetrating the glass wall [Figure 15]. Or perhaps the rock has emerged from the earth and pushed its way through the house, like tree limbs that swallow up suspended utility lines, fences, and other objects. This is not a tender or staged encounter with nature; this is a violent, raw, and highly sensual brush-up of the most dangerous kind. No more planar play, or diaphanous garden-making, this is the real deal, nature clearly and firmly taking possession of architectural space. Did Frey intend to demonstrate the obsolescence of garden space? Is this what Rousseau envisioned? Is nature the garden after all? At first glance, yes. But look closely at the rock; dead-center is a light switch [Figure 16]. Suddenly the monumental rock appears tame, not quite the threatening unpredictable behemoth of nature's wrath. Here, nature has been appropriated, yes tamed, much in the same way that all building materials are scooped from the earth and *manipulated through human intention beyond that which is previously defined.* In Frey House II, the thin glass line separating the boulder from inside and out, a line that seems quite improbable, is the garden.

Figure 15/ Frey House II.
Blurring the line. © J. Paul Getty Trust. Used with permission. Julius Shulman Photography Archive, Research Library at the Getty Research Institute (2004.R.10).

NEW GREEN: LIVING IN THE GARDEN?

If one were to give up a fixed position and abandon oneself to the movement of the sands, competition would soon stop. Actually, in the desert flowers bloomed and insects and other animals lived their lives. These creatures were able to escape competition through their great ability to adjust.
/ Kobo Abé[53]

While it is true that architecture can circumscribe nature or 'nature transplanted', examples being the Eden Project in Cornwall, UK, or the glass houses at Kew Gardens, etc., the resultant enclosed spaces are manifestly gardens. According to Eden's creators, "We built the Eden Project in Cornwall in a disused clay mine, transforming it into a rich, global garden where people can learn about nature and get inspiration about the world around them."[54] Experimental sealed vivariums such as Biosphere 2 in Arizona, USA, where humans participate with nature while it is propagated and observed, remain as docile gardens of science. Yet designers of space occupiable by humans continue to attempt not just to tame, control, or appropriate nature, but like Neutra, to become one with it, effectively exiling the garden as a relic to a cabinet of curiosities. Such was flamboyant Viennese colorist painter, architectural designer, and ecologist Friedensreich Hundertwasser who wrote in 1972, "FREE NATURE MUST GROW WHEREVER SNOW AND RAIN FALL.... THE MAN-TREE RELATIONSHIP MUST ASSUME RELIGIOUS PROPORTIONS."[55] Hundertwasser's work boldly placed gardens on and in several of his projects, most notably in the 'utopian' Hundertwasser House in Vienna, 1986. However, the *substantial* green areas here continue to remain, for the most part, as surface delight, providing shade, adding

Figure 16/ Frey House II.
Nature appropriated. © J. Paul Getty Trust. Used with permission.
Julius Shulman Photography Archive, Research Library at the Getty Research Institute (2004.R.10).

color, and conditioning the air we breathe.[56] Nevertheless, Hundertwasser, who was primarily known as a surface artist and architectural greenist, may have provided the inspiration for many of the new green projects. A series of architectural models that he produced between 1974 and 1975 bear a striking resemblance to Villa Vals and Future System's House in Wales, as well as to several recent projects by other architects.[57] Like Hundertwasser, another 'early' green provocateur, architect Emilio Ambasz, attempts to engage nature and architecture, although with a greater sense of ritual and narrative. Yet unlike Hundertwasser, Ambasz clearly sees a disconnect between human need and nature:

> The ideal gesture would be to arrive at a plot of land which is so immensely fertile and welcoming that, slowly, the land would assume a shape—providing us with an abode. And within this abode—being such a magic space—it would never rain, nor would there ever be inclemencies of any other sort. We must build our house on Earth only because we are not welcome on the land. Every act of construction is a defiance of nature. In a perfect nature, we would not need houses.[58]

Figure 17/ Fukuoka Prefectural International Hall. The boundaries between architecture and nature are remarkably never in doubt. Courtesy of Emilio Ambasz.

In Ambasz's work, naturalistic gestures imitative of nature are formally synthesized within architectural compositions [Figure 17]. While the boundaries between architecture and nature are never in doubt, one suspects that nature could potentially hijack the enterprise without undue harm to the structure or regret on the part of its users. Only when viewing one of Ambasz's cross-sectional drawings, does it become evident that the architecture is well protected by tectonic armor from the real green stuff. The garden here only resembles nature; the garden as such remains intact.

Other strategies to synthesize architecture and nature without the intermediary of a garden are more problematic. The destructive colonizing of certain plants, even when maintenance is performed, is well known. Creepers enveloping building exteriors can cause significant damage to a structure, although they can also provide some weather protection to the wall materials. Bringing flora, fauna, wind, and precipitation further into a building than the exterior wall generally ends in disaster. However, designers are determined to do just that as a strategy for longer-term human survival, not just on Earth, but perhaps beyond. Vertical gardenist Patrick Blanc has developed a second skin for building walls; this method allows the successful adaptation of select plant species to seemingly consume the exterior and interior walls of a building, but these are still modified natural constructions, as Blanc admits: "Inside without wind and rain, a few scale insects may appear and can be taken care of with an application of mild pesticide, though they may also be removed merely with a spray of warm water."[59] Here too, then, is a garden.

Perhaps getting closer to the goal of integrating nature more fully into human habitats is architect Philippe Rahm. Rahm, who defines architecture as the resultant space defined by material assemblies and climate modifications, is challenging the conventional definitional boundaries between nature and architecture: "We consider these intermediary spaces a new landscape, not quite inside nor entirely outside, more natural yet totally artificial, which opens itself to the perfectly isolated interior spaces" [Figures 18,19].[60] Rahm's goal is to create a "meteorological architecture" with socially responsible and ecological objectives.[61] His architecture is composed of a new tectonic language; instead of floors, doors, and windows, Rahm suggests that the new kit of parts available to the designer are "climatic phenomena such as convection, conduction, and evaporation.... Could vapor, heat, or light become the new bricks of contemporary construction?"[62] Rahm's new garden space, the defender of human life within the natural eco-system, seemingly co-exists with architectural space. The garden as meteorology offers opportunities to eliminate the traditional 'greenline'; here "limits fade away and solids evaporate".[63] Rahm's proposals, which remain

Figure 18/ Mollier Houses.

The garden as meteorology offers opportunities to eliminate the traditional greenline; here limits fade away and solids evaporate. Courtesy of Philippe Rahm.

Figure 19/ House Dilation.

A new landscape, not quite inside nor entirely outside, more natural yet totally artificial. Courtesy of Philippe Rahm.

largely untested, certainly challenge the garden construct. At the moment, however, their feasibility lies in the realm of the future.

While we like to imagine that our cities and their architecture are permanent installations, we need only reflect on our own history to realize that our constructions are mere bivouacs. At the same time, the fragile and often forgotten garden, regardless of intended use or aesthetic considerations, is always at hand in some capacity to sustain architecture. This mechanism of protective enclosure allows us to live *with* and to *be* nature. The utopian value of the garden cannot be overestimated; as imperfect as we might be, it is our most perfect invention.

The sand can swallow up cities and countries, if it wants to.[64]

Notes

1. Betsky, Aaron, *Landscrapers, Building with the Land*, New York: Thames and Hudson, 2002, p. 5.
2. Abé, Kobo, *The Woman in the Dunes*, New York: Alfred A. Knopf, 1964, p. 42.
3. *Woman in the Dunes* (*Suna no Onna*), DVD, directed by Hiroshi Teshigahara, 1964; Chatsworth, CA: Image Entertainment, 1999.
4. Abé, *The Woman in the Dunes*, p. 23.
5. *Woman in the Dunes*, DVD, Teshigahara.
6. Abé, *The Woman in the Dunes*, p. 223.
7. More, Thomas, *The Complete Works of St. Thomas More: Vol. 4, Utopia*, Edward Surtz, S. J. and J. H. Hexter ed., New Haven: Yale University Press, 1965, p. 121.
8. More, Thomas, *The Complete Works of St. Thomas More: Vol. 4, Utopia*, p. 121.
9. Smithsonian Institute Human Origin Initiative, "Human Evolution Evidence", July 2011. http://humanorigins.si.edu.
10. Vitruvius, *On Architecture, Books I-V, Vol. 1*, Frank Granger ed. and trans., Cambridge, MA: Harvard University Press, 1931, pp. 34–35.
11. *The Epic of Gilgamesh*, Maureen Gallery Kovacs trans. and intro., Stanford: Stanford University Press, 1985, pp. 78–79. Translator's note: A missing word or line is indicated by three ellipsis points (...). Missing words have been supplied by the obvious demands of context or by conjecture; these are in brackets. If a restoration is more uncertain, a question mark in parentheses follows the word or phrase. A word added to clarify the sense of a passage is enclosed in parentheses.
12. For a discussion of ancient representational and physical garden evidence, see Tom Turner, *Garden History: Philosophy and Design 2000 BC–2000 AD*, London: Spon Press, 2005, pp. 1–80. For discussions of garden archeology and excavation techniques, see John Dixon Hunt ed., *Garden History: Issues, Approaches, Methods*, Washington, D.C.: Dumbarton Oaks, 1992, pp. 5–57. For an archeological account of the Royal Garden at Pasargadae, see David Stronach, *Pasargadae: A Report on the Excavations Conducted by the British Institute of Persian Studies from 1961–1963*, Oxford: Oxford University Press, 1978, pp. 107–112.
13. The Bible, King James Version, Gospel of Matthew 7:15.
14. Ruskin, John, *The Works of John Ruskin, Volume 1*, E. T. Cook and Alexander Wedderburn ed., London: George Allen, 1903, p. 157.
15. Turner, *Garden History: Philosophy and Design 2000 BC–2000 AD*, p. 1.
16. Heidegger, Martin, "Building Dwelling Thinking", *Poetry, Language, Thought*, Albert Hofstadter trans. and intro., New York: Harper and Row, 1971, p. 154.
17. The boundary I am referring to here is not to be confused with the site or property boundary line.
18. The Gospel of Matthew 7:15.
19. Mostafavi, Mostafavi and David Leatherbarrow, *On Weathering: The Life of Buildings in Time*, Cambridge: The MIT Press, 1993, p. 16.
20. Jodidio, Philip, *Architecture: Nature*, Munich: Prestel, 2006, p. 20.
21. The frontispiece of Marc-Antoine Laugier's *Essai sur l'Architecture* (*Essay on Architecture*), 1755, was illustrated with the 'primitive hut'. Although Vitruvius had also posited a primal shelter as the foundation of architectural evolution, Laugier conceived of the hut as the embodiment of what architecture should be. Interestingly, the

earliest evidence of human shelter discovered in 1966 at Terra Amata, France, is thought to be around 400,000 years old; archeological evidence suggests it looked remarkably like Laugier's primitive hut.
22. Betsky, *Landscrapers, Building with the Land*, p. 7.
23. McHarg, Ian L., *Design with Nature*, New York: Doubleday/ Natural History Press, 1971 ed., p. 72.
24. See note 20.
25. McDonough, William and Michael Braungart, *Cradle to Cradle: Remaking the Way We Make Things*, New York: North Point Press, 2002, pp. 16, 156, 186.
26. Koolhaas, Rem ed., *Content*, Köln: Taschen, 2004, p. 163.
27. Hunt, John Dixon, *Greater Perfections: The Practice of Garden Theory*, Philadelphia: University of Pennsylvania Press, 2000, pp. 14–15. Hunt's meaty definition is merely 'provisional'; the remainder of the book is devoted to developing the definition more fully.
28. For a thorough survey of garden definitions, principals, and practices, see Scott J. Tilden ed., *The Glory of Gardens: 2,000 Years of Writings on Garden Design*, New York: Abrams, 2006.
29. *Dictionary of Architecture and Construction*, Fourth Edition, Cyril M. Harris ed., New York: McGraw-Hill, 1975, p. 452.
30. Since Vitruvius there has been no shortage in architectural discourse struggling to define architecture. For a multiplicity of definitions in one source see Manuel Gausa et al., authors, *The Metapolis Dictionary of Advanced Architecture: City, Technology, and Society in the Information Age*, Barcelona: Actar, 2003. For a more comprehensive discussion, see Hanno-Walter Kruft, *A History of Architectural Theory From Vitruvius to the Present*, New York: Princeton Architectural Press, 1994.
31. *Dictionary of Architecture and Construction*, Harris, p. 51.
32. Koolhaas, *Content*, p. 163.
33. For a formal discussion of the Picturesque and the garden, see John Dixon Hunt, *Gardens and the Picturesque*, Cambridge: The MIT Press, 1992. In J. J. Rousseau's 1761 novel *Julie, or the New Heloise* (*Julie, ou la nouvelle Héloïse*), Julie's "Elysium" is a wild garden created to be as authentic to nature as possible without the imitative contrivances found in the Picturesque; this of course reflected Rousseau's complex philosophical positioning on the 'nobility of nature'. See Jean-Jacques Rousseau, *Julie, or the New Heloise: Letters of Two Lovers Who Live in a Small Town at the Foot of the Alps, The Collected Writings of Rousseau*, Vol. 6, Philip Stewart and Jean Vaché trans., Hanover: Dartmouth College, University Press of New England, 1997, pp. 386–401.
34. Adams, William Howard, *Gardens Through History: Nature Perfected*, New York: Abbeville Press Publishers, 1991, p. 299.
35. *Dictionary of Architecture and Construction*, Harris, p. 655.
36. Frost, Robert, "Mending Wall", *North of Boston*, New York: Henry Holt and Co., 1917, pp. 11–13.
37. Jacobs, Herbert with Katherine Jacobs, *Building With Frank Lloyd Wright: An Illustrated Memoir*, San Francisco: Chronicle Books, 1978, p. 4.
38. Ruskin, John, excerpt from "The Two Paths," *Selected Writings*, Kenneth Clark ed., London: Penguin, 1964, p. 199.
39. Bernard Khoury/DW5, "Projects/B018", July 2011. http://www.bernardkhoury.com. Also see, Robert Fisk, *Pity the Nation: Lebanon at War*, London: Deutsch, 1990, pp. 78–79, and William Harris, *Faces of Lebanon. Sects, Wars, and Global Extensions*, Princeton: Markus Wiener Publishers, 1996, p. 162.
40. B018, "Company", July 2011. http://b018.com.
41. Khoury, "Projects/B018", http://www.bernardkhoury.com.
42. Curtis, William J. R., *Modern Architecture Since 1900*, Third Edition, London: Phaidon, 1996, p. 500.
43. The original garden at Centrale was modified; currently, patrons pass through a tunnel of lush 'green' before encountering the dramatic building elevation which faces a simple yet elegant shade garden. The former garden's narrative was far more abstract: linear retractable covers kept unused outdoor tables hidden from view; as the restaurant filled, the covers would slowly retract.
44. Wright, Frank Lloyd, *An Autobiography*, 1932, New York: Horizon Press, 1977, p. 365.
45. Rosa, Joseph, *Albert Frey, Architect*, New York: Rizzoli, 1990, p. 17.
46. Rosa, *Albert Frey, Architect*, p. 16.
47. Rosa, *Albert Frey, Architect*, p. 79.
48. From "Ritratto di Pietra" ("Stone Portrait"), written by Curzio Malaparte in 1940, in Marida Talamona, *Casa Malaparte*, New York: Princeton Architectural Press, 1992, p. 85.
49. Talamona, *Casa Malaparte*, p. 84.
50. Neutra, Richard, *Survival Through Design*, New York: Oxford University Press, 1954, p. 3.
51. Neutra, Richard, *Nature Near: Late Essays of Richard Neutra*, William Marlin ed., Santa Barbara: Capra Press, 1989, p. 11.
52. The earliest evidence of the hearth is at least 790,000 years old. Control of fire led to cooking and the most primal form of 'shelter'. Beyond the 'body' the hearth provided the first intentional separation from nature, and thus became the nucleus of more developed social networks and constructed shelters. See http://humanorigins.si.edu.
53. Abé, *The Woman in the Dunes*, p. 15.
54. The Eden Project, "What's it all about?" http://www.edenproject.com.
55. From Hundertwasser, "Manifesto, Your Window Right, Your Tree Duty", in Harry Rand, *Hundertwasser*, Köln: Taschen, 1991, p. 168.
56. There is no doubt that Hundertwasser's built work co-mingles nature and human intention; Hundertwasser House seemed to fulfill Hundertwasser's utopian schema, saying, "It is much more evident and living—human, part of nature and the universe—than I ever dared to believe that it could be". Rand, *Hundertwasser*, pp. 209–231.
57. Rand, *Hundertwasser*, pp. 172–173.
58. Ambasz, Emilio, Peter Buchanan et al., *Emilio Ambasz Inventions: The Reality of the Ideal*, New York: Rizzoli, 1992, p. 55.
59. Blanc, Patrick, *The Vertical Garden: From Nature to the City*, New York: W. W. Norton, 2008, p. 100.
60. Philippe Rahm, Architectes, "Projects/Mergoscia House", July 2011. http://www.philipperahm.com.
61. Rahm, "Office Agenda/ Towards a Meteorological Architecture". http://www.philipperahm.com.
62. Rahm, "Office Agenda". http://www.philipperahm.com.
63. Rahm, "Office Agenda". http://www.philipperahm.com.
64. *Woman in the Dunes*, DVD, Teshigahara.

CONSUMING BEAUTY: THE URBAN GARDEN AS AMBIGUOUS UTOPIA

/NAOMI JACOBS

What wondrous life is this I lead!
Ripe apples drop about my head;
... Stumbling on melons as I pass,
Insnared with flowers, I fall on grass.
/ Marvell, "To the Garden"

Every garden is a utopian text, expressing the desire for a more perfect world as well as an implicit critique of the less-lovely world in which it is located. A sustainable garden is something more specific: an ecotopian text that attempts to model an ideal realm in which nature and humankind coexist in harmony. To engage in the creation of such a garden is to experience both a utopian way of knowing and a utopian way of doing, for the longer one gardens, the better one understands that a gardener's work is not limited to care of the plants themselves. When well and thoughtfully done, the gardener's practice of care extends to the soil, the insects, the birds, the mice and the groundhogs, and beyond that to the self, the family, the neighborhood, the community, and the planet.

All of this can feel rather a crushing responsibility for a beleaguered urban gardener trying to coax a tomato or two out of less-than-heavenly soil in something less than full sun. Like every utopianist, a gardener must come to terms with the gap between the ideal and the possible—between the perfect garden one can imagine and the local conditions in which one must work. And furthermore, the gardener's many layers of desire and levels of responsibility can never be entirely aligned. One gardener might specialize in the beloved ornamentals: the roses, lilies, rhododendrons, irises and such that were brought from far-away places by European adventurers who risked their lives to collect gorgeous specimens from around the world. Another might prioritize environmental responsibilities and design the garden with an emphasis on native plants, pleasing to the eye, alluring to native pollinators and providing food for native birds and beasts. Yet another might create a flourishing vegetable garden, producing tasty meals for the family from spring through fall. A rural gardener with ample land could do all of these things, if so inclined, while still preserving unaltered woods and meadows.

But for an urban gardener with an over-active conscience, the choices are more stark, for every square foot devoted to ornamental plants (whether native or exotic) is a square foot that might have been devoted to growing vegetables for one's family or for the local homeless shelter. And even in a climate with a long growing season and a range of native food plants, every square foot devoted to food for people represents a square foot taken away from the garden that Mother Nature would plant if we gave back her ground. The very element of design in our gardens can be seen as an imposition of control that does violence to nature. Symbolically, the garden represents a state of innocence. But in reality, every garden testifies to our fallen state, our separation from and opposition to non-human nature, not only as individuals, but as members

Figure 1/ View from South Ridge of Mount Katahdin, Baxter State Park. Photograph courtesy of Nico Angleys.

and heirs of the human communities that have shaped the nature(s) in which we live and garden.

Taking this dilemma as my central problem, I will explore the challenges of sustainable urban gardening as an ethical activity. I will proceed in the personal mode, addressing the interpenetrations of 'utopian' nature and 'dystopian' culture at three loci that frame my own quotidian experiences of nature, utopia and the garden: first, my bioregion, known as "l'Acadie" by the French explorers of the seventeenth century, and still sought out as an Edenic paradise of unspoiled natural beauty; second, my green and quiet city, rich in parks and streams, and bordering the vast North Woods; and third, the small garden I have created on the tainted ground of an old neighborhood in this city. This tightening spiral will bring me to an impasse: a sense that this place I inhabit—like every place of human habitation—is grievously damaged, that many of the choices I have made as a gardener in pursuit of beauty make me complicit in that damage, and that any action I might take in the future will fall far short of what is needed to repair it.

I will be aided out of the ensuing paralysis by the work of contemporary thinkers who ask us to regard with skepticism the notion of 'pure' nature, and to seek instead an understanding of 'natures' in any given place as multiple, as dynamic, and as always in the process of being re-created. Once we relinquish the binary opposition of nature and culture—with its associated opposition of utopia and dystopia—we can begin to conceptualize a garden that functions like what Tom Moylan has theorized as the "critical utopia": a text that acknowledges the dialectic between utopian and dystopian elements in every human endeavor, confronts questions of definitions, and emphasizes process rather than product.[1] With this in mind, I will re-imagine the ideal urban garden as a new kind of *potager* combining food for nature, food for people, and food for the soul. Finally, because one urban plot can accomplish so little on its own, I will envision the city itself as an unplanned collaborative garden, the combined product of all gardeners who create spaces for nature and for beauty in the city. This shared effort honors our competing responsibilities to nurture the natural world, to feed ourselves, and to satisfy the human hungers for beauty, creativity and community.

"THE WAY LIFE SHOULD BE"

I am fortunate to make my home and my garden in Bangor, Maine, a small New England city of 35,000 people. The state of Maine capitalizes on its reputation for clean air, clean water, abundant wildlife, outdoor sports, and gorgeous scenery—a garden of unspoiled natural beauty—to market itself in utopian terms as "The Way Life Should Be". Millions of tourists travel to Maine every year in search of a refuge from urban life, a return to a wild Eden, and many are not disappointed.

Though Maine's wild land was for a time substantially cleared for lumber and agriculture, today 90 percent of the state is again covered in forest, as it was in 1846 when Henry David Thoreau made his first visit. The 12 million acres of the Maine North Woods are said to constitute the largest unbroken tract of forest east of the Mississippi.[2] More than half of the state is so sparsely populated as to have no local municipal government and no paved roads. Only 9,000 people live in this 'Unorganized Territory', at a density of approximately two people per square mile; it would be difficult to find anything more like wilderness in the northeastern United States. At the heart of the woods is the 200,000 acre Baxter State Park [Figure 1]. Bequeathed to the people of the state by a former governor, with the stipulation that it must remain 'forever wild', the park is a mecca for wilderness hikers, climbers, campers, kayakers, canoeists, and back-country skiers. Moose, deer, black bears, and eagles are commonly seen.

Another popular tourist destination is Acadia National Park, which attracted 2.5 million visitors to the Maine coast in a recent year. "L'Acadie" was the name given to this stunningly beautiful maritime region by the French explorers of the early seventeenth century. 50 years earlier, Verrazzano had named the mid-Atlantic coast "Arcadia" because of its lush woodlands. In each case, the reference was to the Arcadia of Greek mythology, a place of beauty and abundance ruled by the great god Pan, where human beings lived a peaceful life in harmony with nature. When Samuel de Champlain came to Acadia in 1604, part of an expedition sent by Louis XIII to establish a fur trade with the indigenous people of the North Atlantic Coast and the St. Lawrence Valley, he found a place far from paradise. The local Mi'kmaq people were thriving in this locale, but the French were ill adapted to its ways; cold and scurvy took almost half of Champlain's 79 men in the first winter, and the expeditions were called back after only a few years as unprofitable. Nevertheless, the region has retained the name "Acadia" and the aura of an idyllic place set apart from ordinary life [Figure 2].

A solitary hiker communing with nature near a pond at Baxter Park or Acadia, breathing the scent of fir and pine, listening to the rustlings of chipmunks and songs of birds, or watching an eagle soar above a remote stream, might feel that she has found a wild utopia. The truth, of course, is more complicated. In Maine as everywhere, human beings and natural forces have together produced the 'nature' that we find, whether we are in a lonely forest, on a rocky shoreline, or sharing a city park with fellow citizens on their way to the methadone clinic nearby. The state's immense wooded tracts contain only a few stands of old growth timber, and large clear-cuts are often concealed behind the so-called 'beauty strip' that borders the interstate highway. About a third of the Maine forest is owned by the wood products industry and criss-crossed by a network of logging roads; the smokestacks of the Millinocket paper mill are visible from the summit of Mount Katahdin. Trailer trucks loaded with pulp logs rumble through remote villages, and sulfurous fumes foul the air of towns where certain kinds of paper are made. Pregnant women are warned not to eat fish from Maine's inland waters, which were long ago contaminated with PCBs, dioxin and mercury from mills, tanneries, and a chemical plant that manufactured chlorine for the paper industry. Despite the state's strong environmental laws, hot summer days often bring warnings of poor air quality, due to elevated levels of ozone and harmful particulates. Maine's location is commonly described as "at the end of the nation's tailpipe", because weather patterns deliver to the Northeast the pollutants generated by coal-fired power plants in the Midwest. These toxic substances not only endanger human health but contribute to acid rain and acid fog, bringing acidification of lakes, resultant damage to fish and amphibian populations, and forest decline. Furthermore, the very hunger for a 'good place' close to nature that draws tourists to the state leads to increased carbon emissions,

Figure 2/ Summer Evening on Gorham Mountain, Acadia National Park. Photograph courtesy of Sam Hess.

Figure 3/ Worn hiking trail atop Chick Hill, near Bangor. Photograph courtesy of Annette Giesecke.

Figure 4/ Pitcher Plant (*Sarracenia purpurea*) in Orono Bog. Photograph courtesy of Sam Hess.

eroded trails, polluted waterways, and degraded habitats for native species—matching the dystopian visions of the most pessimistic of environmentalists [Figure 3].

The same interplay of utopian and dystopian realities is found on a smaller scale in my city and my back yard. Today a center of commercial and financial services for the rural northern half of the state, in the nineteenth century Bangor was the lumber capital of the world and one of the busiest ports on the Atlantic Coast of North America, with as many as 200 sailing ships tied up to its wharves on a typical day. The city's early wealth was drawn from the region's vast tracts of forest. Thoreau described Bangor as "a star on the edge of the night", surrounded by the "howling wilderness that feeds it".[3] Even now, passengers on a night flight into Bangor will see the lights of the city surrounded by an immense darkness.

To a casual summer visitor, this provincial community with its quiet streets, rambling nineteenth century houses, and walkable downtown may recall idyllic visions of a simpler time, a world apart from the Boston–Washington metropolitan corridor that begins 150 miles to the south. Indeed, to a typical New Yorker, the town would not even qualify as urban. We live close enough to the edge of the wilderness that fox kits have been filmed playing at the edge of woods near a busy intersection, and black bears are frequently spotted in the 700 acre Rolland F. Perry City Forest. The opportunity to be alone in what we call "wild" nature is never far away. The forest's nine miles of walking and skiing trails include a boardwalk through a forest wetland, peat bog, and a five-acre 'moss lawn' liberally sprinkled with pitcher plants and other rare species [Figure 4]. The city proper features many small parks; one trail follows the banks of the Kenduskeag Stream for almost three miles past sheer granite cliffs, as well as rapids and waterfalls. As if in continuation with the surrounding forest, lines of mature trees run down the middle of each long block in the older neighborhoods, their green alternating with the grey stripes of asphalt streets. It is not unusual to see a groundhog or a raccoon in residential areas, and a moose occasionally wanders onto the city's streets during blackfly season.

Yet even from the center of the City Forest, one hears the ceaseless traffic on the interstate highway or the activity at the shopping malls just a mile away. Toxic runoff has harmed the amphibians in the stream that runs through the mall's paved area, and local environmentalists fought a mostly-losing battle to prevent a 'Big Box' merchant from building a new superstore that would impinge upon the 300-acre Penjajawoc Marsh, one of the premier bird habitats in the state and nesting ground for several endangered species. There can be no clear boundary between city and nature. Even a protected area like the Bog Boardwalk is created and defined by human activity and marked by such

Figure 5/ Entering the Moss Lawn, Orono Bog Boardwalk. Photograph courtesy of Annette Giesecke.

activity, whether the scientific stations set up in the bog, the rumbling of the jets ferrying tourists to the Bangor International Airport and military personnel to Afghanistan, or the fact that nearly every year, some section of the boardwalk is vandalized and must be replaced [Figure 5].

At every level, then, the natural and the urban infiltrate each other. On scales large and small, the best human efforts to protect and to appreciate nature are vulnerable—not only to human depredation, but to natural processes of wind, water, and growing things. Asphalt streets and sidewalks may restrict moisture to the city's trees; but tree roots also heave asphalt and crack sewer lines. Trees are felled by developers, but also by wind and ice. This is the nature we have. It is one we have made, but one also always making itself. In our own gardens, we seek to balance these simultaneous processes of making and unmaking, to bring into reality our own visions of a good place in which we can work together with those natural processes. But our attempts are always constrained by the history of any given piece of ground.

ON TAINTED GROUND

My own small home garden allows me a regular taste of what Gerard Manley Hopkins called "the dearest freshness deep down things" in the rich flora and fauna just outside the back door [Figure 6].[4] When purchased, the property was nearly bare of plantings. There were a few white lilacs, which someone had cut to the ground in a renewal pruning; a patch of common orange daylilies; and one ancient peony bush, its blossoms white with a creamy center. There was an unkempt barberry on one side of the front steps, a scraggly privet on the other, and a gigantic Norway maple by the gate. The rest was grass, and a smattering of trees that had planted themselves along the property lines. Since then, the lawn has steadily shrunk to make room for flowerbeds, and a kitchen garden occupies the sunny space on the back lot. The original lilacs, now 15 feet tall, fill the spring air with exquisite fragrance. The plantings include over 300 different shrubs and perennials, including multiple varieties of peonies, roses, lilies, and daylilies, as well as sizable stands of native ferns and wildflowers—some gathered from friends' woodlots, some arising on their own initiative. Tending to this flourishing garden gives me great pleasure and solace. It can seem a magical place on a pleasant spring day, with birds twittering, squirrels chattering, lilacs and tulips blooming, pollinators at work, a dragonfly cruising for a mosquito snack, and a fresh breeze rustling the trees. There is no question that the garden provides me with a refuge from the pressures of work and the realities of life outside the fence, or that it creates a nurturing space for nature. More than one visitor, seeing it for the first time, has termed it "heaven". It is what gardening magazines like to call an "oasis" or a "sanctuary". But this backyard Eden is also a toxic site, burdened by the effects of human activity since the land was cleared and houses were built.

First and foremost, my plants do not grow in good earth. Thanks to the inexpensive lumber milled in Bangor in its early history, this city's houses were built from wood. Two thirds of them date from before 1939, a period when most paint contained lead. These large clapboard structures sit close together, typically on one-eighth acre (50 x 100 feet) lots. Due to the harsh climate, houses must be repainted frequently. Although lead-based paint was banned in the

Figure 6/ Lady's Mantle (*Alchemilla mollis*) after a rain shower. Photograph by Naomi Jacobs.

United States in 1978, lead paint chips have fallen to the soil with every round of scraping over the past century and a half.

The oldest part of our house was built in 1885. Lead concentrations in the flower beds that border the long south wall measure over 800 parts per million—nearly three times the levels considered safe for food crops or children. Levels are lower, but still too high for comfort, on the back lot, where we once blithely cultivated a large vegetable garden that we thought was organic. A soil test told us that our urban 'oasis' was inextricably entangled with the natural and human history of our community. To remove the contaminated soil would have exceeded our means. We still grow vegetables in a 20 x 30 feet raised bed filled with clean soil, but the rest of that area has been relegated to flowers.

In addition to the lead contamination, certain areas of our property are actually built upon waste. The L-shaped lot sits at the highest point on the block and slopes down to the streets on either side. The builders created two flat areas: one, on the back lot, for a barn that no longer exists; the other, on the front lot, for the house itself, whose shallow fieldstone foundation sits on a rock ledge. These terraces were built up with random debris and covered with a thin layer of soil and grass. To force a shovel into some parts of this ground is nearly impossible. A grub hoe will turn up lumps of coal, veins of ash, broken window glass, fragments of old china, rusty nails, harness bits, and lost marbles [Figure 7]. In fact, my attempt to remove unsightly chunks of asphalt from one bank ended when I realized the garden shed was likely to slide down the slope if I continued to dig. The asphalt *was* the bank.

Figure 7/ Urban harvest. Photograph by Naomi Jacobs.

In this, my garden continues a long tradition, for it is believed that domestic gardens originated in dump heaps outside dwellings, as "unanticipated consequences" of human habitations.[5] Because of this substrate, some plants I might like to grow simply will not survive, especially when the clay soil and the density of tree roots are factored in. I have tried and repeatedly failed to establish native groundcovers such as the charming bunchberry or wintergreen, both of which would have offered food for birds. Instead, I have resorted to *Vinca minor*, the pretty but much-maligned periwinkle. As I have learned about the importance of native plants to the ecosystem and the dangers of exotic invasives, I have come to see such plantings with more critical eyes. When periwinkle escapes from cultivation into woodlands, this non-native invasive can choke out native growth.

My garden is also contaminated by certain plants that were here well before I took possession. A human being probably planted the large Japanese barberry, a notorious invasive, by the front step. A bird planted another, almost as big, that has sprouted under a maple in the side yard. We cut that one to the ground and dug out what we could of the bright yellow roots, but some were so entangled with tree roots as to be inaccessible. Despite our labor, the plant is even larger than before and has begun to start 'babies' nearby. It seems that nothing short of heavy chemicals will defeat this aggressor. I would gladly rid my garden of barberry and fellow invasives like ground elder and the creeping bellflower that is infiltrating ever-larger sections of my flowerbeds despite many efforts to dig out its fleshy rhizomes. On the other hand, I would be sorry to lose certain other invasives that are problematic on ecological grounds.

Figure 8/ Periwinkle (*Vinca minor*). Photograph by Naomi Jacobs.

When periwinkle cloaks a city bank filled with trash and bounded by a sidewalk, colonizes dry shade in collaboration with a native invasive such as the woodland anemone, or emerges from snow as the spring's first green, it is a very welcome presence [Figure 8].

Similar dilemmas are found in our sidewalk forest. Very few of the city's trees are native maple, beech, birch or conifer. American elms that once lined the streets succumbed to disease decades ago, and the dominant variety is now the Norway maple (*Acer platanoides*), introduced to North America by a Philadelphia nurseryman in 1756. This maple was considered so desirable that George Washington planted a pair at his Mount Vernon estate.[6] Today the Norway maple is on many 'most hated plants' lists and banned for sale in some states. In the wild, it can quickly crowd out the native trees that provide essential food to hundreds of species of caterpillars. It secretes a growth inhibitor to discourage competitors, and few plants other than invasives will thrive under it. Our yard is shaded by a dozen of these trees, which self-seed copiously [Figure 9]. Every year I spend a good deal of time pulling up maple seedlings and cursing the trees as I do. I know all the reasons why I should despise them, yet I also know that their tolerance for poor soil and urban pollution means that they bring cool shade and greenery where other trees might fail. Those we have taken down have provided fuel for our woodstove, giving us the pleasure of warming our house with the product of

Figure 9/ Maple seeds on Judith's ferns. Photograph by Naomi Jacobs.

Figure 10/ Big tree in autumn. Photograph by Naomi Jacobs.

our own little woodlot. All over the city, these trees provide homes to squirrels and birds; they also feed several varieties of *Lepidoptera*, including the caterpillars of the Io and Polyphemus moths, if not the hundreds of varieties that would be fed by an oak.

The gigantic Norway maple next to our front driveway is one of the few large trees remaining on the street. It is not a tree I would plant, but it is the tree I have, and I love it. This majestic specimen has a spread of 70 feet and a height of 50; its trunk is four feet in diameter. It withstood the Great Ice Storm of 1998, when ice-laden limbs crashed on power lines all across town and the night sky was filled with blue flashes as electrical transformers exploded. Its vivid chartreuse flowering is one of the loveliest events of spring, and the shower of gold on the pavements when its blossoms drop presages the brilliance of its autumn foliage [Figure 10]. I've never hugged this tree (or any other), and I don't talk to it, but I do give it the occasional appreciative pat as I pass by. Its days are numbered. Several large limbs have already been taken down for safety, and every year it drops smaller branches.

If I were a native plant purist, I might feel obliged to have it removed immediately, along with the other Norway maples in the yard, and to replace them with native oaks and maples that I would not live long enough to see mature. But when this tree is gone, our house will be exposed to the full force of the summer sun, shade gardens will shrivel, and I will grieve the loss of a beloved presence in our neighborhood ecosystem. I am not prepared to sacrifice this tree, with which I have an intimate relationship extending over 30 years, to a principle, however persuasive. Nor am I prepared to sacrifice other beautiful plants I have fostered, even if they are taking up space that might be devoted to more practical or more ecologically sensitive choices.

Due to this complex of imperfect decisions and contradictory intentions—my own, my predecessors', my community's, even those of the plant-loving daredevils who brought back lilies, rhododendrons, and peonies from China, poppies from the Middle East, irises from Siberia, and lilacs from the Balkans—there is clearly no chance of a perfected realm. Looked at in a certain way, my garden is a tainted site. Even in my efforts to make it more beautiful, I have sacrificed nature to culture, devoting far too much of my precious space to non-native plants that play little part in the local web of life [Figure 11]. I am persuaded by Doug Tallamy's indictment of the harm that our lawns do to the ecosystem, even when grown without chemicals.[7] I take Kerry Dawson's point that "[h]uman aesthetics rarely correspond to ecological principles".[8] I can even entertain Mark Treib's claim that the making of a domestic garden is an act of domination, that "we value the garden because it allows us to maintain control over a piece of land, to shape it, foster it, nurture it, and even punish it, according to our feelings, ideas, and whims. Control also implies power."[9] Such domestic dilemmas play out on a small scale the larger dilemma of the entire human presence in the natural world. We are a part of nature, and yet, our activities change nature and often damage it, whether in our backyards, our towns, our bioregions, or the planet itself.

FROM 'NATURE' TO NATURES

However, at some level I know I am mistaken to set up beauty and pleasure again ethics and utility. Such an opposition replays an equally problematic one between human and non-human nature—between civilization

Figure 11/ Pete's Poppy, "Princess Victoria Louise". Photograph by Naomi Jacobs.

(which involves both human use and human pleasure) and the wild. What do I see if I imagine my garden not as a ruined version of 'pure' nature, but as what Doolittle calls a "hybridized matrix" in which multiple natures coexist?[10] In pursuing this line of thought, I follow geographers and ecologists who have argued for new understandings of nature(s) and of the human relationship to place. Doreen Massey, for instance, asks us to understand places as dynamic entities, with multiple identities and no clear boundaries that could distinguish 'inside' from 'outside'. In her view, a place is a processual entity, "constructed out of a particular constellation of social relations, meeting and weaving together at a particular locus".[11] This is an insight that holds true whether the place in question is urban, rural or wild.

If I adopt this view of the garden and of nature itself as places of multiplicity and process, places whose relations include those between people, plants, insects, voles, birds, and bats, I can see and appreciate the simultaneous natures inhabiting my small plot. The layer I have consciously designed contains ornamental plants both native and non-native: exotic clematis, hybrid shrub roses, hostas, hydrangeas, epimediums and such, but also native ostrich ferns, Solomon's seal, trillium, and bloodroot. As I have become aware of the value of native plants, I have added shrubs and small trees providing food for birds, such as pagoda dogwood and winterberry, whose bright red berries persist into winter; such plants happily coexist with species from distant locations.

The garden also contains an ornamental layer that was designed by natural forces: the birds, the bees, and the wind. A native aster of unassuming aspect seeds itself in a dry corner, and Virginia creeper is blanketing that asphalt-ridden bank. The native buckeye that has sprouted in one garden bed must have been planted by a squirrel. Trout lilies and a Jack-in-the-Pulpit hitched a ride with the duff beneath the fern a friend dug for me. The chokecherry that volunteered by the porch is a scruffy little tree, but robins relish its berries, which glow garnet-red in the late afternoon sun. Spores of moss and hay-scented fern germinated in the woodsy loam where a rotted stump had been; the ferns are now a charming feature there in dappled shade. My responsibility in this aspect of the design is simply to edit the volunteers, weeding out or relocating some, and leaving others to spread at will.

Figure 12/ Kitchen Garden. Photograph by Naomi Jacobs.

Our kitchen garden is another layer without clear boundaries between the wild and the cultivated, the useful and the (merely) beautiful. A milkweed has sprouted in the broccoli row. Self-seeded purple coneflowers infiltrate the garlic, and wayward clematis vines twine up the sunflowers along the fence. Roaming strawberries carpet the ground under a lilac. On the hot side of the house, tomatoes, peppers, and basil in large pots join lilies in the lead-contaminated flowerbeds. Some of these plants feed bugs and birds. Some feed people. Some serve pollinators. Some simply feed the soul. All make up a part of utopian nature in my small urban plot [Figure 12].

As I tend to this 'metropolitan nature', I gain a sense of 'home' that is inextricably bound up in plants, including non-natives.[12] Lilacs from the Balkans are now an iconic element in the New England spring, and in mine. An old-fashioned rose in my garden (perhaps *Rosa spinosissima*?) is a descendant of a plant brought from England by the first European settlers. It was a gift from Bill Chesley, a former student of mine whose family has lived in Maine since the eighteenth century. Bill dug it from the garden of his grandmother, who called it "Thoreau's Quaker's Rose" and said it came from a homestead Thoreau visited on his way to "Ktaadn". I find no reference to true Quakers, or to a rose in bloom, in Thoreau's account, but have no reason or wish to doubt the family lore. The plant is briefly beautiful in flower, then sets equally attractive near-black hips that don't much interest the birds but spark up the slow time of year for humans.

Indeed, my mental map of this garden contains all the people who've given to it. Krista, who lives two doors down, gave me the fragrant lemon thyme and sturdy cotoneaster; when her daughter was married, flowers for the reception were cut from my beds. The fabulous, floriferous apricot daylily came from MaJo's house in the woods [Figure 13]. Judith helped me dig the trillium and ostrich ferns from her family's woods on a spring day when we watched harbor seals from her deck on Penobscot Bay. The "Double Delight" and "*Jardin de Bagatelles*" roses were birthday presents from my sister Ramona, and many of the perennials were grown by bagpiper-nurseryman Pete for sale at an annual peace-and-justice fundraiser. The rhubarb start came from our neighbor Bob, who lets me add my garden debris to his trailer when he's making a

Figure 13/ MaJo's daylily. Photograph by Naomi Jacobs.

run to Public Works. When I mow what's left of the grass, I remember Leo, the elderly neighbor who used to do this for me because, he claimed, he needed the exercise. To give space to these plants and others with similar resonances is to honor the history of the place and the unfolding process that has produced this garden; it is to honor the relationships between gardeners as well as the relationships between people and plants.

I do not, of course, mean to deny that the human history in nature has often been destructive. As William Cronon wrote in his essential article, "The Trouble with Wilderness", "Calling a place home inevitably means that we will use the nature we find in it, for there can be no escape from manipulating and working and even killing some parts of nature to make our home." But, he continues, the solution is not to seek a "flight from history" in some imagined pristine wilderness, untouched by human activity. Rather, "If living in history means that we cannot help leaving marks on a fallen world, then the dilemma we face is to decide what kinds of marks we wish to leave." Our home includes both the garden and the wilderness; we inevitably inhabit a "middle ground" and "need to embrace the full continuum of a natural landscape that is also cultural".[13]

A part of doing so involves accepting the ambiguities and compromises inherent in every choice we make. It can be sobering, but also tremendously freeing, to relinquish the dream of perfection.

BREAD, ROSES, AND BUGS: TOWARD A MORE-THAN-HUMAN POTAGER

Perhaps it is precisely through the utopian model, as understood in contemporary discourse, that we can best imagine a dynamic coexistence of beauty and use, the natural and the human. According to Istvan Csisnery-Ronay, "utopias allow the aesthetic and political attitudes, which are usually mutually exclusive universes of discourse, to play with each other, to spin around, and spin with each other".[14] In such a utopian state of play, I will imagine in this final section an urban garden occupying Cronon's middle ground of sustainable use. Its gardener would follow ecological practices, of course, in seeking to minimize harm to the web of living things. The garden would feed non-human nature as well as people. But the garden would also *of necessity* be beautiful as well as useful. That is, it would not be restricted to native plants or plants with food value for birds, insects, or people. It would assume that the human aesthetic instinct deserves to be fed as well. Thus, this garden would be a reconceptualized version of the *potager*—the ornamental kitchen garden.[15]

The *potager* is that rare endeavor in which productive, aesthetic, and social labor can be integrated. The dream of such integration has long been a strain in utopian discourse: the horn of plenty, after all, spills over with flowers as well as fruits. As women in a 1912 textile strike famously proclaimed, "Hearts starve as well as bodies; give us bread, but give us roses!" Perhaps the most eloquent advocate for beauty as an ethical and political goal was William Morris, who believed that all human beings deserve a "full life to which the perception and creation of beauty... shall be felt as necessary to man as his daily bread".[16] A garden combining the growing of food plants and the growing of flowers is the quintessential practice in which the production of one's daily bread can be simultaneously an act of community and an act of perceiving and creating beauty. Writes Florence Krall,

> The kitchen garden is not a sculptured abstraction symbolic of logical control and domination. Its plans and plantings emerge from an integrated theme based on practical necessity, convenience, and esthetic and sensual satisfaction.... This kitchen garden is a middle ground that centers and encloses.... It cultivates in us a feeling of belonging and a connection to the land, to its creatures and its climate and to the neighbors and neighborhood.[17]

By no means does every *potager* represent an unambiguously utopian enterprise. Some of the most famous began as clear expressions of monarchic power. The nine-hectare Potager du Roi at Versailles was created by Quintinie from 1678–1683, by order of Louis XIV. It included 30 gardens (of which 20 remain), including some 5,000 fruit trees. The heart of the garden was the Grand Carré: 16 large squares in geometric design, arranged around a central pool and surrounded by espaliered pear trees. Other garden enclosures were dedicated to asparagus, melons, and strawberries, to provide the royals with delicacies out of season. The King liked to view the gardens from a strategically located platform, an arrangement that has been described as "agricultural theatre".[18] The politics of this kind of *potager* are not difficult to critique. Such

Figure 14/ Le Chateau de Villandry Gardens. Photograph courtesy of Geoff Livingston © 2009.

Figure 15/ His Holiness Dagchen Rinpoche's hand holds a *vajra*, drawing lines that close the Hevajra Mandala, after the empowerment, Tharlam Monastery of Tibetan Buddhism, Boudha, Kathmandu, Nepal. Photograph courtesy of Wonderlane.

Figure 16/ Young monks clearing the Hevajra Sand Mandala away. Photograph courtesy of Wonderlane.

gardens have historically been maintained by armies of ill-paid workers, to feed the vanity and the luxurious tastes of idle courtiers or landowners. Reportedly, the Sun King even took lessons upon occasion from one of the gardeners —an activity anticipating Marie Antoinette's fondness for dressing as a milkmaid and milking cows that had been carefully cleaned by the servants before the Queen came near. Today, in its post-monarchic manifestation, the king's *potager* has a new life as a tourist destination. Containing about 50 types of vegetables and hundreds of unusual varieties, it is productive as well as beautiful. Locals shop for groceries at a weekly market on the palace grounds, and children are allotted squares for school projects.

Another famous *potager* that elevates the aesthetic dimension to its ultimate degree is the twentieth century creation located on the grounds of the Renaissance Chateau de Villandry in the Loire Valley. Here too, intricate geometric designs with symbolic import are created using vegetables chosen for their visual qualities; the beds are edged with three miles of clipped boxwood, and the design is changed twice a year [Figure 14]. According to garden writer Anna Pavord, "The thought of actually eating any of the vegetables in the vast *potager* at Villandry is quite shocking. Rich ruby chard, metallic blue leeks, shining parsley and frilly lettuce in bronze and green are used like richly textured paint. It's a work of art."[19] In a severe mood, we might feel it an obscenity to devote land, energies and resources to growing food plants as art, while people go hungry and caterpillars find no familiar plants on which to feed.

But once again, we need not see aesthetics and ethics as opposed, nor must we ask every garden to honor every good. The quality of attention that goes along with aesthetic appreciation and creation is distinct from but also compatible with the quality of attention required for good husbandry. As environmental ethicist Roger King notes, "the domesticated is our space. It is from this world that we move out into the wild landscape, either in fact or in imagination. Our ability to do this with respect and attention to details presupposes an education of our moral perception to overcome the habitual and acculturated anthropocentric neglect of nature."[20] The artistic dimension in gardening intensifies such "respect and attention to details" in the relationship between people and plants. A person who loves beauty will be more sharply attuned to color, form, and texture than a person concerned only with function. Thus, a visitor to Villandry may take home a more vivid appreciation of the beauty of her own cabbages.

David Cooper has argued that a garden is not precisely a work of art, but also not precisely a natural phenomenon.[21] Our aesthetic appreciation of a garden falls somewhere between appreciation of a painting and that of a landscape. As an art, the garden is akin to the ephemeral works of British artist Andy Goldsworthy, whose on-site arrangements of found materials such as leaves, twigs, mud, icicles, and flowers are intended to weather and disappear. In many ways, gardens also resemble Tibetan sand mandalas, those intricate patterns painstakingly created grain by grain over a period of days and then ritually destroyed—usually swept up and carried to a stream to be poured out [Figure 15]. The Sand Mandalas are believed to have powers to heal and purify and to "transmit positive energies to the environment and to the people who view them.... A mandala's healing power extends to the whole world even before it is swept up and dispersed into flowing water—a further expression of sharing the mandala's blessings with all."[22] Such beauty is created with the full intention that it be impermanent: it is created *in order to be destroyed* [Figure 16]. Just as the mandala's grains of sand are returned to the sea or river, Goldsworthy's natural materials rot down to humus or erode away to sand. And just so, the elements of the domestic garden are shaped with full understanding that the plants' beauty will be swept away by the seasons.

The kitchen garden differs from these other arts in that it is created to be un-done in a specific way: it is created *in order to be consumed*. In this, it perhaps most resembles the art of baking. Why should anyone bother to make a pie beautiful, or to ornament a loaf of bread with elaborate designs? There's really no answer but pleasure in the making, and love for those who will consume the results. The gardener cultivates these plants so that their roots, seeds and fruits can be taken into human bodies. To the extent that the kitchen garden is an ornamental one, the gardener's hungers for beauty and for the expression of creative energies are also fed. When building a 'more-than-human' *potager*, the eco-gardener will expand this circle of care by consciously cultivating plants that provide food for other creatures, and will learn to regard a tree tattered by caterpillars not as a problem to be solved, but as evidence of abundant life. Such a gardener might give space to a plant for which he has no particular liking, as an act of affection for and collaboration with the butterfly whose caterpillars will devour its leaves and the birds who will eat the caterpillars. With time, the gardener may even gain a liking for the plant and come to regard it as beautiful, for the very reason that it nourishes life.

Unlike Goldsworthy's or the Tibetan monks' materials, the materials of the garden are living, growing things. Thus in a very real sense, the plants are co-creators of this beauty. Charles Lewis conceives of this partnership as grounded in the fact that "Green nature and human nature are both expressions of the pervasive life force that permeates the planet."[23] We can see this relationship at work in the way that many gardeners speak of their plants as having preferences, as 'liking' or 'not liking' a given location or soil; we may even experience gardening as an act in service to the plants, tending to their needs as one might tend a child. Some indigenous peoples sing songs to certain plants, attributing to them personalities of a dangerous lover or intractable child.[24] A gardener with an ecological consciousness will extend this sense of fond relationship to all forms of life that are fed by the plants we encourage to grow in our gardens.

Paying attention to what vegetables like and don't like gives us another reason to bring the beauty of flowers into the vegetable garden. According to folk wisdom, at least some of which has been experimentally confirmed, marigolds discourage nematodes, bee balm improves growth and flavor in tomatoes, geraniums repel cabbageworms and Japanese beetles, nasturtiums serve as traps for some pests and deter others, and petunias discourage the asparagus beetle. Evidence is inconclusive on how well such measures really work, but at the least, the practice of companion planting provides flower-loving gardeners with an ecological justification for devoting precious space to dahlias and chrysanthemums as well as strawberries and squash. William Morris considered art to be "the expression of man's pleasure in labour"; there is no question that the art of a *potager* with its trellises, fanciful designs, color-coordinated lettuce beds, and patches of herbs that are never harvested, is a natural expression of the gardener's pleasure in laboring with plants.[25]

THE GARDEN AS CRITICAL UTOPIA

I began this essay with the claim that a garden is a utopian text, expressing a vision of an ideal relation between human beings and nature, and even embodying aspects of such a relation. After considering dystopian aspects of our relation to nature, both in and out of the garden, I have come to a different formulation. Perhaps our ecological situation demands that we think of the garden not as a utopia in the sense of a vision of perfection, but as what Tom Moylan named the "critical utopia", which "reject[s] utopia as a blueprint while preserving it as a dream". The critical utopia incorporates into its very form the "conflict between the originary world and the utopian society opposed to it... [and focuses] on the continuing presence of difference and imperfection within the utopian society itself" in order to develop "more recognizable and dynamic alternatives".[26] The critical utopias of the 1970s, such as Piercy's *Woman on the Edge of Time*, Callenbach's *Ecotopia*, and Ursula K. Le Guin's *The Dispossessed: An Ambiguous Utopia*, are open-ended, raising more questions than they answer.[27] They present visions of more perfect worlds and set their readers on a productive journey toward that utopian horizon, but also maintain a certain ironic awareness that the horizon is ever-receding.

To understand one's garden as a text of this sort is to devote all best efforts of mind and body to building a home place that enables and embodies a more perfect relation between the human realm and the beings (whether sentient or insentient) of the non-human realm. But it is also to remain aware that such an enterprise can never be pure and will never be completed. We so often do too much, or do the wrong thing, in our relation with nature, and yet we can never do enough to honor the wealth and beauty of its gifts. In this, our care of our gardens is much like our care of each other, and requires the same kind of humility and gratitude.

The urban gardener can find some courage in regarding her own garden as part of a much larger, decentered and dispersed utopian project—one that has no grand plan, no coherent vision, but finds its meaning in process rather than product, and recognizes the impossibility of perfection while yet "preserving it as a dream". In my own city, the sometimes-unwitting participants in this larger project include those families who patiently petitioned City Hall for permission to build and tend raised beds on an abandoned tennis court. The project includes the inhabitants of one dilapidated house who like to sit on their porch on a Sunday morning smoking, cussing, drinking beer, and admiring the flowers and vegetables they have planted on every square inch of their corner lot, including the 'hell strip' between the broken-up asphalt sidewalk and the street. It includes neighbors who swap seedlings and divisions, and passersby who compliment a stranger's plantings. It certainly includes the generous folk who 'Plant a Row for the Hungry' in order to help the local soup kitchen, as well as the bird-lovers who wade through knee-high snow to stock their feeders all winter long. But it does not exclude the gardeners who pursue beauty alone: the rosarians, the peony fanciers, or the elderly gentleman who patrols his tiny lawn for dandelions. All such plant enthusiasts are motivated by a deep love for growing things. And even if they don't grow milkweed for the monarch butterflies or tomatoes for the table, such gardeners are utopianists, for by entering into an intimate relation of care with the natural world—however fallen—in their own backyards, they join the community of gardeners whose zinnias and bean tepees beautify the city's sidewalks and streets, and thus cultivate a larger space of perfection.

A particular house in my neighborhood hasn't been painted in many years, and one of its porch columns is askew. I have never seen its inhabitants. What I know of them is confined to the patch of sunflowers they start from seed every May. When I walk up and down that street, I take pleasure in these bright flower faces. In the autumn, the birds feed there. This too is part of my urban garden.

Notes

1. Moylan, Tom, *Demand the Impossible: Science Fiction and the Utopian Imagination*, New York: Methuen, 1986.
2. http://www.mainetreefoundation.org/forestfacts/Who%20Owns%20Maine's%20Forest.htm.
3. Thoreau, Henry David, *The Maine Woods*, Electronic Text Center, University of Virginia Library, 2000, p. 46. http://etext.virginia.edu/toc/modeng/public/ThoMain.html.
4. Hopkins, Gerard Manley, "God's Grandeur", *Poems of Gerard Manley Hopkins*, W. H. Gardner and N. H. Mackenzie eds., Oxford: Oxford UP, 1973, p. 19.
5. Doolittle, William E., "Gardens are Us, We are Nature: Transcending Antiquity and Modernity", *Geographical Review*, vol. 94, no. 3, July 2004, p. 391.
6. DCNR Exotic Invasive Plant Tutorial, "Norway Maple (*acer platanoides*)". http://www.dcnr.state.pa.us/forestry/invasivetutorial/norway_maple.htm.
7. Tallamy, Douglas W., *Bringing Nature Home: How Native Plants Sustain Wildlife in Our Gardens*, Portland, Oregon: Timber Press, 2007.
8. Dawson, Kerry J., "Nature in the Urban Garden", *The Meaning of Gardens: Idea, Place, and Action*, Mark Francis and Randolph T. Hester, Jr. eds., Cambridge, MA and London: MIT Press, 1990, p. 142.
9. Treib, Mark, "Power Plays: The Garden as Pet", *The Meaning of Gardens*, pp. 86–87.
10. Doolittle, "Gardens are us, we are nature", p. 398.
11. Massey, Doreen, "A Global Sense of Place," *Space, Place and Gender*, Minneapolis: University of Minnesota Press, 1994. http://www.unc.edu/courses/2006spring/geog/021/001/massey.pdf.
12. Gandy, Matthew, quoted in Bruce Braun, "Environmental issues: writing a more-than-human urban geography", *Progress in Human Geography*, vol. 29, no. 5, 2005, p. 640. Braun's essay provides an excellent overview of new work that "unsettles the longstanding separation" of urban studies and environmental studies (p. 635).
13. Cronon, William, "The Trouble with Wilderness: or, Getting Back to the Wrong Nature", William Cronon ed., *Uncommon Ground: Rethinking the Human Place in Nature*, New York: W. W. Norton, 1995, pp. 69–90. http://www.williamcronon.net/writing/Trouble_with_Wilderness_Main.html.
14. Csisnery-Ronay, István, "Notes on Mutopia", *Postmodern Culture*, vol. 8, no. 1, 1997, paragraph 18. http://pmc.iath.virginia.edu/text-only/issue.997/csicsery.997.
15. The phrase "more-than-human" in this context is from Sarah Whatmore, *Hybrid Geographies: Natures, Cultures, Spaces*, London: Sage, 2002.
16. Morris, William, "How I Became a Socialist", *Political Writings of William Morris*, A. L. Morton ed., New York: International Publishers, 1973, p. 246.
17. Krall, Florence, "Spring, Summer, Fall, and Winter", in Francis and Hester eds., *The Meaning of Gardens: Idea, Place, and Action*, p. 144, emphasis added.
18. http://www.potager-du-roi.fr/anglaid/anglais.html.
19. Pavord, Anna, "Square meals", *The Independent*, 14 April 2007. http://www.independent.co.uk/life-style/house-and-home/gardening/square-meals-potagers-are-vegetable-gardens-taken-to-their-ultimate-geometrical-conclusion-and-they-look-just-too-good-to-eat-says-anna-pavord-759438.html.
20. King, Roger J. H. "Toward an Ethics of the Domesticated Environment", *Philosophy and Geography*, vol. 6, no. 1, 2003, p. 6.
21. Cooper, David E., *A Philosophy of Gardens*, Oxford: Oxford University Press, 2006.
22. Freer Gallery of Art and Arthur M. Sackler Gallery, "Tibetan Healing Mandala", http://www.asia.si.edu/exhibitions/online/mandala/mandala.htm.
23. Lewis, Charles A., *Green Nature, Human Nature: The Meaning of Plants in Our Lives*, Urbana: University of Illinois Press, 1996, p. 132.
24. Swanson, Tod Dillon, "Singing to Estranged Lovers: Runa Relations to Plants in the Ecuadorian Amazon", *Journal for the Study of Religion, Nature and Culture*, vol. 3, no. 1, 2009, pp. 36–65.
25. Morris, William, "Preface to *The Nature of Gothic* by John Ruskin", *News from Nowhere and Other Writings*, Clive Wilmer ed., London: Penguin, 1993, p. 367.
26. Moylan, *Demand the Impossible*, pp. 10–11.
27. Piercy, Marge, *Woman on the Edge of Time*, New York: Alfred A. Knopf, 1976; Ernest Callenbach, *Ecotopia: the Notebooks and Reports of William Weston*, New York: Bantam, 1977; Ursula K. Le Guin, *The Dispossessed: An Ambiguous Utopia*, New York: Harper and Row, 1974.

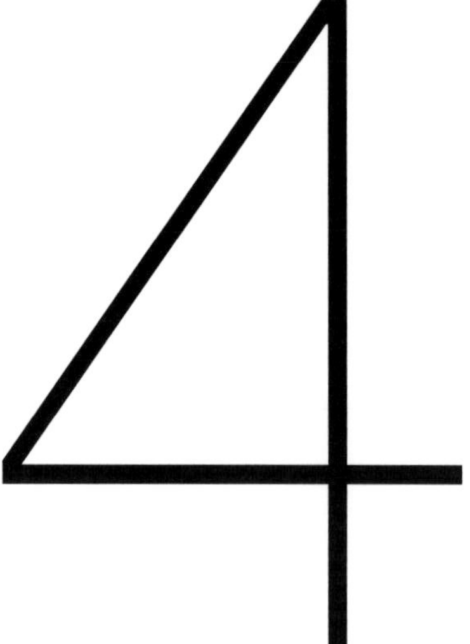

THE GARDEN POLITIC

PLOTS OF PARADISE: GARDENS AND THE UTOPIAN CITY

172 /DENNIS HARDY

Utopias are portrayals of perfection, and when the mind of the utopian is turned to the city there is almost invariably a place for the garden, in one form or another. In the first section of this essay, we ask why this is so, why gardens are so universally favored by utopians. The two subsequent sections review a range of utopian schemes, the first focusing on examples where gardens within the city are given pride of place, and the second looking at depictions of the city itself within a garden. Finally, one has to recognize that there is always a serpent in paradise, and that in some models of perfection the very idea of the garden is anathema. Nothing in utopia should ever be taken for granted.

GARDENS IN UTOPIA

What is a garden for? For the soul, sir, For the soul of the poet! For visions of the invisible, for grasping the intangible, for hearing the inaudible, for exaltations.
/ Anonymous[1]

Architects, planners, political theorists, and social reformers alike have all had a hand in presenting their own versions of the perfect city. Their schemes differ widely in many aspects but most include gardens, both private and communal, as a common element. There seems to be an assumption that individuals require ready access to nature and that gardens offer the best means to provide this. But why do so many utopians share this basic assumption? Why is there an almost universal predilection for gardens?

One reason is that utopians will often regard the Earth itself as a garden, a natural paradise, and if its finer qualities have been lost, perhaps they can at least be replicated in microform. A second reason is that gardens are appreciated as welcome places of retreat, of mental and spiritual repose. Thirdly, an open space of one's own or shared in a community can contribute to better physical health and wellbeing. Finally, in its most basic form, the garden can be a source of food, offering personal satisfaction as well as high rates of yield.

THE EARTH AS A GARDEN

God Almighty first planted a garden; and, indeed, it is the purest of human pleasures.
/ Francis Bacon[2]

Utopians have a tendency to try to repair what is broken, to replace what is lost. In their quest for perfection they will sometimes refer back to a perceived Golden Age, when the Earth was pristine, before damage was wrought by humans. No matter that such an idyll might never have existed (or at least only momentarily), the so-called Golden Age has exercised a powerful and persistent hold on the utopian imagination. Commonly, the Earth is likened to a garden: a natural idyll laced with clear streams, of orchards sweet with the scent of lush fruits, of dense forests stretching to the horizon and wild animals roaming freely but also peaceably:

> Oh, happy Eden of those golden years
> Which memory cherishes, and use endears.[3]

Depending on one's cultural traditions, for many this notion of an earthly paradise is represented by the Garden of Eden [Figure 1]. The story is too well-known to repeat in detail, but suffice it to say that Adam and Eve were installed by God in a place that was, literally, too wonderful to last.[4] Every tree that was "pleasant to the sight and good for food" grew there, four rivers kept the land permanently irrigated, and a plentiful stock of cattle fed from the lush pastures. There was even gold for the taking, but best of all for the human future, there was a Tree of Life and a Tree of the Knowledge of Good and Evil. Freedom abounded, with only one rule to be obeyed, namely, not to eat from the Tree of Knowledge. The rest, as they say, is history, and when Eve bit into the forbidden fruit, the first two humans, not to mention all of their successors, were summarily dismissed from paradise. For the rest of time, the human race has lived in the wilderness, though constantly seeking a way back. The making of utopias is evidence of this constant quest. As such, a return to Eden offers an illustrative metaphor for the whole utopian tradition.

There are other depictions of a similar ilk, like the story of Gilgamesh. Reputed to be the earliest written records, 12 stone tablets tell of a legendary king, Gilgamesh,

Figure 1/ *The Garden of Eden.* Anonymous. Image courtesy of Dennis Hardy, private collection.

in ancient Mesopotamia (now southern Iraq).[5] The tablets themselves date from around 2000 BCE, although they refer to an even earlier period, perhaps a millennium before. Poor Gilgamesh seemed to have everything material a man could wish for but not enough to bring him happiness. Haunted by the death of his good friend, he set off to seek the advice of Utnapishtim, an immortal sage who lived in the faraway land of Dilmun. Overcoming formidable obstacles on his legendary journey, and defying constant exhortations to turn back, he eventually reached his destination. There he found what at first he thought was a true paradise: where precious gemstones grew on trees, while "the croak of the raven was not heard, the bird of prey did not utter the cry of death, the lion did not devour, the wolf did not rend the lamb, the dove did not mourn, there was no widow, no sickness, no old age, no lamentation".[6] In contrast with his own environment, there was a perfect climate, and the land was irrigated by fresh water from rivers and streams. Alas, even these natural riches could not satisfy the king, for their very perfection was overshadowed by constant thoughts of death; as the sage pointed out to him, nothing is permanent and there was no escaping the fact of mortality. We must be slow learners, for this poignant lesson that there is always a dark side to perfection has been persistently ignored.

THE GARDEN AS A RETREAT

A place of submission, of refuge, of sanctuary and of looking inwards for hidden treasures.
/ Jane Brown[7]

In a metaphysical sense, gardens offer a means of escape from the outside world. They have always done so, but especially in modern times when, with cities characterized increasingly by a sense of 'mass'—large numbers, intensity of life, high density of buildings—utopians recognize the garden as a place to recover one's personal sense of spiritual balance. It is somewhere to enjoy the scent of a home-grown rose, somewhere to listen to the birds, somewhere to look at the night sky. Perhaps it will be a backyard, perhaps a roof space, or even a garden shared with others. Whatever its form, for the individual it offers a place "of enchantment and peace, where all our ills can be cured".[8]

We are impressionable souls, and ideas form at an early age. Children's literature is rich in imagery of the garden as a place in which to hide from tiresome adults, a place in which one can create one's own secret world. Emblematic of this theme is *The Secret Garden*. Here the eponymous plot of land is entered through a long-disused door covered with ivy.[9] Finding what was once a walled garden, but at the time of its discovery is little more than a wilderness, Mary, the young protagonist, sets her mind to restoring it. In the process she overcomes her own bitterness as an unwanted child, and also helps the sickly son of the owner to regain his health. Such are the restorative powers of gardens. In another iconic children's book, *Alice in Wonderland*, the main setting is once again a garden.[10] As in *The Secret Garden*, a young girl leads the reader into a hidden world, although this time one that is embellished more decoratively with fantasy. Unlike Mary, who simply steps through a doorway, the whimsical Alice literally tumbles below the ground to discover her own make-believe world. One by one she meets the quirkiest of characters, who challenge everything she takes for granted. Somehow she remains remarkably composed, treating it all as no more than a dream—which it might well have been. Less fanciful but even more widely read by successive generations, another author, Enid Blyton, invited her young readers to indulge in their own adventures, encountering fairies and goblins in gardens where adults are absent.[11] It is only when it is time for tea that a rosy-cheeked aunt appears with a tray of lemonade and buttered scones filled with jam and cream. Fantasy is one thing, but propriety rules that children must not stay in their wondrous gardens for too long.

Figure 2/ Court of the Water Channel, Palacio de Generalife (Jannat al-Arif, the Architect's Garden). Summer palace and country estate of the Nasrid Emirs of the Emirate of Granada, al-Andalus. Constructed 1302–1309. Granada, Spain. Photograph courtesy of César Atanes.

On a more adult theme, one of our earliest images of the garden as a place of escape is to be found in a hybrid of Islamic and Mogul designs.[12] There, one leaves behind all worldly cares to step into a private refuge that is cool and quiet, scented with flowering jasmine and orange blossom. The only sound is of water gently trickling from the fountain that is invariably the centerpiece. Nor are such gardens purely physical retreats, for they are no less renowned for their sensuality. Here both men and women recline seductively, clothed in fine silks, their bodies bathed in evocatively scented oils. Bowls of fruit are placed within reach, filled with ripe peaches, apricots, and fleshy dates. Such gardens can be on a purely domestic scale, typically in the form of enclosed courtyards with a surrounding dwelling, just a step away from a crowded street. In contrast, gardens in this tradition can also be on a monumental scale, offering an exotic setting for a palace, invariably laid out in a strictly geometrical form where symbolism determines its orientation and finer details [Figure 2].

Without the material splendor, not to mention the sensuality, of the above, another example of gardens of refuge can be found in monasteries and convents. Such institutions are by their very nature places of retreat and reflection, and gardens are designed to support their essential principles.[13] Monastic life is an ordered existence, and it is no surprise that garden design is not left to chance. St. Benedict, for instance, specified detailed rules for what became the Benedictine Order, including the pronouncement that gardening was worthy and virtuous. There is evidence that from as early as the ninth century, the Order's gardens were laid out according to a prescribed design. Plots were allocated for vegetables and herbs to serve the kitchen, for medicinal plants to cure ailments, for orchards that yielded blossoms as well as fruit, and for flowery lawns to surround the graves of past devotees [Figure 3]. In the convents, gardens were no less important, and symbolism played its own part in deciding what was grown; the lily, for example, was included as a sign of virginal purity. Together, gardens made their own important contribution to the creation of a particular version of paradise:

> With all these miraculous images, of lily gardens, veiled virgins, flowery meads, the life-saving physic garden, and the Queen of Heaven's beautiful flowers, it seems not at all strange that for pilgrims and ordinary people, these secret gardens of monasteries and convents could fulfill their visions of paradise.[14]

As in the past, gardens continue to offer welcome respite from the pressures of everyday modern life. Although the trend in cities is towards higher densities and greater concentration, allowing less space for private gardens, this has only served to increase appreciation for a personal place of retreat.

Figure 3/ Cloister herb garden.
Gloucester Cathedral, UK. Photograph courtesy of Charlie Beldon.

HEALTHY PLACES

The garden and its summerhouse is the worker's country home.
/ Ligue du coin de terre et du foyer[15]

In addition to being regarded as a sanctuary, the garden is credited with making tangible contributions to health and wellbeing. From the end of the eighteenth century, with the spread of industrialization and consequent urbanization in Western Europe and the United States, the issue of health assumed a particular prominence in the utopian lexicon. Typically, the utopian will look at the world as it is and then turn it upside down, shaking out the most obvious ills and introducing something better. What the utopian saw at this time was an urban population often living under a permanent pall of noxious smoke, without access to fresh water, and with the city's waste running through the streets. Disease was rife and mortality rates were rising. Little wonder that utopian schemes at the time envisaged cities in which all of these ills would be a thing of the past. In their model cities the sun would once again shine through, no one would die of a preventable illness, and nature would be ushered back with the spread of parks and gardens.

Reflecting such hopes, in 1876 a British medical practitioner, Sir Benjamin Ward Richardson, presented to an audience of reformers his vision of a city of health, which he named Hygeia.[16] It would have a population of 100,000, at a density of 25 persons per acre. The houses would be well ventilated and "filled with sunlight", and "planted on each side of the pathways with trees, and in many places with shrubs and evergreens. All the interspaces between the backs of houses [would be] gardens."[17] Additionally, as the houses were to have largely flat roofs, Richardson saw the potential of this upper space for further gardens, "barricaded round with iron palisades, tastefully painted, [to] make excellent outdoor grounds for every house. In some instances flowers [would be] cultivated on them."[18] Anticipating a skeptical response (as utopians usually do), he offered the assurance that "utopia itself is but another word for time; and some day the masses, who now heed us not, or smile incredulously at our proceedings, will awake to our conceptions".[19]

Words were one thing, but in the more developed countries, throughout the second half of the nineteenth century, industrialists (who had the most to gain from a healthy workforce) advanced a number of pioneering schemes of their own. Better housing was the *sine qua non*, but their model communities invariably laid stress on the importance of gardens as well. While these schemes were not strictly utopian, if only because the *status quo* in the form of the capitalist infrastructure was to remain in place, their treatment of individual features like gardens was radically different from what was commonplace at the time. Perhaps they fell short of turning the world upside down, but at least they tilted it sharply in favor of a restored balance with nature.

Illustrating this genre is George Cadbury's Bournville. Cadbury was a Quaker and member of the family of chocolate manufacturers of that same name in Birmingham, England. When the Cadbury factory was relocated to the outskirts of the city, he seized the opportunity to commission a model settlement—which he named Bournville—that would provide family houses with gardens. The housing would be of a much higher standard than his workers had previously experienced in the city, and the new living environment was greatly enhanced by individual gardens. Cadbury could see immediately the value of these gardens and ensured that, before the houses were occupied, the generously-sized plots were planted with fruit trees and laid out with flower beds: "everyone received a generous provision of eight apple and pear trees, twelve gooseberry bushes, a Victoria plum tree and creepers to adorn the house".[20] Tenants were required to agree that they would keep their gardens neat and tidy, and they were encouraged to attend classes in the village on gardening skills. This might all seem very paternalistic now—as, indeed, utopian schemes often do—but Cadbury could at least produce figures to show that the inhabitants of Bournville enjoyed better health than their counterparts in Birmingham.[21]

NATURE'S BOUNTY

Outside my work the thing I care about is gardening, especially vegetable gardening.
/ George Orwell[22]

Finally, the garden appears in some utopian schemes as a rich and often untapped source of food. Certainly, as the above quote suggests, it appealed to at least one critical observer of modern life, George Orwell. Yet the productive garden has certainly not always been a utopian vision. It was one thing to contemplate an exotic garden where the trees were heavily laden with ripe pomegranates and juicy figs, just waiting to be picked, but quite another to have to exert oneself to make things grow. For a peasant population, toiling everyday in the fields, growing vegetables on one's own plot was a necessity rather than an aspiration. Little wonder that in the legendary Land of Cokaygne, a popular idyll in Medieval times, it was enough just to wait for "larks that are so couth [to] fly down into man's mouth, smothered in stew, and thereupon piles of powdered cinnamon".[23] For the hungry peasant, that, indeed, was a true utopia.

Thus, it is only with the separation of the peasant from the land that the idea of a productive garden becomes something of a dream. Utopias come into their own when they can offer a stark alternative to daily living, and it was this change of circumstances—from a basically agricultural to an industrial society—that turned thoughts of a return to the soil into an ideal. In the middle of the nineteenth century, for example, Feargus O'Connor, the radical campaigner for political reform in Britain, urged a renewed attachment to the land.[24] Lamenting the shortcomings of wage labor in industrial towns, he proposed, instead, a society of smallholdings where every family could feed itself. A number of experimental colonies were formed but, by their very nature, these were anti-urban. Other 'back to the land' schemes followed, but it was not until the end of the century that thoughts were turned to a more suburban model of growing one's own food. The context this time was the expansion of the city, replacing the inner core of cramped, unhealthy conditions with more spacious houses with gardens, in which fruit trees could be planted and vegetable beds laid out. There, in the peace of one's own plot, the gardener could reflect on the tenuous restoration of a balance with nature that one might have thought lost for ever with the advent of industrialization.

More recently, productive gardens have come to enjoy a new lease on life in the context of a modern enthusiasm for organic products and a global search for sustainability. From well before communes made their mark in the 1960s, expressing the ideals of the modern alternative movement, growing one's own food has been a constant aspiration. Many intentional communities have stressed the value of working the land, seeing in the process an assertion of their detachment from industrial society. Other advantages include the communal nature of the activity as well as the sheer enjoyment of eating food that is grown through one's own labor and without the use of chemicals. Anyone who has visited a commune will be familiar with the attention paid to the vegetable garden, worked meticulously by hand, the soil constantly enriched with compost from kitchen and other waste. The resultant crops are often remarkable in their abundance and quality, and are soon taken to the kitchen to be used in a variety of delicious dishes; indeed, home-grown food has given a distinctive stamp to the commune menu.[25]

One of various offshoots of this aspect of the alternative movement has been the concept of permaculture, the term combining the words "permanent" and "agriculture", but also "permanent" and "culture". Pioneered in Australia in the 1970s, it first concentrated on ways to achieve a balance between agriculture and nature, but the principles have since been extended to embrace wider issues of designing sustainable human habitats. The most fascinating application of permaculture is to be found in the towns and cities of Cuba and, especially, the capital, Havana, since the early 1990s. With the benefit of advice from permaculture experts, the country instituted a massive drive to encourage urban agriculture. Almost overnight, vacant lots were turned into productive growing areas, and yards and flat rooftops were filled with containers for vegetables and vines, as well as hutches for rabbits and chickens. Out of necessity, the food shortages that had become critical were largely overcome through the people's own inventive production, so much so that Havana can now provide from within its own boundaries an estimated 50 percent of its own vegetables, "while in other Cuban towns and cities urban gardens produce from 80 percent to more than 100 percent of what they need".[26] Comparable examples showing the potential productivity of urban land can be found in the experience of Britain and the United States during the Second World War.[27] Those relatively few instances where it has been tried are enough to reveal the enormous potential of urban land for growing food.

Clearly, there are reasons enough for gardens to find a place in the utopian city and, indeed, they are included in most. Not surprisingly, given the diversity of utopian schemes, the nature of gardens themselves varies. One essential difference is between those cities that contain gardens within their boundaries, and, in contrast—although by no means mutually exclusive—those that are set within a garden matrix.

GARDENS WITHIN THE UTOPIAN CITY

A beautiful house in a beautiful garden and a beautiful city for all.
/ Raymond Unwin[28]

When considering gardens within cities, where better to start than on Thomas More's imaginary island of Utopia, which gave its name to the whole genre of 'utopian' thought? We soon discover that there are "fifty-four splendid big towns" on the island, all exactly alike.[29] Aircastle, the capital of Utopia, is protected from invaders (who might threaten their perfect existence) by high walls and a moat. The citizens of Aircastle, excluding the slaves, live in substantial houses, and behind each one is a large garden that is completely enclosed:

> They're extremely fond of these gardens, in which they grow fruit, including grapes, as well as grass and flowers. They keep them in wonderful condition —in fact, I've never seen anything to beat them for beauty or fertility. The people of Aircastle are keen gardeners not only because they enjoy it, but because there are inter-street competitions for the best-kept garden. Certainly it would be hard to find any feature of the town more calculated to give pleasure and profit to the community—which makes me think that gardening must have been one of the founder's special interests.[30]

It is likely that More found the gardens of Utopia endearing because of the pleasure that his own garden in Chelsea afforded in the troubled times when he stood his ground against the adulterous Henry VIII. But whatever his reason, More's description of the importance of the garden in urban life resonates with later portrayals. Gardens are usually included without question in utopian city schemes; some such gardens are given a place in downtown and adjoining areas, while others reside in suburban areas where they feature more extensively and might even be considered a reason for the outward spread of the city.

THE COMMUNITY GARDEN

The owner of a small garden in a dense urban area has in fact only to lie on his back on a summer's day, and look upwards through foliage to the sky, to realise that he is able to reach back to his origins.
/ Grant Allen[31]

Space is necessarily at a premium in downtown areas, but this has not dampened an inherent enthusiasm for gardens, including the possibility of shared use. This latter option,

Figure 4/ Community plots in Todmorden, Yorkshire, UK. Photographs by Jane Woolfenden.

in turn, reflects an important divergence in utopian thought between ideals based on private property and those favoring a more collective form of society. In fact, the choice is rarely one of total extremes, and, in the case of communal gardens, they make an appearance in various guises. Over the past half-century, often associated with community activism, downtown areas have become home to a variety of garden-based experiments. In the 1980s in the United States the trend was described as "well established and well supported across the country.... Today's community gardens are more diverse and are successful public amenities, many made beautiful by ornamental plantings and public facilities of various kinds. Participants have developed a stronger bond to the land."[32]

Land is not in such short supply as at first appears, and activists have discovered different ways to use vacant lots on street corners, sites recovered from industrial dereliction, and even local parks that are no longer used because of neglect. In such places one can now find urban farms where flowers as well as vegetables are grown and local children help to tend chickens and stock; well-equipped play areas reserved for young children and their minders; and newly landscaped neighborhood parks for communal events as well as relaxation. Todmorden, for example, is a small, former industrial town in Yorkshire, England, that illustrates an inventive use of space to grow vegetables and herbs.[33] Along the streets and lanes one finds hanging baskets and raised beds, and in the yard of the railway station are various growing areas where travellers are encouraged to pick their own fresh produce [Figure 4]. The initiative—under the banner of "incredible edible"—is entirely community driven and everything is freely available, in the hope that it will lead to a greater understanding of sustainable principles and the potential of urban farming.

Amongst those who, I imagine, would have approved of this trend of community-based gardens is Jane Jacobs, the author in the early 1960s of a pivotal work of twentieth-century planning literature.[34] In *The Death and Life of Great American Cities*, she made an impassioned plea for city planners to take note of successful neighborhoods like her own Greenwich Village in New York City, where life was centered on its busy streets and public spaces and on spontaneous community action. In so doing, she helped pave the way for a movement known as The New Urbanism.

Originating in the United States, New Urbanism portrays the modern city in the form of a reconciliation with more traditional, organic, and site-specific forms of town building. Two architect planners, Andres Duany and Elizabeth Plater-Zyberk, were amongst a small but influential group of American architects who assumed a leading role in questioning the inevitability of peripheral urban expansion and helping to shape an alternative approach. Just as Jane Jacobs had advocated several decades earlier, for the New Urbanist, too, life revolves around the street, though narrowed

Figure 5/ Front and back gardens in Poundbury, Dorset, UK. Photographs by Jane Woolfenden.

to a more 'human' scale in hopes of reducing reliance on the car. Although New Urbanism advocates compact housing, there is also a call for gardens, both private and communal, around the city as well as within. It is axiomatic that "farmland and nature are as important to the metropolis as the garden is to the house".[35] Encouraged in response to the excesses of seemingly endless swathes of suburban sprawl coupled with the demise of downtown areas, the New Urbanist town planning movement has spawned a growing number of projects in the United States including Celebration and Seaside in Florida, as well as Kentlands in Maryland.[36]

Demonstrating similar planning tendencies is Poundbury in Great Britain.[37] Based on a master plan by Leon Krier, Poundbury is a mixed-use development characterized by an architectural style based on the regional vernacular. It is intended as a walkable environment and, to make that possible, the houses are close together and gardens are small. In spite of these constraints, the narrow strips to the front of the houses and the 'pocket handkerchief' back gardens are meticulously tended so that each in its own way has become a feature of the community [Figure 5]. Every June, for instance, when the flowers are at their best, residents organize an 'open day' so that neighbors can visit each other's valued plots. Green ribbons are tied to the gateposts to signal which of the gardens can be visited. Given the relative uniformity and unpromising characteristics of the bare plots when purchased, the results are remarkably diverse and enterprising. Some are more contemporary in design: in one of these, for instance, geometric stone slabs are laid across each other in a cruciform structure, with water trickling across the surfaces from a hidden source, the whole set against a backcloth of carefully-chosen shrubs of a distinctly spiky nature. In others, Poundbury's theme of an old market town is enthusiastically picked up, with cottage gardens filled with delphinium and rambling roses, brightly colored poppies and clumps of scabious, orange marigolds and delicate fritillaries.

Patios are universal in these gardens, and conservatories are popular as a means of extending the living room into the garden, or purely as an extension for space-hungry families. Water features, an icon of fashion, are also much in evidence, with fountains mounted on the surrounding walls and ponds sited centrally at the heart of the garden design. Another feature of the contemporary small garden is the use made of metal or stone sculptures and different forms of artwork. Because so many gardens are overlooked, climbing evergreens are grown to provide a constant screen, with trellises mounted along the tops of walls and fences to secure at least a modicum of privacy. Many of the gardens are far from perfect by professional standards, but that is not the point: for those who have made them what they are, these little spaces offer essential space that is truly one's own, a private cosmos.

SUBURBAN PARADISE

The popular semi-detached garden of the early twentieth century became not of the twentieth-century at all, but of the seventeenth, an evocation of middle-class paradise in Tudor England.

/ Jane Brown[38]

It might seem incongruous to portray the suburbs—so often vilified as neither urban nor rural—as a utopian ideal. Yet that is exactly what they were and, for many, still are. The idea of the suburb was born as an antidote to the unhealthy living environment of the industrial city, offering a new type of settlement where residents could live in more spacious surroundings, each house with its own garden. Towards the end of the nineteenth century, campaigners in the more industrialized countries pressed the case for this greener alternative. Ebenezer Howard, a London clerk with a social conscience combined with a penchant for inventions, came up with the idea of the

Figure 6/ The Garden City:
an attractive alternative to urban living. Image courtesy of the Town and Country Planning Association, UK.

"garden city", a form of settlement that would embody the best of town and country [Figure 6].[39] His scheme attracted immediate acclaim (as well as criticism for being unrealistic, a cross that all utopians have to bear) and some of his followers adopted an almost Biblical stance in associating the garden city with the prospect of salvation:

> No more in sunless cities, grim and grey,
> Thro' brick-built conduits shall the nation pour
> Her dwindling life in torment...
> For you in league with sunshine and fresh air,
> With comfortable grass and healing flowers,
> Have sworn to bring man back his natural good,
> Have planned a Garden City, fresh and fair
> When Work and Thought and Rest may ply
> their powers,
> And joy go hand in hand with Brotherhood.[40]

Howard had something very specific in mind when he coined the term "garden city", but the reality is that the term was used loosely by commercial developers—along with the related concepts of garden suburbs and garden villages—to make a wide variety of suburban estates sound more attractive than they really were. In any case, whatever it was called, nothing could stop the suburban explosion that changed the shape of the modern city in the twentieth century. New houses with gardens in Britain, for instance, replaced the countryside that formerly surrounded the big cities, and a whole new lifestyle emerged. It is unlikely that much of this would have been to Thomas More's liking—it was all far too spontaneous for a start—but he would at least have had a soft spot for the attention that was so often lavished on the gardens. Unpromising soils were tamed, and within a few years there was an abundance of fruit trees and flowering shrubs, carefully tended rose bowers, and herbaceous borders that were inauspicious in themselves but, perhaps in the minds of their creators, inspired by some of the great gardens of the eighteenth century. The author of *Utopia* would also have taken satisfaction at the sight of annual competitions that encouraged this new generation of gardeners to display their prize vegetables and perfectly formed flowers.

Although the garden city movement stressed the importance of individual houses, each with its own outdoor space, a number of the early schemes incorporated co-partnership developments where gardens and sometimes other facilities, too, were shared between residents. A variation on this general theme was the inclusion of the likes of communal tennis courts and children's play areas in addition to private gardens. Letchworth Garden City, Hampstead Garden Suburb, Brentham Garden Suburb, and Welwyn Garden City all contained areas of communal space; this, however, was the exception rather than the rule [Figure 7]. Innovation was in short supply in most of the suburbs, and yet there are still gems to be found. Hampstead Garden Suburb, which at the time of its formation was on the edge of London, remains an exemplar of good suburban development where the impact of the individual gardens is augmented by the adjacency of Hampstead Heath, one of London's great natural parks. On the European continent, Germany, Holland, and France, in particular, saw the emergence of their own model developments, mainly garden suburbs.[41] Hellerau, for instance, on the outskirts of Dresden was noted not only for its Arts and Crafts architecture and the greenery of its gardens but also as a vibrant community of artists, craft workers, and intellectuals. Margarethenhöhe was another German garden suburb that attracted praise as a pioneer development, while in France a number of comparable *cités-jardins* sprung up in the environs of Paris. Garden suburb enthusiasts carried their message further afield, to all parts of the world, and another model of their work is to be found in Adelaide, Australia, in the attractive Colonel Light Gardens. Christine Garnaut, the historian of this last development, shows that the proud owners of properties there used their front gardens as showpieces and the rear gardens for more utilitarian purposes.[42]

In the general rush to the suburbs, even those who could not afford to buy a house and garden of their own, or who were not part of a public authority allocation, found ways to connect with the soil. One means was through access to small plots of land where they could grow vegetables and cut flowers, known in Britain as allotments and in Europe by various terms such as workers' gardens, summerhouse

Figure 7/ Bringing back humanity's natural good. Image courtesy of the First Garden City Heritage Museum.

colonies, or leisure gardens. In all of these, working-class gardeners were able to escape from congested living conditions to while away an afternoon or even stay overnight in a self-built hut. The French Congress of Worker Gardeners in 1903 pointed to three advantages of these gardens: it was a healthy way of using leisure time and probably reduced alcoholism in the process; the stock of vegetables helped to keep down the cost of living; and the gardens on a sunny afternoon offered an opportunity to be with one's family.[43] Perhaps surprisingly, these areas of garden plots, often to be seen along railway lines and other marginal locations around cities, remain a feature of modern urban life, surviving as a tenuous link between industrial society and the land.

Taking the suburban ideal to a new level, the American architect, Frank Lloyd Wright in the 1920s looked across the endless American prairies and contemplated a world where everyone could live in large plots, each of at least an acre, that he termed homesteads. In his vision of what he called Broadacre City, he invoked a tradition of sturdy individualism where people could be reconnected with the soil. There, he believed, people would enjoy a sense of pride and identity that had become impossible in the modern city. No more would there be a sharp division between town and country, but instead, a fusion of the two across a wide landscape, held together by the car to which everyone now had access. "Broadacre City", he claimed, "is everywhere or nowhere. It is the country itself come alive as a truly great city."[44] Wright's bold plan to return humanity to a more natural state, more sensitive and in tune with nature, received a mixed reception; vilified by his detractors as intransigent, naïve, and autocratic, he ultimately had to watch as an inferior product took shape, in the form of repetitive rows of houses with gardens that constituted the modern American suburb.[45]

THE UTOPIAN CITY WITHIN A GARDEN

Town and country must be married, and out of this joyous union will spring a new hope, a new life, a new civilisation.
/ Ebenezer Howard[46]

In addition to gardens within utopian cities there is the related concept of a garden setting for the whole urban area. The idea has both practical and metaphysical appeal. Thus, at one level, nearby countryside that serves as a garden offers a fresh source of food and a venue for recreation. At another level, the idea touches on a deeper sense of balance with nature, of ensuring that town and country are in harmony rather than discord. To illustrate what has been a longstanding attempt by utopians to achieve this kind of balance between town and country, three sets of ideas can be considered. The first is broadly a product of utopias grounded in Romanticism; the second draws on specific schemes to ensure that the countryside is never far away; and the third is a unique example of what might be regarded as a folk utopia, where individuals spontaneously looked to the countryside for their own place in the sun.

ROMANTIC ATTACHMENT

I think that we
Shall never more, at any future time,
Delight our souls with talk of knightly deeds,
Walking about the gardens and the halls
Of Camelot, as in the days that were.
/ Alfred Lord Tennyson[47]

The problem with Romantics is that they harbor an inherent dislike of the city. Only grudgingly in some of their schemes do they come to terms with it, and where it cannot be replaced, at least they ensure that nature is never far away. John Ruskin, in the middle of the nineteenth century, was tormented by the sheer ugliness of the new urban landscape and wanted to turn back the clock to the imagined bliss of feudal society. He would have been happy to find himself in the legendary city of Camelot, home of King Arthur and the scene of lost chivalry:

> On either side the river lie
> Long fields of barley and of rye,
> That clothe the world and meet the sky;
> And thro' the field the road runs by
> To many-tower'd Camelot[48]

The idea of a compact city of noble values and its location in such a blissful setting, was compelling, and it is understandable that it has lent itself to utopian imagery. No matter that Camelot (or other such portrayals) is a product of the imagination, there is something about the balance between town and country that remains alluring—the one a nexus of power and intrigue, the other a place of pastoral innocence; the one a human artifact, the other a product of nature. While it would be easy to set one against the other, a juxtaposition of evil and good, of exploiter and exploited, there is a beguiling symmetry and mutual benefit in the relationship. The two are, in fact, complementary, and it becomes only natural to site the city in its own garden, like Camelot itself. Alfred Lord Tennyson, a contemporary of Ruskin, shared this fascination for the lost world of the Arthurian court, with its heroic deeds and chivalrous actions. Tennyson was also responsible for embroidering the legend, putting in his own words the many tales of derring-do that delighted his Victorian readership and then taking it all a stage further to show how the line between reality and imagination can so easily become blurred. Thus, as Gareth (an aspirant knight of King Arthur's round table) and his company approached the "many-tower'd" city of

Figure 8/ An indescribably pleasant impression.
Ashbee's model community at Chipping Campden, Gloucestershire, UK. Photograph courtesy of The Guild of Handicraft Trust.

Camelot across the river meadows, the first sighting of the city was through a morning mist that played tricks, first on their eyes and then their minds:

> At times the summit of the high city flashed;
> At times the spires and turrets half-way down
> Pricked through the mist; at times the great gate shone
> Only, that opened on the field below:
> Anon, the whole fair city had disappeared.[49]

Could this, they asked, be real?

> Those who went with Gareth were amazed
> One crying, Let us go no further, Lord.
> Here is a city of Enchanters....
> There is no such city anywhere
> But all a vision.[50]

Fired by images of this kind of lost idyll, Ruskin dreamed of nothing less than perfection in his own age, a place where every acre would be "under as strict care as a flower garden".[51] It was left to some of his fellow Romantics to rein things back, accepting that urbanization was here to stay but also believing that it need not be as awful as it had become. In particular, the divorce with nature that was by then endemic did not have to be permanent. Thus, Ruskin's contemporary, William Morris, went some way to bridge the gap, although he was himself no lover of big cities. By the time the narrator wakes in Morris' utopian romance, *News from Nowhere*—having gone to sleep in Victorian London—150 years has elapsed. It is enough time to show what could be done. London in its concentrated form (it was even in Morris' time a vast city) has been dispersed and everyone now lives within sight and easy reach of a rejuvenated countryside. People value their gardens and these are everywhere well tended and productive. But it is the change in England as a whole that most of all takes his attention, for in the words of the narrator of his story, "it is now a garden, where nothing is wasted and nothing is spoilt... all trim and neat and pretty".[52]

Ruskin and, to a lesser extent, Morris, both in their way spurned realism in their attempts to reverse the balance between town and country but, in spite of that, their influence on more practical minds was considerable. It was, for instance, only a short jump to the world of Arts and Crafts proponents like C. R. Ashbee, who was no less critical of the modern city, but who sought through his own scheme to create a better balance with nature [Figure 8]. Ashbee started by encouraging the revival of craftwork in East London, before embarking in 1902 on a remarkable

Figure 9/ An exemplary working community.
Ashbee's model community at Chipping Campden, Gloucestershire, UK. Photograph courtesy of The Guild of Handicraft Trust.

experiment that took him and some 150 workers and their families away from the capital.[53] There, in a village setting, they engaged in a variety of crafts and combined their work in the studios with gardening and other pursuits. In the words of a contemporary observer:

> And then looking out of the window, there were lovely views into gardens with their unimaginably lush flowerbeds. The silhouettes of huge trees and high steep roofs with mighty chimneys framed the picture. Here and there, through a gap, a glimpse of distant hills, of hazy-blue rolling country. All this created an indescribably pleasant impression. Presumably it must rain here sometimes, but the impression given by the way the men's work was carried out did not depend on vagaries of rain or sunshine.[54]

For a few years, until ending prematurely because of a shortage of finance, it all seemed to be idyllic, an exemplary model of a working community set in a garden [Figure 9].

GIRDLES AND BELTS

The general intention is to provide primarily for recreation and fresh food... and to prevent further continuous suburban outward growth.
/ Patrick Abercrombie[55]

When Ebenezer Howard proposed the inclusion of an agricultural belt to surround his garden city, he was the first to acknowledge that the idea itself was not new. He paid tribute to the early development of Adelaide in South Australia, where the original city was surround by a ring of "Park Lands".[56] It was later pointed out by one of his garden city disciples, F. J. Osborn, that he might equally have acknowledged a number of other Australasian cities with 'Park Belts' and even the Old Testament, where in Leviticus the people are forbidden to sell the common land belonging to their cities.[57] Thomas More, too, was insistent that each of the towns in Utopia reserved sufficient land for its food supply. Howard, of course, was writing at the end of the nineteenth century, and his own ideal was for a city that would draw many benefits from its own, encircling garden. In one of his finely drawn diagrams, he showed in some detail that such land would include allotments and cow pastures, smallholdings and fruit farms, new forests and large farms. With an eye to the therapeutic nature of gardens, he also designated sites for a farm for epileptics, convalescent homes, and also asylums for the blind and deaf. It was little wonder that Howard—who dwelt at length on some of the practical issues like rent levels—drew on quotes from John Ruskin, who could always be relied on to bring to life the spiritual qualities of such land too:

> No scene is continuously and untiringly loved but one rich by joyful human labour, smooth in field, fair in garden, full in orchard, trim, sweet, and frequent in homestead, ringing with voices of vivid existence. No air is sweet that is silent; it is only sweet when full of low currents of undersound, triplets of birds, and murmur and chirp of insects, and deep-toned words of men, and wayward trebles of childhood. As the art of life is learned, it will be found at last that all things lovely are also necessary.[58]

The city's garden, of course, was just one element of a holistic concept, where town and country are brought together to form a new unity: "town and country *must be married*, and out of this joyous union will spring a new hope, a new life, a new civilisation".[59] It was a message for its time and resonated with others who shared a sense of despair for the sorry state of modern cities and who wanted to do something about it. London, in particular, attracted their attention, already a large city but in the years ahead encroaching on its surrounding countryside at an alarming rate. Ironically, at the time, bus and rail companies were exhorting the public to make journeys at weekends into London's own garden while each year the journey became longer. With few planning powers to stem the flow of new development, local authorities had little option but to buy large swathes of land (like Epping Forest and Burnham Beeches) for the benefit of posterity. This kind of measure could only be partial in its impact and so, in 1927, a public committee was formed to see whether it might be possible to create what they called an "agricultural belt".[60] The technical adviser of the committee, Raymond Unwin, thought that the brief needed to be widened and he proposed what has been likened to a 'green girdle' to safeguard space for Londoners to engage in active recreation and also to enjoy the natural environment.[61]

During the Second World War, when plans were being laid for the anticipated peacetime, an influential report proposed the introduction of a Green Belt Ring (to be known subsequently as a Green Belt).[62] In this ring, development would be precluded and further metropolitan growth would have to leapfrog the preserved land into designated areas beyond. After the war, a Green Belt was formally established around London, and this concept has since been widely adopted, not only in other parts of Britain but also in cities around the world. In only a few places, however, is it totally green or even a complete belt; generally, it looks impressive in plans but is often barely recognizable on the ground.

PLOTS FOR THE PEOPLE

Leave all your troubles in those drab old towns
And fly, fly, fly.
There's still a plot or two upon the Downs
Left for you to buy.
/ George Powell[63]

The First Step towards Peace, a Haven and Happiness.

Figure 10/ Arcadia for all.
Image courtesy of Dennis Hardy, private collection.

Sometimes it is not enough merely to dream of somewhere better, nor to wait for a change of fortune to enable one to find an expensive place in the sun. Instead, as many individuals have shown, change will only come about by taking matters into one's own hands [Figure 10]. Even before the growth towards the end of the nineteenth century of a popular 'back to the land' movement, there is evidence of a great desire (often born of necessity) amongst city-dwellers to work the land. Thus, around the city of Nottingham, England, in the 1830s it was reported that there were "upwards of 5,000 gardens, the bulk of which are occupied by the working class".[64] The contemporary observer warmed to what he saw:

> Every garden has its summer-house; and these are of all scales and grades, from the erection of a few tub staves, with an attempt to train a pumpkin or a wild-hop over it, to substantial brick houses with glass windows.... Many are very picturesque rustic huts, built with great taste, and hidden by tall hedges in a perfect little paradise of lawn and shrubbery... [just the place for the occupants] to go and smoke a solitary pipe, as they look over the smiling face of their garden or take a quiet stroll amongst their flowers.[65]

In a similar vein, early in the following century there were people in London (and, undoubtedly, in many other large cities too) who were not content just to watch their better-off neighbors move to the suburbs.[66] They, too, wanted to dig their own garden and enjoy fresh air and were determined to do so, even without sufficient financial means for conventional transactions. Often through word of mouth, they heard of places in London's countryside where land could be bought for a song. Especially in the 1930s, when farmers were going out of business in the face of falling prices, estates were subdivided and sold in small parcels, with just a small 'down payment' to be found by the aspiring owner.

The hunt was on, and at weekends prospective buyers travelled out of London by train, or even by bicycle along the new arterial roads, to the most likely venues. Some of the more unscrupulous sellers would meet them at the station and take them to a 'hospitality tent' where, with a good filling of beer and meat pies, money soon exchanged hands. Often the land in question was of poor quality, neglected over the years and in a marginal location that was likely to flood, and it probably amounted to no more than a tiny plot. To the new owners, however, these were only details, the only thing that mattered being that they could now regard themselves as 'toffs', in their own minds almost as members of the landed gentry. Instead of the rolling acres of the latter, of course, in this case there was a small patch of waterlogged ground to turn into a country home. Ever inventive, the "plotlanders" (as they were called) bought army surplus bell tents used in the First World War and redundant Victorian railway carriages to live in, and when the sun broke through the digging began.

Every weekend the plots rung with the sound of hammers and saws, as more permanent structures were built, typically with whatever materials came to hand. Spades cut into the heavy clay and potatoes were planted to break up the soil, followed by greens and salad crops such as lettuce and tomatoes. Once they were more settled, and in an increasing number of cases with plots inhabited throughout the year, it was not uncommon to introduce chickens and geese, to add a pig-sty and a typically ramshackle stable, and for the odd goat to be tethered to a gatepost. The children helped with the chores, fetching water from a nearby standpipe, collecting eggs in the morning and buying items from one of the makeshift stores that served the plotholders. Meals were cooked on wood fires and paraffin stoves, and it was a rare treat for city dwellers to eat outside, like this, on their own land. These were self-help communities, where tools were shared and skills learned from each other. Gardening was a new pursuit for most of them, but it was as if an age-old attachment to the soil had been waiting for this release [Figure 11].

The plotlanders were not really harming anyone, and yet they attracted widespread opprobrium. Preservationists feared the whole of the countryside would be overrun in this way; middleclass homeowners resented this downmarket version of their own suburban idylls; and the authorities, fearing contamination of water supplies, saw these developments as a public health risk. In spite of attempts to remove them, so long as they held title to their land, they were, in fact, remarkably difficult to budge. The advent of more effective planning legislation stemmed further development of this kind, and over the years the original plots have been upgraded so that there is no longer anything exceptional about their appearance. All that is left now is the collective memory of an extraordinary episode of self-determination, when a generation of city-dwellers found their own way to return to the land.

Figure 11/ Reconnecting with the soil.
Photograph courtesy of Dennis Hardy, private collection.

THE SERPENT IN THE GARDEN

The serpent had been introduced into Utopia, and from that day to this it has been a struggle between utopian man and the most un-utopian intruder.
/ Bernard Levin[67]

In any study of utopias, one thing becomes clear: there is no such thing as a universal panacea. What might suit one group of people at a particular time can be anathema to others; it might not even appeal to the same group of people at a different time. Even a feature as seemingly benign as a garden should not be seen as a given. In spite of their perceived benefits, there is, in fact, no inherent reason for gardens to be included, in any form, in utopian plans for the perfect city. Indeed, some schemes have studiously avoided their inclusion, portraying an urban future where nature has no place.

Over his lifetime, H. G. Wells tended to change his mind as the world itself changed, but on the eve of the twentieth century he took a gloomy view of what lay ahead. In *The Sleeper Awakes* he looked to the day when London had swallowed up its surrounding countryside and its 33 million people spent most of their lives underground.[68] Streets and squares were placed beneath ground level in deep chasms, shielded from the elements and bathed, night and day, in a white light from powerful electric globes. Most urban dwellers were transported along moving platforms, nearly 100 meters across, with parallel platforms passing at different speeds. The subterranean race seemed perpetually on the move, always in a crowd, and ruled by a world leader called Ostrog: "We are making the future... and here it is!"[69]

Without needing a cue from Wells, but sharing a similarly uncompromising view of what was in prospect, the Italian Futurists barely a decade later advocated the functionalism and modernity of their own, 'high-tech', totally urban environment.[70] Utterly without sentimentality, they wanted to sweep away everything that was the work of past generations—including filling in Venice's canals and demolishing the Classical ruins of Rome—and to start afresh, embracing with enthusiasm new building materials

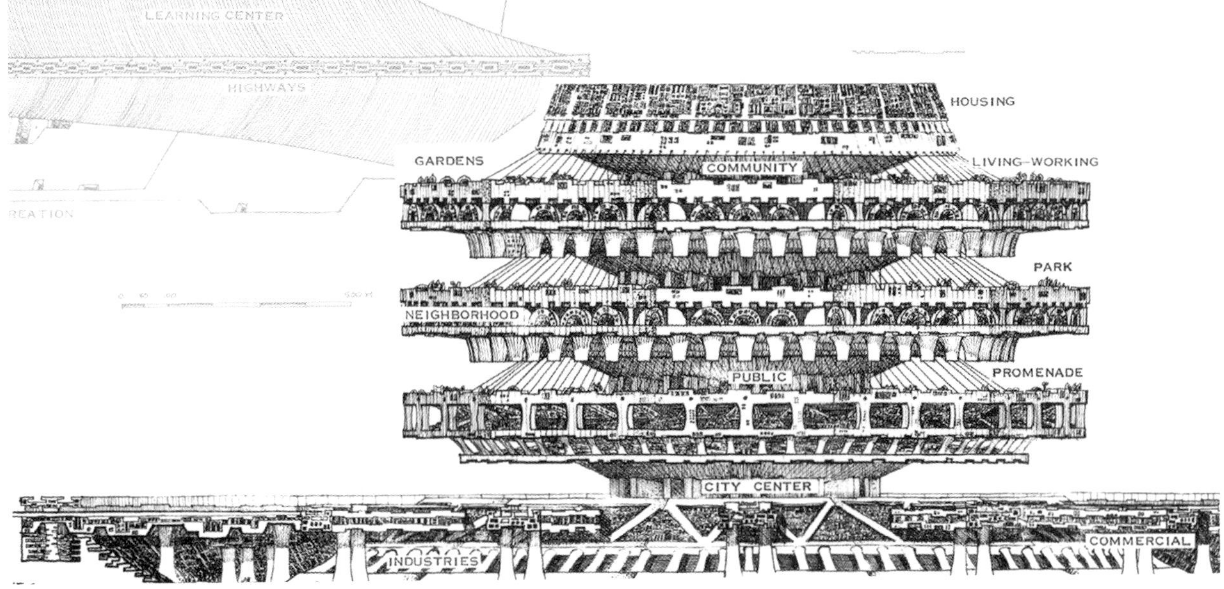

Figure 12/ Babel IIB, Arcology #9, elevation.
Paolo Soleri. The city is a conceptual design for a population of 520,000. Its height is 1,050 meters and its diameter 3,160 meters, with an anticipated population density of 662/hectare. Originally published in Paolo Soleri, *Arcology/ The City in the Image of Man*, Cambridge, MA: The MIT Press, 1969. Drawing courtesy of the Cosanti Foundation.

and techniques to create vast cities of towers. Life would be wholly urban, with human adrenalin flowing like currents of highly charged electricity and the metropolitan population energized by the sheer speed and excitement of it all. Adornment of any kind was irrelevant, and there was no place for individuality. In such a world, where nature was banished, the very idea of a garden was anomalous. Intoxicated by the prospect of a new world of their own making, the Futurists welcomed the outbreak of war in 1914 as a cleansing process that would quickly remove all traces of the past. In one sense they were prophetic; apart from the fact that the war removed a number of their own leading lights, its devastating impact encouraged the kind of totalitarianism that their uncompromising vision embodied.

The interwar period was not a good time for budding utopians and, instead, "the 1920s, 1930s and 1940s was the classic era of the utopia in the negative, the anti-utopia or dystopia".[71] This was epitomized by Aldous Huxley's *Brave New World*, where people are tightly controlled and most of them live in cities that seem to have been designed on the same drawing board as the earlier blueprints of Orwell and the Futurists.[72] There is no need for contact with nature as sensations can be aroused in rooms filled with evocative scents and an array of carefully attuned devices. Only a few pockets of wilderness are left in their original state, and the restricted number of visitors allowed to visit these are invariably horrified by the filth and danger of the natural environment, hastily retreating to the familiarity of their own sanitized and ultra-safe world. In writing a dystopia, Huxley, of course, knew that the scenario he portrayed was not to be sought but avoided. Meanwhile, other visions that are overtly utopian in their intent and geared towards the conservation of natural resources, possess elements that may be disquieting—too alien and therefore construed as dystopian—to those envisioning the lifestyle they project. Such, for example, is the case with Richard Buckminster Fuller (1895–1983), who turned to a functionalist technology that would both aid the conservation of resources such as energy and water as well as protect humanity from the ill effects of a nuclear holocaust. To this end, Fuller further developed engineer Walther Bauersfeld's innovative dome design. The center of a city like New York, he explained, could be totally enclosed within a transparent, air-conditioned 'geodesic' dome, creating, to his mind, a superior environment:

> From the inside there will be uninterrupted contact with the exterior world. The sun and moon will shine in the landscape, and the sky will be completely visible, but the unpleasant effects of climate, heat, dust, bugs, glare, etc. will be modulated by the skin to provide a Garden of Eden interior.[73]

Within this domed area, where nature is strictly controlled, some residents would "live in gardens, or upon garden-terrace skyscrapers".[74] Though relying on an intuitive approach rather than a strictly technological one, architect Paolo Soleri proposed a 'biomorphic', ecological architecture, a manifestation of what he calls "arcology", that is, in the end, not too dissimilar to Fuller's domes.[75] For Soleri, a successful urban future rests on future cities built at enormously high densities as single structures [Figures 12, 13].[76] Again,

Figure 13/ Hexahedron, Arcology #28, front and side elevation.
Paolo Soleri. Morphologically and structurally a pseudo-crystal, the city is a conceptual design for a population of 170,000. Its height is 1100 meters and its diameter one kilometer, with an anticipated population density of 2,984/hectare. In the background is a comparative Arcology, Babel IIC, designed for a population of 340,000. Originally published in Paolo Soleri, *Arcology/ The City in the Image of Man*, Cambridge, MA: The MIT Press, 1969. Drawing courtesy of the Cosanti Foundation.

as in Fuller's urban domes, these cities would be amply equipped with gardens. Although Soleri argued that the countryside would be easily accessible because of this very concentration of urban form, there is little place for an untamed, pure nature within these megastructures. In the end, is a garden within a garden our only prospective Eden?

As the earlier sections of this essay indicate, utopian visions of a world with minimal or no exposure to nature are the exception rather than the rule. Even such limited exceptions, however, should be enough to warn of complacency. Utopias are invariably persuasive but so, one recalls, was the serpent in the Garden of Eden.

Notes

1. Quoted in Jane Fearnley-Whittingstall, *The Garden: An English Love Affair*, London: Seven Dials, 2002, p. 262.
2. See Fearnley-Whittingstall, *The Garden*, p. 53.
3. John Clare's "Helpstone", lines 141–142, collected in Simon Sanada, *John Clare's Poems: The Lifetime Published Poetry*, www.johnclare.info/sanada/, 2009.
4. The Garden of Eden is described in the first book of the Old Testament, Genesis 2. In the Qur'an there is a comparable notion of paradise, but in this case it is located beyond the reach of mortals, in Heaven thereafter.
5. *The Epic of Gilgamesh*, Andrew George trans., London: Penguin, 1999.
6. At the end of Tablet IX, Gilgamesh comes upon Dilmun, a veritable paradise popularly (but not universally) believed to be one and the same as the Garden of Eden.
7. Brown, Jane, *The Pursuit of Paradise: A Social History of Gardens and Gardening*, London: Harper Collins, 1999, p. 50.
8. Brown, *The Pursuit of Paradise*, p. 50.
9. Frances Hodgson Burnett's *The Secret Garden* was first published in serial form in 1910 then in book form in 1911, followed by numerous editions since then.
10. Lewis Carroll's *Alice's Adventures in Wonderland* (subsequently shortened to *Alice in Wonderland*) has gone through numerous editions and film versions since the original publication in 1865.
11. Enid Blyton's prodigious output dates from the middle of the twentieth century. She has never been a favorite of the *literati* but with over 600 million sales was a very successful author.
12. Brown, *The Pursuit of Paradise*, pp. 35–39.
13. According to Brown, *The Pursuit of Paradise*, pp. 50–55, the earliest known plan (for a detailed diagram, see Brown 1999, p. 53) was found at the monastery of St. Gall, Switzerland.
14. Brown, *The Pursuit of Paradise*, p. 55.
15. Quoted in David Crouch and Colin Ward, *The Allotment: Its Landscape and Culture*, London: Faber and Faber, 1988, p. 145. The Ligue du coin de terre et du foyer was founded in 1896 to advocate gardening for French workers.
16. Richardson, Benjamin Ward, *Hygeia: A City of Health*, Project

Gutenberg, 1876.
17. Richardson, *Hygeia.*
18. Richardson, *Hygeia.*
19. Richardson, *Hygeia.*
20. Reid, Aileen, *Brentham: A History of the Pioneer Garden Suburb, 1900–2001*, Ealing: Brentham Heritage Society, 2000, p. 37.
21. Creese, Walter L., *The Search for the Environment: The Garden City Before and After*, Baltimore: Johns Hopkins Press, 1992.
22. Quoted in Crouch and Ward, *The Allotment*, p. 158.
23. Morton, Arthur Leslie, *The English Utopia*, London: Lawrence and Wishart, 1978, p. 282.
24. Hardy, Dennis, *Alternative Communities in Nineteenth Century England*, London: Longman, 1979, pp. 65–119.
25. Madden, Etta and Martha Finch eds., *Eating in Eden: Food in American Utopias*, Lincoln, NE: University of Nebraska Press, 2006.
26. Quinn, Megan, "The Power of Community: How Cuba Survived Peak Oil", *Permaculture Activist*, www.globalpublicmedia.com/articles/657, 2006.
27. Crouch and Ward, *The Allotment*, p.153, where it is claimed that 40 percent of the fresh vegetables consumed in the United States in 1944 were produced in Victory Gardens in backyards and vacant lots.
28. Raymond Unwin, who with Barry Parker prepared the master plan for Letchworth Garden City, in Mervyn Miller, *Letchworth: The First Garden City*, Chichester: Phillimore, 2002.
29. More, Thomas, *Utopia*, Paul Turner trans., Harmondsworth: Penguin, 1965, p. 70.
30. More, *Utopia*, p. 73.
31. Quoted in Fearnley-Whittingstall, *The Garden*, p. 336.
32. Gallup Poll quoted in Crouch and Ward, *The Allotment*, p. 154.
33. Details of the scheme are contained on the website http://www.incredible-edible-todmorden.co.uk/.
34. Jacobs, Jane, *The Death and Life of Great American Cities*, London: Jonathan Cape, 1962.
35. *The Charter of the New Urbanism*, para.3, http://www.cnu.org/charter. For a discussion of New Urbanism, see Robert Steuteville and Philip Langdon, *New Urbanism: Comprehensive Report & Best Practice Guide*, Ithaca, NY: New Urban Publications Inc., 2003.
36. See, for instance, an interesting collection of articles in a special edition of *Built Environment*, vol. 29, 2003, p. 3.
37. Hardy, Dennis, *Utopian England: Community Experiments 1900–1945*, London: Spon, 2006.
38. Brown, *The Pursuit of Paradise*, p. 160.
39. Howard, Ebenezer, *To-Morrow: A Peaceful Path to Real Reform*, Peter Hall, Dennis Hardy, and Colin Ward eds., London: Routledge, 1898.
40. Rawnsley, Rev. Canon, "The Garden City", *Garden City*, vol. 1, no. 2, 1905, p. 9.
41. Ward, Stephen V., *The Garden City: Past, Present and Future*, London: Spon, 1992.
42. Garnaut, Christine, *Colonel Light Gardens: Model Garden Suburb*, Darlinghurst, NSW: Crossing Press, 1999, pp. 100–101.
43. Crouch and Ward, *The Allotment*, p. 145.
44. Quoted in Robert Fishman, *Urban Utopias in the Twentieth Century: Ebenezer Howard, Frank Lloyd Wright, Le Corbusier*, Cambridge, MA: MIT Press, 1982, p. 146.
45. See Stephen Grabow, "Frank Lloyd Wright and the American City: The Broadacres Debate", *Journal of the American Institute of Planners*, vol. 43, no. 2, 1977, pp. 115–124.
46. Howard, *To-Morrow*, p. 11.
47. Tennyson, Alfred Lord, *Idylls of the King: The Passing of Arthur, Complete Poems*, http:www.poemhunter.com/Alfred-lord-tennyson.
48. Tennyson, Alfred Lord, "The Lady of Shalott", *Complete Poems*, http:www.poemhunter.com/Alfred-lord-tennyson.
49. Tennyson, *Idylls of the King: Gareth and Lynette, Complete Poems*, http:www.poemhunter.com/Alfred-lord-tennyson.
50. Tennyson, *Idylls of the King: Gareth and Lynette.*
51. Hardy, *Alternative Communities*, p. 79.
52. Morris, William, *News from Nowhere*, London: Routledge and Kegan Paul, 1970, p. 61.
53. Hardy, *Utopian England*, pp.109–130.
54. Hardy, *Utopian England*, p. 114.
55. Abercrombie, Patrick, *Greater London Plan*, London: HMSO, 1945.
56. Howard, Ebenezer, *Garden Cities of To-Morrow*, London: Faber and Faber, 1902, pp. 140–141.
57. Ruskin, John, *Unto This Last*, 1862, quoted in Howard, *Garden Cities*, pp. 140–141.
58. Howard, *To-Morrow*, p. 12.
59. Howard, *To-Morrow*, p. 10.
60. Greater London Regional Planning Committee, 1927.
61. Second Report of the Regional Planning Committee, 1933.
62. Abercrombie, *Greater London Plan.*
63. From the First World War marching song, "Pack up your Troubles," in *The Peacehaven Post*, 2 January 1922.
64. William Howlitt quoted in Dennis Hardy and Colin Ward, *Arcadia for All*, Nottingham: Five Leaves Publications, 2004, p. 10.
65. See note 64.
66. See note 64.
67. Levin, Bernard, *A World Elsewhere*, London: Jonathan Cape, 1994, p. xiii.
68. Wells, H. G., *The Sleeper Awakes*, London: Collins, 1954.
69. Wells, *The Sleeper Awakes*, p. 70.
70. The best source of Futurist ideas is to be found in Filippo Tommaso Marinetti's original manifesto of 1909, *The Futurist Manifesto*, first published in the Italian newspaper *Gazzetta dell' Emilia* in Bologna on 5 February.
71. Kumar, Krishan, *Utopia and Anti-Utopia in Modern Times*, Oxford: Blackwell, 1987, p. 224.
72. Huxley, Aldous, *Brave New World*, Harmondsworth: Penguin, 1955.
73. Coates, Stephen and Alex Stetter eds., *Impossible Worlds: The Architecture of Perfection*, Basel: Birkhauser, 2000, p. 16.
74. For the quote, see R. Buckminster Fuller, *Utopia or Oblivion: The Prospects for Humanity*, Toronto, New York, and London: Bantam Books, 1969, p. 354.
75. See Charles Jencks, *Architecture 2000: Predictions and Methods*, New York and Washington: Praeger, 1971, p. 99.
76. Tod, Ian and Michael Wheeler, *Utopia*, London: Orbis, 1978, pp. 141–143.

THE PANOPTIC GARDEN

/DAVID BELL

Throughout Western civilization, the garden has been a poignant reminder both of humanity's loss of innocence and its banishment from paradise for eating fruit of the Tree of Knowledge. Alternatively, every prison testifies both to the guilt for that forbidden ingestion and humanity's subsequent fall from grace. Unquestionably, the garden and the prison each have unique ways to shape space, matter, ideas, and experience that signify certain attitudes toward nature and society. Yet, as dissimilar as they appear, the garden and the prison both represent lost ideals that we perpetually and vainly attempt to recover in utopian propositions. Perhaps, more deeply within each of these perennial institutions flicker phosphorescently some unprecedented ideals that can further illuminate the utopian impulse. As they evolved in the Enlightenment's aftermath, each institution in its own peculiar way pursued knowledge virtually without limit. In extending beyond the boundaries tradition had assigned them, both inflated into metaphors of themselves. The finite garden became the boundless landscape, and the prison, renouncing punishment of the individual criminal's body, metamorphosed into a pervasive system to discipline and regulate the amorphous social body. In doing so, the respective ambits of the garden and prison began to merge and overlap unpredictably, the unrestrained power of the eye being their common instrument.

Optimism permeated much of the intellectual climate of eighteenth century Europe. In that Enlightenment atmosphere, it primarily meant an optimal view of reality rather than a hopeful outlook on the future; its foundation was the scientific revolution of the seventeenth century. Culminating in the work of Isaac Newton (1643–1717), the new physics described a reassuringly predictable, reasonable, and elegant clockwork universe that affirmed the sublimity of God's balanced design. Gottfried Leibniz (1646–1716), the philosopher, scientist, and mathematician who was Newton's rival for the invention of calculus, was optimism's principal champion. He conjectured that even if the sublunary world of human affairs was not absolutely the best world, it was optimally the best one possible.

In 1755, the height of the Enlightenment, a powerful earthquake struck Lisbon. The effects of its devastation extended far beyond the great loss of property and 50,000 lives to shake just as violently the century's confident optimism. Nature's seismic rebellion at Lisbon, this most unreasonable event, raised serious doubts that this world was indeed the best one possible. It provoked François-Marie Arouet (1694–1778), more widely known by his pen name Voltaire, in his 1759 satirical novella *Candide: or, The Optimist* to demand of Leibniz's 'optimistic' disciples an explanation for this capricious cruelty in the "best of all possible worlds".[1]

Candide is an irreverent allegory of Adam and Eve's banishment from the Garden of Eden. Its three main characters—the eponymous naïve hero Candide, Cunégonde, the aristocratic heiress he loves, and Pangloss, Candide's teacher, a philosopher, and self-described devotee of Leibnizian optimism—suffer perilous adventures and outrageously tragic misfortunes. Various calamities, notably the Seven Years War and the Lisbon earthquake, repeatedly separate and re-unite them across three continents and many years. Throughout the novella, these characters, especially Candide, find themselves alternating between episodes in various gardens, including the mythical New World utopia El Dorado, and captivity by either imprisonment or servitude to cruel masters.

The story concludes ambiguously, uniting them on a farm in Ottoman Turkey where the hapless Candide finally disavows his teacher's optimistic philosophy. Accepting their fate, they focus on tending their garden while stranded within the alien world of Islamic civilization. Whether we can interpret their Turkish sequestration as imprisonment is moot. Nevertheless, they agree that the only way to cope with their situation and sustain themselves is to cultivate the modest garden they have made.

"LE SILENCE ÉTERNEL DE CES ESPACES INFINIS M'EFFRAIE"

One early consequence of the scientific revolution was the idea that space is boundless. This hypothesis had existed in Christianity at least since the twelfth century in a Hermetic text, *The Book of the XXIV Philosophers*. Of course, established Church doctrine held the universe to be finite and regarded as heretical any idea that it is infinite. Nevertheless, Cardinal Nicholas Cusanus (1401–1464), a mathematician, astronomer, and metaphysician as well as a prelate, speculated that space is not finitely bounded but of indeterminate extent. His position as cardinal, papal diplomat, and celebrated scholar presumably spared him the fate of the Dominican friar Giordano Bruno (1548–1600). The Roman civil authorities burned Bruno at the stake in the Campo dei Fiori for espousing heretical cosmological views, among them his conviction that space is not merely of indeterminate extent but infinite. Two interesting ironies relevant to the present discussion inhabit these stories of Cusanus and Bruno. Cusanus described the indeterminate spatial extent of the universe as having its center everywhere and circumference nowhere.[2] Regarding the latter claim, when Sir Thomas More (1478–1535) wrote his famous book of 1516 about an ideal society, he derived its name as a pun on three Greek words, "*eu*" meaning "good", "*ou*" meaning "no", and "*topos*", meaning "place", i.e., utopia, which effectively means a "good place" that exists "nowhere". The irony of Bruno's immolation, his imprisonment in flame, is that its site, the Campo dei Fiori, "Field of Flowers", received this name because until the fifteenth century, it was a meadow. In a sense, before it was paved, it had been an untended garden within Rome's urban fabric.

René Descartes (1596–1650), in writing *Principles of Philosophy* to supplant the Aristotelian scientific model with his own mathematically based rational system, reasoned that space could not be other than infinite. Though he acknowledged the logical inevitability of Descartes' conclusion, Blaise Pascal (1632–1662) expressed ambivalence and anxiety about the implications of limitless space. Like Descartes, Newton, and Leibniz, Pascal made significant contributions to mathematics and physics as well as to philosophy. However, as a devout Catholic, he faced a dilemma between the impeccable logic of his own scientific and mathematical insights and his deeply felt religious beliefs. In section 205 of his posthumously published *Thoughts*, he wrote:

> When I consider the short duration of my life, swallowed up in the eternity before and after, the little space which I fill and even can see, engulfed in the infinite immensity of spaces of which I am ignorant and which know me not, I am frightened and am astonished at being here rather than there; for there is no reason why here rather than there, why now rather than then. Who has put me here? By whose order and direction have this place and time been allotted to me?

In the following section of *Thoughts*, which is a single sentence, Pascal captures the existential anguish of his quandary: "The eternal silence of these infinite spaces frightens me."[3] It is almost as if Pascal regarded infinite space as a kind of imprisonment.

Indeed, the anxiety Pascal expresses in that single pregnant sentence might easily be a caption for any of the series of engravings, *Carceri d'invenzione*, by Giovanni Battista Piranesi (1720–1778). These haunting architectural *capricci* employ cleverly distorted perspective construction to suggest a simultaneous disintegration of both the form and the space of architecture [Figure 1]. As such, they represent what seems to be an impossible combination of infinite space and the instruments of incarceration. Is it not paradoxical that the prison, the machine to restrict one's being, can exist in a state of infinite spatial expanse?

Figure 1/ *Carceri d'invenzione*, Giambattista Piranesi, Plate VII, "The Drawbridge".

SURVEILLANCE

In the latter eighteenth and early nineteenth centuries, the perfect storm of earthquakes, interminable bellicosity, and the inhumanity that humanity inflicts on itself, all of which Voltaire satirizes in *Candide*, combined with the plethora of knowledge the scientific revolution unleashed to signal a profound reorientation in thought. Coupling reason with the clarifying lens of meticulous observation, Newtonian science promised to expel darkness, superstition, and mysticism from our understanding of the physical world. It provided the most innovative minds of the Enlightenment the armature for a wholesale reconsideration of the institutions that had dominated Western civilization since the fall of Rome. Thus, as the fruits of this new Tree of Knowledge ripened, Enlightenment thinkers applied its rational techniques to the consideration of human affairs and the definition of new values, such as individual liberty, to supplant those defined by Church and monarchy.

Importantly associated with these values was the 'pursuit of happiness', a concrete way to harrow the adventitious injustices of "the best of all possible worlds" by figuratively cultivating one's own garden.

Application of the scientific method to human affairs produced a bewildering abundance of knowledge, which might affirm Pascal's fear of not being able to distinguish between "here rather than there" and "now rather than then". This abundance precipitated a loosening of the relationship between language and the things to which it refers. There could no longer be an unmediated knowledge of reality. With this came the idea that the true nature of human events is change, rather than the perennial status quo of the *anciens régimes*. Thus, the power of things to radiate incontrovertible meaning began to atrophy and an "epistemological consciousness of man as such" came into being.[4] "Man as such", as both an individual and social phenomenon, became the focus of a new discourse, the human sciences.

To accommodate this dramatic proliferation of knowledge and to probe the numerous aspects of this newly discovered entity, 'man', it was necessary not only to create new institutions but also to reconsider established ones—schools, asylums, hospitals, prisons, etc.. In order to improve, cure, and reform more effectively those committed to their care, these institutions had to develop an efficient technology, a power based in measurement and calculation for both observation and discipline. The exercise of this power required intimate access to every detail of the lives of their charges, making those lives transparent to reason.[5]

Sir Francis Bacon (1561–1626), one of the earliest advocates of the scientific method, argued in his *Novum Organum* (*The New Instrument*) that the new science must reason not only deductively but also inductively by rationally drawing conclusions from observation. Through his new method, he claims, "Knowledge and human power are synonymous."[6] This principle informs Bacon's brief work of proto-science fiction, *The New Atlantis*, in which he describes a scientifically advanced utopian civilization, Bensalem, inhabiting an uncharted South Pacific island. 'Knowledge is power' was its governing principle. In applying this credo for the betterment of its citizens and the glorification of God, Bensalem strived to command nature by understanding and obeying its laws. Its central agency for this purpose was "the Society of Saloman's House", which was "the very eye of this kingdom".[7] Although Bensalem scrupulously guarded its existence from the outside world, it trained its watchful eye closely and covertly on all other civilizations, gathering knowledge about them but never interfering in their affairs.

Bacon's synonymy of knowledge and power alloyed with covert observation, surveillance, became a fundamental cornerstone of the incipient human sciences of the late Enlightenment, producing the base metal for many utopian projects. One important outcome of these new ideas was the reformation of the criminal law system. Cesare Beccaria (1738–1794), in *On Crimes and Punishment*, was the first to advocate such reform, proposing that the purpose of the state is to ensure the greatest happiness among the greatest number of people. This ideal formed the core for his principle of utility, which would substantially influence the British legal scholar, philosopher, and social reformer, Jeremy Bentham (1748–1832), whose utilitarian philosophy gave systematic structure to Beccaria's advocacy of the greatest happiness for the greatest number. Bentham believed the prison could play a central role in achieving this end, in part because it provided society with total legal access to its convicts. However, the nature of incarceration must change from the established practice of simply confining criminals until corporal or capital punishment could be administered to them. Society would benefit more by their reformation and repatriation to it. Bentham argued that criminals ought not be thrown together in prison indiscriminately in constant fraternity, which would only reinforce anti-social tendencies. Instead, their isolation from one another was a necessary factor to purge them of their desire to do wrong, control their reformation, inculcate in them a sense of conscience they may never have had, and instill a sense of penitence. The prison as penitentiary was born.

Bentham conceived a particular kind of prison, the Panopticon, as the ideal laboratory to develop the techniques of his utilitarian "felicific calculus" and thereby eventually

Figure 2/ Jeremy Bentham's Panopticon.

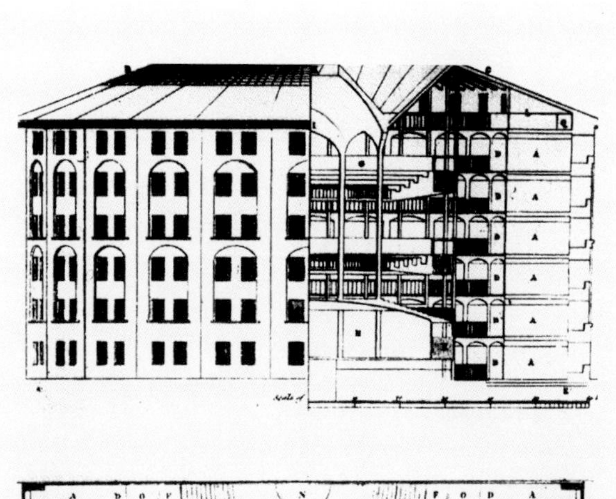

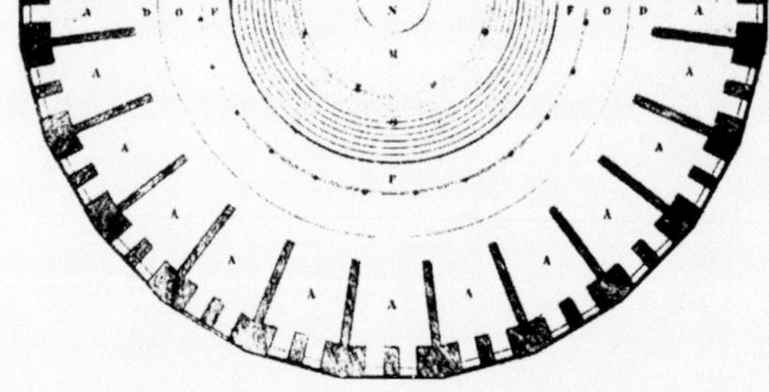

assure the greatest happiness for the greatest number [Figure 2]. The Panopticon was to be the quintessential instrument for applying the necessary techniques of relentless, objective observation and discipline. In the preface to a series of letters he published in 1787 as "Panopticon; or the Inspection House", Bentham described his invention as "a new mode of obtaining power of mind over mind".[8] Ostensibly, the geometry of the Panopticon allows every action of its prisoners to be maximally visible and the motivations of their souls completely transparent to the gaze of whatever anonymous eye occupies the control position afforded by its central viewing platform. Further, the arrangement of this central observation tower is such that the incarcerated never know when they are being watched. Therefore, they must assume that surveillance is constant. The intent was to impress this sense of perpetual surveillance so profoundly that it would stay with prisoners after their reformation and release into society. Those who cannot develop a conscience will at least have indelibly inscribed on their psyches the awareness that an invisible authority scrutinizes their every action. Thus, Bentham's system of surveillance was covert, like that of Bacon's fictional Bensalem. However, unlike Bensalem's policy of non-interference in the world beyond its island, the Panopticon principle insidiously intended to alter human behavior in general.

The Panopticon's insatiable thirst for knowledge about every action and every square inch of the prisoner's body is doubly diabolical. It demands the impression of constant surveillance not only by the imprisoned but also by those who watch them. Theoretically, the agency that empowers the Panopticon is democratic and thus, despite the Panopticon's centralized architectural form, it does not invest observational power in a single individual. Instead, it entraps everyone in its operation, those who exercise power as well as those over whom it is exercised. Because the Panopticon presumes a social order that distributes power with relative uniformity over humanity as a whole, rather than isolating power at a single point, it becomes "an apparatus of total and circulating mistrust".[9] Though designed to assure the greatest happiness for the greatest number, it became the source and symbol of universal human alienation. The system of forces represented by the oppressive observational humidity of the Panopticon located 'man' as a discursive object precisely where the human being was lost as a flesh and blood reality.

Bentham's Panopticon model was never fully realized in England. Nevertheless, it inspired the shaping of several prisons including two small panoptic cell-blocks in Lancaster Castle and some large, semi-circular prisons built in England, Ireland, and Spain.[10] Most nineteenth century prisons, such as Eastern State Penitentiary in Philadelphia, would indirectly incorporate aspects of panoptic surveillance in their radial designs, but the primary basis for those penitentiaries was the isolation of prisoners from one another to instill 'penitence' rather than induce the psychological effects of their continual surveillance. Meanwhile, the principles and techniques that governed the Panopticon's operation received gradual application in many other institutional settings. Thus, the principle of the Panopticon surreptitiously insinuated itself into the world, transforming its human subjects into tokens of knowledge to play out the endless games of disciplinary power with boundless reach. With somewhat different ends, yet sharing the Panopticon's ubiquitous compass of vision, the practice of gardening, heretofore a discrete activity within well-defined boundaries, became synonymous with the boundless landscape.

THE GARDEN

Renaissance gardens, especially those of villas in the Italian *campagna*, were the primary exemplars for most formal gardens constructed throughout Europe from the sixteenth to the eighteenth centuries. The typical villa has two primary components, the *casino* or residence and the *giardino*, the garden. The *giardino* itself consists of several distinct parts: *parterre* (tightly clipped planting beds in geometrical patterns), *bosco* (a grove of trees often with allegorical statuary), and *giardino segreto* (a secret intimate garden derived from the monastic cloister). A clear boundary distinguished all parts of the villa garden from the surrounding wild or 'arbitrary' nature. Leon Battista Alberti (1404–1472), influential architect and the most important theoretician of the Renaissance, had great love for both the Italian landscape and the literature of Classical antiquity. He was certainly familiar with the letters in which Pliny the Younger (first century CE) described in detail his country villas at Laurentium and Tuscany.[11] In *De re aedificatoria libri decem*, Alberti draws upon Pliny and other ancient authors to recommend for villa gardens those values he wished to recuperate from the 'golden age' of antiquity. In particular, he thinks of the garden as a place of delight stimulating the entire human sensorium, especially the sense of sight. With this principle in mind, Alberti advises situating a villa on sloping ground to catch the sun more advantageously and allow both *casino* and *giardino* to have "an elevated position [to afford] a view over sea, hills, or broad landscape" beyond its garden.[12]

A further important aspect of the typical villa garden's adaptation to its site's slope is its arrangement on a series of terraces along a primary axis, for which antiquity provided both literary and architectural precedents. In a letter to his friend Atticus, Cicero describes the organization on multiple terraces of his now lost villa at Tusculum near Rome. Also near Rome in Palestrina are the remains of the Temple of Fortuna Primigenia, which has an axial arrangement of multiple terraces on a steeply dramatic hill.

Although long views are essential, Alberti also stipulates that the garden must have enclosing walls as a "precaution... against wanton recklessness".[13] Such differentiation between the garden and 'arbitrary' nature also emphasizes a pleasing contrast between the work of human hands and the works of nature. For the garden layout, Alberti recommends the same principles of harmonious proportioning: "circles, semi-circles, and other geometric shapes that are favored in the plans of buildings can be modeled out of laurel, citrus, and juniper".[14] Hence, trees should align in rows to form a *quincunx*, i.e., the composition of five objects in a rectangle with an object in each corner and the fifth in the center. In addition to nature and artifices replicating nature, the garden may contain incidental structures of mythological and Classical remembrance such as statues of gods, goddesses, nymphs, etc.; these may include "comic statues... provided they are not obscene".[15] Alberti also recommends the inclusion of artificial grottoes and caves with deliberately roughened massing and surfaces partially covered with "green ochre... to imitate the bearded moss of a grotto".[16] All are essential to the revival of antiquity's 'golden age'.

The general villa typology allows numerous interpretations. Three examples serve well to illustrate how architects adapted this typology to specific sites and programs. The Villa Aldobrandini, perhaps the most splendid among the many villas of Frascati, sited its *casino* in the midst of its surrounding gardens [Figure 3, top]. The Villa Lante, at the edge of the small town Bagnaia, likewise has its main residence amidst its surrounding gardens [Figure 3, middle]. However, unlike other villas, its residence is not a single structure but two identical *casini* separated by part of its gardens, allowing the entire garden space to flow unimpeded from the back of the site to the front gate. In a metaphorical narrative of humanity's progress from its primitive state to the humanist civilization of the Italian *cinquecento*, the gardens transform gradually from the *selvatico*, woodland representing untamed nature outside its walls at the rear of the site, to the highly regularized geometric order of the *parterre* on the town side of the villa. One of the most impressive of the villas in the Italian countryside is the sixteenth century Villa d'Este that Cardinal Ippolito d'Este constructed in Tivoli [Figure 3, bottom]. Its massive *casino* commands the apex of its steep hillside. From there a complex of terraced gardens cascades downward along a central axis from which branch more gardens along secondary and tertiary axes. The Villa d'Este gardens boast an elaborate array of fountains and nymphaea, grottoes, and various constructions that recall antiquity. Among the latter is the Rometta, a fanciful miniature replica of ancient Rome on a terrace looking toward Rome. At the opposite end of the primary axis from the *casino* is a statue of Artemis, the Great Mother Goddess of Greek mythology, in her primitive polymastic form.

Figure 3/ (from top) Villa Aldobrandini. Photograph by Renato Clementi; Villa Lante. © Ehrenfried Kluckert and Könemann Verlag; Villa d'Este. Engraving by Étienne du Pérac.

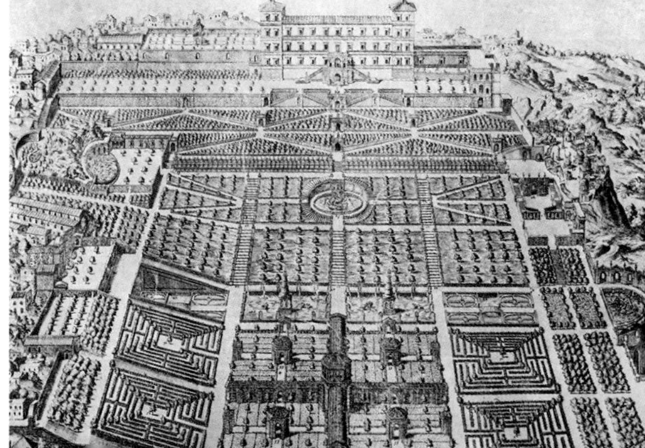

Despite its walled enclosure, the design intent of the Italian villa was neither to separate the villa from nature nor to interrupt the continuity of 'arbitrary' nature. Instead, the villa was more like a brief interlude within nature. Thus, throughout the Italian Renaissance and Baroque periods, the idea prevailed that the garden should have specific limits. A crucial change in the perception of these limits emerges with the garden complex of Versailles. Its unprecedented vastness notwithstanding, it does have specific limits. However, André Le Nôtre (1613–1700) disguised these limits by organizing Versailles' enormous garden complex as a broad, shallow depression, a bowl, in the landscape. Standing within it, one could not see anything beyond its horizon except the sky. This created the illusion that its expanse of carefully manicured vegetation extended infinitely in affirmation of the absolute authority of the king.

Without belittling the marvelous and varied garden works of the sixteenth and seventeenth centuries, the garden during this period was in many ways a diversion, a bibelot plucked out of nature as one might pick a rare flower to display in a vase. But the subtleties of creating such pleasures could have consequences far beyond gratification of the senses. On one rare occasion, the Renaissance garden was the site of a spatial experiment that ultimately influenced developments at an urban scale. In the 1570s, Cardinal Felice Peretti directed his architect Domenico Fontana to design and build his Villa Montalto in Rome. For part of its garden complex, he had Fontana lay out three avenues in the form of a trident diverging from the villa's Viminal gate through the *parterre* gardens. In doing so, he replicated an urban form introduced to Rome by several popes earlier in the century. However, he had Fontana extend the trident's central avenue through the *casino* and *bosco* garden beyond it to end at the *point-de-vue* (viewpoint) in the *selvatico* outside the villa's eastern wall [Figure 4, top]. This simple gesture was an unprecedented attempt at spatial integration on a grand scale. The cardinal would not forget its implications when he ascended to the papacy as Sixtus V in 1585. As pope, he sought to restore monumental grandeur to the once great capital of a global empire by unifying the incremental renovations to Rome's fragmented Medieval urban fabric, projects that had engaged many of his predecessors since the fifteenth century. Making the city legible to its many pilgrims was crucial to his urban unification project. To decorate the *spinae* (middle strips) of their circuses, the ancient Romans plundered many obelisks from Egyptian temples as well as fabricated their own. Those that escaped destruction through subsequent centuries had lain fallow in Vatican storage yards. Thus, Sixtus V had Fontana re-erect many of these obelisks as focal points of critical urban spaces adjacent important monuments, especially Rome's seven major early Christian churches. One of these spaces was the Piazza del Popolo, the first point of arrival to the city after one passes through its important northern gate [Figure 4, bottom]. From here, a trident of three existing major streets diverges to various parts of the city. The design of the Villa Montalto garden served as a rehearsal for the first work of large-scale cohesive city planning in the modern era. Sadly, the construction of Rome's main railroad terminal in the nineteenth century required the villa's demolition. The only part of the Villa Montalto to escape demolition, ironically, was the Fontana del Prigione, The Prison Fountain, which now occupies a site on Rome's Janiculum Hill.

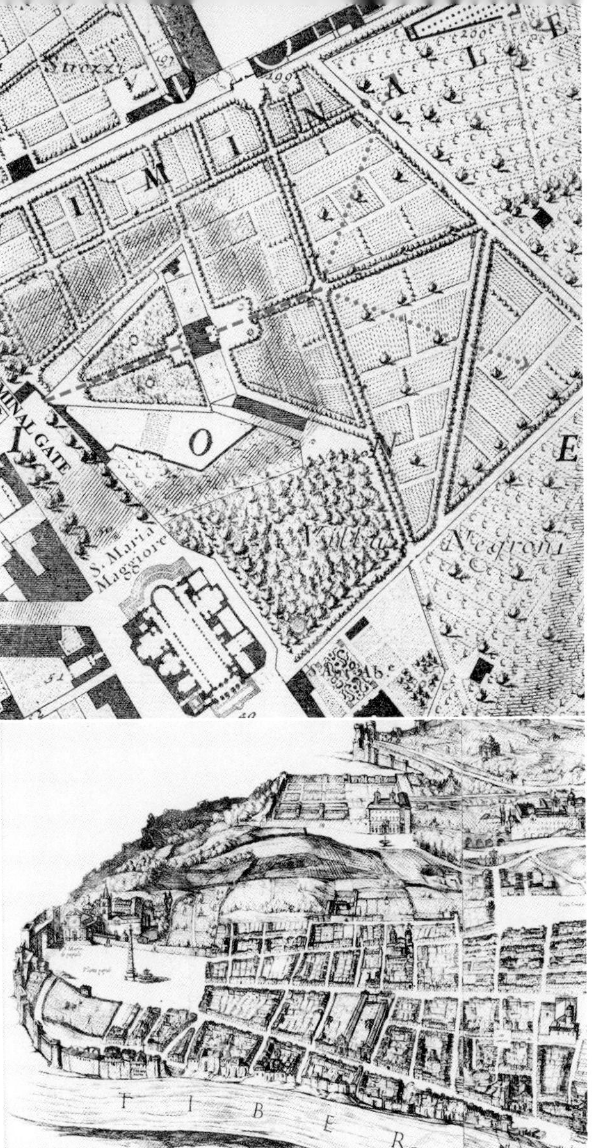

Figure 4/ (from top) Villa Monalto plan. Engraving by Giambattista Nolli; Piazza del Popolo, Rome. Woodcut by Antonio Tempesta.

THE PHILOSOPHICAL LANDSCAPE

Until the eighteenth century, French and Dutch gardens, which derived from the Italian Renaissance typology, provided the model for the design of the English garden. Harmony, balance, and decorum dominated both the formal geometry of its layout and its carefully trimmed topiary, thus maintaining a clear distinction from the surrounding natural landscape. However, early in the eighteenth century, a radically new design approach began to sweep aside the traditional English formal garden. This revolution, like so many others of the eighteenth century, originated in the philosophical thought the new science had cultivated, in particular, the systematic thought of John Locke (1632–1704). One of the earliest and most influential Enlightenment thinkers, Locke was literally a philosopher of common sense. He argued that our reflections on the world around us, especially nature, result from its impingement on our senses, resulting in the formation of ideas. Considering the natural world as essentially a passive object of human inquiry, he drew an important connection between our knowledge of that world and the world of human nature. Just as science had revealed the rational laws that govern nature, Locke's new empirical philosophy reasoned that similar laws must govern civil society. Only the empirical study of human nature will lead to true knowledge; the mysticism of metaphysical speculation and stratospheric hypothesizing of the theologians led to epistemological casuistries incompatible with a rational understanding not only of nature, but also of law and religion. For example, in *An Essay Concerning Human Understanding*, Locke states that "Self depends on consciousness", rather than on substance in the Aristotelian sense, an observation that considerably influenced Bentham's utilitarianism.[17]

Locke does not address questions of aesthetics *per se*. However, in his chapter "On the Association of Ideas" he provides a foundation for understanding aesthetic experience. He stipulates that the ideas arising in our minds through appropriation by the senses associate with other ideas acquired through other sensations. From this network of associations, we begin to form "sympathies and antipathies" and establish priorities among them.[18] Locke's principle of association was crucial to the transformation of ideas regarding nature, landscape, and gardening in early eighteenth century England. These ideas and the practices they affected evolved during that century into two unprecedented categories of artistic experience: the Picturesque and the Sublime. Both categories differed significantly from the orthodoxies of Classical beauty and required a greater integration of natural and human, especially psychological, elements in the garden.

Three individuals during the first third of the eighteenth century, each responding to Locke's thought in a different way, laid the foundational precepts for the evolution of the landscape garden. They were not designers but literary figures with a deep appreciation for the plastic arts. Anthony Ashley Cooper (1671–1713), third earl of Shaftesbury, was a poet and philosopher of some renown. Locke had served as physician and political advisor to Shaftesbury's grandfather, the first earl. He also supervised the education of the younger Shaftesbury, who nevertheless rejected key tenets of his teacher's empirical philosophy, particularly the notion that the mind is a *tabula rasa* (blank slate) upon which the experience of the senses inscribes ideas. Shaftesbury preferred instead Leibniz's optimistic view of the world, which translated for him into a somewhat mystical idealization of nature. In his *Characteristicks of Men, Manners, Opinions and Times*, one of the most popular books in eighteenth century England, Shaftesbury emphatically states that some things have a natural beauty immediately apparent to the mind, independently of the senses. A Neoplatonist and pantheist, Shaftesbury believed that although the senses may perceive truth, goodness, and beauty, they necessarily confirm something already intrinsic to the human mind, i.e., a divine intelligence that endows the universe with an elemental harmony. He describes certain natural milieus as having an inherent, intangible quality that gives them their uniqueness: the "Genius of the Place" or *genius loci*. Thus, he believed that the formality of established English garden design effectively cloaks nature's authentic beauty in a shroud of geometrical artifice. Prefiguring the aesthetics of the Sublime, Shaftesbury's thought would play an important role in the Arcadian and Romantic approaches to landscape garden design later in the eighteenth century that wove together nature, memory, literature, and experience.

Another important advocate for a new approach to gardening was poet and essayist Joseph Addison (1672–1719). Unlike Shaftesbury, he was an avid disciple of Locke's empirical philosophy, particularly the principle of association and its implications for the sense of sight, which, of all the senses, he believed was "most perfect and most delightful".[19] A copy of the pastoral poetics of Virgil's *Georgics* and the contemplation of Locke's ideas were Addison's constant companions on his daily stroll through Oxford's Magdalen Water Walk, now known as Addison's Walk. In the essays he wrote for his daily publication, *The Spectator*, he aspired to present philosophical issues such as Locke's empiricism in concrete, everyday terms. In the series "The Pleasures of the Imagination", especially in *The Spectator* no. 414, he, like Shaftesbury, criticized the established tradition of English formal gardening and defined a set of principles that inaugurated the naturalistic landscape garden's evolution throughout the remainder of the century. Addison compares the effects on the imagination of the works of nature to those of art, and finds the latter wanting. Works of art have nothing of nature's immensity that affords "so great an entertainment to the mind of the beholder" because "in the wide fields of nature the sight wanders up and down without confinement [stimulated by] an infinite variety of images"; this "infinite variety" is a factor of nature's "rough careless strokes" and contributes to its superiority over "the nice touches and embellishment of art".[20] Nonetheless, he concludes his essay by postulating a kind of aesthetic reciprocity between nature and art. The works of nature become even more pleasant the more they resemble works of art, both because of nature's intrinsic agreeableness to the eye and the similitude to nature that art provides. In other words, the work of art should improve upon nature without reforming it. The same is true for landscape design, which should seek a seamless unity of nature with the garden, allowing the eye to wander freely. At the core of Addison's principles are the priorities he assigns to the sense of sight and lack of constraint to its visual field.

Alexander Pope (1688–1744) shared Shaftesbury and Addison's critique of the formal garden. In an essay for *The Guardian* published the year after Addison wrote *The Spectator* no. 414, Pope called for the design of gardens commensurate to the "amiable Simplicity of unadorned Nature that spread over the Mind... a loftier Sensation of Pleasure, than can be raised from the nicer Scenes of Art".[21] In verse, Pope wrote a letter to the classical architect Richard Boyle, third earl of Burlington (1694–1753), that echoed Shaftesbury.

> In all, let nature never be forgot...
> Consult the genius of the place in all;... [because it]
> Paints as you plant, and, as you work, designs.[22]

Of special significance regarding both the experience and extent of the garden, Pope wrote in the same letter:

> He gains all points, who pleasingly confounds,
> Surprises, varies and conceals the Bounds.[23]

Shaftesbury, Addison, and Pope, in advocating a new vision of landscape garden design, all evince an interpretation of nature different from that implicit in Locke's empirical philosophy. Adhering to the principles of the scientific revolution, particularly as portrayed in Bacon's writings, Locke's empiricism considers nature as *natura naturata*. However, when Addison critiques the formal garden and celebrates nature as something that provokes the imagination, or when Pope advises Burlington to regard nature as a collaborator, they are considering nature as *natura naturans*. These two terms have a long and complex relationship in the tradition of aesthetics and the broader discourse of philosophy, most notably in Spinoza's *Ethics*, and they remain centrally important to contemporary environmental philosophy.[24] *Natura naturata* (nature natured) is a concept of nature as the passive object of empirical inquiry, a decidedly instrumentalist predisposition. On the other hand, *natura naturans* (nature naturing) considers nature as active and productive, actively creating reality. Of course, Shaftesbury, who espoused an essentially anti-Lockean position and a kind of pantheism, had distinctly advocated *natura naturans* by connecting nature with the mind's inherent structure. This will become important to the Romantics later in the century when they develop the aesthetic categories of Picturesque and Sublime partly as a reaction to the Enlightenment rationalism of nature. Obviously, the rigorous geometry and manicured hedges of formal gardens such as Versailles exemplify *natura naturata*. Such formality also represented an absolutist monarchy repugnant to Enlightenment political ideals. It is no coincidence that many of the patrons of the new, less formal approach to landscape gardening in England were Whigs, i.e., anti-royalists.

"ET IN ARCADIA EGO"

Before continuing to examine the evolution of the early eighteenth century's ideas about the landscape garden, it is worth considering briefly a rather enigmatic text of the late *quattrocento* Italian Renaissance. The *Hypnerotomachia Poliphili*, bizarre as it is, was one of the most important books to come out of its period. Its strange tale has inspired writers from the sixteenth century to the present. Somewhat shrouded in mystery as to its provenance, the general attribution for its authorship goes to the Dominican monk Francesco Colonna (1433–1527), although evidence exists that Alberti may have written it. An oneiric fantasy, it is the account by its protagonist Poliphilo about a dream he has with a second dream embedded it. On the day before his layered dream, his beloved Polia had spurned his affection and in his troubled sleep that night, he pursues her through a mysterious palace and surreal landscape of its complex of gardens. As he ambles desultorily through the winding paths of these walled gardens, he unexpectedly encounters exotic and mythological flora and fauna, strange topiary, as well as fantastic, colossal, and perplexing works of architecture and sculpture. Through his aleatory wandering, Poliphilo also discovers the ruins of an arcane Classical civilization of a lost 'golden age'. Musing upon nature's power to transform the works of the human hand, *natura naturans*, he appreciates the aesthetic quality of the decaying structures. Colonna's acknowledgement through his protagonist that ruins have power to stir the emotions, especially in this way, is a genuinely non-Classical notion that would eventually influence aspects of the English landscape garden, especially in its Arcadian phase.

Figure 5/ Ha-ha.
Chirk Castle, Denbighshire, North Wales. Photograph by Akke Monasso.

The landscape gardening ideals advanced by Shaftesbury, Addison, and Pope did not have immediate widespread results. Among them, only Pope gave concrete expression to this new polemic by commissioning the architect William Kent (1685–1748), who revived Palladian architecture in England, to design the walled gardens at his estate in Twickenham. By the standards of landscape gardening later in the century, they were quite restrained. Recall that one of Addison's principles for garden design was to create a sense of connection to "the wide fields of nature [where] the sight wanders up and down without confinement". The primary obstacle preventing this was the practical need for some sort of physical barrier, a fence, wall, or thick hedge, to maintain privacy and keep livestock away from the immediate vicinity of the house. In Alberti's words, such a barrier was a necessary "precaution... against wanton recklessness". Although precedents for solving this problem existed in the Middle Ages and seventeenth century France provided the modern origin for its solution, Horace Walpole (1717–1797), the inventor of Gothic fiction, gave credit to the landscape architect Charles Bridgeman (1690–1738). Like many revolutionary ideas, his solution was exceedingly simple. Instead of a barrier like a wall, Bridgeman constructed a ditch separating the house and its immediate surroundings from the pastoral land beyond, thus cleverly meeting Addison's requirement for seamlessness between the two. Bridgeman's invention acquired the name "ha-ha" because of the exclamatory "aha!" its simplicity elicited [Figure 5]. Bridgeman and Kent—developing their work from the precepts of Shaftesbury, Addison, and Pope—are the true fathers of the English landscape garden.

With the innovation of the ha-ha, the development of the English landscape garden proceeded in two distinct phases. The work of Bridgeman and Kent largely defines its first phase, the Arcadian phase, which profoundly engendered a desire to recuperate a lost 'golden age'.[25] Trained as a gardener, Bridgeman pioneered at Stowe, Rousham, and Chiswick the naturalistic, less structured approach to landscape gardening. Nevertheless, he was unable to break free completely from the geometrical order of the formal garden. However, William Kent, who first worked with and then succeeded Bridgeman as the designer for these and other gardens, was successful in doing so.

Kent was a painter who had studied in Italy. While there, he fell under the spell of its villas, their gardens, and the architecture of Andrea Palladio. The Italian landscape made an indelible impression upon him. Its idyllic portrayal in the paintings of Claude Gelée, known as Lorrain (1600–1682), and Gaspard Dughet (1615–1675) amplified his fascination. In them, he saw the juxtaposition of uncultivated but serene nature with Classical temples and ruins from Roman antiquity, especially Lorrain's favorite, the Temple of Sybil at Tivoli [Figure 6]. Returning to England, he continued as a painter but also began to practice architecture and landscape design. The innovation of the ha-ha allowed him to give three-dimensional reality to the Arcadian landscape paintings of Lorrain and Dughet by merging 'arbitrary' nature with the literate refinements he found within the walls of the Italian villa garden. Kent set an important precedent for subsequent landscape garden design throughout England and Europe by punctuating

Figure 6/ *Landscape with the Father of Psyche Sacrificing to Apollo*, Claude Gelée (Lorrain). www.claudelorrain.org.

Figure 7/ (from top) Temple of Modern Virtue; Temple of Ancient Virtue, William Kent, Stowe. Photograph by mym.

the landscape of naturalistic plantings, irregularly shaped lakes, and cascades that he derived from Bridgeman's work with an assortment of incidental structures known as follies. These served as focal points of his pictorially framed views. Among them were grottoes, Palladian-inspired structures, freestanding variations of ancient temples, and even artificial ruins.

Following Lorrain, Kent frequently used the Temple of Sybil as model for his follies. At Stowe, he paired a Sybil-like Temple of Ancient Virtue with a Temple of Modern Virtue. The latter is an artificially constructed ruin and the former is a whole structure [Figure 7, top and bottom]. In addition to the obvious historical references, these two structures had psychological and political motives. The wholeness of the Temple of Ancient Virtue expressed the endurance of ancient virtues. On the other hand, as a ruin, the Temple of Modern Virtue symbolized the vagaries of contemporary morality. The sinuous, irregular profile of the ruin also had its own aesthetic significance, particularly in relation to how nature's "rough careless strokes" create a pleasing diversity in support of Addison's Lockean-inspired associations. Furthermore, Kent was certainly familiar with Colonna's fascination with ruins in *Hypnerotomachia Poliphili*; his friend and patron at Chiswick, Lord Burlington, possessed a copy in his library. The faux ruin was a reminder of the transience of the material world and the power of nature over the works of mortals. In addition, by its juxtaposition to the nearby Temple of Ancient Virtue, it induced in the visitor a sense of nostalgic melancholy for a lost 'golden age'. Politically, Kent's ruined Temple of Modern Virtue was also a sardonic comment by Stowe's patron, Lord Cobham, on the ethics of his fellow Whig and political nemesis, Prime Minister Robert Walpole. The Gothic Temple was another of the Stowe follies with both political and melancholic implications. To Whigs such as Lord Cobham, the Gothic evoked ancient Anglo-Saxon liberties. Thus Gothic follies, both whole and faux ruin, became important inclusions in landscape garden design. In general, most follies evoked a sense of great distance in time and space; others suggested cultural remoteness as well. For example, *chinoiserie*, which emerged in the decorative arts of seventeenth century France, employs motifs inspired by a fanciful interpretation of Chinese art to suggest this remoteness. Kent included at Stowe the first *chinoiserie* folly in England in the form of a small house.

An important tenet of the landscape garden as it evolved in the work of Bridgeman and Kent was that from no single vantage point should one be able to grasp its entirety. Its immensity could only become apparent when one walked through it, acquiring a series of impressions by observing its carefully framed views from different angles and perspectives. Building on this and other principles of landscape gardening, the poet William Shenstone (1714–1763) developed his modest estate The Leasowes as a *ferme ornée*, or ornamental farm, on the concept that the garden is not only an extension of Arcadian landscape painting into three dimensions but also is an epic poem in its own right. He believed its variety of events, emotions, and sentiments should have the structure of a story. In transforming the landscape into a narrative containing various follies among the planting and other natural features, Shenstone provided near every significant view in his park an accompanying literary reference engraved in stone or otherwise displayed. Each was a hint, message, or allusion regarding what one should feel or think while surveying the prospect.[26] The climax of one's journey through The Leasowes garden is a view that merges the foreground, middle ground, and distant landscapes. The use of a narrative, *per se*, as a basis for garden design was not unprecedented. For example, the gardens of Villa Lante are an allegory on the evolution of civilization. Furthermore, it is likely that Henry Hoare, the patron of the landscape garden at Stourhead, which was contemporary with The Leasowes, conceived it as an allegory of Virgil's *Aeneid*. What distinguishes The Leasowes' narrative is that it derives not from an external source but from the direct emotional experience of the landscape and its contents.

THE SYNTACTICAL LANDSCAPE

In 1742, Lancelot 'Capability' Brown (1716–1783) joined Kent's staff at Stowe gardens. While working for Kent, he developed his own approach to landscape garden design and eventually established his own practice. His immensely popular designs made him the dominant figure in landscape gardening. Brown's approach, as revolutionary as was the change from the formal gardens of the seventeenth century, defines the second phase of landscape gardening. Brown considered the framing of Arcadian views as both pretentious and static and had little concern for either creating a painterly landscape or alluding to Greek and Roman antiquity. Thus, his designs rarely included follies to evoke an emotional response, nostalgia, or melancholia. For example, his design for Bowood included only a modest Doric temple to affirm human presence.

Brown was similarly averse to explicit literary analogies like those at The Leasowes. Nevertheless, he explained his work as grammatical in the sense that the elements of the natural landscape have their own inherent syntax or set of rules regarding their arrangement. If one could interpret and give greater clarity to this syntax, one could create a visually coherent landscape that relied solely on its natural order rather than either an imposed geometry, the introduction of architectural artifices, or a literary allegory. Brown acquired the sobriquet, 'Capability', because he often said he could perceive the latent 'capabilities', the *genius loci*, within the syntax of the landscapes he ultimately transformed. In Addison's terms, he improved nature with "the nice touches and embellishment of art" using nature itself as his material. Hence, Brown endeavored to communicate through his syntactical approach a dynamic unification of his landscapes with the natural countryside. He used artificial lakes, rivers, cascades, and belts of trees in order to conceal, reveal, exaggerate, or define those features that supported his primary intentions. The results of his designs at over 170 of Britain's most prestigious estates, including Blenheim and Warwick Castle, were landscapes of simple, large-scale openness, having broad, clear sweeps of lawn and smooth topography [Figure 8].

Brown's successor Humphry Repton (1752–1818) followed the general tenor of Brown's approach, but because he worked mostly with smaller estates, he devised a strategy to imply extent beyond their boundaries. Unlike Brown, who generally placed a continuous belt of trees around the large estates he worked on, Repton would cut a view corridor through the belt to open up and borrow views from surrounding landmarks so they appeared to belong to the property. Despite the differences between the Arcadian and syntactical approaches to landscape gardening, both, like Addison, placed a premium for their appreciation on the wide field of vision, a panoptic-like regime over a seemingly boundless terrain.

PICTURESQUE AND SUBLIME

Although Shaftesbury, Addison, and Pope defined the philosophical and aesthetic bases for the landscape garden, a true theory regarding its practices and principles did not appear until later in the century. At that time, two new aesthetic categories, the Picturesque and the Sublime, arose principally for two reasons grounded in nascent Romanticism. First, they were a reaction against what some considered as the blandly smooth simplicity of Brown and Repton's work. Secondly, and more fundamentally, they emerged to explore how art and the larger natural world might stir the imagination differently than traditional notions of Classical beauty. Classical beauty, especially as Alberti had defined it for architecture, concerned elements of harmony and regularity. Although nature was also Alberti's inspiration, he aimed to distill from it those formal aspects that appeal to the rational mind, more than do those appealing to the emotions. William Gilpin (1724–1804) defined one of these new categories of aesthetic experience as the "Picturesque", a term Pope had derived from a similar French word that described landscape design as having a style like that of a painter. The term "picturesque" in aesthetics of our time often conjures up images of scenic tranquility, charm, and quaintness. It can also be a derogatory epithet meaning superficial, saccharine, or

Figure 8/ Blenheim.
Landscape garden by 'Capability' Brown.

Figure 9/ *Landscape with Tobit and the Angel.*
Salvator Rosa. Photograph by Rama.

banal. However, Gilpin was trying to differentiate Classical beauty from the qualities that moved him in landscape paintings such as those of Claude Lorrain, Gaspard Dughet, and Salvator Rosa (1615–1673). Like Addison, he believed the unique vision of boundless nature these artists expressed was essential to augmenting its appreciation. But Gilpin was less interested in the associative ideas of Picturesque landscapes than in cataloging a set of rules for painting the variety, uniqueness, and quality of nature's shapes, e.g., intricacy, irregularity, roughness, etc..

Uvedale Price (1747–1829) and Richard Payne Knight (1750–1824) were particularly critical of the landscapes of Brown and Repton. Like Gilpin, they were literary figures rather than landscape designers and succeeded him in the following generation as advocates for the Picturesque. Unlike Gilpin, they were true Romantics, interested in the ideas and emotions behind the complexities and asperities of the Picturesque. Gilpin's ideas particularly impressed Price, who wished to apply them to landscape gardening as well as painting. However, Knight believed that a rational set of rules such as Gilpin's was wholly inadequate to grasp these qualities. Moreover, in expressing the ideal Romantic landscape, Knight preferred Rosa's more savage and tempestuous depiction of nature to the placid pastoral qualities of Lorrain and Dughet's work, which characterized Bridgeman and Kent's Arcadian landscape gardens. Rosa infused his painting with a quality central to Price and Knight's Romanticism, i.e., the second alternative to Classical beauty, the Sublime [Figure 9].

The Roman author Longinus introduced the concept of the Sublime in the first century CE to explain the intangible power of great orators to inspire awe in their listeners. The term acquired its modern meaning in Edmund Burke's (1729–1797) 1757 treatise *Philosophical Enquiry into the Origin of Our Ideas of the Sublime and the Beautiful.* Burke clearly distinguishes between the inherent pleasure conveyed by civilized Classical beauty and those things that can affect us in less civilized and even unpleasant ways. In particular, these might induce feelings of terror, awe, gloom, and other sensibilities outside the serene harmony of Classical beauty. Phenomena that are surpassingly gigantic, violent like a savage storm, awe-inspiring like a high, jagged mountain peak, or infinite in the way that so frightened Pascal, could provoke the experience of the Sublime. Perhaps one could even consider an earthquake as Sublime. Burke's notion of the Sublime is an experience that induces a sense of powerlessness in the observer defying rational discursive description. Shaftesbury had written about such sentiments, but until Burke, they did not have unique aesthetic categorization. Although an avid advocate of the Sublime, Knight disagreed with Burke on a key point; he preferred to think of it not in terms of powerlessness but as the exercise of great power to inspire awe, even loathing, but never fear. In developing their theories of the Picturesque, both Price and Knight considered it to lie between the beautiful and the Sublime. Their idea of the Picturesque necessarily infuses the Arcadian landscape with Sublime events.

Figure 10/ (from top) Worlitz, Volcano; Désert de Retz, *La colonne brisée*. Photograph by Ackteon.

Certainly, the seeming endlessness of these landscapes was an important factor, but they must include more immediate moments, radical and exotic singularities, to stir the Sublime sentiment.

Throughout the latter part of the eighteenth century, the English landscape garden and the ideas of the Picturesque and Sublime it embodied seized the imaginations of continental Europeans. Their hyperbolic enthusiasm for English landscape design, known as *anglomanie*, led them to populate their estates with innumerable symbols, indigenous and non-indigenous, of human and natural history. In these gardens, one could confront directly the wild, primitive, frightening, and overwhelming qualities of the Sublime. The landscape park of Hohenheim near Stuttgart involved extensive constructions made to look like the ruins of an ancient city. At Worlitz, near Dessau, Duke Leopold III had constructed a working, smoke and fire-belching volcano [Figure 10, top].[27] Among the many follies that François Racine de Monville had constructed on his one hundred acre estate Désert de Retz, near Marly, were a pyramid implying the presence of ancient Egyptian builders on this site, various examples of *chinoiserie* evoking the mystery of an alien culture, and fantastic grottoes containing sculptures of larger-than-life, torch-carrying satyrs. The most impressive of the Désert de Retz follies is de Monville's summerhouse in the form of a gigantic ruined column, evoking the impression that an immense temple from a lost 'golden age' once occupied the site [Figure 10, bottom].

The proliferation of the English landscape garden ideal led to ever more intricately involved designs, magnifying Kent's requirement that to understand the garden one must walk through it and experience its framed views from differing perspectives. Landscapes became labyrinths of constantly diverging paths circling back on one another in the kind of infinite regression that Jorge Luis Borges portrays in his 1941 short story "The Garden of Forking Paths".[28]

The landscape gardens of England and Europe gradually accumulated objects simulating those of non-Western cultures, replicas of nature, narratives, and antique reconstructions, often inspired by the exaggerated scale of Roman and Greek structures in Piranesi's engravings. They became veritable three-dimensional encyclopedias encompassing all of space and time. Like the Panopticon principle, the ambition of their extent seemed to challenge the infinite and capture the entire world in their orbits.

PANOPTIC UTOPIAS

As the high tide of *anglomanie* washed upon the shores of continental Europe and more than a decade before Bentham devised the Panopticon, Louis XV appointed the architect Claude-Nicolas Ledoux (1736–1806) Commissioner of Salt Works for the Lorraine and Franche-Comté regions. In the 1770s, Ledoux designed and commenced construction of the Royal Salt Works, the Arc-de-Senans, near Chaux in Franche-Comté [Figure 11, opposite second from top]. The *raison d'être* for this worker city epitomized the Enlightenment attitude toward nature: the direct scientific extraction of its wealth. Although not having the rigid program of a prison, this worker city operated under a strict discipline, its design in some ways anticipating Bentham's Panopticon principle. Ledoux developed a series of plans, the first based on a square, then an oval, then a circle, and finally a semi-circle. At its center is the director's house, from which disseminated administrative power. On top of this house was a belvedere, a central observation point for registering knowledge and regulating the activities of the operations. Even after construction stopped, Ledoux continued to develop designs for the Arc-de-Senans as a utopian project. In these explorations, he envisioned highly unorthodox and unprecedented designs exemplifying his idea of *architecture parlante* (speaking architecture), in which a building takes a form that literally expresses

Figure 11/ (from top) Claude-Nicolas Ledoux, Oikema; Arc-de-Senans; House of the Cooper; House of the Water Surveyor.

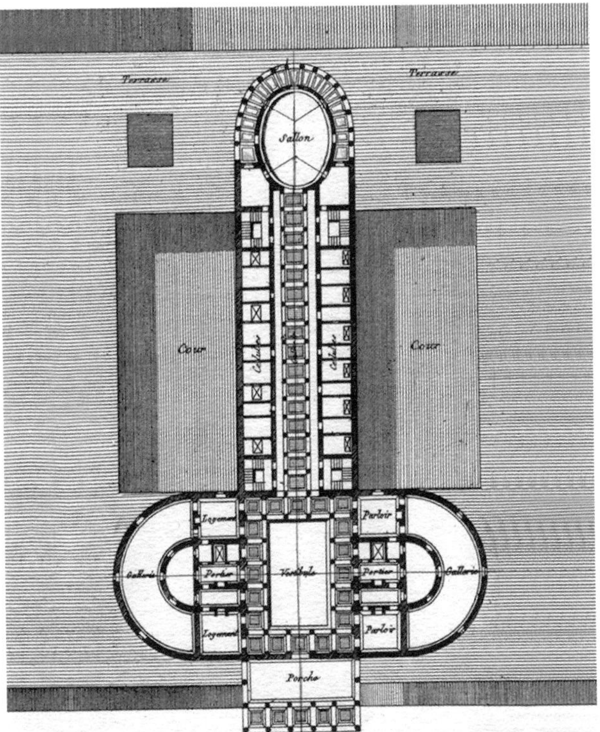

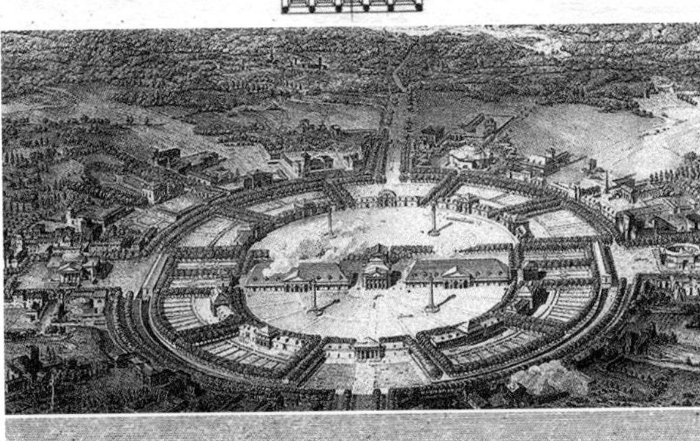

its function. He proposed these buildings almost as if they were follies, sublime in the scale of their metaphor, distributed within the landscape surrounding the main complex. The house of the water surveyor, in the form of an immense overturned bucket in the midst of a stream, and that of the cooper, shaped like an enormous barrel, are illustrative of this unprecedented exercise in metaphorical legibility [Figure 11, third from top and bottom]. Although its massing is rather conventional, the plan he proposed for the Oikema or House of Pleasure makes its purpose explicit [Figure 11, top]. The architectural and administrative legibility of Ledoux's scheme seems consistent with a Panopticon-like program; it was a premonition of future efforts to conceive the city as a planned and completely readable text, an instrument of economic development and social control.

Like Arc-de-Senans, although not as architecturally innovative, numerous ideal worker communities set within an extended landscape began to appear in both theory and practice during the late eighteenth and nineteenth centuries. The developers of these communities—alternatives to the typical urban mills of the day—intended to infuse industrial production with humane working and living conditions predicated upon a rational, progressive, cooperative social structure. David Dale founded one of the most influential of these worker communities, New Lanark, in Scotland. His son-in-law, the prominent industrial reformer Robert Owen (1771–1858), eventually took over its operation. Owen had collaborated with Bentham on several ventures. However, differences in political philosophy ultimately led to the severing of their partnership.

Another early nineteenth century ideal industrial community was the *phalanstère* organized as a secular monastery housed in a massive Versailles-like complex. This idea was the product of Charles Fourier (1782-1837), a prominent philosopher and utopian socialist. He had a passionate interest in architecture and modeled the architectural expression of his *phalanstère* on the Louvre palace, intending it for a rural site. Although Fourier greatly admired Ledoux's work and was a native of Besançon, the capital of Franche-Comté, no definitive evidence exists that he was aware of Arc-de-Senans.[29] As a social utopian dedicated to ending established institutions like marriage, the family, and the Church, it is unlikely he would have subscribed to the strict authoritarian order Ledoux imposed. Fourier never succeeded in building a *phalanstère*. Nevertheless, his ideas were enormously influential even into the late twentieth century.

The founder of French socialism, Claude Henri de Saint-Simon (1760–1825), had substantial influence on progressive thinkers of the nineteenth century, such as Durkheim, Comte, and Marx. He believed it was possible to create an industrialized society founded on scientific objectivity. However, he did not attempt to build a utopian

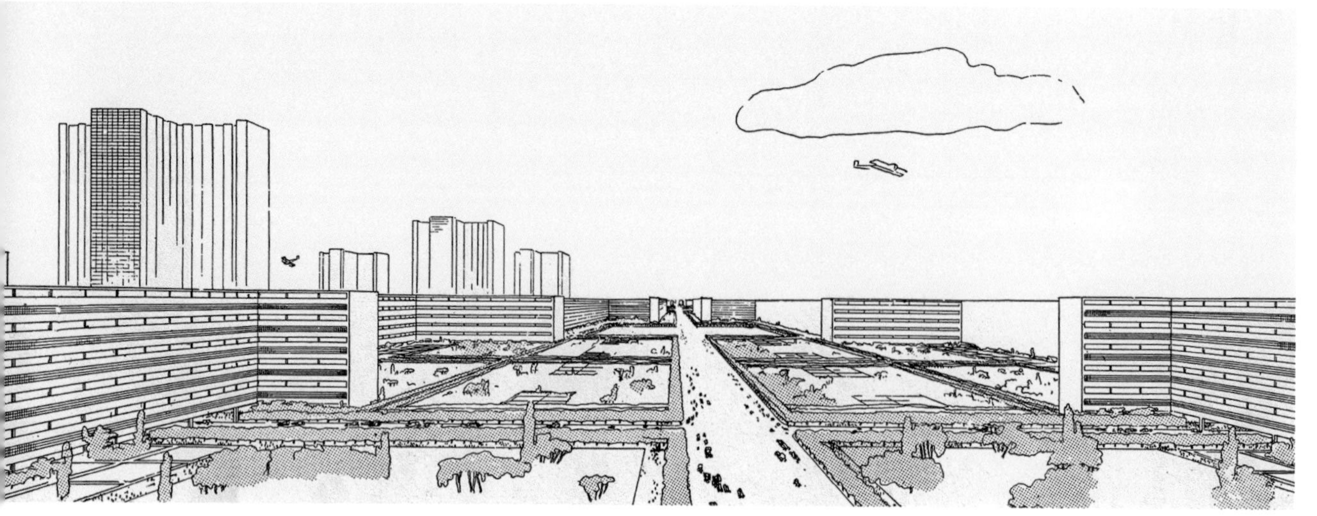

Figure 12/ Le Corbusier, Ville Contemporaine.

industrial community to illustrate his theories as had Owen and Fourier. Saint-Simon's ideal social order had a clear hierarchical structure divided into three generic classes. The first two were workers and owners. The third class, independent of political processes, was a benevolent governing elite so empowered because of the wisdom and artistic insightfulness of its members. All these utopian worker communities, both built and unrealized, had as their end the greatest happiness for the greatest number. In order to achieve this, they presumed that a perpetually watchful administrative eye must oversee the lives of all its members. Furthermore, to prevent the distractions and contaminations of the existing city, location within a pristine landscape was necessary.

Almost a century after Saint-Simon, the Swiss-French architect Le Corbusier (1887–1965) created a vision of the city for the twentieth century by synthesizing the social ideals of Fourier and Saint-Simon with an aesthetic inspired by the pure geometries of modern industry's products. His contemporary, the German architect Ludwig Hilberseimer (1885–1967), proposed a similar strategy for redefining the city on rational grounds. The basis for his proposals was the individual rectilinear spatial cell, reproduced *ad infinitum* to encompass everything from an individual room to the city and eventually the landscape. The dependence of the urbanistic visions of both architects on the rationalism of industry, functional transparency, pure geometries, and political control was analogous to the operations of both the Panopticon and Arc-de-Senans. Both architects also incorporated into their ideal cities, albeit somewhat uncomfortably, abstractly, and indirectly, the sublime romanticism of the Picturesque landscape garden. Their respective initial utopian proposals for the modern city had certain self-imposed geographical limits. However, subsequent models of each, founded upon similar fundamental predicates, sought to break these boundaries by extending indefinitely into the landscape, subsuming it into an urban order. Thus, Le Corbusier transformed the clearly circumscribed boundaries of his Ville Contemporaine of the 1920s into the laterally expanding urbanism of his Ville Radieuse of the 1930s. In the early 1960s, Hilberseimer renounced the barrenness of his 1924 Hochstadt urban ideal for a decentralized order that dissolved city into landscape intertwining urban life with agrarian reform [Figures 12, 13]. Le Corbusier's ideal cities explicitly presumed the total power of a Saint-Simonian elite governing class. Hilberseimer's made no such overt demand, yet an absolute authority was clearly essential and implicit to their realization.

THE INVISIBLE UBIQUITOUS EYE

In discussing the rational basis for determining beauty in architecture, Alberti remarks that the "very same numbers that cause sounds to have that *concinnitas* [i.e., harmony], pleasing to the ears, can also fill the eyes and mind with wondrous delight".[30] In effect, he was stating that the collaboration of vision and rational intellect largely determines aesthetic value for architecture. The progress of landscape gardening throughout the eighteenth century, given its predicate of composing, designing, and perceiving the landscape as a picture, likewise imputes priority to vision. Recall Addison's belief that of all the senses sight was the "most perfect and most delightful". In his recent essay, "Eidetic Operations and New Landscapes", James Corner distinguishes between *landskip*, the contemporary

Figure 13/ Ludwig Hilberseimer, Hochstadt.

impression of landscapes as primarily scenic, and *Landschaft*, which considers landscape as existentially and deeply ingrained into a way of life. The first makes an appeal to the eye alone and objectifies landscape. The second is not only visual but also tactile because it involves a reciprocal relationship between the landscape and those who, by residing in and drawing sustenance from it, are its stewards.[31] Corner's distinction is similar to that between *natura naturans* and *natura naturata*. Yet, when we consider the scenic landscape of the eighteenth century Picturesque, we must acknowledge that its design concerned not only how it affected the emotions through visual experience, but also that the difference between the designed landscape and the landscape of 'arbitrary' nature was ambiguous. Culturally inherent to the visual delight of these landscapes was also the productive purpose they held for their owners as viable agricultural operations. Nevertheless, within the illusory indefinite extent of those eighteenth century Picturesque landscapes is implicit an almost utopian desire to claim and control all that falls within the circumference of the powerful regime of the eye's 'limitless' trajectory.

More than the essential ingredient of an eighteenth century utopian vision, Bentham's Panopticon has become a paradigm of contemporary society. Over time, it evolved to provide a systematic structure for virtually every institution: education, medicine, manufacture, the military, government, etc.. The Panopticon's compulsion to observe, regulate, and normalize what society defines as aberrant made it for Michel Foucault, who examined it critically in *Discipline and Punish*, startlingly like life in the modern world.[32] In its contemporary incarnation, the concreteness of walls no longer defines its limits. Unlike Bentham's architectural model, it has no central viewing tower, but like it, no one person and no single agency controls it. The power of vision, the one sense that distance literally and figuratively can least restrain, is its premise. The Panopticon's penetrating gaze is pervasive and has thoroughly insinuated itself into all aspects of everyday life. Yet, although its operative principle is total visibility, even transparency, the contemporary Panopticon ironically is never visible, never tangible, never concrete, and incapable of containment in a single building, institution, city, or landscape. It itself is opaque. As both

microscope and telescope, it relentlessly scrutinizes, incessantly objectifies, continually inspects and re-inspects, and dissects our lives to provide the knowledge upon which the exercise and maintenance of power in the contemporary world depends. This phenomenon is even more acute now in the adolescence of the digital age, which was embryonic when Foucault wrote about the Panopticon. It has quite comfortably lodged itself in the unprecedented virtual landscapes of cyberspace. The optimism of Leibniz has become the "panopticism" of Foucault.[33] Many large cities, London in particular, now impose pervasive video surveillance, ostensibly for crime prevention purposes. Cookies surreptitiously install themselves on our computers, which also record every keystroke. Most mobile phones have GPS tracking that allow invisible authorities to know one's whereabouts; but these devices also have cameras that allow their owners anywhere in the world to occupy with illusory anonymity a metaphorical version of the Panopticon's central viewing tower. Unlike the earlier utopian visions of Ledoux, Owen, Le Corbusier, and Hilberseimer, the contemporary Panopticon has no hierarchy, explicit or implicit. To paraphrase Cusanus' claim regarding indefinite spatial extent, the Panopticon's center is everywhere but its circumference, though invisible, is both ubiquitous and nowhere. It breathes life into the prisons of Piranesi's febrile imagination. Alberti summed it up concisely: "the only impregnable prison is the eye of the vigilant guard".[34]

If the effect of power is indeed a preeminent factor of the Sublime, whether it is the 'powerlessness' of Burke's Sublime or Knight's exaltation of power, the stealthy Panopticon is the ultimate Sublime machine. It saturates real and virtual landscapes, fusing with them to the extent that, like Poliphilo's agitated night, the one seems like the dream of the other, producing a chillingly immense garden of infinitely forking paths.

Notes

1. Arouet, François-Marie (Voltaire), *Candide: or, The Optimist*, Lowell Bair trans., New York: Bantam Books, 2003, p. 15.
2. Casey, Edward, *The Fate of Place*, Berkeley: University of California Press, 1998, pp. 116–117. With the discovery of the cosmic microwave background in 1964 verifying the Big Bang Theory of the origin of the universe, the paradoxical idea that the center of the universe is everywhere became scientific orthodoxy.
3. Pascal, Blaise, *Thoughts*, W. F. Trotter trans., in *The Harvard Classics*, Vol. 48, Charles W. Norton ed., New York : P. F. Collier and Son Company, 1910, p. 78
4. Foucault, Michel, *The Order of Things*, New York: Vintage Books, 1973, p. 309.
5. Foucault, Michel, *Discipline and Punish: The Birth of the Prison*, Alan Sheridan trans., New York: Vintage Books, 1979, pp. 195–228.
6. Bacon, Francis, *Novum organum, or, True suggestions for the interpretation of nature*, Manchester: George Routledge and Sons, Limited, 1893, p. 11.
7. Bacon, Francis, *The New Atlantis in The Harvard Classics*, Vol. 3, Charles W. Norton ed., New York: P. F. Collier and Son Company, 1909, p. 153.
8. Bentham, Jeremy, "Panopticon; or the Inspection House", *The Works of Jeremy Bentham*, Vol. 4, Edinburgh: William Tait, 1843, p. 39.
9. Foucault, Michel, *Power/Knowledge*, Colin Gordon trans., New York: Pantheon Books, 1980, p. 158.
10. Johnston, Norman, *Forms of Constraint: A History of Prison Architecture*, Urbana and Washington: University of Illinois Press, 2000, pp. 52–53.
11. In his letters, Pliny implies similar gardening principles as those advocated by Alberti but does not specifically articulate them.
12. Alberti, Leon Battista, *On the Art of Building in Ten Books*, Joseph Rykwert, Neil Leach, and Robert Tavernor trans., Cambridge, MA: The MIT Press, 1988, p. 120.
13. Alberti, *On the Art of Building*, p. 300.
14. Alberti, *On the Art of Building*, p. 300.
15. Alberti, *On the Art of Building*, p. 300.
16. Alberti, *On the Art of Building*, p. 299.
17. Locke, John, *An Essay Concerning Human Understanding*, Kenneth P. Winkler ed., Indianapolis, IN: Hackett Publishing Company, 1996, p. 143.
18. Locke, *An Essay Concerning Human Understanding*, p. 174.
19. Addison, Joseph, *The Works of Joseph Addison: The Spectator*, Vol. VI, George Washington Greene ed., New York: Derby and Jackson, 1860, p. 322.
20. Addison, p. 336.
21. Pope, Alexander, *The Works of Alexander Pope*, Vol. 10, John Wilson Croker, Whitwell Elwin, and William John Courthope eds., London: John Murray, 1886, p. 530.
22. Pope, Alexander, "An Epistle to the Right Honourable Richard, Earl of Burlington, Occasioned by his Publishing Palladio's Designs of Baths, Arches, Theatres, &c. of Ancient Rome", *The Poems of Alexander Pope: Epistles to several persons (Moral essays)*, Vol. III, ii, F. W. Bateson ed., London: Methuen and Co. Ltd., 1951, pp. 137–139.
23. Pope, "An Epistle to the Right Honourable Richard, Earl of Burlington", p. 138.
24. See for example Sabine Wilke, "From *natura naturata* to *natura naturans*: Naturphilosophie and the Concept of Performing Nature", *Interculture*, no. 4, 2008, pp. 1–23.
25. The title of this section, "Et in Arcadia Ego" (I am also in Arcadia) is also the title of a painting by Nicolas Poussin (1594–1665). Along with his contemporaries Lorrain and Dughet (the latter a student of Poussin and often goes by Poussin's name), Nicolas was a central figure in the Arcadian school of painters. Although Nicolas was important in this regard, the influence of Lorrain and Dughet on Kent's landscape gardening was more substantial.
26. Shenstone, William, *Unconnected Thoughts on Gardening*, John Dixon Hunt ed., New York: Garland, 1982, p. 128.
27. Gothein, Marie Luise, *A History of Garden Art*, Vol. II, Walter P. Wright ed., Mrs. Archer-Hind trans., New York: Hacker Art Books, 1966, pp. 303–304.
28. Borges, Jorge Luis, "The Garden of Forking Paths", *Ficciones*, Anthony Kerrigan ed., Emece Editores trans., New York: Grove Press, 1962, pp. 89–101. Borges' story obviously addresses the idea of "possible worlds", and as Gilles Deleuze notes in *The Fold: Leibniz and the Baroque*, Borges was a disciple of Leibniz. In addition,

various contemporary writers have compared Borges' narrative structure in his short story to hypertext in cyberspace media. Moreover, Borges' story also bears similarity to Hugh Everett's 1957 "many worlds" hypothesis, which Everett devised to counter the epistemological problems inherent to Heisenberg's uncertainty principle in quantum physics. Borges' story also has some correspondence to the multi-verse hypotheses of the contemporary elaboration of string theory known as M-theory.

29. Beecher, Jonathan, *Charles Fourier: The Visionary and His World*, Berkeley: University of California Press, 1986, p. 245.

30. Alberti, *On the Art of Building*, p. 305.

31. Corner, James, "Eidetic Operations and New Landscapes", *Recovering Landscape*, James Corner ed., New York: Princeton Architectural Press, 1999, p. 154. Corner draws the terms *landskip* and *Landschaft* from Stilgoe, John R., *Common Landscape of America, 1580–1845*, New Haven: Yale University Press, 1982, pp. 12–29.

32. Foucault, *Discipline and Punish*, 217.

33. Foucault, *Discipline and Punish*, p. 218.

34. Alberti, *On the Art of Building*, p. 139.

BENEATH THE RADAR: EXOTICS AND NATIVES IN BOHEMIA'S BORDER GARDENS

/MORNA LIVINGSTON

BOHEMIAN '*TERROIR*'

The particular melancholic beauty of southern Bohemia's landscape has long drawn writers, composers, painters, and photographers seeking solace. In the twentieth century, the landscape was depicted as an antidote to totalitarianism by important visual artists, as if its deep hollows, reflective ponds, woods, and rolling hills—all heavily shaped by man—could salve the wounds of history. For an astounding number of twentieth century artists, the landscape itself, reaching to the Morava Delta into which its waters drain, became the subject of profound study, art, and reflection. To its early settlers in the Middle Ages, the sturdy monks confronting bogs and spongy water meadows left by the last ice age, a solution was to deepen and dam the hollows. In the Renaissance, serfs of the Rozemberk princes in Trebon dug more ponds and stocked them with carp. Draining the bogs left clear pools with dry fields above them, and silt from the ponds helped dress the fields for planting. Completely re-worked though it was, the pond landscape was soon colonized by frogs, herons, and beavers, and came to look as if it had always been there. In fact it is an entirely man-made '*terroir*', a landscape shaped by culture where the earth retains strong characteristics of place. Bohemia's gentle topography holds pockets of the forests that once covered northern Europe. Dark woods, open fields, and old roads connect towns and villages centered on the carp ponds.

The genial aspect of this Bohemia had lent its name by the nineteenth century to artists and their companions all over Europe who lived a casual or roaming life. Placed equally between Prague and Vienna, it drew artists, weavers, and adepts in natural science. During the era of the Grand Tour, Goethe and others came to collect rocks and botanize in towns like the ones I write about: sleepy towns today, whose apogee occurred in the late Renaissance. During Hapsburg rule, Bohemia was part of Austria, but the connection of Slavic and Germanic culture began centuries earlier, when Czech rulers invited German-speaking *Sudetendeutsch* to settle Bohemia. The German town plans, field patterns, and water systems were an important overlay to Bohemia's earlier draining. German speakers further shaped this landscape since the thirteenth century, as did other minorities, like the Jews.

The search for an edge to Bohemia—no matter how blurred—is clear in only one regard, and that is in the path of water flowing through it. Water defines the region. To the west of Slavonice, a line shears two watersheds, splitting, like the fault line of an earthquake, Trebon's waterscape from the waters of Slavonice flowing south east to the Diye River. This strand of the Morava river system takes in the Diye-Thaya watershed as it winds from Czechia to Austria back and forth across the border.

Slavonice's rounded hills, smooth but for a scattering of rocks dragged from Scandinavia by glaciers moving southward to Austria, show on eighteenth century maps as long fields, with hedges between them, extending out from each town; but neither the water nor the land outside the town walls is used now as it was intended in the Middle Ages. Slavonice—despite the Renaissance drawings of princes, the Bible, and Aeneas on its houses, its ancient gates, the velvet darkness of its night sky, the lack of signage, and the smell of wood smoke—in fact speaks more of the shifting current of contested places, than of the Medievally solid and stable. The carp-filled landscape of 1300 and the Renaissance field patterns disappeared some 60 years ago under Communism. The apparent stability—for the town looks really old—was enhanced by the Prague architect, Roman Koutsky, who re-set the town's granite paving more coherently in the late 1990s, lending it a visual unity of the late twentieth century, not of an earlier time. The scouring of that last glacier which softened the region's landforms describes metaphorically what Communist, and before that, Nazi policies did to this town in modern history. While for 1,000 years the well-nigh boundaryless place was fought over, only recently was its surface population scraped away too. In 1939, the Jews who guessed the seriousness of their plight fled if they could. Most thought they would be safe in Prague, a hope soon dashed. There are almost no Jews today, only Jewish cemeteries. Next to be sent away were

Figure 1/ Slavonice. Photograph by Morna Livingston.

the German-speakers, deposited at the border with one suitcase each by the Czechs after World War II. They were blamed for the ease with which Hitler had marched into Czechoslovakia. A third round of change came after the Communists came to power, since they wanted only 'trustworthy' party members living close to the border. A replacement population was chosen by them either from the secret police, or from among highly active Communist-party members, and everyone local fled the country, was moved north, or was put in prison. No person currently living in the town was born there; the few there from childhood came with their Communist parents. The aggression of these successive changes disrupted the cultural continuity of the place. No one cared for sgraffitoed houses of the Renaissance with vaulted ceilings, or managed the tunnels of the town's drainage system. There was such neglect that many roofs caved in, and the tunnels were blocked with mud. Those who knew how things worked had disappeared as if by plague. Worse, their departure is not much mentioned, even today [Figure 1].

LANDSCAPE IN MINIATURE: SLAVONICE'S GARDENS

Gardens have always held a clue to how people dream of a better world. The rigor with which the Communist system discouraged personal liberty, along with the lack of travel opportunities, made the garden a crucial repository of creative energy. Under Communism, farming lost its integrated place in people's lives, becoming a governmental objective with set goals, not a cultural artifact. Food produced by agricultural cooperatives forced everyone to eat much the same diet, while the ribbon-like fields were reworked into an enlarged field pattern. In a metaphorical parallel, everyone now wore similar mass-produced clothes, forcing exotics like the famous Czech embroidered ribbon into history. Often the new life was described as gray. But there is no gray scale in a garden. Gardens could be made on available pieces of earth close at hand. They offset the bland diet; their fruit could be distilled into alcohol, their seasonal activities did not annoy the government, and their social spaces had no political or didactic agenda, unlike the town's Culture Klub.

Far enough beneath the radar to avoid party scrutiny, Czech gardens were initially begun with the perennials, fruits, and nut trees left by previous owners [Figure 2]. Today they are usually densely planted with an eye to color, but not tightly controlled. Espaliers are not trimmed close, as they would be in France; weeds and grass that grow tall can be cut to feed rabbits, as if the gardens longed for freedom. Even today, when the vehement goals of Communism have receded and land ownership is increasingly privatized, the small Bohemian gardens still prize their intimacy. They have room for anything from potatoes to cut flowers, providing shelter for rare trees or botanical specimens. Their social spaces are not necessarily linked to drinking, which is rarely true of the townscape. They provide room to tinker with machines, especially old ones.

Figure 2/ Walled Garden, Mariz.
Photograph by Morna Livingston.

Figure 3/ Cottage with Delphiniums, Dacice. Photograph by Morna Livingston.

Figure 4/ Kolonie Garden, Slavonice.
Photograph by Morna Livingston.

Figure 5/ Greenhouse, Slavonice.
Photograph by Morna Livingston.

The small garden is a '*hortus conclusus*', amid the tangled web of conflicting land rights that continue as legacy of Communism [Figure 3]. A garden wall marks a parenthesis from the insistent communality of the open landscape and of the border itself, whose new identity as a Greenbelt connects it to other borders thousands of kilometers away. Such private spaces as gardens are needed in this otherwise unrelenting public realm, where even the town's air space is so accepted as public that inescapable loudspeaker messages are regularly broadcast a full 19 years after the fall of Communism.

The Bohemian cottage-garden was never so tightly defined as its equivalent in England [Figure 4]. There, cottage gardens took shape when monastic gardens fell apart, and artisans and the nascent middle class adopted them. Beyond that, many parallel pursuits connected the English working class with the wealthy, not least the fact that the entire culture bred plants. The textile-weaver's pinks and the elaborations of auricula breeding should be seen against the background of England's great plant collections. But Czech gardens differ from those in other parts of Europe in their bohemian lack of formality. The once impassable Czech-Austrian border, along with the backwardness of commerce on the Czech side, protected many 'heirloom' varieties of fruit, vegetables, and roses. Omitting castle gardens—which after Communism no longer figured as heated conservatory, botanic garden, or plant reservoir—the smaller southern Bohemian gardens vary as to type. Elsewhere, they might be termed kitchen, vegetable, cottage, or cutting gardens. A Czech assured me they were subsistence gardens, but that does not explain the thousands of trough gardens planted with sedums and saxifrages, the rare geraniums, or the orchids in pots. Some gardens are orchard-like on old farms, walled rectangles amid a tumble of barn ruins that collectivism made worthless and roofless. The only new garden form is the twentieth century's unique *kolonie* garden, a 1960s attempt by the government to grant minute tracts of land to people in Socialist housing. The tracts permitted just a tiny cabin, but old bathtubs for rainwater, tool sheds, and greenhouses walled with pickle jars and plastic water bottles creep in [Figure 5]. Used to ripen hot-house grapes, early tomatoes, and cucumbers, these sheds have been praised by Daniel Ziss as "a pickled cucumber poem... in the shadow of singing combine harvesters, in the shadow of industrial vegetable production policies, and the shadow of agricultural subsidies".[1]

Jiri Skabrada, an expert on traditional Czech architecture, bemoaned the cottages of the Communist period, seeing them as corruptions of tradition rather than amusing variations on historical architecture. To him, the cottages, and perhaps by extension their gardens, lack an inner logic, since no rules control their form, and they bear no relation to one another, unlike the elements of the traditional townscape and farmhouse complex. While miniaturization alone might connect the cottage and the small garden to folk practice, the loss of a unified architectural language prevented that from happening. Skabrada says scathingly of vacation cottages, which with storage barns, industrial buildings, and Socialist housing were the only things the Communists built in quantity: "the knowledge that the author[s] of these imitative creations [had good intentions]... may be... touching, yet [the results are] caricatures".[2] As he watched, the cottages invaded every charming spot, from the slopes of historic sites and important ruins, to the fabric of old villages. This last trend was cynically encouraged by the Socialist government, who wished, in the Sudetenland particularly, to liquidate large farms and reparcel their land. Skabrada resented the cynical insertion of cottages into groupings of genuine folk buildings, especially near the Czech borders.[3]

THE GREENBELT AND THE MACROSCALE

The border... is not so much a line drawn in the sand... but in the imagination, a line across which memory may not travel, empathy may be confiscated, truth held up indefinitely, meaning lost in translation.
/ Rebecca Solnit[4]

On a scale far larger than Bohemia's landscape, the year 2005 saw a new paradise garden formalized, the *Grüneband*, or Greenbelt park, which extends through 23 countries from Scandinavia to the Black Sea along the former Iron Curtain. From the once brutally restricted border, 21 governments signed written agreements to create a single ecological park. It is a grandiose project with so many ramifications, even its planners are still trying to figure out what its existence will mean. To understand its genesis, one must realize that the space between the barbed wire strands had a dimension, in some places up to several kilometers wide, and this functioned as an ecological common ground, or more simply a shared space, like the English 'commons'. While the barbed wire prevented people from crossing, many animals, insects, birds, and plants, having been marginalized in the tightly-farmed landscapes on either side, found a less constricted home in this long empty space. The border dividing Bohemia from Austria lacks a marked geography, and with few hills for lookouts, and no natural barriers, it was all too easy to traverse. When the land was divided into provinces, the boundary shifted like the ox bows of a flatland river delta over time. As mentioned above, the Diye-Thaya River digs and erases its bed in constant meanders, from east of Trebon and the woods of Czech Canada, to the water meadows below Brno in so-called Moravian Brazil, amid vines and jungle-like vegetation.

Because the border tended to shift, the Communists had to reinforce the Iron Curtain with barbed wire, put soldiers on patrol day and night, add lights, raise towers, cut train lines and roads, bury land mines, rig electric fences, let dogs run loose, and even poison the ground occasionally. Current difficulties in defining the Greenbelt as a peaceful park owe something to this painful history. Satellite photographs of the border show how the Communists enlarged the field pattern on the Czech side, but on the border itself, things did not remained static. The Iron Curtain began to serve as a protected area simply because it was not plowed. Weeds, wild plants, and butterflies colonized it; water flowed unobstructed; and plants self-seeded over the hidden landmines. While tame plants and animals stayed put behind barbed wire, the wild ones knew a good open space when they saw it.

The Russian clampdown in 1968, known as the Prague Spring, followed attempts at reform. The reforms were immediately quashed by Soviet tanks and soldiers, depressing the Czechs. Each political change for the next 20 years curtailed more freedoms, reduced diversity further, and made suspect any Czechs who complained about land policies. The Communists kept the border town of Slavonice as a secret zone, as hidden as Oak Ridge was during the development of the atom bomb. Any critics of the police were persecuted. In Brno, the biologist, author, and photographer Milos Spurny was kept in check by being denied equipment for his work, while liberal publishers could not get printing paper. The frustration was incredible. What made Spurny and others so angry was that government land management never took local geography into consideration. One example can stand for the whole: the fertilizer put on cooperative farms washed into fish ponds, contaminating the fish as a food. This was so extreme that removing silt after the fall of Communism was hazardous work, requiring protective clothing and breathing apparatus for the workmen.

WATER MEADOWS AND TWENTIETH CENTURY DREAMS

Many sensitive people realized that the government was inflicting severe damage on the landscape. Spurny hand-built large format cameras and bribed a group of friends with wine and conversation to help him document the riverine landscape of the Morava before the government dammed it. He made photographic panoramas of the beautiful old rivers by carefully splicing several negatives together, and printing them as one long image. Spurny was the sort of person one friend described as "sleeping with the landscape to know it better". Through this identification, he was able to give both voice and image to the watery landscape. His powerful and thoughtful legacy was to document, from a biologist's point of view, the rivers into which the ponds of Slavonice, Dacice, Jhilova, and Brno drain.[5] He focused on the point of the alluvial fan just before it crossed the border one final time into Austria, where the mature Diye, Thaya, Svratka, and Morava join their fractal networks into a single stem. For centuries, this had occurred in fantastic old landscapes of great trees, but the Communists in the early 1970s reworked the drainage to shorten, straighten, canalize, and tie it in fat knots with dams. Spurny wrote:

> Although in periods of spring thaws the rivers frequently turned into giants, in summer they lazily intertwined through the jungle of the South Moravian floodplain. Rivers in their lower reaches are always majestic, robust, versant and composed matrons with wide, deep and sometimes wicked waters, in contrast to the restless sprightlies cheerfully frolicking over pebbles and rocks in submontane canyons. We have enough of these in this country but there are not many matrons left. We have canalized them all.... Make no mistake; every woodsman, canoeist, fisherman and, especially, poacher from the area knows that in the last 50 years things have been going downhill for rivers.[6]

But while Spurny spent the 1970s alternately recording the Morava's beauty and deploring what the Socialist government was about to do to it, the photographer Jan Sagl, after repeated harassment by Prague's secret police, retreated to the relative quiet of Bohemia. Over two decades, he produced color photographs following the seasons. His book *Jihoceska Krahina*, or *Southern Czech Landscapes*, explains that his photographs look:

> at the South Bohemian landscape just as if all the famous towns, strongholds settlements and ruins of castles were missing, as well as all the Renaissance castles, the reds, blues and greens of tourist signs on the trees, together with the white arrows of sign-posts giving the names of villages and ponds, but also stating the distance in kilometers and thus spoiling the poetry.[7]

Rebecca Solnit explains how landscape painting and later landscape photography "evolved out of anthropocentric painting: the banditti or the Madonna got smaller, and the landscape behind the drama got more complex, until eventually the actors left the stage—but the landscape was still composed as stage, as scenery", empty and waiting to be inhabited.[8] This is how Jan Sagl envisioned Bohemia. During the Communist era, coming hard on the heels of World War II and the Czechs' brutal occupation under Hitler, an appreciation of landscape as if it lay outside of history was one of the few ways sensitive people continued to maintain any hope at all. One has only to think of Josef Sudek in his Prague studio, photographing and re-photographing the single tree outside his window in an effort to remain sane. His friend, the artist Anna Farova, explained that Sudek began this in the 1940s and continued for 14 years through the German occupation and the Communist regime. The gnarled tree became his *doppelgänger*, often veiled, through the window. He liked the layering of rain, dew, and frost on the glass. The window was a place for him to meditate for over 15 years, the glass "the dividing line between two worlds, marked by time, by the seasons, by day and night, permeable and impermeable.... Emptied of valuable people and pictures his studio began to expand into the non-material sphere of music and contemplation of the changing surface of the panes of two ordinary windows."[9]

Like Sudek, Jan Sagl had sought this crossover in the arts, when, before leaving for Bohemia, he photographed swallows on telegraph wires after listening to Bach, as if the birds' bodies were musical notes of a score that could be read across the sky. But Sagl's intention was to document the world, not escape from it, and he "retained his romantic desire to record in as much detail as possible the land that had undergone megalomaniacal collectivization and industrialization". South Bohemia "fascinated him with its broad scale of greens, which are so concentrated that from the photos we sense the air imbued with the fragrance of vegetation".[10] Magdalena Jurikova felt that Sagl's photographs grew from a tradition of "landscape painting [that] had gained great authority in Bohemia, particularly when it most intimately related to the milieu in which artists were willing to spend many days and even months in the great outdoors studying its character and symbolism, and to present a summary of their visual experience of it".[11]

Given the intensity of these artists' views, it is not hard to see how the historian Skabrada—just as Sagl wanted traffic signs out of his photographs and Sudek photographed mostly trees—could disdain the eclecticism of the cottage tradition during this bleak time. Belief in the ideal nature of the Bohemian landscape, and an insistence that its values were permanent—Sagl called it the one "reality in which was concentrated everything worth considering" —was not confined to visual artists [Figure 6]. The Jewish writer Marie Bauer, who fled Prague, then Europe days before the war, finally returned to her childhood home the same year Sagl published his photographs. It is probably no coincidence that the only peace Bauer found in her

Figure 6/ Garden near Dobra Voda. Photograph by Morna Livingston.

now empty house and treeless, gateless park where she had played as a child, was a belief in the transformative power of the Bohemian landscape:

> Anton drives... past what had once been our fields and forests. The rustling and bending of the trees in the wind sounds like a lament—first soft and rhythmical, then louder and louder until it turns into music, Dvorak's... *Slavonic Dances.* Whenever I had listened to them... they had always brought me the vision of this familiar landscape. Now it is all around me—and my sadness is gone. The memory of Svinare, my past and our way of life were all illusion. Its time has run out; it collapsed and disintegrated. But the Bohemian landscape, the fields and forests and Dvorak's music, inseparably, have survived, will survive anything.[12]

THE SEARCH FOR AUTHENTICITY IN THE BORDER GARDEN

Often described as an object or a fact rather than a concept, the border is nothing more than a line on a map drawn by war and only occasionally imposed on the actual landscape. It can be imagined as a kind of blueprint for a largely unbuilt public art work....
/ Rebecca Solnit[13]

No simple analogy can capture the difficult history of this borderland, but the water-loving willow is one plant whose pliant use runs a similar gamut of complexity and renewal [Figure 7]. On the one hand, willows were pollarded for making baskets, furniture, and even cradles with a basket weave. On the other it was braided into willow whips with which the boys chased the girls they liked in the spring around Easter. The girls were taught to reward this beating by giving the boys their ribbons. The whips, however, were alive, and after their rough use they were stuck in water, or in the earth, where they could sprout and root; they are thus an emblem of continuing life as much as part of a largely forgotten, but still observed fertility ritual. Single lines of freshly planted willow whips that later will be pollarded line many streams between the ponds. Their stems are brown, but the shoots bright mustard yellow, straight, and thin as arrows. The willow, since its annual use is certainly not of Christian origin, makes the point that elements of older, indigenous religions could come into Bohemia again in the vacuums created by Nazi and Communist disparaging of the Church. And, as before, these elements found their home not inside buildings, but in the landscape and the free space of gardens.

Prominent among these alternative beliefs has been the adoption of American Indian identities, and an attempt to study Indian spiritual practices [Figure 8].

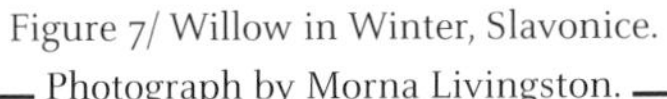

Figure 7/ Willow in Winter, Slavonice. Photograph by Morna Livingston.

Figure 8/ Totem, Stalcov. Photograph by Morna Livingston.

Teepees, totem poles, and moccasined people are often part of the garden and woodland landscape. "The authenticity attributed to nativeness seems to be something everyone can impersonate; as cowboys are to American actors, so are Indians to—apparently everyone, including border or part-time wannabe Indians in Germany and Central Europe."[14] Solnit wrote that Indian identities were taken up like works of art. Real Indians who make it to the Czech Republic on the strength of this may have trouble fitting into this fantasy. Recently, ten Indians from Peru living near Brno who wanted to make a living playing authentic flute music were starving, because people told them they were not Indian enough. With the help of a leather merchant, they constructed 'authentic' Plains Indian outfits and headdresses, took Indian names from American

Figure 9/ Roof tiles in a "Japanese" Garden, Chvalatin. Photograph by Morna Livingston.

Figure 10/ Dish Garden, Mutisov. Photograph by Morna Livingston.

movies, listened to Navaho records, and have been making a living as musicians ever since. The American Indian as well as druidic elements that enliven today's border gardens express a longing for roots in a culture recently taught to mistrust religion, and still troubled over its border history.

A final exoticism among the garden plants themselves is the strong Japonisme of the plant world [Figure 9]. This style had entered the gardens of the wealthy by the end of the nineteenth century, but was only brought into cottage gardens during the Communist period. From tiny and curious bonsai, to curtains of Japanese maple, iris gardens, and yellow and fringed-leaved plants, there has been an explosion of interest in collecting Japanese cultivars [Figure 10]. Many Czech gardeners who plant them are clearly aware that the miniature forms were bred to represent the cosmos in container gardens in Asian temple complexes, so their interest extends to creating curving paths, planting large stones, and building arched bridges over streams in order to create the proper setting.

If there are those who claim that teepees and bonsais create a paradox for today's garden, that they are 'caricatures' to borrow Skabrada's term, at least in the smaller gardens you see people grappling with hard questions on a scale that might lead to something in the way of answers. The tendency to downplay the importance of small gardens by focusing instead on the Greenbelt, or of using other large empty properties as tree parks, shifts attention to the larger picture. It questions where bird populations will breed, or deer cross the border. While larger scale thinking has its good side in terms of the environment, it can usurp the energy needed by those living here to revisit and understand their own history, in a way the garden helps them to do. To limit access along the Greenbelt may be convenient in terms of the wildlife, but there are ghosts of people who once lived there, so it is no blank slate. As the daughter of her nanny wrote, after decades of separation to Helen Waldstein Wilkes, a Czech-born author who was exiled to Canada as a child, "our roots are entwined, but our branches stretch out over separate gardens".[15]

THE GARDEN TODAY

The garden flourished when it lay beneath the radar, unquashed by Communist ideals, but stripped of its traditions. The small garden holds one fact of very great importance: that in it people are drawn to understand their own past. It is one place where issues of family and of history can be laid out in the open. During Communism, the government did everything, and ran everything, making cooperation after their departure when the Czechs could shape their own decisions that much more difficult. Any idea of the public sponsoring benevolent institutions was hard to focus on, and cross-border collaborations even more so, when for so many years, both sides of the border had been fed anti-foreign propaganda, and they no longer spoke the same language. To share plants is very healing, even when a social life cannot be shared.

If southern Bohemia's gardens reflect an irrepressible ability of people to make do in the face of gloomy politics, they do so by creating space for a livable world in the face of an intolerant one [Figure 11]. In gardens, the spirit

Figure 11/ Table with Cherries, Mariz. Photograph by Morna Livingston.

of invention we term vernacular turns grayness into color, resists the monocultures of industrialized tree and farming landscapes, and rethinks discarded industrial products from broken roof tiles to bathtubs with tongue-in-cheek, even black, humor. While these small gardens may lack the close integration with whole village landscape that existed before the 1930s, they pulse with a new life, which has many urban roots. Today they lie in the grander shadow of the Greenbelt, whose park-like presence and environmental significance dwarf them. Yet, the small garden is still one place in which we come the closest to defining an individual paradise. The intense attention gardens receive from their owners, as if their owners really believed in them, is their strong suit. Doing garden chores expresses a confidence that life is good, at least here, in contrast with the glacially slow political processes that effect change in the former Iron Curtain borderlands. In gardens, people grapple with who they are. The garden tradition is the least broken thing about the Czech landscape, and the most healing.

Notes

* The author wishes to thank The Centre for the Future, Telluride and Slavonice, and Philadelphia University, School of Architecture for their support.

1. Ziss, Daniel, *Art and Antik*, 2003, pp. 75–77, quoted in Veronika Zapletalova, *Chatarsvi: Summerhouses*, (exhibition catalogue), Prague, 2007, p. 285.
2. Skabrada, Jiri ,"I do not like Cottages: Cottages vs. Folk Architecture", in Zapletalova, *Chatarsvi*, p. 366.
3. Skabrada, "I do not like Cottages", p. 367.
4. Solnit, Rebecca, *Storming the Gates of Paradise: Landscapes for Politics*, Berkeley: University of California Press, 2007, p. 79.
5. Spurny, Milos, *Sbohem, stare reky: Good-bye, Old Rivers*, Brno: FOTEP, 2007, p. 131.
6. Spurny, *Sbohem, stare reky*, p. 13.
7. Sagl, Jan (photos), Pavel Vrba (text), *Jihoceska Krajina*, Prague: Pressfoto, 1984, unpaged essay.
8. Solnit, *Storming the Gates of Paradise*, p. 243.
9. Farova, Anna, "Josef Sudek: The Window of My Studio", Prague: Torst, 2007, unpaged essay.
10. Jurikova, Magdalena (text), Jan Sagl (photographs), *Jan Sagl*, Prague: Fototorst, 2009, p. 7.
11. Jurikova, *Jan Sagl*, p. 9.
12. Bauer, Maria, *Beyond the Chestnut Trees*, Woodstock: Overlook, 1984, p. 39.
13. Solnit, *Storming the Gates of Paradise*, p. 81.
14. Solnit, *Storming the Gates of Paradise*, p. 33.
15. Wilkes, Helen Waldstein, *Letters from the Lost*, Edmonton: Athabasca University Press, 2010, p. 108.

5

ECONOMIES OF THE GARDEN

ENQUIRY INTO PLANTS, NATURE, UTOPIA, AND THE BOTANIC GARDEN

220 /STEPHEN FORBES

PLANTS, LIGHT, AND LIFE

Our hearts beat utilizing energy that is harvested from sunlight by plants through the agency of chlorophyll. This fundamental truth is rarely acknowledged. The environment that hosted our evolution formed through photosynthesis, resulting in the liberation of oxygen and the capture of carbon. Our daily needs for food, fiber, fuel, shelter, and medicine have been and are still largely met directly or indirectly by plants. A more troubling aspect of our relationship with plants is apparent in the accelerating use of fossil fuels derived from plants. This use is driving the liberation of aeons of captured carbon and leading to climate change. We have now begun to undo the life-sustaining changes in Earth's atmosphere brought about by plants, and we may face an apocalyptic future in which neither plants nor humans will survive.

Our success as a species is based upon the role of plants as a mediation between light and life and the application of plants to human endeavor. Our relationship with plants represents our most profound and intimate relationship after our relationships with each other and with the Divine. The search for knowledge, reconciliation, and even salvation through plants can be seen as a logical response to their transformative power. Significantly, the vital importance of the relationship between light and life, and the notion of a garden as both a literal and metaphorical paradise recur across cultures. Thus, the Biblical Tree of Life and the Tree of the Knowledge of Good and Evil within the Garden of Eden might well be interpreted both metaphorically and literally, for the narrative that drives human endeavor is necessarily a story about harvest.

PLANTS, PEOPLE, AND CULTURE

The systematic exploitation of plants by people provides the foundation for culture and civilization. Indeed, the management, cultivation, and exploitation of plants is both the basis for survival and perhaps the most sublime achievement of culture. We face and overcome manifold challenges in deriving food, fiber, fuel, shelter and tools, medicines and toxins, and compounds for processing, preserving and adhesion from plant sources. Further challenges attend the management of forage and fodder for domestic and wild animals. Meanwhile, our utilization of plants also forms a basis for arts and craft and even for philosophy and spiritual enlightenment. In fact, our enquiry into plants is among humanity's most significant endeavors. Such enquiry is historically established in natural ecosystems and developed as traditional ecological knowledge, even in the absence of gardens. However, the value of cultivating plants in one place to facilitate observation and learning is immediately apparent, and provides the basis for the purpose, origins, and power of botanic gardens.[1]

To arrive at a satisfactory definition of botanic gardens remains a surprisingly challenging undertaking. Definitions for botanic gardens are commonly lists of attributes illustrating contemporary preoccupations. Such definitions emphasize the connection between a plant collection and purposes such as education, science, and conservation, as well as roles in arts and culture, health and well-being, and recreation. According to the organization Botanic Gardens Conservation International, botanic gardens are "institutions holding documented collections of living plants for the purposes of scientific research, conservation, display and education".[2] However, our understanding of the historical purpose of botanic gardens as an institutional framework should not be constrained by a contemporary scientific paradigm.

A definition accommodating a diversity of knowledge paradigms from different cultures and settings is proposed here, reflecting the fundamental nature of a collections-based cultural institution. At its heart, a botanic garden is simply a plant collection established for "enquiry into plants". The phrase, borrowed from the eponymous work of the Greek philosopher Theophrastus, provides a definition for botanic gardens consonant with their central purpose of exploring ideas through the agency of plants. Theophrastus, who succeeded Aristotle as head of the Lyceum in Athens in 322 BCE and

THEOPHRASTI ERESII
DE
HISTORIA PLANTARVM
LIBRI DECEM,
Græcè & Latinè.
In quibus
Textum Græcum variis Lectionibus, emendationibus, hiulcorum supplementis: Latinam GAZÆ versionem nova interpretatione ad margines: totum Opus absolutissimis cum Notis, tum Commentariis: item rariorum Plantarum iconibus illustravit
IOANNES BODÆVS a STAPEL,
Medicus Amstelodamensis.
Accesserunt
IVLII CÆSARIS SCALIGERI,
in eosdem Libros Animadversiones:
ET
ROBERTI CONSTANTINI
Annotationes;
Cum
INDICE locupletissimo.

AMSTELODAMI
Apud Henricum Laurentium.
Anno 1644.

Figure 1/ The frontispiece to an illustrated 1644 edition of *Historia Plantarum* by Theophrastus.
Image courtesy History of Science Collections, University of Oklahoma Libraries.

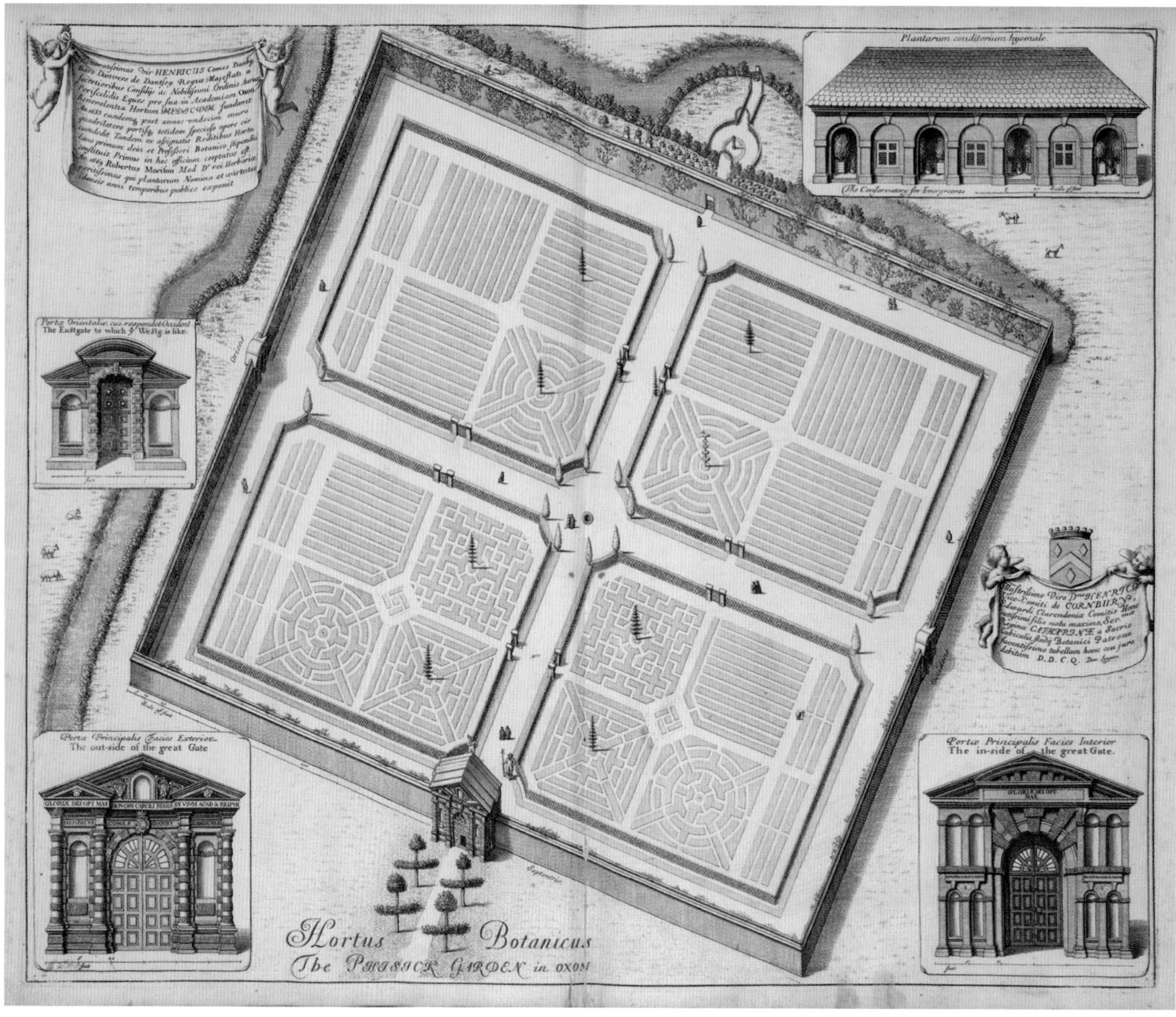

Figure 2/ Plan of the Physic Garden, Oxford, from David Loggan, *Oxonia Illustrata* 1675.
Photograph © The Trustees of the British Museum.

inherited Aristotle's (botanic) garden, engaged in studies of wild and cultivated plants. His Classical tracts *Enquiry into Plants* (*De Historia Plantarum*) and *On the Causes of Plants* (*De Causis Plantarum*) accorded him the title of "Father of Botany" in the Renaissance [Figure 1].

Theophrastus' emphasis on learning in the utilization of a plant collection is hardly unique; two millennia later, the Oxford Physic Garden would be dedicated to the "glorification of God and for the furtherance of learning" [Figures 2, 3].[3] Both Theophrastus and Oxford define botanic gardens by their curation of botanical collections to facilitate learning and the transmission of plant knowledge. In summary, botanic gardens are organized plant collections established and utilized for the enquiry into plants.

PLANTS, PURPOSE, AND GARDENS

Pliny's *Account of The Nature of flax* (*marvellous facts relative thereto*) gives a vivid insight into the relationship between plants, people, and culture:

> To think that here is a plant that brings Egypt closer to Italy! So much so, in fact, that Galerius and Bulbillus, both of them prefects of Egypt, made the passage to Alexandria from the Straits of Sicily, the one in six days, the other in five!... What audacity in man! What criminal perverseness! Thus to sow a thing in the ground for the purpose

of catching the winds and the tempests, it being not enough for him, forsooth, to be borne upon the waves alone! Nay, still more than this, sails even that are bigger than the very ships themselves will not suffice for him, and although it takes a whole tree to make a mast to carry the cross-yards, above those cross-yards sails upon sails must still be added, with others swelling at the prow and at the stern as well—so many devices, in fact, to challenge death! Only to think, in fine, that that which moves to and fro, as it were, the various countries of the earth, should spring from a seed so minute, and make its appearance in a stem so fine, so little elevated above the surface of the earth! And then, besides, it is not in all its native strength that it is employed for the purposes of a tissue; no, it must first be rent asunder, and then tawed and beaten, till it is reduced to the softness of wool; indeed, it is only by such violence done to its nature, and prompted by the extreme audacity of man, that it is rendered subservient to his purposes.[4]

Figure 3/ Great Gate of the Physic Garden, Oxford, with Jacob Bobart the Elder—now known as the Danby Gateway of the University of Oxford Botanic Garden. From Evan Abel (1713), *Vertumnus, An epistle to Mr. Jacob Bobart, botany professor to the University of Oxford and keeper of the physick-garden.* Image courtesy of the Board of the Botanic Gardens & State Herbarium, South Australia.

Pliny's account illustrates the increasing human sophistication in the exploitation of plant materials in art and craft, and in the development of agriculture in a cultural context. Formalized plant collecting and the arrangement of plant collections in gardens to facilitate the development and exploitation of knowledge are perhaps as much hallmarks of civilization as the development of cities and writing. Such endeavors are apparent in the earliest written records, and any gardens based on these plant collections might reasonably be regarded as botanic gardens. A diversity of purposes is common throughout the history of botanic gardens, but while ancient gardens might have been established principally to serve ceremonial, practical, and recreational goals, the defining feature of a botanic garden remains the establishment of a plant collection to facilitate enquiry into plants. Such gardens play a critical role in the evolution of the relationship between people, plants, and culture.

THE ORIGINS OF BOTANIC GARDENS

In his 1915 landmark essay on "The history and functions of botanic gardens", Arthur Hill outlines examples of botanic gardens from ancient China, Egypt, Assyria, Classical Greece, and Central America, but he attests that "these in no way influenced the foundation of modern botanic gardens" grounded in the scientific method.[5] Similarly, Frans Stafleu's 1969 essay presents science as a critical element of the method for botanic gardens.[6] However, these perspectives miss the key point that the institutional framework of botanic gardens continues to be regenerated and reworked across civilizations and through time. The adoption of a scientific methodology in such gardens simply reflects the flourishing of science since the Renaissance. A brief survey of ancient, putative botanic gardens across Asia, Africa, Europe, and the Americas illustrates the recurring themes of plant collecting, curation in gardens, learning, and the transmission of plant knowledge. The enquiry into plants in these early botanic gardens was driven by a range of knowledge paradigms established through philosophical, biocultural, folk, and religious frameworks.

Figure 4/ Fragment of a polychrome tomb-painting representing the pool in Nebamun's estate garden, 1400 BCE. Photograph © The Trustees of the British Museum.

Shennong, the 'Divine Farmer' and the mythological bearer of culture at the beginning of Chinese civilization, might be credited with the first enquiry into plants. Vivienne Lo observes that "Han historians and mythmakers describe his most fundamental task as having led humanity out of a state of hunting and savagery, away from eating raw flesh, drinking blood, and wearing skins, toward an agrarian utopia." Lo also quotes a second century BCE source (The King of Huanan): "In ancient times people ate grasses and drank from rivers; they picked fruit from trees and ate molluscs and beetles. At that time there was much suffering from illness and poisoning. So the Divine Farmer taught the people for the first time how to sow and cultivate the five grains."[7] Shennong is reputed to have tested hundreds of plants to determine their medical value, and in one day consumed seventy poisons. The earliest Chinese herbal, *The Divine Farmer's Herb Root Classic*, is attributed to Shennong, although compiled some time in the Han Dynasty several thousand years after Shennong.[8] Han Emperor Wu-ti (140–86 BCE), for his part, is credited by Hill with the establishment of a botanic garden and the engagement of field collectors in exploring regional China for new agricultural and horticultural crops. Successful discoveries include the vine, pomegranate, safflower, common bean, cucumber, lucerne, coriander, and walnut.[9]

Ancient Egyptian rulers engaged field collectors, and although the focus may have been ceremonial as much as economic, some Egyptian gardens might well be interpreted as botanic gardens [Figure 4]. The Temple of Karnak's 'botanical garden' reliefs illustrate nearly three hundred exotic plants and animals, including those King Thutmose III (1479–1425 BCE) brought from military campaigns in Syria and Palestine [Figure 5].[10] The ancient Egyptian Ebers Papyrus is one of the earliest known herbals; dating back to 1550 BCE and probably based on much earlier sources, it illustrates an understanding of the medicinal values of plants. The illustration of a plant collection or of an herbal is hardly proof of a botanic garden, and no unambiguous evidence establishes the existence of botanic gardens in ancient Egypt. However, gardens certainly played a role in the Egyptians' enquiry into plants, as is evident in the sophistication of their gardens and in their practical application of a deep knowledge of plant materials. Ancient Egyptian literature includes books on the pomegranate and on an oil-producing plant, as well as a later herbal. Therefore, it might be reasonably inferred that some form of botanic garden played a role in expanding knowledge of plants beyond traditional biocultural knowledge.

Ancient Mesopotamian gardens also suggest the establishment of plant collections for an enquiry into plants. Indisputably, plants were collected from military campaigns, for as Assurnasirpal II (883–859 BCE) observed, "From lands I travelled and hills I traversed, the trees and seeds I noticed and collected."[11] Such trees and seeds were certainly planted, as he boasted: "I planted seeds and plants that I had found in countries through which I had marched and in the highlands which I had crossed: pines of different kinds, cypresses and junipers of different kinds, almonds, dates, ebony, rosewood, olive, oak, tamarisk, walnut, terebinth and ash, fir, pomegranate, pear, quince, fig, grapevine."[12]

The resulting gardens would necessarily have served as an enquiry into plants. However, the nature of the enquiry may well have been incidental to the purpose of such gardens for pleasure or for the demonstration of power [Figure 6]. A more specific, if ambiguous, reference to an ordered garden is suggestive of a 'physic' garden of medicinal plants. A cuneiform text for the garden of Merodach-Baladan II (721–710, 703–702 BCE) orders plants in 15 sections and includes highly specialized

Figure 5/ Egypt, Karnak, Temple of Amun, flora and fauna on relief—the so-called Botanic Garden or Cabinet of Curiosities of Thoutmosis III, sixth Pharaoh of the eighteenth dynasty (reigned from 1479–1425 BCE). Image courtesy of the Dorling Kinderley Collection/ Getty Images.

Figure 6/ The 'Garden Party' relief from the North Palace of Ashurbanipal, Nineveh, Iraq about 645 BCE. Photograph © The Trustees of the British Museum.

plants with non-Babylonian names.[13] Further, Babylonian medical texts include a remarkable diversity of plant materials. Cuneiform texts from the reign of Ashurbanipal (668–626 BCE) identify about 250 plant-based medicines including asafoetida, calamus, cannabis, castor, crocus, galbanum, glycyrrhiza, hellebore, mandragon, mint, myrhh, opium, pine, styrax, turpentine, and thymus.[14] The diversity of plant-based medicines, especially exotic ones, suggests that physic gardens may have supported the endeavours of magicians as well as physicians.[15]

Turning to Classical Greece, there remains some dispute about whether Aristotle and Theophrastus had a garden for teaching at the Lyceum in Classical Athens, although the evidence seems reasonably convincing.[16] Theophrastus' *Enquiry into Plants* establishes the central tenet of botanic gardens as an institution, and may well indicate the presence of such a 'botanic' garden.[17] Theophrastus describes plants in *The Causes of Plants* and explores "spontaneous phenomena and phenomena initiated by human art" in *Enquiry*.[18] He seems to accept Plato's view that plants were created to serve man as food, though he notes that plants also ripen (or concoct) seeds in order to reproduce themselves.[19]

Enquiry into plants also seems to have been a key purpose of gardens such as those established by Moctezuma I (Motechzoma Ilhuicamian 1398–1469) at Tenochitlan, Chapultepec (now in Mexico City), and in Huaxtepec (present day Oaxtepec). That in Huaxtepec was apparently established to cultivate tropical medicinal plants that could not be cultivated in the highlands.[20] Nezahualcóyotl's (1403–1473) garden in Texcotzingo (present day Texcoco) is described as a place of study, supporting cosmology, spirituality, philosophy, and the arts; as it supported a purposeful enquiry into plants, it too may be classified as a form of botanic garden.[21] Other Aztec gardens, meanwhile, appear to have had a singular purpose. Cervantes de Salazar described Moctezuma II's (Motechzoma Xocoyotzin 1466–1520) gardens as "provid(ing) great joy, with their variety of flowers and roses and the scents and good aromas they emanated especially in the morning and afternoon.... Moctezuma did not allow to grow vegetables or fruits in those gardens, saying it was not proper of kings to have farms and utilitarian things in the places dedicated to their pleasure."[22]

The success of the Aztec enquiry into plants is evident in a range of Aztec herbals. 251 plants are listed in the Badianus codex, which was translated into Latin by Juan Badiano from a Nahuatl original composed in the Colegio de Santa Cruz de Tlatelolco in 1552 by Aztec Martin de la Cruz [Figure 7]. The sixteenth century Florentine codex manuscript by Franciscan Bernardino de Sahagún lists 123 plants. Francisco Hernández (c. 1514–1580), drawing on Aztec sources apparently including the extensive botanic gardens, listed 1,200 medicinals among a total of 4,043 plants in the index of *Rerum Medicarum*. The Aztecs' "consistent nomenclature, the sheer number of plants utilized—Hernandez described almost seven times more drugs among the Aztecs than Dioscorides (c. 40–90) knew of in the ancient world—and their tradition in therapeutics... bestowed upon the Mexican *materia medica* considerable prestige".[23]

PLATE 8

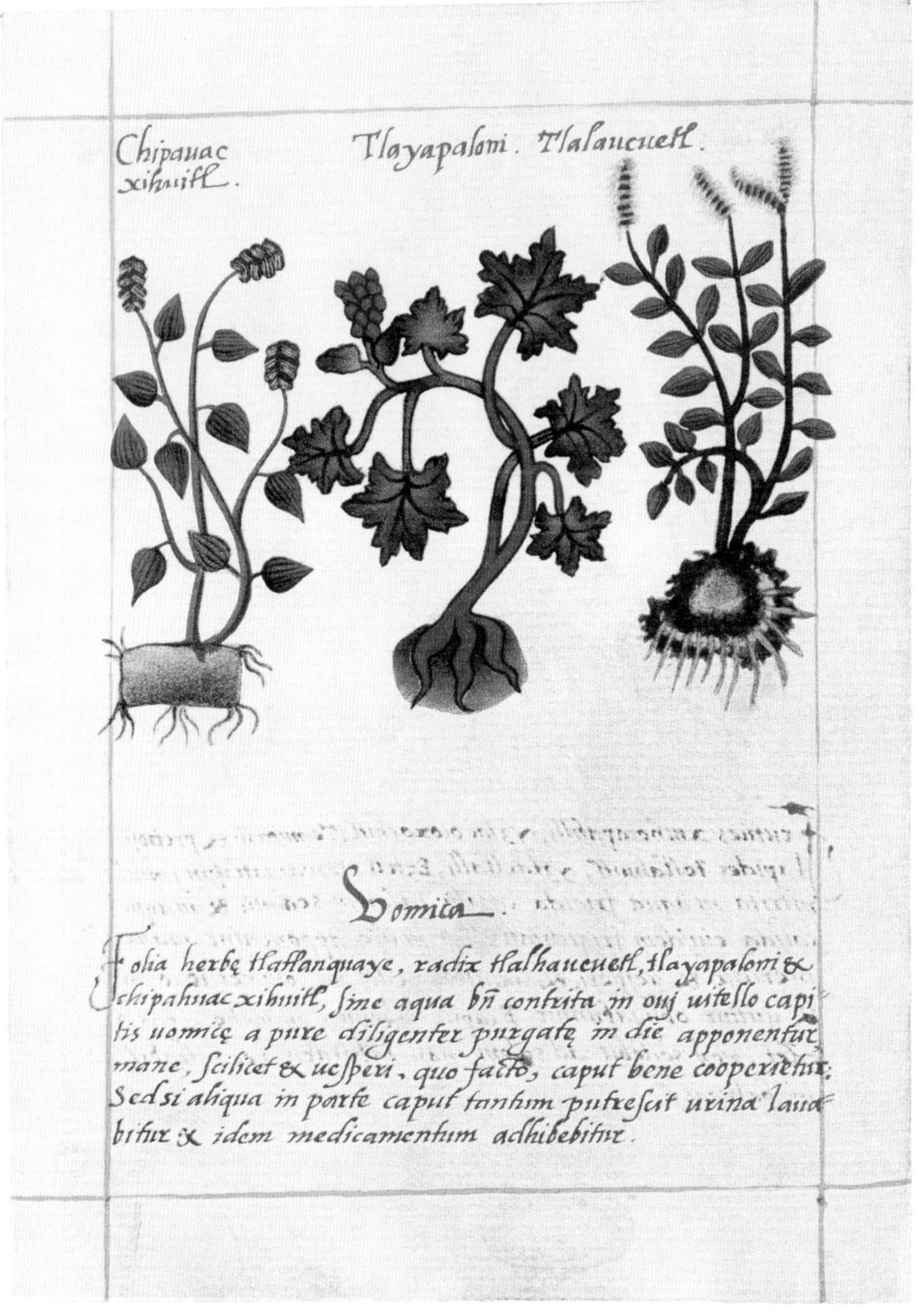

92

Figure 7/ Badianus Manuscript (*Libellus de Medicinalibus Indorum Herbis*), an Aztec herbal from 1552. Image courtesy of the National Geographic Collection/ Getty Images.

Ancient Egyptian, Mesopotamian, and Aztec royal gardens are typically viewed primarily as demonstrations of power, as sacred and devotional spaces, or as places for recreation. And sometimes, secondary roles in exploiting plants for economic purposes, particularly as *materia medica*, are acknowledged. Nevertheless, the clear focus on establishing plant collections, and the development and exploitation of knowledge associated with the collections, suggest gardens that were focused on enquiry into plants. The relationship between magic and science in these gardens was likely complex, and the quest for salvation through exploration of the plant world represents a synthesis of the temporal and the spiritual.

RE-CREATING EDEN

And God said, Behold, I have given you every herb bearing seed, which is upon the face of all the earth, and every tree, in the which is the fruit of a tree yielding seed; to you it shall be for meat.
/ Genesis 1:29

Figure 8/ Garden of Eden from MS illumination with fountain and fruit trees from a fifteenth century French manuscript illumination of the history of the world. God indicates the Tree of Knowledge of Good and Evil from which Adam and Eve are forbidden to eat. In the center of the garden a fountain feeds four rivers, named in Genesis as Pison, Gihon, Hiddekel, and Euphrates (Genesis 2: 10–17). Image © British Library Board.

Figure 9/ *Adam and Eve.*
Albrecht Dürer, Nüremberg, 1504. Adam holds the Tree of Life, here represented as the Mountain Ash, and Eve holds The Tree of the Knowledge of Good and Evil, represented as the Fig. Photograph © Victoria and Albert Museum, London.

And out of the ground made the LORD God to grow every tree that is pleasant to the sight, and good for food; the tree of life also in the midst of the garden, and the tree of knowledge of good and evil.
/ Genesis 2:9

And the LORD God took the man, and put him into the garden of Eden to dress it and to keep it.

And the LORD God commanded the man, saying, Of every tree of the garden thou mayest freely eat: But of the tree of the knowledge of good and evil, thou shalt not eat of it: for in the day that thou eatest thereof thou shalt surely die.

And the LORD God said, It is not good that the man should be alone; I will make him an help meet for him.

And out of the ground the LORD God formed every beast of the field, and every fowl of the air; and brought them unto Adam to see what he would call them: and whatsoever Adam called every living creature, that was the name thereof.
/ Genesis 2:15–19

The search for the Garden of Eden, the interpretation of the Tree of Life and the Tree of the Knowledge of Good and Evil, and the naming of every living creature all have significant resonance in the development of botany and of

European botanic gardens, the establishment of which has been interpreted as both an extension of Classical learning and as an attempt to restore the Garden of Eden on Earth [Figures 8, 9]. Contemporary scholars Richard Drayton and John Prest both observe that Renaissance botanic gardens originated in a literal interpretation of Biblical sources. The purpose of these gardens was to reveal the works of God and recreate in a literal or symbolic way an Edenic utopia, with the aim being to know God in a quest for salvation as much as to further learning. Drayton characterizes the endeavors of Nicholas V at the Vatican (1397–1455), Lorenzo de' Medici at the Villa Careggi (1449–1492), and Alfonso II in Naples (1448–1495) to collect nature into a synoptic *hortus conclusus* as religious and philosophical enterprises entwining Plato's Academy and Christianity. He argues that such endeavors towards the 'gathering in of Creation' contributed to the development of botanic gardens in the fourteenth and fifteenth centuries: "Christian Neoplatonism... directly underlies the Early Modern ideal of the botanic garden as both a resource for healing and a philosophical theatre in which God's truth might be discovered in the diversity of his creations."[24] Similarly, Prest sees the encyclopaedic European botanic gardens of sixteenth and seventeenth century Europe as having been founded "in a context of the re-creation of the earthly Paradise, or Garden of Eden".[25] The Biblical foundation for such an endeavor may today appear abstruse. For example, Drayton quotes Isaiah as an inspiration for the 'gathering in of Creation': "For the LORD shall comfort Zion: he will comfort all her waste places; and he will make her wilderness like Eden, and her desert like the garden of the LORD; joy and gladness shall be found therein, thanksgiving, and the voice of melody" (Isaiah 51:3).

The observation of seventeenth century historian and diarist John Evelyn is perhaps less utopian, in seeking Paradise through the art and industry of agriculture, horticulture, and forestry rather than through the gathering in of Creation. According to Evelyn, "Adam instructed his posteritie how to handle the spade so dextrously, that, in the process of tyme, men began, with the indulgence of heaven to recover that, by Arte and Industrie, which was before produced to them spontaneously."[26]

Even later, in the Enlightenment, Linnaeus (1707–1778) would see his achievement in establishing a natural system for identifying plants and animals as having made it possible for God's Creation to be read in the same way as the Bible. He observed that his scientific system of classification allowed one to "read nature's book as easily as any other tract".[27] In endeavoring to collect and classify the world's flora, Linnaeus' disciples proselytized a scientific and a Christian naming of the Creation. Indeed, Linnaeus' achievement might be viewed as a 'gathering in of Creation', as much as a catalogue. These 'theological' perspectives, evolving with the deepening of scientific knowledge, all share the common theme of recreating an Eden through the efforts of 'Man'.

HOW BOTANIC GARDENS CHANGED THE WORLD

The accelerating development of navigation, global trade, colonization, learning, technology, and science from the Renaissance onwards saw an increasing role for botanic gardens as clearing houses for novel plant material and as incubators for ideas and innovation through an enquiry into plants. The impact of botanic gardens on medicine during the Renaissance, in establishing a universal language for plants during the Enlightenment, in supporting the economic aspirations of colonization during the Age of Empire, and in promoting the greatest diaspora of plants in world history during the Industrial Revolution might indeed support the view that botanic gardens have changed the world. Such an assertion is entirely reasonable if we accept the fundamental importance of plants as a mediation between light and life.

THE RENAISSANCE

Orthodox garden history attributes the origin of botanic gardens (or sometimes of modern botanic gardens) to the physic gardens associated with medical schools in Renaissance universities. This view, which stems from an account of the origins of science and scientific knowledge, perhaps both dismisses the legitimacy of earlier forms of knowledge and oversimplifies the values and purposes that led to the establishment of Renaissance botanic gardens. As we have already seen, these origins may have had as much to do with magic and religion as with science.[28]

Certainly, plants were cultivated for ceremonial, culinary, and medicinal purposes in Medieval monastic gardens. Nevertheless, the unbroken tradition for botanic gardens as an institutional framework for an enquiry into plants begins with the Renaissance medical schools. The most celebrated of these is Padua, which dates from 1545 and remains today the oldest botanic garden in continuous use [Figure 10]. The University of Padua itself had been founded in 1222, and its medical school, which had a chair in 'simples', or medicinal plants, utilized plants as the basis for drugs. By 1543 Francesco Bonafede (1474–1558), Chair of *Lectura Simplicium* at the University, petitioned the Senate of the Most Serene Republic for the creation of a model herbarium and botanical garden, which was established by decree of the Senate on 29 June 1545. Implementation of the project was assigned to Daniele Barbaro, translator of the *De Architectura* of Vitruvius, and work began on a plot belonging to the Benedictines that may already have been a medicinal or simple garden.[29]

The Renaissance saw a flourishing of knowledge associated with the revival of Classical knowledge and the development of a scientific method. In his 1548 dedication

Figure 10/ The Botanical Garden of Padova (Orto botanico di Padova) or Garden of the Simples, founded in 1545. From Antonio Ceni (1854) *Guida all' imp. regio orto botanico in Padova: corredata di sette vedute prospettiche litografate del professore A. Tosini.* Image courtesy of the Biblioteca dell'Orto Botanico dell'Università degli Studi di Padova.

to a contemporary Italian translation of Dioscorides' *Materia Medica*, doctor and naturalist Pietro Mattioli observed that "the garden of medicine had run wild since classical times, through neglect and ignorance".[30] According to Richard Palmer, "Many Dioscoridean plants of immense therapeutic value could no longer be identified. At the same time botanical nomenclature was in chaos, with the result that the wrong plants, in some cases even poisonous ones, were in use in pharmacy."[31] Mattioli's cultivation of the garden of medicine was not without its detractors. Melchiorre Guilandino, who became curator of the Padua Botanic Garden in 1561, offered a particularly harsh evaluation, describing Mattioli's book as "that dung-heap... that lurid rag-bag, constantly being retouched, but never complete, which he calls a commentary on Dioscorides".[32]

While Mattioli had a high opinion of his own botanical prowess, his methodology was criticized for lacking reference to the substantiating collections that characterize a botanic garden, for he had never planted a garden of his own or created an herbal of dried plants. Venetian nobleman and botanist Pietro Antonio Michiel's observed that

> many of the illustrations in the 1554 edition were not drawn from life but were purely fictitious, that Mattioli's work was full of such presumption that students and teachers alike at Padua filled his ears with accounts of its shortcomings. No good could come... from imagining a whole plant on the basis of a twig or dried leaf. What was needed was a labour like his own in raising plants, watching their development from beginning to end, describing the whole in words and illustrations.[33]

The Renaissance debate around the identification and efficacy of Dioscorides' *Materia Medica* is illustrative. While Classical treatises provided a foundation for knowledge, the interpretation of this knowledge was the subject of considerable dispute. The dispute demonstrates

Figure 11/ Dioscorides' *Aconitum* interpreted by Leonhart Fuchs in "*De historia stirpivm commentarii insignes...*", 1542, as *Paris quadrifolia* L. Image courtesy of the Board of the Botanic Gardens & State Herbarium, South Australia.

the development of a scientific approach to medicine. For example, Dioscorides' description of *Aconitum pardalianches* (Leopard's Bane) was generic enough to lead Renaissance botanists to a range of interpretations. In 1542 Leonhart Fuchs suggested the identity of *Aconitum pardalianches* as Herb Paris (*Paris quadrifolia*) [Figure 11], in 1554 Mattioli proposed an indeterminate local species (whose illustration corresponds to Dioscorides' description), and in 1555 Conrad Gesner proposed *Tora venenata*.[34] These proposals were the subject of considerable debate and even acrimony. By 1557 Rembertus Dodonaeus in the Low Countries and the Paduan botanist Giacomo Antonio Cortusio both suggested that Dioscorides' *Aconitum* could be identified as *Doronicum*.

The dialogue was practical as well as academic. Dioscorides' *Materia Medica* observed the medicinal value of *Aconitum* as an analgesic in medicines for the eyes and noted that *Aconitum* "stupified a scorpion that touched it, and that it was poisonous to panthers, pigs, wolves and all wild beasts".[35] However, Arab medicine had introduced *Doronicum* as a drug beneficial to the heart, and it was in current use in internal medicine. As Richard Palmer recounts,

> Cortusio decided to test his idea. He began to administer controlled doses of Doronicum to wolves, dogs and pigs. Each of them died in a short time. He reported his findings to Mattioli, Calzolari, Borgarucci and others, all of whom repeated the experiments with the same result. There began an international slaughter of chickens, pigs, wolves and dogs as the news spread. Sceptical at first, Mattioli gave one of his pet dogs four drachms of Doronicum root in raw meat. At first nothing happened. At supper the dog gobbled up scraps which Mattioli threw from his table, and even mounted several times a bitch which was in the house. But after seven hours it suddenly fell into a fit, and died foaming at the mouth. For Mattioli the moral was clear. "Doronicum" might rather be called "Daemonicum"—the devil had placed it in the pharmacies in the stead of the true Arabic original. This discovery would bring its banishment from pharmacy and save countless lives. How pitiable, wrote Mattioli, were the Middle Ages which had perpetuated such errors, and how glorious the advances of his own day.[36]

While high ideals for botanical research are illustrated through the Paduan garden, there seems to be little to suggest a utopian vision for the University botanic gardens of the Renaissance. Indeed, Guilandino at the Paduan botanic gardens was called upon to support the Venetian Council by supplying a poison for use against an enemy of the Republic.

THE ENLIGHTENMENT

The Enlightenment, or Age of Reason, provides a useful marker for a shift in the nature of enquiry into plants in botanic gardens. Renaissance botanic gardens had served as both *pharmacopoeias* and pharmacies for medical schools, so were necessarily concerned with the accurate determination of plants to ensure the effectiveness of medicines. Enlightenment botanic gardens, meanwhile, saw an increasing focus on natural history and even on the application of natural philosophy as a model for social systems. As Emma Spary writes, the classifications used by naturalists "slipped between the natural world and the social... to establish not only the expertise of the naturalists over the natural, but also the dominance of the natural over the social".[37]

The Swedish botanist, physician, and zoologist Carl Linnaeus is revered by botanists as the "Father of Taxonomy" for his achievement in establishing a universal language for plants. As previously observed, Linnaeus' scientific system of classification meant that "one can read nature's book as easily as any other tract".[38] The ability to read God's Creation as easily as the Bible was more than a theological contribution. A common language was necessary to the establishment of systems of knowledge that could effectively exploit the world's flora through international trade. Linnaeus' new language of botanical classification supported Swedish economic interests in plant exploration and in the exploitation of exotic and novel crops.

Linnaeus also endeavored to revive Swedish power in the absence of colonial expansion through the establishment of new and climatically unsuitable economic crops such as tea, cocoa, rice, coffee, sugar cane, ginger, pistachios, olives, and sago palms in Uppsala. His efforts are today considered naïve and are generally discounted.[39] Nevertheless, such empirical approaches to acclimatization might be interpreted as scientific and, at a stretch, even prescient in terms of what may now be achieved through gene technologies. Linnaeus' scientific *lingua franca* supplanted the values and knowledge associated with the naming of plants within traditional ecological knowledge. The adoption of a universal system for naming plants accelerated the devaluation of traditional ecological knowledge and irreversibly changed our relationship with nature.[40]

Linnaeus' perspective on the natural world was complex, both utopian and informed by a notion of sustainability. His theology encompassed a divine economy of nature served by economics as the science of co-operation with nature. Indeed, Linnaeus may be viewed as:

> one of the major economists of the Enlightenment, not only because of his cameralist policies and success in establishing the science of economics in Swedish universities, but also because of his developed account of the economy of nature. More than anyone of his time he saw the human realm as seamlessly joined to the oeconomy of nature, an exchange system among animals, plants, minerals, and the atmosphere.[41]

Linnaeus was explicit in this regard, observing that "nature's economy shall be the base for our own, for it is immutable, but ours is secondary. An economist without a knowledge of nature is like a physicist without a knowledge of mathematics."[42] In *Linnaeus: Nature and Nation*, Lisbet Koerner observes that, on Linnaeus' instigation, chairs were endowed in "practical economics based on natural science" at every Swedish university bar one.[43] His theological and scientific arguments are distilled in the *Oeconomy of Nature*, ostensibly written by his student Isaac Bilberg in 1749.[44]

Linnaeus' contribution to a dialogue in relation to "practical economics based on natural science" illustrates the reach of the plant collection and the enquiry into plants from Linnaeus' botanic garden at Uppsala. Better known is his ability to engage the community in botanical forays and his indelicate approach to combining botany and sex, which resulted in both popularity and notoriety, and undermined the virtue of flowering plants. Clearly, the importance of Linnaeus' botanic garden extended well beyond the development of his famed binomial system for naming plants and animals [Figure 12]. Linnaeus'

Figure 12/ The botanical garden of Carolus Linnaeus at Uppsala University, Sweden, from a contemporary engraving, 1770. Image courtesy of the University Library of Uppsala.

Figure 13/ Jardin du Roy pour la culture des plantes médicinales à Paris.
Image © Muséum national d'Histoire naturelle, Dist. RMN / image du MNHN, bibliothèque centrale.

own opinion of his work was unencumbered by modesty. Speaking of himself in the third person, he observed,

> God has suffered him to peep into his secret cabinet. God has suffered him to see more of his created work than any mortal before him. God has endowed him with the greatest insight into natural knowledge, greater than any has ever gained. The Lord has been with him, whithersoever he has gone, and has exterminated all his enemies for him, and has made of him a great name, as one of the great ones of the earth.[45]

Linnaeus's pre-eminence was contested in France where a remarkable tradition of botanic gardens provided a foundation for Georges-Louis Leclerc Buffon's achievements. There was likely a garden for simples in Paris before 1577, when apothecary Nicolas Houel established the Maison de la Charité Chrétienne. The École de Pharmacie was later established on this site, and the school's garden, Le Jardin des Apothicaires (Apothecaries' Garden), might be seen as antecedent to the seventeenth century Jardin Royal des Plantes Médicinales (Royal Garden of Medical Plants). It was Guy La Brosse, physician to Louis XIII, who obtained royal assent for a medicinal garden in 1626 and first published the *Dessin du Jardin Royal pour la culture des plantes médicinales* (*Design of the Royal Garden for the Culture of Medical Plants*) in 1628 [Figure 13]. The edict establishing the garden was published in 1635, and the Jardin du Roi in Paris opened in 1640. The purposes for the garden were at this stage unambiguously linked with medicine; the emphasis later changed to a broader exploration of natural history and the alignment of natural philosophy with political and social movements, paralleling Linnaeus' reconfiguration of enquiry into plants. This shift is apparent during Georges-Louis Leclerc Buffon's reign as director or *intendant* from 1739 to 1788. Linnaeus considered natural history as documenting God's law as manifested in the design of the natural world. In contrast, Buffon's celebrated *Histoire Naturelle* certainly promoted the centrality of natural history but rejected "attempts to use living nature to prove God's creative powers and perfect goodness in having ordered the world".[46]

The role of the Jardin, its subsequent reformation within the Museum d'Histoire Naturelle, and its engagement with political, institutional, and social reform during this period is explored by E. C. Spary in *Gardens and Utopia*. Observing the realignment of the Jardin in serving the Revolution, Spary quotes Antoine-Claire Thibaudeau before the Convention Nationale in year III/ 1795:

> Call all men to consider the great and magnificent spectacle of nature, the variety of her productions, and the harmony of her phenomena. She is the source of good laws, of useful arts, of the sweetest pleasures and of happiness.... The *Museum d'Histoire Naturelle* is perhaps the only institution which has remained intact in the midst of the storms of the Revolution; the destructive hand of Vandals, which has broken so many precious monuments of the arts, has respected the temple of nature.[47]

AGE OF EMPIRE

The early endeavors of European colonial powers in establishing colonial botanic gardens were contemporary with the Enlightenment, and in some measure were driven by a similar focus on enquiry; however, the purpose of these colonial botanic gardens was in significant measure driven by practical and economic imperatives. A notable exception was the garden established in Mexico City in 1788, which is significant for its Enlightenment focus on learning. Like the 1755 Royal Botanical Garden of Madrid (Real Jardín Botánico de Madrid) on which it was modeled, this garden would be a locus of education for the public. The garden "employed a botanical lecturer to provide lessons and demonstrations" and enlivened instruction with public performance of "botanical exercises" (*ejercicios públicos de botánica*) "in which top students identified and described plants presented to them before an audience that included local notables".[48] The importance of this garden to trade, agriculture, medicine, and the arts was promoted by its commissioner, Don Martin de Sesse. But unlike most other colonial gardens, this garden "represented an exact equivalent of the Madrid institution and not a subordinate acclimatization center whose entire purpose consisted in furnishing the metropolis with desirable commodities".[49]

The colonial focus on the identification and acquisition of commodities is illustrated in Captain William Bligh's 1787 voyage of HMS Bounty to obtain breadfruit plants from Tahiti for the West Indies as a source of food for slaves [Figure 14]. Bligh observed that "the Object of all former voyages to the South Seas, undertaken by command of his present majesty, has been the advancement of science, and the increase of Knowledge. This Voyage may be reckoned the first, the intention of which has been to derive benefits from these distant discoveries."[50] This represents a significant departure from an Enlightenment focus on natural history collections.

Global trade had previously seen the gradual diffusion of useful plants, particularly staple crops, across civilizations. In the sixteenth and seventeenth centuries, the development of more sophisticated administrative structures, trade, navigation, and cataloguing of observations accelerated the transplantation of economic plants across the globe.[51] Investments in colonial botanic gardens reflected the colonizing powers' aspirations in both scientific and economic arenas, although it is likely that pragmatic and economic purposes predominated. The foundation of early colonial botanic gardens such as the Dutch Old Company Garden, Cape Town, South Africa in 1679 and the Buitenzorg (Bogor) Botanic Garden, Java in 1817; the French Pampelmousses, Île de France (Mauritius) in 1735; the Jardin de l'État Saint-Denis, Île Bourbon (Réunion) in 1769; and Cayenne, French Guiana in 1778 were largely economic in intent. Seeds, plants, specimens, and illustrations for scientific study were repatriated to the colonial powers' own botanic gardens.

Figure 14/ *Transplanting of the bread-fruit-trees from Otaheite* by Thomas Gosse, 1796, illustrating Captain William Bligh's 1787 expedition on HMS Bounty to Tahiti. Mezzotint, hand colored. Image courtesy of the National Library of Australia.

Figure 15/ Sir Henry Wickham standing by the largest original plantation rubber tree grown from seed collected by Wickham in Brazil. Henarathgoda Botanical Gardens, Ceylon, c. 1913. Image courtesy of the Hulton Archive/ Getty Images.

The Calcutta Botanic Garden, created by the British in 1787, was explicitly aligned to the East India Company's economic purpose. Colonel Robert Kyd, subsequently the Garden's first superintendent, wrote to the East India Company:

> I take this opportunity of suggesting to the Board the Propriety of establishing a botanical Garden, not for the Purpose of collecting rare Plants (altho' they also have their use) as things of mere curiosity or furnishing articles for the Gratification of Luxury, but for establishing a stock for the disseminating such articles [as] may prove beneficial to the Inhabitants [of India], as well as Natives of Great Britain and ultimately may tend to the Extension of the National Commerce and Riches.[52]

In Ceylon, the British established botanic gardens at Slave Island in 1810, subsequently relocated to Kalutara in 1813 and to Peradeniya in 1821. A garden was established at Hakgala in 1861 for the introduction of *Cinchona* (quinine), and the first Brazilian rubber tree (*Hevea brasiliensis*) brought to Asia was planted in the Gampaha (Henarathgoda) Botanic Garden in 1876 [Figure 15]. The Georgetown botanic garden was established in British Guiana between 1879 and 1884, and in Australia, botanic gardens were established in Sydney in 1816, in Hobart in 1818, in Melbourne in 1846, as well as in Adelaide [Figure 16] and Brisbane in 1855.

That the establishment of the Rio de Janeiro Botanic Garden in 1808 was aligned to Portugal's economic aspirations is made clear in Prince Regent D. João's instructions to the Governor of Bahia, D. Fernando José de Portugal:

> ... the same activity and intelligence... you will direct toward perfecting and expanding the cultures already present in this captaincy, and animate the new ones that I have sent to recommend to your predecessor, such as pepper, cinnamon, breadfruit, cloves and other spices, the hemp line, and cactus with coxonilha, whose effect can much contribute to the building of an economic botanic garden..., the cultivation of these plants at first being possible in a small way to later spread themselves throughout the captaincy.[53]

The value of linking the plants with cultural systems of knowledge was apparent and sometimes explicit. The Prince Regent later brought to Brazil not only tea (*Camellia sinensis*), but also "Chinese growers with their millennia of knowledge about the culture and enrichment of the product".[54] Later colonial botanic gardens, such as those established in 1902 at Amani in the Eastern Usambara Mountains in German East Africa, continued this clear economic agenda.

As Daniela Bleichmar observes, Spain clearly appreciated the role that might be played by its botanic gardens in bio-prospecting and acclimatization as a catalyst to economic development. The head of the Royal Botanical Garden in Madrid, Casimiro Gómez Ortega, stated that "colonial natural productions could be as profitable to Spain as mines had previously been, and had the added advantage of being easier to obtain".[55]

Figure 16/ *Botanic Gardens, Adelaide*, 1865. James Shaw, oil on canvas. Image courtesy of the Art Gallery of South Australia.

Figure 17/ *Victoria regia*, Lindley and Amerindians —title page from Robert Schomburgk's *Twelve views in the interior of Guiana*, London 1841. Image courtesy of the Barr Smith Library, University of Adelaide.

Figure 18/ *Victoria regia House, Adelaide Botanic Garden*, c. 1876, Engraving. Image courtesy of the Board of the Botanic Gardens & State Herbarium, South Australia.

Indeed, colonial administrators were ordered to identify potentially useful natural resources in their areas for assessment by royal botanists and pharmacists; meanwhile, the governor of the Philippines was ordered "to encourage by all possible means the cultivation of cinnamon, pepper, cacao, cotton, and white mulberry tree (*morera*, to feed silkworms) and the production of silk".[56]

THE INDUSTRIAL REVOLUTION

The Industrial Revolution presented new opportunities for plant collection across the globe while new technology in horticulture, such as the Wardian case, allowed the successful transfer and establishment of new discoveries. An increasing demand for exotic plants for investment, for science, and for public recreation and instruction complemented the increasing supply of novelties in Europe and the United States. The established botanic gardens were at the forefront of plant exploration and repatriation.

The first test of the glazed cases developed by Dr. Nathaniel Ward saw the successful shipping of British ferns and other plants to Sydney in 1833. The arrival of a primrose in full bloom provided a glimpse of the distant Old World for Australian colonists. In fact, "the sensation occasioned by its appearance was so great, that it was necessary to keep the case under constant strict surveillance".[57] Australian plants, in turn, were successfully conveyed to Britain on the return journey. Sir William Hooker, the Director of Kew Gardens, observed that in the 15 years from 1836–1851 the Wardian case had "been the means... of introducing more new and valuable plants to our gardens than were imported during the preceding century".[58]

The discovery and collection for science of the Giant Amazon Waterlily (*Victoria amazonica*) by Sir Robert Schomburgk and his brother Richard in British Guiana perfectly illustrates the catalytic potential of the Industrial Revolution for plant exploration and exploitation [Figure 17]. This plant was described and dedicated to Queen Victoria as *Victoria regia* by John Lindley (based on the specimen collected by Robert Schomburgk) in London in 1837. Advances in engineering and the working of iron allowed Joseph Paxton to envisage, design, and build a conservatory based on the architecture of the waterlily's leaf at the Duke of Devonshire's estate at Chatsworth House. Paxton's conservatory allowed adequate light to penetrate the structure to achieve the first flowering of the lily in cultivation in 1849. This success, and the charismatic nature of the lily, led to the establishment of lily houses in botanic gardens around the world, including the Royal Botanic Gardens, Kew, and Adelaide Botanic Gardens during Richard Schomburgk's directorship [Figure 18]. Further, Paxton's successful adoption of the lily leaf as a model for the Chatsworth House conservatory ultimately resulted in the adoption of Paxton's proposal for the 1851 Great Exhibition in Hyde Park. The Crystal Palace, also based on the lily's leaf, is considered the progenitor of the glass and steel tower blocks that form the fabric of modern cities. The rapid development of glass and steel technology and new approaches to design would see a proliferation of grand conservatories [Figure 19].

With the industrialization of agriculture during this period came increasing attention to the economic exploitation of new plants. Botanic gardens oversaw the greatest diaspora of plants the world has seen, the industrial exploitation of economic plants, and the commodification of showy plants. Botanic gardens also contributed to revolutionary ideas such as Charles Darwin's Theory of Evolution, as John Parker has detailed in his account of the role of John Henslow and the Cambridge University Botanic Gardens in this regard.[59]

Certainly, the publication of Darwin's *Origin of Species* in 1859 was considered a radical departure from the account of Creation in the Bible. However, Darwin might not have seen an irreconcilable conflict, as is indicated by his decision to quote Francis Bacon's *The Advancement of Learning*, 1605, opposite the title page of the first edition:

> To conclude, therefore, let no man out of a weak conceit of sobriety, or an ill-applied moderation, think or maintain that a man can search too far or be too well studied in the book of God's word, or in the book of God's works; divinity or philosophy; but rather let men endeavor an endless progress or proficience in both.[60]

Nevertheless, the Industrial Revolution marked a shift in the relationship between God, Nature, and Man. The new rationalist political economy was coming into ascendancy in Britain. John Stuart Mill encapsulated it in his 1874 essay "On Nature", writing that the "ways of nature are to be conquered, not obeyed".[61] From this point onward, economics and ecology took different paths.

Figure 19/ The 1848 Palm House and the 1852 Waterlily House, Kew Gardens. *The Illustrated London News*, 6 August 1859. Image courtesy of the Mary Evans Picture Library.

BOTANIC GARDENS AND ENVIRONMENTAL RECONCILIATION: A MODERN UTOPIA

An exploration of the history and functions of botanic gardens as an enquiry into plants reveals that botanic gardens have long been effective as innovators or incubators of new plant-based responses to economic, environmental, social, and cultural challenges. And just as botanic gardens have changed the world in the past, they have the potential to significantly influence the nature of our future relationships with plants and the natural environment. Contemporary plant-based solutions to environmental and other issues range beyond the traditional direct application of plant materials. They now include innovation through such approaches as biomimicry, researching seed storage and germination as the basis for landscape restoration, searching the world's flora for applications ranging from medicine to biomass fuels, and re-creating wetlands to manage water reuse. The message of economic botany, a discipline developed in an age of both frugality and exploitation, is perhaps of even greater relevance in contemporary communities that struggle to address sustainability. The achievements of the past and the potential for the future are apparent in botanic garden collections that provide a positive message for innovation and for hope in the relationship between plants, people, and culture.

Since plants provide the basis for life on Earth, civilization needs a new narrative to transform the natural world to reflect this fact. Our challenge in the context of population growth, increasing energy use, and climate change is to achieve sustainability. The contemporary harvest for botanic gardens, then, will be found in environmental reconciliation: the use of plants as a source of energy to fuel a sustainable future. Botanic gardens contribute to such a future to the extent that they help us to recognize processes in nature and to acknowledge that we must draw upon diverse knowledge paradigms to achieve such reconciliation.

Ancient theologies and myths often present a cosmos in balance; the Judeo-Christian Eden provides such an archetype in Western society. Charles Darwin's elucidation of an evolutionary theory and the Industrial Revolution represented a tipping point for the estrangement of religion and knowledge. Science and technology provided both a philosophical basis and the tools to override theological, cultural, and traditional perspectives on environmental stewardship. However, a reconciliation of science and stewardship has been articulated on occasion through both religion and philosophy. Linnaeus' contribution, as presented in Isaac Bilberg's *Oeconomy of Nature*, was to see the stewardship of the lithosphere, the biosphere, and the atmosphere as a theological imperative:

> By the 'Oeconomy of Nature' we understand the all-wise disposition of the Creator in relation to natural things, by which they are fitted to produce general ends, and reciprocal uses.... Whoever duly turns his attention to the things on this our terraqueous globe must necessarily confess, that they are so interconnected, so chained together, that they all aim at the same end, and to this end a vast number of intermediate ends are subservient. [62]

In a contemporary, post-Industrial Revolution setting, James Lovelock's Gaia Theory, arguing that the Earth and its inhabitants work together in a complex self-regulating system to maintain habitability, also provides a unifying narrative that has sometimes been interpreted as quasi-religious rather than scientific.[63] As Stephen Jay Gould observes,

> Gaia strikes me as a metaphor, not a mechanism. Metaphors can be liberating and enlightening, but new scientific theories must supply new statements about causality. Gaia, to me, only seems to reformulate, in different terms, the basic conclusions long achieved by classically reductionist arguments of biogeochemical cycling theory.[64]

Nevertheless, Lovelock's theory and his metaphor illuminate the truth that environmental stewardship is critical for the future of life on Earth. Nobel Laureate Paul Crutzen and Eugene Stoermer define a new geological epoch, the Anthropocene, to acknowledge the profound impact of humans on nature in arenas from climate change to DNA since the Industrial Revolution: "Rather than representing yet another sign of human hubris, this name change would stress the enormity of humanity's responsibility as stewards of the Earth. It would highlight the immense power of our intellect and our creativity, and the opportunities they offer for shaping the future."[65]

In some measure, then, environmental reconciliation is about connecting people with plants and connecting people with the basis of their future: a relationship with the plants that turn light into life. While a dystopian future might seek to bypass this truth through the direct capture of solar energy, or even to bypass solar energy altogether in a nuclear future, our very existence is rooted in plants.

Botanic gardens in the twenty-first century are endeavoring to provide both an inspiring narrative and the technologies to achieve environmental reconciliation. If we take a historical view of botanic gardens, we see both evolution and revolution in their roles, as well as achievements that have changed the world. Twentieth century botanic gardens continued to work on these historic agendas, especially the elucidation and exploitation of the world's flora and the presentation of beautiful and instructive gardens. But the programmatic description of botanic gardens as "institutions holding documented collections of living plants for the purposes of scientific research, conservation, display and education" perhaps fails to properly and successfully place plants at the center of human endeavor.[66] The role of botanic gardens in conservation, while significant, has lacked a coherent and compelling narrative.[67]

A twenty-first century narrative for botanic gardens will resonate with both Theophrastus' *Enquiry into Plants* and biologist E. O. Wilson's observation that "Humanity needs a vision of an expanding and unending future. This spiritual craving cannot be satisfied by the colonization of space.... The true frontier for humanity is life on Earth, its exploration and the transport of knowledge about it into science, art and practical affairs."[68] As the only contemporary institutional framework with a charter to consider the whole plant kingdom (as opposed to the limited charters of, for example, conservation, agricultural, horticultural, forestry or medical institutes), botanic gardens are uniquely placed to connect and reconcile people and plants, and to seek a sustainable future through environmental reconciliation.

Botanic gardens in the twenty-first century must continue major programs from the past, as well as adopt new programs to address contemporary challenges. Ways of seeing the natural world remain remarkably constrained. Perceptions of taxonomy, for example, are largely determined by culture and use. The exclusive adoption of Linnaeus' binomial taxonomic system facilitated the scientific catalogue of life, but at the expense of the documentation of cultural taxonomies and associated traditional ecological knowledge. Perhaps unwittingly, Linnaeus' apostles and their successors have sought to illustrate his conception of the Creation, rather than to chronicle indigenous biocultural knowledge or to seek a new understanding of the relationships between plants, people, and culture. Charles Darwin's real achievement was *seeing* a pattern of adaptation in the catalogue of life; the Theory of Evolution followed. Contemporary botanic gardens are also exploring new ways of seeing the plant world.

Wilson's exhortation that we transport to practical realms the knowledge of life on Earth clearly applies to the exploration of the natural world as a source of innovation as well as a model of sustainability. Through hundreds of millions of years of evolution, a myriad of past and present plants (and animals) have seen remarkable adaptations to environmental and competitive challenges. The challenge of *seeing* plants (and nature) and of adopting systems, processes, and elements from nature has developed as the field of biomimicry. A celebrated story for biomimicry comes from the University of Bonn botanic garden, whose director Wilhelm Bartholett observed that the leaves of the lotus lily (*Nelumbo nucifera*) remained clean while neighboring plants exhibited the residue of atmospheric pollutants on their leaves. The observation was hardly new, for the lotus has long been venerated in Eastern religion as a symbol of purity. Bartholett's achievement was to have understood the opportunity provided by the leaf's form and function. His research led to the development of a self-cleaning coating and paint with the potential to significantly reduce lifecycle maintenance costs for the built environment.[69]

Such industrial applications for botanic gardens had been championed by Sir William Hooker and his successor, Sir Joseph Hooker, at the Royal Botanic Gardens, Kew, in the nineteenth century and were widely adopted, especially through the development of Museums of Economic Botany.[70] Although the rise of forestry, agricultural, and horticultural institutes superseded these educational industrial museums, the thread of this endeavor has been retained in some botanic gardens. For instance, the Technical University of Delft Botanic Garden was established in 1917 to research novel tropical crops and products from the Dutch colony of Indonesia. While this research waned by the 1960s, Bob Ursem's appointment in 2001 saw the regeneration of the Garden's role in materials science under the Center for Materials Science. Ursem's guiding philosophy is that "those 'technologies' that have been 'developed' in the natural world offer by definition the best, strongest and most sustainable solution". Observation is again a key element of the enquiry into plants.[71] In one case, Ursem observed that *Pinus mugo* leaves lack the thick layer of wax typical of other pines in alpine environments as a protection from ultraviolet light. Ursem discovered instead a thin wax layer capable of converting ultraviolet light into blue light usable for photosynthesis. The principle of a biological ultraviolet filter has the potential for application in other systems.

Globally, the future functioning of native ecosystems continues to be compromised by exotic pests. The rate of spread of pest species is exacerbated by climate change, as well as by increasing volumes of global trade and personal travel in which species are carried, intentionally or unintentionally, to new environments. Botanic gardens have envisioned an International Plant Sentinel Network to contribute to international biosecurity by using the richness of the living collections as the basis for an early warning system to help predict and prevent the incursion of new pests (insects, pathogens, or plants).[72] Some have partnered with biosecurity agencies on such matters.

One particularly ambitious instance of this new role for the botanic garden in the twenty-first century is the "Breathing Planet Program" of the Royal Botanic Gardens, Kew. The program presents seven actions developed in response to the findings of the Stern Review Report on the Economics of Climate Change, prepared by Sir Nicholas Stern for the British Government. The report noted that,

> the cost of doing nothing about climate change is vastly greater than the 1% of GDP needed for effective action. The human cost is already undermining political and economic stability in the developing world.... Sustainability needs plant science. Kew holds the world's greatest concentration of knowledge about plants. We work globally with other botanic gardens and partners to help reduce the extent and impact of climate change, and to rescue species and habitats from destruction. The Breathing Planet Programme has seven key actions: driving discovery and global access to essential information; identifying highly threatened species and regions; helping global conservation programmes on the ground; safeguarding 25 percent of species through the Millennium Seed Bank partnership; building a global network to restore damaged habitats; growing locally appropriate species for a changing world; using botanic gardens to inform and inspire.[73]

The Millennium Seed Bank partnership exemplifies the focus on conserving plant resources through an ambitious international collaboration to secure 25 percent of all plant species in seed banks. The partnership can be seen as a new incarnation of the 'gathering in of Creation'. In the face of catastrophic climate change, habitat loss and degradation, and the invasions of pest plants and animals, it aims to recreate a Garden of Eden containing "every herb bearing seed, which is upon the face of all the Earth, and every tree, in the which is the fruit of a tree yielding seed" (Genesis 1:29). The conservation of the world's flora in seed banks represents both an insurance policy against extinction and an investment in understanding seed biology as the foundation for landscape function and ecosystem services, as well as for food, medicine, shelter, clothing, and fuel [Figure 20].

The Eden Project in Cornwall, a multiple greenhouse complex housing flora from around the world, scrupulously avoids categorization [Figure 21]. However, the Project clearly inhabits some of the same space as botanic gardens, as "an educational charity aiming to promote the understanding of the vital relationship between plants and people".[74]

Figure 20/ Botanic gardens seed collector and *Ptilotus macrocephalus*, Moomba, South Australia. Photograph by Andy Rasheed. Image courtesy of Santos.

Figure 21/ Biomes at Eden Project, St. Austell, Cornwall, England, UK. Photograph by Tamsyn Williams. Image courtesy of the Eden Project.

The Eden Project's purpose goes beyond education, recreation, conservation, and research to advocate and even catalyze change. Chief Executive Tim Smit observes,

> Progress has come at such a price to our sense of wellbeing and to the condition of our planet, our moral compass has been disoriented by over-respect for the free market. Our democratic processes are overridden by the needs of 'now' and a misplaced belief that the past was a better place. It wasn't and never has been. It is simply a wailing of [those who are] weak and frightened by a future which is ours to make.[75]

Botanic gardens now endeavor to secure the world's plant resources and to achieve a reconciliation between people and plants, and through this route to secure the future of humankind.

A FINAL WORD

The four pillars that provide the foundation for our Life on Earth—food, water, energy, and biodiversity—are all intimately linked. The contemporary dialogue around the conversion of food crops to biomass fuels, the challenges of increasing food production that currently utilizes 70 percent of developed freshwater, and the potential impact that reforestation programs aimed at reducing carbon dioxide levels in the atmosphere could have on groundwater availability to surrounding farm production, all illustrate the interconnectedness of these pillars. A utopian vision in modern botanic gardens must connect people with plants so they can recognize the value of plants and of the ecosystem services that sustain plants and ourselves.

Franz Kafka observed, "we are separated from God on two sides: the fall separates us from God and the Tree of Life separates God from us".[76] Our relationship with plants resonates with the tensions inherent in the story of humanity's eviction from the Garden of Eden. Clearly, we have not fulfilled our charge to "dress and to keep" the Garden that was given to us (Genesis 2:15). As was made apparent in the Millennium Ecosystem Assessment, unsustainable exploitation has stretched ecosystem resilience to the breaking point.[77] The collapse of oak and elm forests through the agency of plant pathogens; increasing deforestation, desertification, and ecosystem collapse; as well as increasing levels of atmospheric carbon dioxide liberated from fossil plant fuels all provide a counterpoint to the successes apparent in medicine and the improved farming yields achieved by the 'Green Revolution'.

From a missionary perspective, contemporary botanic gardens are focused on conserving plants' genetic resources and on promoting ecological literacy and environmental reconciliation. This is a utopian vision upon which the future of humanity might well depend.

Notes

1. Hill, A. W., "The History and Functions of Botanic Gardens", *Annals of the Missouri Botanical Garden*, vol. 2, no. 1/2, February 1915, pp. 185–240.

2. Botanic Gardens Conservation International, *Definition of a Botanic Garden*, viewed 5 August 2011, http://www.bgci.org/resources/1528/.

3. University of Oxford, *A History of the Gardens*, Oxford: University of Oxford, Botanic Garden and Harcourt Arboretum, viewed 16 August 2011, http://www.botanic-garden.ox.ac.uk/Garden/History%20Sub/obg-history-2.html.
4. Bostock, John and Henry Thomas Riley trans., "The Nature of Flax–Marvellous Facts Relative Thereto", *The Natural History of Pliny, Pliny the Elder*, Vol. 4, Book XIX, *The Nature and Cultivation of Flax, and an Account of Various Garden Plants*, London: H. G. Bohn, 1856, p. 129.
5. Hill, "The History and Functions of Botanic Gardens".
6. Stafleu, F., "Botanical Gardens Before 1918", *Boissiera*, vol. 14, 1969, pp. 31–46.
7. Lo, Vivienne, "Healing and Medicine", *China: Land of the Heavenly Dragon*, E. Shaughnessy ed., rev. ed., London: Duncan Baird Publishing, 2000, pp. 148–162.
8. Farlex Inc., *The Free Dictionary*, Pennsylvania: Farlex 2011, viewed 18 August 2011, http://encyclopedia.thefreedictionary.com/Shen%20Nong.
9. Hill, "The History and Functions of Botanic Gardens".
10. Beaux, N., *Le Cabinet de Curiosités de Thoutmosis III: Plantes et Animaux du "Jardin botanique" de Karnak*, Orientalia Lovaniensia Analecta 36, Leuven: Uitgeverij Peeters, 1990.
11. Wiseman, D. J., "Mesopotamian Gardens", *Anatolian Studies*, vol. 33, 1983, pp. 135–144.
12. Dalley, S., "Ancient Mesopotamian Gardens and the Identification of the Hanging Gardens of Babylon", *Garden History*, vol. 21, no.1, 1993, pp. 1–13.
13. Leach, H. M., "On the Origins of Kitchen Gardening in the Ancient Near East", *Garden History*, vol. 10, no. 1, 1982, pp. 1–16.
14. Janick, J., "Herbals: the Connection Between Horticulture and Medicine", *HortTechnology*, vol. 13, no. 2, 2003, pp. 229–238.
15. Biggs, R. D., "Medicine, Surgery, and Public Health in Ancient Mesopotamia", *Journal of Assyrian Academic Studies*, vol. 19, no. 1, 2005, pp. 1–19.
16. Thanos, C. A., "The Geography of Theophrastus' Life and of his Botanical Writings (Περι Φυτων)", *Biodiversity and Natural Heritage in the Aegean*, Proceedings of the Conference 'Theophrastus Eressos', Sigri, Lesbos, 6–8 July, 2000, A. J. Karamanos and C. A. Thanos eds., Athens: Frangoudis, pp. 113–131.
17. Theophrastus, *Enquiry into Plants, Vols. I–II*, A. F. Hort trans., London: William Heinemann, Loeb Classical Library, 1916.
18. Theophrastus, *De Causis Plantarum, vol. I*, B. Einarson and G. K. K. Link trans., London: William Heinemann, Loeb Classical Library, 1976, p. xi.
19. Theophrastus, *De Causis Plantarum*, pp xviii–xix.
20. Granziera, P., "Concept of the Garden in Pre-Hispanic Mexico", *Garden History*, vol. 29, no. 2, 2001, pp. 185–213.
21. Leszczyńska-Borys, H. and Borys, M. W., "Splendor of Mexican Prehispanic Gardens", *Acta Horticulturae*, 881, 2010, pp. 891–898. See also P. Aviles, "Seven Ways of Looking at a Mountain: Tetzcotzingo and the Aztec Garden Tradition", *Landscape Journal*, vol. 25, nos. 2–6, 2006, pp.143–156.
22. Leszczyńska-Borys, "Splendor of Mexican Prehispanic Gardens".
23. Guerra, F., "Aztec Medicine", *Medical History*, vol. 10, no. 4, 1966, pp. 315–338.
24. Drayton, Richard, *Nature's Government: Science, Imperial Britain, and the 'Improvement' of the World*, New Haven: Yale University Press, 2000, p. 6.
25. Prest, John, *The Garden of Eden: the Botanic Garden and the Re-creation of Paradise*, London: Yale University Press, 1981.
26. Prest, *The Garden of Eden*, p. 54.
27. Koerner, Lisbet, *Linnaeus: Nature & Nation*, Cambridge, MA: Harvard University Press, 1999, p. 25.
28. Tomasi, L. T., "Projects for Botanical and Other Gardens: a Sixteenth Century Manual", *Journal of Garden History*, vol. 3, no. 1, 1983, pp. 1–34.
29. UNESCO, *Botanic Garden (Orto Botanico), Padua*, France: UNESCO, viewed 23 May 2011, http://whc.unesco.org/en/list/824.
30. Palmer, Richard, "Medical Botany in Northern Italy in the Renaissance", *Journal of the Royal Society of Medicine*, vol. 78, February 1985, p. 151.
31. Palmer, "Medical Botany in Northern Italy in the Renaissance", p. 151.
32. Palmer, Richard, "Pharmacy in the Republic of Venice in Andrew Wear", *The Medical Renaissance of the Sixteenth Century*, Roger Kenneth French and Iain M. Lonie eds., London: Cambridge University Press, 1985, pp. 100–117.
33. Palmer, "Medical Botany in Northern Italy in the Renaissance", p. 153.
34. Delisle, C., "The Letter: Private Text or Public Place? The Mattioli-Gesner Controversy about the *Aconitum Primum*", *Gesnerus*, vol. 61, 2004, pp. 161–176.
35. Palmer, "Medical Botany in Northern Italy in the Renaissance", p. 155.
36. Palmer, "Medical Botany in Northern Italy in the Renaissance", p. 155.
37. Spary, Emma, "The 'Nature' of Enlightenment", *The Sciences in Enlightened Europe*, William Clark, Jan Golinski, and Steven Schaffer eds., Chicago: University of Chicago Press, 1999, pp. 281–282.
38. Koerner, *Linnaeus: Nature and Nation*, p. 103.
39. Koerner, *Linnaeus: Nature and Nation*, p. 122.
40. Ashmore, L., *Harmless, Useful, Interesting and Ornamental—Perceptions of Diversity in Nature*, Honours Thesis, University of Adelaide, 2002.
41. Schabas, Margaret, *The Natural Origins of Economics*, Chicago: University of Chicago Press, 2005, p. 40.
42. Koerner, *Linnaeus: Nature and Nation*, p. 103.
43. Koerner, *Linnaeus: Nature and Nation*, p. 107.
44. Biberg, Isaac, "Linnaeus, Carl, *The Oeconomy of Nature, 1749*", *Miscellaneous Tracts Relating to Natural History Husbandry and Physick*, Benjamin Stillingfleet trans. and J. Dodsley ed., London: Arno Press, 1791.
45. Farber, Paul Lawrence, *Finding Order in Nature: the Naturalist Tradition from Linnaeus to E. O. Wilson*, Baltimore: John Hopkins University Press, 2000, p. 13.
46. Spary, Emma C., *Utopia's Garden: French Natural History from the Old Regime to the Revolution*, Chicago: University of Chicago Press, 2000, p. 30.
47. Spary, *Utopia's Garden*, p. 10.
48. See H. W. Rickett trans., "Sesse: Establishment of the Royal Botanical Garden, from Archivo General de la Nació (Mexico)", *Chronica Botanica*, vol. 11, no. 1, 1947, pp. 5–20. Quoted material is from Daniela Bleichmar, "Atlantic Competitions: Botany in the

Eighteenth-Century Spanish Empire", *Science and Empire in the Atlantic World*, James Delbourgo and Nicholas Dew eds., New York: Routledge, 2007, p. 240.
49. Bleichmar, "Atlantic Competitions", p. 240.
50. Bligh, William, *A Narrative of the Mutiny of the Bounty*, London: W. H. Smith, 1838, p. 3.
51. de Vos, Paula, "The Science of Spices: Empiricism and Economic Botany in the Early Spanish Empire", *Journal of World History*, vol. 17, no. 4, 2006, pp. 399–427.
52. Thomas, A. P., "The Establishment of Calcutta Botanic Garden: Plant Transfer, Science and the East India Company, 1786–1806", *Journal of the Royal Asiatic Society*, vol. 16, no. 2, 2006, pp. 165–177.
53. da Costa, Maria, Lucia M. Novan, and Tania Sampaio Pereira, "Activities of Botanical Gardens", *Jardim Botanico do Rio de Janeiro, 1808–2008*, A. Lirio ed., Rio de Janeiro: Jardim Botanico do Rio de Janeiro, Ministeìrio do Meio Ambiente, 2008, p. 16.
54. Bediaga, Begonha, Haroldo C. de Lima, et al., "Two Centuries of Scientific Activities", *Jardim Botanico do Rio de Janeiro, 1808–2008*, A. Lirio ed., Rio de Janeiro: Jardim Botanico do Rio de Janeiro, Ministeìrio do Meio Ambiente, 2008, p. 18.
55. Bleichmar, Daniela, "Visualizing Nature: The Production and Uses of Natural History Images in Colonial Science", prepared for delivery at the 2003 meeting of the Latin American Studies Association, Dallas, Texas, March 27–29 2003, p. 5, viewed 26 May 2011, http://lasa.international.pitt.edu/members/congress-papers/lasa2003/files/BleichmarDaniela.pdf.
56. Bleichmar, "Visualizing Nature", p. 5.
57. Ward, Stephen H., *On Wardian Cases for Plants, and their Applications*, London: John van Voorst, 1854, p. 17.
58. Taylor, Patrick ed., *The Oxford Companion to the Garden*, Oxford: Oxford University Press, p. 506.
59. Parker, John S., "The Origin of the Origin: What Henslow Taught Darwin", *Proceedings of the Bath Royal Literary and Scientific Institution*, vol. 10, viewed 10 September 2011, http://www.brlsi.org/proceed06/lecture0206.htm. See also D. Kohn, G. Murrell, et al., "What Henslow Taught Darwin: How a Herbarium Helped to Lay the Foundations of Evolutionary Thinking", *Nature*, vol. 436, 2005, pp. 643–645.
60. Darwin, Charles, *On the Origin of Species by Means of Natural Selection*, first ed., London: John Muray, 1859.
61. Mill, John Stuart, *Three Essays on Religion*, second ed., London: Longmans, Green, Reader, and Dyer, 1874, p. 28.
62. Biberg, "Linnaeus, Carl, *The Oeconomy of Nature*, 1749".
63. Lovelock, James, *Gaia: A New Look at Life on Earth*, 3rd edition, Oxford: Oxford University Press, 2000.
64. Gould, Stephen Jay, "Kropotkin was no Crackpot", *Natural History*, vol. 106, June 1997, pp. 12–21.
65. Grutzen, Paul J. and Christian Schwager, "Living in the Anthropocene: Toward a New Global Ethos", *Yale Environment 360*, New Haven: Yale University Press, 24 January 2011, viewed 28 August 2011, http://e360.yale.edu/feature/living_in_the_anthropocene_toward_a_new_global_ethos/2363/.
66. Botanic Gardens Conservation International, *Definition of a Botanic Garden*, viewed 29 July 2011, http://www.bgci.org/resources/1528/.
67. Forbes, Stephen, "Science and Policy: Valuing Framing, Language and Listening", *Botanical Journal of the Linnaean Society*, vol. 166, no. 3, 2011, pp. 217–226.
68. Wilson, Edward O., *In Search of Nature*, Washington D.C.: Island Press, 1996, p. 178.
69. Staffler, Boris F., Manuel Spaeth, et al., "The Dream of Staying Clean: Lotus and Biomimetic Surfaces", *Bioinspiration & Biomimetics*, vol. 2, no. 4, 2007, pp. S126–S134.
70. Emmett, Peter and Tony Kanellos eds., *The Museum of Economic Botany at the Adelaide Botanic Garden: a Souvenir*, Adelaide: Board of the Botanic Gardens & State Herbarium, 2010.
71. Boeten, P., "From Soles to UV-filters to Dikes", *Delft Centre for Materials Newsletter*, issue 4, 2006, pp. 1–3, viewed 25 August 2011, http://home.tudelft.nl/fileadmin/UD/MenC/Support/Internet/TU_Website/TU_Delft_portal/Onderzoek/Kenniscentra/Delft_Research_Centres/Materials_Science/Newsletter/doc/DCMat_newsletter_may.pdf.
72. Botanic Gardens Conservation International, *International Sentinel Plant Network*, viewed 8 August 2011, http://www.bgci.org/usa/sentinel/.
73. Kew Botanic Gardens, "Helping the Plant Breathe", London: Kew, 2008, viewed 18 August 2011, http://www.kew.org/ucm/groups/public/documents/document/ppcont_013437.pdf.
74. Eden Project, *Annual Review 2008/09*, Cornwall: Eden Project, 2010, viewed 24 August 2011, http://www.edenproject.com/documents/Annual-review-2008-2009.pdf.
75. Eden Project, *Annual Review 2008/09*.
76. Kafka, Franz, "The Third Notebook—January 18, 1918", *The Blue Octavo Notebooks*, Max Brod ed., Ernst Kaiser and Eithne Wilkins trans., Cambridge: Exact Change, 1991, p. 37.
77. Millennium Ecosystem Assessment, Guide to the Millennium Assessment Reports, Millennium Ecosystem Assessment, 2005 viewed 28 August 2011, http://www.maweb.org/en/index.aspx.

ZOOTOPIA: UTOPIA AND DYSTOPIA IN THE ZOOLOGICAL GARDEN

/IRUS BRAVERMAN

In his book on utopianism, Krishan Kumar delineates several common types of utopia, including paradise, a golden age in which people live simply and in harmony with nature; the ideal city, the good society designed by a rational plan; and Cockaigne, the land of abundance, enjoyment, and pleasure.[1] While utopia is more than an amalgam of these conceptions, each makes an elemental contribution to it. Paradise contributes the element of harmony, the ideal city provides design, and Cockaigne adds desire.[2] All of these types of utopia are manifest at the zoological garden. However, each element contains the seeds of its own destruction, and as such is equally dystopian. I adopt the term "zootopia" to express the utopian and the dystopian impulses at work in the zoo and to allude to their tightly intertwined nature.

My first section explores zootopia as a paradise, a place where people may enjoy the illusion of living in harmony with a romanticized nature. Although situated at the heart of the modern urban project, the zoo exposes city dwellers to wild nature and educates them about the proper human relationship to this nature. "It's an oasis. It's Eden. It's a place where you can get away from the dust, the dirt, the grime, the buildings", says Susan Chin, Vice President of Planning and Design and Chief Architect of Bronx Zoo, in an interview. Indeed, the zoo is constructed as a space of lost paradise; it is an enclosed and protected place of wildness, where humans can safely observe and 'connect' with their 'other'. That this process has been accompanied by nostalgia for lost nature and for the animals that have progressively been removed from the everyday life of the urban dweller is evident in the ambivalent human responses to nature that persist to this day.[3] Utopian nostalgia thus arises out of the dystopian elements of contemporary life.

However, zootopia is not only an exhibit of the wild and untouchable other, idealized into a harmonious and romantic nature. Simultaneously, it is a rational project that involves careful planning and detailed control over both animals and their habitat. This notion has commonalities with Kumar's ideal city, the good society designed by a rational plan. Indeed, the modern zoological garden developed as an urban institution. From the late nineteenth century, cities have come to be read as monuments to the human capacity for progress and order. Every large city was expected to have its own collection of life on Earth. It follows, then, that zoos—where nature was introduced to the metropolis and converted into a domesticated spectacle—have come to represent the ultimate triumph of modern man over nature, of city over country, of reason over nature's apparent wildness and chaos [Figure 1].[4]

At the zoo, animals are taxonomically categorized and exhibited to produce desired outcomes in terms of spectatorship and pedagogy.[5] The zoo organizes nature according to physical geographies and habitats that are confined within linear and taxonomic divides. The recent introduction of ZIMS–the Zoological Information Management System—feeds directly into this construction of the zoo as an intensely planned environment. Zoo animals are named and recorded into global databases, where sophisticated computer software systematically organizes and centralizes information about them. Finally, animals are selected for breeding according to human notions of endangerment and preservation. At the heart of this system lie both the human urge for classification and a strong utopian assumption that the world *can* be neatly and exhaustively ordered. The zoo, then, is a *protected* garden (indeed, the Hebrew word for garden—*gan*—derives from the root "to protect"), in the sense that it is a site for the protection of both nature's wildness and human orderliness. But the conflicts between these two utopian impulses always invite their own destruction in the form of dystopian realities.

Finally, the zoo is a theme park: as a garden for human entertainment and consumption it evokes Cockaigne—the land of abundance, enjoyment, and pleasure. Indeed, consumption of animal-related products significantly shapes the visitor's experience of the zoo. In order to survive, the zoo must sell tickets, animal figurines and sponsorships, crackers for feeding the elephants, giraffe art, and the like. The consumerist expectations of zoogoers must be met. The small acts of consumption spread along the space of the zoo inform the visitor about how to buy, and thereby also about how to save, this nature. When zoo animals are adopted by corporations or by individuals, the

Figure 1/ Zootopia, nature as domesticated spectacle. Iconic, Modernist zoological architecture, Berthold Lubetkin, 1934. Penguin Pool, the London Zoo. Photograph courtesy of the Zoological Society of London.

plight of their wild counterparts is turned into a marketing scheme. The zoo must present, in other words, a nature that is both desirable and consumable. This is ironic, given that excessive consumption is typically deemed a major cause for the vanishing habitats of these animals.[6]

The role of humans at the zoological garden is also idealized. Usually absent from traditional exhibit spaces, humans travel through the zoo as passive spectators. At the same time, they are constantly called upon to play an active role in preserving the endangered animal world, which, according to the zoo's narrative, has reached its miserable state as a direct result of humanity's irresponsible behavior. In addition to its particular productions of nature, then, the zoo promotes a vision of omnipotent humans who have destroyed this nature and who are therefore now obliged to rescue it. At the zoo, modern conservation messages rely upon heightened forms of capitalism, guilt, and redemption. Indeed, apocalyptic claims about the death of nature underlie the very existence of the zoo.[7]

Ultimately, the zoo's presentation of nature is utopian, in the sense that it confirms current ideals and makes room for hope about nature's future. Pointing an accusing finger toward humans at large, and toward the consumption habits of the individual zoogoers in particular, the zoo aims to change the latter's behavior. Messages about the 'right' way to consume are spread along this space, disciplining the zoo visitor into more ecologically responsible modes of consumption. The awe and amusement that this visitor experiences at the utopian zoo are often overlaid with the fear and guilt implied by the dystopian message that is also present in this space.[8]

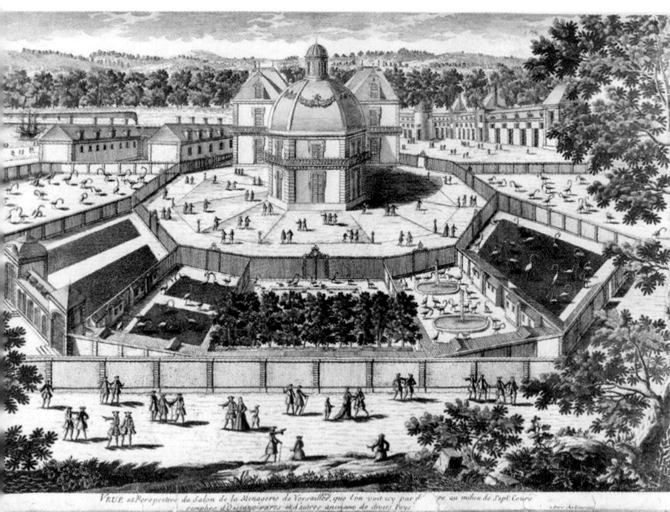

Figure 2/ Collecting nature as a luxury and curiosity. The menagerie at Versailles, filled with rare birds. seventeenth century engraving. Bibliothèque Nationale, Paris, France. Photograph © Snark/ Art Resource, NY.

Figure 3/ Herd of elephants, Central Park, New York. c. 1865–1901. Stereographic card, Underwood and Underwood, Baltimore MD and Ottawa KA. Robert N. Dennis collection of stereoscopic views, the New York Public Library. Miriam and Ira D. Wallach Division of Art, Prints and Photographs. Accession number MFY Dennis Coll 91-F230.

PLACING WILD ANIMALS IN THE URBAN GARDEN: A HISTORY

As contrived meeting places for the most urban people and the most exotic animals, zoos have often been the places for negotiating these relationships. They display the diversity and complexity of human ideas about animals. In a changed world... this may be their most enduring value.[9]

Contemporary North American zoos are products of a long process of institutional evolution. Some trace the origin of the zoo back to exotic animal collections managed in ancient kingdoms, under rulers such as King Wen of China, King Solomon of Judea and Israel, and King Nebuchadnezzar of Babylon. Zoos also existed in most of the Greek city-states, and the Roman emperors kept private collections of animals for study or for use in the arena. This type of zoo is often referred to as the "menagerie": an aristocratic or royal animal collection that exhibited the power and wealth of the ruler. Rather than serving scientific or educational agendas, the menagerie formed an "establishment of luxury and curiosity" [Figure 2].[10]

The next major phase in the zoo's institutional evolution was the zoological garden (from which derives the abbreviated term "zoo"). Zoological gardens were designed as living museums intended for the promotion of scientific agendas and for the education of the general public in the city. The oldest such existing institution, the Vienna Zoo in Austria, evolved from the Imperial Menagerie at the Schönbrunn Palace in Vienna, and was opened to the public in 1765. In 1795, the Jardin des Plantes was founded in Paris with animals from the royal menagerie at Versailles, primarily for scientific research and education. The London Zoo was established as a research collection in Regent's Park in 1828 and opened to paying visitors in 1847. Central Park Zoo, arguably the first public zoo in the United States, opened in New York in 1860 [Figure 3]. One of the distinct features of the zoological garden was its taxonomic allocation of animals. Classification and scientific knowledge were the primary concerns at this stage of the zoo's evolution, and animals were, accordingly, mostly exhibited in cages [Figure 4].[11] While early zoos conveyed a message of separation between humans and nature, the twentieth century saw a move on the part of many zoos toward ideologies of interconnectivity and unity within biological

Figure 4/ The cage as nature's stage.
Fairmount Park, Zoo. Llama ("Peru"), Philadelphia, PA. c. 1860–1910. Stereographic card, C. R. Webster, Rochester NY. Robert N. Dennis collection of stereoscopic views, the New York Public Library. Miriam and Ira D. Wallach Division of Art, Prints and Photographs. Accession number MFY Dennis Coll 91-F375.

Figure 5/ Simulating nature. Hagenbeck Tierpark.
Alfred Brehm, "Die Gartenlaube", *Bilder aus dem Tiergarten*, Leipzig: Alfred Kröner, 1863.

diversity.[12] The initial steps in this direction are commonly attributed to Carl Hagenbeck of Germany. Considered the father of the modern zoo, Hagenbeck opened the world's first bar-less zoo in 1907 [Figure 5]. Whereas in traditional zoos the means of achieving separation and enclosure were highly visible, Hagenbeck contrived to make them invisible. Inspired by the bucolic longings of the 1700s, Hagenbeck attempted to make all apparatuses, all attempts at classification—indeed, any trace of human intervention—vanish in favor of seeing the animals themselves, presented in a manner that simulated nature.[13] In his "zoo of the future, nothing more than unseen ditches were to separate wild animals from members of the public".[14] The design of the exhibits attempted to recreate the natural habitats of animals, promoting more naturalistic behavior on the part of zoo animals and enabling the public to view them in a context similar to their native environments.[15]

European zoos served as a model and an impetus for building zoos in the United States. At the same time, American zoos were also products of the broader movement to create public parks.[16] Late nineteenth century anxieties about moral and social order in the city led to the creation of large parks in the outskirts of cities, as well as to the creation of national parks. American zoos came into existence during the transition of the United States from a rural and agricultural nation to an urban and industrial one.[17] For the most part, they were founded as divisions of public park departments.

The father of American landscape design, Frederick Law Olmsted, was influenced by English garden theory of the informal landscape. He believed that nature could offer psychic recreation to tired city workers. Nature, according to Olmsted's interpretation, was to be represented by winding paths, an apparent absence of human artifice, and wide vistas to picturesque spots. Zoos added a variation to this theme by placing animals in the pastoral landscape.[18] But while Olmsted opposed the London Zoo for consuming

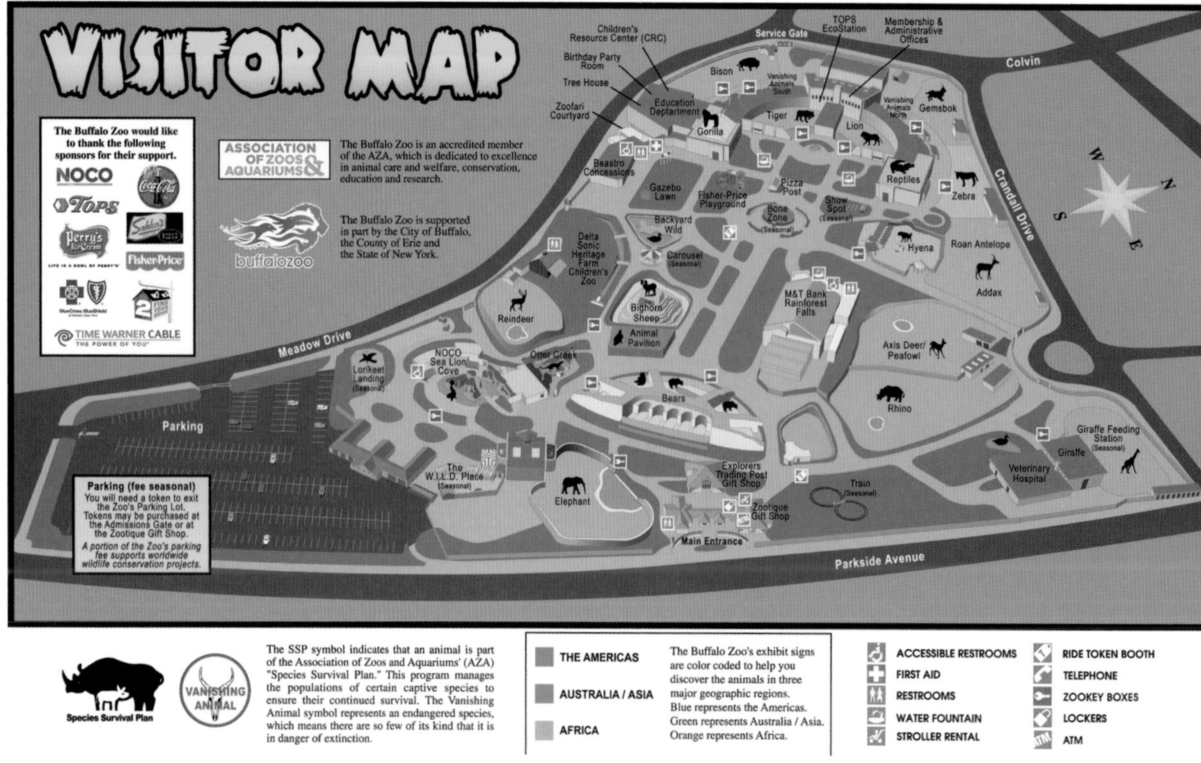

Figure 6/ Ordering nature. Buffalo Zoo Visitor Map. Courtesy of the Buffalo Zoo, Buffalo, New York.

precious space that could be better used for green recreation, in the United States there was no shortage of space, and parks needed to attract visitors. As a result, American zoo planners conceived of their parks in different terms from the formal urban gardens that were European zoos.[19] The zoo was set against the theater as a moral diversion; the scripture was even evoked to attract respectable audiences to the zoo. American zoos also opposed the common European use of colonial architecture in the design of zoo buildings. Indeed, American zoo designers usually preferred buildings that they thought blended with, rather than distracted from, the visitor's experience of nature.

The atmosphere of the country park and the reform goals of the parks movement supported the educational goal of zoos. Claiming a measure of scientific truth, zoological parks encouraged popular natural history studies and used their landscape layout to advance this mission. Like other public parks, they provided a retreat for city dwellers and a balance of nature and culture where a middle class ethos could be enforced.[20]

When ecology emerged as a matter of public interest in the 1970s, a few American zoos started shifting their focus toward conservation. This brought about the most recent stage in the zoo's institutional evolution: the zoo as a biopark or a conservation society.[21] Nowadays, the American Association of Zoos and Aquariums (AZA)—the central organization of contemporary American zoos—considers conservation to be a fundamental ethical concern. In its Preamble to the Code of Professional Ethics, originally adopted in 1976, the AZA states accordingly that: "Members of the American Association of Zoological Parks and Aquariums... have an important role in the preservation of our heritage."

Today's zoos bear the traces of their convoluted history. They contain physical evidence of the pre-modern cage phase and its taxonomic approach. The naturalistic design associated with Hagenback's zoological parks is still a prevalent feature in contemporary exhibit design. At the same time, the zoo has shifted drastically from a space for animal spectacles geared toward the entertainment of the public into a vehicle for the preservation of species and habitats. Whereas the education of the public remains a prominent feature of zoos, the contents of education by zoos have changed. Both utopian and dystopian elements are evident in the zoo's current stage of development as an institution for conservation.

PARADISE: UTOPIAN NATURE AT THE ZOO

Nature in the zoo presents all sorts of contradictions. What could be more unnatural than polar bears in Miami or giraffe in New York City? Zoos present a peculiar blend of nature and culture... they are parks that constitute a middle ground between the wilderness and the city, specially constructed meeting places for wild animals and urban Americans.[22]

The zoo produces a harmonized, sanctified, and sanitized nature that is expressly juxtaposed to modern urban life. This section explores two major design methods through which this nature is constructed at the zoo: zoogeography and immersion. First, however, comes a more general discussion of zoos as natural spaces.

Modern zoos developed as urban institutions.[23] Located in the metropolis, the zoo enables an affordable escape from urban life. To constitute such an escape, the zoo had to offer something other than the familiar city experience. Indeed, contemporary American zoos try to create what some of my interviewees refer to as an "illusion of nature". Says Jim Breheny, Director of Bronx Zoo, "My job is to instill in these people—that have absolutely no connection whatsoever to nature anymore—the appropriate sense of awe, respect, and appreciation for animals."[24]

The illusion that the zoo provides for its visitors, according to Breheny and others interviewed for this project, is one of transplantation into a different space from the urban world in which they reside, a space that is both natural and wild. In the words of Susan Chin, Vice President of Planning and Design and Chief Architect of Bronx Zoo, "Our guests come here to get that respite from the urban environment.... You have places to go where you can see trees and squirrels and ducks and muskrats."[25] Paul Harpley of Toronto Zoo similarly states that "without the city, there would also not be a zoo in the way we think about zoos, because we wouldn't need to bring the other to the urban." In other words, the zoo aspires to afford its visitors an escape into a utopian space, presented as natural but governed by the human ideals of unity, order, and simplicity.[26]

Such a utopian nature, however, is not constructed in the abstract. It is geographically situated, and sometimes even modeled after particular sites in faraway lands. This nature is also scientifically mapped and classified. At the Buffalo Zoo, which will serve as my main example in this essay, different sites highlight three distinct modes of mapping and classification. Overall, whereas the zoo itself is loosely organized according to a continent-based scheme (the Americas, Australia/Asia, and Africa—but, interestingly, not Europe), specific exhibits are modeled according to habitats (e.g., the rainforest). Additionally, signs posted on plants and near most animal exhibits across the Buffalo Zoo display their taxonomic names.

Each of these three mapping schemes—continent-based, habitat-based, and taxonomy-based—highlights a different aspect of the human-nature relationship. Geographic ordering maps animals according to their physical location. For this sort of ordering to exist, one must acquire synoptic control over the world and map it as such, exercising skills that have been especially pertinent since the colonial age. According to this traditional form of mapping, animals and humans are arranged by their geographic affiliation, as classified by European colonizers. This sort of mapping highlights human domination over the entire world.

The second type of arrangement—by habitat—stresses the general idea of the world as an ecosystem, which in fact highlights human/animal interdependence. Thirdly and finally, the taxonomy-based system derives from Linnaeus' *Systema Naturae*, 1735, in which the world is organized into animal, plant, and mineral kingdoms.[27] The kingdoms are divided into classes, and they, in turn, into orders, genera, and species. This form of ordering highlights scientific and objective ordering along with the human power to name, and, more generally, to know all things. At the Buffalo Zoo, the three forms of animal classification are used interchangeably. This, perhaps, is not so surprising, as the different forms of mapping all reflect a strong desire for order and an ideal of complete synoptic control [Figure 6].

IMMERSION DESIGN

Two major design principles are used by contemporary zoos in North America to facilitate the illusion of geographically-situated natures: immersion design and zoogeography.[28] Immersion design attempts to create an illusion of nature in the midst of modern urban space. "By immersion I mean that you're really designing a space that [makes] people feel like they are part of the habitat", explains Bronx Zoo designer Chin. In other words, immersion design is not simply a matter of showing animals in the context of nature rather than in the context of architecture. It also creates experiences that make people feel part of nature, rather than external observers of it. This requires paying close attention to the minute details of exhibit space.[29] According to Jim Breheny, Director of the Bronx Zoo:

> It drives me crazy: you go to certain zoos and you'll see a fence or you'll see a stainless steel food pan. You're going to spend 16 million dollars on this exhibit to make people think that you're transporting them to the Congo Basin and then they're going to go there and see a gorilla picking sliced carrots out of a stainless steel food pan?! Doesn't make any sense to me. That's the kind of

> attention we give to detail. At no point do you see the apartment that's 300 feet away. You don't see that because that would make you forget that you are in the Congo.[30]

Though much less pronounced than sight, sound is also utilized in the immersion-designed zoo. Here, from the website of the Saint Louis Zoo:

> Have you ever noticed that in almost every habitat you hear an amazing variety of insect drones and chirps, birdcalls, and frog choruses? The Zoo has recreated these sounds of nature in its exhibits, thanks to a state-of-the-art audio system installed along the visitor pathways. Keep your ears open for the chatter of macaque monkeys in the trees, the high-pitched squeaks of bats in the cave, and the sudden rattle of a Missouri rattlesnake coming from the undergrowth.[31]

When walking with Bronx Zoo Director Breheny through the zoo's Congo Exhibit, which has won numerous national and international awards, I was informed that the birds' chirping, like most of the trees and rocks, was artificial [Figure 7]. The artificial has been disguised so well that I had to ask Breheny to distinguish it from the natural. Designer Chin further notes,

> We want to blur the line so you feel like you're in nature. We don't want you to feel like you're in a contrived space, though sometimes it's going to be pretty obvious, like in Madagascar. But even then, as you walk through Madagascar... you might forget for a little while that you're in a building in the Bronx Zoo. When you're looking at those lemurs and they are leaping about and they're doing their thing, you might actually forget.[32]

When I asked whether the zoo ever installs signs that indicate which materials in the exhibit are artificial, Breheny replied: "Why would we want to do that? For 90 percent of the people who come here, this is as close as they are going to get to a field experience."[33] Artificial elements are used because they are so much easier to manage and maintain than certain natural elements. However, exhibit designers and architects go to great pains to hide the artificiality of the exhibited artifacts [Figure 8]. Architect Gwen Howard of the Buffalo Zoo speaks to this aspect of zoo design:

> The fake is very prescribed. You're going to build me one tree; it's going to be this diameter, this kind of species; it's going to have six primary branches, and off of each of those would have a minimum of three to five secondary branches.[34]

Figure 7/ Congo immersion.
Congo Exhibit, the Brox Zoo, New York.
Photograph courtesy of Adriana Lopetrone.

Despite the incredible efforts required to construct nature-like exhibit spaces, the nature performed at the zoo is not an exact simulacrum of wild nature, and intentionally so. On many grounds, the zoo distinguishes itself from the wild, providing a safe and sanitized environment for its visitors and for its animals. Perhaps most importantly, predatory relationships are largely eliminated from the exhibit space. "You don't see animals killing animals", says Breheny of the Bronx Zoo. "Our visitors could never see that", he adds. "They make no connection between a piece of hamburger on a styrofoam plate and a cow." Cindy Lee, Curator of Fish at Toronto Zoo, similarly explains:

> You wouldn't want that seal to do what it does in the wild, which is balance a fish or a penguin on its head and rip it up into pieces while throwing it into the air. You wouldn't want your child to see a lion tear up a goat. It's inhumane. They do eat animals here but the animals are killed humanely.[35]

According to scholar Paul Shepard,

> The extension of the human idea to the wild... will see in the behaviours and interrelationships among animals infinite cruelties and will seek to prevent

them.... [H]umane action will try to prevent dogs from eating cats and men from eating dogs.[36]

Clearly, the humane nature performed at the zoo is an idealized nature: nature as humans would want it to be.

Yet certain predatory relationships *are* included in this idealized vision. Lee Ehmke of the Minnesota Zoo tells me, for example, that "fish are murdered on a daily basis in front of the public.... The further down the food chain they are..., the less people are concerned about these animals."[37] The one event in most modern North American zoos that comes closest to hunting is the feeding of snakes with whole prey. So as not to offend zoo visitors, this event is usually relegated to holding areas that are inaccessible to the general public.[38]

For a successful geographical and mental transportation from the urban to the natural to occur, it is not enough to blur the lines between the natural and the artificial. Human artifacts and activities must also be made invisible. The Jungle Exhibit at the Bronx Zoo, for example, depends upon the constant labor of architects, zoologists, botanists, graphic designers, construction workers, welders, carpenters, painters, electricians, plumbers, audio specialists, gardeners, cabinet-makers, and glaziers.[39] This labor too is made to seem natural and transparent. It is especially important to ensure the invisibility of buildings. "The most dangerous animal in the zoo is the architect", former director of the Bronx Zoo William Conway has been quoted saying. His remark illustrates the suspicious attitude of many zoo officials toward buildings and their designers.[40]

Yet again, in some important respects the zoo explicitly refrains from imitating wild nature. Anything that threatens the pleasant feelings prompted by the zoo's image of nature is rendered unseen, including disease, competition, and, above all, aging and death. Breheny provides an example:

Figure 8/ Exhibiting nature naturally. Polar bears, Berlin Zoo. Photograph courtesy of Chris Joseph.

We have animals here that get old. Sometimes they don't move as good or their coats aren't as shiny and they may be blind in one eye. They're not attractive to look at. You'd be surprised that we get letters [complaining] about that. So which is it? Do you want us to kill everything when it's in its prime and breed more so that everything is bright eyed and bushy tailed, or is it okay for us to exhibit older animals or animals with handicaps?[41]

The zoo not only attempts to avoid any reminders of human fragility, it also avoids the exhibit of humans altogether. Although masses of people frequent the zoo at any given time, humans are strikingly absent from the zoo's exhibit space. Lee Ehmke, Director of the Minnesota Zoo, is adamantly opposed to any inclusion of humans in zoo exhibits. "At the Vienna zoo", he explains, "human artifacts are injected into natural themes to try to tell a story about the relationship [between] people and animals.... However, I think it can be very confusing to people to have the human element mixed with the animal."[42]

At the zoo exhibit, the human role in nature is framed quite carefully. On the one hand, humans are frequently referred to as the cause for animal extinction and for habitat destruction. This reference is made only in the abstract; the finger rarely points to specific corporations or individuals. At the same time, humans are presented as those who have the power to make a difference. This time, the appeal is made to a concrete human: the individual zoogoer. By presenting a strict dichotomy between humans and animals, the zoo's exhibit space systematically reinforces the human/nature divide. Such a binary presentation furthers the image of a 'first nature' that is at the mercy and at the disposal of man.[43]

As I have shown, zoo directors constantly make decisions about what kind of nature to reproduce. Strong believers in animal preservation, they attempt to balance animal population considerations and individual-oriented animal welfare approaches, on the one hand, with the public's desire to witness a performance of nature and be awed, on the other hand. The image of nature displayed at the immersion design exhibit is, accordingly, of a very particular kind: it is harmonious and pleasant, a nature that excludes certain sights that might emotionally unsettle or physically threaten the zoo visitor. It is also a nature that must not distract its visitors from the central educational message of the zoo: animal preservation. Nature is intentionally designed into a manicured performance that elicits compassion and awe rather than alienation and fear. A view of a harmonious, yet human-absent, nature emerges. Constructed at the heart of the city, the zoo's nature is designed to bring its visitors closer to wild nature. At the same time, it makes nature remarkably inaccessible and remote: a paradisiacal utopia.

ZOOGEOGRAPHY: COLOR-CODING NATURE

We've spent hundreds of millions of dollars creating illusions to transport people to far off places of the world to... instill in them the appropriate sense of awe, appreciation, and respect for animals.[44]

The zoo, to which people go to meet animals, to observe them, to see them, is, in fact, a monument to the impossibility of such encounters.[45]

Zoogeography is the study of the distribution patterns of animals in nature and the processes that regulate these distributions.[46] Like immersion design, design based in zoogeography creates the illusion of a whole and unified nature. Visiting the zoo "is like a family vacation", suggests designer Chin of the Bronx Zoo, for "who can afford to go to Africa right now?" Indeed, for the most part, the zoo's presentation of nature is geographically specific. The zoo appeals to the public by providing a vicarious journey into a distant and exotic nature in a faraway land. Like other vehicles of mass communication, including *National Geographic* magazine and nature programs on television, the zoo provides its visitors with a vivid local experience of a disappearing global nature.[47]

Zoogeography constructs a specific interpretation of nature in that it creates pockets of nature that are identified by their geography, rather than by their habitat (say, desert or rainforest) or through other classificatory schemes. This approach manifests in the frequent organization of the zoo according to continents. The Toronto Zoo was the first in the world to introduce zoogeography design on a large scale, says Paul Harpley, Manager of Interpretation, Culture, and Design at Toronto Zoo. "We basically had the whole world represented", he explains. Today, continent-based designs are common in many North American zoos.

The ambition to render the entire world, as represented in assemblages of animals and habitats, subordinate to the controlling vision of the spectator is not a new thing. It was already present at the Great Exhibition of 1851 by Wylde's Great Globe, a brick rotunda that the visitor entered to see plaster casts of the world's continents and oceans. This design strategy afforded an elevated vantage point over a micro-world that claimed to be representative of a larger totality [Figure 9].[48]

The zoo's heightened focus on geography entails an erasure of both space and time. Within the walls of the average zoo, enormous spatial and temporal distances are eroded, and the most profound variations in climate and landscape collapse. Penguins from the Arctic swim a few yards away from Kenyan lions, giraffes roam near polar bears, and dinosaur exhibits feature alongside living animals. The zoogoer moves through species, landscapes, and temporalities in whatever pattern and pace she chooses. It is like switching television channels at random. Anything is possible.[49] As mentioned earlier, one technique for mapping the world—and animals and plants in particular—according to geography is color-coding. At the Buffalo Zoo, visitor maps and brochures explain that "exhibit signs are color-coded to help you discover the animals in three different geographic regions: Blue represents the Americas. Green represents Australia and Asia. Orange represents Africa."

Although the zoo aims to create an escape from rational urban life into a paradisiacal nature, nature at the zoo is also organized to conform with urban life, and in this sense it also contains dystopian elements. At the same time, the nature that the urban dweller finds at the zoo presents a utopian image of an improved and mapped nature that can easily be read and consumed by the average zoogoer.

UTOPIAN ORDERINGS AT THE ZOO

Zoos tell us something not only about the making of Western popular culture but about the complex construction of metropolitan cultures and identities; of what it was, and is, to be a city-dweller.[50] Indeed, the zoo has been identified as a product and symbol of the alienation of urban life: over-crowding, anxiety, aggression, and nervous disorders characterizing both.[51] If the city is a human zoo, the zoo is a reproduction of the modern city.[52]

Humans have classified, measured, and standardized just about everything: animals, human races, books, taxes, jobs, and diseases.[53] The underlying assumption of scientific taxonomies is that all living species can be compartmentalized into systemic and hierarchical categories. Such categories present themselves not only as mutually exclusive but also as exhaustive, and therefore as constituting a system

Figure 9/ Nature in a micro-world.

James Wyld's Great Globe, situated in London's Leicester Square between 1851 and 1862. Cross section of the Great Globe, *Illustrated London News*, 7 June, 1851. Unknown artist.

Figure 10/ A comprehensive collection of nature. Rainforest exhibit, the Buffalo Zoo, Buffalo, New York. Photograph courtesy of the Buffalo Zoo.

that is consistent and complete.[54] The zoo uses three such taxonomic mechanisms: lists, sites of spatial separation, and database systems.

LISTS

Director of the Buffalo Zoo Donna Fernandes lists the categories that she used in developing educational programs for the Prospect Park Wildlife Center in New York and in mapping out the Buffalo Zoo's animal collections. These categories include "habitat—where an animal lives; mode of locomotion; type of shelter; activity cycle; feeding behavior; seasonal behavior; activity cycle; predator avoidance; mating system; parental care; social organization; and method of communication".[55] Fernandes explains that the purpose of such listing was "to see if there were obvious gaps in our representation of animal life".[56] The need to neatly arrange the world, as expressed in Fernandes' list, is very much in line with the utopian desire to create a better, more orderly world.

Buffalo Zoo's rainforest exhibit provides an even more pronounced example of the desire to know thoroughly in order to render complete. A comprehensive list of animal and plant species organizes them according to their common and scientific names as well as their conservation status (courtesy of Dr. Fernandes of the Buffalo Zoo):

Pink-toed tarantula *Avicularia magdelenae*/ **Brazilian red and white tarantula** *Lasiodora cristata*/ **Brazilian salmon tarantula** *Lasiodora parahybana*/ **Colombian giant tarantula** *Megphobema robustum*/ **Blue poison dart frog** *Dendrobates azureus* **CITES II, PMP**/ **Bumblebee poison dart frog** *Dendrobates leucomelas* **CITES II, PMP**/ **Red piranha** *Pygocentrus nattereri*/ **Giant South American river turtle** *Podocnemis expansa* **CITES II, US Endangered, studbook**/ **Yellow-spotted Amazon river turtle** *Podocnemis unifilis* **CITES II, US Endangered, studbook**/ **South American red-footed tortoise** *Geochelone carbonaria* **CITES II**/ **Dwarf caiman** *Paleosuchus palpebrosus* **CITES II**/ **Green crested basilisk** *Basiliscus plumifrons*/ **Monkey-tailed anole** *Polychrus marmoratus*/ **Green anaconda** *Eunectes murinus*/ **Boat-billed heron** *Cochlearius cochlearius ridgwayi* **PMP, studbook**/ **Scarlet ibis** *Eudocimus ruber*/ **Roseate spoonbill** *Ajaia ajaja* **PMP, studbook**/ **Fulvous whistling duck** *Dendrocygna bicolor*/ **Sunbittern** *Eurypyga helias* **PMP**/ **White-tailed trogon** *Trogon viridis*/ **Blue-crowned motmot** *Momotus momota* **PMP, studbook**/ **Chestnut-mandible toucan** *Ramphastos ambiguus swainsonii* **SSP, studbook**/ **Linne's two-toed sloth** *Choloepus didactylus* **PMP, studbook**/ **6-banded/ yellow armadillo** *Euphractus sexcinctus*/ **Giant anteater** *Myrmecophaga tridactyla* **CITES II, PMP, studbook**/ **Southern tamandua** *Tamandua tetradactyla*/ **Brown capuchin** *Cebus apella* **CITES II, PMP, studbook**/ **Common squirrel monkey** *Saimiri sciureus* **CITES II, PMP, studbook**/ **White-faced saki** *Pithecia pithecia* **CITES II, PMP, studbook**/ **Black howler monkey** *Alouatta caraya* **CITES II, PMP, studbook**/ **Capybara** *Hydrochaeris hydrochaeris* **PMP, studbook**/ **Vampire bat** *Desmodus rotundus* **PMP**/ **Ocelot** *Leopardus pardalis* **CITES I, US Endangered, SSP, studbook**/ **Collared peccary** *Pecari tajacu* **PMP, studbook**

A much longer list of plants displayed at the rainforest exhibit follows. Again, the deep desire to create the fullest, most complete representation of the world is essentially utopian; it is linked to the desire to create an ideal design [Figure 10].

THE HERITAGE FARM: DISTINGUISHING DOMESTIC FROM WILD NATURE

In addition to its wildlife exhibits, the Buffalo Zoo exhibits domesticated animals, although pets, and non-wild animals in general, are prohibited from entering the zoo. Domesticated animals are limited to a particular space—the children's (or petting) zoo. This exhibit embodies yet another example of animal ordering with utopian implications.

Replacing the older children's zoo, the Heritage Farm is Buffalo Zoo's newest exhibit. It purports to take the visitor back in time to the nineteenth century by displaying an actual farm with pigs, cows, hens, a mule, and sheep the way they were supposedly raised and fed during that period. The exhibit includes interactive signage. Children are asked, for example, "what products come from this animal?" and are instructed: "leather shoes", "meat", and "milk" for the cow; "pigskin football" and "meat" for the pig; "pillow feathers", "meat", and "eggs" for hens; and "wool yarn" and "meat" for sheep.

Other signs feature personalized narratives by children who are seen performing various tasks such as collecting and cleaning eggs at the farm. During visiting hours, one or two zoo instructors are usually present to enable children to pet or feed the animals. Finally, sinks and hand sanitizing machines are situated at several locations, along with signs that encourage visitors to wash their hands after touching the animals.

Clearly, the rules of conduct that pertain to the exhibit of domesticated animals are quite different from those that pertain to captive animals. First, in contrast to the multiple projects of mapping and classifying wild animals, domesticated animals are not assigned geographic color codes, nor are they affiliated by scientific names or habitat. Instead, they are only identified by their common name (e.g., cow, chicken) and by their uses for humans.

The zoo's displays of captive and domesticated animals also differ in the level of human involvement depicted. Unlike in the immersion design exhibit of the rainforest, human involvement in both the life and the exhibit of domesticated animals is not minimized but, rather, emphasized and highlighted. The zoo's wild animal exhibits are accompanied by dystopian narratives of extinction. By contrast, at children's zoos it is deemed morally appropriate for humans to use domesticated animals: to eat them and use their skins and fur for dress or entertainment (e.g. the pigskin football).

Finally, whereas the zoo visitor is commonly allowed only to look at, not to touch, wild animals, this prohibition does not apply to domesticated animals. Visitors, especially children, are encouraged to experience the domesticated animals through their multiple senses, not only through seeing. By contrast with the spectacular, and, at the same time, flat image of wild animals, a more sophisticated understanding of domesticated animals can emerge. This distinction reinforces the uniqueness of wild animals and ensures their separate legal protection.

But why would one desire to touch or feed a cow? Biophilia, the instinctual human bond with other living systems, is one possible answer.[57] Since urban dwellers are not only alienated from wild nature but also from rural life, if they desire to connect with animals other than pets they must visit either the zoo or the farm. Because the farm is less and less accessible to the urban child, zoos are stepping up to the challenge, providing this child with an opportunity for an intimate connection with nature, broadly defined.[58]

What should one make of the zoo's differing approaches toward domesticated and wild animals? Perhaps most obviously, wild animals are precisely that: animals in a 'state of nature', and thus potentially in a predatory relationship with humans. In this case, both the safety of humans and that of the animals call for a separation between humans and animals. This form of gazing at the other from a safe distance is also what establishes and enables the thrill of the spectacle. By contrast, domesticated animals have, for centuries, been tamed by man for his domestic needs. These animals are therefore not considered dangerous and can be touched and fed directly, even by urban children.

Above all, the divergent methods of display used by zoos for wild and domesticated animals reinforce the initial distinction between domesticated and wild animals and serve in the end to elevate the status of wild animals, even to the point of sanctifying them. Whereas we are morally allowed to kill and consume certain animals for daily use, we are prohibited from consuming or using most wild animals, and can even be criminally prosecuted for doing so. A hierarchy between animals is thereby established and reinforced. Under this interpretation, the zoo's domesticated animals are underclass citizens, undeserving of proper scientific recognition and of the ecological protections that do exist for the full-status animal citizens of the zoo: wild, and especially endangered, species.

At the same time, the zoo's uses of domesticated animals can enhance familiarity and intimacy toward wild animals. Indeed, instead of alienating visitors from wild animals, the familiarity established toward domestic animals may extend to include care about the wellbeing of wild animals, which in turn promotes a harmonized human/animal relationship.

One way or the other, the existence of farm animals at zoos points to the human need to establish domination of *all* living beings. Farm animals are merely one segment of an array of animals that have been successfully subordinated to human management. The human desire to organize and classify animals motivates this practice of differentiating between wild and domestic animals through their separation within the zoo's space. By distancing the farm and its animals from the wild nature of the rainforest, the zoo reifies the nature/culture binary and undercuts the idealized nature displayed in other zoo exhibits.

The Buffalo Zoo's Heritage Farm—and children's zoos in general—carries unwitting assumptions about humans. The reality that certain humans do not eat cow or pig, or do not consume any animal parts for that matter, is made invisible in this space, which assumes a particular set of Christian and Western ideals. Hence, whereas the zoo carefully distinguishes between different animals, it does the opposite with regard to humans: a homogenous human approach toward using animals prevails here above all others.

DATABASE MANAGEMENT

I have explored the role of lists as well as the zoo's use of physical space to demarcate various animals from each other. I have also shown how, in the process, human/animal and animal/animal divisions are both naturalized and legitimized. Herein, I explore another type of animal ordering performed at the zoo: database management.

For the past several decades, ARKS—which stands for Animal Records Keeping System—has served as the central animal database for zoos worldwide. Established by ISIS—the International Species Information System—the ARKS database system records the basic information about all zoo animals: their scientific and common names and identifiers, their sex, and their birth and death dates. This database contains records of 2.4 million animals (374,000 currently living) and more than 10,000 species.[59] The ARKS database has enabled global public access to basic information about zoo animals worldwide. Using this system, anyone could find out, in a matter of seconds, how many Rocky Mountain Bighorn Sheep are held in zoos in the North American region and around the world.

Since 2000, zoo professionals have been joining efforts in the creation of ZIMS: the Zoological Information Management System. ZIMS is a state-of-the-art global animal management database that is web-enabled and contains up-to-the-minute, accurate, and secure information.[60] Over 800 zoos worldwide—the majority of accredited world zoos—are expected to participate in ZIMS.[61] This broad-based collaboration will generate multiple possibilities for the enhanced management of zoo animals.

The development of the ZIMS database system is tied to the recent transformation in the grand mission of zoos.[62] Whereas the traditional zoo did not require much animal management outside the zoos' gates, an evolving global conservation ethos and the legal limitations on taking animals from 'the wild' have resulted in the use of large database systems, studbooks, and animal management structures to create a sustainable zoo animal population.

Based on animal records and on genetic and demographic input by AZA's population management center, different animal programs that work within the AZA decide which animal species should be prioritized for preservation efforts and which individual animals to breed within these populations.[63] Hundreds of animal programs in North America enable broad-based partnerships for breeding and maintaining certain zoo animals. Jean Miller explains about the AZA animal programs that they

> know the pedigrees of all these animals and they have all these genetics people and population managers and all that stuff and they look at the genetics and make a plan for sustainable population in X number of years, with the broadest genetic diversity. So they do all these calculations and say, "okay, this animal needs to pair with this animal".[64]

The aim of AZA's animal programs is to collectively manage the zoos' animal populations so that they are neither under- nor over-represented. The recommendations issued by AZA's animal programs translate into routine practices of animal loans between zoos and to the physical transportation of zoo animal bodies across the country and around the globe.[65] Animal management by zoos has become sophisticated enough that zoo professionals now calculate the identity and the number of animals to interbreed or to phase out.[66] In effect, zoos actively shape the identity of zoo animals, creating their own futuristic Noah's ark.

Whereas the classification of zoo animals into scientific categories such as species and type presents itself as simple and solid—and thus implies that human management can be absolute through space and time—this is hardly the case. In fact, the definition of species is far from intuitive and is still hotly debated within biology.[67] Beyond its inherent instability, the language of species masks both the importance and the extent of human discretion in making zoo decisions. Based on factors such as perceived attractiveness, physical size, resemblance to humans, and the degree to which a species is considered 'a higher form of life', conservation efforts are biased toward particular species. Unfortunately, such bias may lead researchers to "concentrate resources on species that breed relatively poorly and that are expensive to keep and difficult to return to the wild".[68] Additionally, the pragmatic need to build public attendance by featuring 'attractive' species can outweigh conservation concerns.[69]

Consequently, the role of captive breeding is increasingly under scrutiny, even among zoo professionals. Some have named it "a topical treatment for an epidemic", arguing that "intensely managed 'species parks' or 'megazoos' may be the only option for a long time to come".[70] Others have pointed out that captive breeding programs can only be appropriate for a small subset of endangered species, that they are costly, and that they do not provide adequate solutions to deal with the large problem.[71] Yet others have argued that these programs are "a harmful delusion", suggesting that major resources should be channeled directly into wild population and ecosystem preservation efforts, instead of into "ill-conceived recovery captive breeding".[72] Finally, studies have also suggested that the current absence of criteria for species selection by zoos must be replaced with a set of rational criteria.[73]

The utopian urge to neatly classify and arrange animals according to rational criteria is, in fact, less rational and less benevolent than it presents itself to be. Databases and animal programs not only rearrange the world of captive animals according to human forms of classification; they also create an 'improved' version of this animal world.[74] In this way, humans transcend their Biblically allotted role as 'namers' to become 'creators', with potentially dystopian results.[75]

McTOPIA AT THE ZOO

I have explored the zoo as a site of a wild and harmonious nature, where both realized and idealized images of nature and of the animal kingdom are shaped and reinforced. I have also examined the zoo as a space for ordering and managing nature, whether through classifying and categorizing zoo animals into distinct categories and spaces, or through the zoo's virtual project of knowing its animals through extensive database systems. My final section considers the utopian and dystopian implications of zoos as spaces of consumption. To save animals, the zoo must first survive in a world of competing recreational sites and increasingly limited public budgets. For this reason, it must generate revenue.

Gift shops are the zoo's most apparent spaces of consumption. They are strategically situated at the zoo's entrances and exits, and sometimes also scattered throughout. Four different companies compete over the zoo gift shop market across the United States, which results in an identical gift shop experience in almost every zoo in the country.[76] T-shirts, mugs, stuffed animals, and numerous other animal gadgets are a standard part of what is in effect another of the zoo's exhibits.

Yet unlike in the traditional zoo exhibit, at the gift shop little attention is paid to how animals, humans, and their relationships are represented and displayed. Conservation-oriented puzzles are displayed alongside hunting gadgets, and Curious George books stand side by side with the conservationist "Panda Bear What Do You See?" The Director of the Buffalo Zoo confirms that the zoo has no set guidelines to determine which products to sell at the gift shop. What enters this space, arguably, is what sells. "But we wouldn't want to sell only candy, in the same way that we wouldn't want to sell cigarettes and alcohol", adds the Director, who is now considering selling green products.

Although the gift shop is the zoo's most apparent space of consumption, acts of consumption are also scattered throughout the zoo. At the Buffalo Zoo, visitors are invited to buy crackers to feed the elephants for a dollar each and pressed-penny machines are conveniently located at various spots. Additionally, signs posted in numerous places across the zoo declare corporate sponsorships of particular animals and exhibits. For example, Buffalo Exterminators sponsors the otter exhibit, and Time Warner sponsors the two Amur tigers, which are named, accordingly, "Thyme" and "Warner". As in Susan Davis' account of San Diego's theme park, a virtual maze of advertizing, public relations, and entertainment renders this zoo an exhaustively commercial space.[77] Indeed, the zoo is a site of controlled sales of goods (foods and souvenirs) and experiences (architecture, rides, and performances), all themed to fit the zoogoer's image of nature.

Yet the zoo presents the acts of consumption carried out in its space as a higher form of consumerism than those performed elsewhere. "Whatever you spend goes into saving animals", I was told by the employee behind the counter at the Buffalo Zoo's gift shop. Fernandes explains that by supporting the zoo, one indirectly also supports the zoo's conservation efforts. The moral legitimacy of the zoo, and its conservation mission in particular, are thus presented as flowing into the acts of consumption performed there.

Zoogoers are also called upon to consume in more ecologically responsible ways in their daily lives. A sign posted at the Buffalo Zoo's polar bear exhibit advises readers of "10 ways to consume wisely". Similar notions are expressed at the rainforest exhibit. "Be a Rainforest Protector! Doing our part to save rainforests", reads the sign at the entrance: "Buy baskets, jewelry and clothing made by native groups living in and around rainforests. By earning money this way they can stop cutting down the rainforest for fuel or crops.... Refuse to buy anything made from old-growth rainforest woods.... Cross off foods made with palm oil...."

The product offered by the zoo is nature itself. This way, zoo consumption is distinguished from shopping at the mall. According to commonplaces of Western culture, nature denotes a sphere of authenticity and purity that stands in stark contrast with contemporary consumer society. As a place of nature, then, the zoo represents the anti-commercial world outside the marketplace.[78] Perhaps in an attempt to bridge these two contrasting notions—of recreational consumption, on the one hand, and of an anti-commercial nature, on the other hand—acts of consumption performed in this space are configured as acts of virtue. More than merely selling a product, the zoo also sells the ideal of conservation. "Buy a panda bear, save a panda bear", is the zoo's implicit message. As Jennifer Price argues in *Uncommon Ground*, shopping for nature commodities is a safe way to express environmental concerns within the familiar satisfactions of consumerism, even while this activity may dampen awareness of the environmentally exploitive aspects of mass consumption itself.[79]

The zoo, then, is not only a space for encountering nature; it is also a place for consuming nature. Brown and Stern have contended that, more than any other contemporary social institution, marketing—with its boundless ability to invent imaginary worlds of perfect appearances—is the keeper of the late twentieth century utopian flame.[80] One might even claim that the consumerist aspects of the zoo already turn it into a utopian space, in the most elementary sense that marketing builds on the desire for a better future. But the zoo is also utopian in the particular consumer experience it offers. Unlike in many other places of consumption, here the act of consuming is made to seem responsible. By buying, one is necessarily participating in building a better world, as zoo professionals imagine it: a world of biodiverse habitat filled with wild animals. In this world of the future, responsible and green choices govern commercial decisions.

For many utopians, however, commercial life in all its forms comprises the complete antithesis of the utopian ideal. Twentieth century consumerism has been referred to as "McTopia", and, as such, depicted in nightmarish terms.[81] Indeed, many commentators consider the twentieth century in general, and the late twentieth century in particular, to be characterized by a wholesale retreat from utopia, creating a mood of dystopian negativity. Dystopias, anti-utopias, counter-utopias, kakotopias, and sub-topias, comprise a complete inversion, a sort of grotesque mirror image, of the paradisiacal original.[82] Such imagined societies are invariably desolate, terrifying, hostile, barbaric, and pessimistic. They relocate utopia from a point in time to a point in space, thus abandoning the high modernist notion of a future paradise.[83]

Equally dystopian imagery informs the apocalyptic message delivered at the zoo. If we continue to destroy habitat and to kill animals at such alarming rates, so goes the zoo narrative, our children will no longer be able to experience anything even remotely related to the wild. This grand apocalyptic narrative legitimizes the zoo's animal exhibits and its breeding operations. But in the midst of such dystopia—the death of nature, if you will—a utopian message also emerges: there are still ways to save this planet through acts of responsible consumption. In the modern zoological garden, then, utopia and dystopia go hand-in-hand, undermining while also balancing and necessitating each other.

UTOPIA OR APOCALYPSE? THE ZOO AND THE FUTURE OF NATURE

With so many imaginative variations on the theme of animals, do we really need real ones?[84]

This essay adopted the term "zootopia" to refer to the overall manifestations of both utopia and dystopia at the zoo. I have identified three main ways through which zootopia is performed. The first is naturalization. Nature at the zoo is hardly a simulacrum of wild nature. Instead, the zoo designs a sanitized nature, in which certain relationships exist while others are made invisible, and in which humans and animals may appear to live in harmony. It is also an image of a geographically specific nature, mapped and controlled, where the visitor can immerse herself without danger.

At the same time, the zoo presents an ordered nature. Here, the urge for the rational classification of the world is highlighted, fitting the utopian image of the ideal city. The extensive listing of animals and plants, as well as the distinction between domesticated and wild animals, demonstrate the zoo's project of classifying animals. With increasingly elaborate models of database management developed recently by zoo professionals, and the ZIMS database in particular, taxonomic, genomic, and demographic classifications of zoo animals serve to further the zoo's preservation ideals. The zoo, then, has moved beyond the scientific management of information about animals into the realm of selective breeding, which in turn shapes the face of present and future nature.

Finally, as a space of consumption and a site of urban recreation, the zoo strongly participates in what some have called "McTopia". Yet beyond this relatively traditional role of consumption, the zoo presents the act of buying as an act of redemption, a step toward constructing a better world. Simultaneously, the zoo project conveys a dystopian warning and an almost sacred apocalyptic message. If the zoo fails to represent this nature and put it into order, if humans will not consume responsibly, and if the human/nature relationship will not change radically—so the zoo narrative goes—we will soon witness the end of nature as we know it. Zootopia is thus at once both 'the good place' and 'the bad place', evoking utopian hopes and dystopian fears in equal measure.

Notes

1. Kumar, Krishan, *Utopianism*, Minneapolis: University of Minnesota Press, 1991.

2. Capps, Donald, "Melancholia, Utopia, and the Psychoanalysis of Dreams", *The Blackwell Companion to Sociology of Religion*, Richard K. Fenn ed., Malden, MA: Blackwell, 2001, p. 96.
3. See Raymond Williams, *The Country and the City*, Oxford: Oxford University Press, 1973; John Berger, "Why Look at Animals?", *About Looking*, New York: Vintage International, 1989; and Kate Soper, *What is Nature? Culture, Politics and the Non-Human*, Oxford: Blackwell, 1995.
4. See Chris Philo, "Animals, geography, and the city: Note on inclusions and exclusions," *Environment and Planning D: Society and Space*, vol. 13, no. 6, 1995, pp. 655–681 as well as Thomas Birch, "The incarceration of wildness: wilderness areas as prisons", *Environmental Ethics*, vol. 12, no. 1, 1990, pp. 3–26.
5. Willis, Susan, "Looking at the Zoo", *The South Atlantic Quarterly*, vol. 98, no. 4, 1999, p. 617.
6. Aldridge, Alan, *Consumption*, Cambridge: Polity Press, 2003, p. 53.
7. See Bill McKibben, *The End of Nature*, New York: Random House, 2006.
8. This essay relies on interviews and observations conducted at the Buffalo Zoo in New York between 2009 and 2010. More generally, I rely on 55 open-ended, semi-structured interviews conducted between May 2009 and November 2010 with zoo professionals from a range of American zoos. I quote directly from 11 of these interviews.
9. Hanson, Elizabeth, *Animal Attractions: Nature on Display in American Zoos*, Princeton: Princeton University Press, 2002, p. 186.
10. *Methodical Encyclopaedia* (1782) quoted in "Menagerie", *Wikipedia*, http://en.wikipedia.org/wiki/Menagerie.
11. Zuckerman, Solly, *Great Zoos of the World: Their Origins and Significance*, Boulder, CO: Westview Press, 1980; interview with Paul Harpley, Manager, Interpretation, Culture & Design, Toronto Zoo, Toronto, Canada, 17 June 2009.
12. Mullan, Robert and Garry Marvin, *Zoo Culture*, Illinois: University of Illinois Press, 1999, p. xiii.
13. Baratay, Eric and Elisabeth Hardouin-Fugier, *A History of Zoological Gardens in the West*, London: Reaktion Books, 2002, p. 263.
14. See "Hagenbeck Zoo", *Zoo and Aquarium Visitor*, 2009. http://www.zandavisitor.com/forumtopicdetail-411-Hagenbeck_Tierpark_und_Tropen-Aquarium-Zoos.
15. Veltre, Thomas, "Menageries, Metaphors, and Meanings", *New Worlds, New Animals: From Menagerie to Zoological Park in the Nineteenth Century*, R. J. Hoage and William Deiss eds., Baltimore: Johns Hopkins University Press, 1996, p. 22.
16. See Hanson, *Animal Attractions*.
17. Hanson, *Animal Attractions*, p. 2.
18. Hanson, *Animal Attractions*, p. 2.
19. Hanson, *Animal Attractions*, p. 24.
20. Hanson, *Animal Attractions*, p. 24.
21. Kisling, Vernon, *Zoo and Aquarium History: Ancient Animal Collections to Zoological Gardens*, Boca Raton, FL: CRC Press, 2000.
22. Hansen, *Animal Attractions*, p. 2.
23. Anderson, K., "Culture and Nature at the Adelaide Zoo: At the Frontiers of 'Human' Geography", *Transactions of the Institute of British Geographers*, vol. 20, no. 3, September 1995, p. 279.
24. Interview with Jim Breheny, SVP Living Institutions and Current Director of Bronx Zoo, New York, 15 July 2009.
25. Interview with Susan Chin, Vice President of Planning and Design, and Chief Architect of Exhibition and Graphic Arts Department, Bronx Zoo, New York, 17 July 2009.
26. Sargent, Lyman Tower, "The Three Faces of Utopianism Revisited", *Utopian Studies*, vol. 5, no. 1, 1994, p. 28.
27. See Polaszek, Andrew, *Systema Naturae 250: The Linnaean Ark*, Boca Raton, FL: CRC Press, 2010, p. 6.
28. Coe, Jon, "Trends in Exhibition", *Jon Coe Design Pty Ltd.*, 2009, http://www.joncoedesign.com/trends/exhibit_trends.htm#immersion.
29. Coe, "Trends in Exhibition"; see also Hanson, *Animal Attractions*, 160.
30. Interview with Jim Breheny, 15 July 2009.
31. "What is an Immersion Exhibit", *St. Louis Zoo*, http://www.stlzoo.org/yourvisit/thingstoseeandde/riversedge/immersion.
32. Interview with Susan Chin, 17 July 2009.
33. Interview with Jim Breheny, 15 July 2009.
34. Interview with Gwen Howard, Buffalo Zoo, Buffalo, New York, 31 July 2009.
35. Interview with Cindy Lee, Curator of Fishes, Toronto Zoo, Toronto, Canada, 17 June 2009.
36. Shephard, Paul, *Thinking Animals: Animals and the Development of Human Intelligence*, Athens, GA: University of Georgia Press, 1998, p. 248.
37. Interview with Lee Ehmke, Director, Minnesota Zoo and Former Director of Design at Bronx Zoo, 21 & 22 July 2009.
38. Ludwig, E. G., "People at Zoos: A Sociological Approach", *International Journal for the Study of Animal Problems*, vol. 2, no. 6, 1981, p. 316.
39. Mullan and Marvin, *Zoo Culture*, p. 54.
40. Mullan and Marvin, *Zoo Culture*, p. 52.
41. Interview with Jim Breheny, 15 July 2009.
42. Interview with Lee Ehmke, 21–22 July 2009.
43. Smith, Neil, *Uneven Development: Nature, Capital and the Production of Space*, Oxford: Blackwell, 1984.
44. Interview with Paul Harpley, 17 June 2009.
45. Berger, "Why Look at Animals?"
46 Brown, James, Theodore Brown, and Mark Lomolino, *Biogeography*, 2nd ed., Sunderland, MA: Sinauer Associates, 1998; Interview with Paul Harpley, 17 June 2009.
47. See Alexander Wilson, *The Culture of Nature: North American Landscape from Disney to the Exxon Valdez*, Cambridge, MA: Blackwell, 1992; Anderson, "Culture and Nature at the Adelaide Zoo", p. 282; and Scott Montgomery, "The Zoo: Theatre of the Animals", *Science as Culture*, vol. 4, no. 21, 1995.
48. Bennett, Tony, "The Exhibitionary Complex", *New Formations*, no. 4, Spring 1988, p. 97.
49. Montgomery, "The Zoo: Theatre of the Animals", p. 589.
50. Anderson, "Culture and Nature at the Adelaide Zoo".
51. Morris, Desmond, *The Human Zoo*, New York: McGraw Hill, 1969.
52. Baratay and Hardouin-Fugier, *A History of Zoological Gardens in the West*, p. 224.
53. Bowker, Geoffrey and Susan Star, *Sorting Things Out: Classification and Its Consequences*, Cambridge, MA: MIT Press, 1999, p. 17.
54. Bowker and Star, *Sorting Things Out*, p. 10; See also Bowker and Star's discussion in "There's No Such Thing As a Rodent", p. 45.
55. Interview with Donna Fernandes, Director, Buffalo Zoo, Buffalo, New York, 8 May 2009.

56. E-mail exchange with Donna Fernandes, 7 October 2010.
57. Wilson, Edward, *Biophilia*, Cambridge, MA: Harvard University Press, 1984.
58. Interview with Donna Fernandes, 8 May 2009.
59. See *International Species Information System*, http://www.isis.org/Pages/zims.aspx.
60. Dubois, Sue, Kevin Johnson, and Brandie Smith, "Building Better Information Systems for Zoos and Aquariums", *The Zims Project*, 2002, http://www.iadisc.org/reports/building_better_info_systems.htm.
61. Interview with Jean Miller, Registrar, Buffalo Zoo, Buffalo, New York, 5 and 13 June 2009.
62. Braverman, Irus, *The Institution of Captivity: Governing Zoo Animals in North America*, Stanford University Press, forthcoming.
63. See "Population Management Center", *Association of Zoos and Aquariums*, http://www.aza.org/population-management-center/.
64. Interview with Jean Miller, Registrar, Buffalo Zoo, Buffalo, New York, 5 and 13 June 2009.
65. Braverman, Irus, "States of Exemption: The Legal and Animal Geographies of American Zoos," *Environment and Planning A*, vol. 43, number 7, 2011, p. 1693.
66. Interview with Robert Wiese, Chair, AZA Task Force on Sustainability, 9 November 2010; Interview with Paul Boyle, AZA Animal Programs, 24 November 2010.
67. See Robert Wilson, *Species: New Interdisciplinary Essays*, Cambridge, MA: MIT Press, 1999.
68. Balmford, Andrew, GM Mace, and N. Leader-Williams, "Designing the Ark: Setting Priorities for Captive Breeding", *Conservation Biology*, vol. 10, no. 3, 1996.
69. Marešová, Jana and Daniel Frynta, "Noah's Ark is Full of Common Species Attractive to Humans: The Case of Boid Snakes in Zoos", *Ecological Economics*, vol. 64, no.3, 2008, pp. 554–558.
70. Conway, William, "The Role of Zoos in the 21st Century", *International Zoo Yearbook*, vol. 38, no. 1, 2003, p. 11; Interview with William Conway, Former Director of Bronx Zoo, New York, 14 July 2009.
71. Balmford, Mace, and Leader-Williams, "Designing the Ark".
72. Snyder, Noel, Scott Derrickson, Steven Beissinger, et al., "Limitations of Captive Breeding: Reply to Gippoliti and Carpaneto", *Conservation Biology*, vol. 11, no. 3, 1997, pp. 808–810.
73. Balmford, Mace, and Leader-Williams, "Designing the Ark".
74. Braverman, "The Institution of Captivity".
75. Ritvo, Harriet, "Possessing Mother Nature: Genetic Capital in Eighteenth-Century Britain", *Early Modern Conceptions of Property*, Susan Staves and John Brewer eds., London: Routledge, 1995, p. 424. See also Vicki Hearne, *Adam's Task: Calling Animals by Name*, New York: Skyhorse Publishing, 2007.
76. Interview with Donna Fernandes, 30 September 2010.
77. Davis, Susan, *Spectacular Nature: Corporate Culture and the Sea World Experience*, Berkeley: University of California Press, 1997.
78. Davis, *Spectacular Nature*, p. 8.
79. Price, Jennifer, "Looking for Nature at the Mall: A Field Guide to the Nature Company", *Uncommon Ground: Rethinking the Human Place in Nature*, William Cronon ed., New York: W. W. Norton and Company, 1995, pp. 186–203.
80. Brown, Stephen, Pauline Maclaren, and Lorna Stevens, "Marcadia Postponed: Marketing, Utopia and the Millenium", *Journal of Marketing Management*, vol. 12, 1996, p. 676.
81. Brown, Maclaren, and Stevens, "Marcadia Postponed", p. 675.
82. Kumar, *Utopianism*; Brown, Maclaren, and Stevens, "Marcadia Postponed", p. 673.
83. Brown, Maclaren, and Stevens, "Marcadia Postponed", p. 674.
84. Willis, "Looking at the Zoo", p. 70.

COMEDIES OF SURPLUS: REPRESENTING THE GARDEN IN CONTEMPORARY AMERICAN LITERATURE

/JENNIFER ATKINSON

If you say "gardening" to someone familiar with horticultural publications—or even literary fiction in which gardens appear—it is unlikely that radical politics and revolutionary agendas will immediately come to mind. Gardening, after all, is something many of us do to *escape* the messy, exhausting, and often bitter worlds of political struggle and social strife. Jamaica Kincaid learned this lesson some years back during her lecture at a prominent garden-conservatory, where audience members attacked her for focusing on political history and race relations in Southern gardening practice.[1] While the intensity of their response seems unwarranted, their reluctance to turn from talk of soil and seeds to political issues is hardly surprising. Many enthusiasts are so accustomed to thinking of the garden as a refuge from life's shocks and setbacks—from injustice, disappointment, or simply the routine pressures and frustrations of everyday life—that they find something almost perverse about dragging our social and political baggage into this small utopian haven.

Yet this association of gardens with the escapist and apolitical goes beyond mere personal justifications for puttering around in the flower beds; it pervades a good deal of Western literature as well, even appearing in texts that have nothing, ostensibly, to do with garden matters *per se*. The famous final lines of Voltaire's *Candide*, of course, express the desire to stay at home and "cultivate our garden"—a resolution that effectively releases the story's characters from reformist efforts. That equation of the garden with retreat was also familiar to those of George Orwell's readers who sent angry letters shaming him for keeping a rose garden—an activity, as one put it, that "encourages a sort of political quietism".[2] It is precisely this cultural association that allows us to 'get' the humor and absurdity of a novel like Jerzy Kosinski's *Being There* (along with its 1979 filmic adaptation), where a *gardener* unwittingly finds himself at the hub of American politics, and then accidentally becomes a presidential advisor. In *The Constant Gardener*, John le Carré similarly uses gardening as a device to signal the deactivation of political impulses. The story's heroine, a social-justice activist decidedly more concerned with saving *people* than tending her neglected and under-watered houseplants, uncovers a pharmaceutical conspiracy of global proportions; meanwhile, her unwitting doormat of a husband (the appropriately named Jason "Quayle") tinkers away in his plot of rose bushes, oblivious to the political corruption intensifying the poverty and exploitation of people in Africa. Scholars also play off this association, whether examining gardens in the historical novel that "articulate [the] desire for withdrawal from civil strife",[3] or arguing, as historian Keith Thomas does, that the "preoccupation with gardening" may help "explain the relative lack of radical and political impulses among the British proletariat".[4] In any random sample of English or American literature and popular media, the formula is repeated again and again; from outdoor catalogues and horticultural journals, to advertising copy and fiction in which the garden makes a mere cameo, the connection appears ubiquitous enough to warrant its own archive.[5] And sure enough, if readers skim the index of Martin Hoyles' horticultural history, *The Story of Gardening*, they will find the following entry: "Politics, incompatible with gardening".[6]

The formulation may, in part, have origins in the link between paradise and the restful garden as imagined in many world religions—as well as in secular counterparts like Thomas More's *Utopia*.[7] Here, despite being an ideal setting for dreamy fantasies of the good life, the garden did not necessarily belong within more explicitly political strains of utopianism that challenge and critique the dominant structure—let alone those aimed at overturning it.

Yet as common as it is, the trope of the escapist garden is not without rival concepts. In fact, we find this formula turned upside down in a significant number of American literary texts and artworks—in projects like *Oxygen Bar*, for example, a 2005 installation by Chicago artist Laurie Palmer that featured a miniature garden housed within a "mobile breathing machine" [Figure 1]. This interactive device—one of two that plied the streets of Pittsburgh—included oxygen masks through which the public could breathe air produced by the plants' photosynthetic work and thereby participate in an exchange dramatizing the intimate relation between plant and human life. Yet on closer inspection, *Oxygen Bar* presented more than a simple reminder of our dependence on kingdom *Plantae*; its tiny garden also staged an indictment of neoliberalism's commodity logic and resource privatization schemes. As the plants went quietly about their work, converting light into oxygen and organic matter, the public read a message stenciled in bold letters across the installation's face: "FREE". On one level, of course, the statement summarizes a basic fact of photosynthesis, which supplies terrestrial life with an essential source of energy at no apparent cost. Yet at the same time, the text also parodies free-sample promotional schemes that stimulate interest in new products by offering complementary samples to potential consumers. And so, in simply pairing garden life with an everyday emblem of market-based economics, Palmer's installation raises a profound set of questions about our current biopolitical predicament: with all of human life dependent on the products of plants' work (as producers of both food and oxygen), how are justifications constructed for privatizing, commodifying, or withholding any of the myriad products they generate? What are the implications for life when the commodity principle comes to subsume our most fundamental relations to nature?[8]

Figure 1/ *Oxygen Bar*.
Photograph courtesy of Laurie Palmer.

Such questions appear all the more relevant when one considers the production history of *Oxygen Bar*.[9] The plants it housed were gathered from a wooded site near Pittsburgh that had been singled out for real estate development, launching yet another debate in the ongoing saga of land and natural resource privatization. In light of this history, Palmer's installation may have prompted its audience to imagine the commodification of our air supply as the next (and, arguably, the ultimate) phase in the privatization of our planet's resources.

So much for the apolitical garden.

I include the case of *Oxygen Bar* because it provides a useful index for the extent to which critical—and explicitly political—garden tropes increasingly appear in American culture. While it is true that presumptions about gardening's escapist nature remain legion, one can also find an ever-growing number of writers, artists, and gardeners who frame horticulture as a kind of utopian *praxis*: from growers' cooperatives that challenge the ascendancy of corporate agribusiness; to bands of 'guerilla gardeners' who fight for open space and squatters' rights in the city; to urban farmers who are hauled away in handcuffs for violating the private property rule; to utopian manifestos like Peter Lamborn Wilson's "Avant Gardening", which frames the planting of tomatoes and turnips as an outright act of rebellion.[10]

These more progressive modes of garden imagination are not entirely new in Western literature and thought; indeed, many of them draw on ideas about cultivation that can be traced back to the writings of John Locke and earlier texts. Yet this political strain in garden writing has gained increasing traction in recent decades within the context of growing environmental crisis, the globalization of corporate-industrial agribusiness, and the emergence of oppositional movements involving agrarian elements and DIY practice.

Some of the most compelling instances of the changing meaning surrounding the garden can be found in twentieth and twenty-first century American literature—the focus of the present essay—where gardens function as a tool for reimagining problems of waste, value, and surplus. From Richard Powers' novels to essays by popular garden writers like Michael Pollan and Ruth Stout, these works use gardens to challenge—even present figurative alternatives to—the commodity logic dominating our everyday experience in late capitalism. These texts embody the premise of Palmer's

Oxygen Bar by foregrounding the 'free' nature of gardening's most basic process, thus calling into question the laws of capitalist exchange that may otherwise appear as the natural order of our world. Our daily economic and environmental experience, after all, is largely structured by arrangements where every form of 'increase' requires a parallel act of subtraction. Such trade-offs may even be said to embody the structural condition of capitalism itself, where the wealth and privilege of one class are secured through the reciprocal impoverishment of another; where more industrial production means less biodiversity, and each uptick in consumption exacts some new ecological price; where gains in personal and state security for the West frequently mean more vulnerability for those in the developing world; and where 'cheap' oil translates into tremendous costs for our atmosphere, oceans, and other habitats.

Yet against such 'zero-sum' relations, the gardening practices depicted by writers like Powers, Pollan, and Stout stand out as a unique model for the 'net gain' in contemporary life. Generating new value without depleting it from somewhere or someone else in the world, the garden presents a template for non-parasitic increase that disrupts the seeming inevitability of capitalism's subtraction-based accounting. And in so doing, this figure allows writers, artists, and activists to pry open the doors to a wider zone of utopian counter-imagining, one positioned squarely in the midst of everyday life.

These progressive strains of garden representation compel us to question the thinking of those growers who prefer to imagine their activity as untainted by politics, along with any such appraisal of the garden as a zone from which economic debate, environmental controversy, class struggle, and other forms of political agitation can be shut out. Indeed, to the extraordinary extent that gardens magnetize the efforts and fascination of growers and writers, they reveal a broader structure of desire that touches on the very matters we supposedly sidestep in the act of coming to these plots. As the following essay will show, gardening has an uncanny way of throwing into relief a network of social concerns left unaddressed—and personal desires left ungratified—in other spheres of everyday life. In fact, several cases I examine here do not consciously set out to address gardens at all; their explicit subject may instead lie with the way people work and recreate, manage money, envision waste and value, or merely survive the day in the early twenty-first century. In the process, however, these authors come to draw on the meanings and mechanisms of cultivation, and project into the garden's midst their desires for less alienated forms of work, a different pacing of everyday life, less fragmented and instrumentalized relations to place, and an alternative way of imagining and ascribing value to the things that constitute our built and natural environment. In this way, the reciprocal transactions and encounters in cultivated space open new vistas for utopian studies, as well as for political and aesthetic projects that may initially seem remote from the world of roses and radishes.

. . .

While all of this may seem like an overblown way to frame the meaning and utopian possibility embedded in a patch of dirt with plants, consider how powerful the mechanics of natural increase appear when situated against the history of industrialism in Richard Powers' novel *Gain*, 1998. In this work, the garden's economy effectively overturns the logic of capitalist accounting that otherwise frames the story, because the garden generates value without creating zones of depletion or loss in the process. *Gain* presents this dialectic at the structural level itself, exemplifying our society's zero-sum arrangement through a double-helix narrative that alternates between two stories: on the one hand, the spectacular two-hundred-year rise of Clare Chemical Company, which comes to dominate the chemical industry on an international scale, and on the other hand, the present-day demise of a small-town woman, Laura Bodey, who develops cancer in her early 40s.[11] While the two accounts are separated by a substantial period of time, we ultimately perceive them as fatally connected. Not only does Laura live in the shadow of one of Clare's chemical plants; she also fills her life with a bewildering array of the consumer products it manufactures—from household cleaners and insecticides to skin creams, home perms, and soap. The braided stories allow Powers to present the 'costs' or 'externalities' accompanying economic progress in advanced capitalist societies.[12] With the zero-sum mechanism presiding over *Gain*'s double narrative, characters fatalistically assume the sacrifice of human lives and nature's well-being to be inherent to the advancement of American business—from the founding days of Clare Chemical, where industrialists escaped prosecution for fatal factory explosions "on the grounds that their works had done more cumulative good than harm",[13] to Laura's present-day attempt to reconcile herself to her impending death by focusing on the blessings that have accrued from the very industrialization that caused her cancer.[14] As she is ravaged by the disease, Laura feebly reminds herself that one must ultimately "pay the check for the meal you've eaten".[15]

Yet as the gains depicted in the corporate narrative feed off the life at the center of Laura Bodey's portion of the novel, two counter-figures point beyond the seeming inevitability of this subtraction-based arrangement. The first emerges in the story of Clare Chemical Company's origins as a producer of common household soap. Both the economic and molecular attributes of this product constitute a net gain in the wider economy of life, for soap is made when substances without discernible use or value—waste fats and ashes—are turned into waste's immaculate 'other': soap, in other words, is "[d]irt's duckling transformed to salve's swan, its rancid nosegay rearranged into aromatic garland".[16]

Laura Bodey's story has its own analog to this simple yet miraculous bar of soap and the waste-converting chemistry that produces it: here, the alchemical possibility of 'gain' is embodied by the garden, Powers' second counter-figure to the zero sum model. The present-day narrative opens with an image of the sun, which philosopher Georges Bataille has described as an embodiment of "ceaseless prodigality", something that "dispenses energy—wealth—without any return".[17] Laura marvels at the sun's ability to "lift new growth from out of nothing": to draw value from this solar economy, she has only to coax each plant in her garden to "catch a teacupful of the two calories per cubic centimeter that the sun, in its improvident abundance, spills forever on the Earth for no good reason except that it knew we were coming".[18] And so in the midst of a life-depleting (yet stupendously profitable) late twentieth century corporate business world, Laura's solar-powered garden, like the Clare brothers' original bar of soap, presents a decided exception to the gain-loss relations structuring the rest of the story. In short, it becomes a living prototype for non-parasitic increase.

In the context of Powers' historically-embedded portrait of the expansion of corporate capitalism, this rendering of Laura's transaction with nature summarizes the very gestalt of those modes of representation aimed at reinventing what gardening might mean. Far from suspending history, politics, and economics, the garden can become a central arena within which to challenge our existing economic system. Powers' treatment of the garden directs the reader's attention to an alternative form of exchange based on broadly dispersed, exponential increase—a form of increase whose mechanisms do not presume the necessity of depleting one party in order to enrich another.

Figure 2/ Pumpkin grown by James Gerhardt, Mertztown, Pennsylvania. Photograph courtesy of David Bednarski.

In this, Powers does not so much invent as *reaffirm* an idea that has grown increasingly prominent in American literature. The genre of garden writing proper, for instance, wanders with remarkable frequency into the very territory Powers explores, as the grower's conventional understandings of cost/gain mechanics are overturned by his or her experience working the soil. In a historical moment heavy with the sense that we live in an unreplenishable, entropic world, Michael Pollan imagines himself stumbling across a unique instance of the 'net gain' one afternoon in the form of a homely squash. Having been overlooked earlier that summer, the squash has quietly morphed into a 30 pound colossus, and when Pollan at last uncovers it beneath the tangle of vines and leaves he finds himself wondering:

> Where did this thing, this great quantity of squash flesh come from? From earth, we say, but not *really*; there's no less earth here now than there was in May when I planted it; none's been used up in its making. By all rights creating something this fat should require so great an expense of matter that you'd expect to find Sibley squashes perched on the lips of fresh craters. That they're not, it seems to me, should be counted as something of a miracle.[19]

In short, the process of garden cultivation allows Pollan to discover an extraordinary phenomenon: up to this moment he has reflexively imagined gardening to be like any other form of production in a world ruled by market forces, where—unless one replenishes the materials or value used up in the process of creation—one inevitably leaves behind less of whatever existed prior to that transaction. Pollan, in other words, embarks on his project conditioned by the assumption that enrichment will require some element of subtraction. And yet in his garden, only a negligible amount of value (in the form of minerals) is consumed to bring this massive squash into being. Moreover, as Pollan explains, were he to leave his squash to decay where he finds it, "there would actually be a surplus in the garden's accounts; the soil would be both richer in nutrients and greater in total mass than it was before I planted it". Admittedly, much of the increase generated here comes from water; and yet as Pollan reflects, "considered from the vantage of the entire planet's economy of matter, [the squash] represents a net gain. It is, in other words, a gift" [Figure 2].[20]

. . .

Many would regard the transformations depicted in Pollan's and Powers' gardens—and found in any garden, for that matter—as wondrous in their own right. And yet, to understand the full force of the garden's cultural appeal—

along with its implications for utopian thinking—one must also consider gardening's great counter-figure of capitalist agriculture, a practice that produces value by sapping the resources of both workers and nature. Indeed, while garden enthusiasts like Pollan celebrate their activity as the wellspring of a broadly dispersed, exponential increase, critics have long indicted the complicity of corporate agriculture with the extractive and subtraction-based accounting of capitalism itself.[21] Karl Marx, for instance, described the market system and agriculture in ways that are nearly interchangeable: the latter, as he explains, violates every principle we might associate with a "conscious and rational treatment of the land as permanent communal property, as the inalienable condition for the existence and reproduction of the chain of human generations". In *Capital*, he depicted commercial farming as a practice that nurtures the growth of predatory market systems rather than of life as such, "exploit[ing] and... squandering... the powers of the earth" and "the vitality of the soil". Conversely, Marx's definition of capitalism itself reads something like a sketch of imprudent farming: in a frequently-quoted passage, he wrote that capitalism develops "only by sapping the original sources of all wealth—the soil and the laborer".[22]

Classic twentieth century critiques of the American farm system—perhaps best exemplified in the works of John Steinbeck and James Agee—add yet another dimension to this critical tradition by appraising one of history's most misguided horticultural experiments: the cross-breeding of industrial capitalism with nature's reproductive principles. *The Grapes of Wrath*, as most readers remember, dramatizes the tragic results of our attempt to make nature's cycles conform to those of the market. When agricultural prices fall, Steinbeck's landowners must prop them up by destroying the fruits of their orchards and fields. Nature's ability to survive drought or frost cannot protect it from an inauspicious financial climate—a force sufficiently powerful to devastate California's otherwise plentiful growing season. Thus in one of the most memorable scenes of the novel, growers spray kerosene over mountains of perfect oranges while hungry workers look on.[23]

Although the crops grow abundantly, and both labor and the means of production are available in excess to meet existing need, what counts is that the commodity is not sufficiently valued in the current market to produce a desired rate of profit. Industrial agriculture thus stands in for the madness and waste of capitalism itself: "Men who have created fruits in the world cannot create a system whereby their fruits may be eaten", writes Steinbeck; this is a failure "that topples all our success", and culminates in the absurd arrangement where children die of pellagra "because a profit cannot be taken from an orange".[24]

While Steinbeck's sketch of capitalist agriculture focuses upon starvation amid surplus, journalist James Agee presents an inverted farm system by staging scenes of humans consumed by crops, and of dehumanized laborers serving the needs of deified commodities. In his portrait of Southern cotton cultivation, a plant that sharecroppers "cannot eat" nonetheless demands the "greatest expense of strength and spirit" from growers, and even assumes a total power over their lives—a power precisely the opposite of the life-giving powers of food crops celebrated in gardening accounts. Rather than giving sustenance, this paradigmatic capitalist crop, vampire-like, drains the life force directly from its growers. And in the process, cotton cultivation comes to embody the very "doubleness" characterizing "all jobs... by which one stays alive and in which one's life is made a cheated ruin" [Figure 3].[25]

This is the story of American farming as Agee tells it. Commercial agriculture develops the natural conditions of production precisely by "tearing them away from the individual independent labourer", causing nature and science to undergo the very mutation that Marx predicted within an industrial model: these now return to "confront the individual labourers... as something *extraneous* and *objective*", as forces that are "independent of them and control them".[26] The result is the creation of a class of growers who must feel toward the cotton crop and

> toward each plant in it, toward all that work, ... a particular automatism, a quiet, apathetic, and inarticulate yet deeply vindictive hatred, and at the same time utter hopelessness, and the deepest of their anxieties and of their hopes: as if the plant stood enormous in the unsteady sky fastened above them in all they do like the eyes of an overseer.[27]

The paradox characterizing these scenes of starvation and servitude among surplus helps us see why gardening's mechanisms of increase have assumed such extraordinary traction in American literature. As progressive and socialist critiques of the farm reveal the waste and contradiction inherent in systems designed for producing exchange value, they create an opening for the gardening genre to reappropriate and entirely reimagine the notion of 'crises of overproduction'. Within the horticultural sphere, agribusiness' tragedy of waste becomes the gardener's comedy of surplus; here in the garden plot, where market values do not trump all other values and considerations, the grower's dilemma commonly revolves around how to *distribute* outrageous surplus among those not similarly oversupplied.

Gardening books like Ruth Stout's *How to Have a Green Thumb*, 1955—a work that is part instructional tract and part comedic memoir—typify this preoccupation with the problem of managing excess: in marked contrast to Steinbeck's landowners, who battle nature's surfeit with kerosene, Stout launches a campaign to *integrate* the exuberance of her garden into the collective metabolism of her community of family and friends. Like many

Figure 3/ *Bud Fields Standing in Cotton.*
Walker Evans, gelatin silver print, 1936. Courtesy of the Harry Ransom Humanities Research Center, The University of Texas at Austin.

Figure 4/ Free Veggies: Comedy of Surplus.
Block Island, RI. Photograph courtesy of Matthew Ebel.

subsequent horticultural publications, her book is replete with tips and tricks for keeping things from going to waste as the garden's excessive output moves from one seasonal stage to the next. In fact, this emphasis often leaves the impression that Stout spends significantly more time soliciting people to accept her superfluous vegetables than she invests in the garden's cultivation. In one of her more colorful anecdotes, Stout recalls the summer when tomatoes overwhelm the capacity of her own household's metabolism, giving rise to heroic efforts to distribute this surplus before everything rots. To her dismay, Stout discovers her predicament to be common as dirt at this frenzied time of year: neighbors facing the same midsummer dilemma won't accept her goods, and the local produce vendor is virtually buried in a glut of his own. Finally, after several failed attempts and "a good deal of telephoning", Stout reports that she has at last "located the neighbor of a friend who reluctantly consented to accept them *if* we would deliver them. She would make some catsup with them, although she [had] already made more than she wanted" (italics added).[28]

Summer squash, in particular, lends itself to garden writing's mock crisis of overproduction with a unique humor and frequency. Radio personality Garrison Keillor maintains that summer is the only time country people lock their cars in church parking lots, a measure they take to prevent gardeners from leaving zucchinis on the seats. Barbara Kingsolver finds herself on both ends of this horticultural caper in *Animal, Vegetable, Miracle*. Her family resorts to customizing its dinner invitations around guests who will not only eat, but also take home boxes of garden-surplus (i.e. individuals without their own plots); yet one day the tables turn as the author finds sacks of zucchinis from an unknown source hanging on her mailbox: "The perpetrator, of course, was nowhere in sight. 'Wow', we all said—'what a good idea!'" As summer progresses the situation grows critical, and Kingsolver starts securing the perimeter before she leaves to make sure no one can "break in and put zucchinis in our house" [Figure 4].[29]

Yet in many respects, the real significance of these accounts of abundance may not be the mere use of gardens as a device for imagining *alternatives* to the dominant structures epitomized by Powers' chemical corporation or Steinbeck's agricultural empires; even more important, this mode repositions nature's process as *the* fundamental structure of production, and capitalism as the great exception and aberration. In *The Accursed Share*, Georges Bataille challenges the basic tenets of conventional (or "restricted") economic theory, wherein particular operations are "carried out with a view to a limited end, that of economic man". In its place, Bataille proposes a more comprehensive understanding of economy, one foregrounding the fact that "[o]n the surface of the globe, for *living matter in general*, energy is always in excess; the question is always posed in terms of extravagance. The choice is limited to how the wealth is to be squandered." In other words, within the total balance of life's activity, it is "outrageous expenditure" (rather than conservation or scarcity) that constitutes the norm. And while Bataille does not concern himself with gardening *per se*, his meditations on surplus bear an uncanny resemblance to those we find in garden writing; both, ultimately, identify the source of our world's "indefinite exuberance" as the sun.[30] In radiating the Earth's surface with an energetic superabundance that exceeds life's ability to absorb it, the sun not only generates the natural proliferations we see in garden reports from high-summer; it also gives rise to countless forms of social excess, epitomized for Bataille in the lavish gift-giving practice of Native American potlatch—a practice bearing no small resemblance to the episodes depicted throughout our gardening accounts, where Kingsolver's neighbors try to out-zucchini each other, and where Stout, worked into a state of semi-panic, spends her days "dashing about trying to find someone to give [the surplus] to".[31]

Bataille distinguishes such 'non-productive expenditure' from those conventional forms of consumption that are bound to the cycles and mechanics of capitalist production. And here again, the logical overlap with gardening literature is instructive: living organisms, he argues, generally receive more energy than is required for maintaining life, and whatever "energetic remainder" is not used for growth must necessarily be lost, "willingly or not, gloriously or catastrophically".[32] Since this excess demands to be released, we are presented with a choice: either it can be spent luxuriously and deliberately, or—as we see in capitalist regimes based on accumulation—it will periodically erupt in conflagrations of waste and war. In cultivation literature, these two possible outcomes are manifested in the contradiction between capitalist agriculture burning mountains of produce (*à la* Steinbeck), and the quasi-potlatch practices into which Stout and company are thrust.

This split, I would argue, suggests that a significant degree of garden writing's appeal proceeds from the comparatively balanced social outcomes it depicts: with the commodity principle effectively removed from the exchange dynamic, value must be realized in a more collective fashion. In fact, insofar as nature's urgent temporality makes it nearly impossible for a single person to absorb the season's excess by spreading consumption evenly over time, these portraits would seem to imply that the value of garden surplus cannot even be realized *unless* and *until* it is distributed among others. Thus, the meticulously cultivated plants that growers "cannot eat"[33] in Agee's portrait of cotton production take on a radically different meaning in the gardener's economy, where growers like Stout orchestrate distribution schemes to release them from "worry[ing] over what to do with what we couldn't use".[34]

...

Yet the utopian implications pervading these garden episodes ultimately involve more than just whimsical speculations about better forms of resource distribution; moreover, the 'free gifts' they feature animate our fascination for reasons more complex—and more relevant to issues of environmental crisis and utopian thinking—than those I have already laid out. This is because those writers who become seriously engaged with gardening tend to represent it not only as an enterprise that creates *new* value in the world, but also as an arena where one discovers the possibility of generating value from *negative* value. The garden's mechanisms, in other words, do more than just transcend the need to subtract value from one social or environmental sphere in order to enrich other zones; quite often the gardener's process works in the opposite direction altogether, converting noxious and useless elements back into the useful and wholesome. Like the soap in *Gain* that quietly challenges the novel's entire structure of predatory economics, gardens provide an instance and ethos of "waste turned inside out".[35]

As defined in John Scanlan's cultural history, *On Garbage*, waste has traditionally been understood as "what remains when the good, fruitful, valuable, nourishing and useful has been taken"; it includes "the entrails, the bits and scraps, the mountain of indistinguishable stuff that is in its own way affirmed by a resolute dismissal: it is *refuse-d* (not accepted, denied, banished)".[36] Well before Powers and Pollan celebrated their gardens' ability to transform waste into value, a long lineage of American writers had imagined real and fictional gardens as a kind of "counter-waste" technology. Ruth Stout, for instance, expresses frustration with dictionaries for defining "refuse" as "worthless matter" when her own gardening experience has transformed her understanding of these concepts, rendering waste as "something valuable instead of as something worthless".[37] Popular garden-writer Eleanor Perényi inventories a multitude of things routinely tossed out, all of which the compost heap "devour[s]... and return[s] in a form that is priceless while costing nothing".[38] Nineteenth century author Charles Dudley Warner reflects that, despite our practice of burying "decay in the earth" and feeding it with "offensive refuse", "nothing grows out of it that is not clean; it gives us back life and beauty for our rubbish".[39] And prefiguring all of these, Walt Whitman's poem "This Compost", 1855, recognizes soil as a medium that "grows such sweet things out of such corruptions". After Whitman calculates the negative values "deposited" into the earth—rot, excrement, and whole generations of "distemper'd corpses"—he demands a fuller accounting of the bio-economy at work here: "how can it be that the ground itself does not sicken?" "What chemistry!" he exclaims,

> That all is clean forever and forever,
> That the cool drink from the well tastes so good,
> That blackberries are so flavorous and juicy,
> That the fruits of the apple-orchard and the orange-orchard, that melons, grapes, peaches, plums, will none of them poison me,
> That when I recline on the grass I do not catch any disease,
> Though probably every spear of grass rises out of what was once catching disease.[40]

This economy of transmutation allows writers like Pollan to see the garden's products as tokens of "entropy undone", providing a culture conditioned by zero-sum ideologies with "reason enough to garden". "Living as we do in the autumn of a millennium", Pollan reflects, "and feeling somehow that we've come very late into this world, this strikes me as the harvest's most salutary teaching.... Here in my garden the second law of thermodynamics is repealed."[41]

Such reflections highlight the profound manner in which gardens have shaped some of our most fundamental notions of value and waste. Many of the oldest Western constructions involving 'wasteland' versus 'good land' drew on cultivation practices to secure their distinctions. In Old and Middle English the term "waste" indicated an environment that was "unsuitable to sustain human habitation", and the

equivalents that eventually replaced it in English—"desert" and "wilderness"—came to serve as inverse symbols to the garden across a wide spectrum of religious beliefs, mythologies, and cultures.[42] John Locke brought this antinomy to bear on the question of property in the *Second Treatise of Government*, where he elaborated on the wastefulness of soil left uncultivated: "Land that is left wholly to nature, that hath no improvement of pasturage, tillage, or planting, is called, as indeed it is, *waste*; and we shall find the benefit of it amount to little more than nothing."[43]

Here, Locke's use of "waste" points us toward a second tier of meaning: not simply a remainder or refused part, as Scanlan describes it, but rather a failure to maximize potential or to use a thing in the best way. This meaning pertains not only to things and places, but also to human ability, talents, and capacities ('wasted potential', a 'wasted mind', a 'wasted life'). In these earlier uses, "waste" thus stood decidedly against the garden—and against cultivation more precisely. As Raymond Williams explains in *Keywords*, in its earliest use, the term "culture" operated as "a noun of process: the tending of something, basically crops or animals".[44] Beginning in the early sixteenth century, "cultivation" came to refer to the process of human improvement as well—the cultivation of intellect, character, or talents. Thus to waste one's potential became, by definition, the failure to cultivate it. Yet owing to what Williams calls one of the strangest etymological developments in Western thought, the idea of 'culture'—originally inseparable from soil cultivation—grew increasingly distinct from the concept of 'nature' over the past several centuries, with the two eventually becoming distinct conceptual poles. As Lawrence Buell puts it, the relation evolved "from an understanding of the two domains as symbiotic, to the notion of culture as a marker of the divergence of the social from the natural".[45] And through this same process, the horticultural roots of the binary between waste and culture were largely undone as well.

American gardening literature has been an important medium for reviving that historical connection between self-cultivation and soil-cultivation—along with the dynamic relation this bears to our notions of waste. At a historical moment when waste seems less like that which is banished to the margins than something constituting the very fabric and substance of daily life—a time when garbage haunts the collective unconscious with an unprecedented intensity—we can hardly be surprised by the tremendous resonance surrounding ideas of the garden as an agent of waste's undoing.[46] Indeed, the very scale of this waste has helped garden writing proliferate far beyond traditional manifestations in the backyard plots like those Stout and Perényi depict. Today, both guerrilla gardening and mainstream community growing programs expand on the garbage-to-gardens trope as they reclaim waste spaces (generally abandoned or unwanted lots in low-income neighborhoods) for growing flowers and food.[47] These plots, moreover, are often created out of the toxic soils of former industrial sites. One community garden recently established in San Francisco is literalizing this idea of the transmutation of trash by installing a replica of the Hanging Gardens of Babylon—made from dumpsters.[48] And the idea evidently resonates with mainstream film studios as well as urban activists. The 2008 Pixar film *WALL-E*, which opens in a planetary garbage-dump (Earth itself eight centuries from now), features a hero in the form of an animated trash-compactor who discovers a single plant, pots it in an old shoe, and in so doing sets the film's entire plot into motion. The scenario that unfolds during the film's credit sequence depicts humankind ultimately rediscovering the lost art of cultivation, and tells a rebooted version of its historical development beginning with the (re)invention of the plow.

Given the broader meaning that underpins this tradition of representing the 'uncultivated', waste is often understood to involve nearly anything deemed worthless in a social as well as strictly material sense: homeless and criminal populations, unused or derelict spaces, diseased and impoverished bodies, social outcasts, and so forth. Today, ex-convicts, the unemployed poor, and at-risk, inner-city youth—the officially unwanted or human 'waste' elements of modern society[49]—are increasingly recruited into urban gardening programs across the United States, where they can develop work skills that rejoin them to local economies in which they sell their produce.[50]

Homeless individuals often operate independently from such organized growing programs, constructing their own 'gardens' out of trash within the city's interstitial spaces, a practice that helps soften the desolation and insecurity of daily life in the street [Figure 5].[51] Much like the Rock Garden of Chandigarh—the four-acre sculpture garden that Nek Chand built from discarded toilets, broken ceramics, street rubbish, and demolition materials—these gardens, at first glance, appear to involve a kind of generic category-mistake. A garden made *of* trash (as opposed to one that has *processed* or *transformed* it), would seem to necessarily disqualify itself from counting as a garden in the first place. Yet in fact, insofar as these sites are comprised of refuse, their garden-ness—their status as waste-undone—is not at all invalidated, but rather directly affirmed. Precisely by rendering waste valuable, beautiful, or wanted, the sites operate as gardens in the purest sense of the word. Kevin Lynch provides a useful insight for unraveling this paradox: in responding to historians who lament that gardens do not last as buildings and other architectural forms do, he remarks that "[g]ardens depend on constant maintenance; they are easily remodeled and quickly abandoned. But it is this very impermanence, this dependence on constant care and use, that is their finest quality. While they exist, they are wanted."[52]

Figure 5/ *Jimmy's Garden.*
Photograph courtesy of Margaret Morton.

What is most striking about these practices and representations, perhaps, is not just their reaffirmation of horticulture as a vital link between nature, culture, and utopian or reformist efforts; such notions of gardening also re-imagine the implications of 'waste' (in the sense of a failure to actualize potential) for a whole host of social, economic, and environmental issues. If nature and culture are framed as a binary, the garden simply stands *opposite* to waste in its material, social, and spatial manifestations. Yet, as many contemporary instances of garden imagination would suggest, the fantasy and topos of the garden today is not one where waste ceases to exist because undesirable elements are singled out and eliminated; rather, it is one in which these elements cease to be considered 'waste' or 'garbage' in the first place, as their value is at last apprehended, reintegrated, and reaffirmed. This understanding of the garden as an occasion to 'go beyond' waste undoubtedly draws on twenty-first century ecological principles that involve a more broadly-conceived biological interdependence, but it is not limited to them; in fact, the idea's ramifications inform and involve utopian literature, environmental justice movements, struggles for meaningful forms of work, movements against the privatization of resources, and more.[53] To construct the garden in this way, writers, growers, and activists imagine an eco-social order that would utilize the value already inherent in *everything*, a system where everything would 'count', so to speak. They draw on the garden as a way of demanding a more honest and comprehensive social accounting, wherein nothing—neither 'valueless' humans nor 'useless' aspects of nature—can be left off the balance sheets or dismissed as externalities. They recognize true waste as a mode of production that makes life into a "cheated ruin" (as Agee describes the plight of his sharecroppers), or that mandates the destruction of food while people go hungry (as Steinbeck depicts). And thus, this form of garden practice and imagination embraces the recognition, as Lynch puts it, that "[w]asting is useful where it supports life and its development, and wasteful where wasting is blocked, accumulates in toxic form, or causes a loss of organic material".[54] In short, as these cultural forms have reinvented the garden, they likewise reinvent the idea of sustainability as such—not as a departure from death and waste, but rather as an unyielding insistence on the fundamental interdependence of all things natural, social, and economic.

. . .

These intricate connections between cultivation, accounting, and value return us once more to Richard Powers, who encodes all of their implications into the opening and closing scenes of *Gain*. Yet Powers' novel also brings these more fully into the present by elaborating the relation of each element to waste—in all its dimensions—and by constructing the garden as indispensable to the ethical project at the heart of his tale of life and death in late capitalism.

In the opening scene of *Gain*, the protagonist is working in her garden, and Powers uses this setting to underscore the waste and insufficiency that have been made of Laura Bodey's life—a life otherwise structured around trips to the supermarket, managerial to-do lists, carpool rotations, and the routine duties of a dead-end career in real estate. Along with the abrupt intrusion of death in mid-life, it is the activity of gardening that throws into relief these wasted days and the endless postponement of genuinely fulfilling production. As Laura digs among the flowers beneath a brilliant sun, gardening is established as an emblem for labor experienced not as wasted time, but rather as an end and a pleasure in itself. Thus, despite the cheerful image of Laura in her garden, a sense of loss and wasted potential pervades this opening scene, a silent admission that the real object of her passion has been relegated to the spare time of a single free day. As Powers describes Laura's gardening, "[t]he work is play; the labor, love. This is the afternoon she slaves all week for", the one fulfilling pursuit to "complement the way she makes a living on week days".[55]

The relation between waste and the garden is given an even fuller expression in the waste that has been made of Laura's body by a cancer whose source, ultimately, traces back to poisons she absorbed from this very same plot of flowers and vegetables. The astonishing and complex implications coded into this fact, which cannot fully be grasped without further tracing their source back to the history and triumph of corporate capitalism, are revealed only gradually. And curiously enough, the key to reading their meaning ultimately resides in a disposable camera that sits unused and forgotten beside Laura's hospital bed near the story's end. As Powers' story suggests, both Laura and the camera—each embodying something intricately complex and wondrous, an astonishing potential that is nothing less than the product of all human and natural history up to this moment in time—are unceremoniously disposed of in order to sustain capitalism's imperatives for endless accumulation. They are a mere means and externality to the larger order. As Powers writes of the camera, "[T]he entire engineering magnificence was designed to be pitched. Labor, materials, assembly, shipping, sales markups and overheads, insurance, international tariffs—the whole prodigious creation costs less than ten dollars." This wonder must be "cheap enough to jettison", Powers explains. "You cannot have a single-use camera except at a repeatable price."[56]

Assessed against the principles of interconnection that gardening has come to represent, the camera and the poisoned body (which itself develops from the poisoned garden) together form an indictment of the logic underpinning a social and economic system that leaves so much off its accounting ledgers. Echoing the portrait of the garden, the sun, and the 'free gift' in the opening scene, the story of this camera's production also "starts in sun". Its disposable cardboard case traces back to "a sunny upland stand of southern yellow pines. A thing that once lived for light."[57] The device is a miracle of interconnected parts, a globalized orchestration of nature and people in their mutual dependence, all of which Powers elaborates in a breathless, four-page *tour de force* rendering of the myriad aspects it comprises—geographies, economies, individuals, workers' collectives, and business conglomerates; the intricate and mind-numbing handwork of factory laborers, the elements in the flash battery, whose metals will one day "leach into runoff and gather in the fat of fish", and much, much more:

> The camera jacket says: "Made In China With Film From Italy Or Germany". The film itself accretes from more places on the map than emulsion can cover. Silver halide, metal salts, dye couplers, bleach fixatives, ingredients gathered from Russia, Arizona, Brazil, and underwater seabeds, before being decanted in the form of DDR. Camera in a pouch, the true multinational: trees from the Pacific Northwest and the southeastern coastal plain. Straw and recovered wood scrap from Canada. Synthetic adhesive from Korea. Bauxite from Australia, Jamaica, Guinea. Oil from the Gulf of Mexico.... Design and color transfers drawn up in New York. Assembled and shipped from that address in California by a merchant fleet beyond description, completing the most heavily choreographed conference in existence.[58]

This dizzying testament to the interdependence of things evokes the very principles present in that opening scene of Laura working her garden under the sun, along with all the wisdom and social possibility inherent in the discoveries of garden enthusiasts as they participate in a bio-economy that refutes zero-sum principles. As this masterfully rendered device—this pocket-sized artifact and critique of capitalist modes of production—sits quietly next to an unfolding death that is itself the product and culmination of the principles that camera embodies, the whole, two-hundred-year-plus drama of *Gain* unfurls before us, setting forth what the garden means now, and what that meaning suggests about our market-centered ways of life. This garden embodies the impossibility of factoring anything out of the total social and environmental equation, the impossibility, in the end, of separating life into distinct spheres of value and waste. The garden poisons us—spiritually, socially, physically—when (and as long as) the present order regards waste as something that can be counted out of the total social equation, and as long as it pursues a narrow version of gain by depleting value everywhere else, acting as if that social and environmental impoverishment weren't really the ultimate and unambiguous fruits of capitalist wealth cultivation as such.

Yet in the end, the fact that Laura's garden is poisoned does not mean it must fail as an agent of ethical transformation. Already, its principles have pointed Laura beyond the structure of endless and self-perpetuating exploitation. Once her cancer begins to consume her, Laura finally apprehends the significance of her relation to the garden, a relation in which she may act as a steward of life and flourishing. The implications of that dynamic become particularly suggestive as she lies ailing at home and begins to let go of her life at the novel's end. "Everything else, she learns how to shed. It's weight off her, almost. A clarification, a spring cleaning.... Things will do their work without her. Things will do their work without her." This final phrase is repeated with a mantra-like intent, giving Laura comfort in the thought that, insofar as she purportedly plays no part in the broader life of things, her passing will not interrupt its continuation. That thought, however, is at once interrupted by thoughts of her garden:

> Things will do their work without her. Things will do their work without her.
>
> All except her one good thing. [Laura] can no more relinquish it than she can leave her own children. If she could just get the soil ready again, sink her hands in wrist deep, she might be all right. She lies in bed, twelve feet away from that plot. She obsesses over that perfect ground, the richest soil in the world, lying there going to waste.[59]

Unlike all other things, which "will do their work without her", this particular garden comes into being, and thrives, through and because of her effort. And reciprocally, through the garden, Laura is made over into a source of wellbeing, a partisan of life. One can only imagine the possibilities were this principle to become the governing structure of the political economy that caused Laura's demise.

As Robert Harrison writes, the gardener does not simply hand herself over to work or sheer productivity; rather, she "is committed to the welfare of what [s]he nourishes to life in the garden".[60] The Czech author Karel Čapek perhaps describes this best. When Labor Day arrives in his memoir, *A Gardener's Year*, 1929, he decides to celebrate the occasion in the way that gardeners are particularly wont to do. He goes from plant to plant, addressing the needs of each: "and you would like to go deeper in the ground, wouldn't you? And the little alyssum will say 'Yes,' and I shall put it deeper in the soil." He reflects on the merits of this activity, and why people like himself are so compelled to do it:

> Work! Even this messing with the soil you may call work, for I tell you it strains your back and knees; you are not doing this work because it is beautiful, or because it ennobles, or because it is

> healthy, but you do it so that a campanula will flower and a saxifrage will grow into a cushion. If you wish to celebrate anything, you should not celebrate this work of yours, but the campanula or saxifrage for which you are doing it.[61]

For Laura, setting to work on behalf of life unfolds as its own virtue, and gains a special intensity when structured in such an intimate way—when she can commit herself to a utopian enterprise by "sink[ing] her hands in wrist deep". Even after Laura can no longer rise from bed, she is invigorated by the possibilities of gardening, and her thoughts turn from cancer back to life: "The ripples in her plaster ceiling deepen into furrows as she studies them. She drifts from visualizing her T cells, finds herself getting the visualized poppies in. She decides to do all blooms this year, to leave the vegetables for another life."[62] Laura's garden has allowed her to experience fulfillment in being the source of life and flourishing for something outside of herself. And given what we see of capitalist production in *Gain*, this possibility is not just a consoling thought to lessen the bitterness of Laura's poisoning. It offers an ethical and political alternative to the very system that has killed her.

Notes

1. Kincaid, Jamaica, "Sowers and Reapers", *The New Yorker*, 22 January 2001, p. 41.
2. Orwell, George, "Some Thoughts on the Common Toad", *Facing Unpleasant Facts*, Peter Davison ed., Orlando: Houghton Mifflin Harcourt, 2008, p. 217.
3. Boccardi, Mariadele, "Beyond the Garden: Liminality and Politics in the Twenty-first Century Historical Novel", *The Twenty-First Century Novel: Reading Contemporary Fiction*, Lancaster University Conference, September 2005: p. 6.
4. Thomas, Keith, *Man and the Natural World*, New York: Pantheon Books, 1983, p. 240.
5. See also Christopher Thacker, *The History of Gardens*, Berkeley: University of California Press, 1985, p. 51.
6. Hoyles, Martin, *The Story of Gardening*, Concord, MA: Journeyman Press, 1991, p. 311.
7. Even when representations of an ideal society shifted from a mythological register ("paradise") to secular constructs ("utopias"), gardens retained their revered status. In More's *Utopia*, 1516, the home of every townsperson includes a garden.
8. This problem has been central to the critique of market instrumentality since Marx; what makes Palmer's project relevant to our own moment is its expression of the new scale of capital's bio-regulatory capacity. In his own day, Marx saw limits to the market's ability to manipulate natural phenomena, citing forestry and agriculture as cases where capital's production time was suspended or subordinated to "organic laws" as crops slowly matured (*Capital* III, pp. 119–121). In that moment, capital primarily looked to increase the productivity of human labor; today, however, technoscience seeks to directly reengineer the rhythms and productivity of nature (e.g. genetic modification). Against this intensification, then, *Oxygen Bar* suggests the extension of bio-regulation taken to the atmospheric level.
9. See Mary Thomas, "CMU's 'Groundworks' is a complex show with local and international reach", *Pittsburgh Post-Gazette*, 24 November 2005.
10. Wilson, Peter Lamborn, "Avant Gardening", *Avant Gardening*, Peter Lamborn Wilson and Bill Weinberg eds., Brooklyn: Autonomedia, 1999, pp. 9–10.
11. Clare serves as a thinly veiled stand-in for Dow Chemical or Proctor & Gamble. See Richard Powers, *Gain*, New York: Picador USA, 1998.
12. These "costs" manifest as cancer, environmental depletion, meaningless work, off-shored jobs and a general sense of social alienation. In a significant early scene, Jephthah Clare (father of Clare Soap & Chemical's founders) wonders at the networks of exchange that do not appear to enrich any party at another's expense, arrangements where "[h]e, the Oregon trapper, the Chinese Hong,... everyone prospered. Each of them thought he'd gotten the better end of the deal. Now, how could that be? Where had the profit come from? Who paid for their mutual enrichment?" (Powers, *Gain*, p. 10). Powers resolves these speculations by paying the balance in the form of a toxic twentieth century and Laura Bodey's poisoned body.
13. Powers, *Gain*, p. 68.
14. Powers, *Gain*, p. 320.
15. Powers, *Gain*, p. 40.
16. Powers, *Gain*, p. 34.
17. Bataille, Georges, *The Accursed Share*, New York: Zone Books, 1991, p. 28.
18. Powers, *Gain*, pp. 3, 7.
19. Pollan, Michael, *Second Nature*, New York: Delta, 1991, p. 171.
20. Pollan, *Second Nature*, p. 172
21. See Andrew Kimbrell, *The Fatal Harvest Reader*, Washington: Island Press, 2002; Wilson and Weinberg, *Avant Gardening*, pp. 7–34; Vandana Shiva, *Stolen Harvest*, Cambridge, MA: South End Press, 2000.
22. Marx, Karl, *Capital*, New York: International Publishers, 1967, Vol. III: pp. 948–949; Vol. I: p. 475.
23. Steinbeck, John, *The Grapes of Wrath*, New York: Bantam Books, 1969, p. 385.
24. Steinbeck, *The Grapes of Wrath*, p. 385.
25. Agee, James and Walker Evans, *Let Us Now Praise Famous Men*, Boston: Houghton Mifflin, 1960, pp. 325–326.
26. Marx, Karl, *Theories of Surplus Value*, Moscow: Progress Publishers, 1963, pp. 390–392.
27. Agee and Evans, *Let Us Now Praise Famous Men*, pp. 326–327.
28. Stout, Ruth, *How to Have a Green Thumb Without an Aching Back*, New York: Cornerstone Library, 1976, pp. 27–28, 42.
29. Kingsolver, Barbara, *Animal, Vegetable, Miracle*, New York: Harper Collins, 2007, pp. 188–189.
30. See Bataille, *The Accursed Share*, pp. 22–23, 23, and 28 respectively for the quotations.
31. Kingsolver, *Animal, Vegetable, Miracle*, p. 46.
32. Bataille, *The Accursed Share*, p. 21.
33. Agee and Evans, *Let Us Now Praise Famous Men*, p. 325.
34. Stout, *How to Have a Green Thumb*, p. 46. Such accounts, in other words, do not exactly present wish-scenarios where growers

inexplicably commit outrageous acts of generosity; rather, the dynamics are a function of nature's urgent process and unique temporality, its randomness and resistance to the "science" of economic control. These crises of overproduction are thus framed by both wonder *and* dismay, since the temporality of the garden becomes excessive and burdensome when nature's productivity erupts all at once. Thus in many accounts of the garden as some better, more "balanced" version of accounting, we also find an acknowledgement that surplus itself has its own economy of waste, overintensity, and negative value. Annie Dillard, who clearly appreciates nature's economy, understands how radically its process can depart from the tidy eco-cycles featured in many gardeners' accounts. As she observes:

> Nature is, above all, profligate. Don't believe them when they tell you how economical and thrifty nature is, whose leaves return to the soil. Wouldn't it be cheaper to leave them on the tree in the first place? This deciduous business alone is a radical scheme, the brainchild of a deranged manic-depressive with limitless capital.... This is a spendthrift economy; though nothing is lost, all is spent. (*Pilgrim at Tinker Creek*, New York: Harper Perennial, 1998, p. 66.)

35. Powers, *Gain*, p. 34.
36. Scanlan, John, *On Garbage*, Chicago: University of Chicago Press, 2005, pp. 13–14.
37. Stout, *How to Have a Green Thumb*, p. 61.
38. Perényi, Eleanor, *Green Thoughts: A Writer in the Garden*, New York: Modern Library, 2002, p. 39.
39. Warner, Charles Dudley, *My Summer in a Garden*, New York: Modern Library, 2002, p. 99.
40. Whitman, Walter, "This Compost", *Leaves of Grass*, Bradley Sculley and Harold Blodgett eds., New York: W. W. Norton and Co., 1973, pp. 368–369.
41. Pollan, *Second Nature*, p. 173.
42. See Roderick Nash, *Wilderness and the American Mind*, New Haven: Yale University Press, 2001, pp. 1–22, and Max Oelschlaeger, *The Idea of Wilderness*, New Haven: Yale University Press, 1991, pp. 1–30.
43. Locke, John, *Second Treatise of Government*, Joseph Carrig ed., New York: Barnes and Noble Publishing, Inc., 2004, p. 25.
44. Williams, Raymond, *Keywords: A Vocabulary of Culture and Society*, New York: Oxford University Press, 1976, p. 77.
45. Buell, Lawrence, *The Future of Environmental Criticism*, Malden, MA: Blackwell, 2005, p. 136.
46. Paul Hawken, *Nature Capitalism*, Boston: Bay Back Books, 2008, notes that Americans cause the waste of nearly one million pounds of materials per person per year, a figure that includes household trash as well as hundreds of millions of square yards of landfilled carpet, construction debris, CO_2 emissions, chemicals for manufacturing, etc. Out of this trend, contemporary US fiction has increasingly shifted away from representing a culture defined by production to one defined by waste. (See Cynthia Deitering, "The Postnatural Novel: Toxic Consciousness in Fiction of the 1980s", *The Ecocriticism Reader*, Cheryll Glotfelty and Harold Fromm eds., Athens: University of Georgia, 1996, pp. 196–203; and Lawrence Buell, "Toxic Discourse", *Writing for an Endangered World*, Cambridge: Belknap Press of Harvard University Press, 2001, pp. 30–59).
47. See Laura Lawson, *City Bountiful*, Berkeley: University of California Press, 2005, and H. Patricia Hynes, *A Patch of Eden: America's Inner City Gardeners*, White Junction River, VT: Chelsea Green Publishing, 1996.
48. Rosenberg, Jay, "18th and Rhode Island Community Garden", Personal Communication, 11 April 2009.
49. In *Wasting Away*, San Francisco: Sierra Club Books, 1990, Kevin A. Lynch traces the connection between garbage and class, citing the prevalent waste-motif in Friedrich Engels' study of Manchester class relations, Charles Dickens' use of the device to distinguish characters in *Our Mutual Friend* and *Bleak House* (e.g. the dustman Boffin and ragpicker Krook), and the outright conflation of the two within the work of V. S. Naipaul. Lynch cites the following excerpt from Naipaul's *An Area of Darkness* to illustrate this relation:

> Study the four men washing down steps of this unpalatable Bombay hotel... After they have passed, the steps are as dirty as before.... They are not required to *clean*. That is a subsidiary part of their function, which is to be sweepers, degraded beings, to go through the motions of degradation.... Cleaning the floor of a smart Delhi café, they will squat and move like crabs between the feet of the customers, careful to touch no one, never looking up. (Quoted in Lynch, *Wasting Away*, p. 17.)

50. While these programs may call to mind the old bourgeois notions of gardening as a moral tonic for the urban underclass, they differ significantly from those "rehabilitative" initiatives (as well as government-sponsored victory and relief gardens) insofar as they are now overwhelmingly organized at the grassroots level. Rather than being state-created, they are grown in response to the state's withdrawal and neglect. See Sarah Ferguson, "A Brief History of Grassroots Greening on the Lower East Side", Wilson and Weinberg, *Avant Gardening*, pp. 80–90.
51. See Diana Balmori and Margaret Morton, *Transitory Gardens, Uprooted Lives*, New Haven: Yale University Press, 1993.
52. Lynch, *Wasting Away*, p. 28.
53. See Jennifer Atkinson, "Seeds of Change: The New Place of Gardens in Contemporary Utopia", *Utopian Studies*, vol. 18, no. 2, 2007, pp. 237–260.
54. Lynch, *Wasting Away*, p. 159–160.
55. Powers, *Gain*, p. 7.
56. Powers, *Gain*, p. 348.
57. Powers, *Gain*, p. 345.
58. Powers, *Gain*, p. 348.
59. Powers, *Gain*, p. 318.
60. Harrison, Robert Pogue, *Gardens: An Essay on the Human Condition*, Chicago: University of Chicago Press, 2008, p. 170.
61. Čapek, Karel, *The Gardener's Year*, London: Continuum, 2005, p. 42.
62. Powers, *Gain*, p. 318.

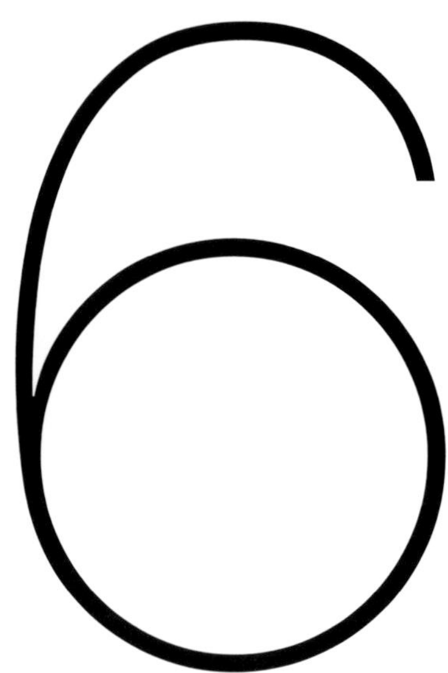

HOW THEN SHALL WE GARDEN?

BITTA-BLUE FARM AND THE SUMMER OF BP

/SUSAN WILLIS

20 April 2010
Explosion and fire on the BP-licensed Transocean drilling rig Deepwater Horizon in the Gulf of Mexico. 11 people are reported missing and approximately 17 injured. A blowout preventer, intended to prevent release of crude oil, failed to activate [Figure 1].

On 20 April I was on my hands and knees planting leeks—a little late for leeks, but I was late getting the soil ready. Leeks require the skill of a surgeon. Each is a fine green hair—not stiff like a toothpick, but pliant and difficult to manage. The tiny blades stick to my fingers then enter the soil askew. It's a tedious job and the row is very long.

I had taken a break mid-row and gone to the house for a snack where I caught a few minutes of radio news. Back on my hands and knees with nothing before me but inch after inch of leeks, I mulled the report of an oilrig explosion. How odd, particularly as the report had been extremely brief, tucked in amongst the more expected bad news on our wars and economy. An oilrig—I visualized one of those Star Wars contraptions that stand thigh-deep in the water.

Subsequent reports had the rig listing; two days later it sank into the Gulf. This was not the end, but just the beginning. The explosion of the Deepwater Horizon that precipitated British Petroleum's catastrophic oil leak in the Gulf of Mexico would cast a pall over the entire growing season.

I work a small New England farm far from the Gulf, but not so far that a hurricane in Mississippi doesn't flood my fields some three or four days later. Thus, as April of 2010 folded into May, then June, I found myself playing, then replaying, a mental image of oil spewing out of BP's damaged well—the same image that continually played on TV. It was as if my brain and the television were both plugged into BP's live action video feed. All summer long, my efforts to manage my farm and Community Sponsored Agriculture (CSA) of 25 member families were punctuated by reports of oil slicks; then plumes; befouled marshes; blobs on the beaches; dead birds, turtles, and dolphins; and a series of failed attempts to cap the broken well, involving unimaginable equipment such as a containment dome, more blowout preventers, and finally 'junk' and 'mud'.

Summer on the farm rolled into fall with all the predictable uncertainties that spell success or failure. I keep a farm journal to better map the choices I make from one growing season to the next. Now, as I read my 2010 farm journal alongside the timeline of the BP Gulf oil disaster, I am struck by the dramatic polarity between BP and me. What could be more different: at one end of the spectrum, a global corporation at the forefront of the world's most crucial economic sector, with profits in the billions; and at the other end, a small organic farm devoted to sustaining the land and its member community. Everything BP does and represents impacts my farm project, either directly or indirectly, while my farm doesn't signify so much as a grain of sand for BP. So, then, does my farm matter in this our world, where tremendously powerful corporations accrue immense profits at the price of minimally regulated risks and catastrophic environmental degradation? The answer may lie in what the reader gleans from my account.

. . .

My spring begins deep in the unrelenting cold of February. I start many seeds indoors in trays huddled against sunny windows. Some will not germinate unless the potting soil

Figure 1/ Deepwater Horizon Oil Spill.
Burning oil, Gulf of Mexico. Photograph courtesy of Dr. Oscar Garcia, Florida State University.

Figure 2/ Chard. Photograph by Susan Willis.

is a consistent 85ºF. These—the trays of peppers, tomatoes, and eggplant—sit atop electric heating pads. Like many New England market farmers, I try to get a jump on the seasons. Imagine the anticipatory pleasure when I sow leeks and onions in pots placed near the wood stove. Imagine, too, the flurry of activity when in the slow wet days of March I drag all my potting materials indoors and begin the meticulous process of poking individual—sometimes tediously small—seeds into the potting cells. I'm impatient. I can't wait for the day when I will be outdoors planting in the real soil. But in February and March, my impromptu household greenhouse allows me to live the incipient spring.

Notwithstanding my desires and efforts, Nature will prevail. In New England it's unwise to set tomato plants out much before the third week of May, if not Memorial Day weekend. So I spend much of April transplanting the now large but still delicate tomatoes, peppers, and eggplants into bigger pots, then ferrying these outdoors to get acquainted with the sun and back in at night to shelter from the frost. What brinksmanship! All to defy the seasons. Of course I'm caught up in the friendly neighborhood rivalry to see who will produce the first tomato. Then too, I fret over my CSA. Will the members be chafing for the bounty of midsummer? Can I expect them to be patient when I'm so clearly doing everything I can to speed things up?

Slow down. Look around. Spring and early summer luxuriate in greens. Arugula's peppery leaves taunt the frost and thrive in the clammy cold as do the plump spinach and mustardy leaves of tat soi and yukina savoy. The shockingly chartreuse black seeded simpson—earliest of the lettuces—shouts crispness. Radishes break the surface of the soil. Beet greens beckon, and the first harvests of kale and chard [Figure 2].

22 April
Deepwater Horizon rig sinks in 5,000 feet of water. Reports of a five-mile-long slick. Search-and-rescue operations by the US National Response Team begin.

25 April
US Coast Guard remote underwater cameras report the well leaking 1,000 barrels per day (bpd) of crude oil. It approves a plan for a remote underwater vehicle to activate a blowout preventer and stop the leak.

26 April
BP's shares fall 2 percent amid fears that the cost of cleanup and legal claims will hit the London-based company hard. Roughly 15,000 gallons of dispersants and 21,000 feet of containment boom are placed at the spill site.

I've been building the soil for decades, piling on wheelbarrow loads of leaf and grass clippings, cleaning the henhouse and goat stalls, turning the manure and hay mulch into the soil.

Building is not an upward process. There is no mountain or mound to testify to the great quantity of material I've added to my fields. Rather, the soil builds downward as organic matter is broken down and rendered accessible to the root systems of the crops. If I endeavor to expand my cultivated areas by incorporating a parcel that previously supported only pasture or scrub, my shovel turns up not soil, but dirt. The color of toast, dirt is dense and clings tenaciously to compacted root hairs. It offers no aroma, but instead harbors stones and the tough roots of sumac and bittersweet. I know such dirt is not inert, but its marginal fertility can be measured in direct proportion to its unyielding rejection of my spade, notwithstanding the pounding of my boot-clad foot.

Soil begins with the labor of the initial tilling. But my efforts to dig the ground, spread manure and turn it into the dirt are secondary to time and process. There is no quick fix when it comes to the production of rich soil. Yes, I might grow vibrant tomatoes if I pour on the Miracle-Gro or vigorous corn if I treat the rows with a hefty dose of granular 10-10-10 fertilizer, but my soil will be the poorer for its chemical bath—each year rendered more inert until only ever-increasing doses of chemicals will produce a crop. To appreciate rich soil is to learn the patience of the earthworm, whose life is the essence of time inseparable from process. I recall the red wrigglers I kept when the kids were small. The worms were housed in a lidded plastic container stowed under the kitchen table. Banana skins, orange peels, coffee grounds, and eggshells went straight from the plate into the worm's abode. How quickly the raw matter of waste transformed into fluffy soil. To call it magic is to deny the life-giving reality of organic process. Magic is instead the property of the inorganic—the prestidigitation of Miracle-Gro's inert elements whose combination quickens on the basis of the soil's depletion.

In April the soil is heavy, waterlogged by the thaw and saturated with spring rain. I'm covered with mud. My hands are cold and soil caked. Only my feet are dry, encased in rubber boots. Moving along on hands and knees, I plant the cold-hardy seedlings—kale, chard, broccoli, cabbage, and cauliflower—that I had started from seed so that I could set them out in neat and uniform rows. The direct seeded crops—lettuce, carrots, turnips, beets—afford me the luxury of standing to hoe a furrow and then lightly rake the soil to cover the seeds. Regardless of the hours of work, the April fields are no more than potential. I look across the rows and see the soil sculpted into furrows and studded with fresh seedlings. In April there are no weeds.

27 April
The Coast Guard announces it will set fire to the leaking crude to slow the spread of oil in the Gulf.

The Minerals Management Service approves a plan for two relief wells.

BP reports a rise in profits, due in large part to oil price increases, and shares rise again.

28 April
A third leak is discovered and the Coast Guard says the flow of oil is 5,000 bpd, five times greater than first estimated.

29 April
President Obama talks about the spill at the White House, his first public comments on the issue. He pledges "every single available resource" including the US military, to contain the spreading spill, and also says BP is responsible for cleanup.

Growing food for a local market and cultivating a clientele willing to be 'locavores' means recognizing and accepting the seasons. This flies in the face of the globalized food industry and America's peculiar economy that preaches and depends on consumerism. Why would anyone want to conform to the seasons when we can have fresh strawberries every day of the year? Why try to figure out how to shape a fall meal around rutabagas when there's that interesting asparagus dish you've been wanting to try? Isn't it indeed quite utopian to have every fruit and vegetable always at hand? And isn't it absolutely Calvinist to want to do without?

The answer is really not about the values and desires that motivate our individual choices, because at rock bottom, the limits of our food system are not about the seasons. They derive from the fossil fuels that enable us to plant, feed, harvest and distribute our food. Do we really believe that jets and cargo vessels will forever ply the sky and seaways with deliveries of apples from New Zealand, lettuce from China, blueberries from Mexico, and peaches from Chile? Do we really think that an entire planet given over to monocultures is sustainable?

The trick is to set aside the notion of limits and live the seasons, instead, as distinct periods of possibility. 'Locavores' savor what's special about each season—even the preserves that are winter's remembrance of times past.

9 May
BP says it might try to plug the undersea leak by pumping materials such as shredded tires and golf balls into the well at high pressure, a method called "junk shot".

11 May
At a hearing before the Senate committee on energy and natural resources, oil company representatives blame each other for the accident. Halliburton, which cemented BP's well, claims to have met BP's requirements and cites the failure of Transocean's blowout preventer. Transocean's CEO says the blowout preventer was successfully tested a week before the accident; he blames BP and Halliburton for the inadequate cementing believed to have led to the

Figure 3/ Row covers. Photograph by Susan Willis.

explosion. BP's president says that Transocean, as owner/operator of the drilling rig, is responsible for safety.

I'm an organic grower. This doesn't mean I simply let nature take its course. Besides all the organic amendments I work into the soil, I draw on a vast arsenal of traps, ruses, tactics, and products to deter or subdue all the organisms that want to eat or blight my crops. Indeed, organic farming is a lively, problem-solving pursuit. Unlike my neighbor who dons his backpack sprayer loaded with Sevin at the least sign of a beetle or loper, I don't rely on a single, all-purpose toxic elixir. In fact, after observing my neighbor from across the road that constitutes a buffer between our fields and seeing how much Sevin he uses to quell an invasion of cucumber beetles, I've grown increasingly skeptical of the safety of so-called "conventional" vegetables.

So what's in my arsenal? Most notable are the giant inflated plastic eyes—balloons really—that float above the rows to scare bunnies and birds. There's also a scarecrow, which is most effective if I move it about and change its clothes. Rubber garden hoses festooned with scraps and coiled to look like snakes help deter mice and voles. These also can be trapped in a deadfall jug trap if I ferret out the rodents' tunnel and set my trap without disturbing the terrain. Or, they can simply be caught by the cats.

Most practical in my arsenal are the floating row covers that I buy by the bolt and unfurl down the rows of newly planted seedlings. Made of a micro-mesh so fine, these row covers block the tiniest flea beetle, while allowing ample sun and rain to reach the tender plants [Figure 3].

Then there are the herbaceous solutions—flowering and aromatic plants that either deter or attract insect pests. While I like the idea of deterrence and typically plant marigolds amongst my crops, I'm put off by the practice of planting a vegetable 'sacrifice', a plant that's adored by a particular insect and set out in a field to be attacked and devoured while the preferred crop goes unscathed. Then there are all the plant-based sprays and powders approved by the Organic Materials Review Institute—products made of neem oil, and pyrithrin, and others that deliver Bt. And there are the mineral-based products that prevent fungal blights. These include the invaluable copper spray that saved many organic growers from the devastating late blight that can decimate tomatoes. And there are powdery clays that don't hinder photosynthesis, but do make a plant's leaves inhospitable to fungal growth.

And finally, there are the beneficials. Imagine a shipment of praying mantis or stick insects set loose in your garden—or even a troop of ladybugs. More subtle are the nematodes bought as a powder and sprinkled on the ground. These work underground to attack those nasty grubs that are the larval form of all those squash, bean, and Japanese beetles that appear unbidden and relentless in the spring.

13 May
Steve Wereley, a researcher at Purdue University, tells the press he believes the well is leaking 70,000 bpd.

My dog pokes her nose into the rough that borders a cultivated row and begins to dig. Fluff flies as she pulls out a supple young rabbit, bites to sever its spine, then leaves it squirming on the ground. She pulls out another. And another. A fourth escapes through the pasture fence. With three paralyzed bunnies lined up, my dog chomps them down one by one—fur, bones, ears—everything in three bites each.

I no longer think of bunnies as cute, and I regret that one of these got away. The early May escapee would plague me throughout the summer. Older and much wiser, it would maintain a burrow somewhere in the goat pasture—out of bounds to my dog—and nightly venture out to raid the rows of vegetables.

Bunnies are the natural born predators of young broccoli. Before my dog's discovery of their burrow, I had watched as my 100 foot row of broccoli disappeared section by section, night by night. At first, I thought cutworms were to blame, as often I found the tiny seedlings lying on the ground beside their severed stems. In fact, these were bunny rejects—plants deemed not as tasty as one previously devoured, and so discarded as the bunnies made their way down the row—tasting and sometimes dropping until the entire row was trashed. No! Bunnies are most definitely rodents, as are those pesky chipmunks, who chirp incessantly from atop their rock walls, then dive in a flash to scurry under the narrow mesh fence that supposedly protects the blueberries. Chipmunks bedevil my dog, since no amount of digging or nosing will allow her to breach the chipmunks' rock fortress. Only my svelte, undersized cat can squirm in after them and prize them out of their tight crevices. Unlike my dog, the cat doesn't immediately eat her rodent trophies, but carries them into the house where she plays chaos with the chipmunk on her own turf.

Farming is not nature. It may have to do with plants, animals, climate, and seasons. A farmer may be cognizant of environmental impact, but in the end farming wholly redefines natural ecologies. My farm is a microcosm of border skirmishes carried out between the cultivated space and the forested or grassy areas that surround my fields. The borders are pretense, marked as a distinction between tilled and untilled. Exchanges are rampant as invasive plants migrate into the fields or are sown there in the manure I use. Transformations prevail. Certainly, the rodents who have learned to prefer garden plants are no more natural than I the farmer, who seeks to keep her tract of land rodent free.

I'm beginning to take on the mentality of my neighbor, whom I've long maligned for his quick and incontrovertible categorization of birds and animals as either 'good' or 'bad'. Deer, fisher cats, raccoons, opossums, weasels, coyotes, foxes, chipmunks, squirrels, voles, moles, mice, shrews, and rabbits are all bad. That leaves only his dog as a good animal (although he might be tempted to include the bears and panthers that people talk about but have never actually seen). As for the birds: grackles, blue jays, and most definitely, English sparrows are bad. These can be blasted off the face of the Earth. On the other hand, bluebirds are super good. They are to be given houses and mealworms, especially if they arrive too early in the spring to dig their own worms. Robins are nice; but one has to monitor the mockingbirds, as they might be too territorial and, hence, drive the good birds away. As for orioles, they're special; so you better not chop down that near-dead linden, as it's the only place they've nested for the past four years. And don't forget to leave your barn door open for the swallows.

Though scorning my neighbor's policing of the bird population, I've adopted some of his practices. I begin to leave the barn door open in April and I make sure the bluebird boxes are clean and ready. I bust up the sparrow nests, thus sending them into a summer of hormonal overdrive. But what to do with the catbirds? Here's where I slide precipitously into the policing of birds. Catbirds are marvelous. Alert and social, they flit about the arbor where we sit for lunch. Their cat cries chide as I weed the rows. I know they're watching—not me—but the ripening blueberries. Catbirds have the knack of plucking the berries just days before they're ripe. Greedy and quick, they'll eat every one. My solution: a berry patch imprisoned in an ugly Guantanamo structure, covered with netting and festooned with anchoring clothespins. The catbirds watch and chide and study the net. Not three days after it's up, I find one inside. Berry season will be spent shooing the interlopers out. Now, no longer the policeman, I'm the Darwinist, willing to share the harvest with the smartest individuals of the species.

When it comes to bugs, I'm the exterminator. Squashing them by hand is the only foolproof method. Notwithstanding row covers and sprays, I spend many a summer's day on leaf inspection duty. Painstakingly, I search the undersides of bean and squash leaves, my thumb and forefinger a ready pincer. Sadly, I can't capture the cucumber beetles. They are far too small, hard-bodied, and quick to fly. But the bean and squash beetles are fat and easily crushed. Some days, out of tedium, I count as I squash. Am I developing an obsessive-compulsive disorder? Or am I astutely monitoring the infestation? 27 crushed beetles. My fingers are an iridescent yellow. Meanwhile, across the road my neighbor relentlessly sprays Sevin. We both know that one beetle will lay hundreds of eggs, which will mature into grotesque yellow larvae capable of devouring a squash plant in days. The best organic cure for beetles is crop rotation. But that would mean a season without melons, squash, cucumbers, and beans. Might as well call off the summer. So I deploy the row covers, use pyrethrin, inspect, and crush.

30 May
BP chairman Tony Hayward causes outrage after telling reporters, "There's no one who wants this over more than I do. I would like my life back."

3 June
BP begins an advertising campaign in the USA aimed at boosting opinion. Hayward features in the first.

BP faces political flak over its decision to pay out more than $10 billion in dividends to shareholders, despite the deepening crisis.

20 June
Photographs of Hayward attending a yacht race on the Isle of Wight with his son provoke anger in the USA.

Summer's solstice finally arrives. The ground heats up, the days are drenched in sun, and squash ripens. Zucchini, patty pan, and yellow crookneck transform sunlight into buttery goodness. Snap beans lengthen and plump out. Eggplants double in size overnight. Tomatoes and peppers yearn to be red. Now that summer's onslaught brings such a bounty of starch and juice, does anyone miss the tender greens of spring?

In principle, I understand the arguments for monocultures—the claims for their efficiency based on the maximization of productive technologies, the privatization of crop science, the elimination of labor, and the rationalization of distribution.

In reality, I rail against the large scale destruction of habitats wrought by cotton, rice, sugar, soy, corn, wheat, alfalfa. Even lettuce and blueberries are fast becoming monocultural commodities, not to mention pigs and chickens.

I recoil at the wholesale degradation of soil, water, and air brought about by the wanton use of chemically produced nitrogen and petroleum fuel technologies. I quake at the terminator crops whose genes infiltrate traditional varietals, making us all either consumers or infringers of patented materials. And I bemoan the mind-numbing uniformity of landscapes that signal death to creativity, death to beauty, death, finally, to all but the prized 'mono-crop'.

So I wonder if economies of scale can challenge industrialized agriculture. Can farmers' markets, food co-ops, community gardens and CSAs flourish as viable alternatives to agribusiness? Can organic practices put a lie to the claims made by industry? Indeed, can local small scale organic farming enable consumers to question the products and practices associated with organic when it becomes global and industrial?

Rather than compete with the 'too big to fail' logic of monocultures, local organic farming undermines by example. Diversity is the most disruptive aspect of farming for a local market. Not only can I grow beets and carrots, I can beguile with yellow beets and purple carrots. I can offer not one, but three types of kale and lord knows how many varietals of squash. My tomatoes include Black Russians, red and yellow heirlooms, and even green tomatoes. My plots offer a controlled riot of tastes, colors, aromas, all of it growing, then peaking, and changing as I rotate new crops for spent ones.

The bounty surprises even me and makes me wonder if a half-acre of Monsanto soybean is truly more productive than my multicrop half acre. Does Monsanto's half-acre produce more by weight? Or feed more people? How do I calculate outcomes if Monsanto farms for profit and I for the cost of living? How might I factor in experiential and emotional considerations? Does Monsanto's half-acre gratify? Certainly mine tips the scale with equal portions of satisfaction and worry.

7 July
There are more than 27,000 abandoned oil wells in the Gulf of Mexico, according to an investigation by the Associated Press, which describes the area as "an environmental minefield that has been ignored for decades". Some wells date back to the 1940s. State officials estimate that tens of thousands are badly sealed.

11 July
BP begins its latest attempt to seal the leak. Robots remove a leaking cap from the well, to allow a replacement containment system to be installed.

With this attempt reportedly going well, BP shares rise again.

Distribution is the biggest problem that every small-scale farmer confronts. When I was a teenager, already dabbling in the art of farming, I simply brought my pints of strawberries to the local Safeway supermarket, whose produce manager regularly bought truckloads of seasonal vegetables from local farmers. In contrast, today's chain store supermarkets have hammered out ironclad relationships with international suppliers, who offer product uniformity—whatever happened to small apples, twisted carrots, and gritty lettuce?—as well as the ideology of food safety balanced precariously against the reality of eggs laced with salmonella and spinach with *E. coli*.

If I were a bigger small producer—say, if I cultivated three, four, or even ten acres—I might market through a local food co-op or a handful of restaurants whose menus feature local or regional ingredients. I'd trade the certainty of an up-front contract against the woe of a crop failure, and I'd find myself pressed by the demands of the buyer. Do I really want to supply a steady stream of baby arugula to a local restaurant? And what if the chef doesn't like my juicy, cat-faced heirlooms and instead wants a more manageable tomato?

The privilege of a truly small producer is autonomy—but there's still the problem of distribution. Farmers' markets offer a solution for many small growers, with the most successful making a circuit of five, even six, markets per week. From the consumer's point of view, a farmers' market is a wholesome weekly carnival. Some offer bluegrass bands and crafters. Most include prepared 'value added' foods like breads, jellies, and cheeses. And some allure with a heady blend of ethnic cookery.

Now imagine the market from the farmer's point of view. Many farmers pack, wash, and bundle their produce the night before market day. Others get up in the wee hours to pick and prep. Vans and trucks must be packed, with care given not only to the vegetables, but the canopy, tables, and tasteful display cloths and banners. Then there's the milling crowd, the smiling outreach to potential customers—or worse yet, the lack of a crowd. Finally, there's the waste—all those bundles of shiny red radishes that no one wanted, all that limp basil that couldn't withstand the mid-day heat, and the crates of summer squash rendered redundant by every other farmer's crates of squash.

I hate waste! If I grow something—invest my skill and intellect in the choice of seeds, labor over each and every plant, and provide fresh wholesome food—then I want it to be eaten. And if I discover tomatoes too blemished for sauce or a zucchini that escaped my attention and grew to the size of a baseball bat, then I want my chickens to eat them. The broken under-leaves of chard? not so bad, I'll put them in a soup. A wounded eggplant? cut around the scar and throw it in the ratatouille.

Because I hate waste, a CSA is my solution. Every week, everything the farm produces is divided equally amongst the community of members. Everything goes. Of

Figure 4/ Harvest. Photograph by Susan Willis.

course, I agonize over supply. The lettuce seems too small. What can I substitute if there aren't enough green beans? If everyone got an eggplant last week, can they handle some more this week? Sometimes it's difficult, even for me, to step outside of a supermarket mentality and realize that a CSA is precisely a share of the harvest. As such, it truly reflects the seasons; and at the height of summer the lettuce will be small and the eggplant prolific. To placate my worries over how my vegetables are received—after all, my clientele is the community that supports me—I remind myself that every leaf, fruit, and root is 100% organic, and it's all picked the day my community members arrive to claim their shares [Figure 4].

15 July
Secretary of State Hillary Clinton pledges to look into claims that BP lobbied for the release of the Lockerbie Bomber.

22 July
BP admits to using Photoshop to exaggerate the level of activity at the Gulf oil spill command center.

I stomp the shovel deep into the ground, raise and turn the load of dirt, stoop to remove weeds and rocks. Stomp. Turn. Stoop. Stomp. Turn. Stoop. Stomp. Turn. Stoop. It's mid-summer and I'm in the Zen of digging. No need for ear buds and an I-Pod, I meditate at one with my body's motion. Over the years, I've become extremely efficient and can dig for hours, heedless of fatigue.

Hoeing requires more attention. I use a scuffle hoe, a flat triangular blade fastened to a long handle. With a scuffle, hoeing is a thrusting motion, unlike traditional hoeing where the movement is pulled back towards the body. The scuffle suits my smaller frame and fosters precision rather than strength. Deft turns of the wrist or hand drive the scuffle between and around young plants, unearthing weeds while avoiding the vegetables.

Hand weeding brings me close to the earth on hands and knees. Here, I'm not in the Zen, but engrossed in the task of pulling the weeds by their roots. Chickweed eludes my grasp, clover drives its roots deep, and witch grass casts long runners. I poke, gouge and pull barehanded to be thorough.

I love to work and wake each morning during the growing period reviewing the day's tasks. Like a kid in galoshes, I like my big boots. They enable me to trod like an elephant and then float at night when I finally take them off. I also like my dirty jeans. They feel like a second skin. My gloves make me feel tough and stronger than I am. I like to sweat and drink water from my thermos. I pretend I'm impervious to rain, although a full day's soaking sends me to the aspirin. And I like to see the results of my efforts spread out before me—clean rows, healthy plants—and a host of tasks yet to be done.

Work is easy. I know it and do it and find it gratifying. Labor is something else. It's an economic construct that turns work into an abstraction. My labor power, or ability to do work, is what I would offer an employer in exchange for a wage. Labor enters into a particular calculus of value, which in everyday terms has to do with the cost of commodities, the price of goods, the level (or lack) of profit, and people's standing in society. If I tried to define my work on a scale of value determined by labor, I'd be pitifully underpaid. And if I tried to market my vegetables in accordance with the minimum hourly wage, they would be woefully expensive.

Because small plot farming makes very little economic sense, it risks being construed as an isolated and idealistic—even utopian—endeavor. In fact, my CSA is stitched into lines of supply and exchange that define the economy at large. I buy seeds, supplies, and implements, and I hire a farm intern one day a week. I devise marketing strategies. And I pay taxes. Nevertheless, small plot farming for a CSA requires a different calculus of value. Indeed, it tests the logic of the larger system where value is all but synonymous with price. How then, to imagine value differently? Rather than wax poetic about community and fresh food, I suggest we locate the CSA's value in its quality of being alternate—a sort of anti-matter to the glut of commodified matter that surrounds us. Alternative food and farming practices represent instances of a world that certainly doesn't exist; but might be something we strive to attain.

Figure 5/ Manny. Photograph by Susan Willis.

26 July
BP chief executive Tony Hayward is to leave the company, to be replaced by Bob Dudley, a veteran overseeing the clean-up.

27 July
BP plunges into the red. The company is to book a $10 billion tax credit against the cost of cleaning up the oil spill and is making a provision of $32.2 billion towards the cleanup. Part of the bill will be picked up by UK and US taxpayers.

1 August
BP will attempt to stem the flow of oil with a 'static kill' in the next 24 hours. The procedure involves pumping heavy drilling mud and cement into the well.

This is New England. Rocks are everywhere. Giant boulders rim my fields in broken, but precise lines. These are the legacy of the eighteenth century colonists who cleared the woods and built my house on solid, rough-hewn granite. The goats think the rock walls were built expressly for them. The kids frolic from rock to rock while the adults stake a claim to the largest boulders, where they chew cud and doze [Figure 5]. The dominant doe presides from the biggest boulder. On a good day she'll share it with the buck. As for me, I marvel at the giant rectangular cut stones that form the steps from the pond up to the house. Others pave the dooryard. Then there are the impressive hearthstones and all the ones that form the central chimney. Most charming are the precisely set stones that line the hand dug well.

Did the colonists see the stones for their beauty, or just something that had to be dealt with in order to farm the land? More than two centuries after their labors, I'm still gouging out stones. The bigger ones join the rock walls, while the smaller are dumped into potholes in my unpaved drive. Year after year, more rocks appear, to test my resolve and the strength of my back. My neighbor thinks my complaints are unfounded. After all, his father farmed my field 80 years ago—plowed it yearly and removed all the stones. Still the earth heaves them to the surface. The farm's aesthetic bears the imprint of coping.

Now at the height of summer, the under-performing broccoli raab has gone to seed, as have one or two lettuces. The summer squash are leggy. They put all their energy into the tips of their vines, which produce a few small fruits and leaves while the central stem twists like a gnarled bristlecone pine. The giant sunflowers offer bounteous seed heads to droves of finches while their leaves crackle and crumble like potato chips. Many of the crops that thrived in the spring and early summer now await shovel and hoe [Figure 6]. They'll be cleared to make way for fall's tender seedlings. Rotating the crops reiterates the passage from seed, through growth, to harvest. Fresh and new rows parallel the tattered and spent. The farm's aesthetic embodies mortality.

Volunteers prosper in my plots. The sunflower that sprouted from a seed dropped by a bird, winging away from last year's bird feeder, will certainly be allowed to grow. I adore sunflowers even when they pop up in the middle of a cultivated row, as did the singular stalk of corn that cropped up amongst the chard. The corn, born of a kernel that I scattered in the chicken yard, made its transit to the garden in a wheelbarrow load of enriching chicken soil.

Morning glories climb the fence round my lettuce rows. I remember my elation a full decade ago when I discovered the original morning glory, its two telltale cloven leaves innocently sprung from the earth. Now prolific, morning glory is a menace. Still, the purple-blue flowers are a delight. So I allow them to twine the fence, but I draw the line when insidious upstarts vie with the pole beans for climbing rights. Hoeing and weeding are discretionary tasks. When I come upon dense clusters of marigolds and calendulas that sprout from last year's spent flower heads, I diligently transplant them to flower beds and borders. Soon the entire place will be carpeted in yellow and gold. Will I develop a more ruthless approach to weeding? Not likely. Witness the annual hibiscus that clutter the rows. The farm's aesthetic orchestrates orderly disorder [Figure 7].

3 August
A whistleblower group reveals that scientists within the US Environmental Protection Agency have raised concerns with superiors over a chemical dispersant approved for use in the Gulf. BP sprayed almost two million gallons of Corexit on the slick and at the leak site on the seabed.

Figure 6/ Height of Summer. Photograph by Susan Willis.

4 August
BP says the 'static kill' attempt to stop the leak has been successful, though more mud may still have to be pumped into the well to close it permanently.

The US government announces that the majority of oil from the BP spill has been cleaned up.

Spring drenched the earth with rain and flood—an onslaught that brought FEMA compensation to my small town. The soil, waterlogged and heavy could not be worked for many weeks. The so-called 'growing season' was set back. When drier weather finally came, it loosened the soil, then quickly gave way to months of drought. Now I'm pained by the withered, turned-back-on-itself look of drought-stressed plants—the lilacs worn and limp, the dust-blasted oregano. Fragile ribbons of moisture chart the paths of my soaker hoses while all around, the desiccated earth cries for rain. The spring-planted crops struggled and failed. I had to stall my CSA members with a start up date in late June. This means the promised 20-week CSA will run through the first week in November. Will the frosts hold off? Or will my entire operation crash and freeze in late September? I struggle from week to week, barely able to accept the successes for fear of looming failures.

My daughter berates me, saying I make everyone's life a living hell during the growing season.

Diligence and toil are bulwarks against adversity, but no amount of skill and effort can eliminate uncertainty. And notwithstanding the almanac of mean temperatures and rainfall, there is never a 'normal' year. Thus, I watched with anxiety and dread as an entire row of broccoli bolted. Taller and taller it grew, then finished with miniscule heads hardly sufficient for a Chinese stir fry. Meanwhile, the Brussels sprouts grew into great bushy plants whose kernel sized sprouts quickly exploded into more bushiness. The tomatoes thrived, but only so long as I stayed ahead of the blight. Reports had it appearing in backyard gardens not 20 minutes away.

Booby traps to certainty are the norm. The chicks sent day-old from the hatchery and 'sexed' as pullets grew into a flock with a dozen roosters. The seeds from a packet labeled "cauliflower" matured into cabbages. The beets failed to germinate, as did half the carrots.

On a farm where uncertainty prevails, I should have expected the arrival of Attila and his Hun—a pair of ducks that my neighbor found and loosed on my pond. Appropriately named, Attila made everyone's life a game of leap and run during the period when his Hun was laying eggs and attempting to sit on her nest. We learned to exit the house armed with a broom, tennis racket, or golf club, until the day when Hun stopped laying eggs, and both became adored pets. With certainty, their nesting season will come round again, unless that other certainty—the stealthy coyote—carries them off. Thus, we devise duck protection tactics, attempting to check one certainty against another.

5 August
The White House is accused of spinning a report about the amount of oil cleaned up from the Gulf oil spill.

15 August
Barack Obama goes for a swim with his daughter in the Gulf.

It is revealed that BP has yet to update its oil spill emergency plan, more than three months after the Deepwater Horizon rig exploded. Errors include the identification of the sea walrus as an animal in need of protection, despite there being none in the Gulf, and the citation of a wildlife expert who died four years before the plan was approved.

Figure 7/ Flowers. Photograph by Susan Willis.

My husband bought me a new freezer this year. I was ecstatic and greeted the summer with intensions of freezing everything. Now, vats of tomato sauce bubble on the stove. Like maple syrup, it reduces over time to its vital essence. My daughter helps —not the one who blamed me for the living hell, but the one who doesn't mind skinning buckets of tomatoes. She's surprised by the way their acid finds the tiny cat scratches on her hands. I like to make sauce because everything in it comes from the farm—tomatoes, onions, peppers, basil, garlic, oregano—all preserved for those days in winter when it's hard to remember the glut of summer.

When the apples ripen, I vow to save every one, happy to find this year's crop almost worm free. At night I peel and core, then simmer the apples with just enough sugar and spice to make another rich sauce. Now, their pungent aroma displaces the tomatoes and engulfs the house.

Soon the freezer fills with neatly stacked and labeled containers. Besides the sauces, there are slivered peppers, sliced and breaded eggplant, chopped chard, diced peaches, and dainty cubes of pesto. Next year I'll do more. And I'll remember to use the food dehydrator as well. There's nothing like the zing of a dried tomato slice when it plumps up on a pizza.

My parents were in their teens during the Great Depression, and as young adults they weathered the Second World War. Me, I'm a Baby Boomer—one of that spendthrift generation that thinks only of itself, aims to be perpetually young and endangers our children's futures with our unwillingness to depart the planet before we bankrupt Social Security. Why, then, am I such a saver? Am I some sort of throwback to my parents' generation? Or did I just imbibe their example and learn to take pleasure in saving for winter's rainy day? Indeed, my father taught me how to make jams and jellies. He grew every fruit imaginable, even persimmons. But he never went so far as to cultivate shell beans. Black, white, brown, mottled, spotted and striped—they make a carnival of color neatly sorted and labeled, jar by jar on the shelf.

7 September
The world's smallest seahorse faces extinction following the BP oil spill. The Zoological Society of London's seahorse team warns that the destruction of so much of the dwarf seahorse's habitat could lead to a dangerous drop in population levels.

20 September
The day after it confirmed that the leaking well has been successfully and permanently plugged, shares in BP rise. The US campaign group Public Citizen calls off its boycott.

23 September
Scientists estimate that a total of 4.4 million barrels of oil were released into the Gulf of Mexico during the nearly three months the well leaked.

The cruciferous vegetables of fall cleanse the palate and offer a new range of tastes and textures. Mellow cauliflower, nutty broccoli, bold turnips, and cabbages—all improve in flavor as October brings frost back into the world [Figure 8]. I harvest the rows and feed the headless plants to the goats and chickens, who adore big crunchy cabbage and cauliflower leaves. Fall is the time to clean the fields, removing as many pesky perennial weeds as possible; to put away the implements, soaker hoses, and row covers; and to prepare the fields for winter's replenishment with freshly spread manure and mulch. My movements are slow. I work doggedly and without enthusiasm. Has the year caught up with me and made me just plain tired, or do I miss the excitement of spring and summer? Luckily, I won't be wallowing in despair. Ten pounds of seed garlic just arrived in the mail. Haul out the shovel and hoe! Tomorrow I'll be planting again! Garlic is spring's promise made in the fall.

By early December, I've put the growing plots to bed. Dusted with lime and covered with mulch and manure, they will soon be blanketed with snow. They look content, but I am not. I've not learned the torpor of the moles deep in the frozen ground or that of the fish and frogs in their ice-locked bubbles. I reason that the soil needs to rest and replenish; but I'm from southern California, where a year-round growing season made the notion of torpor the stuff of myth. There, the soil never rested; indeed, my father took pride in the oranges and avocados he grew in topsoil deep and rich. Now his topsoil is paved and covered over with a subdivision where people vacuum their three-car garages and chemically manicure their miniscule lawns. So I'll take my New England farm where deep in the torporous beds, rocks move, then heave, eager to blunt my shovel in the spring.

. . .

So, then, does my farm matter? Certainly not to BP. In a world driven by market-based solutions to environmental degradation and destruction, my tiny farm—notwithstanding its organic output and sustainable practices—would probably

Figure 8/ Cabbage. Photograph by Susan Willis.

Figure 9/ Wages of Destruction. Oil-polluted marshlands south of Houma, Louisiana. Photograph courtesty of Frank McMains.

not garner even a single pollution trading credit. Imagine the magnitude of the BP spill. Measure the square miles of surface water affected by the spill. Now, measure the tidal inlets and estuaries. Now, the barrier islands and finally the seafloor. Then there's the water by volume, and the subsoils beneath the seafloor. Finally, calculate all the life forms and their impacted progeny. How many farms like mine would it take to trade equal measures of viable against toxic? The fallacy of cap and trade strategies is that caps blow like so many blowout preventers and there are no trades that can erase the awful reality of a toxic event. A million small sustainable farms will neither negate the BP spill nor mitigate its consequences.

But the problem with asking if Bitta-Blue Farm matters is that the criteria for assessing significance have been determined by the dominant economy. Even if we shift from the logic of trade and profit to a calculus based on carbon—as many environmentalists urge—we are still trading in units. BP's carbon footprint flies off the chart; whereas my farm's negative or neutral reading is infinitesimal and therefore inconsequential. The farm's value resists quantification. If my farm journal captures and conveys the farm as a place where the pleasures of the senses meet the gratification of productive activity, then the real question to be asking is how to make that experience a commonly held reality.

As I write in the last weeks of 2010, there are reports of dead and dying deep-sea coral on the floor of the Gulf. The wages of destruction may well outpace the impetus for utopia [Figure 9].

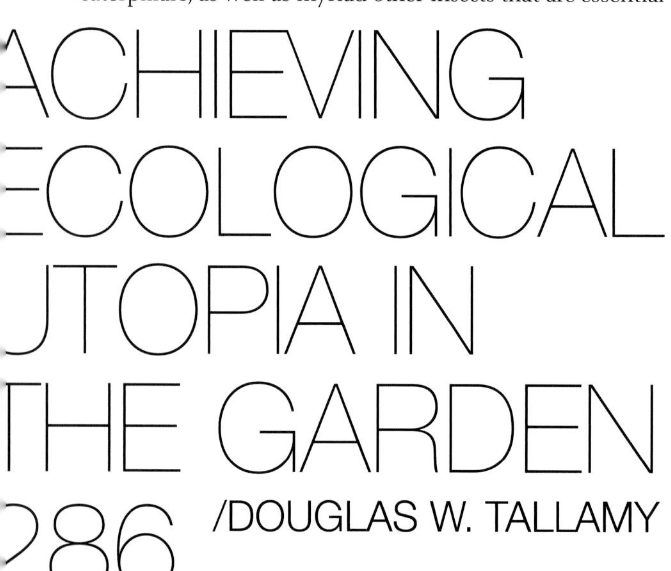

ACHIEVING ECOLOGICAL UTOPIA IN THE GARDEN

286 /DOUGLAS W. TALLAMY

A male blue grosbeak flexes his azure crest as he searches the ground from his perch on an ironwood tree. He has been singing for hours each of the past six days within the territory he claimed after returning in May from his wintering grounds in southern Mexico. He has chosen this site to raise his young because it is dotted with the small trees and shrubs that are perfect for concealing his nest. Even more important, the insects needed to feed his nestlings are plentiful here [Figure 1].

The grosbeak sings for two reasons: to warn off intruding males, and to attract a mate. Today he has found romance; a chocolate-colored female, attracted to his melodies, has found the site to her liking and has started to construct a nest deep within a dogwood tree. Blue grosbeaks are among the few birds that use snakeskins as nesting material [Figure 2]. The task of locating a suitable skin has fallen to the male, and he is in luck; a black rat snake has recently left a perfectly usable skin near a groundhog hole. Soon the skin is woven into the nest that will become the home for three nestlings. This will be his only successful bout of reproduction this year but he will sing every day in celebration until mid-September when he and his mate return to Mexico.

What I have described did not take place in a national park, or even in a small county preserve. It happened in my yard. It happened in my yard because my wife and I have built our landscape with all of the bits of nature that blue grosbeaks require to make more blue grosbeaks. Our yard, once mowed for hay, is now planted with young oaks, birches, and viburnums; gray dogwoods, flowering dogwoods, and alternate-leaf dogwoods; red cedars, winterberries, and inkberries; American elms, American chestnuts and American beeches; silverbells, fringetrees, black cherries, red maples, and more. Cindy and I have planted our yard with a diversity of native plants that make the food necessary for grosbeak reproduction. Our woody plants alone support well over a thousand species of caterpillars, as well as myriad other insects that are essential foods for young grosbeaks. After the fledglings leave the nest, these same plants supply the grosbeak family with seeds and berries to supplement their continued diet of insects.

Figure 1/ Blue grosbeak, male (top) and female (bottom). Gardeners over much of the USA can attract breeding pairs of blue grosbeaks to their yards if they provide food and shelter for these beautiful birds. Photographs by Douglas W. Tallamy.

We have the snakeskins our grosbeaks use to build their nest because we have black rat snakes, black racers, milk snakes, ribbon snakes, ring-necked snakes, and garter snakes in our yard. We have these harmless snakes because we have the mice, voles, shrews, and toads they eat, and because we have groundhog dens that are perfect places for snakes to avoid the weather extremes of winter and summer. And we have snake food because we have the

Figure 2/ Blue grosbeaks prefer to make their nests with snakeskins. Photograph by Douglas W. Tallamy.

plants that supply the insects and seeds eaten by mice, voles, shrews, and toads, and because we leave refuges for them so they can avoid being decapitated during Saturday mowings.

We have nesting blue grosbeaks in our yard, as well as chipping sparrows, field sparrows, song sparrows, common yellowthroats, willow flycatchers, Carolina chickadees, cedar waxwings, robins, cardinals, mockingbirds, bluebirds, brown thrashers, titmice, woodpeckers, wrens, and others because we have redundancy in each of their ecological requirements. If a mockingbird has already built a nest in a suitable dogwood, our grosbeaks can find an unoccupied dogwood, because we have many. If our black cherry trees do not produce enough larvae of the Promethea moth, white furcula, and small-eyed sphinx to satiate the baby grosbeaks, our oak trees will fill the void with unicorn caterpillars, red-humped oak worms, and white-dotted prominents. If our black rat snakes shed their skins within a mole tunnel where the grosbeaks can't find them, our black racers will leave their sheds in plain view on one of our mowed paths.

Our native plants are not riddled with insect damage because the insect herbivores they support attract a large and diverse community of natural enemies that keep their populations in check. We have built a landscape that guarantees a steady supply of all of the resources needed by blue grosbeaks to successfully reproduce: a landscape with enough complexity to promote long-term balance and stability in the food webs it creates. Such a landscape approaches utopia for grosbeaks and for us as well [Figure 3].

UTOPIA: SUSTAINABILITY THROUGH BALANCE

Variations on political, economic, and religious utopias have been envisioned through the ages, but a cornerstone common to all is the concept of perfection through balance and equality. In political utopias, happiness is achieved through balance of power; economic utopias promote a balance in the distribution of resources: equal wealth, and therefore equal status for all. Members of religious utopias accept the common good in all religions and thus happiness through symmetry and balance in philosophy. Utopias of all types are achieved through sharing: the sharing of power, wealth, or philosophies. Nowhere is sharing more critical to success than in ecological utopias: societies founded on life in harmony with nature. Rather than usurping them for their own use, humans in ecological utopias share physical and biological resources with other species and thus can live together indefinitely. An ecological utopia is the only truly sustainable society because it protects the species that run the ecosystems on which humans depend.

UNDERSTANDING THE BALANCE OF NATURE

The concept of an intrinsic 'balance of nature' has been a popular misconception since Herodotus. Its primary tenet is that if an ecosystem is disturbed, it will eventually return to its original state. Though still promoted in popular literature, the notion that nature, left to its own accord, would settle into an unchanging and predictable series of interactions has long since been discredited.[1] Numerous studies now suggest that nature is in a constant state of flux, the details of which are impossible to predict over long periods. Ecologists no longer view balance in terms of lack of change, but instead focus on factors promoting ecosystem stability. Today, 'balance' in nature might better be described as resilience against disturbance. How long can an ecosystem remain productive before it tips into a downward spiral of species loss and collapse? Diverse ecosystems—that is, ones with many interacting species—have been shown to be more stable and more productive in the face of perturbation than simplified ecosystems.[2] Populations may fluctuate, dominance hierarchies may shift, and even the composition of the species present may change over time, but the system as a whole is more likely to remain 'balanced' in a stable state of productivity when more species interact than when fewer interact. Species diversity, therefore, is the key to ecosystem stability and thus to ecosystem sustainability.

DIVERSITY IS KEY TO SUSTAINABILITY

Species diversity leads to the stability and productivity required for long-term sustainability of ecosystems in two different ways. Stability is created by redundancy: several species doing the same job.[3] Redundancy is a back-up system inherent to diverse ecosystems. Just as a football team has a back-up quarterback ready to lead the team if the first string quarterback is injured, stable ecosystems contain many species that perform the same ecosystem service. If one species is lost, the others quickly compensate. Pollinators provide a nice example. 80 percent of flowering

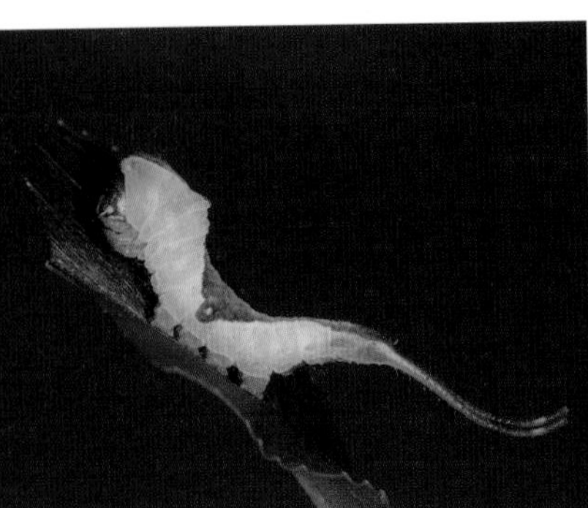

Figure 3/ If birds cannot find enough larvae of white furculas (left) on black cherry trees, they can look for streaked dagger moths (middle) and white-dotted prominents (right) on oak trees. Photographs by Douglas W. Tallamy.

Figure 4/ Ruby-throated hummingbird. Pollinators provide a good example of the value of ecosystem redundancy. Photograph by Douglas W. Tallamy.

plants depend on animal pollinators to carry their pollen to the female parts of conspecific flowers—that is, flowers belonging to the same species. The morphology of a flower dictates which pollinators will have access to its pollen. Flowers with deep corollas (long necks) attract pollinators with long tongues, because they are the only species that can reach the nectar reward at the bottom of the corolla. In the tropics, many of these pollinators are hummingbirds, but in the temperate zone sphinx moths with tongues considerably longer than their bodies perform this function. An ecosystem that supports a dozen species of sphinx moths has redundancy in long-tongued pollinators, whereas an ecosystem with only one species does not. If the lone sphinx species were to disappear, as it would if its larval host plant succumbed to a new shopping center, flowers dependent on long-tongued pollinators would also disappear because they would no longer set seed. In contrast, if one moth species is lost in a redundant system, the others would compensate for its loss, and long-necked flowers could persist [Figure 4].

In contrast to stability, an ecosystem with many species promotes productivity not through redundancy, but by chance.[4] Ecosystem productivity is a function of plants—the first trophic level—because only plants have the ability to capture energy from the sun and prevent it from radiating back into space. Through photosynthesis, plants lock the sun's energy in the carbon bonds of simple sugars and carbohydrates. Plants keep some of this food for their own growth and reproduction, but the rest is reluctantly passed to higher trophic levels every time an animal eats a plant part [Figure 5]. Thus, food generated by plants enables the existence of all food webs on Earth, with the minor exception of sulfur-based food webs at deep-sea hydrothermal vents, in essence becoming the stuff of animal biomass. An ecosystem that captures much

Figure 5/ Trophic Levels. Courtesy of K. Shropshire.

energy and converts it to plants and animals is more productive than one that converts less energy into plant and animal biomass. Because all plants are not created equal, some plant species are inherently better than others at converting sunlight to biomass under particular environmental conditions (e.g. acid soil, moderate rainfall, high altitude, frequent fire, etc.). This is where chance determines ecosystem productivity. An ecosystem with many species of plants has a higher probability of containing one or more species of highly productive plants, strictly by chance, than an ecosystem with fewer plant species. Thus, with few exceptions, diverse ecosystems are more productive than ecosystems that are species poor.

PARADISE LOST

The message that diversity is good for our ecosystems and therefore good for humans has been both poorly delivered and poorly received. A perfect example lies right outside your nearest window. Nearly everywhere, a glance outside reveals a close neighboring building, or a savannah-like landscape of turf grass dotted with a few

Figure 6/ Current suburban landscapes are biologically barren.
Photograph by Douglas W. Tallamy.

non-native trees and shrubs. What animals do you see? A squirrel perhaps, a bird or two? More likely, you will see no animals. We have become so accustomed to our lifeless landscapes that we are not alarmed by the absence of what is no longer there. Our baseline knowledge of what ought to exist there, of what was once normal, has shifted so dramatically over the years that now there are few people still alive who have experienced the rich diversity of life that once flourished where our *PlayStations* now stand. In fact, if we see life in our gardens—an insect, a rabbit, a groundhog—we usually do our best to exterminate it [Figure 6].

Recently, my students and I measured the traits of suburban landscapes built between 1992 and 2005—that is, during the height of sprawl in the Mid-Atlantic states.[5] We chose neighborhoods built by 26 different developers in Delaware, Pennsylvania, and Maryland, and we measured the landscapes of three randomly chosen properties from each development. Our goal was to compare the diversity of plants in suburban landscapes with that of the ecosystem the suburbs replaced, the Eastern deciduous forest.

Even I was shocked by our results. After subtracting areas that could not be landscaped (the driveway, house footprint, etc.), we found that 92 percent of the landscape was barren lawn. There were very few plants in these suburban yards, but 79 percent of the plants that were there were from Asia or Europe, and nine percent were highly invasive. The invasive species were not in the yards we measured because they had moved in of their own accord; they were there because the homeowner had planted them! Our suburban landscapes are now so barren that they contain only ten percent of the tree biomass of the mature Eastern forests they have replaced.

This statistic bears repeating. We have removed 90 percent of the trees from our living spaces—not because we had to in order to live comfortably, but because we did not think we needed to share our yards with other species. We could double the number of trees in suburbia and still only have 20 percent of what used to grow there. There are 23,671 species of plants indigenous to North America, but for the past century we have been busy replacing them with a handful of non-native ornamentals and vast expanses of European turf grasses. We have insisted that the few plants in our gardens be species from somewhere else, with no thought to the effect of such plants on local food webs. In fact, we have forgotten all of the many essential ecological roles that plants in our landscapes play every minute of every day and have focused on only one of their attributes: their appearance. In short, we have reduced the organisms that keep us and all other animals on Earth alive to mere ornaments.

FOR THE LOVE OF 'NEAT'

There are many reasons that barren landscapes nearly devoid of animal life have become the status symbol of the Western world. One of these, our love of neat, highly manicured landscapes, has deep-rooted psychological underpinnings that stem from our ancestral fight against nature for survival. A neat landscape is one in which we have won that fight. We have beaten back the encroaching vegetation that historically threatened our crops and hid dangerous predators. In neat landscapes, we, rather than nature, are in control; we feel safe and secure.

We also love 'neat' because we love order.[6] If you empty a bag of blocks onto a tabletop, soon the people sitting at that table will start to sort and arrange the blocks into an orderly design. They will do this with no direction or encouragement from the outside. Our urge to order a disorderly world is innate; we make sense of the complexity of the world by rearranging it into an order we can understand. Because neat landscapes make us feel safe and satisfy our desire for order, we make subconscious value judgments about landscapes based on their appearance. A neat landscape is inherently good in our minds; we see it as beautiful. And if a neat landscape is beautiful, people who maintain their properties by these standards are people we respect, trust, and admire. To own a neat landscape, a tidy garden, is to have high status.

This historical process has led us to evaluate landscapes and gardens solely on the basis of what they look like. What landscapes do, particularly in an ecological sense, has lost all meaning and importance in today's world. Nothing epitomizes order and control over nature better than a monoculture of manicured turf grass; but nothing conflicts more directly with the need to maintain a diversity of organisms in our managed ecosystems—that is, to share our spaces with other species—than large expanses of lawn [Figure 7]. Our myopic obsession with the aesthetics of our landscapes has spawned a global, multi-billion dollar horticultural industry with the single purpose of painting our properties with beautiful plants. Horticulturists are artists, and the garden is their medium. If they select landscape plants from all over the world, horticulturists have a larger palette with which to paint. The public has enthusiastically embraced this approach to landscaping because it elevates status, but the cost of such a landscaping paradigm to biological diversity has been enormous.

Figure 7/ We have replaced over 40 million acres of native plant communities with ecological deserts of turf grass. Photograph by Douglas W. Tallamy.

FOOD WEBS AND NON-NATIVE PLANTS

Landscaping with plants that evolved elsewhere would not degrade the ecological function of our gardens if non-native plants were the ecological equivalents of the native plants they replace. We could move plants all over the world with impunity and rest assured that our ecosystems were still functioning as well as they ever did. If one of our favorite ornamental plants spread from our gardens to natural landscapes and excluded native vegetation, we might bemoan the change of the natural world we once knew, but this would be an emotional loss, not a functional one. In several ways, alien plant species are, indeed, functionally similar to native plants. They photosynthesize at similar rates, they often prevent soil erosion and water runoff as well as native species, and they sequester carbon, shade the land, and filter pollution from the air as well as plants that evolved in North America. Unfortunately, however, non-native plants are not the ecological equivalents of native plants in one critical contribution to ecosystem sustainability: they are poor at supporting local food webs.

Plants form the foundation of stable, complex food webs only if some of the sugars they manufacture during photosynthesis are eaten by herbivores in the second trophic level. Although diverse plant communities enable the existence of diverse communities of herbivores and the omnivores and predators that eat them, this is not why plants evolved the ability to generate food. Plants generate food for their own use; energy that is taken from a plant by an animal can no longer be used by that plant for its own growth and reproduction. Plants, therefore, have evolved a number of mechanisms for deterring herbivores.[8] They grow spines and thorns on their stems. They cover their leaf surfaces with inedible hairs or load their tissues with silica and lignin that can quickly grind down tooth enamel. But the most pervasive and effective defense that plants deploy against herbivores is chemical in nature: all plants produce distasteful or toxic secondary metabolic compounds that are always in their leaves (constitutive defenses) or are mobilized to particular leaves as soon as an herbivore starts to eat them (inducible defenses).[9]

Chemical defenses are extremely effective in preventing most species of herbivores from eating most species of plants. That is one of the reasons the world is green; most of the vegetation is unpalatable to the animals that would otherwise eat it. It is important to note that insects are the plant-eaters that are most sensitive to plant chemical defenses. Gardeners tend to think that insects can and do eat any plant they choose, but this is urban legend. Plant chemistry has made most insects extraordinarily picky eaters. Insects typically cannot use a particular plant lineage for growth and reproduction unless they have first developed the physiological and behavioral means with which to circumvent that lineage's cocktail of defensive chemicals.[10] Such complex adaptation takes a long evolutionary interaction with a prospective host plant [Figure 8].

Monarch butterflies provide an excellent example. Long ago milkweed plants in the genus *Asclepias* made the evolutionary 'decision' to protect their foliage with deadly cardiac glycosides and with copious amounts of latex sap that glues shut the mouthparts of insects that bite the plant. These defenses are very effective at excluding nearly all species of herbivorous insects from using milkweeds as host plants. In contrast to most insects, however, monarchs and their close relatives, the queen butterflies, have evolved specialized physiological and behavioral adaptations that allow them to circumvent milkweed defenses.[11] Milkweed specialists like the monarch and queen, as well as two species of *Tetraopes* long-horned beetles, a weevil, and a chrysomelid leaf beetle, have evolved the ability to produce a series of enzymes that detoxify cardiac glycosides and sequester the end products in the hemolymph (insect blood) and exoskeleton of these insects. Monarchs have beaten the latex sap defense of milkweeds with a fascinating behavior; before eating a leaf, a monarch larva will chew through its midrib to sever the canals that deliver the latex sap throughout the leaf. Once the canals have been snipped, the larva can then eat any portion of the leaf that is distal to the broken vascular bundles [Figure 9]. Other milkweed specialists have converged on similar vein-snipping behaviors that prevent exposure to sticky latex sap.[12]

Figure 9/ Monarch larvae block the flow of sticky latex sap in milkweed leaves by first snipping through the latex canals in the leaf's midrib. Photograph by Douglas W. Tallamy.

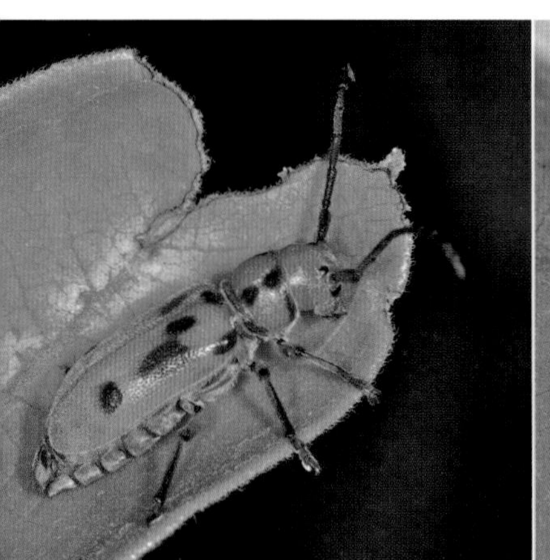

Figure 8/ Milkweed Tetraopes beetles (left), Labidomera chrysomelid beetles (middle) and Queen butterflies (right) can develop on milkweed plants because they have adapted to milkweed defenses. Photographs by Douglas W. Tallamy.

Specialized adaptations are very effective means by which insects can circumvent plant defenses, but they impart one important disadvantage. An insect that specializes in one type of defensive chemical becomes restricted in its ability to eat plants that deploy other types of chemical defenses. In our milkweed example, monarchs and queens and milkweed beetles have evolved the ability to circumvent tough defenses that deter most other insect herbivores, but in doing so they have given up the option of eating any other type of plant. There are 1,385 plant genera in the Mid-Atlantic states of the USA, yet milkweed specialists can only eat species in one, *Asclepias* milkweeds.[13] This trade-off is worthwhile for milkweed specialists as long as there is milkweed available. But if our landscaping preferences eliminate milkweed from our landscapes, milkweed specialists disappear. They do not have the physiological ability to eat plants with which they did not evolve and to which they did not adapt. When we landscape with plants from Asia and Europe, we guarantee the loss of monarchs, and queens, and Pandora sphinx moths and luna moths and red-spotted purple butterflies and all of the specialists that have never before encountered the defenses of those plants [Figure 10]. Unfortunately, this is the overwhelming majority of our insect herbivores; it is estimated that 90 percent of insect species that eat plants are specialists in a limited number of plant lineages.[14]

Figure 11/ Coreid.
Humans would not last long on Earth without insects to provide ecosystem services. Photograph by Douglas W. Tallamy.

INSECTS ARE ESSENTIAL

One of the most difficult concepts for humans to accept is our dependency on other living things—not just those species we have domesticated for our convenience, but the millions of species that enable our ecosystems to function. When they hear that their gardening practices are causing large reductions in insect populations, most gardeners celebrate. After all, the elimination of insects from our gardens has always been an important goal of gardeners. We equate 'insect' with 'pest', and when we go to a nursery, we typically seek plants labeled "pest free", meaning that insects will not eat this plant. We have been taught to create gardens that are as close to a perfect portrait of beauty as possible; sharing our gardens with insects has not seemed consistent with this ideal. We have been manipulated by the pest control industry to believe that the aesthetic aspects of gardening conflict with gardens as living systems, and so we have done our best to kill the life that our landscape plants attract. The explosion of the silk flower industry attests to our willingness to trade life for perfection [Figure 11].

Figure 10/ Without its native hackberry host, the tawny emperor would disappear. Photograph by Douglas W. Tallamy.

The landscaping paradigm that favors form over function has been enormously successful in ridding our gardens of insects. In the USA we have created tens of thousands of square miles of managed landscapes that are largely free of native insects. The insect species we still battle are those we have imported, often along with our non-native ornamental plants. Insects such as hemlock woolly adelgid, Japanese beetles, gypsy moth, emerald ash borer, Asian long-horned beetle, many of our scale insects, soybean aphid, and many more have been brought to the USA without their associated communities of natural enemies, their specialized parasitoids, predators, and diseases. Because they exist in enemy-free space, their populations often erupt, giving our native insects an unearned reputation

Figure 12/ 96 percent of our terrestrial bird species rear their young on insects. Photograph by Douglas W. Tallamy.

Figure 13/ Summer tanager. Imagine a world without birds. Photograph by Douglas W. Tallamy.

for being garden pests. Thus, all insects are targeted for indiscriminate elimination from our gardens, regardless of their contributions to garden function and sustainability.

Because the only insects most people encounter on a daily basis are those few species that bite us (mosquitoes), annoy us (house flies and cockroaches), or nibble on our garden plants, it is often a surprise to learn that insects are essential to the ecological integrity of terrestrial ecosystems. E. O. Wilson called insects "the little things that run the world" because so many vital ecological processes would not occur if insects disappeared.[15] In an effort to interpret the ecological importance of insects in terms of a value system everyone can relate to, John Losey and Mace Vaughan estimated the economic value of the ecosystem services insects provide humans in the United States. Familiar services such as pollination ($3 billion), pest control ($4.5 billion), and biodegradation ($380 million) totaled $57 billion worth of services delivered annually by the same creatures we kill at every opportunity.[16] No one, however, has put a dollar value on the most important ecosystem service performed by insects around the world: insects are the primary means by which most animals gain access to the energy fixed by plants. By developing the ability to eat well-defended plants, insects convert nutrient-poor plant tissues into convenient packets of food—their bodies—rich in protein and lipids.[17] Without insects to link animals in higher trophic levels to the plants of the first trophic level, animal diversity would be restricted to the few species that are solely vegetarians. Without insects, food webs would become simplified and highly precarious.

Birds provide an excellent example of animals that are heavily dependant on insects for protein, particularly while they are rearing their young. People typically think of birds as seed- and berry-eaters because many birds do eat seeds and berries during the fall and winter. Baby birds, however, need the high-quality protein and energy-rich fat bodies produced by insects to reach maturity. This is why 96 percent of the terrestrial birds in North America rear their young on insects and spiders.[18] Since spiders themselves use insect protein to become spiders, birds would not be able to reproduce without insects. That's right: no insects, no baby birds [Figure 12].

Try to imagine, as did Rachel Carson, a world without birds.[19] We are rapidly creating such a world by constructing landscapes that do not support insects. 127 species of neotropical migrants, such as wood thrushes, warblers, catbirds, hawks, wrens, vireos, flycatchers, kingbirds, nightjars, swallows, tanagers, orioles—species that fly thousands of miles to Central or South America to spend the winter—have declined an average of one percent per year since 1966.[20] Add up those percentages and you're looking at a 50 percent reduction in the populations of many bird species over the past 50 years. Our birds are declining for many reasons, but the reduction of insect food throughout much of their breeding range ranks high among them [Figure 13].

Birds are hardly exceptional in their need for insects. Frogs, toads, and salamanders also depend on insects for food. Rodents, themselves an important part of vertebrate food webs, eat as many insects as they can find. Opossums eat insects, raccoons eat insects, as do bats, foxes, and bears. There is no escaping the fact that if you want your kids to develop an emotional connection with the wonders of nature; if you want your landscape to do something, rather than just look like something; if you want to build a sustainable ecological utopia in your garden, you must put the plants that support your local insects back in your yard.[21]

THE IMPACT OF SCALE

The degradation of natural diversity in the suburban/urban matrix would not threaten ecosystem function and thus our own sustainability if such landscapes were small and localized—we could rely on life in undisturbed areas to compensate. However, the human footprint is now so enormous that in most areas of the globe, and especially in the lower 48 states of the USA, humans have compromised the ecological integrity of 95 percent of the land.[22]

Agriculture, including crops, monoculture tree farms, and ranching, occupies 41 percent of the land: and 54 percent of the lower 48 states has been carved into a giant matrix of cities, suburbs, and degraded habitat islands.[23] We worry about the destruction of the Amazon rainforest, 15 percent of which has already been logged: but, by comparison, an astounding 70 percent of the forests along the Eastern seaboard of the USA are gone and no one seems to notice.[24] Only five percent of the USA is relatively pristine [Figure 14].[25] Although this includes space allocated to our national parks (about one percent of the country) most of our remaining pristine areas have little biodiversity because they are too high (e.g., the highest peaks of the Rockies and Cascades) or too dry to sustain much life. This, of course, is why we haven't already developed them ourselves.

That 54 percent of our lower 48 states is in a biologically compromised patchwork of cities and suburbs is an environmental statistic that most people simply do not believe. That patch of woods at the end of the street and the seemingly endless trees that line many of our highways look like pristine habitats to most people. But those tiny patches are unable to sustain many species for several reasons. First and foremost is that the patches of habitat in fragmented landscapes are too small to sustain the number of species they supported when they were part of large contiguous habitats. There are both evolutionary reasons and ecological reasons that small, isolated habitat patches lose species after fragmentation.[26] On an evolutionary time scale, the rate at which new species evolve is much slower within small habitat islands than within large habitats. The mechanisms that promote the evolution of new species, such as physical barriers to gene flow, scarcely exist in small spaces, thus limiting the opportunity for the evolution of new species in isolated habitat islands.

Most people have great difficulty relating to the enormous time spans over which evolution occurs, but the loss of species from fragmented habitats can easily be understood within short ecological time frames as well. When a large habitat is chopped up into a series of small, isolated habitats, the large populations of plants and animals that once inhabited that area are reduced to several small populations that are isolated from each other. Therein lies the problem, because small populations are highly vulnerable to local extinction.[27] All populations fluctuate over time: under favorable conditions, they increase in size, and in unfavorable times, they decrease in size. Large populations can absorb these natural fluctuations without disappearing from their habitat, but small populations typically decline to zero within a local patch the first or second time they are stressed. Once they disappear from a habitat fragment, they rarely have the opportunity to re-colonize it because source populations are too far away.

The birds on Barro Colorado Island, an island in the middle of the Panama Canal, provide an excellent example.[28] In 1914 this patch of tropical forest was the top of a small mountain rather than an island and was surrounded by hundreds of square miles of undisturbed habitat. When the canal was completed, the Chagres River was dammed, and the rising waters of what is now called Gatun Lake turned the mountaintop into an island isolated from the adjacent forest. Barro Colorado Island may not seem that isolated to us; the distance to the nearest shore in most places is less than a mile. But to most of its animals and plants, it may as well be in the middle of the Atlantic Ocean. As soon as Barro Colorado Island was formed, its isolation from the

Figure 14/ What was once 960 million acres of virgin forests in the eastern USA has been reduced to tiny isolated patches of secondary growth. Photograph by Douglas W. Tallamy.

Figure 15/ Natural areas in the USA are fragmented by four million miles of paved roads. Photograph by Douglas W. Tallamy.

greater surrounding forest began to take its toll on the number and kind of animals that would survive on the island. Because most forest animals are reluctant to leave the forest, they were cut off from any interactions with the mainland. They would not swim or fly to the mainland to find food or mates or to disperse to new territories. Even though the island is 3,700 acres in size, a sizable chunk of real estate compared to most of the habitat islands we have created in North America (the average size of a woodlot in Delaware, a state once entirely forested, is now ten acres), it is too small to sustain the populations of many of its original inhabitants.[29] Since 1914, 65 of its original 283 species of birds have disappeared from the island, and many others are on the brink of local extinction. Nearly a century has passed since Barro Colorado Island was cut off from the mainland, yet the extinction debt has only been partially paid. No one knows how long it will take before the island community reaches its final equilibrium number of species that is balanced between extinction and immigration. What is clear, however, is that the number of species that can be sustained on the island is a fraction of what existed on that same acreage before it was isolated by water.

Area effects are no less devastating on habitat islands —forests surrounded by developments rather than by water —than they are on real islands. The creatures that depend on the resources found only in forests cannot make a go of it on manicured lawns criss-crossed by paved roads. Just as on islands surrounded by water, the loss of species from habitat islands takes time, but it inevitably happens. For example, Ashdown Forest in Sussex, England, the inspirational setting of A. A. Milne's *Winnie the Pooh*, has become entirely isolated by development since Milne wrote in the book in the 1920s. In the ensuing 90 years the forest has lost 47 plant species.[30] Ashdown Forest is over 6,000 acres in size, yet it is still too small to sustain its species over time.

My point is simple: the most destructive part of suburbia is not the space occupied by houses and roads, although that is substantial. For instance, the paved surface area of the four million miles of roads that criss-cross the USA now covers an area over five times the size of New Jersey.[31] Instead, it is the way suburbia fragments large chunks of habitat into areas too small to sustain nature that so threatens our biodiversity [Figure 15]. David Quammen draws a superb analogy between a Persian carpet and an intact ecosystem.[32] A Persian carpet is an exquisite piece of art with both form and function. If you were to cut it into 36 pieces, it loses both. It does not become 36 new carpets; instead, it is reduced to 36 worthless scraps of fraying material. Ecosystems are similarly degraded in both form and function when they are fragmented. Unlike Persian carpets, however, ecosystems have no optimal size at which they function best; their diversity, and thus functional capacity, increases linearly with their size.[33] In the case of ecosystems, bigger is always better.

THE CRITICAL ROLE OF SUBURBAN ECOSYSTEMS

In the past we have viewed conservation as an either/or enterprise: nature or humans, but never both at the same time in the same place. We have focused our efforts almost entirely on preserving natural habitats, a worthy goal to be sure: but once that woodlot was cut and that housing development built, we looked elsewhere to save biodiversity. We did not consider the possibility that we could share 'our' land with other species—that we could actually live with much of the nature that used to occupy the spaces we have taken for ourselves. Since the 1950s we have done our best to eliminate the natural world from our spaces because it is easier to build in a cleared area, and it is easier to create an artistic landscape on a clean canvas. We have not worried about the loss of nature from human-dominated spaces because we have clung to the historical perception that the world is still largely untamed and unoccupied; no matter what we destroy locally, we believe nature is still intact someplace else. Unfortunately, in a world with *seven thousand million* people and no political discussion of the ecological limits of the earth, nothing could be farther from the truth.

Although we have not recognized it in the past, the landscapes of the places in which we live and work —those highly managed expanses of savannah-like lawn and ornamental plants—determine the degree to which our ecosystems are fragmented by the human enterprise. If the animals and plants found in natural habitat fragments can also make a living within the suburban landscapes that are the cause of fragmentation, then fragmentation as a phenomenon ceases to exist. Diversity can thrive everywhere. But if we landscape in ways that exclude most living things, the diversity of life required to run our ecosystems becomes unsustainably confined to isolated habitat fragments. We can and must make human-dominated landscapes effective biological corridors that connect relatively undisturbed habitats with each other by sharing the spaces we need for ourselves with other species. Michael Rosenzweig has called this approach to conservation "Reconciliation Ecology"; its cornerstone philosophy is *sharing*, sharing in the true sense of ecological utopia.[34] Our gardens and the landscapes that surround them are now the essential keys to a sustainable future on this planet.

Figure 17/ The spun glass caterpillar, a resident on native oak trees, is one of the most exquisite species that will come to your garden. Photograph by Douglas W. Tallamy.

Figure 16/ Big lawn. It's not just the type of plants we use in suburbia that is eliminating nature, it is the amount of plants in our landscapes as well. Photograph by Douglas W. Tallamy.

ATTAINING ECOLOGICAL UTOPIA

To achieve our vision of gardens as functional ecological utopias we must change our current landscaping paradigm in two ways. First, we need to put plants back into our managed landscapes. Barren, sweeping views may have an aesthetic appeal for some, but we can no longer afford to denude the Earth to achieve them. Second, to restore the ecological integrity of our landscapes we must not only use *more* plants in our landscape designs, but they must also be the *right* plants [Figure 16]. The right plants for our gardens are not just the ones that provide the particular look we are after; they are the species that support our local food webs: our regionally native plants.

For those who have only known gardening with the standard non-native ornamentals offered in nurseries, switching to native species may seem daunting, or worse, boring. Yet, increasing the percentage of native plants in our landscapes is easy. We can replace non-natives with more functional natives that are similar in habit, flower type, and fall color by digging up the old and putting in the new, or through attrition: simply replacing plants from Asia and Europe as they die. Landscaping with natives may seem unimaginative only if we continue to think of plants just as decorations. If, however, we notice and enjoy the web of life associated with our native plants species—the stunning cecropia moth produced by our black cherry trees, the fascinating spun glass caterpillar found on our oak leaves, the beautiful indigo bunting that breeds in our patch of meadow—our gardens will provide a unique and fulfilling experience every day of the year [Figure 17].

Figure 18 and Figure 19/

(top) The traditional approach to landscape design has been to clear the land of most or all existing vegetation, plant the entire property in lawn, and then carve out small spaces for flowerbeds. (bottom) Instead of designing where our plantings will go in a sea of lawn, our new approach will be to carve out necessary lawn spaces from a property that is otherwise entirely planted. This schematic suggests ways to use lawn for social spaces and paths for movement, while planting the rest of the property with productive native plant communities. Illustrations by Douglas W. Tallamy.

The real challenge in attaining ecological utopia is to increase the amount of plant life on your property without losing control of your landscape. Perhaps the best way to accomplish this is to flip on its head the landscaping paradigm that has dominated our culture for the past century. The traditional approach to landscape design has been to clear the land of most or all existing vegetation (properties built on farmland have already been cleared), plant the entire property in lawn, and then carve out small spaces for flowerbeds [Figure 18]. This approach renders most of the property an ecological wasteland. But if we do the opposite, we can use lawn as it should be used, while turning most of our property into a vibrant landscape. Instead of figuring out where our plantings will go within a sea of lawn, our new approach will be to carve out necessary lawn spaces from a property that is otherwise entirely planted [Figure 19].

Where do we need lawn? The cool season European grasses comprising our lawns are ideal spaces for walking because they can bear our weight without being crushed to death. Start by deciding where you will need grass paths to allow movement from one place to another: a path to the backyard vegetable garden, paths on either side of the house to allow passage from the front yard to the back, and so on. Next, decide where you would like spaces for small social gatherings. These are often positioned in a private, cozy place near the house in the backyard, but can just as easily be placed in the front or side yard, depending on your property size and shape, and on your personal preference.

The biggest change in our new approach to landscaping will occur in the front yard. Today it is almost universally accepted that the front must be entirely lawn. Real estate agents tell us that we need to see the entire house from the street to preserve curb appeal. Knowledgeable landscapers say "hogwash" to that notion. Our properties can have curb appeal whether one can see all, part, or none of the house from the street if we use our plantings to direct the eye to the most aesthetically pleasing parts of our yards. That may be our front door, our front flowerbed, or a magnificent oak off to the side of our house. Less appealing areas of our properties can be screened with dense plantings of natives. Where these plantings are developed will be defined by where we build a view (a landscape 'window') with lawn. Our lawns will no longer be the landscaping default—what we do with our yards when we don't know what else to do—rather, they will become a useful landscaping tool that help define the use of various parts of our properties.

What should we do with all of those spaces that are not in lawn? If you are lucky enough to build on property that already has native plant communities, take care to protect them from the start, although reshaping existing growth to work with the design of your lawn spaces may be necessary. Most yards are already in lawn, however, so you will need to restore the plant communities that once thrived there. Planting large areas can be daunting tasks; I recommend making your restoration a long-term project. Move from one manageable area to the next, as time and resources permit. You will start to reap the benefits of your new plantings almost immediately as you begin to share your living spaces with other species.

My research has shown that, in areas of the country where there is enough water to support them, woody plants like trees and shrubs serve as hosts for many more species of Lepidoptera (moths and butterflies) than herbaceous plants and in doing so provide more types of food for birds and other insect-eaters.[35] Supplying birds with the caterpillars they need while they are nesting will bring just as many birds to your yard during the spring and summer as a bird feeder does during the winter.[33]

PLANT DENSELY

We are so used to landscapes nearly devoid of the plants that support life that dense plantings such as those typically found at forest edges may seem too 'wild' for many gardeners. But remember: plants equal life. The more plants we put in our yards, the more food and shelter we provide for other living things. A garden that requires yards of mulch and constant weeding is one that wants more plants. When you are restoring nature in your yard, keep your focus on the animals that will come to your plants, not on the individual plants themselves. This means that all trees don't have to be treated as specimen trees, isolated from other trees by seas of grass. Trees planted close enough to create a closed canopy are exactly what most of our charismatic animals prefer. Garden beds edging your property should be so packed with high-value plants that you cannot see the ground. This reduces maintenance effort by leaving little room for weeds in your beds. It also protects the ground from the extremes of summer heat and winter cold, prevents the soil from drying out, improves water absorption and retention, and allows a complex community of soil organisms to flourish [Figure 20].

BUILD A BALANCED COMMUNITY

A community of plants and animals that is in balance is one that will persist, and a community that is not in balance will cease to exist in its current form. Thus, in the parlance of environmentally conscious societies, sustainability cannot be achieved without balance. Ironically, many gardeners reject native plants because they fear they are not sustainable. There are many misconceptions about using native species as landscape plants, but one of the most pervasive is the fear that natives will be defoliated by the very insects we are trying to attract with them. After all, that is one of the reasons 'pest free' plants from Asia and Europe appeared to be the logical choice for gardeners in the first place. No gardener wants her favorite plantings to be riddled with insect damage. However, the notion that diverse native plant communities are more susceptible to insect damage than non-native species is neither logical nor correct. If this were the case, insects would have destroyed all of the plant communities in North America long before Europeans arrived with their non-native plants.

It may seem paradoxical, but planting natives that are part of local food webs is the best way to prevent insect outbreaks. It is true that native plants attract more species of insect herbivores than non-native ornamentals—15 times more species by some measures.[36] Nevertheless, all of those insects attract their own enemies in the form of numerous species of predators, parasites, and diseases that keep insect populations in check. Natural enemies are essential components of balanced gardens, and to have a diverse community of natural enemies present in your yard at all times, you must have a diversity of prey available at all times. This is the principle behind conservation biological control.[37] When one prey species, say, a caterpillar that nibbles oak leaves, becomes too uncommon to support a particular predator, other species of caterpillars that develop on maples, for example, will be present for that predator to eat and will prevent it from leaving the area. Of course, this scenario will only occur if you have oaks and maples in your garden. The key to controlling insect outbreaks is to nip them in the bud. This can only happen if natural enemies are present in gardens whenever an insect begins to become too numerous [Figure 21].

Figure 20/ Best landscape. The more plants you put in your yard, the more food and shelter you are creating for other living things. Nearly all of the plants in this yard belong to a native plant community. Very little space is devoted to lawn or heavily mulched beds. The result is a beautiful, highly functional landscape in which nature is happy. Photograph by Douglas W. Tallamy.

Figure 21/ This fawn sphinx larva has been attacked by numerous Cotesia parasitoids, common natural enemies of caterpillars. Photograph by Douglas W. Tallamy.

Problems arise when we landscape with plants that support very few herbivores, because then there usually is not enough food to keep insect predators and parasitoids, as well as hungry birds, nearby. When there is an outbreak of one of the many insects we have imported along with our Asian ornamentals—like the Japanese beetle, hemlock woolly adelgid, azalea lace bug, or the Euonymus scale—there are not enough natural enemies to control them. This helps explain why as much as four times more pesticide by weight is applied each year to suburban landscapes than to agricultural fields in the USA.[38]

Predicting that a diversity of native plants will create an ecological community in your yard that will maintain a balance between herbivores and their enemies is one thing, but providing convincing evidence for this prediction is another. Although there is growing support for this approach in agricultural settings, "conservation biological control" as I have described it is a new concept for suburban ecosystems and has yet to be thoroughly tested.[39] A good start, however, has been made by Erin Reed, one of my recent graduate students at the University of Delaware.[40] Erin compared the amount of damage sucking and chewing insects made on the ornamental plants at six suburban properties landscaped primarily with species native to the area and at six properties landscaped traditionally with a preponderance of non-natives. After two years of measurements Erin found that less than five percent of the leaves on either set of properties were damaged at the end of the season. Earlier studies have shown that homeowners do not notice or react to insect damage until about ten percent of the leaves are damaged, so the damage levels in Erin's study were well below the aesthetic injury level in both native plantings and traditional plantings.[41]

Erin's most important result was that there was a small but statistically significant difference in the amount of damage between the two landscape types. Although there were more insects present on the native landscapes, there was actually less insect damage to the native plants on those landscapes.[42] The diversity of native plants supported enough insects to maintain large and diverse communities of natural enemies that, in turn, ate most of the insects before they became large enough to cause noticeable damage. If Erin's study proves to be the rule and not an exception, we need not worry that our native plants will be destroyed by insects. The bluebirds and chickadees, parasitic wasps and toads, assassin bugs and ladybird beetles, fireflies and hover flies, and lacewings and ground beetles in our yards will all keep our plant-eating insects in check before they cause perceptible damage to our beautiful gardens. Native plantings can give us balanced, pesticide-free landscapes that function sustainably without human intervention, as nature has done from the beginning: a gardener's utopia, to be sure.

CONCLUSIONS

Allen Hershkowitz, a senior scientist with the Natural Resources Defense Council, recently said, "A lot of people think that conservation means you have to diminish your lifestyle."[43] No wonder. We are asked daily to forego the consumptive and lavish lifestyles to which we have become accustomed in the name of conservation and sustainability. Yet, conservation through the creation of ecological utopia in our landscapes can counter such feelings. No one feels diminished by close interactions with the marvels of nature. If we garden with the plants that sustain food webs, we will invite the participants in those food webs—the natural world itself—into our lives. The very existence of zoos, of nature shows, of domesticated pets, of a child's fascination with tadpoles, and of millions of dedicated bird watchers attests to our inner biophilia.[44] Gardeners no longer need to wage war on nature to practice their passion. They can create attractive gardens that enrich their lives, not just through the beauty of the plants themselves but also with the fascinating life forms those plants attract. Unlike the pursuit of other utopias, creating ecological utopias in our landscapes with native plants is not an esoteric experiment conducted by a few idealists; it is an imperative for us all if we want to be sustained by our planet.

Notes

1. Wu, Jianguo, and Orie L. Loucks, "From Balance of Nature to Hierarchical Patch Dynamics: A Paradigm Shift in Biology", *The Quarterly Review of Biology*, vol. 70, no. 4, December 1995, pp. 439–466.
2. Duffy, J. Emmett, "Why biodiversity is important to the functioning of real-world ecosystems", *Frontiers in Ecology and the Environment*, vol. 7, no. 8, October 2009, pp. 437–444. See also Nick M. Haddad, Gregory Crutsinger, Kevin Gross, John Haarstad, and David Tilman, "Plant diversity and the stability of foodwebs", *Ecology Letters*, vol. 14, no. 1, January 2011, pp. 42–46.
3. Ehrlich, Paul R., and Anne H. Ehrlich, *Extinction: the Causes and Consequences of the Disappearance of Species*, New York: Random House, 1981.
4. Tilman, David, Peter B. Reich, Johannes Knops, David Wedin, Troy Mielke, and Clarence Lehman, "Diversity and productivity in a long-term grassland experiment", *Science*, vol. 294, no. 5543, October 2001, pp. 843–845. See also David Tilman, "Niche tradeoffs, neutrality, and community structure: a stochastic theory of resource competition, invasion, and community assembly", *Proceedings of the National Academy of Sciences*, vol. 101, no. 30, 27 July 2004, pp. 10854–10861.
5. Tallamy, Douglas W., Jules Bruck, Sarah Walker, Kelly Pippins, Sarah Shpak, and Anne Lucey, "The abundance, diversity and geographic origin of suburban landscape plantings". Submitted to *Conservation Biology*.
6. Daniel Nadenicek, personal communication.
7. We have replaced over 40 million acres of native plant communities with ecological deserts of turf grass according to C. Milesi, S. W. Runnng, C. D. Elvidge, J. B. Dietz, B. T. Tuttle, R. R. Nemani, "Mapping

and modeling the biogeochemical cycling of turf grasses in the United States", *Environmental Management*, vol. 36, 2005, pp. 426–438.
8. Rosenthal, Gerald A., Daniel H. Janzen, and Shalom W. Applebaum, *Herbivores: Their Interaction with Secondary Plant Metabolites*, New York: Academic Press, 1979. See also Douglas W. Tallamy, "Behavioral adaptations in insects to allelochemicals", *Molecular Aspects of Insect-Plant Associations*, Lena B. Brattsten and Sami Ahmad eds., New York: Plenum Press, 1986, pp. 273–300.
9. Berenbaum, May R. "Coevolution between herbivorous insects and plants: tempo and orchestration", *Insect Life Cycles: Genetics, Evolution, and Co-ordination*, Francis S. Gilbert ed., New York: Springer-Verlag, 1990, pp. 87–89.
10. Ehrlich, Paul R., and Peter H. Raven, "Butterflies and Plants: a Study in Coevolution", *Evolution*, vol. 18, no. 4, December 1964, pp. 586–608.
11. Brower, Lincoln P., "Understanding and Misunderstanding the migration of the monarch butterfly (Nymphalidae) in North America", *Journal of the Lepidopterists' Society*, vol. 49, no. 4, 1995, pp. 304–385.
12. Dussourd, David E., and T. Eisner, "Vein-cutting behavior: Insect counterploy to the latex defense of plants", *Science*, vol. 237, no. 4817, 21 August 1987, pp. 898–901.
13. Tallamy, Doug W., and Kimberley J. Shropshire, "Ranking Lepidopteran Use of Native versus Introduced Plants", *Conservation Biology*, vol. 23, no. 4, August 2009, pp. 941–947.
14. Bernays, Elizabeth, and Michelle Graham, "On the Evolution of Host Specificity in Phytophagous Arthropods", *Ecology*, vol. 69, no. 4, August 1988, pp. 886–892; see also Douglas J. Futuyma, and Fred Gould, "Associations of Plants and Insects in a Deciduous Forest", *Ecological Monographs* vol. 49, no. 1, March 1979, pp. 33–50.
15. Wilson, E. O., "The Little Things that Run the World (The Importance and Conservation of Invertebrates", *Conservation Biology*, vol. 1, no. 4, December 1987, pp. 344–346.
16. Losey, John, and Mace Vaughan, "The Economic Value of Ecological Services Provided by Insects", *BioScience*, vol. 56, no. 4, April 2006, pp. 311–323.
17. DeFoliart, Gene, "Insects as Human Food", *Crop Protection*, vol. 11, no. 5, 1992, pp. 395–399.
18. Dunn, Jon L., and Jonathan Alderfer, *National Geographic Field Guide to the Birds of North America*, 5th edition, National Geographic Society: Washington, D.C., 1999.
19. Carson, Rachel, *Silent Spring*, Boston: Houghton Mifflin, 1962.
20. Sauer, J. R., J. E. Hines, and J. Fallon, *The North American Breeding Bird Survey, Results and Analysis 1966–2004*, Version 2005.2, Laurel, Maryland: USGS Patuxent Wildlife Research Center; see also Jeffrey Wells, *Birder's Conservation Handbook*, Princeton, NJ: Princeton University Press, 2007.
21. Louv, Richard, *Last Child in the Woods: Saving Our Children from Nature-Deficit Disorder*, Chapel Hill, NC: Algonquin Books, 2006.
22. Rosenzweig, Michael, *Win-Win Ecology: How the Earth's Species can Survive in the Midst of Human Enterprise*, New York: Oxford University Press, 2003.
23. *USDA Census of Agriculture*, 2002. http://www.nass.usda.gov/census/
24. Brown, William P., "On the Community Composition and Abundance of Delaware Forest Birds", Ph.D. Dissertation, Newark, DE: University of Delaware, 2006.
25. Kershner, R. T., and B. T. Leverett, *The Sierra Club Guide to the Ancient Forests of the Northeast*, San Francisco: Sierra Club Books, 2004.
26. Rosenzweig, *Win-Win Ecology*.
27. Mace, Georgina M., and Russell Lande, "Assessing Extinction Threats: Toward a Reevaluation of IUCN Threatened Species Categories", *Conservation Biology*, vol. 5, no. 2, June 1991, pp. 148–157.
28. Robinson, W. Douglas, "Long-term Changes in the Avifauna of Barro Colorado Island, Panama, A Tropical Forest Isolate", *Conservation Biology*, vol. 13, no. 1, February 1999, pp. 85–97.
29. For the information on Delaware specifically, see Brown, *On the Community Composition*.
30. Marren, Peter, "What time hath stole away: local extinctions in our native flora", *British Wildlife*, June 2001, pp. 305–310.
31. Hayden, Dolores, and Jim Wark, *A Field Guide to Sprawl*, New York: W. W. Norton, 2004. See also Chris Elvidge, Christina Milesi, John Dietz, et al., "U.S. Constructed Area Approaches the Size of Ohio", *EOS: Transactions, American Geophysical Union*, vol. 85, no. 24, June 2004, pp. 233–234.
32. Quammen, David, *The Song of the Dodo: Island biogeography in an age of extinctions*, New York: Hutchinson, 1996.
33. Rosenzweig, Michael, *Species Diversity in Space and Time*, New York: Cambridge University Press, 1995. See also Rosenzweig, *Win-Win Ecology*.
34. Rosenzweig, *Win-Win Ecology*.
35. Tallamy and Shropshire, "Ranking Lepidopteran Use of Native Versus Introduced Plants". A complete list of all plant genera in the Mid-Atlantic States, ranked by their potential to support nature, can be found at: http://copland.udel.edu/~dtallamy/host/index.html.
36. Tallamy and Shropshire, "Ranking Lepidopteran Use of Native Versus Introduced Plants".
37. Landis, D. A., S. D. Wratten, and G. M. Gurr, "Habitat management to conserve natural enemies of arthropod pests in agriculture", *Annual Review of Entomology*, vol. 45, 2000, pp. 175–201.
38. Pimentel, D. D. Andow, R. Dyson-Hudson, et al., "Agricultural and Economic Impacts of Reducing U.S. Agricultural Pesticide Use", *Handbook of Pest Management in Agriculture*, 2nd edition, D. Pimentel ed., Boca Raton, FL: CRC Press, 1991.
39. Landis, Wratten, and Gurr, "Habitat management".
40. Reed, Erin B., "Bottom-up Effect on Top-down Control in a Suburban Landscape", M.A. Thesis, Newark, DE: University of Delaware, 2010.
41. Sadof, Clifford S., and Michael J. Raupp, "Aesthetic thresholds and their development", *Economic Thresholds for Integrated Pest Management*, Leon G. Higley and Larry P. Pedigo eds., Lincoln: University of Nebraska Press, 1996.
42. Burghardt, K. T., D. W. Tallamy, and W. G. Shriver, "The impact of native plants on biodiversity in suburban landscapes", *Conservation Biology*, vol. 23, no. 1, February 2009, pp. 219–224.
43. Quoted in L. Lehrer, "At 96, White House Correspondents' Association goes Ecological", *Politico*, 30 April 2010.
44. Wilson, Edward O., *Biophilia*, Cambridge, MA: Harvard University Press, 1984.

LET
FLOWERS
SPEAK
302 /JOSEPH BEUYS

EARTH PERFECT?

VIOLETS

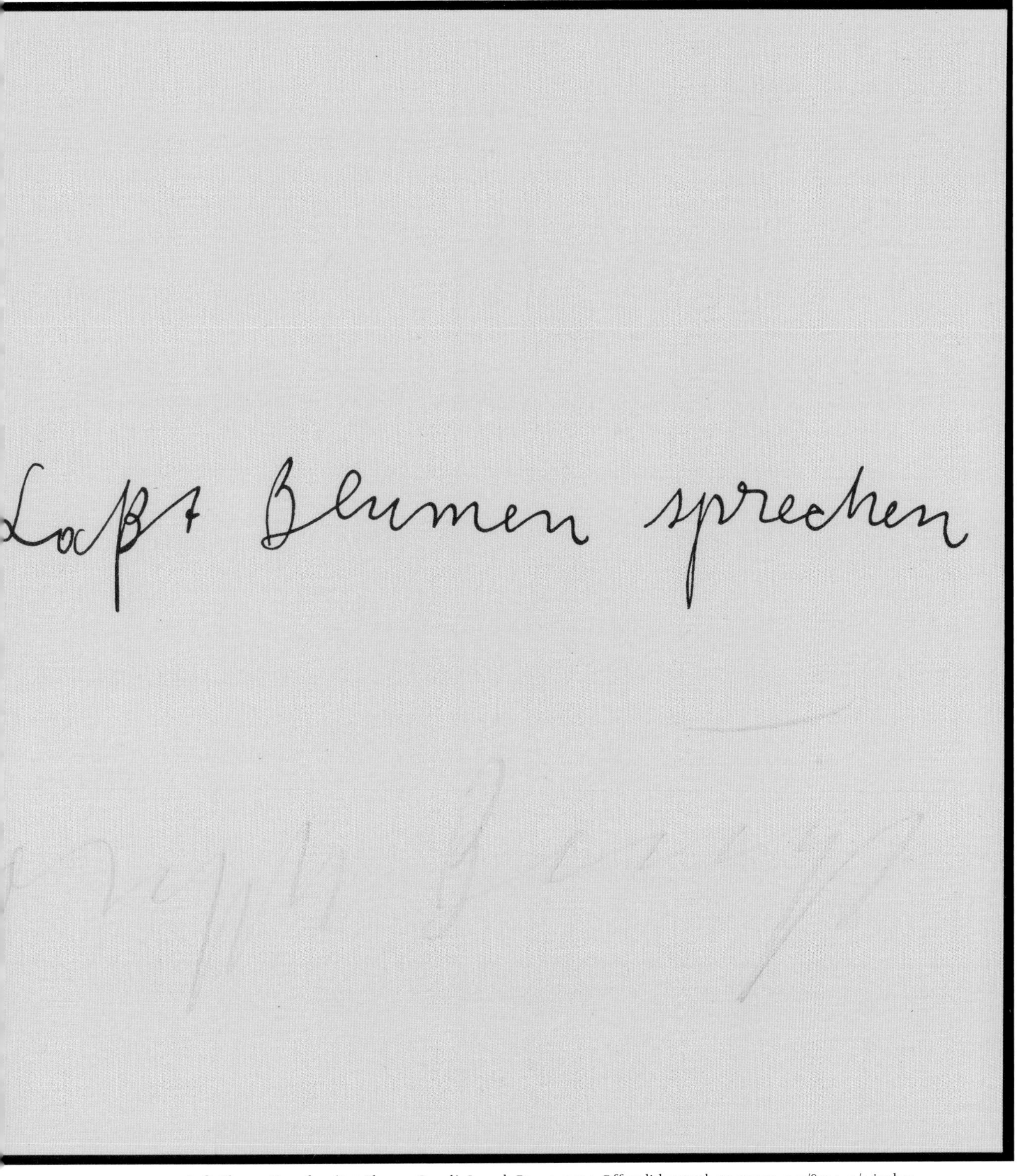

Laßt Blumen Sprechen (*Let Flowers Speak*), Joseph Beuys, 1974. Offset lithograph on paper. 5–7/8 x 4–1/4 inches. Walker Art Center, Minneapolis. Alfred and Marie Greisinger Collection, Collection Walker Art Center, T. B. Walker Acquisition Fund, 1992. Accession number 1992.332. Image @ 2011 Artists Rights Society (ARS), New York / VG Bild-Kunst, Bonn.

EDITORS

ANNETTE GIESECKE

Annette Giesecke is Professor of Classics and Chair of Ancient Greek and Roman Studies at the University of Delaware. With a background in the art and literature of the Classical world, she has written on a variety of subjects ranging from Epicurean philosophy and the poetry of Homer and Virgil to ancient attitudes towards the natural environment. She is author of *The Epic City: Urbanism, Utopia, and the Garden in Ancient Greece and Rome* (Harvard University Press, 2007).

NAOMI JACOBS

Naomi Jacobs is Professor of English and Chair of the English Department at the University of Maine. She is past president of the Society for Utopian Studies, and was founding member of the Advisory Board and Editorial Committee to the journal *Utopian Studies*. Professor Jacobs is the author of *The Character of Truth: Historical Figures in Contemporary Fiction* as well as of many articles on utopian and dystopian writers of the nineteenth and twentieth centuries, including William Morris, George Orwell, Ursula K. Le Guin, and Octavia Butler.

CONTRIBUTORS

JENNIFER ATKINSON

Jennifer Atkinson is Lecturer in American Studies and Environmental Studies in the Interdisciplinary Arts and Sciences program at the University of Washington, Bothell. Her article on gardens in literary utopias, "Seeds of Change," won the Society for Utopian Studies' Arthur O. Lewis Award for the best paper from an untenured scholar.

DAVID BELL

David Bell is an architect and Director of Undergraduate Architecture Programs at the Rensselaer Polytechnic Institute in Troy, New York. He has written essays on a variety of theoretical concerns in architecture and the arts. His most recent work has addressed issues from a dialectical analysis of the architecture and criticism of Adolf Loos to a comparison of the works of Marcel Duchamp with the conceptual foundations of quantum physics.

IRUS BRAVERMAN

Irus Braverman is Associate Professor of Law and Adjunct Professor of Geography at the University at Buffalo, State University of New York. Her unique interest in law, landscape, and the politics of planting is reflected in her book *Planted Flags: Trees, Land, and Law in Israel/Palestine* (Cambridge University Press, 2009).

STEVEN BROWN

Poet and critic Steven Brown is a doctoral student in the field of American utopianism at Harvard University. His poems have been published with ten silver gelatin prints by Jerry Uelsmann as *Moth and Bonelight*, a limited edition from 21st Editions.

U WE CLAUS

Environmental artist U We Claus collaborated with iconic twentieth century artist Joseph Beuys on projects such as *7000 Eichen* (*7000 Oaks*) and *Piantagione Paradise* (*Planting Paradise*) in Bolognano, Italy. He is the creator of the Sommer Berger Garden in Amorbach, Germany. The garden, which was awarded the status of Geotop of the UNESCO Geo-Naturepark Bergstrasse Odenwald, became the subject of his film *The Way Up Is the Way Down.*

DAVID E. COOPER

David E. Cooper is Professor Emeritus of Philosophy at the University of Durham. His extensive writings on the history of Eastern and Western philosophy, environmental ethics, the philosophy of language, and aesthetics include *A Philosophy of Gardens* (Oxford University Press, 2005) and *Buddhism, Virtue and Environment* (Ashgate, 2005) with Simon P. James.

DONALD DUNHAM

Architect and theorist Donald Dunham is Assistant Professor of Architecture in the College of Architecture and the Built Environment, Philadelphia University. His published projects include "Modulating a Dialogue between Architecture and Nature," in J. Gauer, ed. *The New American Dream: Living Well in Small Homes*, pp. 65–77 (Monacelli, 2004) and "Inclusivity, Objectivity, and the Ideal: The Museum as Utopian Space", which received the 2011 International Award of Excellence from the *Journal of the Inclusive Museum*.

STEPHEN FORBES

Stephen Forbes is Director of the Botanic Gardens of Adelaide, South Australia. His diverse interests include landscape management, urban nature conservation, and 'placemaking' in the interest of health and wellbeing. Recent papers exploring the role of botanic gardens in social innovation include: "How botanic gardens changed the world", "The audacity of man and the oeconomy of nature", and "Science & policy: valuing framing, language & listening".

ARIE GRAAFLAND

Founder of the Delft School of Design, Arie Graafland is Antoni van Leeuwenhoek Chair of Architecture and Professor of Architecture Theory at the Faculty of Architecture, Delft University of Technology, the Netherlands. Widely published in the field of architectural theory, he is editor of the Delft School of Design Series on Architecture and Urbanism with 010 Publishers.

DENNIS HARDY

Dennis Hardy is Emeritus Professor of Urban Planning and Utopian History and former Pro Vice Chancellor of Middlesex University. His books include *From Garden Cities to New Towns, From New Towns to Green Politics* (Spon, 1991), *Utopian England: Community Experiments, 1900–1945* (Spon, 1991), and *Cities that Don't Cost the Earth* (TCPA, 2008).

PATRICK HEALY

Philosopher, aesthetician, and poet Patrick Healy is Lecturer at the Delft School of Design, Delft University of Technology, and Professor of Interdisciplinary Research at the Free International University, Amsterdam. His recent publications include *Images of Knowledge: an Introduction to Contemporary Philosophy of Science* (SUN, Amsterdam, 2005) and *The Model and its Architecture* (010 Publishers, 2008).

MORNA LIVINGSTON

Photographer and architectural historian Morna Livingston is Associate Professor of Environmental Design and Visual Studies at Philadelphia University. Specializing in ancient and Medieval water systems as well cultural landscapes, her published works include *Steps to Water: the Ancient Stepwells of India* (Princeton Architectural Press, 2002) and *La Foce: A Garden and Landscape in Tuscany*, co-authored with Benedetta Origo, Laurie Olin, and John Dixon Hunt (University of Pennsylvania Press, 2001).

LYNDA H. SCHNEEKLOTH

Lynda H. Schneekloth, ASLA, is Professor Emeritus of the University of Buffalo School of Architecture and Planning. Her scholarly research is focused on the idea of placemaking, that is, how people preserve and transform the world, including natural processes and built form. She is author of *Placemaking: The Art and Practice of Building Communities* with R. Shibley; *Olmsted in Buffalo and Niagara* with R. Shibley and T. Yots; *The Power Trail* with B. Gawronski, J. Kasilove, and T. Yots; and co-editor of *Ordering Spaces: Types in Architecture and Design* with K. Franck.

DOUGLAS W. TALLAMY

Douglas W. Tallamy is Professor and Chair of Entomology and Wildlife Ecology and Director for the Center for Managed Ecosystems at the University of Delaware. He is also author of *Bringing Nature Home: How Native Plants Sustain Wildlife in Our Gardens* (Timber Press 2007, 2nd edition 2009).

SUSAN WILLIS

Susan Willis is Associate Professor in the Literature Program at Duke University and proprietor of Bitta-Blue Community Supported Agriculture in Killingworth, Connecticut. Her recent publications include "Forensics of Spinach", *South Atlantic Quarterly* 107.2 (Fall, 2007).

Black Dog Publishing Limited
10A Acton Street
London
WC1X 9NG

t. +44 (0)207 713 5097
f. +44 (0)207 713 8682
e. info@blackdogonline.com

Designed by Rachel Pfleger at Black Dog Publishing.
Edited by Annette Giesecke and Naomi Jacobs.

British Library Cataloguing-in-Publication Data.
A CIP record for this book is available from the British Library.

ISBN 978 1 907317 75 0

Black Dog Publishing is an environmentally responsible company. *Earth Perfect?: Nature, Utopia, and the Garden* is printed on FSC accredited paper.

Cover/ *The Garden of Earthly Delights.*
Hieronymus Bosch, Flemish, 1500–1505. Oil on wood, 220 x 389 cm. Museo Nacional del Prado, Madrid. Photograph courtesy of the Museo del Prado.

art design fashion
history photography
theory and things

www.blackdogonline.com